Praise for Peter Guralnick's

Dream Boogie: The Triumph of Sam Cooke

"The splendors of [Guralnick's] book — its percolating narrative, meticulous research, and profound identification with its subject — make it a worthy successor indeed to the Presley twofer. . . . Guralnick's got more empathy in his pinky than most writers have in their entire bodies and has always displayed an amazing gift for putting himself in the subject's shoes."

— James Marcus, *Newsday*

"Guralnick writes prose like Cooke wrote songs, with a minimum of outward fuss belying a fanatical attention to detail. Both singer and biographer, in short, make it look easy."

— Matt Konrad, *Ruminator Review*

"Unsurpassable. . . . The writing is as relaxed, graceful, and affecting as a superior Sam Cooke performance. . . . The author is equally at home with the fine points of the gospel road, the machinations of the record industry, and the sweeping political and racial tumult that was a backdrop to Cooke's meteoric career. . . . To use a gospel-music term Guralnick turns the house out."

— *Kirkus Reviews* (starred review)

"A masterpiece of research and writing, *Dream Boogie* gives us a Sam Cooke [who is] glorious, flawed, but remarkable in his capacity to keep going back into a creative space, no matter what loss hovers around him. In that space, he becomes an alchemist of the most remarkable type, turning even his anguish into art."

— Warren Zanes, *San Diego Union Tribune*

"Guralnick casts a penetrating eye into the darkness. . . . He makes all other music historians look like skimmers."

— Michael Corcoran, *Austin American-Statesman*

"Guralnick, as in his biography of Elvis Presley, displays a feel for the culture that gave rise to the musician, and his account is a revelatory portrait of the rough-and-tumble yet familial world of black show business before and during the civil rights era."

— *The New Yorker*

"This is simply the best music book of the year."

— Greg Haymes, *Albany Times-Union*

"Guralnick, American popular culture's most passionate, rigorous and eloquent biographer, chronicles Cooke's life and career . . . with the grace and consideration that his subject so richly deserves."

— Laura Miller and Hillary Frey, Salon.com

"Engrossing. . . . A respectful, vibrantly human picture of a widely influential, multilayered man. . . . The book really crackles in the chapters that detail Sam's time with the famed Soul Stirrers and his crossover into the secular field. [Guralnick] pulls you onstage and backstage during the chitlin-circuit tours. . . . You feel the energy of the shows, inhale the funk."

— Roshod Ollison, *Baltimore Sun*

"Rich in detail, deeply insightful, sensitive to the complexity of both Cooke's triumphs and tribulations. Peter Guralnick has illuminated the spiritual and cultural world of gospel and soul in which Sam Cooke thrived and pioneered."

— Leon Litwack, Pulitzer Prize–winning author of *Been in the Storm So Long: The Aftermath of Slavery*

"To Guralnick 'what was most extraordinary about Sam Cooke was his capacity for learning, his capacity for imagination and intellectual growth,' which means he was always in transition, best understood by what he had not yet become. [At his death] he had built an empire on myth, pride, and suspended antagonisms, and without Sam it was all gone. All but the music."

— John Leland, *New York Times Book Review*

"Peter Guralnick tells the story like it really is. *Dream Boogie* is the truth."

— L. C. Cooke

"Guralnick's writing is like Cooke's music. You want to follow him down the highways and byways of American music just to see . . . where he leads you. Like his landmark biography of Elvis, *Dream Boogie* illuminates and explicates our culture and history and sets our toes to tapping."

— Susan Larson, *New Orleans Times-Picayune*

"Guralnick makes clear throughout the book [that] in the end Sam Cooke's life, unlike the lives of many of his peers, was not about weakness, hedonistic surrender, or merely being a co-opted victim but about a certain kind of moral and artistic strength built on a sense of pride that was simultaneously sinful and glorious. . . . Someone has finally written a book worthy of him."

— Gerald Early, *Chicago Tribune*

"Scintillating. . . . You will not be able to put *Dream Boogie* down."

— Jeff Guinn, *Fort Worth Star-Telegram*

"There's no real substitute for the sound of Sam Cooke's music, but the detailed descriptions of his recordings throughout this masterful biography are the next best thing to wearing headphones while you read."

— *Publishers Weekly* (starred review)

"Meticulous, thoughtful, driving; Guralnick has done it again, perfectly conveying the essence of American popular culture by immersing us in the irresistible story of this remarkable artist."

— Ken Burns, producer-director of *The Civil War, Unforgivable Blackness: The Rise and Fall of Jack Johnson,* and *Jazz*

"Guralnick brilliantly describes the music [and] plumbs the mystery of Cooke's enthralling charm, intelligence, talent, and ambition. . . . From the richness of his research, he captures an extraordinary, flawed life that — like the music and the era that produced it — is uplifting and suffused with heartbreak."

— John Holman, *Paste*

"Dense, detailed, and utterly captivating."

— David Kirby, *Boston Phoenix*

"Eloquently written and brilliantly researched, *Dream Boogie* is a landmark study of the electrical connection between soul music and the civil rights movement. A stunning achievement."

— Douglas Brinkley, author of *The Great Deluge: Hurricane Katrina, New Orleans, and the Mississippi Gulf Coast;* editor of *Windblown World: The Journals of Jack Kerouac*

"*Dream Boogie* highlights the author's diligent attention to the small details that made his Elvis biographies so impressive [and] in some respects even improves upon those achievements. . . . A model of good biography."

— David Cantwell, *Nashville Scene*

"Guralnick writes like a dream. . . . The prose delivers — through it, Cooke dazzles and disarms with his liquid grace and that impossible voice, just as he did in real life. He sends us."

— Sam Rosenfeld, *American Prospect*

"One can almost taste the fried chicken and poundcake his mother makes for [the family's] summer trips back to Mississippi. . . . The reader is with Cooke at every step as he follows his dream."

— Gail Mitchell, *Billboard*

"Guralnick's storytelling skills are up to the task of tracking a figure as charming, lustful, ambitious, and ultimately inscrutable as Cooke. . . . [*Dream Boogie*] also serves as an illuminating look at America as it reluctantly embraced soul power."

— K. Leander Williams, *Time Out New York*

"Too much pop criticism no longer seems even interested in talking to an audience beyond the small one that will already know what the writer is talking about. . . . I can't imagine how exhausting it must be to work on the scale that Guralnick does, [but] our past needs the love and respect he continues to show it."

— Charles Taylor, Salon.com

"No doubt about it, Guralnick's mammoth, meticulously researched bio of the late gospel-cum-pop singer Sam Cooke is an awesome achievement."

— Tom Sinclair, *Entertainment Weekly*

"An All-American dream set to sweet soul music. . . . The book succeeds thanks to Guralnick's magnificent storytelling powers, which dance right to the edge of a biographer's bailiwick and occasionally shimmy over."

— John Freeman, *Atlanta Journal-Constitution*

"Guralnick describes live shows with such clarity you'll feel you were in the audience. . . . A thorough portrait of a man who, whenever obstacles arose in his path, never faltered in keeping his eyes on the prize."

— Gillian Gaar, *Harp*

"The book is first and foremost the story of a phenomenal individual whose majestic voice and innovative personality helped fuel the rise of a new era. . . . Guralnick doesn't sanitize Cooke's life nor excuse his relationship failures or occasional career missteps. Most important, he links Cooke's stylistic evolution to other major changes within the community, providing a vivid and rich portrait of African American life and culture."

— Ron Wynn, *Book Page*

"Cooke emerges here as a force of nature, extraordinary in his musical ability but even more in the breadth of his ambition and the energy he spent fulfilling it."

— Merrell Noden, *Mojo*

"Guralnick . . . is that rare critic whose writing is as compelling as the music he raves about."

— *Details*

Dream Boogie: The Triumph of Sam Cooke

Peter Guralnick

BACK BAY BOOKS
Little, Brown and Company

New York | Boston | London

Back Bay Books / Little, Brown and Company
Hachette Book Group
1290 Avenue of the Americas, New York, NY 10104
littlebrown.com

Originally published in hardcover by Little, Brown and Company, October 2005
First Back Bay paperback edition, October 2006

PAGE I: *Courtesy of Country Music Hall of Fame and Museum/Hatch Show Prints*
TITLE PAGE: *Photograph by Jess Rand, © Michael Ochs Archives.com*
PAGE XII: George McCurn (Oopie), probably Jesse Whitaker (also of the Pilgrim
Travelers), Sam Cooke, ca. 1957. *Courtesy of Carol Ann Woods*
PAGE I: Sam Cook. *Courtesy of ABKCO*

Permissions to quote from copyrighted material appear on page 748.

Library of Congress Cataloging-in-Publication Data

Guralnick, Peter.
    Dream boogie : the triumph of Sam Cooke / Peter Guralnick. — 1st ed.
       p. cm.
    Includes bibliographical references (p. 707), discography (p. 715), and index
      ISBN 0-316-37794-5 (hc) / 0-316-01329-3 / 978-0-316-01329-1 (pb)
   1. Cooke, Sam. 2. Soul musicians — United States — Biography.
3. African American sound recording executives and producers —
Biography. I. Title.
ML420.C665G83 2005
782.421644'092 — dc22   2005000077

10 9 8 7 6 5 4 3

LSC-C

Designed by Susan Marsh

Printed in the United States of America

For J. W. Alexander and Doc Pomus, mentors in music and life

Good morning, daddy!
Ain't you heard
The boogie-woogie rumble
Of a dream deferred?

Listen closely:
You'll hear their feet
Beating out and beating out a —

      You think
      It's a happy beat?

Listen to it closely;
Ain't you heard
something underneath
like a —

      What did I say?

Sure
I'm happy!
Take it away!

      Hey, pop!
      Re-bop!
      Mop!

      Y-e-a-h!

— Langston Hughes, "Dream Boogie"

Contents

Author's Note   xv

Prologue: "The QCs Are in the House" *(1948)*   3

The Singing Children *(1931–1947)*   7

"The Teen Age Highway Que Cees, Radio and Concert Artists"

   (1947–1950)   29

Soul Stirring *(December 1950–1952)*   65

The Further Education of Sam Cook *(1953–1955)*   94

"Lovable" *(1956–May 1957)*   130

How He Crossed Over *(June 1957–January 1958)*   171

The Biggest Show of Stars for 1958 *(1958)*   218

Sam, Barbara, and Linda *(Christmas 1958–1959)*   268

Having Fun in the Record Business *(1960)*   315

Another Country *(1961)*   355

Boogie-Woogie Rumble *(January–July 1962)*   393

Another Saturday Night *(July 1962–February 1963)*   416

Scenes from Life *(March–June 1963)*   463

Independence Day *(June–December 1963)*   503

Long Time Coming *(December 1963–June 1964)*   537

The Piper *(June–November 1964)*   576

Uncloudy Day *(November–December 1964)*   609

Aftermath   639

Notes   653

Bibliography   707

A Brief Discographical Note   715

Acknowledgments   717

Index   720

Author's Note

S AM COOKE was born into a world defined, but not limited, by its separateness, a world of "twoness," as W. E. B. DuBois wrote in *The Souls of Black Folk,* in which it was impossible to avoid "this sense of always looking at one's self through the eyes of others, of measuring one's soul by the tape of a [predominantly white society] that looks on in amused contempt and pity." It was a world, as DuBois also recognized, so rich, so vibrant, so colorful that, thrown back on its own resources, it created a culture that has in many respects, both with and without acknowledgment, *defined* the American cultural mainstream. This was a community in which imagination and self-invention trumped pedigree, in which, as James Baldwin wrote, there existed "a zest and a joy and a capacity for facing and surviving disaster . . . very moving and very rare. Perhaps we were, all of us," Baldwin reflected in *The Fire Next Time,* "pimps, whores, racketeers, church members, and children — bound together by the nature of our oppression, the specific and peculiar complex of risks we had to run." If so, it was that inescapably shared heritage, Baldwin went on, that helped create the dynamic that allowed one "to respect and rejoice in . . . life itself, and to be *present* in all that one does, from the effort of loving to the breaking of bread." It was that freedom, that "presentness," that vitality which Sam Cooke sought to celebrate. It was that experience which he sought both to embody and transcend.

I have tried to portray a little bit of that world, the world of Dorothy Love Coates and the Gospel Harmonettes and Langston Hughes, Duke Ellington and Zora Neale Hurston, a community whose closeness was reinforced, as Baldwin underscores, not simply by a cultural legacy but by a cruel and systematic exclusion that led nearly all African-Americans to find refuge in the same neighborhoods, the same schools, the same eating establishments and hotel accommodations. That is one of the reasons that Malcolm X and Muhammad Ali, Jim Brown and James Baldwin, Louis Armstrong, Martin Luther King Jr., Jimi Hendrix, James Brown, Jackie Wilson, and Fidel Castro all play greater or lesser roles in this story. My aim, my hope, is to suggest some of the richness and diversity of this proudly self-contained society, some of the sense of self-delight and self-discovery that Sam Cooke's own life and work continue to embody, even set against a bitter backdrop of prejudice and discrimination. At the heart of the story is a man who, while creating some of the most memorable pop songs of a generation, in addition to a universally recognized civil rights anthem, was himself as complex, uncategorizable, and sometimes unreadable as his work was transparent. Exploring this hidden side of Sam Cooke was as much of a challenge, and as rewarding in its own way, as seeking out some of the vanished touchstones of a world all but lost to mainstream history.

"There is one terrible thing," said the filmmaker Jean Renoir, speaking ironically of the imperative of art in *The Rules of the Game,* "and that is that everyone has his reasons." But that, of course, is the one glorious thing, too. It is the human comedy (the human *drama*) that continues to fascinate both in life and in art. The Sam Cooke that I discovered was a constant surprise, as charismatic, as charming and adroit as the man that I had imagined but no more without flaws than anyone you might happen to meet. People sometimes ask: don't the flaws bother you? But I had no interest in whitewashing either Sam Cooke or his surroundings. In the words of Lithofayne Pridgon, a friend of Sam's who was later celebrated for her relationship with Jimi Hendrix, I wasn't looking for any "wonderful white picket fence" or picture-postcard view. I don't think real life, or real art, stems from that. I wanted to be true to a world that celebrated life in all its variegated glory, to a community that never failed to acknowledge that without sin there is no salvation, that if we deny human nature we deny the only truth to which we have access.

What was most extraordinary about Sam Cooke was his capacity for learning, his capacity for imagination and intellectual growth. With his friend J.W. Alexander he started his own record label and publishing company, probably the first such enterprise fully controlled by a black artist. Toward the end of his life he set out to develop young African-American talent in South Central L.A. with what was intended to be a series of rehearsal studios, the first of which he dubbed Soul Station #1. His success was predicated on what his brother L.C. called "second sight," which might be another way of describing his ability to read people and situations with both an empathetic instinct and an analytic cast of mind. He absorbed every lesson that was put in front of him, but his pride in where he came from would not permit him to be defined in anyone's terms but his own.

"I don't even know why I do what I do," Sam said to the young singer Bobby Womack. "When I do it, it just comes." And that's the way his music still sounds: as fresh, as elegant, as full of mirth, sadness, and surprise as when it first emerged, translating somehow across the ages in ways that have little to do with calculation or fashion and everything to do with spontaneity of feeling, with a kind of purity of soul. That's the Sam Cooke I've sought to describe: that rare individual whose horizons kept expanding right up till the day he died. He was always moving on to the next thing. He was always looking forward to the next chapter. And he was always looking to take anyone with him who was ready to go.

Dream Boogie

Prologue: "The QCs Are in the House"

There is no music like that music, no drama like the drama of the saints rejoicing, the sinners moaning, the tambourines racing, and all those voices coming together and crying holy unto the Lord. . . . I have never seen anything to equal the fire and excitement that sometimes, without warning, fill a church. . . . Nothing that has happened to me since equals the power and the glory that I sometimes felt . . . when the church and I were one.

— James Baldwin, *The Fire Next Time*

SIX NEATLY GROOMED, well-dressed young men, sixteen, seventeen years old, the oldest might have been eighteen, slipped quietly into the back of the church.

There they stand, poised, looking out over the heads of the congregation, with only the teenage five- or six-member gospel quartet onstage (with two lead singers, a modern gospel "quartet" rarely limits itself to four) aware of their presence.

The Sunday program that is under way is the same one taking place at any number of Chicago's nearly one thousand black churches large and small, from humble storefronts to cathedral-like edifices; the music that swells the air is the same music you might hear at any one of the hundreds of thousands of Negro churches across the country. But Chicago is the hub of the brand-new gospel movement sweeping the nation. Mahalia Jackson, whose Christmas 1947 release, "Move On Up a Little Higher," has for the first time won her national recognition and established her indisputably as the "Queen of Gospel," calls Chicago her home and may be seen every Sunday at Greater Harvest or Greater

Salem Baptist Church or the First Church of the Deliverance or St. Luke Baptist, where for a time she coached the choir. She may, in fact, be in the house on this particular Sunday afternoon.

The most influential gospel quartet in the country, the Soul Stirrers, so called not just for the effect they have on their audience but for the emotion they reach down for in themselves, have been permanent residents of the South Side for most of the past decade. Robert Anderson, Sallie Martin, Thomas A. Dorsey (father of the new, more emotive gospel style and composer of such classics as "Precious Lord, Take My Hand" and "The Lord Will Make a Way Somehow"), the Roberta Martin Singers, and a host of others, including dozens of eager young teenage quartets whose dreams of stardom center not on the secular stage but on the church, have all flourished in Chicago, their numbers fed by the stream of black migrants from the South that has poured in steadily since the twenties and in ever-increasing numbers in the three years since the end of the war. Indeed, the Soul Stirrers' lead singer, R.H. Harris, whose characteristic delivery, a falsetto "yodel" of unrelenting drama and intensity, has been said to have moved more souls than the weight of scores of uninspired Sunday sermons, is so prominent a figure that he was elected "Mayor of Bronzeville," an honorific proclamation of self-identity, by Chicago's South Side in 1945.

With or without material reward, with or without popular renown, this is a music that seeks at once to embrace and rise above earthly experience. It is the music that has provided hope and succor in the face of what has seemed at times a cruel and hopeless burden, "good news in bad times," as it has been characterized, "a new song," in W. E. B. DuBois' vivid evocation, "America's one gift to beauty [and] slavery's one redemption, distilled from the dross of its dung."

The six boys who have taken their place at the back of the church know nothing of this — or perhaps they do, perhaps they know it all — but they would never attempt to articulate it, they would be embarrassed to hear it described in such abstract, intellectual, and highfalutin terms. The "fire and excitement" is what they feel; it's what they set out to draw from their audience whenever they take the stage, teasing the congregation with practiced, easeful moves, teasing something out of themselves by digging deeper, and then deeper still, until they, too, are transported by what one-time boy preacher James Baldwin described as "a freedom . . . close to love."

Three are preachers' boys themselves; two of these are brothers whose father assistant-pastors the Highway Missionary Baptist Church in a storefront on Thirty-third Street. Little Marvin Jones, the baritone singer with the lopsided grin, has the kind of pugnacious tenacity that would be necessary to persuade a quartet to take on a second baritone voice when the father of the first, Charles Copeland, founded and continues to coach the group. Marvin's own uncle, Eugene Smith, is manager and co-lead singer of the highly influential Roberta Martin Singers. Jake Richard, the older of the two brothers, has matinee-idol good looks and cuts a broad swath through the growing company of teenage girls who follow the group from church to church. They are all polite, clean-cut, fresh-faced, dressed in matching gray suits and carefully knotted ties, with patterned handkerchiefs peeking out from their breast pockets. It is no wonder that they are everybody's darlings, young and old, "Mahalia's boys," recognized and frequently called upon to sing a number whenever they show up at one of her programs. But there is one boy in particular who stands out, one boy who, without saying a word, clearly exerts authority — by his calm, by his bearing, by the quiet self-assurance that emanates from his person. He seems at the same time to offer an invitation to anyone within range of his warm, inviting smile, he clearly possesses the kind of easy grace that cannot be practiced or assumed. This is Sam Cook, the other preacher's son, boyish, slender, his pomaded hair rising in carefully gathered waves.

It is at his signal that the six boys leave their place at the back of the church, march briskly up the aisle, and take their seats, arms defiantly crossed, in the very front row. Throughout the building the cry goes up, "The QCs are in the house, the QCs are in the house." The hapless group onstage — perhaps it is the Crume Brothers or the Holy Wonders or the Teenage Kings of Harmony (And Their Queen) — know that they will have to call the unwanted arrivals up for a song, but they are not even given the chance. The six boys in the front row take advantage of the momentary lull and, at the prompting of their leader, hit a number while still sitting down.

It is all over the instant they take the stage. The group's harmonies are like the Soul Stirrers' in many respects, and they sing much of the older group's repertoire. But the warmth and magnetism that the principal lead singer brings to the songs, the disarmingly seductive tone that he establishes from the start, is something altogether different from anything that has been heard in quartet singing to date. He *caresses* the songs with a voice that is at once smooth, insistent, and utterly beguiling, despite its occasional adolescent tendency to break. The six voices blend and separate, creating intricate harmonies that set off the lead and fill the church with music, in classic quartet fashion, without benefit or need of any instrumental accompaniment. But it is clear that all eyes are focused on the lead singer, even in between songs as he stands poised for a moment biting his lower lip, then leans his head back, closes his eyes, and launches into the familiar melody of "There Is a Fountain Filled With Blood," "The Lord's Prayer," or "He Knows How Much We Can Bear." Somehow the atmosphere is transformed, and the sensuality in the air is almost palpable. As one young girl who saw him a few years later would recall, "He was just singing from his heart, not trying to get you to shout all over the place. He was there to sing and give you the word of God, and you just knew it, you felt it. You didn't have to scream and carry on" — you just kind of *melted*. "Sam was like a magnet," Lou Rawls, one of the Teenage Kings of Harmony, could reflect with perhaps greater appreciativeness in later years. "Wherever he went, whether or not he was singing, the minute he walked into a room, you knew he was there. You always wanted to be around him, just for the fall-out."

The Singing Children

Let me tell you a story on Sam. Sam was always ambitious. He always knew exactly what he wanted to do. When we was very little boys, we were playing, and he had these popsicle sticks — you know them little wooden sticks? He had about twenty of them, and he lined them sticks up, stuck 'em in the ground, and said, "This is my audience, see? I'm gonna sing to these sticks." He said, "This prepare me for my future." Another time he said, "Hey, C., you know what?" I said, "What?" He said, "I figured out my life, man." He said, "I'm never gonna have a nine-to-five job." I said, "What you mean, Sam?" He said, "Man, I figured out the whole system." He said, "It's designed, if you work, to keep you working, all you do is live from payday to payday — at the end of the week you broke again." He said, "The system is designed like that." And I'm listening. I'm seven and he's nine, and he's talking about "the system"! I said, "What are you gonna do, then, if you ain't gonna work, Sam?" He said, "I'm gonna sing, and I'm going to make me a lot of money." And that's just what he did.

— L.C. Cooke, on his brother's early ambitions

S AM COOK WAS A GOLDEN CHILD around whom a family mythology was constructed, long before he achieved fame or added the *e* to his last name.

There are all the stories about Sam as a child: how he was endowed with second sight; how he sang to the sticks; how he convinced his neighborhood "gang" to tear the slats off backyard fences, then sold them to their previous owners for firewood; how he was marked with a gift from earliest childhood on and never wavered from its fulfillment.

He was the adored middle child of a Church of Christ (Holiness) minister with untrammeled ambitions for his children.

Movies were strictly forbidden. So were sports, considered gambling because the outcome inevitably determined a winner and a loser. Church took up all day Sunday, with preparations starting on Saturday night.

They were respectable, upwardly mobile, proud members of a proudly striving community, but they didn't shrink from a fight. Their daddy told them to stand up for themselves and their principles, no matter what the situation was. Respect your elders, respect authority — but if you were in the right, don't back down for anyone, not the police, not the white man, not *anyone*. One time neighborhood bullies tried to block Sam's way to school, and he told them he didn't care if he had to fight them every day, he was going to school. He lived in a world in which he was told hard work would be rewarded, but he could see evidence to the contrary all around him. Their father told them that their true reward would come in heaven, but Sam was unwilling to wait. He was unwilling to live in a world of superstition and fear, and even his father's strictures and homilies were subject to the same rational skepticism, the same unwavering gaze with which he seemed to have been born. He was determined to live his life by his own lights and no one else's.

H E WAS BORN JANUARY 22, 1931, in Clarksdale, Mississippi, the fifth of the Reverend Charles Cook and his wife Annie Mae's eight children (the oldest, Willie, was Annie Mae's first cousin, whom they took in at three upon his mother's death). Charles and Annie Mae met at a Church of Christ (Holiness) convention at which he was preaching, and they started going to church together. He was a young widower of twenty-three with a child that was being raised by his late wife's family. Born to sharecroppers in Jackson, Mississippi, in 1897, he had been baptized into the Holiness church at the age of eight, and when the church split in two a couple of years later (its founders, Charles Price Jones and Charles Harrison Mason, differed over the importance of speaking in tongues as certain confirmation of "spirit baptism," with Mason declaring this surrender to a force that overcomes recognizable human speech to be a sure sign of grace), the Cooks remained with the Jackson-based Reverend Jones, while Reverend Mason's followers became the better-known, more populous (and more prosperous) Memphis-based Church of God in Christ.

All Nations Pentecostal Church, 3716 Langley Avenue, Chicago, Easter Sunday, 1941. *Russell Lee, Farm Security Administration Archives, Library of Congress*

Just fourteen when she met Charles, Annie Mae was fair-skinned, round-faced, with hair she could sit on. She was sixteen when they married in November of 1923. She had grown up in Mound Bayou, a self-sufficient all-black township founded in 1887 and known as "the negro capital of Mississippi." The granddaughter of a businessman reputed, according to family legend, to be "the second-wealthiest man in Mound Bayou," she was raised by an aunt after her mother died in childbirth. She was working as a cook when she met her future husband and by her husband's account won him over with her culinary skills, inviting him home from church one day and producing a four-course meal in the forty-five minutes between services.

They had three children (Mary, Charles Jr., and Hattie), spaced eighteen months to two years apart, before Sam was born in January of 1931, with his brother L.C. ("it don't stand for nothing") following twenty-three months later.

Within weeks of L.C.'s birth Charles Cook was on the road, hitchhiking

The Reverend Charles Cook
and his wife, Annie Mae.
Courtesy of ABKCO

Right: L.C. and Agnes Cook,
ages five and two. *Courtesy of
Agnes Cook-Hoskins*

Far right: L.C. alone.
Courtesy of ABKCO

to Chicago with a fellow preacher with thirty-five cents in his pocket. It
was the Lord who had convinced him he couldn't fail, but it was his children's education, and the opportunity he was determined to give them
to get ahead, that provided the burning motivation. He had sharecropped, worked on the railroad, and most recently been a houseboy in
one of Clarksdale's wealthiest homes while continuing to do the Lord's
work as a Holiness circuit preacher — but he was not prepared to con-
sign his children to the same fate. He was thirty-five years old at the
time, and as certain of his reasons sixty-three years later. "It was to educate my children. It was a better chance up here. In Mississipi they
didn't even furnish you with the schoolbooks. But I didn't put nothing
ahead of God."

Charles Cook preached his way to Chicago, "mostly for white folks,
they give me food and money," he said, for a sermon that satisfactorily
answered the "riddle" of salvation, "proving that man could pray his self
out of hell." Within weeks of his arrival, he had found work and sent for
his wife and children, who arrived on a Greyhound bus at the Twelfth
Street station, the gateway to Chicago's teeming South Side.

It was a whole different world in Chicago, a separate self-contained
world in which the middle class mingled with the lowest down, in which

black doctors and lawyers and preachers and schoolteachers strove to establish standards and set realistic expectations for a community that included every type of individual engaged in every type of human endeavor, from numbers kings to domestics, from street players to steel workers, from race heroes to self-made millionaires. It was a society which, despite a form of segregation as cruel and pernicious as the Southern kind, could not be confined or defined, a society of which almost all of its variegated members, nearly every one of them an immigrant from what was commonly referred to as South America, felt an integral part. It was a society into which the Cook family immediately fit.

From the moment of his arrival, Reverend Cook found his way to Christ Temple Cathedral, an imposing edifice which the Church of Christ (Holiness) had purchased for $55,000 six years earlier, just ten years after its modest prayer-meeting beginnings in the Federal Street home of Brother Holloway. He preached an occasional sermon and served as a faithful congregant and assistant pastor while working a number of jobs, including for a brief time selling burial insurance, before he found steady employment at the Reynolds Metals plant in McCook, Illinois, some fifteen miles out of town, where he would eventually rise to a position as union shop steward.

The family lived briefly in a kitchenette apartment on Thirty-third and State but soon moved into more comfortable surroundings on the fourth floor of the four-story Lenox Building, at 3527 Cottage Grove Avenue (there were five separately numbered entrances to the Lenox Building, with the back porches all interconnected), in the midst of a busy neighborhood not far from the lake. There was a drugstore on the corner, the Blue Goose grocery store was just up the street, and directly across from the Blue Goose was a chicken market where you could select your own live chicken and have it killed and dressed on the spot. Westpoint Baptist Church was on the other side of the street, all the players hung out at the poolroom on Thirty-sixth, and Ellis Park, an elegant enclave of privately owned row houses surrounding a park with two swimming pools in the middle, ran between Thirty-sixth and Thirty-seventh across Cottage Grove.

The new baby, Agnes, was almost two years old when Reverend Cook, through the intervention of one of his original Jackson mentors, Bishop J. L. I. Conic, finally got his own congregation at Christ Temple Church in Chicago Heights, some thirty miles out of town. This quickly became the focus of the Cooks' family life.

We was in church every time that church door was open. That was a must, no ifs, ands, or buts about it. Saturday night Mama would cook our dinner. Then we'd all get up about 6:30 Sunday morning, 'cause everyone had to take their bath — seven children, one bathroom! — so we could be dressed and be at church at nine o'clock for Sunday school. After Sunday school you had eleven o'clock service, with prayer and singing, and Papa would do the sermon for the day. Then Mama would take us to the basement and heat up our food in the church kitchen. Then we had afternoon service, and after that BYPU, which is a young people's service, then the eight o'clock service until about 10 o'clock, when we would go home. Plus Wednesday night prayer meeting! One time Mary, our oldest sister — she was used to doing what she wanted — decided she wasn't going to go to church. She said, "I know what I'm gonna do. I'm going to wash my hair, and then I'm going to tell Papa, 'I can't go to church 'cause I just got my hair washed, and I haven't got it done.'" Well, she washed her hair, and she told Papa, but he just said, "That's all right, just come right on." So she had to go to church with her

*hair all a mess. Papa didn't play. You had to either go to church or get
out of his house.*

— Hattie, Agnes, and L.C. Cook in a spirited chorus of voices recalling
their early religious training

THE CHICAGO HEIGHTS CHURCH, which had first been organized
in 1919, grew dramatically under Reverend Cook's stewardship. The
"seventeen" previous ministers, he told gospel historian David Tenenbaum, had been able to do nothing to increase the size or fervor of a congregation made up for the most part of workers from the local Ford as-
sembly plant, but, Reverend Cook said, "I worked up to one hundred and
twenty-five, I filled the church up. You had to be sure to come there on
time if you wanted a seat."

He was, according to his daughter Agnes, a "fire-and-brimstone
country preacher" who always sang before he preached, strictly the old
songs — two of his favorites were "You Can't Hurry God" and "This
Little Light of Mine." He took his sermon from a Bible text and was
known to preach standing on one leg for two minutes at a time when he
got carried away by his message. The congregation was vocal in its
response, shouting, occasionally speaking in tongues, with church
mothers dressed in nurse's whites prepared to attend to any of the congregation who were overcome. The Cooks didn't shout, but Annie Mae
would cry sometimes, her children could always tell when the sermon
really got to her and her spirit was full by the tears streaming down her
cheeks. The other ladies in the congregation were equally moved, for
despite his stern demeanor, the Reverend Cook was a handsome man —
and despite his numerous strictures, as his children were well aware, the
Reverend Cook definitely had an eye for the ladies. Annie Mae sang in
the choir, which was accompanied by a girl named Flora on piano, and
different groups would come out occasionally to present spiritual and
gospel music programs. One group in particular, the Progressive Moaners, became regular visitors — they always got a good response — and
that is what gave the Reverend Cook the idea for the Singing Children.

THE COOK CHILDREN were all musical, but Charles, the next-to-oldest,
was the heart and soul of the family group. He was eleven, "and I
had to sing every Sunday in church, my daddy used to make me sing all

the time, stop me from going out in the street and playing with my friends."
He and his big sister, Mary, sang lead in the five-member quartet. Hattie,
who was eight, sang baritone; Sam, already focused on music as a career
at six, sang tenor; and L.C., the baby of the group, was their four-year-old
bass singer.

They practiced at home at first but soon were "upsetting" the church
on a regular basis, taking the Progressive Moaners' place at the center of
the service and in the process reflecting as much on their father, Reverend Cook, as on themselves. They sang "Precious Lord, Take My
Hand" and "They Nailed Him to the Cross" with Flora accompanying
them. "We just practiced our own selves and decided what songs we was
going to sing," recalled Hattie. "Every time the church doors opened we
had to be there."

Before long they were going around to other churches and leading off
their father's out-of-town revivals in Indianapolis and Gary and Kankakee.
The entire family traveled together, all nine of them, generally staying
with the minister, but not infrequently having to split up among various
church households due to the size of the group. Each of the Singing
Children had a freshness and charm. They were a *good-looking* family,
even the boys had pretty, long bangs, and the church ladies used to cluck
over that baby bass singer who put himself into the music so earnestly,
and the handsome lead singer — he was a big boy who carried himself
in a manly fashion — but no one missed the little tenor singer, either, the
one with the sparkle in his eye, who could just melt your heart with
the way he communicated the *spirit* of the song. Sometimes, when he got
too many preaching engagements, Reverend Cook would send them to
sing in his place. "When they'd come back, the people would tell me, say,
'Anytime you can't come, Preach, just send the children to sing.'"

All the children were proud of what they were doing, both for themselves and for their father. And their father was proud of them, not only
for causing the Cook family sound (*his* sound) to become more widely
known but for adding substantially to his store of entrepreneurial activities: the church, the revivals, the riders he carried out to Reynolds each
day for a fee in his nearly brand-new 1936 Chevrolet, soon to be replaced
by a Hudson Terraplane, and, when Charles was old enough to drive, a
pair of limousines ("Brother, I made my money!" he was wont to declare
in later years with unabashed pride).

But Charles, a gruff, sometimes taciturn boy with a disinclination to show his sensitivity, soon grew disenchanted with the spotlight. "Aw, man, my daddy used to make me sing too much. I used to get so tired of singing I said, I'm gonna get up there and mess up, and he won't ask me to sing no more, but once I got up there, that song would get so good, shit, I couldn't mess up. I couldn't mess up. But I said, if I ever get grown, if I ever make twenty-one, I'm not going to sing for nobody. And I didn't."

Meanwhile, Sam, the irrepressible middle child, made no secret of his own impatience for the spotlight. Even L.C., who slept in the same room with him and appreciated wholeheartedly his brother's wit and spark, was taken aback by Sam's undisguised ambition. Charles could easily have resented his brother's importunity, but instead he retained a strictly pragmatic point of view. "Well, he had such a pretty little tenor — I mean, it was kind of undescribable, his tone, his singing. But we didn't have nobody to replace him. So we wouldn't let him lead. We were the lead singers, my sister and I. We pretty much had the say-so."

IT WAS A BUSY LIFE. The children all went to Doolittle Elementary School just two blocks west of the Lenox Building, and they were all expected to do well. Both parents checked their homework, though even at an early age the children became aware that their mother possessed more formal schooling than their father, and she would even substitute-teach at Doolittle on occasion. Reverend Cook, on the other hand, conveyed a kind of uncompromising rectitude and pride, which, in all of their recollection, he was determined to instill in his children. "He had a saying," said his youngest daughter, Agnes, "that he would write in everybody's course book when they graduated, and he would recite it to you constantly: 'Once a task is once begun / Never stop until it's done / Be the labor great or small / Do it well or not at all.' He always told us, 'If you're going to shine shoes, be the best shoe-shine boy out there. If you're going to sweep a street, be the best street sweeper. Whatever you strive to be, be the best at it, whether it's a small job or working in top management.' He always felt that you could do anything that you put your mind to."

Everyone was expected to contribute. The girls did the housework. Willie, the oldest, the adopted cousin, was already sixteen and working for the Jewish butcher at the chicken market across the street. At eleven, Charles went to work as a delivery boy for the Blue Goose grocery store. Even the little boys helped their mother with her shopping.

Charles joined the Deacons, a neighborhood gang. Sam and L.C. freely roamed the streets, but there was only so much you could get away with, because the neighborhood functioned, really, as an extended family; if you got too out of hand, the neighbors would correct you, even go so far as to physically chastise you, and Reverend and Mrs. Cook would certainly do the same.

There were still white people in the neighborhood when the Cooks moved in, but by now almost all its residents were black, the shopkeepers uniformly white — and yet the children for the most part thought little about segregation because their exposure was limited to the fact, but not the experience, of it. Reverend Cook, on the other hand, was unwilling to see his children, or anyone else in the family for that matter, treated like second-class citizens. One time the police confronted Charles on the street, and Reverend Cook, in his children's recollection, came out of the house and said, "Don't you mess around with my kids. If there is something wrong, you come and get me." And when the policeman touched his holstered gun, their father said, "I'll whip that pistol off you." He meant it, according to his children, "and the police knew he meant it. Our daddy wasn't bashful about nothing. He always told us to hold our head high and speak our mind. 'Don't you all run from nobody.'"

IT WAS A FAMILY ABOVE ALL, one that, no matter what internal frictions might arise, always stuck together. Charles might feel resentment against his father and long for the day when he could find some escape; the girls might very well feel that it was unfair that the boys had no household responsibilities; Sam and L.C. might fight every day just in the course of normal events. "We was always together," said L.C. "We slept together, we grew up together. Sometimes we'd be in bed at the end of the day, and Sam would say, 'Hey, we didn't fight today,' and we'd fight right there in the bed — that's how close we were!" But the moment that the outside world intruded, Cooks, as their father constantly reminded them, stood up for one another. Mess with one Cook, mess with all.

The children all took their baths before their father came home from work ("We could tell it was him by the lights of his car"). Then they would sit down at the round kitchen table and have dinner together, every night without exception. They weren't allowed to eat at somebody else's house ("If you had a friend, bring them home"). Their mother, who addressed her husband unfailingly as "Brother Cook," never made them eat anything they didn't like and often cooked something special for one or another of her children. Chicken and dumplings, chicken and dressing, and homemade dinner rolls were the favorites, along with red beans and rice. None of them doubted for a moment that Mama loved him or her best of all. She lived for her children, as she told them over and over, and she prayed every night that she would live to see them grown, because "she did not want a stepmother over her children."

After dinner, in the summertime especially, they might go for a drive. They might go to the airport to watch the planes take off; they might go to the park or just ride around downtown. On weekends they would all go to the zoo sometimes, and every summer they had family picnics by the pavilion at Red Gate Woods, part of the forest preserve, family picnics for which their mother provided baskets of food and at which attendance was not optional.

Once a year the family attended the national Church of Christ (Holiness) convention in Annapolis, Detroit, St. Louis, and every summer they drove to Mississippi, spending Reverend Cook's two-week vacation from Reynolds shuttling back and forth among their various relatives all over the state, with Reverend Cook preaching (and the Singing Children accompanying him) wherever they went.

The preparations for the trip were always busy and exciting, with Mama staying up the night before frying chicken and making pound cake because there was nowhere on the road for a black family to stop. Papa did all the driving, at least until Charles turned fifteen, and after the first hour or so, everyone started to get hungry and beg Mama for a chicken leg or wing out of the shoe boxes in which she had packed the food. They all sang together in the car, silly songs like "Merrily, We Roll Along," and read off the Burma-Shave signs that unspooled their message sign by sign on the side of the highway. They all remembered one sequence in particular year after year. The first sign said "Papa liked the shave," the next "Mama liked the jar," then "Both liked the cream," and, finally, "So there you are!" One time, Agnes recalled, they ran out of bread for the cold cuts, and Papa sent her and her sixteen-year-old sister, Mary, into a grocery store — she couldn't have been more than five or six at the time. "Well, Mary went in and picked up the loaf of bread and put it on the counter just like she do anywhere else, just like she would do at home, and the man said, 'You're not from around here, are you?' So she says no, and he said, 'When you come in here, you ask me for what you want, and I'll get it for you.' So she said, 'I'm buying it. I don't see why I can't pick it up. I'm taking it with me.' "

It was a very different way of life. Charles and Mary went out in the fields to pick cotton, but, L.C. said, he and Sam had no interest in that kind of work ("We were out there playing with the little girls, trying to get them in the cotton gin"), and Hattie, who did, was forced to take care of Agnes. One time Sam and L.C. were watching their grandfather pull up some logs in a field, "and he just throwed the horse's reins down when he seen us coming," said L.C. "Well, Sam got tangled up in the reins, and they had to run and catch the horse. And we got Sam back to the house, and he was all right, but I never will forget, he said, 'That horse tried to kill me.' I said, 'No, Sam, the horse was just spooked. She wasn't trying to kill you.' He said, 'No — Nelly tried to kill me!' "

They met far-flung relatives on both sides of the family who had never left Mississippi, including their mother's cousin Mabel, who lived in Shaw and was more like a sister to her, and their father's brother George, who sharecropped outside of Greenville. Their grandmother, L.C. said, was always trying to get Sam and him to stay with her. "She would say, 'You got to come live with us,' but I had a little joke I'd tell her. I said, 'You know what? If Mama and them hadn't of moved and left Mississippi, as soon as I'd gotten big enough to walk, I'd have walked out!' They used to laugh at me and say, 'Boy, you're so crazy.' "

Papa preached and they sang all over the state. To Hattie, "It was really a learning experience," but from Charles' point of view, "We was glad to get there, glad to leave."

THEY SAW THEIR FATHER as a stern but fair man, but their mother was someone they could tell their secrets to. She treated their friends with the same kind of gentle consideration that she showed all of them, never reluctant to add another place to the table or take a mattress and lay it on the floor. "I don't know where one of you all might be," she told them by way of explanation, "maybe someone will help you some day in the same way." If any one of them was in a play and just said "Boo," why, then, to their mother, they were "the best booer in the world."

None of them was ever really singled out. Papa whipped all of them equally, and Mama rewarded them all the same — but even within the family Sam stood out. To L.C., bright-eyed and bushy-tailed, someone who by his own account, and everyone else's, too, "always thought like a man," Sam was similar — but at the same time altogether different. "Hey, I thought I had a personality. But *Sam* had the personality. He could charm the birds out of the trees."

If you tried to calculate just what it was, you would never be able to figure it out. There were other little boys just as good-looking, and there were undoubtedly others just as bright — but there was something about him, all of his siblings agreed, whether it was the infectiousness of his grin, or his unquenchable enthusiasm, or the insatiable nature of his curiosity, he possessed a spark that just seemed to light a fire under everyone he was around. He was a great storyteller and he always had something to tell you — but it was the *way* he communicated it, the way he made you feel as if you were the only person in the world and that what he was communicating to you was something he had never told anyone else before: there was a seemingly uncalculated spontaneity even to what his brothers and sisters knew to be his most calculated actions. He was always calling attention to himself. "He loved to play little pranks," his sister Agnes said, "and he could think of more jokes than anyone else." But why his actions failed to cause more jealousy or resentment than they did, no one could fully explain. Unless it was simply, as L.C. said, "he was just likeable."

To his older sister Hattie, Sam always had his own way of doing things. Sam and L.C. and Charles all pooled their collection of marbles, "but Sam liked to be by himself a lot, too, and he would take those marbles and have them be like boxers in the ring — he made up all kinds of things."

For that same reason, to his ninety-eight-year-old father looking back on it all thirty-two years after his son's death, "Sam was a peculiar child. He was always headman, he was always at the post, from a kid on what he said went. He'd just be walking along the street and make a song out of it. If he said it was a song, it was a song all the way through."

The others could see the contributions their next-to-youngest member made even to such familiar spirituals and jubilee numbers as "Deep River," "Swing Down, Chariot, Let Me Ride," and "Going Home," not to mention the more modern quartet style of Birmingham's Famous Blue Jays and the Five Soul Stirrers from Houston, both of whom had recently moved to the neighborhood. Spiritual music was at a crossroads, with the older style of singing, which the Reverend Cook favored — "sorrow songs" from slavery times along with the more up-tempo "jubilee"-style rhythmic narratives of the enormously influential Golden Gate Quartet — giving way to a more direct emotional style. This was the new quartet sound, with five- or six-member groups like the Stirrers expanding on the traditional parts while featuring alternating lead singers who egged each other on to a level of histrionics previously confined to the Pentecostal Church. Their driving attack mimicked the sound, as well as the message, of gospel preaching, and their repertoire, too, frequently sprang from more accessible personal testimony, like the "gospel blues" compositions of Thomas A. Dorsey. To the Singing Children it made little difference, they sang it all. Their repertoire was aimed at pleasing their audience, but they were drawn to the exciting new quartet sound. Anything the Soul Stirrers or the Blue Jays sang, they learned immediately off the record. But Sam's ability to rearrange verses or rhyme up familiar Bible stories to make a song was not lost on any of them, least of all the Reverend Cook.

It wasn't long before the Singing Children had a manager of their own, a friend of their father's named David Peale who owned a filling station and had plenty of money. He set up church bookings for them, established a firm fee structure ("We charged fifteen cents' admission, and we wouldn't sing if we didn't get paid"), drove them to their engagements in a white Cadillac limousine, and collected the money at the door. They had quite a following, according to Agnes, still too young to join the group. "Everywhere they went, they would turn the church *out*."

Sam accepted Christ at eleven, in 1942, just after America had entered the war — but like all of his brothers and sisters, the religion that he embraced seemed to have less to do with the Church of Christ (Holiness) or their father's strictures than the simple precepts that Reverend Cook had taught them: show respect to get respect, if you treat people right, they in turn will do right by you. At the same time, as Reverend Cook was equally quick to point out, there was no prohibition in the Bible against worldly success; in fact, there were many verses that endorsed it, and as proud as he was of his ability to put enough food on the table to feed a family of ten — *and* to have recently acquired two late-model limousines, a radio, a telephone, and a brand-new windup phonograph — he was equally determined that his children should learn to make their own way in the world.

Sam took this lesson in the spirit, but perhaps not quite in the manner, that his father intended. He established his *own* business with a group of neighborhood kids, with his brother L.C. serving as his chief lieutenant and himself as CEO. "Yeah, tearing out people's fences and then sell it back to them for firewood at twenty cents a basket. *We* did that; Sam didn't do it — he get the money. Sam would have me and Louis Truelove and Slick and Dan Lofton (there was about five of us) to go tear out the fence and chop the wood up — naw, they didn't know it was their fence — and then as soon as we get the money, he take half of everybody's but mine."

He was a mischievous, inquisitive child, always testing the limits but, unlike L.C., not inclined to measure the consequences of his every action. He went to the movies for the first time at around thirteen, at the Louis Theater at Thirty-fifth and Michigan, somehow persuading his younger brother to accompany him. "I said, 'You know Papa don't believe in it.' He said, 'Nobody gonna say anything, and you ain't gonna tell anyone.' I said, 'Noooo . . .' 'Then how he gonna know?'"

"After that we went all the time — me and Sam had a ball. One time there was no seats, and Sam called, 'Fire!' Shit, they wanted to put our ass in jail. But we got a seat. We used to get tripe sandwiches at this little place on Thirty-sixth, they be all covered with onions and pickles, and you get in the theater and just bite down on it, and everybody in the show want to know, 'Who got them tripe sandwiches?'"

Their older sister Hattie still hadn't gone to the movies herself. "I wanted to go so bad, but I was scared of a whipping. Everyone in our group was going to the show, and I had to tell them I couldn't. They even offered to pay for me, 'cause I was too embarrassed to say, 'My daddy won't let me.' But then I finally do go, and who do I see first thing in there? Sam and L.C. And they said, 'Girl, we was wondering when you was going to wake up!'"

Sam, as L.C. saw it, "said just what he thought, whether you liked it or not. If Sam thought something, he would tell you, it didn't make no difference. One time we was going to the movies at the Oakland, on Thirty-ninth and Drexel, and we stopped to get some caramel corn. We come out of the store, and here are these three fellows, and one of them says, 'Hey, man, give me a quarter.' And Sam just looks at him and says, 'Hey, man, you too old to be out here mooching. Why don't you get a job?' He say, 'Hey, man, what you say?' Well, Sam and I put our popcorn on the ground and get ready to fight. But then one of the other boys say, 'Hey, man, don't mess with them. Don't you know they're Charlie Cook's brothers?' Said, 'Charles'll come down here and kill everybody.' So that's what made the boys back up. But Sam didn't care. He said, 'I got a quarter, and I'm going to the show with my quarter. You need a job!'"

His imagination was inflamed by the cowboys-and-Indians movies that ran at the Louis and at the Oakland Theater, too, and when they got home, he and L.C. played at all that "cowboy jazz," which, of course, inevitably led to yet another brotherly fight. There was no question that Sam lived in the world as much or more than any other member of his family: he was bright, he was daring, he was driven by ambition. But at the same time, much of the vision that fueled that ambition came from an interior view, a life of the mind, that was very different from his brothers' and sisters', that was almost entirely his own. Radio, like the movies, offered a vehicle of escape; he was completely caught up in the comedies, dramas, and ongoing serials. But books were his principal refuge from the humdrum reality of everyday life. He and Hattie (and later Agnes) were the readers in the family, each one taking out five books at a time, the maximum you were allowed, from the Lincoln Library on Thirty-ninth. They read everything — adventure books, mysteries, the classics (Sam's favorite was *Huckleberry Finn*) — and they swapped the books around, so that in one week, by Hattie and Agnes' account, they might read as many as ten books apiece. "We would all sit down and read," said Hattie, "we would take turns. Our parents didn't go far in school, but they [valued] education." "But Sam was really the bookworm," said Agnes. "He was a history buff, but he would read just about anything."

H E STARTED HIGH SCHOOL at Wendell Phillips, just a ten- or fifteen-minute walk from home, over on Pershing near the library, in the fall of 1944. His big sister Mary had recently graduated, Charles was entering his senior year, and Hattie was a junior, but Sam, despite his slight stature and some initial reserve, quickly made his mark. It was impossible, his classmates would later acknowledge in the *Phillipsite*, the high school yearbook, to imagine Sam Cook "not being able to make a person laugh." His teachers described Sam as "personable and aggressive," which might charitably be taken as a stab at summoning up something of his bubbling good nature, his vast appreciation of life in all of its dimensions. But whatever his schoolmates' or teachers' opinions of him, however much or however little he may have impressed them, he was probably better known as big Charlie Cook's brother than for any accomplishments of his own. And although he sang in the glee club, where sufficient notice was taken of him that he was given a solo at the Christmas show in his junior year, few of his classmates seem even to have been aware of the existence of the Singing Children, let alone their celebrity in certain circles.

He took over his brother's job at the Blue Goose when Charles started driving for a fruit-and-vegetable vendor. According to his little sister, Agnes, "Sam always drew a crowd, the kids would go in the grocery store just to talk to him." And he joined one of the local "gangs," the Junior Destroyers — more like a teenage social club, according to his brother L.C., which served as a badge of neighborhood identification and mutual protection. "We had to belong to a club to go to school," according to Sam, but he enjoyed the growing sense of independence, the thrill of confrontation not infrequently followed by unarmed combat, above all the camaraderie of belonging to a group that was not defined by his father's church. Everyone's memories of Sam at this time come back to his laugh, its warmth, its inclusiveness, the way he would indicate, simply by timbre, that for him there was no such thing as a private joke. There was another boy in the gang, Leroy Hoskins, known to everyone as "Duck," whose laugh was so infectious that Sam vowed he would one day capture it on record.

For all of his social skills, he continued to insist on his own idiosyncratic way of doing things, no matter how trivial, no matter how foolish this might sometimes make him seem. Charles had by now started working the 3:45 to 11:45 P.M. shift out at Reynolds ("I lied about my age. I got the job because I loved clothes; I was always the best dresser in the family"), and L.C. was working as Charles' assistant on the fruit-and-vegetable truck and pestering Charles to teach him to drive. "I was eleven, but Charles taught me, put me on two telephone books in my daddy's car so I could see. He was gonna teach Sam at the same time, but Sam said, 'No, man, I'll learn myself.' You couldn't tell Sam nothing — he had to do it on his own. He tried to put the car in gear with his feet on the brakes instead of the clutch, almost stripped the gears in my daddy's car. Charles said, 'Sam, you gonna strip the gears.' He said, 'No, man, don't disturb me now.' You know, sometimes I think he thought he was the smartest person in the world."

THE WAR IMPINGED in various ways. Most directly because Willie was in the Army Corps of Engineers overseas — he was in one of the first units to cross the Rhine, and they eagerly followed the news of his division's movements and looked forward to his letters home. Sam and L.C. explored the city, roaming far beyond the confines of the neighborhood, sometimes walking along the lake all the way to the Loop and back, a distance of some three miles, and observing a hub of activity, a sense of entitlement and economic well-being, from which they knew black people were systematically excluded. They read the *Chicago Defender*, too, the pioneering Chicago journal that served as a kind of Negro national newspaper, and took a job selling the weekend edition of the paper on the street every Thursday night when it came out. Their growing interest in girls took them to the skating rink up by the Regal Theater on Forty-seventh Street, where all the big stars of the day appeared — but, true to the strictures of their father, while they may have gazed longingly at the marquee, they never ventured inside to see the show.

They continued to sing every chance they got, going from apartment to apartment in the Lenox Building, with Sam performing pop numbers by the Ink Spots he had learned off the radio and L.C. taking care of the business end. "Sam would do the singing. I just get the money."

The Singing Children continued to perform all around town, wherever their father was preaching or their manager could get them bookings. For all of his reluctance, Charles was a more and more compelling performer who was not about to be distracted from his song. One time when he was little, L.C. watched in amazement as "this lady got happy and jumped up and grabbed Charles — I mean, she was shaking and wiggling him all around — but he never stopped singing. She wouldn't have had to shake me but one time, brother, and I'd be gone, but Charles was bad." At the same time, Sam's gift was increasingly apparent to Charles, who couldn't help but recognize the gulf that existed between a God-given but unwanted talent like his own and the wholehearted commitment that Sam brought to his music. But each of the children, with the possible exception of Hattie, was at this point disaffected in his or her own way. Charles at eighteen couldn't wait to get out of the house and out from under his father's rule. Mary, a year and a half older and working at Reynolds now, too, was going with a young minister at Westpoint Baptist across the street whom she would soon marry, and simply felt that she was "too old to be getting up there singing": it was, in a sense, embarrassing to her.

Even Sam seemed tired of living so much in his father's shadow. "This Little Light of Mine" was the Reverend Cook's favorite song, the one he would sing almost every Sunday before he would preach, and one day, when he was around fifteen, Sam announced, "Papa, I can beat you singing that song." Reverend Cook, never one to take a challenge lying down, said, "Son, I beg to differ. That's my song." But he agreed to let Sam test his theory.

When Sunday came, Reverend Cook announced that his son was going to sing with him, and Sam strode confidently to the pulpit in front of the whole congregation. "All right, Papa," he said, "you start." No, Reverend Cook replied, it was his song, and Sam could start. Then, just as Sam got the people right where he wanted, his father held up a hand and said, "Okay, boy, you can back up now." Bewildered, Sam said, "What you talking about, Papa?" But his father just said, "You can stop singing, it's my song, and it's time for me to sing." And so he did, according to L.C. "Papa took that song, and he wore Sam out with it. Afterwards, Sam said, 'You know I was getting ready to turn it out.' And Papa said, 'Yeah, you was getting ready, but I turned it out. Like I told you, it's my song.' And Sam laughed and said, 'Yeah, Papa, it's your song.'"

To his brothers and sisters it was one more example of Sam's stubborn belief in himself, perhaps the closest that any of them could come to their father's sense of divine mission. And while they chuckled among themselves on those rare occasions when Sam got his comeuppance, no one ever thought to question his good intentions, merely his common sense.

The one time they saw his confidence falter was when the whole family went to hear the Soul Stirrers at a program at Christ Temple Cathedral, the Church of Christ (Holiness)'s mother church at Fortyfourth and Lawrence. It was the first time that any of the Singing Children had seen the Stirrers in person, and they were expecting to get up and do a number themselves. But when they heard R.H. Harris' soaring falsetto lead, and upon its conclusion second lead James Medlock just matched him note for note, they looked at one another with a combination of astonishment and fear. "I mean, we thought we were *bad*," said

L.C., "but that was the greatest sound we ever heard in our lives." They were mesmerized by the intricate patterns of the music, the way in which Harris employed his patented "yodel" (a falsetto break that provided dramatic counterpoint to the carefully worked-out harmonies of the group), the way that he interjected his ad libs to visibly raise the spirit of the congregation, then came down hard on the last bar of each verse without ever losing the thread of the song. That baldheaded old man just stood up there flat-footed and delivered his pure gospel message, with the women falling out like the Singing Children had never seen. After a couple of numbers, Sam shook his head sorrowfully and turned to his younger brother. "Man, we ain't got no business being up there today," he said. And though the others all tried to persuade him otherwise, Sam remained resolute in his refusal to sing.

IT WAS DURING THE WAR that they first heard their parents talking openly about segregation, about what you could and couldn't do both inside and outside the neighborhood. Their father was growing increasingly impatient with the lack of visible racial progress, and he was beginning to grow impatient with his own little ministry as well. More and more he was drawn to the traveling evangelism with which he had started out in Mississippi and which he had never entirely given up. "He was just kind of a freelance fellow," Church of Christ (Holiness) bishop M.R. Conic told writer David Tenenbaum, and soon Charles Cook started traveling again in ever-widening circles, shifting his exclusive focus away from his little flock. He thought he could do better for himself and his family.

The Cooks by now had moved around the corner to 724 East Thirty-sixth, and David, the baby of the family, who was born in 1941, would never forget his fifteen-year-old brother Sam getting in trouble with the neighbors, not long after they moved in, when the couple downstairs became involved in a noisy altercation. "We was all up there having fun, and [heard] this commotion on the floor below, so Sam goes out and leans over the bannister and calls out, 'What's all this noise out here?' The guy shot upstairs — I mean, he was serious — but we all went back inside, and Sam said, 'Well, that's all right, he won't make any more noise.'"

With the war over, Willie went back to work at the chicken market, Mary settled into married life, and Charles enlisted in the air force at the age of nineteen. He was stationed in Columbus, Ohio, and despite his unwavering determination to quit singing altogether the moment he turned twenty-one, he joined a chorus that traveled widely with a service show called Operation Happiness.

But that was the end of the Singing Children, and the extension of another phase of Sam's singing career. Just as he and L.C. had gone from apartment to apartment in the Lenox Building, serenading the various tenants with one of the Ink Spots' recent hits, they had begun in the last year or so to greet passengers alighting from the streetcar at Thirty-fifth and Cottage Grove, the end of the line, in similar fashion. Sam's specialties continued for the most part to derive from the sweet-voiced falsetto crooning of Bill Kenny, the breathy lead tenor for the group that had dominated black secular quartet singing (and in the process enjoyed a remarkable string of number-one pop hits) for the last seven years. Among Sam's favorites were Kenny's original 1939 signature tune, "If I Didn't Care," the group's almost equally influential "I Don't Want to Set the World On Fire," and their latest, one of 1946's biggest hits, "To Each His Own." As in the apartment building, Sam would sing, and L.C. would pass the hat. "People would stop because Sam had this voice. It seemed like he just drew people to him — he sang the *hell* out of 'South of the Border.' The girls would stop, and they would give me dimes, quarters, and dollars. Man, we was cleaning up."

Sam and L.C. harmonized with other kids from the neighborhood, too ("You know, everybody in the neighborhood could sing"). They sang at every available opportunity — Johnny Carter (later lead singer with the Flamingos and Dells), James "Dimples" Cochran of the future Spaniels, Herman Mitchell, Johnny Keyes, every one of them doing their best in any number of interchangeable combinations to mimic Ink Spots harmonies, "singing around [different] places," as Sam would later recall, just to have fun.

His mind was never far from music; one day, he told L.C., he would rival Nat "King" Cole, another Chicago minister's son, whose first number-one pop hit, "(I Love You) For Sentimental Reasons," was one of Sam's recent favorites. But somehow he never seemed to contemplate the idea that he might have to leave the gospel field to do it. Nor did he allow the music to distract him from his main task of the moment, which was to finish high school. Reverend and Mrs. Cook were determined that each of their children would graduate from Wendell Phillips — and it seemed as if L.C. was the only one likely to provide them with a real challenge ("Everybody else liked school; I didn't"). Sam saw education as a way to expand what he understood to be an otherwise narrow and parochial worldview. Reading took him places he couldn't go — but places he expected one day to discover for himself. He was constantly drawing, caught up in his studies of architectural drafting at school but just as quick to sketch anything that caught his interest — he did portraits of his family and friends, sketches to entertain his little brother David. In the absence of inherited wealth, he placed his faith in his talent and his powers of observation, and despite an almost willful blindness to his own eccentricities, he was a keen student of human nature. Which was perhaps the key to his success with girls, as his brother L.C. saw it, and the key to his almost instant appeal to friend and stranger, young and old alike.

His father had full faith in all his children, but perhaps most of all in his middle son. He was focused in a way that none of the others, for all of their obvious intelligence, ambition, and good character, appeared to be — and Reverend Cook had confidence that neither Sam's mischievousness nor his imagination would distract him from his mission. It was Sam's mark to sing, as his father was well aware. "He didn't bother about playing ball, nothing like that. He would just gather himself on the steps of buildings and sing."

It was a gift of God, manifest from when he was a baby, and the only question in Charles Cook's mind was not whether he would achieve his ambition but *how*.

Then one day in the spring of 1947, two teenage brothers, Lee and Jake Richard, members of a fledgling gospel quartet that so far had failed to come up with a name for itself, ran across Sam singing "If I Didn't Care" to a girl in the hallway of a building at Thirty-sixth and Rhodes. He was singing so pretty that Lee and his brother started harmonizing behind him, and it came out so good that they asked him who he was singing with. "I don't sing with nobody," Sam told them, and they brought him back to the apartment building where they lived on the third floor, at 466 East Thirty-fifth, just a block away, and where Mr. Copeland, the man who was training them, and the father of their fourteen-year-old baritone singer, Bubba, had the apartment at the back.

"The Teen Age Highway Que Cees,

Radio and Concert Artists"

THE GROUP THAT SAM was about to join consisted of four boys between the ages of thirteen and sixteen. There were the three Richard brothers: Lee, who sang first lead; Charles ("Jake"), the oldest, who sang bass; and Curtis, whose tenor was the shakiest element in the mix. Creadell Copeland ("Bubba"), the baritone singer, was two years behind Sam at Wendell Phillips and sat next to him by alphabetical arrangement in gym class — "but I didn't know he sang." There had been a fifth boy, Junior Rand, whom they had tried to make into a second lead, but he moved away. And then there was a boy named Raymond Hoy who lived in the same building and was always hanging around. He couldn't sing at all, so they named him MC and let him introduce them at their very infrequent church appearances. They had been singing together for more than two years now, brought together when the Copeland family moved into the same building as the Richards and the boys subsequently became friends. Mr. Copeland worked nights, and when they woke him up one too many times running in and out of the house, he responded with a suggestion that surprised them all. "Let's make singers out of you guys," he said, " 'cause you're making too much noise." He had sung in a quartet himself, and he quickly tuned them up, gave them their voices, taught them to blend, and instructed them in some of the old-time songs, like "There Is a Fountain Filled With Blood" and "Old Ship of Zion."

They scarcely left the house for the first year, said Creadell Copeland. "Then my father took us up and down State Street, all the little storefront churches. We would just walk in right off the street, and sometimes

The Highway QCs. Top, left to right: Gus Treadwell, Jake Richard, Marvin Jones. Bottom, left to right: Sam Cook, Creadell Copeland, Lee Richard. *Courtesy of Barbara Cooke and ABKCO*

there'd be more people in the quartet than in the audience. But we were getting experience."

The experience was not all that satisfying, though. Lee by his own admission was not really strong enough to sing solo lead, and for all of Mr. Copeland's coaching, they could never get the group to "sound together" like their models, the Soul Stirrers and the Famous Blue Jays. They were not even sure enough of themselves to give a name to their quartet. That was the group's situation when Lee and Jake first met Sam Cook.

Mr. Copeland started working with Sam right away. There was no question of the boy's talent, his breadth of knowledge, or his aptitude for music, but Mr. Copeland worked hard with him on his breath control and raising his natural pitch so he wouldn't get hoarse after singing four or five songs. The emphasis was on both precision and passion. Mr. Copeland had the whole group rehearsing their scales, some days for an hour or an hour and a half at a time. And he had Sam and Lee singing off each other, trading leads just like Harris and Medlock with the Soul Stirrers, learning to translate their emotions into the kind of controlled vocal intensity and seemingly adlibbed interpolations pioneered by Harris and standing as the mark of the new "gospel" quartet movement. Soon they were able to match the Stirrers almost note for note on much of their most familiar repertoire, and by the time they were ready to start going out again, they had acquired not only a new sound but, for the first time, an actual name, a name with an undeniable ring to it but one that none of them could fully explain.

They were the Highway QCs. The "Highway" part was obvious enough. Mr. Copeland said, "What are we gonna name ourselves?" And someone said, "The Highways," because they all went to the Highway Missionary Baptist Church, where the Richards' father was assistant pastor. They kicked around different names to go with "Highway" for a little while, but Mr. Copeland said every one of those names was taken, and then out of the blue he just came up with "QCs." Everyone thought that sounded all right, but they asked him what did it stand for? "Quiz Kids," he said. "That ain't no Quiz Kids," said Jake, and Mr. Copeland conceded that maybe it wasn't, but that was the name they stuck with, even though Creadell was a little embarrassed for his father.

He was not at all embarrassed for the group, though. "After Sam joined, we started to make the rounds that we had previously made, but then each time naturally the crowd would get bigger because our reputation became better with the type of lead singer that we had. We started going up on Forty-third. We'd take a PA system with us, and people would let us sing in the barbershops, the barbershops and beauty shops — we'd sing in the window and put the speaker outside, and all the people would congregate and put money in a hat. That's how we bought our first uniforms."

After that they started to move from the storefront churches into some of the larger ones. Some Sundays they would do two programs, one at three, one at seven o'clock in the evening. Then in the summer, when school was out, they began to travel further afield. Mr. Copeland had an old truck, and they'd take half the neighborhood with them — to churches in Joliet, Illinois; South Bend and Gary, Indiana; Detroit; and Muskegon, Michigan. They'd stay out sometimes for as many as three or four days, playing on programs that Mr. Copeland had set up and showing up at others just to "chop some heads." Nobody got paid, Mr.

Copeland supplied all the money for gas and travel, they were just young boys out having a good time, each and every one of whom loved to sing. But of them all, Cope's son, Bubba, was convinced, Sam was probably the most dedicated. "That was just his character. There was never a time he didn't want to sing." He was, as the other boys might or might not have recognized, committed to a long-term goal that was not necessarily confined to the Highway QCs. And now he was on his way.

I N THE SPRING of his senior year, Sam finally got his license. L.C. was already driving and had a duplicate key made so he could steal the car from Sam whenever he was using it. One day Sam busted him to Papa, "and Papa just said, 'Give me that key,' and I said, 'Yes, sir, Papa,' and handed him the key. And went right out and had another one made."

Either Sam or L.C. took their mother shopping on weekends. Every Saturday they would go to Hillsman's downtown, where the quality of the food was better than in the neighborhood groceries, and it was cheaper, too. They got a chocolate milkshake and a hot dog as a reward, and their twelve-year-old sister, Agnes, resented it. "The boys didn't have any [other] chores to do. They were really spoiled by my mother. What made it so hard on me, one of my sisters was seven years older than me, the other ten, so that meant they were out of the house, and all the work fell on me. I used to say, 'I wish I was a boy, I wouldn't have to do this.'"

Agnes resented the way her older brothers felt like they had to protect her all the time, too. "My fondest memory of Sam is when my mom and dad would go out of town [on a revival] and they would take my little brother — so we would have the house to ourselves, because we never did want to go with them. We would just have a ball. But as far as boys were concerned, he would just let them know right away, 'This is my sister. Respect her.' As a matter of fact, all of my brothers were like that. *Leave her alone!* They made sure no one [ever] talked to me!"

He couldn't control who talked to her at a QCs' program, though. Agnes was one of their most faithful fans. "You could always count on a church full of girls, and I was one." She nearly always went with her girlfriend Reba Martin, along with other kids from the neighborhood, and she was enthralled by the way that Sam could captivate an audience by the sheer force of his personality. "He just drew everyone to him. And it made me feel great, because this was my big brother. He wore his hair straight back, and he had waves in it, the top was long and the bangs were close to his head. He was learning, and as he continued to sing, his performance got much better. All the boys had a role that they did outstandingly. They were unique, I think, because they were so young. And everywhere they went, they upset the house. The older groups wouldn't even call them up, because they knew they would turn the house out. I mean, the QCs were the baddest thing out there."

Sam was unquestionably the key. As Creadell Copeland put it, "All we had to do was stand behind Sam. Our claim to fame was that Sam's voice was so captivating we didn't have to do anything else."

What made that voice so captivating to some extent defied analysis. For all the comparisons to R.H. Harris and the Soul Stirrers, there was something different in the young man's approach, there was something about his manner, and the manner of his singing, that was altogether his own.

He had clearly studied Harris. His diction, his phrasing, his gift for storytelling, the way in which he would make extemporaneous "runs" and then end up right on the beat with an emphatic enunciation of the word or phrase that would bring the whole verse into focus — these stylistic traits all echoed the older man's. But where Harris was in the end a "hard" singer, who, for all of his precise articulation, the controlled drama of his delivery, and the soaring sweep of his falsetto flights, bore down relentlessly in his vocal attack, Sam, unlike many of the new breed of quartet singers, sang in a relaxed, almost deceptively simple fashion that reflected not just the breathy intimacy of Ink Spots lead Bill Kenny but the relaxed, almost lazy approach of Bing Crosby, or even Gene Autry, whose "South of the Border" was a staple of his secular repertoire. He was a crooner in a field which, however much the aim of each group was to cause every one of its female followers to fall out, had not put much stock to date in the subtleties of seduction.

He was also, like Harris, a straightahead stand-up singer. Not for the QCs or the Soul Stirrers the acrobatic antics of some of their more flamboyant counterparts, running all over the stage, falling to their knees, tossing the microphone about like a football — maybe the strongest point of similarity between the Soul Stirrers and the Highway QCs was that, sex appeal aside, they were about pure *singing*, first, last, and always.

Sam's older sister Hattie was amazed that he never betrayed nervousness of any kind. To QCs baritone singer Creadell Copeland, what was even more surprising was how well Sam dealt with all the local fame and adulation. There were always girls around clamoring for his attention, but Sam handled them with deference and respect. He never got carried away with his own image and appeared to be genuinely interested in other people. "He was the kind of person who even as a youth, he would always put his hands on you — he would be touching you all the time, and this was long before it became fashionable. He liked to get right in your face if he was talking to you; if he walked up to you, he didn't stand away from you. He had a lot of strange habits that I scrutinized pretty good — because of his talent, and because of the fact that he was so successful in all of the things that he tried to do."

T HE QCs MIGHT MAKE as much as $30 or $35 on a good night, generally less, but the money didn't really matter. After a while they got to the point where they could draw people to a program on their own, but mostly they worked with three or four other young quartets. Their repertoire continued to grow as they took advantage of their newest member's talent not just for delivering a broad range of material but for rearranging some of the old "way-back" numbers and telling familiar stories in new ways. They sang "When You Bow at the Cross in the Evening" and the Golden Gate Quartet's "Our Father," Lucie Campbell's brand-new composition "Jesus Gave Me Water," "Steal Away," and "Nearer My God to Thee," Sam's mother's favorite. When Mahalia Jackson's "Move On Up a Little Higher" came out that winter, they adopted it as their theme song. Sam would turn out the church with it every time — *unless* Mahalia happened to be on the same program.

They spoke constantly of achieving the celebrity and success of groups like the Soul Stirrers or the Famous Blue Jays, they dreamed of escaping the neighborhood — going all over the country, like the Soul Stirrers, with five different changes of uniform and their own limousine. They even talked about singing pop because they knew "that was a fast way to get out there in the world," Creadell observed. "Of course we never did it, but we would talk about it."

They didn't really need to sing pop, though, to see their reputations growing. Or to see the gospel world expanding far beyond the limits that might previously have been imagined. Mahalia's hit single focused attention not just on the majestic voice of the woman who would some two years later headline the "first all-Negro spiritual gospel concert ever

to be presented in famous Carnegie Hall" but on the commercial potential of the music as well. The speaker above the door of the Blue Jays'
record store at Thirty-sixth and Cottage Grove broadcast not only their
own recordings but the recordings of such well-known local figures as
Sallie Martin, the Roberta Martin Singers, and the Soul Stirrers, not to
mention the nationally known groups who appeared on the Stirrers' regular bimonthly programs at DuSable High School, including Cleveland's influential Wings Over Jordan Choir, the Spirit of Memphis, the
Fairfield Four out of Nashville, Detroit's Flying Clouds, and Los Angeles'
Pilgrim Travelers, whose first release on the Specialty label, "I'm
Standin' On the Highway," was outselling even the Stirrers.

Chicago was a hotbed of gospel activity, as the Travelers' new manager and tenor singer, J.W. Alexander, appreciatively recognized. "The
competition was *very* strong. You had Robert Anderson and the Willie
Webb Singers, Silas Steele was singing lead with the Blue Jays, and
Rebert Harris was with the Soul Stirrers. Groups would walk in on other
groups and get called up to do a guest number, and they would try to take
over the program. So it was very competitive." But, as Alexander was
quick to point out, the spirit of cooperation offstage was just as prevalent, and it was the Stirrers who took the Pilgrim Travelers out on their
first national tour and the Travelers who returned the favor by introducing the Soul Stirrers to California. Onstage, said J.W., it was nothing
short of open warfare, with each group doing everything in its power to
wreck the house, but offstage there was a sense of shared enterprise, the
clear knowledge that they were all doing their best to make their way in a
world fraught with dangers, a world in which they were thrown together
not just by choice of vocation but by the unavoidable accident of race.

It was in this spirit that sometime in the winter of 1947–1948,
Rebert Harris and Charlie Bridges, the lead and second lead singers of
the Soul Stirrers and the Famous Blue Jays respectively, along with an
Oakland, California, gospel singer and entrepreneur named Abraham
Battle, put together an organization conceived as a kind of clearinghouse
for the advancement of quartet singing in general and the training and
education of gospel groups in particular.

The National Quartet Convention was, in Rebert Harris' words, an
attempt to "professionalize" the field. "I listened to other groups, and I
felt, along with the other Soul Stirrers, that they needed a change from
what they were doing at that time. They wasn't being accepted by the

public because of their language, their pronunciation, their diction — all of that was completely out of order." What Harris and Bridges and their respective groups did was to establish an organization, and an annual convention, at which courses of instruction would be offered not just in singing technique but in how to present yourself to the public, how to meet people and book and publicize your appearances, how to carry out the business of music in a dignified way, in a manner, as Rebert Harris saw it, that was "spiritually educational," not the scattered "vaudeville-type" approach that he felt at the time was all too prevalent.

The first convention was held at the St. Paul's Church of God in Christ at 4528 South Wabash, and seven states were chartered. Not long after that, the association established its "national headquarters" in the same storefront location at 3838 South State out of which the Young Men's Christian Club had long operated as an interdenominational gathering place. It rapidly became a focal point for the teenage gospel movement, a drawing card every weekend and a kind of central casting call which the Stirrers and Blue Jays frequently attended, along with any other well-known quartet that might happen to be in town. J.W. Alexander would always recall the first time he saw Sam singing with the Highway QCs on one such occasion. The QCs did not impress him all that much — in his view they didn't yet have their own sound — but the young lead singer, for all of the evident influence of Harris upon him, had "something special, he had a particular charisma. People just liked the guy, they could relate to him. I thought to myself: *this guy's a jewel.*"

The Soul Stirrers appeared to have something of a different reaction to the brash young quartet, at least as the QCs saw it. From their point of view, Harris and the other Stirrers were just jealous. They never heard a word about it directly from the older group. But every time they showed up at a Soul Stirrers program and the people would clamor for them to sing, naturally — because what else would they be doing there? — the Stirrers acted as if they didn't even know their young protégés were in the house, and then, when the QCs' fans started to chant their name, Harris would call them up for one song, and one song only. It may well have been that the Soul Stirrers simply didn't choose to interrupt their program — they were on top of the gospel field, after all, and Harris was a supremely self-confident, some might say an almost arrogant individual — but the QCs to a man were convinced that the Stirrers were scared of them, that they could begin to see the handwriting on the wall.

Fifteen-year-old Lou Rawls, a regular at the "singing battles" at 3838 South State, would almost certainly have agreed. He sang with the West Singers out of his grandmother's Greater Mount Olive Baptist Church, along with any number of pickup quartets of his own, but he saw the QCs as representing the kind of unassailable professionalism to which all the young quartets aspired. And he saw Sam Cook as possessing the kind of suave assurance, easygoing manner, natural good looks, and irresistible charm that any one of the quartet singers would have given his eyeteeth for. "We figured if we could all dress alike, that would give us an edge, but Sam just stood out. He didn't have to call attention to himself. It was just there."

Rawls ran into L.C. first at 3838, with his new group, the Nobleaires (Sam had given them the name; the Nobles were L.C.'s gang). He met Sam and the QCs not long afterward, and soon he got to know the whole family. A grave, somewhat taciturn youth whose life had been marked by the absence of both parents (his father's mother had raised him over by the Ida B. Wells Project on Thirty-eighth after his father had left and his mother had gone out to the Coast for war work), he envied the Cooks their relative affluence and stability. "They had a big flat, not one of them little kitchenette apartments, and we'd just go up there and hang. They were just a normal family, you know, children of a preacher, with the usual restrictions, but Sam's mother, if you came around with Sam or L.C. or any of the others, then you were just part of the family. She would feed you, if she saw you doing something wrong, she would chastise you — but you knew she was doing it out of love." He was crazy about Mrs. Cook, he was crazy about the whole family, really, but most of all he was taken with Sam. L.C. he recognized as a player, someone with his eye out for success just for the sake of success — it didn't really matter how it was achieved. But Sam was single-minded in his vision: whatever else was going on in his life, he was going to express himself through his music. There was lots of talent at 3838, but Sam, in his mind, overshadowed everybody, not just for his talent but for his determination. He had no doubt that one day Sam and the QCs would make records and be known throughout the world. Just like the Soul Stirrers.

THE QCs' FIRST REAL EXPOSURE to the Soul Stirrers' world came about in a curious fashion. R.B. Robinson was one of the Soul Stirrers' three baritone singers, a "utility" voice who could sing a number of

different parts. Two years earlier, at the age of thirty-two, he had married
nineteen-year-old Dora Walder in Los Angeles, her hometown, and they
had subsequently made their home in Chicago, where the rest of the Soul
Stirrers all lived. He had known Creadell's father for some time, and
through him he began to hear all about this quartet that Cope was training and in particular about the group's new lead singer. He also met Cope's
daughter, Georgia ("Babe"), who was about to graduate from Wendell
Phillips with Sam, and before long, he was coming around to the house
both to see Babe and to hear the quartet.

From that point on, whenever R.B. came back into town, Cope would
call a rehearsal, and R.B. soon was actively coaching them, teaching
them the songs that the Soul Stirrers sang and giving them the Stirrers'
own arrangements and voicings. It seemed odd to them at first that R.B.
should be "training" them, and odder still when R.B. told them not to
say anything to anyone because he would get in trouble. But they took
him for a friend and listened entranced as he told them tales of the road,
of making as much as $700 or $800 for a single program. The Soul Stirrers' booking policy was scientifically worked out, he explained: if they
played Chicago on a Sunday afternoon, they played Gary that night, if
they played St. Pete on Sunday, it was Tampa on Monday — and everywhere they went, they went first-class. If there had been any question
previously, there certainly was room for none now. With R.B. in their
corner, there was no doubt in any of the QCs' minds of where they were
heading. It was only a matter of how long it would take to get there.

IN THE MONTHS before Sam's high school graduation, the fortunes of
the group rapidly improved. They were booked on a big Mother's Day
musicale presented by the Gay Sisters at Holiness Community Temple
that ran directly up against the Stirrers' annual presentation at DuSable
with the Pilgrim Travelers as their special guests. They were traveling
more frequently to Detroit, Gary, even Indianapolis. And they were gaining more and more public recognition as the up-and-coming young group.

Sam was going with a girl named Izetta who was in L.C.'s class at
school and who was responsible for what turned out to be L.C.'s last
whipping. At fifteen L.C. was no more enthusiastic about formal education than he had been as a child. "So this one time I ditched school, and
Izetta was over the house. She said, 'L.C., we had so much fun at school
today, you should have been there.'

"I mean, we're all at the table eating, and I'm saying, 'Shh, girl,' but Papa heard. He said, 'Annie Mae, did L.C. go to school?' She said, 'He left out of here going to school, Brother Cook.' So he asks me, 'L.C., did you go to school?' I said, 'No, sir, Papa' — 'cause whatever you did, Papa taught us, don't lie. I said, 'Mama sent me out of here, but I didn't make it.' He said, 'What you mean you didn't make it?' And he started whupping me. And everything he would whup me for, I was supposed to say, 'Yes, sir' to. So he asked me, 'Are you gonna be good?' and 'Are you going to do everything your mother tell you to?' And I said, 'Yes, sir, Papa. Yes, sir, Papa.' But then he tricked me.

"He said, 'You think you a man, don't you?' And I said, 'Yes, sir, Papa.' And then he really whupped me. Afterwards, I sat down with my father, and I said, 'Papa, I can't stand no more whuppings.' He said, 'What you mean?' I said, 'Papa, if you whup me any more, I'm just gonna have to leave your house.' He said, 'You are going to leave the house?' I said, 'Papa, I'll do whatever you tell me to, but I can't stand no more whuppings.' And he never whupped me no more again."

Sam had girls everywhere he went — in his friends' and family's observation, he had more trouble fighting them off than he did attracting them — but there was one girl in particular, Barbara Campbell, not quite thirteen and just finishing up eighth grade at Doolittle, to whom, to everyone's astonishment, he seemed inextricably drawn. According to L.C.: "She was my girl first — when we were in grammar school — we wasn't nothing but kids. But then she moved away." She moved back because her mother had just gotten divorced and was about to marry her fourth husband, and her Grandmother Paige, her father's mother, said enough was enough, she was going to keep these poor children together for a while. So they all moved into Grandmother Paige's comfortable, two-story home at 3618 Ellis Park, Barbara and her twin sister, Beverly, and their older sister, Ella, and before long, she began meeting up with all her old friends from the neighborhood.

She ran into the Richards' sister Mildred, whom she had originally met through QCs "announcer" Raymond Hoy when she was living with her other grandmother over on Rhodes. Mildred, whom everyone called "Mook," told her about her brothers' new singing group, and then a friend named Sonny Green reintroduced her to Sam standing in front of the chicken market, where Sam's brother Willie worked.

Sam said, "I know her!" And Sonny Green reacted with surprise. But

she repeated her name, reminded Sam that she was one of the twins, and when he asked, "How old are you now?" at first she said, "Oh, I ain't gonna tell you." Then, when he pressed her, she told him fifteen, and when he challenged that, she compromised on fourteen. Sonny raised an eyebrow, but he didn't say anything, and she told him afterward, with that peculiar mix of flirtation and intimidation that always seemed to fascinate men, "You better not tell on me — 'cause I really like that guy." She knew she loved him from the moment that they first met.

Mildred was the one who helped facilitate the first stumbling steps of their love affair. Barbara would meet Sam over at the Richards' house — they would sit out in the hall and smooch once they were able to get rid of Mook's brother Curtis. Then Barbara started going to church at Highway Baptist, where Mildred led the children's choir. Her grandmother encouraged the friendship because the Richards were preacher's kids, and Barbara started sleeping over at their house on Saturday night and walking to church with Sam on Sunday, stealing kisses along the way. Even though she had other "boyfriends," she had never really cared about anybody before. But they didn't do anything else, because there was nowhere else to do it. Soon Sam started coming around every day, and Mildred helped Barbara sneak out of the house a few times at night, telling her grandmother that she needed to speak with her, giving Sam and her a few minutes to smooch on a park bench. Barbara's grandmother was very strict, so they had to be careful, but with Mildred's help they were able to carry on their "play" affair right under her nose, and before long, Barbara's older sister, Ella, joined them at church when she started going out with Mildred's brother Jake.

Anyone looking at them from the outside might have thought that Barbara was being ensnared by this sophisticated "older man," but to Barbara it was a case of the hunter being captured by the game. She loved Sam, she thought he was so cute with his marcelled hair and pug nose, and she knew he liked it when she told him so. She didn't like it at all herself when he would tease her about her height or the fact that she had no breasts — but she could tell by his impish smile that he didn't really mean it, and anyway, they would grow. And, of course, he never stopped coming around. She knew he had lots of other girls at his beck

3618 Ellis Park. Inset: Barbara Campbell, age eight. *Courtesy of Barbara Cooke and ABKCO*

and call, but with her determination, Barbara felt, for all of his supposed sophistication, he didn't stand a chance.

S AM GRADUATED FROM WENDELL PHILLIPS in June of 1948. He was clearly a young man with a future but not necessarily a future that any-one around him could clearly discern. He had announced his intentions to friends and family: he was not simply going to sing for a living, he was going to be a star. But how exactly he was going to achieve that stardom, whether gospel music would be the vehicle, the QCs the engine of his suc-cess, not even he could have said for certain, even though no one who knew Sam Cook could imagine him singing anything but spiritual music.

He was, in a sense, what they all wanted him to be, providing girl-friends and friends, casual acquaintances, mentors, and fans with the sense that they were "the one," that however little time he might have available for them, all of his attention, all of his intellect, emotion, and charm were theirs for that moment. That was undoubtedly the key to his remarkable ability, both onstage and off, to communicate a message as sincere as it was convincing. And yet at some point inevitably he disap-peared, he would vanish into a world of his own — whether the unex-plored vistas that reading revealed to him, the vast territory of his unrealized ambitions, or a vision of the future that none of them was vouchsafed. For the most part he did it with a grace that minimized resentment, and few doubted that he would get where he was going — but they all felt his absence at one point or another, the elusiveness, the gulf between his apprehension of the world and their own.

That summer, with everyone out of school, the group really started to travel — on programs with the Flying Clouds, the Meditations, the CBS Trumpeteers, and the Fairfield Four. With R.B.'s encouragement, there was more and more talk about making a record. The Soul Stirrers recorded for Aladdin in Los Angeles, and R.B. was always telling them that he was going to set them up with this guy or that guy, but nothing ever came of it. On their brief tour with the Trumpeteers, they cut some dubs one afternoon in a church auditorium in Detroit, but no one knew what to do with the acetates, Cope had no earthly idea, and they just played them once in a while for themselves.

Cope was becoming more and more of an embarrassment, not just to the group but even to his own son. "My dad was the kind of person that Saturday nights he would go out and do a little too much. And Sundays we'd have a program, and he just couldn't make it. So we had to do them by ourselves. That began to happen with more and more frequency, so after a while, we were just sort of out there." He was hard on Bubba, too, forbidding him to travel to any of the weekday programs that would interfere with his education and refusing to even entertain the idea of his son quitting school like some of the rest of them were now talking about doing.

Charles saw them during this time when he was on leave, and he couldn't believe what he was hearing. "They was singing down on Thirty-first and Cottage, and Sam said, 'I want you to come hear us.' I walked in, and it was just so amazing; Sam was singing 'Swing Down, Chariot, Let Me Ride,' and there was something that went through me. I said, 'Man, this boy can sing!'"

Even so, change was inevitable. Cope just wasn't carrying himself right, and Jake and Lee's little brother, Curtis, was becoming increasingly undependable, failing to appear at rehearsals and showing less and less interest in the quartet's fortunes. Not only that: Bubba would soon be going back to school, and that would be the end of touring for a while.

That was how Marvin and Gus came into the quartet.

Marvin Jones and Gus Treadwell had first encountered the QCs at their Mother's Day program. They were both singing with the Gay Singers, an outgrowth of the widespread popularity of the piano-playing Gay Sisters (Evelyn, Mildred, and seventeen-year-old Geraldine), who had sponsored the all-star musicale at Holiness Community Temple in May. Marvin, a small, feisty youth of fifteen, sang lead baritone with the group; Gus, more stolid both in appearance and temperament, sang tenor; and the two Farmer sisters, Doris and Shirley, filled out the group.

Marvin had been singing all of his life. "At five I used to sing this song, 'Pennies From Heaven,' on the stage of the Avenue Theater on Thirty-first and Indiana — I had this little umbrella, and at the end of my song, I would open my umbrella up and the people would be throwing pennies onstage." His uncle, Eugene Smith, was the new manager and dramatic baritone voice with the Roberta Martin Singers, whose classic "gospel blues" composition, "I Know the Lord Will Make a Way, Oh Yes, He Will," had been particularly influential in the new movement. Marvin idolized his uncle. "I wanted to be just like him." And, he was pleased to be able to say, "God gave me the gift to do so."

Marvin and Gus had been partners from childhood on. They were like "two peas in a pod," with their talent for singing and their passion for gospel music. But neither of them had ever encountered the QCs before, even though Marvin had been baptized by the Reverend Richard at Highway Missionary Baptist and Gus' father had known Reverend Cook down South.

From the moment that Marvin heard the QCs sing their first notes, "I vowed that I would not die before I got in that quartet. I had to get in that quartet! Now, they didn't need me. I was a baritone singer, and they *had* a baritone singer already. They were actually looking for a tenor singer, 'cause Curtis Richard just wasn't acting right — so they wanted Gus. But I just started showing up at their rehearsals, and I would grab Sam in the hallway and hit a song. 'Cause I knew if I had that song, Sam would hit it, too, and then Gus would join in, and the next thing you knew, we were singing."

Marvin was convinced that, if it came down to a choice between him and Bubba, he would prevail. "The difference between Bubba's voice and mine was obvious. Bubba had a very light baritone, which did not give the Highway QCs the depth that they wanted, because with a deeper baritone, you sound more like men, more like adults. That's what they were looking for."

That may very well have been so, but in the end, it was Creadell's school situation that gave Marvin the break he was looking for. "It went on for maybe two or three months, and then Bubba couldn't make the program one day, for whatever reason, and we were standing on the corner, talking about the program, and Cope was telling the guys to get their white shirts and things and get them on 'cause they had to go make this church. Anyway, I said, 'You want me to go, too?' And he said, 'Yeah, you can go, too.' That's how I got in the group. I had stopped going to school, and Bubba was still in school. From that point on, I wasn't worried about Bubba. He was worried about me."

As Lee Richard saw it: "That's when we became dangerous — with Gus and little Marvin." When they had Bubba, too, they could field two baritone singers and two strong leads, just like the Soul Stirrers. And even without Creadell, in L.C.'s view, "they had a more stable background." They just sounded more like a real professional group.

Marvin never looked back. As far as he was concerned, the QCs, not the Stirrers, were the number-one group in the city ("We never wanted to be like them; we wanted to be where they were"). And Sam was the number-one attraction. "He was one of the most outgoing individuals that you could ever meet. And everybody liked him. There was no conceitment at all. But he wasn't the kind of guy that you could trick. He always knew how to work it. Even when we was kids, he knew whether we should do it this way or that, spend this or hold on to that — he just always had that kind of talent.

"We went to bed singing, and we got up singing. We couldn't live without it. We'd get done rehearsing at Cope's at Four-sixty-six East Thirty-fifth, across from Doolittle, and then we'd go over to my girlfriend Helen's and eat and rehearse all over again. We were doing what we loved to do, and we did it everywhere, and everybody knew us."

ONE OF THE PEOPLE who got to know them was Louis Tate. Tate was thirty-three and working in a Gary, Indiana, steel mill, with a wife and nine children to support. He had had an early encounter with the gospel business when as a teenager he did some local promotion for the Big Four, a Birmingham quartet, in the area around Covington, Louisiana, where he grew up, and he had been very much involved in the Gary gospel scene from the time of his arrival in that city some fifteen years earlier. He was unprepared, though, for the reaction he felt the first time he heard the Highway QCs. "I just sat there, and I was spellbound," he told writer David Tenenbaum, "'cause I didn't know no kids could sing like that."

As Marvin Jones remembered it, "He approached us at a church program, and he indicated that he had the resources that were necessary for the Highway QCs to make it and he wanted to be our manager. And at that time we were looking for a manager, because Cope — well, Cope drank quite a bit, and a lot of the programs, he didn't go with us, because he was just always in his own world. So we moved on with Tate."

Tate, they soon found out, did not have all the resources that he claimed. His money, as Marvin Jones put it, turned out to be "very limited," but whatever money he had, Marvin and the others quickly realized, he was more than ready to spend on them. "He was very sincere. I mean, this guy sacrificed his family, he practically forsaked his family and quit his job for the Highway QCs."

He went to their parents for permission to manage the group and even obtained Reverend Cook's help in purchasing a '37 Olds to take the group out on the road. Soon they were traveling all over, not just the Midwest but Texas and Louisiana and throughout the South, struggling to make the gigs in their raggedy old car, which according to Marvin broke down "every twenty miles. And Tate would get out in his white shirt and tie and get up under the car and fix it. I remember we was on our way one Saturday to this southern Indiana town for a program and had a guarantee of so much money — the car broke down, and we couldn't get it fixed till Monday, and we missed the program. We set in that car and sulked for two days, eating oranges and apples and bread and you name it. We went down to Tallulah, Louisiana, where Lee Richard had a grandmother. It was the first time this Chicago boy had seen cotton. We did quite a bit of stuff with the Five Blind Boys out of Jackson, Mississippi, with Archie Brownlee; they were the one group that ever 'turned out' on the Highway QCs, but next time we paid them back!"

Tate, as Lee Richard said, put the QCs on the map — literally. "He may not have had a lot of education, but he had a lot of know-how. And he loved us." And Sam took to the road as if he were born to it, which in a way he was. His father was, as Church of Christ (Holiness) Bishop Conic had said, "a kind of wanderer," and just around this time he rededicated himself wholeheartedly to his wandering, giving up his pastorship at the Chicago Heights church for a life committed to the freelance saving of souls. It was a clear choice, according to L.C. The church was "too much of a burden, family-wise. It didn't pay enough. And it was too confining."

Sam was no more inclined to confinement. He loved the gospel road. "He'd eat it, sleep it, walked it, talked it. Singing was his life," Tate said. "He'd wake up at twelve [midnight], one o'clock, two o'clock, and say [of an idea that had just come to him], 'Tate-y! Listen at this! How this go?'" And after Tate had listened and was struggling to get back to sleep, Sam would not be satisfied until he had awakened the rest of the group and rehearsed them in his new approach. It was a great adventure, an experience for which he was voracious in every respect. There were more women than he could ever have dreamt of — but he still couldn't get enough. Tate didn't try too hard to monitor his young protégé, but when he thought "he'd did his thing long enough," he might interject a mild homily on the value of pacing yourself, with little hope of actually influencing Sam. As his fellow QCs by now well knew, for all of his easy-going manner and the breezy assurance of his singing, Sam *always* had his eye on the prize.

None of them really took it amiss. Sam was of a different order from the rest of them, and different rules applied, whether it came to girls or popular recognition (not infrequently one and the same thing). In the observation of Creadell Copeland, still an integral member of the group whenever he was able to make the program: "We all got individual pictures to sell, and we'd try to sell them during the break. I'd sell one on occasion. Gus — I don't think Gus ever sold any. But Sam would sell all of his. He was the handsome boy, and he was the best singer, and he conducted himself that way. But he never got carried away [with himself]. And we didn't have no people we were ashamed of."

Sam never failed to apply himself to his craft, either. He was, as Tate quickly recognized, the group's principal source of material; he had a genuine gift for making old songs new. And he *studied* music. He learned to control his voice better; he was quick to suggest new harmonies and new approaches that the group might try; he found different ways to project his personality in a more professional manner. To L.C., still struggling to achieve a similar degree of success in the same field: "The QCs were the best group I ever heard in my life. As a matter of fact, the QCs had a better sound than the Stirrers. They were more versatile — they could [even] sing pop. The Stirrers couldn't sing no pop. The QCs were so popular, man, look here, those cats could go into a church, and that church be full of kids. Sam *brought* those kids to church. See, Sam revolutionized everything by bringing the kids. *That's* when the Soul Stirrers noticed them."

THE QUARTET UNION OF INDIANA, of which Tate was president, presented its first state program of 1949 on Friday night, May 20, at the Antioch Baptist Church in Indianapolis, where the Pilgrim Travelers had played the month before. It featured the QCs, the Harmony Kings of South Bend, "and all groups of the local union of Indianapolis. Fail to hear this great program, and you will miss the great treat of the new season."

The notice ran accompanied by the QCs' new picture, all six of them (including Bubba), baby-faced and hopeful, looking as if they couldn't wait to grow into their new uniforms.

Through Tate and his Quartet Union connections (the union served as a local branch of the organization that R.H. Harris had founded a year and a half earlier), the QCs were working at least once a month in Gary. Twenty-year-old Roscoe Robinson, who was singing with a local group,

Joiner's Five Trumpets, first met the QCs at one of those programs and was immediately won over. "The first time I heard Sam, he was shouting with the pretty voice. He was killing with that pretty voice — but he was controlling it. And all the young girls — they just couldn't stand it, they were going crazy. So I come up to him and started talking to him and he said, 'Well, man, I like your singing.' I said, 'I just can't sing like you!' He said, 'Man, you ought to come over to Chicago sometime.' And from then on I started coming over, and I rehearsed with them and stayed at Sam's house. His mama would cook for everyone!"

The QCs' following just grew and grew. In every city, they had a group of young ladies who showed up wherever they appeared. In Chicago, Marvin's girlfriend Helen ("Sookie") was at every program, and so was her aunt Gloria — "we used to call her 'Queen.' She was going with Lee, Sam was going with Barbara [Campbell]," and Gus was going with Agnes' girlfriend Reba.

In almost every respect, things couldn't have been better. The only cloud on the horizon was Tate's inability, no matter how great his efforts, to get them a record deal. The Five Blind Boys of Mississippi, still known more commonly as the Jackson Harmoneers and featuring the forceful delivery and bloodcurdling screams of twenty-three-year-old Archie Brownlee, R.H. Harris' most extroverted disciple, were making records for the Coleman label in Newark. So were the Happyland Singers of Alabama (soon to be rechristened the Five Blind Boys of Alabama), four of them graduates of the Talladega Institute for the Deaf and Blind and all in their teens to early twenties. But no matter what he did, Tate couldn't seem to make the right connections. All the record companies would tell him, he explained to the group, was that the QCs were too young, or that they were afraid the boys' voices might change. They all had their excuses, he told his impatient young charges, even as the evidence existed right in front of their eyes to contradict what Tate was saying. Other young quartets were getting contracts: why not them?

They had internal problems as well, not so much stemming from their lead singer's stardom as from lack of leadership on Tate's part. "We *were* young," Marvin recognized. "We were talented. But we were dumb. We didn't have any professional sense. We didn't realize that what you have to do is to utilize all of the resources that you have to make your group better. Which meant that if I could lead on certain things, I should lead on that song. If Jake should lead, let him lead. Because that made the group better. But the rivalry between Lee and Jake, the rivalry between the two brothers — that's where the [problem] was. Because Lee knew that Jake could outsing him, and he never given him any opportunity. And Lee was the kind that was — oh, Lee was bodacious, he'd punch you out in a minute." But Tate was never willing, or able, to intervene.

That was the summer, the summer of 1949, that they went to Memphis. They barely made it, as Tate's car gave out by the time they reached the city limits. The original idea had been to do a program, or a series of programs, sponsored by the Spirit of Memphis Quartet and then move on, but when they found themselves temporarily without transportation, they made the decision, for the time being at least, simply to try to live off the land.

To sustain themselves they went on the radio at the invitation of the Reverend Gatemouth Moore, a flamboyant thirty-five-year-old recent arrival in Memphis himself. Moore, a noted blues singer and composer of the blues standard "Did You Ever Love a Woman," had experienced a public conversion onstage at the Club DeLisa in Chicago earlier in the year in the middle of a song. He had arrived in Memphis on July 31 for a revival at the Church of God in Christ's seven-thousand-seat home church, Mason Temple, sponsored by the Reverend W. Herbert Brewster, the great gospel composer, preacher (at his own highly influential East Trigg Baptist Church in South Memphis), and early civil rights leader. Moore was billed as the man who "turned his back on a million dollars" and sang and preached on an all-star bill that included the Spirit of Memphis, Queen C. Anderson, the soloist at East Trigg who had originated Reverend Brewster's composition "Move On Up a Little Higher," and the Brewster Ensemble Singers, among others.

Off of the success of that revival, Gate, a familiar figure on Beale Street, where he had gotten his start in the thirties and was seen, in the words of the *Memphis World*, as "the Memphis boy who skyrocketed to world fame," was offered a job at the city's (and the nation's) first — and so far only — all-Negro-staffed radio station. WDIA had gradually introduced its new approach to programming from the previous November, and Gatemouth Moore's arrival pretty much completed the process. He called his noontime show *Jesus Is the Light of the World* and not only played records but dispensed counsel and sold advertising ("I'm the first that brought them national accounts"). He had been on the air for barely a month when the QCs arrived in town. "I'm the one that took care of them," he boasted. "Somebody else brought them down, but I was the only religious disc jockey, and I put them on my radio program and advertised them, advertised their appearances, so they could get a chance."

"That's when Memphis fell in love with us," Marvin's memory concurs, "when we did that show on WDIA. B.B. King was on the air then, too, sang that Pepticon jingle. And Gatemouth wanted to manage us, [but] we wasn't interested."

He did help them find living quarters at Mrs. Annie Brown's rooming house, across the street from LeMoyne Gardens, the black public housing project in South Memphis, where he lived. Mrs. Brown furnished them with free room and board, recalled Essie Wade, who had just moved into the Edith Street rooming house with her new husband, Spirit of Memphis "organizer"-manager and sometime singer Brother Theo Wade. "People just helped them. They didn't have any money, so Mrs. Brown just let them stay there. She fed her family, and she would feed all of them — I don't remember how many there were, but there were quite a few!"

They got help from the Southern Jubilees, too, a local quartet whose members were a little older than the QCs and who presented them at a program at New Allen AME on Third Street, where a fifteen-year-old named Cornelia Lee, who was going with the Jubilees' bass singer, was so affected by Sam's performance, by the way he scrunched up his little face and, she thought, sang right at her, that she stuck her finger in her nose. "I never figured why I did it except that I seen somebody else do it and Sam was messing with me." But then Sam went and told her grandmother when he and the other QCs came by after the program, and her grandma scolded her, and she jumped all over Sam as soon as her grandma left the room. The QCs used to come over to her grandmother's house all the time — "they were just little old boys" trying to show off, as Sam would tell her girlfriends and her all about Chicago and act like he was so proud of his "big-city" ways.

Dan Taylor, the Jubilees' twenty-two-year-old tenor singer, was very much taken with the quartet as a unit, but Sam stood out for him almost as much as he did for Cornelia Lee. "I was living on Porter Street, so they was living close around. I knew Marvin and Lee and Charles [Jake] and Gus, I mean I knowed *all* of them — but Sam was a brilliant fellow.

Always fast — talked fast, moved around fast, he was a manic little ras-
cal. But he was a nice dude, and a *good* singer, one of the clearest speakers in any lead or feature singer that I ever heard in my life. You know,
there are a lot of singers that could sing as good as Sam, but they didn't
have the speech he had. He was always a noticeable fellow."

The Southern Jubilees started taking the newcomers around Memphis and then into Arkansas and Mississippi, both out of friendship and,
as Dan Taylor acknowledged, for a specific practical reason. "They had a
manager, and he had a car." For the QCs it was a whole new world. None
of them had been away from home before for any extended period of
time, and they made the most of it in every imaginable way. Sam, of
course, was the main attraction, but there was not a single one of the
QCs, as Marvin pointed out proudly, who was not resourceful. "In those
days you were always invited to dinner. And if one of the girls at a program took a liking to any guy in the group, it didn't matter who it was —
if she would say, 'Why don't you come over for dinner?' our line was
always, 'Well, you know, I can't leave the guys.'" They got a lot of free
meals that way and didn't sacrifice any romantic associations.

The QCs found an even more prominent place for themselves on the
Memphis gospel scene than they had been able to make at home. Perhaps it was their status as out-of-towners. None of the Memphis groups
had yet begun to travel widely outside the mid-South, not even the highly
influential Spirit of Memphis Quartet, who had just begun to make
records themselves. With a number of local gospel unions, though, and
a tight-knit church community, there was an extensive network of booking connections, fueled by a dawn-to-dusk radio station that became
known as the "Mother Station of the Negroes," and the QCs soon found
themselves in the midst of a thriving youth-oriented market that offered
considerably more opportunities for recognition and remuneration than
3838 South State. Other groups their age were just beginning to make
their mark. The Gospel Writer Junior Girls, who had made their Chicago
debut in June on a Women's Day program sponsored by R.H. Harris'
wife Jeanette's group, the Golden Harps, had recently begun broadcasting on WDIA as the Songbirds of the South, and Sam was taken with the
singing of Cassietta Baker (later to become famous as Cassietta George
in the Caravans), one of the group's distinctive leads. He was greatly
impressed by the Reverend Brewster, too, an extraordinary preacher and
polymath whose *Camp Meeting of the Air* was regularly broadcast live

from East Trigg Baptist Church and who presented the QCs at a number of programs at his church. Brewster had not only written many classic songs in the new gospel vein ("Surely God Is Able" was his latest), but he wrote and produced "sacred pageants" every year, often with uplifting racial themes. With his scholarly dignity, wide-ranging intellectual curiosity, and emphasis on elocution ("Anybody could be on the pulpit and beat on the Bible [but I was] taught . . . to stand up there and say my thing just like I was reading Caesar on Gaul, orations of the crown, and the Shakespearean plays that I loved so much"), he proved a natural model for Sam, to whom he taught another of his recent compositions, "How Far Am I From Canaan?," expounding upon it both musically and textually to his eager young pupil. Tate even got them what Marvin took to be a real record audition at a recording studio in town. "The Soul Stirrers had just put out a number, and we were asked to sing that song in the studio. They said, 'If you do it as good as the Soul Stirrers, we'll record you.' Well, as fate would have it, that day we was off track. You know you have [those kind of] days. We didn't make it, and they would not record us."

As disappointing as that failure was, however, it was not their darkest moment in Memphis. Their cocky self-assurance, their prideful attitude, almost guaranteed a succession of falls. The next came when Sam and Lee and Jake took the car one night, leaving Marvin and Gus behind. "They had some girls," said Marvin, "and they took them to the park, and when they got there, the girls were telling them, 'This is a white park. We got no business in here. We're going to get in trouble.' Well, naturally, the guys are from Chicago, and they're not used to this sort of thing, and they thought these girls were just trying to get out of doing what they was going in there to do. Anyway, after they got in the park and settled down, they discovered these lights on them — the police had driven up behind them and put the spotlights on them and told them to get out of the car. Well, everybody got out, and they lined them all up, but Sam was the only one who had his hands in his pockets. And as they went down the line to each person and asked them where they were from, when they got to Sam, the officer got angry because he had his hands in his pockets, and he slapped him and called him a nigger and said, 'You are not in Chicago. We will hang you down here, and they'll never find your body.'

"I'll never forget that. Because when they came home that night, they told us. That was a sad part in our lives. But I told them, 'You didn't have no business leaving me and Gus behind. *That's* why you got messed up!'"

It was another kind of misunderstanding, this one, as Marvin recalled it, over a song, along with a sudden, sharp break with the Spirit of Memphis Quartet, their original sponsor, that ultimately led to their departure from town. "I don't remember the essentials of what occurred, but they literally ran us out." One of the local groups, evidently, had an old syncopated "jubilee"-type number, "Pray," that they had arranged along the lines of the Golden Gate Quartet, "and we heard it one time, and that was it. We took it." Then, according to Marvin, the two Memphis groups entered into a concerted alliance, "they put out insinuations and innuendos about the police looking for the Highway QCs, which was not true." It was all, Marvin said, on account of the way that "we were taking their programs from them." But it created a climate in which it was no longer tenable for them to stay.

It didn't really matter. It was time to go. They had been away now for more than two months and accomplished all that they could. Everyone was a little bit homesick, and Tate, it seemed, was out of ideas.

BACK HOME, SAM GOT A JOB at the Sears warehouse and rekindled his romance with Barbara Campbell. She was fourteen years old, still, in her own words, "green as a cabbage" — her grandmother had never told her anything about sex other than that if she lifted up her dress, she could have a baby — but everyone knew she was Sam Cook's girl. At night Mildred would help her sneak out of the house, and when it got cold, Sam would show up looking so handsome with his broad-brimmed felt hat and belted black trench coat and turned-up shirt collar — he was her "shining knight," and they would walk and talk and smooch till her lips hurt. On Saturdays she would go to the show — he knew exactly where she would be sitting — and they would sit and kiss in the dark all afternoon long.

Barbara never doubted that he loved her, but for all her innocence, she was shrewd enough to recognize that she was not the only one. One time she caught him out in an affair with a girl who hadn't missed anybody in the neighborhood, and when she told him that she knew what he had done, he was so embarrassed that he actually said, "Oh, I wasn't up to that." She was not about to let him off the hook. "Oh, Sam, how could you?" she said with her best impression of wounded teenage innocence.

But she could understand it. It would be easy for any woman to fall for Sam, she realized, with his "beauty" and his "gift of gab" — and, anyway, she had another boyfriend of her own.

For the QCs it was a time of some frustration. They were local heroes upon their return, bigger certainly than when they had left, and back to doing all their regular church programs in Chicago, Gary, Indianapolis, and Detroit. But somehow after the unanticipated adventure of their Memphis sojourn, the free and easy life they had led, it all seemed stale, dull, and unprofitable, in every sense of the word, to go back to living at home. Tate clearly had run out of money and luck, and if he remained as dedicated to them as ever, having named his tenth child Sammie Lee for the two lead singers of his group, they were not necessarily as dedicated to him.

Then Itson showed up, "another unsavory type," as Creadell would later describe him, but with money, influence, and power at his disposal. "Itson impressed us," Marvin Jones recalled, "with the way he dressed, the car that he drove, and the things he could do. Itson came along with his slick-talking ass —" "Yeah, but he really loved the QCs," declared Creadell with a laugh.

Marshall L. Itson had a real-estate company with offices at 5005 South Indiana in the heart of Bronzeville's business and entertainment district. He had a brand-new black fish-tail Cadillac, and he bought the group one of their own so they could ride around town in style. Sam would come and pick Creadell up at school. "I was in my senior year, and the police used to stop us going up and down South Parkway. 'What are you youngsters doing in this car? Get out.' We'd say, 'We're spiritual singers.'" But the police would make them get out every time before they would let them go on their way.

Their new manager bought them brand-new uniforms, too, a double-breasted black suit for each of them and a pair of double-breasted blue ones. They would rehearse behind a one-way mirror at the back of his office, and Marvin and the others got a big kick out of the fact that they could see everybody who came through the door, but the customers couldn't see them. "So they would come in, and we would be singing, and they would be looking around, trying to figure out where the music was coming from."

Itson used to love to hear them sing "When We Bow Our Knees at the Altar" — that was his favorite — and, in fact, when he got them their own Sunday-morning radio spot on WIND early in the new year, they adopted it as their theme song, coming in behind him as he solemnly intoned, "When we bow our knees at the altar" ("At the altar") / "And the family have all gathered there" ("Gathered there"). Itson was crazy about them, and he was crazy about the entertainment life. He was their biggest fan.

It seemed like they were finally beginning to get somewhere. To have their own program on the radio, just behind the Soul Stirrers — now, that was really something. And radio time, as Itson was constantly pointing out, wasn't cheap. Only the most successful quartets could afford to spend $85 for what amounted to a quarter of an hour of advertising. Because that, as they well knew, was the whole point. Even when they were out of town, they maintained the program. Itson had them make transcriptions, big prerecorded sixteen-inch acetates that could be played in their absence to announce where they would be appearing the following weekend, in addition to presenting a regular program of their music.

Itson had business cards made up for them, too, with all of their names listed and a different title assigned to each. Sam was President, naturally; Lee was Group Manager; Marvin was Secretary and Jake Assistant Secretary, while Creadell was appointed Treasurer and Gus named to the position of group Chaplain. "The Famous Radio Teen-Age Highway Q.C. Singers, Heard Each Sunday Morning 8:15 to 8:30," it announced at the top, with Itson's name above the title and all contact information included.

For the first time they were beginning to feel like the full-fledged professionals that they had always wanted to be, a feeling that was only reinforced when Itson scheduled their first big headlining program at DuSable in what was billed as a showdown with their one real rival on the teen gospel circuit, the Teen Age Valley Wonders of Cincinnati, Ohio. The Valley Wonders "mocked" the Pilgrim Travelers as much as the QCs "mocked" the Soul Stirrers — they were a family group made up of two brothers, their sister and father, and the boy singing lead sounded just like Kylo Turner, the Travelers' lead singer. They had done a number of programs with the QCs — both groups tore the show up so bad "they had to open up the doors," said Marvin, "to let the women out of there" — but this time the QCs had a surprise in store for their rivals. The Valley Wonders' big new number was a song the Travelers had just put out called "Something Within Me," and the QCs were determined to take it from them. They rehearsed and rehearsed and rehearsed, and Itson took out a big ad in the March 25 issue of the *Defender,* the same size the Soul Stirrers used to announce their programs. It had their new picture prominently displayed in the upper-left corner and declared:

THE TEEN AGE HIGHWAY QUE CEES
RADIO AND CONCERT ARTISTS

Presents
THE NATION'S FAVORITES

TEEN AGE
VALLEY WONDERS

of Cincinnati, O.

and the one and only
nationally known

Phillip Temple Juniors
OF TOLEDO

It was a confrontation to which they looked forward as eagerly as their fans. But, unfortunately, by the time it took place, their lead singer was in jail.

IT HAD TO DO WITH ANOTHER OF Sam's girls, whose fifteen-year-old sister, a student at Doolittle, brought a "nasty book" that Sam had given to his girlfriend to school. One of the girl's teachers intercepted the "obscene and indecent handwritten pamphlet," and an arrest slip was made out on February 23, the day after Sam was picked up at his parents' house at ten o'clock in the morning. On the arrest slip, which presumably followed a night in jail, he was listed as a nineteen-year-old colored laborer, five feet nine inches tall, 148 pounds, and the object of an obscene-literature investigation. Two weeks later, on March 9, he pleaded guilty before Judge John R. McSweeney in municipal court and, despite his father's testimony as to his good character and decent upbringing and the QCs' belief that Itson had somehow or other fixed it with the judge, got ninety days in Cook County House of Correction. It was, L.C. insisted, more like a reformatory than a prison. "I went out there once or twice.

My dad wasn't too upset, 'cause we didn't really give it nothing. You know, we were good kids; we didn't go to jail for killing nobody. It wasn't such a big deal."

It *was* a big deal to the QCs, though, as even L.C. would concede. "My group, the Nobleaires, really whipped the QCs' ass more than once while Sam was in jail. I mean, we always made the QCs work, but without Sam, we took the program without a fight."

There were other, more immediate repercussions. The big showdown with the Teen Age Valley Wonders took place as scheduled just two and a half weeks after Sam's trial, but with their lead singer "incarcerated," in Marvin's rueful recitation, the QCs made a sorry showing, singing "jubilee-type songs instead of those gospel, 'spiritual' numbers where you [could] go out and excel and get a shout from the audience. The people knew the QCs was in the room — but Sam was surely missed." He was certainly missed by S.R. Crain, the Soul Stirrers' manager, who had come to the program to check out the two groups. He put his money on the QCs, "and I get there and — no Sam. Boy, that hurt me. Those little boys from Cincinnati whipped the QCs so bad I lost everything I had!"

It was a difficult time, as everyone saw it, for both Sam and the QCs. The QCs did the best they could to keep Sam's spirits up, and the authorities even let them rehearse at the jail. But it was, as someone remarked, a "lonely time" for Sam, and it seems doubtful that his mother's and father's prayers made him feel any better. The way he and everyone else figured it, he was the one who was never supposed to get caught; he saw himself, as he told his brother L.C. impishly, as "the all-American boy," a guise he believed that provided the perfect cover in a society predisposed to cherish deference and charm. And yet here he was languishing in jail, unable to convince a red-faced old judge that he was anything more than some little nigger.

His immediate experience when he got out in June was no less unsettling. Itson had booked the group on another tour with the Fairfield Four, and Sam caught up with them in Birmingham. But when he arrived, he made the same kind of mistake he had made in Memphis — he drank out of a water fountain marked "Whites Only" — with the same result. The police assaulted him, he told Marvin and Gus, they dismissed him once again as just another nigger, and his spirits were so cast down he could scarcely even bring himself to perform.

But his spirits were not cast down for long. Itson continued to do everything he had promised he would, the QCs became more and more well known, and soon the time in jail seemed like no more than a temporary setback on the path that had been marked out for them from the start. In the view of Lou Rawls, now a member of the Holy Wonders (with L.C. soon to follow): "When they pull up in that Cadillac, whoa, who's that? That's the QCs, man, you know. The rest of us was driving cars that looked like they was going to fall apart. And they did! They could travel all over, and we was riding on rubber bands."

They even had a "rematch" with the Valley Wonders, and this time it came out the way it was supposed to have the first time around. "We murdered them!" recalled Marvin with open glee. "Sam walked on them that day, and that's a fact." The entire Cook family was there to witness the QCs' triumph. "That boy was bad," L.C. said of the Valley Wonders' lead singer. "He just about fell out singing." "Yeah, but we murdered them, didn't we?" said Marvin with undiminished satisfaction.

Things might have gone on like this indefinitely. The QCs occasionally felt a twinge of conscience ("We really misused Tate," said Marvin, voicing a regret they all came to share in later years. "We walked away and left him stranded without even an explanation"), and they all continued to feel the economic pinch ("We really excelled under Itson, but one of the problems, unfortunately, was that we [still] didn't have any money in our pockets"). But there was little doubt in any of their minds that they were headed for surefire success. Itson still had the connections, he evidently had the wherewithal, and, as they were well aware, he was fully prepared to use it. There was, in fact, no telling where it all might have ended if Itson hadn't disappeared just around Christmastime.

The trouble he got into had to do with apartment rentals. There had been a spate of stories in the *Defender* all through the fall about unscrupulous landlords swindling people through the "rent racket" — which depended on a combination of an acute housing shortage and an abundance of naïveté on the part of renters and included every form of fraud and chicanery, from taking deposits for nonexistent apartments to renting the same apartment to multiple tenants to failing to provide promised amenities and services. M. L. Itson's most egregious crime, it was revealed sometime later, involved a case of outright kidnapping, whereby he had not only taken possession of the assets and property of a wealthy elderly widow, he had imprisoned the widow herself in the basement apartment of his own home. But the QCs knew nothing of this at the time. They only knew that on December 4, without a word of warning, he simply disappeared.

It came as a tremendous shock. They had always suspected he was a little "shady." They *knew* he was a "slickster" who was not above taking advantage of a situation or bending the rules in his favor. But to discover one day that his office was closed up and he was irrevocably gone. . . . Rumors flew all through the neighborhood; it turned out that there were something like forty "rent racket" warrants hanging over him at the time of his disappearance, and there began to be speculation about the fate of the widow whose property he was administering (and who was not actually found for well over a month, "sleeping on a filthy cot" in Itson's basement, her personal needs and hygiene unattended to). Whatever their doubts about Itson, though, none of them had ever expected anything like this. And none of them had expected, with Christmas rapidly approaching, to find themselves in limbo once again.

For all of the QCs it was a bitter disappointment, but for Sam in particular, who at this point could almost taste stardom, it was almost unbearable. To his brother Charles, a player by now who made his living from shooting pool and rolling dice, it was more a matter of "making money and owning Cadillacs. They was little teenagers." Lee Richard, Sam's co-lead, saw it pretty much the same way. "We hadn't made any money. Christmas was coming, and Sam wanted an outfit. Sam [always] wanted to be sharp." But to L.C., there was something else involved. It was not just the economics but the status and the opportunity that making records afforded a gospel quartet. Sam had always envisioned something more.

Whatever the case, something happened at this point that no one could have foreseen. Sam was asked to join the Soul Stirrers as R.H. Harris' replacement.

HARRIS HAD QUIT THE SOUL STIRRERS some two months earlier after what appears to have been a period of considerable turmoil. He had been the heart and soul of the group from the moment he first joined, in 1937, eleven years after the group's original founding in Trinity, Texas, by fifteen-year-old S. Roy Crain, and six years after its reformation by Crain in Houston. With his falsetto yodel, his passionate conviction, his revolutionary approach to quartet voicings (it was Harris who had introduced the concept of two contrasting vocal leads to the classic quartet formation, thereby extending membership from the conventional four to five and sometimes even six), his singing represented, as cultural historian Tony Heilbut has written, "art almost immune to criticism." But he was also, from the time that he first joined the group, a volatile element within it, a virtuoso performer whose own opinion of himself was scarcely less than that of the most extravagant of his admirers and who, without any of the need that less accomplished individuals might be understood to feel, often shaded history to exclude or diminish the contributions of others. Still, he remained almost universally revered within the gospel community, and it would have been virtually impossible for anyone with any knowledge of that community to imagine the Soul Stirrers without their principal lead voice, particularly at this moment in their history.

The Soul Stirrers in 1950 stood at a commercial crossroads. Newly signed to the Specialty label in Hollywood through the good offices of Pilgrim Travelers manager and tenor singer J.W. Alexander, the group had put out three releases on the label by the fall of 1950, with the first, an intense two-part version of the 1905 Charles Tindley gospel classic, "By and By," selling twenty-six thousand copies, and the second, the equally uncompromising "I'm Still Living On Mother's Prayer," up to eighteen thousand on their latest royalty statement. These were good, if not great, sales figures (the Travelers by comparison had sold over 270,000 copies of all their Specialty releases in the first three quarters of 1950), but Specialty owner Art Rupe cautioned patience, pointing out that their old label, Aladdin, had sold no more than five or six thousand apiece of the last few Soul Stirrers releases and that "as you get more records out on the SPECIALTY label, you will build your name up again to where it once was."

Specialty had just set up its own booking agency, Herald Attractions, and with the promise of better-paying dates and the addition, in late 1949, of a new second lead, Paul Foster, as hard-driving as anyone other than Archie Brownlee (and capable of stirring Harris on to even greater heights), the Soul Stirrers appeared to be facing the prospect — or at least the possibility — of a second golden age. That was why Harris' departure was as much of a shock to his own group as it was to the general public.

There were three principal theories for that departure. The first was the one propounded by Harris himself, who was generally recognized as

being among the most "conscientious" and strictly religious of the spiritual singers. As J.W. Alexander, who would almost certainly have characterized himself as a more worldly man, said, "Harris really believed in
what he was doing; he didn't like to joke about it." Or as Harris himself
said to Tony Heilbut, "The moral aspects of the thing just fell into the
water. The singers . . . felt they could do anything they wanted."

Others viewed the matter somewhat differently. Some opined that
with a paternity suit hanging over him in Cleveland, Harris was in no
position to be self-righteous about the moral pitfalls of the road and that
Cleveland was too important a market to be shut out of.

A third opinion took heed of both of the others and, without necessarily negating either, suggested that, as in almost everything else, politics was at the bottom of it all. Harris, as the acknowledged star of the
Soul Stirrers and the single element anyone might view as indispensable, was "pulling a power play" in the eyes of more than one of his contemporaries, quite simply angling for a bigger piece of the pie for
himself.

Harris certainly knew as well as anyone that gospel was at the dawn
of a new, and considerably more affluent, age. On October 8 gospel
music had come to Carnegie Hall for the first time in the person of
Mahalia Jackson and the Ward Singers — but with offers having been
tendered to the Soul Stirrers and the Pilgrim Travelers as well. An article
was just about to come out in the December 1950 issue of *Ebony*, the
Afro-American version of *Life* magazine, which would characterize the
Soul Stirrers as "the top gospel group in the country" in a text that celebrated gospel music culturally and historically as not only "the greatest
contribution of the Negro to the rich musical lore of the U.S." but also a
commercial format in which "gospel singers are earning more today
than many crooners or blues singers." In such a climate it would not
have been difficult for Rebert Harris to imagine that he was holding a
winning hand in seeking merely to be rewarded in a manner commen-
surate with his talents.

Whatever the explanation, and however exactly it was done (Harris
always remembered announcing it at a program at DuSable in the fall,
though, he was quick to point out, he had told the other members of the
group a year earlier, "but they didn't believe me"), Harris' resignation,
once proffered, was immediately accepted. And S.R. Crain, the no-
nonsense founder and business manager of the Soul Stirrers, wasted no

time finding a replacement. After trying out Paul Foster as first lead singer for no more than two months, Crain determined that for all of the passion of his singing and for all of his brilliance in the second lead's role as instigator and foil, Foster lacked both the temperament and imagination to keep the Soul Stirrers on the path that Harris had first set for them. That was when he got in touch with Sam.

It no longer mattered at this point whether he and the other Soul Stirrers had ever actually been jealous of the QCs, as the brash young quartet always believed. The idea that Crain might have planted R.B. Robinson in their midst as a hedge against the day when Harris' ego would inevitably overcome his talent had never even occurred to them. What Crain was first and foremost, though, the QCs all recognized, was a good businessman. And, not surprisingly, he came to their lead singer now, unbeknownst to the rest of them, with a straightforward business proposition.

It was certainly a logical avenue to pursue. Sam knew all of the Soul Stirrers' songs, not just from R.B. Robinson's coaching but because of his own unqualified love for the music. And the timing was certainly right, with Itson on the lam and the QCs in turmoil. Crain invited Sam to his apartment at 542 East Forty-fifth Street almost surreptitiously in the dead of night. They ran through a few numbers, and then Crain asked him to sing W. H. Brewster's "How Far Am I From Canaan?," a number the Soul Stirrers were thinking about recording that Crain was unaware Sam had learned in Memphis from the Reverend Brewster himself. Crain started the song, the other Soul Stirrers fell in behind, and then Sam took it, "he did it precisely and better," in Crain's recollection, "and with his own style!" In Crain's further recollection, there was a second audition that same evening, with Reverend Leroy Taylor, a long-time member of the Norfolk Singers who had sung on and off with the Soul Stirrers for the last couple of years, but if there was, it was a perfunctory affair. There was no longer any question about it: Sam Cook was Crain's boy.

The next day Sam came back to the house in the Stirrers' new Packard with five suits Crain had just bought him for their upcoming tour. L.C.'s reaction was one of unrestrained admiration. "I said, 'Man, you're looking good. I wish I could go with you.'"

The reaction from the QCs and their fans was nowhere near as benign. Even Sam's fifteen-year-old sister, Agnes, felt more than a little betrayed. "Oh, I was hurt, because the QCs were my group — I really related to them. We were all about the same age, we went to the same school, we grew up together. I felt that he was deserting them, and I really didn't like it."

The QCs liked it even less. They saw R.B. as a turncoat, someone they had trusted as a friend but who, they now felt, was nothing but a back-stabber. More than that, they were disappointed and puzzled by Sam. They could understand the profit motive — even Agnes could concede that — but they felt almost as betrayed by the secretive manner in which Sam had come to his decision as by the decision itself. They simply couldn't fathom how someone as articulate as Sam Cook, someone as sure of himself and his actions, almost to the point of arrogance, could fail to even inform them that he was leaving. Instead, he came to them one at a time under cover of confidentiality and discussed the possibility of his departure as if it were no more than a theoretical proposition.

To Marvin he posed the question outright. "We had a program at 3140 South Indiana, Reverend Childs' church. We were sitting in the car talking, and he said, 'Hey, Marvin, if you had a chance to go to the Soul Stirrers, what would you do?' Well, I didn't know it was a loaded ques-tion, so I said, 'Man, if I had a chance to go with the Soul Stirrers, I'd leave in the morning.' And that's exactly what he did. And we were very, very close, we was [practically] in the same skin."

He approached Lee and Jake Richard in much the same way. Lee always remembered how Sam showed up in a brand-new pair of cowhide shoes and a new pair of pants that Lee later presumed the Soul Stirrers had bought for him. "He said, 'I got something I got to ask you on. I want y'all's opinion.' He said, 'What y'all think of me singing with the Soul Stirrers?'" But he never came right out and said he was going to do it.

Creadell, like the rest of them, knew that Harris had left the Soul Stirrers, and he had even heard that Sam was rehearsing with them, "but I didn't give much credence to that, because the Highway QCs were the center of Sam's life — we were a group, and none of us ever thought beyond the group. Then Jake came and told me. That's about all I can remember — I don't remember Sam ever coming to the group and say-ing anything. But I know we were all just devastated."

Reverend Cook alone saw no ambiguity in the situation. Sam came to him for advice, "and I told him, 'Anytime you can make a step higher, you go higher. Don't worry about the other fellow. You hold up for other folks, and they'll take advantage of you.' The only way that he could prove [himself] was to get with somebody that was going somewhere. And the Soul Stirrers were, boy, they *were* — no matter that they tried to snub him, wouldn't let him sing [when he was with the QCs]." To Reverend Cook it was a simple matter of economics. It was a question of making a living. Sam wasn't singing to save souls. There was only one way to save souls, and spiritual singing was not it. Spiritual singing, like every other earthly pursuit, was only a means to an end.

Soul Stirring

The Soul Stirrers were very well named. They tried to get [that] feeling, emphasized and built themselves up on soul-stirring — slower singing, very melismatic. That's why Sam was the way he was. Sam was shaped in large measure by the Soul Stirrers during their rehearsals. He reacted to them as they pushed him, like a good rhythm section inspires an instrumentalist . . .

— Art Rupe

S AM COOK HAD EVERY REASON to be nervous, but he didn't overtly betray it. He remained silent, watchful, polite, while label owner Art Rupe and Soul Stirrers manager Roy Crain debated his presence in the small rehearsal studio at Specialty Records, at 8508 Sunset Boulevard in Hollywood, a day or two before the Soul Stirrers' scheduled March 1 recording session.

Rupe, a balding, bespectacled, tautly controlled and ambitious man with a passion for organization and an unwavering belief in his own carefully worked-out plans and principles, was furious. Despite the fact that the Soul Stirrers had been out on the Coast for the past two and one-half weeks for a series of programs with the Pilgrim Travelers, the thirty-two-year-old Rupe had heard not one word from Crain about changes in the group's lineup. Where was Harris? he demanded of Crain again and again. It was Harris who had signed the contract; it was *Harris* who was the draw. Surely Crain could understand that. The group's record sales on the Aladdin label were at a standstill when they first came to him a little more than a year ago, but he had signed them because of his belief in their lead singer. Who was this kid Crain had brought into the studio?

Crain was crazy to have permitted Harris to leave. Maybe they should just postpone the session until Crain could get him to return.

Crain, a stolid-looking, full-faced, dark-complexioned man of thirty-nine with an abundance of "mother wit" and a pragmatic streak that led him never to challenge authority in a situation in which he did not hold the upper hand, explained patiently that it wasn't a matter of his letting Harris go, that he had, in fact, argued against it, but Harris had plans of his own — and, besides, this kid could sing. And if Art didn't want to believe *him*, he should ask Alexander, who had been out with them off and on for the last three months.

Thirty-five-year-old J.W. (James Woodie) Alexander, variously known as J.W., Jim, Jimmy, Alex, Alec, or Elec, depending on race, gender, occasion, or regional accent, was not as reluctant as Crain to interpose himself in the argument. A tall, soft-spoken, elegantly dressed man with a polished bearing, a deceptively deferential manner of speech, a pealing, high-pitched laugh, and a shock of prematurely gray hair, Alexander had in effect served as advisor and scout for Rupe ever since bringing his group, the Pilgrim Travelers, to the label on the eve of the Musicians Union strike that began on January 1, 1948. Like every other label owner, Rupe frantically stockpiled all the sides he could in the weeks preceding the announced strike, but a cappella quartet singing, he quickly realized, could be a way of getting around the recording ban altogether, since singers were subject to neither union membership nor rules. For the full year that the strike continued, Rupe added to his gospel catalogue and discovered to his surprise that gospel music sold — perhaps not in numbers that could match a big r&b hit, but with a steadier buildup and a longer life span — to an audience whose loyalty ensured that they would not only buy the latest record release but continue to purchase a favorite quartet's back catalogue for years to come.

Alexander had proved himself to the young record company owner again and again, first with the label's two biggest-selling gospel numbers up till that time, "Jesus Met the Woman at the Well" and "Mother Bowed," both of which had sold over 120,000 copies, then by steering such gospel stars as the Soul Stirrers, Brother Joe May, and the Gospel Harmonettes in Specialty's direction. Alex never directly challenged his label "boss," but he always got his point across. And Rupe always listened.

Sam and Lou Rawls, ca. 1952. *Courtesy of Barbara Cooke and ABKCO*

Alexander's message on this occasion was very simple. He had been out with the Soul Stirrers since early December, he had witnessed the kid's very first performance in Pine Bluff, Arkansas, an inauspicious debut by some standards but a program that proved not only the kid's talent but his mettle. He had faith, he told Rupe, in the unique qualities of communication that this boy had exhibited from the time that Alexander had first spotted him two years earlier at the Young Men's Christian Club in Chicago, Illinois.

But he had a contract on Harris, Rupe persisted stubbornly. And he wanted Harris to honor that contract.

J.W. was unfazed. "I said, 'Art, Harris has left the group.' I said, 'You haven't even heard the kid. Why don't you give him a chance?'"

R UPE WAS STILL NOT altogether convinced when they entered the Universal Recorders studio on Hollywood Boulevard on March 1, but, he told Alexander, only half joking, he was willing to allow him one mistake. He hadn't gotten this far in a hard business without learning to trust his instincts. It continued to bother him that Crain had given no advance warning — that was no way to do business. And while there was no question that the kid could sing, he didn't have Harris' authority, he didn't have Harris' command, and there was a real question, it seemed to Rupe, of whether he would ever have Harris' fans. Still, with the group assembled and rehearsed, it seemed like it was worth the gamble — and, in fact, it didn't compare with all the calculated gambles he had already made in setting up and establishing his company.

He had first come to California in 1939 as Arthur Goldberg, from McKeesport, Pennsylvania, with the idea of going into the motion picture industry, but he soon discovered that the record business offered a far greater window of independent opportunity. In 1944 he put several hundred dollars of his savings into a company called Atlas Records, which had advertised in the newspaper for "investor partners." What he got from this experience, as he often liked to say, was an enduring lesson in how *not* to run a record company. One of the principal elements of that lesson was that there was no point in trying to challenge the mainstream record companies — RCA, Columbia, Decca, with their vast catalogues of popular songs — on their own turf. So, having grown up in a mixed neighborhood with a broad exposure to both blues and black church music, he settled on "race music" as his field and invested $200 of his remaining $600 in a selection of 78s, which he played "until they got gray" in order to discover exactly what went into a race-records hit. With a stopwatch and a metronome he made a detailed study of length, beat, feel, and lyrical content, "and I established a set of rules or principles which I felt would enable me to make commercial records. Some of the music moved me so much it brought tears to my eyes."

At this point the logical next step was to establish a company of his own, and this he did, first with the Juke Box label, then with Specialty in the fall of 1946. His study of what constituted a hit paid off with a string of Top 10 chart entries by Roy Milton, Joe and Jimmy Liggins, Camille Howard, and, in 1950, Percy Mayfield, whose inspired plea for racial understanding, "Please Send Me Someone to Love," had hit number one just three months prior to the Soul Stirrers' session and was still riding high on the r&b charts. This number represented not just the commercial culmination of Specialty's efforts to date but the marriage of retail and aesthetic success for which Art Rupe had always striven (Mayfield, a homegrown poet from Minden, Louisiana, was in Rupe's view "as great as Langston Hughes" in his own way). At the same time, his guiding principle in business remained, necessarily, to stay in business. He prided himself on his ability to make the best deal possible from the standpoint of both survival and self-interest (he saw the competition as fierce and, frequently, unprincipled) and then, uncompromisingly, to adhere to it. His guiding principles in the studio were to be well rehearsed, use the best equipment, place the vocals up front in order to emphasize the words — and, above all, bring out the *feeling* in the music. "Gospel was my favorite type of music, not for religious reasons but because of the feeling and the soul and the honesty of it. To me it was pure, it wasn't adulterated, and that's why I reacted to it." As for his own role: "I guess my talent was having empathy for what they were doing and truly feeling it, and also, I guess, being discriminating to a degree, being a hairsplitter. To me the performance was the thing. Making a record to me was analagous to producing a play, with an introduction, development of a plot, even acts and a coda, or an ending. That was the principle that I followed."

T HEY BEGAN THE THURSDAY-afternoon session with what Art considered to be eminently sensible choices. Among the songs the group had presented to him at rehearsal were two by Thomas A. Dorsey, the acknowledged father of contemporary gospel music. The new singer took the chorus on the first one, "Come, Let Us Go Back to God," a morality tale decrying today's sinful ways, his high, plaintive voice coming perilously close to breaking at times as he seemed determined to impress everyone present with the intensity of his feelings. His voice did, in fact, break and even go out of tune a little on the second, a 1939 composition called "Peace in the Valley," which Dorsey had written for Mahalia Jackson but which neither Jackson nor any other gospel singer of note had yet recorded. As the Soul Stirrers did it, the song, with its relaxed, almost country-and-western flavor, turned into a vehicle perfectly suited to showcase the contrast between Sam's lilting gift for melody and Paul Foster's unreservedly exhortatory second lead. They ran through four full takes of the song, each hovering right around the two-minute-forty-second mark that Rupe believed to be optimal for airplay, as Paul doubled the chorus and took the song home while the group chanted hypnotically in the background.

The session continued with varying degrees of success over the next couple of hours. The kid could certainly sing, but Rupe took exception to the easygoing, almost lazy way he sometimes went about it. On the fourth song, "I'm on the Firing Line," which amounted to virtually a solo vehicle, he sang his lead as though he were crooning a pop song, while the group offered little more than the restrained prompting you might find on an Ink Spots record. If this was meant as some kind of new "intimate" approach to gospel, it was clearly one with which the producer had little sympathy, and he cut the group off after one take while writing "nothing happens" on the session sheet.

They quickly did two takes each of three more songs, the highlight being an original Sam Cook number called "Until Jesus Calls Me Home," which once again showed off not only the boy's oddball approach but his capacity to project the kind of warmth that Alexander and Crain swore put him across with the sisters in the amen corner. They had done seven songs at this point, with four, maybe even five, in Art's judgment, usable. He had no complaints about the session. The group had, as always, come in well rehearsed, and he was satisfied that the newcomer at least brought something different to the table. He might even have been tempted to call it a day, except that both Crain and Alexander were insistent that Cook have a chance to do his showpiece number, "Jesus Gave Me Water," which, against all common sense, was the same song the Pilgrim Travelers had had a hit with just five months earlier.

Art argued against it to no avail. Crain and Alexander wouldn't let go of the fact that it was the number that went over at all of their programs, it was one of the songs that Sam had brought with him from his old group, the Highway QCs. Art said he didn't give a damn about the Highway QCs, Alex ought to realize they had just sold twenty thousand copies of the song in a heavily promoted package of five Pilgrim Travelers singles that had been released the previous October.

"You will think that we have gone crazy," Specialty had announced at the time in a publicity release that detailed "an arrangement with Randy's Record Shop of Gallatin, Tennessee to give these five numbers . . . concentrated promotion over a 50,000 Watt Station, WLAC, in Nashville, Tennessee." WLAC operated on a "clear channel," with an unimpeded signal enabling it to reach more than half the country at night. Because it sold much of this time to advertisers like Randy's, which in turn sold its own advertising and used the programming to serve a huge mail-order business, this was perhaps the single forum on which rhythm and blues and gospel records could get national exposure, similar to the Grand Ole Opry's more conventional outreach to country music fans on Nashville's other fifty-thousand-watt clear-channel station, WSM.

Rupe's unconventional strategy had worked, selling nearly 115,000 copies of the five simultaneously released records and validating his promise that they all had a "profit pedigree." How much more profit was to be mined from any of the songs, let alone "Jesus Gave Me Water," which had already seen competing versions by Clara Ward and the Ward Singers and the Famous Blue Jays as well? Crain and Alex were adamant, though, that he should at least give Sam's version a chance. And in the end he relented.

From the very first notes, as Sam's tenor wafts over the Soul Stirrers' repeated background chant, it is obvious that he is singing with a confidence and flair that have not appeared so unambiguously until now. With the introduction of the narrative itself, as the first verse kicks in behind the chorus, it is equally obvious that here is something completely different from the Pilgrim Travelers' funereal presentation, that Sam is here to tell a joyful *story*, that he will relate the entire text of the Bible tale in three richly diversified verses and four choruses — and all in the same length of time it took the Travelers to complete the single verse and chorus that made up their record. The brisk, almost dancing vocal arrangement gives free rein to the most flexible and *playful* elements of Sam's voice, and the melisma that Rupe sought to encourage in all his singers here is used to draw out the story line in much the same way that the insertion of additional adjectives into the basic text ("Living, loving, lasting water") postpones resolution to bring home the point. Several times in the course of the song, Sam fully develops that lilting manner of teasing out the melody that he has only experimented with before, elongating the pronunciation of the central element of the story until it becomes a kind of patented ululation ("wa-a-a-a-ter") that occupies the listener's attention in a manner that becomes its own text. There are moments in the performance in which there is evidence of strain — there are a lot of words, Sam has a lengthy story to tell, and he becomes breathless and a little hoarse here and there. But all in all it is a bravura piece, a startlingly bold performance from the fresh-faced twenty-year-old, and it was clear that for all his doubts Art Rupe was finally won over. Only two takes of the song (with one second's time difference between them) were necessary to get it right, and there was little question, in Rupe's or Roy Crain's or anyone else's mind, what the next Soul Stirrers single was going to be.

The rest of the session was anticlimactic for the producer. The group did a couple of takes of "He's My Rock," a showpiece for Paul Foster, but Art didn't see any commercial potential in it, and he dismissed "How Far Am I From Canaan?," the song Sam was proudest of, the one he had learned from Reverend Brewster in Memphis, as lacking the kind of unrestrained spirit or drive that he was looking for from all of his spiritual singers. "Put all the showmanship that you can in your voices," he wrote to one of his gospel groups. "SING LIKE YOU ARE IN A BATTLE WITH THE BLIND BOYS, THE SPIRITS, AND THE PILGRIM TRAVELERS, and you are following them and they have done such a good job that they already tore the building down, and it looks like you all can't do much more. Then you all come on and really shout and make everybody happier and make the old sisters fall out and REALLY TEAR DOWN THE BUILDING!!! NOW, THAT'S THE WAY YOU MUST SING ON THESE RECORDS!"

Sam, in contrast, sang the familiar Brewster number with an ease that set the song apart, with even more of the casual insouciance that he had brought to "Jesus Gave Me Water" — but it ran to nearly three min-utes, too long by Rupe's exacting standards, and the producer clearly did not recognize the intensity that was imparted by the very effortlessness of its performance. For the first time the seductiveness of Sam's voice is showcased — it is a truly masterful performance replete with all of his most accomplished vocal curlicues and embellishments — but Rupe never seriously considered it for release. Still, even as they ran out of time on yet another demonstration of the kid's peculiar inclination toward melodic delicacy and fancy filigree, and on a number ("Christ Is All") that Art almost certainly felt the Harris-led Soul Stirrers had done stronger and better at their last session, he and everyone present had reason to feel proud and optimistic about the future. In the face of the most daunting adversity, as even Rupe himself would have had to admit, young Sam Cook had come through.

IT HAD NOT ALWAYS SEEMED so certain, even to Crain and Alexander, Sam's staunchest supporters. Crain in fact had had his gravest mo-ments of doubt when the Soul Stirrers and the Pilgrim Travelers had played their first few dates together, starting in Pine Bluff in early December. Alexander's quartet was one of the most flamboyant groups on the road, self-described "Texas cowboys" who, in J.W.'s own words, would stop at nothing to get the crowd: "We'd jump off the stage and run up the aisles, we got to moving and people got to shouting [while] the Stirrers would stand and put one hand in their bosom and just sing." The Travelers had two superlative lead singers, Kylo Turner and Keith Barber — the first could mesmerize an audience like Bill Kenny of the Ink Spots while bending his notes with all the intricacy of R.H. Harris; his cousin, Barber, could scream with the best of them. And the two of them together could always be counted on to wreck the house.

The Five Blind Boys of Mississippi were on the same bill, and while the Highway QCs had generally managed to hold their own against the Blind Boys when the two groups were just starting out, the Blind Boys' lead singer, Archie Brownlee, probably the most intense of all the screamers, had come a long way since then. "You could stand next to Archie onstage," J.W. Alexander said, "and he could shake you." The Blind Boys' other lead singer, Reverend Percell Perkins, who functioned as their sighted manager, was a screamer, too, and, according to Crain, "Perkins could make Archie jump offstage quicker than the boys could see." With their latest release, "Our Father," the kind of hit the crowd started calling for even before they reached the stage, the Blind Boys were a force to be reckoned with, and their entrance alone, with the five of them trudging down the aisle, each with his hand on the next one's shoulder amidst a mounting crescendo of screams from the audience, was pure theater in and of itself.

"In Pine Bluff, Archie and Turner and them Travelers just [tore] the house down," Crain always liked to recount, as if it were a treaty-signing ceremony that he was recalling at which the Stirrers, like Robert E. Lee at Appomattox, were forced to admit defeat. "We sang 'Jesus Gave Me Water' and 'How Far Am I From Canaan?,' but they just whipped us about the ears. They was glad to get back at us, because we was tumbling on them when Harris was there." It didn't stop with the end of the program, though. Both of Alexander's lead singers and the Five Blind Boys stayed on Sam, ragging him as a "lightweight" and calling him "the rookie." Percell Perkins even went so far as to say, "Boy, don't you try to holler with us, we gonna lay the wood on you," and Crain was so disturbed that he went to Alexander and asked if he had made a mistake. Alex just looked at him gravely and shook his head. "Crain, I like him," he said, "and if you don't mind, I'd like to talk to him."

So he took Sam aside and told him not to pay those fellows any mind — they were just jealous of the way the young girls had flocked around him after the program. "You don't have to holler with those guys," he said. "Just be sure you're singing loud enough for the people to hear you — and then be certain they can understand you." It was all, J.W. said, about getting your message across. And Sam accepted it. "He soaked it up like a sponge. Because [he could see] that I was not a screamer, but I could come up behind the screamer and always get the house." That, said J.W., with his calm, imperturbable manner, was what Sam, too, would be able to do. He simply had to be patient.

But it was at times an extraordinarily painful process. Every night, it seemed, he faced the same humiliation. The Blind Boys and the Travelers killed him. No matter what he did or how hard he tried, they showed little compassion for his youth onstage, even as they warmed up to him in the midst of all the camaraderie, hardship, joy, danger, and outright prejudice that they inevitably shared offstage. "Archie could make an audience cry," said another young singer just coming up in that world. "I mean, the whole place would be shouting and falling out, and he would tell Sam, 'See, that old pretty shit you doing ain't about nothing.'" Sam took it even more to heart because Archie was the only singer out there who could make *him* cry. Archie made him look bad — and the audience kept on calling for Harris. It was "devastating," Sam told a friend, to have to get up onstage when he knew the people didn't want him. It challenged his very belief in himself.

But he persevered. He gave no thought to quitting, as Alex and Crain continued to reassure him, and Crain coached him patiently day after day. It was Crain's gift, as he saw it, to train singers — he didn't have the voice to lead himself, but he had trained Harris to fit into the Soul Stirrers' *system,* and now he was determined to train Sam. "It might seem a little braggy-like, but it's no brag. S.R. Crain could see something in singers," he declared self-referentially. "It wasn't a matter of me fitting into Sam's life, it was a matter of Sam fitting into mine. Of course he was a good learner in every respect. He kept an armful of books. [Whatever you tried to teach him] he could learn."

Some of the other Stirrers were more dubious. In fact, with the exception of R.B. Robinson, who had so effectively trained the QCs himself, they were almost as doubtful at first as the Blind Boys and the Pilgrim Travelers. Some ten to twenty years older than their new lead singer, they cast a baleful eye on both his youth and what they viewed as his stylistic immaturity. "Sam started as a bad imitation of Harris," commented J.J. Farley, the baritone singer from Crain's hometown of Trinity, Texas, who had joined the group in 1936. And even Paul Foster, the thirty-year-old second lead who fully recognized that the group needed a "seller" out front, worried at first that Sam didn't have either the weight or rhythmic intensity of Harris. "'Jesus Gave Me Water' — that's easy. You can sing that without even perspiring. [But] you get up there and sing 'By and By,' you got to *work* that number to get something out of it, because there ain't nothing in there to sell. 'Peace in the Valley,' 'Love the Lord,' all those hard gospel numbers — you got to lay off them [sometimes] because you can hurt your own self." Sam, as Foster saw it, was too inclined to lay off. Paul would be looking to Sam to lift him, just like Harris always had, and Sam would just try to turn it back over to him. "I was slow, draggy, I had the voice, but I wasn't in no hurry until I could see I had it to do. Sam would say, 'Come on, help me, man, we're going to get in the house.' I said, 'I done give it up. You go on in it.' He'd keep working, and he'd keep begging me. [But] if I didn't want to do it, I wouldn't do it." Gradually, though, they worked out an accommodation, and Paul came to see that Sam had the potential to be even better than Harris at selling, if he could just absorb some of the lessons that Crain, not to mention Archie and the rest of them, was teaching him.

Crain, who conceived of himself as the boy's only true "guide and protector," emphasized deportment as well as singing technique. "You could never get him up in the morning, but I devised a plan. If the program was at eight o'clock, I'd tell him it was seven, so maybe we'd get him there on time." When Crain was pleased with his pupil's progress, he called him "Sammy-o." If he felt compelled to deliver a lecture, he began with "Now, son," knowing he could no more maintain a stern tone with Sam than anyone else could, least of all the teenagers who were flocking in growing numbers to their programs and occupying the front rows of every church. "They didn't go to Archie, they didn't go to Kylo Turner. They came to Sam."

By the time they arrived in Los Angeles on February 11 for the series of West Coast programs J.W. had set up in advance of their recording session, Sam was a full-fledged member of the group. To Alex's relief he went over well at their first concert, at the Embassy auditorium in downtown L.A., but when they went up to Oakland, the promoters protested loudly that they had assumed they were getting R.H. Harris when they booked the Soul Stirrers. To show his confidence in Sam, J.W. offered to waive both the Stirrers' *and* the Travelers' guarantee if the promoters were not fully satisfied with the program. "Fortunately [he] went over well, and the people liked him! He did have that type of charisma."

But it wasn't until the first Soul Stirrers record with their new lead singer came out some two months later that J.W.'s and Crain's faith in Sam was fully vindicated.

"JESUS GAVE ME WATER," backed with "Peace in the Valley," was released on April 21, after a series of cheerfully hectoring letters from Crain to Art Rupe on his new "Nationally Known Soul Stirrers of Chicago, Illinois" stationery. "Hi Art," Crain saluted his boss in a May 8 follow-up that thanked Rupe for finally releasing the new single and assured him that "the People will like and buy my Records with the young feller (Sam)."

He was right. From the day the record came out, Sam Cook was a star. Everywhere the Soul Stirrers and Pilgrim Travelers appeared together, "Jesus Gave Me Water" was the single most requested number —

The Soul Stirrers, ca. 1952. Top, left to right: Sam, J.J. Farley, Paul Foster, R.B. Robinson. Foreground: S.R. Crain. *Courtesy of Specialty Records*

and nobody was interested in hearing it by its originators, the Pilgrim Travelers, either. When the Stirrers gave their annual Mother's Day homecoming program at DuSable High School on May 13 (with both the Travelers and the Spirit of Memphis as their special guests), former QCs Marvin Jones and Gus Treadwell sat in the back and listened to Sam do the song that had been his calling card in the last few months he had been with them. "We both just cried because that young boy was devastating. That was the day I told Gus, 'You know, we ought to go get Harris and put the Highway QCs back together [behind him].' That would have been something." But, Creadell Copeland acknowledged, Sam had developed so fast that "Jesus Gave Me Water" was no longer a QCs song. "He [had] just got progressively better. He learned to control his voice more. As good as he was with the QCs, he just [became] much better."

The Cook family, too, was out in full force, Reverend Cook as always in a dignified dark suit, with Sam's mother, her broad face wreathed in smiles, wearing her best Sunday-go-to-meeting dress and one of the many elaborate hats made for her by a friend named Belle. Half the neighborhood turned out, as Mrs. Cook made it her personal mission to sell more tickets than all the other Soul Stirrers combined, and fifteen-year-old Agnes transferred her allegiance once and for all from the QCs to her brother's new group. "It was the first time I saw him with the Soul Stirrers, and he turned it out." Sam, her brother L.C. concurred, unquestionably took the show.

But perhaps it should be left to Rebert Harris, about to debut his new group, the Christland Singers, at DuSable the following week, to put his finger on the mysterious source of Sam's charismatic appeal. Harris, never one to downplay his own accomplishments or shrink from the kind of direct comparison that Marvin Jones envisioned (but with a lineup of former Soul Stirrers behind him, not unknown QCs), observed to gospel historian Tony Heilbut some years later that Sam "did it in a different way. He didn't want to be that deep, *pitiful* singer, like, 'My mother died when I was young,' you know, Blind Boys, Pilgrim Travelers stuff." Sam, he said, adopted a different kind of approach, even as he was still evolving a style of his own. "He was a singer who could just stand and within the process of just singing create without throwing the background off." And, without pausing for breath, Harris concluded, as so many others had, and would, over the course of Sam's career, "I taught him that."

He was a hometown hero, and he basked in the attention that every hometown hero duly receives. The Famous Blue Jays' record store couldn't keep his record in stock. His best girl, Barbara Campbell, nearly sixteen now, was growing up and attracting attention whenever they went anywhere in public. They talked about the future, they even talked sometimes about getting married — but Barbara knew that was just a fantasy as long as Sam had all these other girls who wanted to give him anything (a car, clothes, money) they had. He talked all the time about how he just wanted a room for himself, where they could go to be alone — but she was cynical about that, too. He gave his mother money to fix up the apartment, to get herself a new stove and a nice hideaway bed, but Barbara knew he was as likely to give his money away to strangers, or other girls, and even though his family didn't approve of her — she didn't know if they would think *anybody* was good enough for their son — she tried to get him to put things in their proper perspective. She knew he had other girlfriends, she still had her other boyfriend, Clarence Mayfield — he was her "financier" — and, even though he knew she was not in love with him, he cared for her, and took care of her, every bit as much as Sam.

WHILE THE SOUL STIRRERS WERE AT HOME, they had rehearsals twice a week, Tuesdays and Fridays at 2:00 P.M. at Crain's house, with meals provided by his wife, Maude. Rehearsals were important — they were a part of the whole "business" of music, with fines attached for any infringement of a set of rules that ranged from tardiness to public misbehavior — but the most important thing about them from Crain's point of view was that they kept the group together. Because to stay together, as he recognized, "you had to care for each other first." That was the basis for their entire enterprise. Everyone drew a nominal salary, everyone shared equally in record and songwriting royalties, but the bulk of the money went into a common fund that took care of everything from the $1,400 they had to pay out for a new Chrysler to carry them well over fifty thousand miles every year to the purchase of uniforms, the photographs they sold at concerts, even medical bills as they came up. If you were a Stirrer, the whole world knew it, and you carried yourself as a Stirrer wherever you went: clean, dignified, someone for older folks to be proud of and young people to look up to. That was no problem for the newcomer. With just a few hints from Crain about maybe being a little more discreet about his "affairs of the heart" (after all, they all had affairs of the heart) and staying away from some of the "bad boys" he had grown up with (he was no longer a fighting Junior Destroyer, Crain reminded him, but a singing Soul Stirrer), Sam not only fit the image — he defined it.

Crain became a proud "papa" in September, and the group enjoyed a brief respite from the road. But for the most part the road was their home, as they traversed the country, playing everywhere from Las Vegas (at former Soul Stirrer Walter LaBaux's church on the "colored" West Side) to Foster's hometown of Grand Teton, Louisiana, from the West

Coast swings that J.W. Alexander set up to bookings in Philadelphia, New Jersey, and New York under the auspices of veteran gospel promoters Ronnie Williams, Brother Thermon Ruth, and Reverend Frederick D. Washington. They played Atlanta, St. Louis, New Orleans, and Palm Beach, staying in the few small colored hotels that dotted the landscape if there was room and in private homes when, more often than not, there wasn't. "Those were rough days," said Jesse Whitaker, the Pilgrims' melodically inventive baritone singer, "but it didn't bother us. We'd get hungry, man, we'd have to find a grocery store, buy some bologna, cheese and crackers, what we could get. Groups today, they can stop anywhere to eat and sleep. We couldn't. We had a rough time, but we didn't let it bother us. We knew when we went down through there what to do and how to do, we didn't let it rob us, it just made us more careful."

It was like being in a brotherhood of disaccommodation. There were so few places where they could count on being able to stay — the Foster in New Orleans, the Crystal in Houston, the Claxton Manor in Tampa, promoters Herman Nash and B.B. Beamon's Savoy Hotel in Atlanta — that at one time or another you were bound to run into virtually every other black entertainer, or even sports stars like Joe Louis and Jackie Robinson who were out there on the road. And if you didn't actually run into them, you knew you shared the same situation, so everyone in the world of black entertainment was more or less on a first-name basis, and if you read about Duke or Count or Louis in the *Defender* or Atlanta's *Daily World*, you felt just as much common cause with them as if you had been invited into their own homes.

The touring was mapped out under the auspices of Herald Attractions, which Art had set up in 1950 with the idea of expanding the opportunities for his gospel acts and no doubt exercising some degree of control over the manner in which they were presented. In charge was Specialty's former publicity director, Lillian Cumber, "a well-educated Negro lady," as Art described her to one of his acts, who was "only interested in handling top-attractions which I recommend." Mrs. Cumber for her part referred to her employer as "a young liberal who doesn't [just] preach liberalism, he practices it," while Specialty was the one label "that has ever attempted to create a position [such as her own] for a Negro" and expressed its resolute determination not to "tolerate a distributor who is prejudice[d] even if it means the loss of sales."

The immediate result, as Rupe saw it, was a professionalization of services, an opportunity for the groups "to realize more money for their performances" and, not coincidentally, a chance to "boost record sales." Nonetheless, for all of Mrs. Cumber's dedication to the task, there remained glitches to be worked out, and the Soul Stirrers in particular were reluctant to pay an agency commission on the Chicago bookings they had so painstakingly established as the core of their economic operation over the years.

J.W. Alexander attempted to intercede on the Stirrers' behalf. "I can see your point of view from the agency angle," he wrote to Lil the day after the Mother's Day program, while stressing that Crain was "quite unhappy" and that J.W. could see *his* point of view as well. They had all had to educate themselves in various aspects of the business, was the implicit message of J.W.'s letter. More important, they were all in this *together*. Wouldn't it be better to lose a little commission but have a happy group of Soul Stirrers than to risk "a lot of personal feeling and strife"? "There are a lot of Groups singing, and no doubt many have written you, but very few [like the Soul Stirrers] that people are paying to see consistently. So please give it thought." Which she undoubtedly did — as much perhaps for J.W.'s courtly manner as his carefully chosen words.

Everyone recognized Alex as a good businessman and a really "shrewd" man. "Even Crain would ask questions," said Travelers baritone singer, Jesse Whitaker. "Alex taught him a lot. Mostly about traveling and the different promoters, you know. Because a lot of times promoters would get to you if you didn't be careful. Alex was the type of guy who didn't hold a grudge, he was just that type of person. If he could help you, he help you. But if you cross him, you had a problem — and he let you know you crossed him. The promoters knew him, and they knew what would happen if they didn't do right. [It wasn't that he was better educated], he just know how to use it."

Alex had even gone so far as to announce the Travelers' incorporation in April, declaring in a publicity release on Specialty Records stationery that his "ace religious group" would issue stock, to be "jointly owned by the five singer-members," and that "on the eve of Alexander's fifth anniversary as manager . . . plans are readying for a European tour," another example of visionary forward thinking that, unfortunately, never came to pass.

All of this had little to do with Sam directly — he was a Soul Stirrer first, last, and always, a participant in group decisions, a beneficiary of group success, certainly, but the business aspects tended to escape him. At the same time, he could scarcely miss the way Alex commanded the respect of both black and white, the suave, smooth manner that was so different from Crain's blunt stolidity, and the interest the older man took in him and his career, providing him with helpful encouragement, giving him little tips all the time without ever seeming to criticize or step on Crain's toes. For the most part, though, he was just thrilled to finally be caught up in the life. The record was selling like crazy — he would have known it even if Crain hadn't told him, simply by the way the girls all called for it, and the older women, too. There were dozens of girls in every little village and town, big-legged yellow gals who crowded up into the front pew, sisters just shouting out his name, he told his brother L.C. — and you didn't even have to lift a finger to get them to do it. In some of them little country towns in Mississippi or Alabama, there might be some old grandmama who would offer you a place to stay and then apologize for the fact that there wasn't enough room for you to sleep by yourself, would you mind sharing a bed with her fifteen-year-old granddaughter if she put up an ironing board in between? And you couldn't even be sure what she meant, what was in the grandmother or granddaughter's mind, until the girl made a move in the middle of the night. But they always made a move.

He would joke about it with the other Soul Stirrers while they were in the car traveling on to the next town. They were all married, of course, but, he quickly discovered, no one was married on the road. And no one was attached past the date of the program or, geographically, beyond the city limits. They rehearsed in the car as they drove; Crain would give them a pitch, and they would all chime in, working out new arrangements, perfecting their harmonies, trying out new material. They still weren't able to take the program from the Blind Boys, but with J.W.'s encouragement and Crain's coaching, Sam was able more and more to establish his own tone — it was a matter, as Alex said, of lowering the volume to the point where people almost had to pay attention. Sam studied the audience as much as they studied him; he fixed on a girl and tried to get her until he could feel the rest of them starting to come across, he could feel the thrum start to build in the church or auditorium as he took out a comb and ran it through his carefully processed hair or played with what he knew to be the seductive sound of his own voice.

In St. Petersburg, five-year-old Ann Thompson, whose father, Rev-

erend Goldie Thompson, promoted all the gospel shows in the
Tampa–St. Pete area, fell in love. All the gospel groups used to stay with
the Thompsons in their public housing unit in Jordan Park, and she was
used to the neighbors coming around and gawking at all these out-of-
town "celebrities," but Sam was different — and it wasn't just that he
was so much closer to her own age than all these men she had gotten
used to calling "uncle." He had a way of *communicating* that no one else
had. It was like he himself said. "Now, listen, Cheese," he told her, using
her family nickname, "I'm not your uncle, I'm not your cousin. I'm your
guardian angel." And he was, too, protecting her from the imaginary
monsters she was afraid of, taking her on his shoulders sometimes
when he sang, reading to her so the familiar Bible stories came alive in a
language that was both fresh and respectful and that developed the story
line in a way that kept you in total suspense. She was a sickly child, but
she felt safe around him, and as much as she loved to hear him sing,
what she loved most about him was the way he took her *seriously,* the way
it seemed he "could adapt to anything or anybody and make them feel
comfortable."

"WE ARE VERY PROUD of the group," Art Rupe wrote to Crain in September. "As a matter of fact, we want to thank you for suggesting
that we put out 'Jesus Gave Me Water' and keeping on us until we did."

The single had sold thirty-five thousand copies by this time, eight
thousand more than "By and By," the Stirrers' greatest success with Harris,
though considerably less than the Pilgrim Travelers' biggest sellers or
Brother Joe May's "Search Me Lord," which had sold almost seventy
thousand copies in 1950 alone. Gospel music was clearly making great
strides in terms of both sales and public acceptance, though privately
Rupe continued to doubt that the record-buying audience would ever
"reward gospel singers the way popular stars were rewarded [because]
the business had a quasi-religious tone and the public was not yet condi-
tioned to financially support [it]." Still, as the *Chicago Defender* pointed
out the same week that it advertised the Soul Stirrers' annual fall program, with the Five Blind Boys, at DuSable, "gospel singing is not only
popular but very lucrative." As proof the article cited sales of over a million copies of the Blind Boys' "Our Father" on the Peacock label, a mark
that *Defender* columnist Charles Hopkins must surely have been aware
was apocryphal but nonetheless was indicative of an accomplishment

"the Blind Boys can be proud of, especially when you consider the limited market."

It was a time of expansive plans and heady optimism, in which J.W. Alexander, less of a skeptic perhaps than Art, foresaw a day when gospel would be promoted just like pop. In fact, he felt, you could already see it beginning to happen, with Mahalia's popularity reaching into new areas every day and the wedding that summer of flamboyant gospel shouter and guitar player Sister Rosetta Tharpe attracting a crowd of twenty thousand at Griffith Stadium, home of the American League Washington Senators, where tickets were sold at prices of up to $2.50 and the turnout far outdrew the Senators' usual attendance.

It was, as many in the community saw it, part of a too-long-delayed recognition of Afro-American culture, with downhome blues emerging as a potent sales force, hailed self-consciously in another *Defender* article as "a part of our American heritage . . . that we should be proud, not ashamed, of," and John Lee Hooker, one of the subjects of the story, "personif[ying] a way of life familiar to many of our older citizens who have migrated from the south."

And yet even as that way of life was being recognized, it was being overtaken, too, by the arrival of a new kind of music that incorporated elements of both blues and gospel and that had only recently been dubbed "rhythm and blues" by *Billboard* correspondent Jerry Wexler, who introduced the new nomenclature as "more appropriate to more enlightened times" and would join Atlantic Records to produce some of the best new rhythm and blues records not long afterward. The music itself eschewed the sophisticated voicings of Lucky Millinder's and Billy Eckstine's big bands, while at the same time sidestepping both the sly hepness of Louis Jordan's Tympany Five and the directness of John Lee Hooker's and Muddy Waters' blues. It was all about emotion, just like gospel music, but in the case of groups like the Orioles and the Dominoes, whose second single, "Sixty-Minute Man," topped the rhythm and blues charts all that summer, it was a quivering kind of emotion that combined sexual explicitness with unabashed declarations of romantic love. Gospel-trained voices like those of the Orioles' Sonny Til and the Dominoes' arresting falsetto lead, Clyde McPhatter, suggested a different kind of ecstasy than anything they had sung about in church, one that the quartet singers might well identify with but could never publicly admit. More and more, the new music infiltrated their world, and the visible rewards which its more worldly practitioners so often enjoyed were all around them, mocking the meager "offerings" that they took from their programs.

THE SOUL STIRRERS' SECOND SINGLE from the March 1951 session, "Come, Let Us Go Back to God," and "Joy, Joy to My Soul," which Art issued at Crain's recommendation at the beginning of October ("The public is crazy about them," Crain wrote in advocating the release of the two titles), didn't sell anywhere near as well as their unexpected hit, but it was a measure of Crain's new standing with his employer that Art took the recommendation seriously, and it gave the Stirrers a nice point of contemporary reference in their programs.

By the time that Art saw the group again for their next session at the end of February 1952, he was astonished at the improvement the young man had made under Crain's guidance in just one year. However confident he may now have been of Sam's talent, though, not to mention the Stirrers' surprising burst of popularity, he did not trust either one enough to allow the group to explore the intimate sound they had experimented with behind Sam's quiet lead toward the end of their last session. In fact, in a bow to the kind of "modernization" that had contributed to the success of the Five Blind Boys and many of the other acts on black Houston nightclub owner Don Robey's Peacock label, Art added drums after the first two takes of the first number, the chief effect being to coarsen the group's careful harmonic blend along with an occasional rushing of the beat. Sam contributed one original, "Just Another Day," a pretty melody on which he and Paul traded increasingly insistent verses, and then, after a couple of indifferent numbers, they revisited "How Far am I From Canaan?," the W. H. Brewster composition with which Art had been so dissatisfied at their previous session. They got it down to two minutes and forty-seven seconds this time, ten seconds off the previous version, and Art was so enthusiastic about their rehearsal performance of the song that he noted, "Best number that we did today. Three As and a plus!" It probably *was* the best number they did, along with Sam's original, but it somehow missed the mark — it missed the aching sense of loss, of *lostness,* that was the unique center of Sam's voice. More to the point, it made clear that Art still did not have full confidence in the particular properties of his new lead singer's appeal, the sinuous, almost sexual nature of his style.

None of the releases in the first six months of the new year sold espe-cially well. Art rushed out "How Far Am I From Canaan?" within a couple of weeks of the session, but it sold only fourteen thousand copies by July, when sales began to dwindle. It was a matter of relative indifference to the group from a financial point of view. With royalties established contractually at two cents a record, the difference between fifteen thou-sand and thirty thousand total sales (representing the sum of all Soul Stirrers releases in a quarterly royalty period) was very little, and there was virtually no likelihood of ever having more than $600 to divide among five group members at any given time. Records, in fact, were little more than a means to keep the public's interest alive — record *sales* were merely important in order to maintain the record company's interest and thereby ensure money and promotion for personal appear-ances. By the end of 1952, the Soul Stirrers had five singles out with Sam singing lead (Art released Sam's composition "Just Another Day" in late August, and it sold somewhat better than "How Far Am I From Canaan?"), but it was still "Jesus Gave Me Water" that audiences called for every time.

Art meanwhile had discovered a new market whose potential he had suspected from the day he first went into the music business but whose existence no one had ever been able to actually verify until now. With New Orleans–born Lloyd Price's "Lawdy Miss Clawdy," Specialty Records had the first bona fide industry-wide crossover hit.

RUPE HAD SET OUT FOR NEW ORLEANS in March of 1952, some two weeks after the Soul Stirrers' session, not with the idea of crossover success but in hopes of discovering an artist who could match twenty-four-year-old New Orleans piano player Fats Domino's notable record of commercial success — and thoroughly disarming musical charm — in the r&b market. He set up a series of auditions at Cosimo Matassa's J&M Studio on North Rampart Street, where Fats had recorded all of his re-gional and national hits, but after a week in which nearly every one of the singers sounded to Rupe "amateurish and quite poor," he was about to give up when this "young fellow showed up just as I was getting ready to leave."

The young fellow was twenty-year-old Lloyd Price, and he had heard about the audition through Fats' bandleader, Dave Bartholomew. He practically had to beg Rupe to listen to his song ("I thought he was going to cry when . . . I told him it was time for me to go"), but when Art heard it, he was knocked out by both the song, which the boy called "Lawdy Miss Clawdy" after a Maxwell House Coffee commercial that local DJ Okey Dokey had put together in his style of rhyming patter ("Lawdy, Miss Clawdy, drink Maxwell House Coffee and eat Mother's homemade pies!"), and its delivery. "It was," Rupe recalled, "very emotional, very fervent." It also had a freshness, a kind of optimistic vulnerability that was reminiscent both of gospel music and of B.B. King's new gospel-influenced blues. At the same time, though, it possessed a *flair* that, it seemed evident, no one but this kid, with his engaging manner and wide, open grin, could put across.

Art quickly organized a session, using Dave Bartholomew as the leader plus the core of the Fats Domino band, with Fats himself laying down those immediately recognizable rolling piano triplets that had established his style. They recorded three additional titles, but "Lawdy Miss Clawdy" was clearly the one, and Art released it without a lot of fanfare a month and a half after the New Orleans session. It entered the r&b charts on May 17 and stayed there for much of the remainder of the year, occupying the number-one spot for seven weeks in the summer of 1952 and becoming Specialty's first bona fide million-seller without any official acknowledgment in the pop marketplace. But it was white under-the-counter sales that raised it from the status of just another "race records" hit.

"The white retail shops began to carry it because market demand dictates where the product goes," Rupe summed up years later with the irrefutable logic of the financial analyst. In fact, one of the biggest obstacles to getting the kind of sales for a gospel or rhythm and blues hit that a pop record could achieve was the very absence of conventional retail outlets. Race records promotion was still based primarily on word of mouth within the community, and merchandise was sold at least as often at barbershops, shoe-shine parlors, and taxi stands as at the kind of record store where you might be able to find a wide variety of choices carefully set out in neatly ordered bins.

The widespread growth of radio, increased teenage buying power after the war, and changing social and racial mores were suddenly beginning to affect record-buying habits, particularly in the white community, something that was not lost on the independent labels that operated on the margins of the business. "As far as we can determine," wrote

Atlantic Records executives Jerry Wexler and Ahmet Ertegun in *Cash Box* in 1954, "the first area where the blues stepped out . . . was the South. Distributors there about two years ago began to report that white high school and college kids were picking up on the rhythm and blues records — primarily to dance to — [and] conservative old line . . . record stores in southern cities found themselves compelled to stock, display, and push rhythm and blues recordings." They went on to cite numerous examples of this trend which had "swept the rhythm and blues markets and [gone] on to become favorites with many, many young white record fans," and "Lawdy Miss Clawdy" appropriately — from the standpoint of both chronology and sales — led the list.

The percentage of white teenagers in this new consumers' pool was impossible to calculate precisely, but there was no question they were present in ever-increasing numbers, and from this point on, Art Rupe's attention would turn more and more not so much to reaching them directly as to providing the kind of rhythm and blues with a gospel tinge that was susceptible to crossover success. It was not that he lost his love for pure gospel music — he saw the new hybrid in fact as something of an adulterated derivative, and if it came down to personal taste, there was little question of which he would prefer. But there was equally little question which, as a businessman, he felt it incumbent on him to pursue.

THE COOK FAMILY SHOWED UP en masse when the Stirrers played Detroit. There was a family group on the program called the United Five, made up of two sisters and three brothers, the youngest of whom was fourteen. Twenty-one-year-old Mable John thought nobody could beat her baby brother, who was known as "Little" Willie John because of his impish face and diminutive stature. Willie could really "sell," to the young girls and older women alike — the older women would take their hats off sometimes, those big wide hats that Mahalia used to wear, and throw them at his feet. But Sam, she soon realized, was at least his equal, as much for his cool demeanor and his refusal to enter into the common fray as for his undeniable gifts.

"It didn't matter who he was up against," Mable said, "because he didn't do it as a competitor. All these Baptist sisters would sit down at the front, and they would scream. We would laugh at them because we were kids, but they were serious. They would yell things like, 'Sing, honey. Sing, child,' and I often wondered what was going on in some of their minds. Maybe I didn't need to know. But you know what? Sam never allowed it to distract him. If he saw he had your attention, he could sing directly to you and almost be whispering. And when he got through, you would feel that he was talking to no one else in the room but you. [But then] the whole building would go up in smoke!"

Sam was so excited driving his family back to Chicago that he kept turning around to tell his sixteen-and-a-half-year-old sister Agnes stories until, finally, she had to tell him that if he turned around one more time, she would never ride with him again. What irritated Agnes even more was the way he continued to try to protect her, as if she were still twelve years old rather than the mother of a one-year-old child herself. Not only did he insist on keeping her away from all the other singers on the program, he kept her away from his own group as well. It was as if he thought she was going to *embarrass* him in public, even though he would have said that he was just doing it for her own good, she didn't know these guys like he did.

To ten-year-old David it was just exciting to see his brother onstage, especially "when he would get into a song and the people started shouting. Everybody loved Sam — he was a lot of fun, always telling jokes and making people laugh. I remember when he used to come off the road we would sleep together [in the same bedroom], and he would wake up in the middle of the night and start humming a tune and then write it down — and I would get peeved sometimes, because I had to go to school the next day. He always exuded confidence. I really admired that. And he was a very good artist, too. He drew all the time."

Sam's older brother Charles started going out on the road with the group around this time. Twenty-five years old, an army vet, and an independent operator who had added drugs and women to his portfolio of convertible assets, he cut a dapper figure, with his draped suits, carefully trimmed mustache, and elaborate process, and the other Stirrers were glad to have him as their driver. Charles for his part found that he loved the road, and he was as mesmerized as everyone else by his brother's accelerating poise and self-assurance. Sam had grown up with them all, he looked like they did, he even *sounded* like they did (Papa said it was the "Cook sound" that made him), but for all of the undeniable family resemblance, there was simply no telling where Sam's compelling power came from.

Unlike Sam, Charles was a good driver. "They was glad I was along, because they could relax, and I could do the driving while they slept. And they had a big fine car, so that was right up my alley. We stayed in these little small hotels — maybe twelve, fifteen rooms. This one man in Texas built a place up over his garage just for the Soul Stirrers, and his wife cooked for us and everything. Sometimes they had [other] special places for us to eat. This was all new to me, but it wasn't new to them. They had traveled this road before. I remember we went back to Clarksdale, we played all different places [with] the Blind Boys and the Pilgrim Travelers — but when they announce the Soul Stirrers, Sam would be standing at the back of the church, and they'd come down the aisle, and, man, people would just start in to shouting when they'd start singing their theme song. The house would almost come down then, just by them walking in. Them young girls, man. It was quite a scene when Sam would get to town."

IN AUGUST REVEREND AND MRS. COOK, Sam, Charles, L.C., and Sam and L.C.'s closest friend, Duck (Leroy Hoskins), all set out for Los Angeles to attend the National Interdenominational Singers Alliance, an umbrella organization virtually interchangeable with the National Quartet Convention. L.C. and Duck rode with the elder Cooks; Charles drove Stirrers' utility singer R.B. Robinson and his family; Lou Rawls, whom L.C. had now joined in the Holy Wonders (sponsored by the Quartet Convention to attend the Alliance festivities), drove out with Farley, the Soul Stirrers' bass singer, while Sam rode with Crain and the rest of the group. The convention took place at the famed St. Paul Baptist Church at Forty-ninth and Main, where Professor J. Earle Hines, widely credited with having brought gospel music to L.A., served as music director, and the morning service was broadcast by Joe Adams, the Mayor of Melody, over KOWL. It was Reverend and Mrs. Cook's first trip to California, and they planned to combine it with the annual Church of Christ (Holiness) convention a few days later. Five thousand singers from all over the country were expected to attend, announced the *Los Angeles Sentinel,* and the Soul Stirrers and Pilgrim Travelers were featured, along with two of the founders of the National Quartet Convention, the Famous Blue Jays and R.H. Harris with his Christland Singers, on the program that kicked off the festivities.

It was the "nationally known" Soul Stirrers who were pictured with the news item in a recent publicity photograph that showed them grouped in three rising pairs around a mike. Sam is left front beside a bespectacled Paul Foster. His hair is longish and lightly processed, his mustache still not fully grown in, and he has the same half smile as all the other Stirrers save for Crain, whose immaculate center part is his most distinctive feature and whose broad lips are tightly pursed while still conveying a kindly expression. They are all wearing light-colored, lightly patterned suits with broad lapels, each with a white handkerchief and a striped tie with a boldly colored vertical pattern that appears almost to be licking at the stripes. They look like *stars,* and to nineteen-year-old Lou Rawls, who had "never been out of Chicago in my life, it was overwhelming. It was a church full of egos — I mean, this was the elite. I knew who they all were, I had seen them all in Chicago at one time or another, but to be in the same place with all of them at the same time. And Sam was the new kid on the block, he was something they'd [never] heard."

"Sam was singing," recalled L.C., almost as carried away by Sam's success as Lou, "and this lady two rows in front of me threw her baby up in the air. And, I mean, lucky some man caught that baby, 'cause she really threw it, man!"

It was an exciting time for them all, and everyone in the extended Cook family was on their best behavior. There were lots of fine-looking women at the convention, both on the program and in the audience, and everybody strutted around wearing their uniforms and bragging about whose version of "Dig a Little Deeper" was the best. Leroy Hoskins introduced himself to everyone as Duck Cook, and, L.C. noted with mock chagrin, "Some girl come by and told my father, said, 'Reverend Cook, all your sons are nice, but that Duck is the nicest.' Papa just said, 'What he do, honey?' He didn't say, 'That ain't my boy.' He just said, 'Yeah, that Duck Cook is really something.' Duck's own family would get mad at him, his brother Lester would say, 'You think you're a Cook,' and Duck would say, 'I am.' The rest was just acquaintances, but Duck was all of our best friend."

Just as the convention was about to start, Mahalia Jackson announced the details of her latest European tour, which would begin in November, take her on a swing of seven European countries, and earn something like $100,000. She appeared on Ed Sullivan's top-rated Sunday-night television variety show now as "the queen of the Gospel singers" and would sell out Carnegie Hall once again in October two weeks after the Travelers and the Stirrers played DuSable with the Blind Boys on a tour that

J.W. had announced would take in "101 cities." J.W. was still trying to figure out how to get his quartet and the Stirrers onto the more lucrative circuit that Mahalia and Clara Ward and the Ward Singers were blazing.
Nothing had ever come of the European tour he had announced the previous year, and, with record sales flat (the Travelers sold 153,000 records
from their entire catalogue in 1952, the Soul Stirrers a sharply reduced
78,000), he was chafing at his inability to break out of the endless round
of small churches and segregated southern auditoriums that he and
Crain knew so well.

BARBARA DISCOVERED that she was pregnant toward the end of the
summer of 1952. She and Sam had been messing around for the last
couple of years, first at a friend of Sam's house, then at the Evans Hotel
whenever Sam had the money, sometimes even at Sam's house when his
mother and father were out of town and the coast was clear. She was living
with her mother and her mother's husband, Mr. Cornelius, working a little
job and paying $15 a week rent for her room, but when she was finally
forced to admit that she was pregnant that fall, her mother did the worst
thing she could possibly have done: she called up Sam and invited him to
dinner. He showed up with his brother L.C., and everything was going
pretty well until her mother announced, as if this was something he would
want to know about and take care of right away, that her daughter was
expecting his child. At that point L.C. just said, "Man, I'll see you later,"
and bailed. Then her mother, to Barbara's eternal embarrassment, kept
on about it with Sam, refusing to let up until Sam finally stormed out, saying he didn't think it was his child and he wasn't ready for marriage now,
anyway — he had a career to think about. Barbara tried to tell herself that
he didn't really mean it, this wasn't her knight in shining armor, and she
knew what boys were like, the way they needed to impress not so much
others as themselves — she knew how good Sam was at that. He maintained his own little impenetrable world. But still she couldn't help but
admit to herself that she was simply "outdone." For all of the ups and
downs of their relationship, she had never doubted up till now that she
would somehow "get her man." But now she was at a loss as to what to do.

Her mother tried to make up her mind for her.

After Sam left, her mother forbade her ever to see him again. Which
was a joke, given her mother's own history with men and virtual abandonment of the responsibilities of parenthood. But she wasn't sure what

choice she was going to have in the matter. The Cook family was going to welcome her departure from their son's life. With the exception of L.C. (and she wasn't so sure of him now), they had never thought she was good enough for Sam. She couldn't go to her other boyfriend, Clarence, the one her Grandmother Paige denounced as a racketeer, because he was in jail on what he termed one of his frequent "vacations" from drug dealing. He had tried to warn her about Sam, he had told her Sam was not the man he appeared to be — in Clarence's view, Sam was not a man at all. But she was always inclined to put that down to jealousy, even though Clarence knew she was not in love with him and said it didn't matter, he would always protect her, anyway. But right now he was in no position to protect her. And for the first time she doubted that Sam really loved her. She felt like she couldn't believe any of that shit ever again.

Barbara wasn't the only one of Sam's worries. His Cleveland girl-friend, Marine Somerville, had gotten pregnant probably during the same week as Barbara on a trip she had made to visit him in July, and there was another girl in Chicago who said she, too, was going to have his baby in the spring. Crain clucked that Sam was going to have to learn to take better care of his business, that even though this was the kind of thing that could happen to any of them, there were lots of girls out there who just wanted to have your baby — but, son, Crain told him, you've got to learn to deal with the *situation*, there was no reason to "call it trouble, it was just a way of life." *Unless* you let it interfere with the group.

He was twenty-one years old, and he felt like all of a sudden he was being asked to grow up in a hurry. His parents moved to Cleveland that winter with his little brother David when his father got a new church to pastor. Then L.C. went into the army in February; Charles and Willie were on their own; the two older girls were married; and Agnes by now was married, too. For all of his success, he felt a little bit at loose ends, and he was impatient for change, although in the absence of having encountered it, he might have found it difficult to define. He knew in many ways just what he was capable of: he had the power to make people fall in love with him, both onstage and off. But in his adeptness at allow-ing each person to see whatever it was he or she wanted to see, in his seemingly effortless ability to play whatever role was assigned to him, he had yet to discover a voice of his own.

The Further Education of Sam Cook

SAM'S STYLISTIC BREAKTHROUGH, like all great discoveries, has been variously ascribed to accident, necessity, invention, and the illumination of genius — and it was undoubtedly a combination of every one of those elements. According to Crain, it took place in Fresno, according to J.W. Alexander in San Jose, where "Sam pitched the song a little high, kind of out of range, and when he got to the highest note in the song, he couldn't make it, so he bent it, and the 'trick' went over so well that Crain told him to keep on doing it."

"He just floated under," Crain said, describing the first appearance of what would almost immediately become Sam's most recognizable vocal trait, a lilting "yodel" ("whoa-oho-oh-oh-oh") that he could interpolate at will into the body of any song, thereby lending it an altogether different flavor, a yodel that, unlike R.H. Harris' daunting octave leaps, softened rather than intensified the thrust of the song, evoking once again the crooning style of Bing Crosby and the Ink Spots to which Sam had been drawn since childhood.

"What I was doing wrong," he told his old friend and teenage quartet rival Leroy Crume, who would join the Soul Stirrers himself just three years later, "I was trying to sing too high, I was killing myself." And, Crume added, "He might not have liked to admit it, but he was [still] trying to sing like R.H. Harris." Once he hit upon this new device of his own, he was "Sam Cook all the way."

Exactly when or where it happened will continue to be subject to debate (Crain sometimes ascribed the transforming moment to a program with the Five Blind Boys of Mississippi in Chattanooga, Tennessee, and various QCs insisted that he sang that way all along), but there is no question that it came into full flowering sometime before the

The Soul Stirrers, late 1953–early 1954: June Cheeks on the floor, as Sam, Paul Foster (with glasses), and the other Stirrers look on. *Courtesy of Ray Funk*

Soul Stirrers' February 27, 1953, session in Los Angeles — because that is where you can hear Sam's yodel clearly manifest itself for the first time.

The session was unusual in a number of respects. To begin with, Art Rupe was not present and put J.W. Alexander in charge, writing to Crain two and one-half weeks earlier: "I am indeed very sorry that I can not be with you for your recording session but Alex assured me that you two will put your heads together and really make us some hits. I have all the confidence in the world in you Roy, and I want you to know that I am very particular when it comes to letting groups record on their own without me being present. You and the fellows should consider this a very honor of my esteem of your wonderful talents and ability." And he enclosed a check for $300 (and four copies of the group's contract renewal) both as proof of that esteem and as proof, too, that "we are not dropping the Soul Stirrers (Smiles), but are continuing our very pleasant relationship."

Alex took his duties seriously, bringing a Pentron tape recorder to the Stirrers' hotel to monitor their material and picking out one song, Alex Bradford's "He's My Friend Until the End," to concentrate on. It offered, as he saw it, a good opportunity for Sam to demonstrate his newfound approach and, like a number of compositions by the Chicago-based twenty-six-year-old Bradford (whom he was about to recommend to Art as a recording artist in his own right), it was an exceptionally well made combination of passionate belief and skillful homiletics in a style well suited to Sam's long-standing strengths.

That was the first song they recorded when they went into the studio, and J.W.'s faith was immediately rewarded. Sam's singing was as supple as ever, his manner easy and unforced, and the number worked very much like a romantic pop song, with Sam breaking into an occasional falsetto and the Stirrers chirping away in the background much in the manner of the Orioles, the Ravens, or one of the other "bird" groups who were so popular on the r&b charts. The piano and organ that Art had contracted for in an effort to modernize the Stirrers' sound competed clumsily for space, and the drums were no more necessary for establishing the beat than at the previous session, but Sam's vocal performance could not have been improved upon in either of the two takes that have survived.

The leads on the next few songs were, surprisingly, divided between Sam and Paul, and the instrumental accompaniment did not improve, but Sam's singing was of a new standard, in which the interplay of the voices was consistently guided by his growing confidence and the skimming lightness of his fluid, all-purpose yodel. Probably the single most arresting moment of the session was his interpretation of a 1948 Mahalia Jackson number, "I Have a Friend Above All Others," that in his version stands as a beautifully modulated cri de coeur in which "Whoa, Lord" is incorporated into his yodel, then apostrophized, first as "Savior divine," then, with the voice dropping to an almost romantic level, as "Friend of mine." But it is on a much more literal presentation of Lucie Campbell's "He Understands, He'll Say, 'Well Done'" (retitled "End of My Journey" by Crain) that Sam for the first time unveils his own original yodel, no longer simply a melismatic variation on melody or the acrobatic elongation of vowels, but a *Sam Cook* yodel, which, however shyly it may declare itself at first, will almost immediately become the hallmark of the Sam Cook sound.

"I Have a Friend Above All Others" remained unissued for twenty

years, and, in the aftermath of the session, one wonders if Art's uncharacteristic willingness to relinquish control momentarily stemmed not so
much from his esteem for the group as from his increasing uncertainty
as to what to do with them. In any case, no single from the session was
issued for six or seven months, and it was a full year before "He's My
Friend," the number in which J.W. so strongly believed, was finally
released, achieving a degree of success that vindicated J.W.'s judgment —
but by then any number of other events had intervened.

The world of music, Art Rupe felt, sometimes gloomily, sometimes
with real excitement about the commercial possibilities that were opening up, was rapidly changing. With the remarkable breakthrough of
Lloyd Price's "Lawdy Miss Clawdy" the previous year and a growing
recognition on the part of the record industry that this was turning into a
"full-fledged trend," everyone was looking for their own crossover hit,
and Art was not about to be left behind. He continued to have some
degree of success with Price, though nothing like the cataclysmic success of that first record, but he needed to expand his horizons. With
Lloyd about to be drafted, and with the boy and his mother more trouble
sometimes than they were worth, he needed to open up the New Orleans
territory in a way that he could not achieve simply by occasional visits
from California. So he hired a flamboyant young record entrepreneur
from Laurel, Mississippi, named Johnny Vincent to serve as a regional
distributor and talent scout, and to act as a location producer, attempting
to pass on all the lessons he had learned in the business in a detailed
memo that covered everything from "General Policies in Distributor
Relations" to "How to Sign Up a Recording Artist." "Remember," he
wrote to Vincent in the spring of 1953, "that a recording session costs
money." And at the conclusion of a set of specific production tips ("The
most important thing is to bring out the words. . . . However, at no time
shall the rhythm be lost"), he stressed that "All of the above technique
does not mean anything if the song is not sung . . . WITH FEELING
AND SOUL. . . . Never show anger or disgust. KEEP PRAISING
EFFORT . . . KEEP THEM RELAXED."

Art had recently remarried, he was thinking of starting a family with
his new wife (and longtime secretary), Leona, and he was also doing
something that he absolutely detested: like every other independent
label owner, he was paying money to get his records played. This was at
total odds with his business ethics, his belief in economic determinism,

and his sense of fair play, not to mention his respect for the dollar — but there was nothing he could do about it, it was no longer a level playing field, and the only way for Specialty to remain competitive was to pay like everybody else.

All of these factors undoubtedly entered into his asking J.W. Alexander to take on full-time a&r (artist and repertoire, or "production") duties at Specialty at around this time. The label had been pretty much of a one-man operation up until now. By Art's estimate he had produced, "I'd say ninety-five percent or more of everything — that was the part of the business that I really enjoyed." So, to offer Alex the opportunity not simply to recommend gospel groups but, with Art's approval, to sign and produce them, too, was a tremendous concession on the label owner's part. But it would have meant Alex having to leave his group, and this J.W. was not prepared to do. For the time being, then, things remained pretty much as they were, with the recently signed Five Blind Boys of Alabama, whom J.W. had recommended off a strong showing at a Detroit program the previous year, getting the lion's share of the label's gospel sales with their debut release, "When I Lost My Mother," in March. The single, delivered with the powerhouse punch of the better-known Five Blind Boys of Mississippi, sold so well that it easily outstripped sales of all current Stirrers' and Travelers' singles combined over the first nine months of the year and eventually went on to sell nearly a hundred thousand copies.

The Stirrers and the Travelers remained a strong draw on the road, nonetheless. They were out with the Five Blind Boys of Mississippi all through April and May of 1953 and then in June set out with the Blind Boys of Alabama and the Spirit of Memphis on a Herald Attractions–sponsored "Gospelcade" that ran head-to-head with Clara Ward's far better known Gospel Cavalcade but, according to Herald's own publicity apparatus, set "attendance records" everywhere it went.

The Blind Boys, whose four-man nucleus had originally met at Alabama's Talladega Institute for the Deaf and Blind in 1938, had started out their musical life as the Happyland Jubilee Singers. A 1948 program in Newark with the Five Blind Boys of Mississippi, then known as the Jackson Harmoneers, was their defining moment, both nominally and stylistically, as promoter Ronnie Williams billed a Battle of the Blind Boys, and the overwhelming power of Harmoneers lead singer Archie Brownlee was persuasive in converting the Happylands from a group that featured gospel and the older jubilee repertoire in almost equal measure to an up-to-date quartet that performed almost exclusively in the hard-hitting gospel style. Their lead singer in that style, Clarence Fountain, was, in fact, so close to Archie, as J.W. wrote to Art in April, that "most people think that 'When I Lost My Mother' [the Alabama group's big hit] was done by . . . Archie [and the Five Blind Boys of Mississippi] and that helps the record sell." It was Clarence's scream that did it, J.W. observed, and as he saw it, the confusion could only help both groups.

Clarence Fountain and the Blind Boys of Alabama took pretty much the same view of Sam that Archie and Percell Perkins had two years earlier: "He was young, stylish, and the girls liked him — but, hey, we'd tear the house down on him in a minute because we was the Blind Boys, and we knew how to sing." They were so hot at the time, the other groups all let the Blind Boys close, but one time, bass singer Johnny Fields said, Crain insisted that they open for the Stirrers, and when Sam expressed misgivings, Crain said, "No, let them. They can't go but so far." As it turned out, the Blind Boys killed the crowd that night and wouldn't turn them loose — the Soul Stirrers, according to Fields, didn't even get a chance to sing. "Boy, Sam jumped on Crain like he had stole something. 'I told you, man, not to call them Blind Boys first.' Boy, we set there laughing, [but] when it was over everybody was shaking hands. It wasn't an envious thing."

Sam was different, the Blind Boys all agreed. He had qualities, both musical and personal, that made him stand out. Some people, said Johnny Fields, thought Sam was stuck up because of the way he carried himself — some of the other singers were jealous because of the way he attracted all the young girls. "But he had such a nice personality, and [you] didn't never have to guess about Sam. It wasn't a game. If he liked you, he was just down-to-earth, and if he didn't like you, or something happened, he would let you know where he was coming from."

One of the most likeable things about him, said Blind Boys lead singer Clarence Fountain, was that he was the same with everyone, young, old, sighted, blind. "He was an all right cat, he had a good, solid mind, and he could just stop and read you a book. He'd ride with us all the time, and he'd read us westerns and things of that nature, and he could almost put you there, right back in the same time when the book was wrote and how things were going on — he had a good eye for reading, a good eye for everything. See, he liked the Blind Boys. We was all right with him. He didn't mind taking you to the bathroom, doing things with blind people that a lot of people don't like to do. Sam was all right when he was all right."

As far as Sam's singing went, Clarence took the only slightly grudging view that he was improving all the time. "He learned how to sing because he had to come out of all these holes. We'd get on that stage, and we'd put something on him, and he knew he had to come out from under that — to be good you had to come out and beat the other man." Sam had sufficient power, Fields conceded, to put a number across, but his greatest strength was his ability "to make up a song as he was singing along. He just put verses in, and it come out right. Hey, that was my boy. I loved him, because he was a lovable guy. We run across the same girls sometimes, 'cause I was just as good as he was in that day. He had good records going, we had good records going." It could be, in its own way, a little bit like the Wild West out there, with showdowns every night and sometimes even violent confrontations. One night after the program, Johnny Fields recalled, they were all sitting in the restaurant on the ground floor of the town's only colored hotel, "and this guy come in off the street and saw Sam and started a whole lot of talking about, 'Hey, man, you think you more than everybody else. You mess with all our women, and we're gonna fix you.'" At this point, R.B. Robinson and one of the other Soul Stirrers slipped out the back, "and they went upstairs and come back to the head of the steps. Each one had a gun in his hands and tell the guy, 'Look up. Look up. Look up here.' The guy looked up, and he cut out. But that type of thing, that type of jealousy — the group was his group, man, they got a little conflict and there was a lot of conflict!"

The Gospelcade reached the West Coast just around the same time as Lloyd Price's scheduled June 27 session at Universal Recorders in Hollywood. Art Rupe had been telling Lloyd about Sam for over a year, he kept saying that the two of them had a lot in common and ought to meet. "So I made a point of it," Lloyd said, "and we started talking right there in the [Specialty] office, and I liked Sam right away, that big smile, 'Hey, welcome, man' — but I hadn't seen him perform."

Lloyd went out to the program in San Jose that weekend, and his eyes were opened. Unlike the Blind Boys, he had no reservations whatsoever about Sam's talent; in fact, he was thunderstruck by the cool confidence and seemingly effortless charm with which he carried off his performance. "I had never seen nothing like it! I mean, I was the hottest thing in the country, I thought I was the only lightning on the road, and here was this handsome, good-looking young guy, he just stood there and sung, that's all he did, and that's all he had to do — and he *rocked* them, he just rocked them."

Lloyd, who himself had a well-deserved reputation as a "big playboy," recognized immediately in Sam a kindred, if considerably quieter, spirit. He could certainly understand Sam's appeal. He was personable, persuasive, "had that big, bright smile and laugh," he conveyed gentlemanliness and "genuineness" with every fiber of his being.

After the program, they talked some more, about show business, about Mr. Rupe, about the hazards of travel in the South, they talked about all kinds of things — "I told him about this girl in Fresno, she came to one of my dances, and I took her to breakfast, and we started meeting. I told Sam she was a nice girl, and when he got to Fresno he should meet her. And I told *her* she should meet Sam." Her name was Dolores Mohawk, and she was his girlfriend, Lloyd explained, but she was his *Fresno* girlfriend, which didn't require explanation for any other entertainer on the road.

The Gospelcade played Fresno the following Sunday, July 5, and Sam didn't have to look for Dolores when he got there: she was at the program, and she introduced herself to Sam.

Dolores Mohawk was born Dolores Milligan in Lubbock, Texas. She was twenty-two, just a few months older than Sam, and, like him, raised in the Holiness church. She moved to Fresno with her family as a teenager and had a child by a Mexican boyfriend at seventeen. She left her child to be raised by an aunt and pursued a career as an entertainer, singing Dinah Washington material with the local Kirk Kirkland Quintet, obviously drawn to the life. Which was how she had come to meet Lloyd. "I didn't know she was a singer. I didn't even know she had a son — you got to understand that on the road you don't ask those questions, and ladies never tell. They just meet you. I just knew she was a very serious person and wanted to perhaps get married or something like that, but at that time I was not interested. I was fresh out of Louisiana and flying high."

Sam obviously was interested. He was at least heavily smitten and asked Crain's permission to stay with Dolores that night as the other

Stirrers moved on to Bakersfield. Crain had his misgivings, and J.W. Alexander, who knew Dolores by reputation, felt strongly that the Stirrers' manager should have acted on them, but the girl promised to get Sam to the Bakersfield program on time, and, as Crain told biographer Dan Wolff, "She was a pretty girl. If it was me, I'd sure want to go. [So] I put myself in his stead, and I relented."

That was how Sam fell in love. Two weeks was all it took. As Lloyd Price said, "I was kind of shocked on the one hand — but, on the other hand, Sam got a nice girl. She was a very, very nice girl. And I always respected Sam, so I figured she was absolutely in good hands." The surprise to Lloyd was not so much that the two of them should have hit it off (he would have bet on that) but that Sam, whom he took to be a brother in the chase, should have been caught so easily by the snares of love.

Barbara, meanwhile, had had her baby, a beautiful little girl, eight pounds at birth, whom she named Linda Marie, the middle name the same as her mother's. She continued to live with her mother and step-father for a while, sharing a room with her mother's mother, Grandma Beck — but she grew tired of all their rules and strictures, most of all she grew tired of what she came to see as her mother Mamie's hypocrisy. Here was a woman, blond-haired, blue-eyed, who had carried on all kinds of affairs, married four times, and passed for white much of her life — and she was trying to tell *her* what to do. So she went off with her boyfriend Clarence again once he got out of jail. He took care of her, he made very few demands of her, in the end he even married her just to give the baby legitimacy, though Barbara never took Clarence's last name, and the baby kept the name "Campbell," too. Clarence truly loved her, he proved it in every way, he even claimed the baby as his own, going around to the old neighborhood and showing her off, saying, "Look at my baby, ain't she cute?" even though everybody knew she wasn't his. Clarence educated her, he gave her the life she wanted, and he was no hypocrite, either. He and the people he did business with were principled, moral people who lived by their own code — everyone knew the code, but if you stepped outside it, look out, you were a dead man! She thought of him as her brother, her husband, her friend — but she could never think of him as her lover, and then he had to go back to jail, and the baby got sick with bronchial pneumonia and had to stay in the hospital for three weeks while Barbara worked two jobs just to try to support herself and her child in the world.

She never heard from Sam during this time, but she never stopped thinking about him either, and sometimes she thought about the one time he had made oblique reference to getting married before she had even gotten pregnant, talking about it as if it were a theoretical "what if?" question that scarcely demanded — and certainly didn't get — a response. Maybe that was why when she thought of his coming back, she imagined riding off with him on a white palomino, like that made-up story of Sleeping Beauty and her prince. In her heart she knew she still loved him, but she no longer knew what that love was based on. She didn't understand what had happened any more than she understood him — or herself.

Dolores Mohawk kept her promise to Crain and made sure that Sam arrived in plenty of time for the rest of the California programs and for the July 10 recording session for which the group briefly broke its tour.

The session was once again of a somewhat experimental nature, though it would be difficult to say what was the source, or even the point exactly, of that experimentation. The Stirrers for once did not come in well prepared, and their lack of fresh material was probably the principal reason for the truncated length of the session, which produced only four complete tracks, as opposed, for example, to the eleven at Sam's first Soul Stirrers date. Other than lack of material, the most pronounced difference was the substitution of Hawaiian steel guitar for the piano and organ of the previous session, or the a cappella approach which the group still took in live performance. Its most interesting utilization came on the first, and only issued, number, "Come and Go to That Land," where the soaring lines of the out-of-tune guitar played off in oddly dissonant harmonies with the floating freedom of Sam's new, almost scatting style. The words "go," "peace," "find," and even "joy" were all occasions for his syllable-lengthening yodel, with evidently spontaneous interpolations recurring effortlessly, and enchantingly, at the same point in each take. Art was drawn in enough by the sound to create a "composite take" in which the guitar was virtually silenced by an overdubbed bass and drums, and the gentle swing of Sam's voice was undercut, and overpowered, by a speeded-up, more predictably accented beat.

Otherwise Rupe was obviously not very taken either with the steel guitar player, who might as well have wandered in off the street, or with any of the other material. He must have been left, in fact, with something of a queasy feeling about a group he had always considered as meticulous in their preparation as he was himself, a group that he saw as "a basketball team [who] when they throw a note, someone will be there to respond to it. [It was] a beautiful thing the way they worked, even when they sang songs that weren't interesting or didn't sell, they had it really polished." He had always been able to handle Crain, but now, as Sam seemed to be taking on more and more of the lead role, he found the group increasingly unpredictable, and he found it increasingly difficult to sell them in the contemporary market.

Which was particularly frustrating because he knew the gospel sound was in the air. You couldn't miss it: it was everywhere. Not just in the sales that Specialty was chalking up with the Five Blind Boys of Alabama, and the sales expectation he had for Alex Bradford, whom he had recorded for the first time just three weeks earlier, but on the r&b charts, where both Sonny Til and the Orioles' "Crying in the Chapel" and Faye Adams' "Shake a Hand," two undisguisedly gospel-based numbers, established themselves in August and alternated at the number-one spot for fifteen weeks before eventually relinquishing it to the Drifters' "Money Honey" sung in the purest of falsettos by *their* gospel-trained lead, Clyde McPhatter. As *Billboard* would comment in somewhat wonderstruck fashion in the aftermath of this gospel-driven success, " 'Shake a Hand,' a common greeting among followers of spiritual and gospel music, is being uttered more so today by other facets of the entertainment industry largely because the religious field continues to gain recognition as a growing bonanza." At the same time, the story went on, without bothering to point out that the expression "Shake a hand" had been popularized by a secular, not a religious, recording, spiritual record sales were actually suffering because "religious platters are not the fast moving items that r&b wax is." How to resolve that discrepancy between substance and style was the dilemma not just of Art Rupe but of every independent label owner, and of the music industry at large, and more and more Rupe, in conjunction with J.W. Alexander, was wondering if crossover sales were not the only answer.

In any case, he put out just one more release by the Soul Stirrers for the rest of the year, with both sides stemming from the February session and neither capturing the attention of either the spiritual *or* the crossover audience. The Stirrers and the Travelers remained on the road almost constantly, with Herald Attractions reporting a year-end gross of $100,000 for the Travelers (on a reported 173 dates) and $78,000 for the

Stirrers versus an astounding return of $130,000 for the Five Blind Boys of Mississippi's forty weeks on the road. Even the Five Blind Boys, though, as earthshaking as their presence could be, were unable, according to Durham, North Carolina, gospel DJ Jimmy "Early" Byrd, to create the effect that Sam now had on his audience. "He had a little aura about him. He was better, dressed sharper than the other guys and had bigger fan response. Sam was the only guy whose voice would sound like an instrument, he made it sweet like nobody had before, and he was so pretty, and so dynamic, that he would mesmerize the women, women would faint, actually fall out, when he would walk down the aisle."

Byrd knew whereof he spoke, because "I'm a pretty boy, too, we used to date the same broads. See, every quartet in every town, they have a book — like the athletes do. You know who the quartet Janes are, and we had a list. So Sam would come to my town, he'd say, 'Man, I want some snow and some shoveling coal' — you know, 'snow' means a white girl, we'd sneak them in the back — and sometimes we'd get two at a time and have orgies, man. That's how close we were."

THAT WAS WHY it came as such a shock to nearly everyone of his acquaintance when Sam married Dolores ("Dee Dee") in October. Not even L.C., or anyone else in the Cook family, was prepared for it. "Yeah, we were surprised," said L.C. "Sam had a *school* of girls. We didn't think Sam was going to marry nobody, especially not that quick." The elder Cooks, still in Cleveland with twelve-year-old David, did not choose to attend the wedding, which took place in Chicago on October 19 after Dolores and her little boy rode the train out from the Coast. Geography did not appear to be the operative factor, since none of the other Cooks attended the ceremony, either. It was, in the view of Reverend and Mrs. Cook, just as it had always been with Barbara: this woman who had set her snares for Sam was simply not good enough for their son.

For Barbara, of course, it was the greatest shock of all. It hurt her deeply, altogether destroying whatever illusions she had been able to preserve. It undoubtedly hurt eighteen-year-old Marine Somerville in Cleveland, too, who had delivered her baby, Denise, on April 23, just two days before Linda was born. And it probably struck a chord with Evelyn Hicks, another of Sam's Chicago girlfriends, who had had her daughter, Paula, a couple of weeks before that. But it was Barbara who had put her faith in Sam, it was Barbara who had believed him when he said he

Sam, Dolores, and her son, Joey.
Courtesy of Specialty Records

didn't want to settle down or make a family life because he was trying to make a career for himself. It was Barbara who now had to rethink not just her life but her dreams.

Sam moved out of the old neighborhood for the first time with his new wife and family, into the basement apartment in Soul Stirrers baritone R.B. Robinson's building at 6505 Langley. R.B.'s wife, Dora, with a five-year-old of her own, soon befriended Dee Dee. "Sam was a man about town and the women did like him," she told writer Daniel Wolff. "I always tried to comfort her, if there was any comforting to be done."

Barbara brought the baby over one time at Sam's request so that he could see her. She didn't really know how to respond when Sam's wife said how pretty Linda was, that she looked just like Sam, and that she, Dee Dee, wished she could have some children by Sam herself. "I said, 'Well, you got a boy, you got a son — you know, that's his stepfather. I guess I'll let you have some more.' And that was it. I had a long conversation with her, and I told her that I was gonna go on and live my life. And I would never interfere or interrupt her marriage — she never had to worry about me, is what I wanted to say. [Because] if I couldn't be the one, I certainly wasn't going to be the second lady." But what Sam thought neither Barbara nor anyone else had any idea. As in so many other matters, he simply maintained an inscrutably cheerful and impenetrable calm which, for all they knew, might merely have masked the simple fact that it was all as much a mystery to him as it was to them.

J UNE CHEEKS' ARRIVAL in late 1953 kicked the Soul Stirrers and Sam into high gear. Cheeks, the electrifying lead singer for the Sensational Nightingales out of Philadelphia by way of the Carolinas, represented an even more flamboyant version of Archie Brownlee's vocal theatrics combined with the kind of physical routines that, according to gospel historian Tony Heilbut, got him thrown out of some churches. "I was the first," he told Heilbut, "to run up aisles and shake folks' hands. Man, I cut the fool so bad, old Archie started saying, 'Don't nobody ever give me any trouble but June Cheeks. . . . That's the baddest nigger on the road.'" Born in Spartanburg, South Carolina, he joined the Gales in 1946 and would stop at nothing to wreck house, but according to Cheeks, there was no money to be made with the Gales, with the nadir occurring at a program in Miami when, after paying their hotel bill, "we wound up with fifty cents apiece. I just went and threw mine as far as it could go into the Atlantic." The other Gales took a somewhat less charitable view of his departure. "He and his wife got a little bigheaded," said guitarist JoJo Wallace. "Folks were telling him he was the Nightingales by himself." So he left them after a program with the Dixie Hummingbirds in Jackson, Mississippi, "he left us there at the hotel and took the car with him!"

He was a strange fit for the Soul Stirrers, who prided themselves on their ability to get the crowd to listen without gimmicks and who already had their own strong second lead in Paul Foster. JoJo Wallace felt that he "disfigured their ministry with too big of a forceful sound." But to Pilgrim Travelers' bass singer Jesse Whitaker, Cheeks provided a lesson that Sam Cook still needed. "June really got Sam going. He sung hard and moved with it, you know, with gestures and stuff. When he joined, he sat down and talked to Sam about what he should do and how he should do it. A lot of times he'd [even] show him. Julius Cheeks was a strong singer, man."

"I was the one," Cheeks told Tony Heilbut, "[who] caused Sam Cook to sing hard. I gave him his first shout. We was working in the San Francisco Auditorium. Sam used to stand real pretty on stage. I pushed him, and he fell off the stage. People thought he was happy. I said, 'Move, man,' and the two of us fell into the audience. We were doing 'How Far Am I From Canaan?,' and things just came together."

There is a photograph from this period that conveys some of the spirit of that moment. In it the Soul Stirrers are all immaculate in matching white suits, dark ties and handkerchiefs, and *sharp* two-tone saddle shoes. In this photograph it is Cheeks who has leapt off the stage, and the look on the other Soul Stirrers' faces matches the expressions of the audience, as amusement, appreciation, attentiveness, encourage-ment, and pure curiosity vie with each other for primacy. Sam and Paul seem to be exhorting June to go ahead on, and Sam in particular seems engaged in a way that leaves any pose of cool reserve long since aban-doned — he was no longer, as nine-year-old Bobby Womack, whose fam-ily group sometimes shared a bill with the Stirrers in their hometown of Cleveland, observed, just a "pretty boy that everybody could dump house on." Cheeks, said J.W. Alexander, just wouldn't quit. "The group [the Soul Stirrers] would sit down, and he wouldn't go sit." Dumping house meant everything to June, J.W. said — it was the same goal Sam had set for himself from childhood on, but now he was learning a different way to accomplish it.

They went into the studio together in March of 1954 for the Stirrers' annual recording session. Three of the completed numbers, with Oak-land gospel stalwart Faidest Wagoner accompanying the group on piano, are essentially Sam Cook solos, sung in that lyrical style that had by now become his trademark, but with an elaboration of that style that you can attribute either to growing maturity or, possibly, deeper commitment. The first, "Jesus, I'll Never Forget," is a lightly swinging up-tempo num-ber with lots of "oh-oh-oh"s and "no-no-no"s for Sam to practice his ascending and descending yodels, and a confident, practiced touch that leaves no question of his vocal mastery. The second, "He'll Make a Way," by Cleveland gospel singer Clinton Levert, an accomplished songwriter and performer whom Sam had met and grown close to in the course of his travels, has Sam singing at the top of his range, with the Soul Stirrers backgrounding him all the way through. His falsetto here is an effortless extension of his natural delivery, carried off with a smoothness that the raw, untrained vocalist of his first Soul Stirrers sessions could never have achieved but with a poignancy, too, that R.H. Harris' more unre-lenting attack could not suggest. He employs his intricate melisma on words such as "please," "weakness," and, of course, "I," which is characteristically elongated to "I-I-I-I" — but it is his patience and deliberation that are most noticeable throughout the five takes, the manner with which he has established a style so much his own that he can issue an understated and highly effective scream at the end without for a moment suggesting either imitation or lack of inspiration.

It is the song with which he begins and ends the session, though, the piano player Faidest Wagoner's "Any Day Now," that under any other circumstances would have had to be considered the highlight of the session. It was, said Wagoner, based on "The Bells of Saint Mary's," the title song of the 1945 Bing Crosby movie, and it is written with a devotional purity that climaxes in a vision of transcendent joy. Wagoner played with the Stirrers whenever they came to Oakland — she played with every major gospel group that came to town because she served as an assistant to the promoter, James Wilks, and her father, Reverend McKinley McCardell, was one of the founders of the Oakland Church of God in Christ. She had come to know the Stirrers well, even going on the road with them occasionally with her group, the Angelairs, and what she loved most about Sam was his ability to make a song's meaning absolutely clear. He was a crowd-pleaser, there was no question about it, "all the women went wild. You know, he was always smiling, had that lovable smile on his face. [But] he was a different man from most of the singers, he had such a talent that he could just sit up and create something, make a poem out of something, and the way he did the songs was different. They had words, they had meanings — you could understand what he was talking about."

"Any Day Now" is a masterful performance by any standard. But perhaps more significantly, it achieves a profundity that none of Sam's previous recorded performances had approached, with a somber piano arpeggio to announce its serious and stately intent, a beautifully articulated, carefully developed vocal by Sam that starts with the lowest and ends with the highest notes in his range, and a deeper meaning, which he seems to communicate with restrained but undeniably passionate fervor. When at the conclusion of the song he declares, "Any day now, I'm going home," his voice trails off in an almost wistfully ascendant falsetto that conveys all the heartbreak, all the hope, and all the fragility of faith.

It is, all in all, an astonishing performance, and the capstone of a remarkable session that, despite producing only four finished songs, suggests a level of discipline and control, a subordination of style to content that Sam had never before been fully capable of. But if you are looking for any sign of June Cheeks in these three songs, you will have to look elsewhere. In fact, the only overt evidence of Cheeks, at least to the untrained ear, comes with "All Right Now," the fourth number of the day, the kind of incantatory extemporization that was commonplace for Cheeks but not for the Stirrers, at least not up until now.

Sam plays the role of setup man here, offering a perfectly modulated Bible lesson in the second verse before June Cheeks roars in and takes the song away. Here you have all the power of live performance, with June unleashing his full-throated scream and chuffing like a preacher, his expelled breath rasping both to punctuate the sermon and raise it to higher, more ecstatic ground. It goes on for at least three takes, two of which are well over three minutes, with each yielding the same ecstatic conclusion and Art merely suggesting that the other Stirrers sound their *t*'s a little more clearly in the background. "Ri*ght*," he says, carefully enunciating and biting off the ending exaggeratedly to illustrate his point. "This is 'All Ri*ght* Now,'" he pronounces, only to be met with the immediate rejoinder — by whom and in what spirit it is impossible to tell — "You don't sing it and say 'All ri*ght*."

With or without the *t*'s, it is clear that Rupe was excited about the performance, and subsequent to the session, he edited down the best take by almost a minute, presumably for single release. But fate intervened in the person of Don Robey, the light-skinned Houston nightclub owner and reputed numbers boss who owned Peacock Records, the label for which the Sensational Nightingales, the Five Blind Boys of Mississippi, and R.H. Harris' Christland Singers all recorded. "Dear Mr. Rupp [*sic*]," he began his letter of March 25, "I had occasion to talk with Mr. Crain and Mr. Farley of the Soul Stirrers a few days ago regarding the services of [Julius] Cheeks," the upshot of the talk being Robey's reminder to his Specialty counterpart that Mr. Cheeks was "under exclusive contract to Peacock Records, Inc., and monies have been spent on the artist [whose] services . . . are extraordinary." He felt sure, nonetheless, that a happy medium could be struck, for as Robey declared philosophically, "one man's loss is another man's gain."

And yet, for whatever reason, that middle ground was never found. It may simply have been that Art resented the fact that Robey was looking for financial compensation when, as he noted on Robey's letter, at the time Harris went to Robey, following his departure from the Soul Stirrers, "we said nothing about it." Or it could have been, as Jesse Whitaker of the Pilgrim Travelers surmised, that Paul Foster saw his position threatened by June Cheeks' more extroverted approach and the Soul Stirrers elected to go the tried-and-true route rather than gamble on Cheeks' more volatile personality. The association in any case was soon sundered, the track remained unissued for nearly twenty years, and Cheeks returned to the Sensational Nightingales before long, leaving Sam with the lessons he had learned and a close personal connection that would survive, and thrive, on many fierce musical battles still to come.

Art finally issued "He's My Friend Until the End," the Alex Bradford song in which J.W. Alexander had shown such belief a full year earlier, around the time of the new session. It almost immediately rewarded that faith, with sales of over twenty-five thousand for the first half of 1954, by far the Stirrers' best showing since Sam's debut single three years earlier. Around the same time, J.W. Alexander put Herman Hill and Associates, a public relations firm, on retainer at $75 a month and shortly thereafter issued a press release saying that the Travelers had had their new Cadillac outfitted with "a white piano installed in the trunk and a midget record player in the glove compartment." To J.W. it was just a way of stirring up excitement, even if the piano didn't exist: "I had searched around to see if it was possible [to install the piano], I felt I could use it with my songwriting, but they couldn't do it at the time. However, I did *want* it done and, all through the South especially, people would come to see the eggshell-white Cadillac with the piano in it."

The Pilgrim Travelers had their virtual miniature piano, the Soul Stirrers had Sam. "We were doing very well," J.W. said. "We were a good drawing card [on the road], and we would get a new Cadillac every year." But at the same time, record sales were coming harder and harder (only "I've Got a New Home," a Whitaker composition with a catchy, almost pop feel, came close to matching previous Travelers' bestsellers), and, in J.W.'s view, they were all going to have to work just a little bit harder, and perhaps come up with new and more up-to-date methods, if they were to sustain their success in the long term.

For Art Rupe the new year was only providing further proof of his recent revelation. His faith in the dramatic, swooping style of Alex Bradford had paid off as "Too Close," Bradford's initial single for the label, continued to sell well into 1954, with eventual sales of nearly two hundred thousand copies, Specialty's highest mark for gospel sales and more than enough to qualify it as a solid r&b hit. But that, of course, was the exception, not the rule, and while Mahalia Jackson was continuing to develop a widescale white audience with her Carnegie Hall concerts and European tours, signing a five-year deal with Columbia Records in August for the kind of money (a reported $25,000 a year) that up till now had been available only to a popular recording artist, Rupe could see that the day of pure gospel, the music that had most inspired him and to which he owed so much of his success, was past and gone. Continuing with the quartets, he now knew, was going to be as much a matter of faith and hope as anything else — though he was not prepared to offer outright charity. He was, as always, committed to a hardheaded business approach and unstinting efforts on behalf of every act signed to the Specialty label.

At the same time, his deal with Johnny Vincent, the young New Orleans record hustler to whom he had issued such explicit instructions on sales and production methods, was paying off with undreamt-of results. Art didn't much like Vincent or trust his work ethic, either, but one of his first signings, a twenty-seven-year-old New Orleans–based bluesman named Eddie Jones, who dressed in a fire-engine-red suit and occasionally dyed his hair blue, delivered Specialty's all-time bestseller to date with his very first release, issued under the name of Guitar Slim. The song, a fiery gospel-laced number called "The Things That I Used to Do," which Slim claimed had been auditioned for him by the devil in a dream, hit the charts in January and remained there for the first five months of 1954, occupying the number-one r&b position for fourteen weeks and becoming one of the biggest-selling blues records of all time. More significantly, it established a style, blues with an unashamed dollop of soul, as Slim's strong church-inflected voice set the tone while the piano and simple but elegantly voiced instrumental arrangement by fellow New Orleans resident (and Atlantic recording artist) Ray Charles supplied the undeniable gospel underpinnings.

"The Things That I Used to Do" was followed almost immediately on the charts by the record debut of Roy Hamilton, a big-voiced, church-trained singer out of Jersey City, New Jersey, by way of Georgia. Hamilton applied *his* unmistakable vocal talents to an openly gospelized version of the Rodgers and Hammerstein inspirational showtune "You'll

Never Walk Alone," which vied with "The Things That I Used to Do" for eight weeks at the top of the r&b charts and even reached number twenty-one on the pop charts. Most remarkable of all, Hamilton, a clean-cut, strictly stand-up singer with no suggestive moves or lyrics and no suggestive instrument other than his voice, played to mixed crowds whose "predominantly [white] femme audience," reported *Cash Box* on the occasion of a riot in Revere, Massachusetts, "went beserk and stormed the stage."

From this point on, there was absolutely no question of the course that Rupe, and Specialty, would follow. Art soon severed his connection with Johnny Vincent because of what he saw as Vincent's maddeningly undisciplined approach and questionable business ethics, but he was determined to find the key to the crossover sales that he had stumbled upon almost inadvertently, first with Lloyd Price, now with Guitar Slim. It was clear to him that it lay somewhere in the cracks between blues and spiritual music, he suspected that it might exist in the "crying style" of rising blues star B.B. King, but one thing he was certain of: it was, like all the music he had recorded, somehow rooted in rhythm, and with the crack recording unit that he had found in Cosimo Matassa's Rampart Street studio (and with the crossover recognition that Crescent City native Fats Domino was beginning to enjoy), he was convinced that its geographical locus was New Orleans, and its spiritual heart was gospel music.

Just how convinced can be seen in a series of letters he wrote in early 1955 to the singer he had dubbed "Sister" Wynona Carr from the time she first arrived in the Specialty studio in 1949 on J.W. Alexander's rec-ommendation. Carr had enjoyed solid gospel sales and had even had something of a hit the previous year with "The Ballgame," a self-penned number pitting Jesus against the Devil in — what else? — a ballgame. This was followed in rapid succession by "Dragnet For Jesus" and "15 Rounds For Jesus," both of which remained unissued, as Art urged her instead to consider recording secular material or, barring that, to "try to write words in the blues field to songs in the Gospel field that have been hits in the past. For example, you know what Ray Charles did with 'I Got a Woman' [his end-of-the-year groundbreaking single in which Charles took Guitar Slim's approach one step further by basing the song directly on the Southern Tones' "It Must Be Jesus," a popular gospel release in the summer of 1954]. Also, Little Walter took [Sister Rosetta Tharpe's]

'This Train' and made it into 'My Babe,' and it was a big hit. That seems to be what the people are buying today, and even if you cannot sing these numbers in your style, we certainly need them desperately for our other artists."

T HE STIRRERS HAD THEIR ANNUAL SESSION in February of 1955, but this time in Chicago and, for the first time, without the supervising presence of Art or even Alex. No outtakes appear to have survived, but the four master takes would constitute the group's next two singles, as sure an indicator as you could get of Art's wholehearted approval (there was nearly a year and a half, by way of contrast, between Wynona Carr's recording of "The Ballgame" and its release in the fall of 1953).

It was a different kind of session in other respects as well, with the meticulous manner in which each song was built serving as testimony to the continuing perfectionism of the Stirrers' approach. In addition, the quietly stated interplay on organ and piano of Willie Webb and Eddie Robinson, longtime stalwarts on the Chicago gospel scene, for the first time provided the group with the kind of accomplished professional backing on which other quartets had long since capitalized.

The first number was a finely measured composition by twenty-two-year-old James Cleveland, onetime boy soprano and Mahalia Jackson accompanist, currently musical director of Reverend C. L. Franklin's New Bethel Baptist Church in Detroit and the only male member of the Caravans. Taken at a grave, almost stately pace, "One More River to Cross" has the simple classic construction that gives a pop song like Irving Berlin's "Always" its unforgettable impact. Jesse Farley's burbling bass introduces the chorus' initial harmonizing of the title phrase, with Sam's delicate tenor wafting over it and offering the variations that fill out its meaning. There is just one more river to cross before, he declares, he reaches his journey's end, there is just one more river to cross "before I'll be free from sin." The imploring hesitancy of his delivery, the contrast between his fervent desire for release and the Stirrers' forcefully voiced reiteration of the theme only serve to bolster the artful construction of the song, and when Sam brings the message home with the kind of hypnotic repetition that is at the heart of gospel music's evocation of spiritual transcendence, there remains that same gentle, almost quizzical but disarmingly eloquent touch that will always set him apart from Archie, June, or even his chief second, Paul Foster.

"Nearer to Thee" represents the pinnacle of Sam's songwriting to date, the kind of narrative skill that J.W. considered to be Sam's mark and that so many of Sam's gospel peers saw him create nightly in the extended live extemporizations that were the bell note of any gospel program. But where others created fervor through their "shouts," Sam created fervor by telling a story — and here the thematic centerpiece of the story was the familiar hymn "Nearer My God to Thee," which in the first verse the congregation is singing "in a voice that was loud and clear," in the second represents a measure of Christian faith, and in the concluding verse offers comfort and consolation to the singer. Like "One More River to Cross," Sam's song is thoughtfully constructed, but in that middle verse an interesting thing happens, as you feel Sam's imagination for a moment take flight, with impersonal moral lessons suddenly yielding to personal illumination, as the singer delares: "Songs have a feeling / There's a story in every song that we sing / Songs have been known to lift heavy burdens / If all of our troubles to God we ought to bring." And for once you feel as if you might be peering into Sam's own soul.

The last two songs of the session, "Be With Me Jesus" and "I'm So Glad (Trouble Don't Last Always)," were equally well performed but more conventional in approach, with the first, an original by Sam, building on Paul's preaching exhortations, and the second, a sixteen-bar spiritual also known as "When Death Comes Creeping In Your Room" or "Run, Sinner, Run," distinguished from its innumerable predecessors primarily by the confident curlicues of Sam's voice. In fact, what is most remarkable about the entire session is the manner in which Sam takes charge. Even on "Be With Me Jesus," on which Paul's robust tenor takes the nominal lead, it is Sam's voice that deliberately breaks the logjam of emotion that Paul establishes, it is Sam's unmistakably idiosyncratic, lightly swinging, and graceful style that resolves the tension and takes the song to new and higher ground.

"Dear Art," Crain wrote the Specialty label owner a day or two after the session from his new Woodlawn Avenue home in Chicago, "Please release 'Nearer My God to Thee' [sic] and 'Be With Me, Jesus' right away." And in a follow-up letter a week later, he added, "I trust that I made a good session. The songs go over big with the audiences wherever we appear. . . . Which one do you think is best? 'Nearer to Thee' is a house reaker [sic], SMILE. I set them up with 'I'm So Glad Trouble Don't Last Always.'" And he concluded by recommending that "Be With Me

Jesus" and "One More River to Cross" should come out "just after the other two sides."

As indeed they did. Perhaps sensing a hit, Art followed Crain's instructions to a T, giving up on their current single, "Any Day Now," which had failed to sell in any great numbers, and releasing "Nearer to Thee" within two months of the session. It took off immediately, selling almost twenty-five thousand copies in its first three months on the market and forty-three thousand by the end of the year. As per Crain's suggestion, the label owner followed up with "One More River" in June, while "Nearer to Thee" was still cresting, and *it* sold twenty-two thousand over the next six months. So the Soul Stirrers found themselves commercially resurrected, surpassing the Pilgrim Travelers for the first time (the Travelers sold a paltry fifty-three thousand records overall for the year), despite the controversy that J.W. deliberately ignited with the use of a saxophone on one of the Travelers' new releases. But whether their fortunes were waxing or waning, for all of Art's unambiguous intentions to keep on recording gospel music, neither group could miss the vast gulf that separated success in the gospel world and success in the uncharted land of rhythm and blues.

"WE COULD SEE how it was affecting us," said the Pilgrim Travelers' Jesse Whitaker. "Say there was a club down the street, church up here. You go by the club, you can't find a parking space. Go up to the church, and you can. We could see it." It didn't tempt Whitaker to make a change any more than it tempted Clarence Fountain of the Five Blind Boys of Alabama, because, as Fountain said, "You don't turn your back on God." A promise had been made, and it was not one to be easily broken. But neither man failed to recognize the temptations set out along the way, and both acknowledged how natural it was to feel envy for the rewards that others were reaping, for the "big dollar" and "the swimming pool in the backyard" that were held out as enticements merely for singing different words to your song.

Sam seemed more and more sure of himself and his ground. "He ruled Crain," Clarence Fountain observed of the power shift that had taken place within the group. Sam was now the unquestioned star, and where the older man might once have instructed, or even reprimanded, his young protégé, he now seemed content to follow wherever Sam chose to go. Which for the most part was fine because, as virtually all of

his peers were prepared to admit, Sam's instincts were good, his character almost unfailingly cheerful, and, whatever circumstances he found
himself in, he rarely surrendered his winsome appeal. But as Clarence
Fountain pointed out, he didn't take a backseat to anybody, either. "He
always thought highly of himself. He had confidence that he could do as
good as anybody." And Jesse Whitaker certainly recognized, from having
been on the road with him for nearly five years now, that he wasn't all
sweetness and light. "He had a temper. Oh, he'd let you know. When
somebody would do something to him, or somebody didn't do something right, you go to the café and [the meal] wasn't fixed right, boy, he'd
get on them."

To L.C., on the other hand, out of the army now and with little else to
occupy him as he cast about for a musical career of his own, the picture
was unclouded, the transformation in his brother's fortunes complete.
"Everybody loved him. Sam said to me, 'I don't have to turn out the
church [the way Archie Brownlee does], because I am going to sing
pretty to them, and my personality and everything are going to get me
over.' And he was right! I would go out on the road with him a lot of
times with the Stirrers, and the Blind Boys would be turning out the
house. Crain would go get Sam then. 'Come on, Sammy-o, it's time for
you to walk down the aisle.' See, Crain was a very shrewd man. And Sam
would say, 'L.C., walk with me,' and we would walk down that aisle, and
the people just forget all about Archie, the Blind Boys would be *over* —
because all the attention goes to Sam. Well, that was Crain's strategy.
And as we walk down the aisle, everybody who touch Sam would be giving him money, people would just put twenty-dollar bills in his hand,
and he would pass them right back to me. I said, 'Don't go down that
aisle too fast now, Sam, wait for me!' I mean, he could mess up a whole
program just by walking in."

To J.W. Alexander, observing it all with something more than dispassionate curiosity, "The young girls would scream, the old women would
scream. *In the churches.*" What, J.W. naturally asked himself, if Sam were
singing about love?

BARBARA SCARCELY SAW SAM anymore, her other boyfriend (and husband of convenience) Clarence Mayfield was in jail, and she had taken
up with Fred Dennis, a childhood friend of all the Cooks who had grown
up in the Lenox Building and whose aunt Edna was Annie Mae Cook's

best friend. Fred, known as "Diddy" (for "Diddy Wah Diddy") was a "prominent man about town" who owned a pool hall between Thirty-sixth and Thirty-seventh, sold reefer and cocaine, and had various other business interests on the side. She ran into him one day in a club, and he recognized her right away. "Hey, you're Sam Cook's chick," he said, and she said she had *been* Sam's chick, but Sam was married now, and one thing led to another — they had some drinks, they got high, and he told her he was married, that he had two sons and a baby by another girl but that he was separated from his wife and didn't have a girlfriend now. As she got to know him better, Barbara could see he had money — and he was crazy about her little girl, plus he was living the fast life, to which she was more and more drawn. She knew if she played her cards right, she could go places with Diddy, with the right man, she knew she could really "soar." So she told him he could support her, but she was going to work for her money so she wouldn't be obligated to him. Diddy picked up on it right away, he asked her if she could cook and clean. And so she cleaned house for him and cooked him steaks until he asked her to move in, and before long she had dyed her hair blond and was wearing it in a ponytail, just like a movie star. She may not have had Sam, but she was in the life.

Charles, too, had gotten more and more caught up in the life ("None of us," L.C. noted with sweeping disregard for civics class–defined virtue, "was following the law strictly") — but not with the same degree of impunity as Diddy, whom he continued to know as much from his various side ventures as from the pool hall. Charles had found his own way to pay for his dapper look, his slick wardrobe, and his jitterbug life, and with his truculent manner it was perhaps not surprising that he came to the attention of the law and was sentenced to two years in the pen for dealing marijuana.

Sam, meanwhile, was still ducking and dodging, as Jesse Whitaker saw it. "He was kind of sneaky, had to be careful, with all these girls coming up pregnant." It was, as Crain said, the price of fame. Once, earlier, J.W. had upbraided Stirrers' baritone singer R.B. Robinson for not protecting Sam better from the snares of his female admirers, but R.B. just chuckled and said, "Well, let him get his head bumped." But if he did on occasion experience a bump or two, the bumps were scarcely felt, and, as Barbara and the mothers of his other children might have pointed out, they didn't change his life any, just theirs — and their children's.

And yet, like so many other "sudden success" stories of his own and

other generations, he returned almost compulsively to the old neighborhood. He sought out old friends and associates, kept track seemingly of
everyone he had ever known, and, for the brief moment that he bestowed
the focus of his attention on them, made them feel, his brother L.C.
observed wonderingly, as if they were the most important person in the
world. It was as if he had the sense that he was going somewhere they
could never go and, whether out of guilt or obligation, simply didn't
want to leave any of them behind.

He ran into Lee Richard one time when he was home, and Lee told
him some of the QCs had gotten back together — himself, his brother
Jake, Bubba, too — and they had found this new lead, Johnnie Taylor,
who had been singing pop music with the Five Echoes at the Squeeze
Club. Johnnie was an arrogant little fellow who strutted around like a
banty rooster, but there was no question he had talent, he had been
rehearsing with them for a little while — *and he sounded exactly like Sam.*

Sam knew Johnnie from the neighborhood; Johnnie had been raised
by an aunt and spent a lot of time around the Cooks when he was growing up. And even though Sam remained uncertain whether the bad feelings surrounding his departure from the group four years earlier had
entirely dissipated, he started coming around to the QCs' rehearsals on
the pretext of checking out their new lead singer.

Johnnie *was* a feisty little man with a long, lantern-jawed face, full
mustache, and high pompadour, and — there was no doubt about it —
he really did sound like Sam. Far from being cowed in his idol's presence, though, his entire reaction seemed to be that he was going to kick
Sam's ass. Which Sam appreciated — Johnnie's bristling pugnacity was
probably nearly as much of a motivating factor for his recurring visits as
his fondness for the other QCs, and he encouraged them to the point
that when Bubba informed him they had gotten a recording contract
with Vee Jay but had no original material, "he said, 'Okay, when you
going to rehearse, Bub?' And he gave us a song, 'Somewhere to Lay My
Head,' and was teaching Johnnie runs, you know, he just stayed there
with us for about four hours."

They recorded the song in May, around the same time that June
Cheeks, reunited now with the Sensational Nightingales, recorded his
version of the song. The Gales' version came out first and, not surprisingly, offered a more driving, apocalyptic sound, but when the QCs'
record was released in August — slower, more plaintive, with Johnnie

Taylor's voice virtually indistinguishable from Sam's — Sam, according to Bubba, did everything in his power to promote their record, with the exception, said Lee Richard, of really going to bat for them with Crain to get them on a Stirrers program. When the record became a hit, Sam told Lee, "I sure in the hell wish I hadn't given you all that knowledge!" But Lee was sure he was joking, and Sam never asked for any credit or money for the song, either.

That was the summer that twenty-seven-year-old guitarist Bob King joined the group. Bob King was a Philadelphian who had grown up with both Sensational Nightingales guitarist JoJo Wallace and Howard Carroll, one of the founders of the Gales and currently guitarist with the Dixie Hummingbirds, whose wife was King's wife's sister. All three had played together as teenagers, at house parties as well as churches, and all three shared a bluesy style which in Bob King's case was fueled by a particular enthusiasm for the music of North Carolina bluesman Blind Boy Fuller. King had been playing with the Southern Tones, whose hit number was the recent inspiration for Ray Charles' "I Got a Woman," but the Tones had curtailed their travel, and when Howard Carroll told his brother-in-law that the Stirrers were looking for a guitarist, Bob jumped at the chance.

Clarence Fountain of the Five Blind Boys of Alabama, whose guitarist, George Scott, had always been an integral part of their sound, took credit for the addition. "We made them get a guitar," said Fountain. "We kicked them so bad they had to get music [accompaniment]. We was in Passaic, New Jersey, one night making so much noise onstage, they said, 'We got to get us one of those noisemakers, too.'"

Whether or not this account paints a picture that the Stirrers themselves would have recognized, there was no question they had felt pressured for some time to "modernize." Their experiments in the studio with drums, keyboards, and steel guitar were transparent attempts to escape the stigma of being just another one of those "old-timey" a cappella groups, and while the very distinctive vocal subtleties of their style clearly did not require overpowering instrumental accompaniment, the straightforward approach of a guitarist like Bob King, with his bluesy little flourishes, could only add to the excitement of their sound. "I was so proud of him," said JoJo Wallace, who first saw King with the Stirrers at a program in Mobile, Alabama. "He stayed harmoniously with the Soul Stirrers' style. That really impressed me a lot, because I knew he could do it once he got a break."

King was with them that summer on their extended tour of the West, with the Travelers, Brother Joe May, and Dorothy Love and the Original Gospel Harmonettes. He was certainly present when Art recorded the program at the Shrine Auditorium in Los Angeles on Friday evening, July 22, 1955. It was billed as gospel DJ Brother Clarence Welch's First Annual Summer Festival of Gospel Music and, despite the disruption of a bus and streetcar strike, drew almost a full house to the sixty-five-hundred-seat auditorium, whose cavernous stage had once served as the home court for the University of Southern California basketball team.

ART HAD HIS NEW A&R MAN, Robert "Bumps" Blackwell, at the Shrine to record the event. Bumps, a light-skinned thirty-seven-year-old Seattle native with a dapper look and a bad eye, was an indifferent musician but a tireless hustler who seven years earlier had recruited fourteen-year-old Quincy Jones and seventeen-year-old Ray Charles to his Seattle big band. He booked four or five shows a night sometimes for his various aggregations and was able, according to one of his trumpet players, Floyd Standifer, to "talk his way into anything" and not infrequently talk his way out. "He had an inventive mind," said Standifer, as well as a barbershop, a butcher shop, a jewelry business, a booking agency, and, he told Art Rupe when he showed up at the Specialty door earlier in the year, both a working knowledge of Yiddish and an advanced degree in music.

Bumps had settled in Los Angeles in 1953 after several brief earlier visits. "When I got there," he told *Melody Maker* correspondent Michael Watts, "the sun was shining, everything was happening, and I met musicians. I went home, and it took me two weeks to sell out and liquidate." He supported himself working club dates and hustling various music-related jobs, which included cutting some sides on a singer named Sonny Knight for the Messner brothers' Aladdin Records, one of Specialty's principal L.A.-based r&b rivals, who put out "But Officer" in the summer of 1953. Nothing much came of the record, but Bumps continued to cut demos on Knight, and it was one of those demos that served as his ticket of introduction to Art, who wasn't crazy about the singer but was impressed by the arrangement. Bumps went to work for Specialty on February 1, 1955, in his own mind as the label's newly designated head of production, in Art's as a "trainee a&r assistant" whom Rupe would school to do things the right way.

It took Art a while to warm to his new employee, who was by turns almost perversely peculiar, ingratiatingly sycophantic, and disturbingly transparent in his need to convey the impression that he already knew it all. But he was full of energy and eager to learn, and in the first six months of his employment, he recorded music of considerable diversity, from the driving zydeco accordion blues of Clifton Chenier to the romantic doo-wop-based balladry of twenty-two-year-old Jesse Belvin, a handsome young trendmaker who had already written "Earth Angel," "Dream Girl," and a host of other r&b hits (some under his own name, many of which he simply sold outright) for a tight nucleus of talented young L.A. musicians who had no doubt that Jesse was going to be the first in their ranks to achieve mass crossover acceptance.

It was very much of an education for an outsider who liked to consider himself sui generis (his family in North Carolina, he claimed, had its own family crest, and neither white people nor black people knew quite what to make of him) and who placed great emphasis on his "sophisticated" musical thinking and "conservatory" training. All of a sudden he was being thrown into situations in which that thinking and training were of little value. Art had him recording strictly *untrained* musicians but discovering, to his surprise, a wealth of emotional profundity that he had never previously recognized. Some, like Sonny Knight, might see him as a pure bullshit artist, but Bumps had a more exalted opinion of himself, and he saw his mission now as "organizing the ignorance and bringing the science to it," an undertaking which he embraced with typical flair.

But he had not up to this time recorded "spiritual" music of any kind, and outside of his childhood exposure to organized religion, for whose hypocrisy he had nothing but scorn, he had little awareness of gospel music, either. That was why the Shrine Auditorium concert was such a revelation to him, in almost every way.

The First Annual Summer Festival of Gospel Music would have been a revelation to *anyone* unused to the shouting, straining, sweat-soaked catharsis that gospel music offered up night after night for the modest price of admission in churches and auditoriums in city after city across the land. It was, like so much else in the black community, a *shared* experience in which the audience was fully as participatory as the performers and in some ways even more invested in the spirit. For the performers were just that — performers — and if on a particular night they did not feel the spirit, they could almost as effectively mime it ("We were making up songs to make folk shout," declared Gales' guitarist JoJo Wallace with what seems like almost undue harshness, "and [at the time] nobody was saved"). But for the audience there was no question of "faking it"; salvation occurred precisely in the manner in which they were caught up in the moment, and the whoops and cries of the crowd, the testifying and talking in tongues of men and women who came not so much to be entertained as to be carried away, became as much a part of the program as the ear-splitting screams emanating from the stage, the energetic choreography of the more acrobatic groups, and the naked show of passion, pride, exaltation, humility, invincibility, and joyful celebration that lay in equal measure at the heart of the gospel experience.

To Bumps it only served as a reminder of the human life force. "People were screaming, throwing purses and umbrellas and stickpins. You were liable to get yourself killed!" he related of his first extended exposure to the music.

In the absence of any filmed record of the performance, we can only imagine some of the more extravagant visual details, and, because of the way in which the tape boxes were labeled and stored, it is impossible to reconstruct the exact order of the program. But it is not difficult to summon up the pandemonium that greeted the little "skip and hop" of Birmingham native Dorothy Love as she sang the Harmonettes' big hit, "Get Away Jordan," and impishly stared down all the groups sitting up onstage awaiting their turn to go on who thought "they didn't need us women. And we just kept showing up!"

Brother Joe May showed up, too, the "Thunderbolt of the Middle West," in his black preacher's robes and gold cape, with nothing but a piano to bolster a voice that scarcely needed amplification, just roaring out his faith, staking out his belief in modulations, both vocal and emotional, that you would think would tear out a man's guts, not to mention his vocal cords, when repeated night after night. They were aware of it, every one, spectator and performer alike: how could they not be? Everyone warned June Cheeks that he was going to blow out his voice if he didn't learn to hold back — and what about Archie with the Five Blind Boys? How long before *his* voice was little more than a scarred and ravaged instrument? But there was no holding back, it seemed, when the spirit took you, whether the spirit was the spirit of the moment or, as so many insisted, the spirit of the Holy Ghost.

Most of the songs were far longer than they were on record, extended by both an elevation of feeling and an absence of commercial constraints. Whether it is the Pilgrim Travelers performing their "Straight Street," the Caravans, with James Cleveland's hoarse imprecations setting off Albertina Walker's commanding lead and Cassietta George's distinctive stylings, or the touching sincerity and bluesy conviction of Brother Joe May's seventeen-year-old daughter Annette and gospel veteran Ethel Davenport, there is a rising and inexorable tide of emotion, a wave of feeling on which everyone is carried, until it reaches a crescendo no longer dependent upon the performance itself but upon the spirit of every person in the auditorium. It's as if the room is lifting off and everyone in the room with it — it lifts the performers higher, it lifts the audience higher, and if you have ever been there, you will never forget it, nor will you ever again be able to imagine summoning it up by artificial means.

But at the center of the evening, and at the center of the whole emotional experience, is the Soul Stirrers', and Sam's, performance, different from any other Sam Cook performance on record because for once there appears to be no artifice, no calculation, and if there is, it is so artfully concealed as to reinforce the hyperreality of the moment.

The first number, "I Have a Friend Above All Others," is a reworking of the song that Sam sang with such breathy intimacy in the studio two years earlier as a kind of inspirational love song in which "Savior divine" was paired with "Friend of mine." Here it is not so much transformed in structure as intensified in style, as even the gentle lilt of Sam's yodel takes on a preacher's rasp altogether absent not just from the original but from any of Sam's studio efforts.

"Be With Me Jesus," from the most recent session, a nearly eight-minute-long duet between Sam and Paul Foster, only reinforces this sense of urgency, as Sam seconds Paul's extended extemporizations with both chanting repetition and emphatic exhortation ("Come on, Paul," "Sing it, Paul"), until the tension becomes almost unbearable and Sam reenters with his own only slightly more modulated voice. At the end, after declaring "I can breathe" and repeating "Now, Lord" over and over, Paul embarks upon a fervent recitation of the Twenty-third Psalm, with the calming words delivered in a way that both intensifies and crumbles meaning, as Paul enters into a state where he is practically speaking in tongues. "Oh, oh, oh, oh, surely, surely, surely, oh oh oh oh oh, GOOD-

NESS AND MERCY SHALL FOLLOW ME ALL THE DAYS OF MY LIFE," he shouts, and you begin to think it is going to go on forever until, finally, Sam's voice enters once again, resolving the tension once and for all and allowing the crowd a collective sigh of relief.

But not for long, as Sam bears down on the familiar opening notes of "Nearer to Thee," his current hit single, delivering the lines with a forcefulness that immediately elicits a crowd response. "The minister was preaching," he declares, "and the congregation was standing near," and from the start there is an atmosphere of palpable expectation, a thrill of recognition that runs through the house as Sam spins his familiar tale, but this time in the phlegmy gargle of the preacher himself. Emphatic hand claps push the song along, lift it with that note of irregular encouragement so different from the stolid timekeeping of most secular music to a higher note of anticipation, until, for the first time, the crowd really breaks loose as Sam reaches the words that will form the resolution of every verse, the old familiar spiritual that each person in the song is singing, "Nearer My God to Thee."

From that point on, he is home free, as singer and audience challenge each other to ever-greater exchanges of emotion, and the intensity of the singing, complemented by Bob King's barely audible chording and bluesy fills, generates an onrushing avalanche of feeling from which there is no turning back. When Sam sings "Songs have a feeling / There's a story in every song that I sing," the crowd clearly feels a surge of sympathy for the singer, but when, after acknowledging in the first of a series of new verses that "Trouble is one thing / That comes into everybody's life some time," he concludes with a determined reaffirmation of his faith ("I'll never give up / Every day I'm going to get nearer / Father, let me get nearer to Thee"), the room spontaneously explodes. The song builds and builds — it is as if he is extending not just its length but its breadth and scope — and when Paul comes in behind him with his fervent support, the momentum is unstoppable.

"Nearer to Thee," Crain said, was the group's "stick." That and "Be With Me, Jesus" were "how we put the hammer on." And what made it work, from Crain's point of view, was the interplay between Sam and Paul, with the congregation hollering "and Paul talking in tongues [until] they formed a line out in front of us to keep Sister Flute [Crain's term for the old lady in the congregation who started the shouting] off of us. Because she came for us, she meant it, she wasn't playing. She just wanted to [touch] that boy. Everybody loved that boy. I wish I was educated enough to tell you what that boy was."

You can hear it. You can feel it. There's no doubt about the ecstatic exchange, as Sam introduces yet another new verse in which he is characterizing not just an abstraction now but *himself*, a self who can be lonely and vulnerable ("Sometimes I like to be in the company / And then again I like to steal off all alone") but who can always be consoled by the familiar message of the song ("I know God will make my burdens all right / If I tell him, 'Lord, I've got a desire / Just to be nearer, NEARER TO THEE'").

Then, amidst the roars of the crowd, he expands the territory even further. "Do you know, do you know that bad company," he declares, "will make a good child go astray," and the heart of every mother, and many a father, in the audience goes out not just to that child gone astray but to the beautiful child up on the stage of the Shrine Auditorium who is preaching this lesson of sin and redemption.

> But I don't care what that child may do
> That mother, she'll pray for, pray for him, night and day
> When they bring that child to the mother,
> No matter, it's no matter what the problem may be
> When they say, Who is that child?
> The mother say, That child is mine
> I've been praying to Jesus to let my boy,
> To let my boy
> Get nearer, Father, let him get nearer to Thee.

And now Paul comes racing back, and the crowd gives an evocative roar of recognition mixed in with ecstatic whoops as Sam and Paul duel back and forth and Sam builds up to his final verse, the verse that is clearly intended to suggest his own mother, Annie Mae, though no one in the audience is likely to know that "Nearer My God to Thee" is, in fact, her favorite song. "I remember when I was a little boy," Sam sings, cannily measuring the crowd's emotional response but at the same time abandoned to it:

> Mother used to steal off, steal off all alone
> I used to wonder

What my mother was doing (help me, Lord)
I crept out one morning
I found Mother with folded arms
And Mother had her eyes up,
She was looking up toward the sky
And I, I saw the tears
As they fell down [from] my mother's eyes
But I could still hear the song Mother was singing,
Nearer My, Nearer My God to Thee

It is almost too much. Just Sam and Paul are left, Paul testifying, as Crain has described him, Sam echoing, guiding, touching, trading off word for word until at last they reach the almost wordless peroration of the song, a grace note, a singular manifestation of purity, a momentary glimpse of transfiguration, but one that is almost immediately abandoned for the transforming experience all over again, to be offered this time perhaps by Dorothy Love and the Original Gospel Harmonettes, at another program by June Cheeks or the Blind Boys, but always a new challenge to rise up to, a new lesson to be learned.

For Bumps it truly did represent a transcendent experience and an epiphany that had little to do with the rational plan for getting ahead on which, with a healthy dose of self-promotion thrown in for good measure, he had so far based his life. "It was awesome, phenomenal: [Sam] was like a black Billy Graham. Shit, the girls were following him around like the pied piper. Girls and young guys . . . but the chicks would just be completely gone." He saw something else, too, though. He saw that Sam Cook was bigger than the world in which he was living. He saw with the blinding force of revelation that Sam Cook should go pop.

That was what he told Art the following night at the celebratory dinner that the label owner held for all the groups at the Watkins Hotel on Adams Boulevard in the elegant "Sugar Hill" section of black Los Angeles. J.W. just sat and quietly seethed as this slick interloper who had taken the job that J.W. had turned down without any of the knowledge that should have gone with it, suggested to Art that they should test the market and try this kid that he had barely met on some popular tunes. Art was dead set against it, and so, for that matter, was Sam. Crain was, naturally, horrified and would have had Bumps thrown out on the spot if he could. But J.W., who always tried to rise above personalities and prided himself on taking the long view, sought out Art after the dinner. "I told him Bill Cook [the Newark DJ who managed the enormously successful Roy Hamilton] had been trying to get Sam to change over. And I had been working with Sam, too, and he was damn good. I said, 'Art, this kid is going to want to change over.' And he said, 'I don't know. I'm selling records on the Soul Stirrers.' I said, 'Art, if you don't do it, someone else will.'"

With the exception of the Gospel Harmonettes, each of the Specialty acts had recording sessions scheduled following the July 22 program: Brother Joe May on August 2, the Travelers on the fourth, and the Soul Stirrers two weeks later. In the wake of the concert's success, and what would appear to have been a renewed commitment to the future of gospel at Specialty, Rupe's approach to the Soul Stirrers' session was peculiarly limited, with Bob King's guitar for the most part underutilized, the addition of drums doing nothing for the pulse of the music, and, in the aftermath of the session, not a single song selected by Art for release. It's hard to understand why. "Last Mile of the Way," a 1950 Mahalia Jackson recording, was inspiringly sung, and, when Sam finally took over the lead exclusively from Paul on the ninth take, Sam's composition "He's My Guide" became one of their better simulations of a live performance, with Sam's throatily strangled screams a new contribution to his rapidly growing vocabulary of vocal techniques. "Pilgrim of Sorrow" was probably the session's highlight, with Bob King's shimmering tremolo-laden guitar suggesting the kind of blues feeling with which Roebuck "Pop" Staples was just beginning to make a name with his family group, the Staple Singers, and Sam's moody, bluesy, melancholically triumphant vocal providing a distinctive counterpoint to the more conventional gospel fare.

There is no record of Art's reaction, though there was certainly no question of his intention to have the group back in the studio again (he would rerecord two of the songs at their next two sessions). Perhaps he simply felt their hearts were not in it. Or perhaps his mind was on other things, as, not long afterward, the live recordings were permanently shelved and it seemed as if the gospel catalogue was once and for all relegated to secondary status in the label owner's commercial calculations, if not in his heart.

Bumps in any case was getting ready to go to New Orleans on his first independent a&r expedition. The primary goal was to record a singer who, on Lloyd Price's recommendation, had sent Art a tape back in February just after Bumps' arrival at the company. "Mr. Art Rupe," the singer announced at the front of the tape, "you are now going to hear Little Richard and his Upsetters . . . "

Art might have ignored it, but Richard kept calling every four or five days, from Atlanta, Albany, Georgia, Fort Lauderdale, and Jacksonville, and while the label owner didn't hear the crying voice of B.B. King, he heard something like it, "the same [kind of] feeling, and that, coupled with a gospel sound and a little more energy, was the basis for [my] being interested." By March 10 he had tried to set up a recording session in Atlanta, only to find out that once again there was a contractual issue with Peacock label owner Don Robey. By May those problems had been ironed out by means of a judicious loan to the artist of $600 with which he could buy out his contract, and in September Art dispatched Bumps to New Orleans to record Richard at Cosimo Matassa's studio (where both Lloyd Price and Guitar Slim had been recorded) with the most extensive set of instructions he had drawn up to date. "I had to literally make blueprints by writing out every little detail of what we expected. [Bumps] had been through quite a brainstorming session with me. This was his big chance." On September 13 Little Richard and Bumps entered the studio together for the first time, and five days later ("Sunday evening — Rainin' hard — Thinking of You-All") Bumps mailed back the session sheets and signed contract, along with an account bursting with the kind of carefully worded enthusiasm he had learned to adopt around the boss he called "Pappy." All nine songs, he wrote, "were exceptionally good — meaning it was difficult to pick a release." He had his own choices in mind, he admitted, "but I hate to prejudice [your] judgment." Then, after specifying Richard's preferences — "all real tough" — he came right out and revealed himself. "'Tutti Frutti Au Rooney,'" he said, "is our answer to [Chuck Berry's] 'Mabelene' . . . Richard is a great artist with loads of soul. He actually covers [rivals] 'Ray Charles' and 'Clyde McPhatter' on these nine [tunes]."

Time would only prove how right he was.

"Lovable"

Some girl was trying to turn him, make a pimp out of him. He said,
"Bumps wants to manage me, and Bill [Cook] still wants to manage
me." He said, "I need to get me another car." I said, "Man, once the
record comes out, you'll be able to get any kind of car you want."

— J.W. Alexander on a conversation with Sam at the Cecil Hotel in
Harlem, spring 1957

B Y THE TIME THAT LEROY CRUME joined the Soul Stirrers as their
new guitarist in the spring of 1956, it seemed as if Sam's future
was already inescapably upon him. Roy Hamilton's manager,
Newark DJ Bill Cook, had been courting Sam even before the Shrine
concert the previous summer, and he remained indefatigable in his pursuit. With his encouragement, Sam had started writing some little pop
songs, and Cook got them to some of the r&b groups that he dealt with
in the course of his deejaying duties as well as to Hamilton, whom Sam
admired as much as anyone in the r&b world for his emotion-laden, near-
operatic gospel style. Cook, a "slickster" in the not unadmiring opinion
of fellow DJ Jimmy "Early" Byrd, never pushed too hard, never
demanded a commitment that might elicit a rejection, but whenever the
Soul Stirrers were in the New York area, he took Sam around first to the
Apollo to meet his colleagues in the secular world, then to the West Fifty-
seventh Street offices of Atlantic Records, home of Ray Charles, Clyde
McPhatter, Ruth Brown, and just about every other high-class r&b act
you could name, where he and Sam would wait in the reception area for
no more than a minute or two before co-owners Jerry Wexler and Ahmet
Ertegun ushered them right in.

Wexler himself was perplexed by what exactly was going on. "They

The Stirrers, 1956: R.B. Robinson, Leroy Crume, Sam, J.J. Farley, S.R. Crain, Paul Foster. *Courtesy of LeRoy Crume*

would just drop by the office and hang out. There was no question they were affiliated in some way. And, of course, Sam was so hip. I kept begging him to sing the 'devil's music,' but he was a Soul Stirrer, and he just wasn't ready." As Ahmet recalled, Bill Cook put the price of their interest in Sam at helping him to get out of his Specialty contract, but "we were just waiting for things to develop."

Then in June something did develop. Whether as a result of Bill Cook's promises of stardom or Atlantic's eagerness to record him, Sam finally appeared won over, and with Bill Cook he worked out a plan to win over Art Rupe in turn. In clear, plain prose and touchingly elegant block letters, Sam wrote Art the kind of letter whose format he might have learned in a high school business course. "Dear Sir," it read:

> I write this letter to ask your consideration in a matter that's very important to me. A fellow I've been knowing for quite a while asked me if I would consider recording some popular ballads for one of the major recording companies if he could arrange it. I told him yes. So he arranged it for me. But it's my understanding that I would have to get permission from you before I went through with the deal. I'm planning on doing the recordings under another name. And I would continue to record and sing with the group. I have my material ready

and all I need is an okay from you. I wish you would give it your utmost consideration. Awaiting your immediate reply.

Rupe, who was not unaware of all the plots and machinations swirling around Sam but remained ambivalent about the prospect of breaking up the Soul Stirrers ("I was in the middle of a tense situation"), did not fail to respond to the urgency of Sam's tone. After consulting with Bumps, who was unabashed in his predictions of success and had no interest whatsoever in seeing Bill Cook reap any benefit from it, he wrote to Sam care of the Soul Stirrers on July 3 in somewhat cool and disingenuous terms:

Dear Sam,

I received your letter concerning your recording under a different name for a different company.

We appreciate your honest intentions in this matter — even though we do have you signed to an exclusive recording contract.

However, we must advise you that we are not interested in having you record for anyone other than us at the present time; and, we most certainly would be very happy to record you in the Pop field ourselves — and we feel that we can offer you considerably more success.

Therefore, we suggest that you call us immediately so that we can discuss the matter further.

With kindest personal regards, we are
Yours very sincerely,

SPECIALTY RECORDS

Art Rupe

P.S.: We sent you some song contracts which we'd appreciate having you sign and return to us.

And there the matter rested for the time being.

WITH THE EXCEPTION of their newest member, the Soul Stirrers did not seem to be taking this threat to their livelihood particularly seriously. To Crain, "A lot of things was going on that I didn't know, and

I'm glad I didn't. The Soul Stirrers was all I was thinking about, because that was my creation." To Foster, as fervent in his faith as he was in his singing, it was almost inconceivable that anyone would ever leave the gospel world, whatever the temptation. But to Leroy Crume, not yet twenty-three and on the road for the first time, everything that Sam said reverberated, and even if he was not necessarily convinced that everything Sam said would come true, he believed that Sam Cook was capable of looking into the future in a manner that none of the others either could or would.

Tall, handsome, with a prominent gap between his two front teeth and a quiet, almost courtly manner that never failed to attract the ladies, Crume had practically grown up with Sam and L.C. on the teenage gospel circuit in Chicago. He and his brothers had had a group, the Crume Brothers, who had played all the same places that the QCs played but with nowhere near the same degree of success, and when Sam joined the Soul Stirrers five years earlier, Crume had joined R.H. Harris' newly formed group, the Christland Singers. But not before his father asked Harris, "Are you going to take care of him?" And when Harris said that he would, "My daddy looked at me and said, 'Boy you better mind him.' Here I am, eighteeen years old, and I thought I was a man!"

Crume had played with the Soul Stirrers, too, off and on, "they used to have me play an acoustic guitar, just set on a chair behind them when they would come around Chicago. But then when they decided that they wanted to get a [permanent] guitar player, they got this guy out of Philadelphia, Bob King, and I was hurt."

Bob King had gotten sick, though, in early 1956, and his rapidly worsening health created a crisis for the group. Following their February 2 session, he was in and out of hospital with a kidney condition that appeared to be irreversible, and his periods of remission became briefer and further between. Crain wanted to replace him with Arthur Crume, Leroy's older brother, but Sam, who had always liked Leroy, was adamant that Leroy was the one, and, in fact, if that was what it was going to come down to, the choice was not so much between the Crume brothers as it was between himself and Crain.

As L.C. understood it from Crain years later, "Sam told him like this. He said, 'Okay, fine, we'll get Arthur. But you just gonna have to get someone else to sing lead.' Crain said, 'What you mean, Sammy-o?' Sam said, 'If we get Arthur, I'll just sing tenor, you can sing lead.' Crain said, 'Sam, you know I can't sing no lead.' Now Crain is the one who told me this, Sam never mentioned it to me. And Crain told me, 'L.C., you know Sam wasn't playing. And I wasn't gonna have Sam quit the group about singing no tenor. So I said, "Sam, you're right."' But, you know, Sam was right. Arthur may have been a better guitar player, but Leroy was better for Sam. Him and Sam communicated, they were on the same page."

That may well have been so, but Crume, who had little knowledge of the political intrigue surrounding his invitation, had misgivings of his own. He had a job at the five-and-dime, where he made $46 a week, every week, with his future guaranteed. He wasn't married, but he had an infant son to take care of. Nor had he forgotten how good R.H. Harris had been to him or how bad he had felt when the Soul Stirrers passed him over the first time. So it was little wonder that when J.J. Farley, substituting one night for the Christland's bass singer, sidled up to him onstage and said, "Hey, fucker, you want to make a change?" his first reaction was that the Soul Stirrers' secretary-treasurer, a notorious "jokester," was putting him on, his second that the decision was not his but that of the man who had given him his opportunity. So he went to Mr. Harris, but even after Harris told him he would be a fool to turn down a chance like this, Crume was still reluctant to give up the security that he had for the uncertainty of life on the road — until, finally, Sam came by and got in his face and told him that he was looking at a "career opportunity." And even then he only agreed to go out on a short-term basis, getting a temporary leave of absence from his boss.

One of the first shows that they did was in Philadelphia at the Met (more formally, the Metropolitan Opera House), an ornate hall on the corner of Broad and Poplar that seated fifty-five hundred and took up almost an entire city block. "It was an all-star show with all these heavyweight groups — I'd never been on a show like this, and I was shaking in my boots. And we was riding down the street, on our way to the auditorium, and Sam said, 'Oh, look, there's Bob.' Just walking down the street, on his way to the concert — he had just gotten out of the hospital, and I was happier to see him than they were! He didn't even have a guitar with him, he played mine the first half, and then he left and went back into the hospital, and I played the last half. We were in Florida the week after when we got the word that he had passed.

"Sam came to me then, and he says, 'You going to stay with me now, aren't you?' I said, 'No, man, I can't stay.' Well, he got all excited, so to get him off my case, I told him, Yeah, I'd stay. And he kept talking about,

'We going to have some fun,' and all that kind of stuff. But I just wanted to get back home.

"So when we got home, I went back on my job, and then the group got ready to leave and Sam came by my house, and they told him where I was. And when I came home that evening, oh, man, he got on my case. He said, 'Man, you told me you was going to stay with the group,' and I won't say what he said, but he was using all kinds of four-letter words, he was really upset. Then he asked me, 'How much money you making?' and when I told him, he just laughed out loud. Now that made *me* mad, but that got him out of his mood, he just started cracking up about it, and he said, 'I'll tell you what. You come with the Soul Stirrers, and we'll give you $125 a week and pay all of your expenses. We'll pay your rent. We'll buy you food. We'll have your clothes cleaned.' I said, 'Sam, there's not that much money in the world.'"

TRAVELING WITH THE SOUL STIRRERS was different from anything Crume had ever experienced on any of the little weekend trips he had made with R.H. Harris and the Christland Singers. And traveling with Sam as his friend and advocate was different from anything that simply being a member of the group could ever have offered. It was only a matter of weeks before he was taken off salary and made a full-fledged participating partner in Stirrers business. But it was only a matter of days before he knew that he had embarked upon an adventure that would provide him with a kind of fellowship, and education, that he had never known before.

"Every night after the show, Sam knew someplace to go. And I don't mean just one or two nights of the week, I mean *every night*. No matter how big or small the town was, Sam could find them little after-hours joints, even way out in the country. He just knew so many people, and he remembered every one, even if he didn't see them from one year to the next. You know, we met everybody at them little small hotels — r&b, blues, gospel — because we all had to stay there. Here we are, six guys in a Cadillac, with all of our clothes — I had a guitar and amplifier, and Sam was a camera bug, he had a little portable radio, too, and eventually Paul Foster and I got a little portable twelve-inch TV, because even if you could find a room with a TV or radio, that was a 'deluxe,' and that would cost you extra, probably three dollars, three and a quarter a night instead of the two dollars you paid for a regular room. And we got all that stuff in one car!

"Sam used to run my legs off. I was so tired, being up all night, and then we got to go on to the next town. One particular time, I remember, it was in Raleigh, North Carolina, and we had two ladies — well, Sam knew the one he was with, and he introduced me to mine — and I said, 'Sam, I want to go back to the hotel.' Because I wanted to get intimate with my girl. But Sam says, 'Oh, Crume, let's go one more place. Just one more place.' And we had already been to lots of places already. I said, 'Look, Sam, let me tell you something . . .' Because he was driving, you know, so I couldn't leave. I said, 'This is the last time I'm gonna run with you. After tonight, don't never ask me again.' Well, he got right up in my face with that Sam Cook look on his face, and he said, 'Crume, you just said that because you're upset. You know you don't mean it.' He just laughed and said, 'You know, man, we're partners.'

"It didn't mean nothing to Sam, he never got tired, and when we would travel the next day, Sam and I would jump in the backseat to get some sleep. Man, I'd be laying there, and Sam's sitting in the middle, and all of a sudden he'd punch me and say, 'Crume, you awake?' I'd say, 'No. I'm not awake. Let me sleep.' He said, 'Well, let me just tell you this one thing, and then you can go back to sleep.' And he'd say that one thing, but then he'd be talking for hours — about what we were going to do the next night, and who he knew where we were going, all kinds of things.

"He'd call himself whispering, but he can't whisper, and now I'm *never* going to get back to sleep. Because once he started talking, his story would never end. One time he woke me up to tell me, 'You know, someday I'm going to be rich.' He said, 'One of these days I'm gonna be so rich I'm gonna buy me a white convertible Cadillac.' I said, 'Sam, did you wake me up to tell me that? Man, get outta my ear.' He said, 'I got a plan.' I said, 'Sam, I don't want to hear nothing about what you have to say.' 'Cause he went through money like water, he threw it away. I said, 'Sam, you will never in your life accumulate anything. Because you can't hold on to anything.' But Sam was thinking way ahead, I was thinking of him, you know, doing this with the Soul Stirrers, but he was looking into the future, he was thinking way beyond the Soul Stirrers."

S AM SAW HIS WAY OUT, it slowly began to dawn on Crume, through those little pop songs he was writing all the time. None of the other Soul Stirrers paid any attention to them, they didn't even seem to notice as Sam half hummed, half sang, making up what sounded for all the world like nonsense verses in the back of the speeding Cadillac. J.W. Alexander certainly knew about Sam's ambitions and, as someone who had started out in pop music himself, even encouraged them. Alex, newly remarried, had temporarily moved to Houston and was doing some work for Don Robey, producing gospel sides on Reverend Cleophus Robinson for Robey's Peacock label and working with Robey's r&b stars Bobby "Blue" Bland and Little Junior Parker, whose "Next Time You See Me" he had just helped polish for a fee of $250.

"Sam and I got ukeleles," said J.W., "and we'd be singing pop songs. Then Sam began to write, and I got a book in New York on How to Write a Hit Song and Sell It — I forget who wrote the doggone thing. But I just told Sam to make it simple, to where little children could hum it. Housewives or truck drivers or what have you. You write that kind of melody, and lots of people will remember it. And make it danceable, that's really the key."

Crume at first saw the songs primarily as vehicles that Sam would use to entertain the ladies. "We'd get in a room and rehearse, sometimes we'd have a roomful of people, he'd get on my guitar and I'd sing backup — all he knew were three changes, but we'd sing those songs to the girls, try them out and see if they were acceptable. And they accepted them mostly!"

It didn't take long, though, to realize that the songs were intended as more than just social diversion. Sam was working on them constantly, coming up with new ones all the time. The idea, he told Crume, who was as unaware of Bill Cook's interest in Sam as the other Soul Stirrers were of the songs themselves, was to sell them to a top group like the Platters, who had just written crossover history with their number-one pop hit, "The Great Pretender," and whom Sam had somehow gotten to meet in New York. "There's money in songwriting," he declared in the face of Crume's skepticism that Sam even knew what money meant.

"He used to make me so angry. He'd go out, and, you know, he's going to buy for *everybody*. He didn't want *nobody* to spend their money. I said, 'Sam, let me spend my own money.' 'No, no, I got it.' Everywhere we'd go, he'd do that. The next day he'd say, 'Let me have ten dollars.' I said, 'I told you to let me pay for myself.' 'Hey, man, let me have ten dollars.' I say, 'All right, but it's the last time —' He says, 'Crume, you know you lying, don't you?' And he was right. I always let him have the money!"

It was an education for Crume in every respect. While he had scarcely led a sheltered life, and his father had brought him up on harsh tales of slavery and racial mistreatment, he had had little personal experience of the South since moving from Missouri to Chicago with his family at the age of nine, and the daily insults, the habit the others had all picked up of falling in almost instinctively with local laws and customs were things he simply was not used to. In Alabama they had a problem with the generator, and while they waited for the man to fix their car, they could hear the patrons of the diner next door cracking jokes about the niggers in the Cadillac that had broken down. The one thing they hated worse than niggers, they declared loudly, seemingly determined that the group would not miss out on the joke, was niggers with Mexicans traveling with them.

"And Paul Foster nudged me, and he said, 'Crume, those people are talking about you.' I said, 'I hear 'em.' Because at that time I had a process, and my hair was real brown, and I looked a little like a Mexican. One of our guys, R.B. Robinson, was born in Troy, Alabama, and he was deathly afraid, so he got out of the car and walked away, way down a dirt road. But I roused up, and one of them yelled, 'That's not a Mexican. He's a nigger. That one's a nigger, too.' And boy, oh boy, we didn't say anything. We just sat there, and they just talked about us like we were animals."

Another time, they were late for a show in Tyler, Texas, when the universal started to make noise, but the mechanic wouldn't even look at it that evening, telling them they could suit themselves, but he was going home for supper and wouldn't be back till seven the next morning. It was hot and sticky, they hadn't had anything to eat all day, "and there wasn't no hotel or motel where we could put down in this little town, but we were parked right across the street from a store that had watermelons stacked up on the porch. Man, I kept looking at those watermelons. I was going to get one and leave some money, but Sam said, 'Crume, don't do that. First thing they're gonna say, even though you got money, they'll say you're stealing.' So I didn't, and we finally settled down, all six of us, and went to sleep in the car." And when the mechanic finally put the car up on a lift the next morning, "all it was was a little bolt that was loose. He said, 'You guys could have tightened this up yourself.' Can you imagine, we missed the gig and suffered through all that because he couldn't even take the time to look at it."

For the most part, though, race rarely intruded directly, because for the most part they rarely left their own segregated world. Everyone knew about the White Citizens Council attack on Nat "King" Cole on the stage of the Birmingham Municipal Auditorium in April, but the attitude of many in the black community was that he should have known better than to have sung for an all-white audience in Alabama. "He was born there," was the sardonic refrain of one column in the *Amsterdam News*. "He should know how those old peckerwoods are." On a more serious note, J.W. Alexander was reported by the *Los Angeles Sentinel* to have "electrified audiences everywhere" on the Pilgrim Travelers' big March tour, "when he fervently ask[ed] that prayers be offered for both Miss Autherine Lucy, embattled University of Alabama coed [whose court-ordered admission in February 1956 provoked a student riot that led to her suspension, and then expulsion, by university trustees before she was even able to enroll], and the [black] citizens of Montgomery, Alabama," whose boycott of the segregated city bus system had started the previous December. But even J.W. conceded that the quartets' role in the civil rights struggle was a limited one — and would probably have to remain so if they wanted to retain the harmless anonymity that allowed them to operate just beneath the redneck radar. The fact that they were *gospel singers* was the one thing that made it all right for them to be driving around in their brand-new Fleetwood Cadillac. If they'd been Bobby "Blue" Bland or Junior Parker, with their flashy looks, flaunting sexuality, and aggressive new musical styles, J.W. knew they would have encountered far more frequent challenges, and far more open hostility, to their very ability to go about their business. The Pilgrim Travelers did sing for the Movement one time in Montgomery after the police canceled their show at the City Auditorium in a generalized reprisal against any kind of gathering that might sustain the spirit of the boycott. They sang at a local church, donating the proceeds to the boycott fund, but the police came into the church and put a stop to that, too.

It was three weeks out, five days at home, regular as clockwork, a *business*, Crume learned, with Crain in charge and J.J. Farley not just the practical joker but the "disciplinarian" and chaplain in the group, who levied fines and started off each rehearsal with a prayer. If you were late for rehearsal, it could cost you $10, and you had to change your wardrobe within ten minutes of getting offstage because you never met your fans with your stage uniform on or you faced another fine. Due to

Sam's habitual dilatoriness, Crain would always be telling them that the program started an hour earlier than it actually did, just as he had ever since Sam joined the group, but Crume took exception to being treated like that. "I'd tell him, 'Hey, man, we're grown men.'" Even though he could understand why Crain might have thought he had to do it, since Sam was always running late and might even miss a show once in a while.

"Sam liked to act like he knew everything, and I would bug the heck out of him sometimes. Sam used to say, 'I don't agree with your ass all the time, Crume, but at least I know you're telling me the truth.' You know, you could needle him because he would get so serious, and then when you'd say something to him, he'd think, you know, you were serious, too. Sometimes I'd tease him about something or other when he'd be driving, and he'd start to turning around, because he always liked to look at you when he was talking. And R.B. Robinson would say, 'Crume, why don't you leave him alone?' Because Sam would be going all over the road. I wouldn't laugh till R.B. said, 'Leave him alone,' but then I'd smile, and Sam would say, 'You fucker, Crume, I'm gonna get you for that.'"

But mostly it was Sam who led the way, even for these men who had been in the business in some cases since before he was born; it was Sam, Crume realized, whose charm, vision, insistence on personal and professional growth, and, above all, natural ease set the tone for the group, and for Crume's own experience with the group. "He made me grow up. Sam was a reader because he always wanted to learn. He was always stressing [the need] for more knowledge, even with his singing. When I came into the group, I liked to read comic books — Superman, Dick Tracy, Captain Marvel. And Sam was always in the backseat with a magazine or some kind of book. And he said, 'Crume, damnit, you're with the Soul Stirrers now, you got to read something educational, you got to put those damn comic books away.' So I did. But when I'd get in the hotel, I'd curl up on the bed, man, and get my comic books out until there was a knock on the door, and then I'd hide them under my pillow until he'd leave!

"But that's the way Sam was. He was an educational-type guy. He was the kind of guy who if you didn't know something and Sam thought he could help you with it, he was johnny-on-the-spot! He wasn't a moody person, but he could fly off the handle real quick, and if he thought he was right, he'd argue you down. That's just the way he was, kind of headstrong. He would listen to you, he would listen to anybody, but after he listened to you, if he thought he was right, he'd say, 'Hey, I'm gonna do it my way.' But if he thought about it and [decided] he was wrong, he'd come back to you and say, 'Damn, man, I was wrong. Hell, I was wronger than shit.' And, you know, most of the members in the group was like that. I think Sam instilled that in us. He didn't show his [emotions] very long. You wouldn't see him in any extended bad moods. R.B. Robinson, our baritone singer, used to say Sam was 'The Great Pretender.' Just like the song."

CRUME NEVER REALLY got to know Dolores. In fact, he was no more able to understand why Sam had gotten married than anyone else. But maybe that was what R.B. meant when he called Sam "The Great Pretender": from Crume's point of view, Sam was almost flawless in his portrayal of this "happy-go-lucky, free-spirit type of guy," but maybe he just never chose to fully reveal himself to any of them.

If that was the case, it would have been hard to say who Sam did reveal himself to. In many respects it seemed as if even without all of his reading and all of his restless exploration of worlds that were otherwise foreclosed to him, he would have had every reason to feel displaced. The church that had been the center of his childhood was long gone, and his parents, after two years in Cleveland, were once again traveling the evangelical trail. His brother Charles was in jail. The hollow shell of his marriage and his wife's consequent isolation and depression were evident to everyone around him, and his daughter by his childhood sweetheart was growing up without a real father, just as his other children elsewhere saw him only when his travels happened to bring him to their town.

The rest of the Soul Stirrers, for all of their own "happy-go-lucky" ways, owned property and had settled families of their own, while Sam had just moved out of R.B. Robinson's basement apartment for a flat around the corner from Crain's spacious new home on Woodlawn Avenue. And, while there was no question, even within the group, that he was the principal drawing card and "star," he had to share his income equally with all of the others, even his songwriting royalties, which, while they belonged to him by contract and by law, according to a long-established Soul Stirrer principle were treated as just another by-product of the group's shared labor.

There was a distinct feeling of dissatisfaction on every front. He had joined Clay Evans' Fellowship Baptist Church the previous fall both because he knew Clay from his days as a spiritual singer and because all the other Stirrers except Paul belonged. It appeared to his brother L.C., though, to be more of a social obligation than a source of spiritual solace. In fact, while few in the gospel world doubted his *sincerity,* many might have questioned the depth of his faith, and clearly it was not salvation that was on his mind so much as the disparity between what he had and what he wanted — and his own inability, for all of the strength of his rational impulse, to define exactly what that was. His wit, his charm, his instinctive kindness and shining intellectual gifts were qualities lost on no one, and he was well aware of his capacity to draw upon vast reservoirs of trust and love, but it was his own ability to give love back that weighed on him, it was his own ability to bestow the kind of unqualified love that some gave to a woman, some gave to God, that was of increasing concern to him as he continued to ponder the future course of his life.

FOR THE TIME BEING it was the road that would have to serve as his only refuge and the strangers that he met along the road as his closest friends. To Bobby Womack, the twelve-year-old middle child of the Womack Brothers, a family group consisting of five siblings managed by their father, Friendly, and largely confined to the Cleveland area by their father's job in the steel mills, "Sam brought a whole new element to gospel. He started bringing young people into the church to the point where it was like a rock 'n' roll show, chicks pulling up their dresses, and he's going out in the crowd and rubbing some girl's leg while he's singing, and she jump straight up in the air!

"And the preachers all *hated* it. I mean, the preacher's sitting up there, [preacher] has a limousine, he's got all the mothers and he's hitting on their daughters, and he's saying, 'It's disgusting. Who do [this gospel singer] think he is?' But *I'm* saying, 'Damn, this is great. That cat right there is cold. Yeah, that's what I want to do.' I didn't think Sam was putting on no show. He was just enjoying himself."

He always got them with his new song, "Wonderful," which the Stirrers had recorded at their February session, just before Crume joined the group. Composed by Chicago gospel pioneers Virginia Davis and Theodore Frye and well known from a raw 1952 treatment by Sister Jessie Mae Renfro accompanied by the Five Blind Boys of Mississippi, "Wonderful" was transformed in Sam's velvety version into a love song whose divine subject, while unmistakably referenced, could understandably be mistaken by the girls to whom Sam directed his seductive reading. "Whoa-oa-o, He's so wonderful," Sam crooned, returning again and again to the vocal mannerism that had become his signature and evoking again and again sighs, screams, and ululations of their own from his new teenage fans and their mothers. From the perspective of seventeen-year-old Mavis Staples, whose family gospel group, the Staple Singers, had just signed with the Vee Jay label, "He had an air about him, you know, just a little slick young man. I loved to see him because he was so handsome. And I loved to hear him laugh. That was all the talk with the ladies, how good-looking this man was. And when the time came for the Soul Stirrers to sing, the people would just go wild." The new song became his calling card, and Dorothy Love, whose group, the Gospel Harmonettes, always gave the Stirrers stiff competition, took to calling him "Mr. Wonderful" in joking recognition of the effect that it had predominantly on his female audience.

There was a humid air of sexual excitement almost everywhere that he appeared. Whatever form of sublimation had previously served as its disguise was gone now, replaced by the kind of naked avidity that might have been more threatening had Sam not been, as Dorothy Love suggested, "so good-looking and charming," so undeniably *boyish* in his appeal. Perhaps that was what allowed him to skitter back from the edge of outright vulgarity, to get away with things that would have simply seemed coarse in the presentations of others. What he couldn't get away from were the feelings that he aroused, the kind of pansexual hysteria that future r&b star Sam Moore witnessed as a member of a gospel quartet called the Mellonaires in Miami and, like Bobby Womack, compared to a rock 'n' roll show. "This man was so smooth, so good, and such class," Moore told writer Daniel Wolff, "I've seen women just pass out trying to get to him." Even the gospel promoter in Miami, "an open gay" in a field in which homosexuality, while not uncommon, was mostly hidden, was so inflamed by Sam's "pretty-boy" appeal, according to Moore, that he was affected in exactly the same way as the women. "I know," Moore said of the promoter's reaction, while stipulating that he was certainly not aware of any reciprocity of feeling on Sam's part, "[he] loved himself some Sam Cook."

It was not just the preachers who disapproved of the erotic atmosphere, either. Some of the other singers tut-tutted about Sammy getting the "big head." "I think it was mainly that the young ladies was just crazy about him," said Five Blind Boys bass singer Johnny Fields, "because I've never known Sam to willfully do something to somebody that would cause a conflict. But they drew their own impression." Even his sisters looked somewhat askance at Sam's new "jitterbug" image, while his brother L.C. took it as his model. Sam had started wearing his hair in a high pompadour that was processed to the bone, "and we didn't like it at all," said his older sister Hattie, "and we told him. He had too good hair to be having any process on it. We thought it was terrible."

Sam, on the other hand, couldn't tear his gaze away from the exploding crossover success of some of the new r&b rages. Thirteen-year-old Frankie Lymon, whose "Why Do Fools Fall in Love" had just gone to number six on the pop charts. Former Drifters and Dominoes lead singer Clyde McPhatter, out of the army now and on his own, whose ethereal gospel-laced falsetto was just crashing the pop charts with "Treasure of Love." Eighteen-year-old Little Willie John, whom Sam had known as a pre-teen with his family gospel group in Detroit, was now knocking out audiences all over the country with his seductive "Fever." Ray Charles had just had his third number-one r&b hit with a gospel sound no less pronounced than the Soul Stirrers'. Fats Domino was pulling in up to $2,500 a night playing to audiences of predominantly white teens. The Platters were well on their way to their second number-one pop hit of the year with the Ink Spots' 1939 standard, "My Prayer," propelled by Tony Williams' spectacular lead tenor. And Bumps' new protégé, Little Richard, had sold nearly two million records in just eight months and was in the midst of his third straight hit in a row (his second number one r&b) with a sound straight out of Alex Bradford and the Clara Ward Singers' Marion Williams.

He ran into them everywhere he went, at the diners and hotels in the "colored" section of town to which they were all consigned, driving their Cadillacs, flashing their wads, surrounded by all the emblems and appurtenances of success. These were his colleagues, these were his peers, young men his own age or younger, on their way to the kind of success he had dreamt about since he was a child. He was not the sort to be jealous, but he *knew* he could compete with them in everything but material reward — and there was no question in his mind that he was equally deserving of that.

"RETURNED BY POPULAR DEMAND," announced the nearly one-quarter-page advertisement for the Soul Stirrers' July 22, 1956, program in Atlanta, just three months since their last. "This concert will bring two stylists of lead singing together for the first time," declared the *Atlanta Daily World*. "Years ago the Christland Singers [led by an un-named R.H. Harris] were the Soul Stirrers. Then the group reorganized. From the revitalized group came Sam Cook, who sings the lead in 'It's Wonderful,' 'Nearer My God to Thee [*sic*],' and other hits." In separate squibs two and five days later, the paper cited Sam as "the inimitable lead singer" of the "No. 1 [group] in the nation's gospel song popularity polls" and pointed out that the Christland Singers had "originated the lead singer technique used so effectively" by Sam. The program, put on by veteran gospel promoter Herman Nash, would mark the two groups' "first battle of song."

For Crume, "all that father against son business" was just to build up the box office. "People still fall for it, they always come out if they think there's bad blood between two groups, in sports or anything else. But R.H. Harris was strong. And Sam was strong. I remember Crain was worried, because he was always afraid of R.H. Harris. He said, 'That's the singingest man in the business.' But I checked with Sam. I said, 'Do you feel all right?' He said, 'Hey, man, don't worry.' And I didn't."

It was just exciting to be back in Atlanta, where Nash and his promotion partner, B.B. Beamon, a former Pullman car porter who had started putting on rhythm and blues shows in the late forties, had most of the popular black entertainment business, both gospel and secular, to themselves. The last time the Stirrers had come to town, in April, B.B. King, Muddy Waters, and a new group called the Flames (whose uncredited lead singer, James Brown, was rapidly becoming known for crawling the floor and crying out the one essential word of their hit song, "Please Please Please," over and over again) had all recently appeared under B.B. Beamon's auspices at the Magnolia Ballroom on the West Side, while Little Willie John played the Magnolia just three days before their City Auditorium appearance this time. With the Royal Peacock, the brand-new Auburn Avenue Casino, Henry Wynn's Stairway to the Stars, and all the little after-hours joints and nightspots that dotted "Sweet Auburn," the temptation was to be on the go every night of the week, and it was Crain's understandable intention to make sure that his "inimitable lead singer" did not do just that on their brief sojourns in town. As a result, Crain always booked the group into Herman Nash and B.B. Beamon's hotel, the Savoy, where someone could keep an eye on Sam, and where his clear instructions were: "Check in. I don't want you guys to go out on the street. Just send out for anything you want."

Naturally that didn't sit too well with Sam. They were free agents, Sam declared with some spirit to Crume, his designated "running buddy." "He told me, 'There's another hotel, the Forrest Arms, not too far from here. Let's go down there, 'cause we got to have our freedom!' " The Forrest Arms, Sam explained to Crume, was "where all the action was," all the show-business people stayed there — and, indeed, it lived up to its reputation.

The program itself may well have been something of an anticlimax. Crume simply didn't want to see Sam or his mentor, Harris, embarrassed, and he would have thought that Sam, for all of his bold proclamations, would have felt some misgivings, but he never saw him waver. Both groups acquitted themselves well, but, Paul Foster said afterward, "all them tricks that Harris was making, Sam made every bit of 'em, that's what tricked it all." The way Paul saw it, Harris was lacking an effective second lead to set him off. "He didn't have nobody to top him out. Me and Sam was stronger than he was, and that was too bad. The booking agent, Nash, said, 'Y'all shouldn't have done the old man like that.' I said, 'Pops ought to stay in his place.' And Harris was standing right there, and he said, 'Boy . . . ' " Then the next night, they went on to do it all over again in Birmingham.

Barely one month later they returned to Atlanta top-billed over both sets of Blind Boys, June Cheeks' Sensational Nightingales, the Swanee Quintet, Edna Gallmon Cook and her Singing Son, and even Mahalia Jackson's near-rival in popularity, Clara Ward, in an event "celebrating Herman Nash's six years of Gospel Promoting." Because they were scheduled to be in New York the following day, Nash flew them in, while R.B. Robinson, who was afraid to fly, skipped the program and drove straight from Chicago to New York. For Crume it was an eye-opening experience. They had never played this big a show in Atlanta before, and the crowd was so huge they opened up the small auditorium as well as the big one and there still wasn't room for everyone to get in. Crume had been needling Sam since the beginning of the summer that the only reason he was getting all the attention was that he was always introduced last. "I said, 'That's why people have been clapping their hands. Really, they're yelling for me.' Sam said, 'Man, you must be crazy!' I said, 'No, you let me go last, and I'll show you that that hand is for me.' "

Crume had provoked Sam to the point that they started switching off, and each night he would goad him against all dictates of reason to argue over who had gotten the bigger hand. "This particular night, in Atlanta, they had five beautiful girls to introduce us and escort us all the way from the back up to the stage, and Sam and I were bickering about who was going [to go] in last. I said, 'Hey, it's my turn.' So Sam was ahead of me, ahead of Sam was Paul, then J.J. Farley, then Crain leading the way. And when they introduced the Soul Stirrers, we started walking down the aisle, real slow like, with these beautiful ladies escorting us, and the people just went crazy [over Sam], yelling and screaming, you know, and rubbing him on the sleeve just to touch him. And Sam just couldn't resist. He looked back at me, and I'm throwing my head up in the air, pretending I didn't even see him, but when we got onstage and stood there for our little ovation, Sam was punching me, saying, 'Now did you see that, fucker, all them people touching me?' And I said, 'I didn't see a thing, man. All I know, they was screaming at me!'"

They went straight from there into the Apollo Theater, on 125th Street in the heart of Harlem, the mecca of black entertainment, which had had its grand reopening two weeks earlier, "after a month of renovation and preparation," with Clyde McPhatter and Buddy Johnson headlining. The presentation of a full gospel program had been introduced on the Apollo stage some eight months earlier for a Christmas 1955 show, when gospel singer, DJ, and promoter Thermon Ruth had persuaded theater owner Frank Schiffman that not only was there an audience for the music but that audience would come to the Apollo to hear it. Ruth, something of a pioneer in the fields of both gospel and pop (his gospel group, the Selah Jubilee Singers, had first recorded in 1931, when he was seventeen years old, and his pop group, the Larks, was one of the first gospel-based crossover acts, in 1951), had recently returned to New York from a two-year stay in North Carolina and immediately reestablished himself with the city's first-ever daily gospel program, *The Old Ship of Zion,* on WOV from six to seven every morning. Once he convinced Schiffman, he had to convince the groups that "you could sing spirituals anywhere," in other words that this was the best way to "reach all kinds of people. [And] that this would be the first time they would ever be presented in a great way. Beautiful stage, great lighting and acoustics. Above all [that] Mr. Schiffman guaranteed the money [and that] they were going to get it regardless of whether the show was a flop or not," a promise they knew well from bitter experience not every gospel promoter could afford to keep.

J.W. Alexander for one hadn't needed any convincing. He seized on the opportunity for the Pilgrim Travelers to be among the first quartets to appear on the Apollo stage, joining the Five Blind Boys of Mississippi, Brother Joe May, the Sensational Nightingales, the Harmonizing Four, the Caravans, and Alex Bradford in what could have been billed as a World Series of Gospel. The Soul Stirrers, certainly, were courted for the weeklong booking, but S.R. Crain held out when he was offered no more than $1,000 for the entire group. And he continued to hold out when Thermon Ruth booked Clara Ward, the Dixie Hummingbirds, and the Davis Sisters for his second Gospel Caravan at the end of March. Ruth, and the Apollo, upped their offer to $1,800, but Crain just told them, "When you got some money to spend, you come back and talk to me."

Later that spring, Crume was present when the offer for the next Apollo bill was raised to $2,000. "Crain said, 'Two thousand dollars for a whole week, an entire week, four shows a day?' He said, 'Let me show you something, mister.' Crain brought out three contracts. One for Newark. One for New York. One for Philadelphia. He said, 'Do you see what I get for one show? We only sing for about fifteen or twenty minutes?' And each of them was a thousand or twelve hundred dollars. He says, 'I only have to be onstage for twenty minutes. And you mean to tell me you want me to sing a whole week for two thousand dollars? Mister, get out of my face with that.' And he walked away. I went up to Crain and said, 'You know we don't get that kind of money every night.' He said, 'Yeah, but he don't know that.'"

It was frustrating to Crume, because both he and Sam wanted so badly to go into the Apollo. "I told Crain, 'Think of the prestige.' He said, 'Wait a minute, Crume. Let me tell you something.' He said, 'You can't go across the street and buy a hamburger and say, "I'm going to pay with prestige." You can't do that.' He says, 'I promise you, we will go into the Apollo, but when we do, we gonna get paid.'"

They opened on August 31, at the top of a bill that included both Clara Ward and the Caravans but that clearly had been pared down to accommodate the financial needs of its headliners. Sam was so excited he lost his voice. "He wasn't used to four shows a day. He didn't know how to pace himself," Crume observed. "He was singing hard, just like it was a one-nighter. But with a one-nighter, you got all day to rest. At the

Apollo you only got a few minutes." He was enthralled, too, by all there
was to do in New York, all the sights, all the glitter, all the girls. Fats
Domino and Frankie Lymon were headlining Alan Freed's "Second
Anniversary Rock and Roll" show at the Brooklyn Paramount, which in
nine days grossed $220,000, while Fats got national exposure with an
appearance on Steve Allen's Sunday night television show.

Bobby Robinson, the proprietor since 1946 of Bobby's Happy House
record shop, just one block down from the Apollo and described by its
owner as "the first black [-owned business] on the street from the Hudson to the East River," saw in Sam a quality he had never seen before.
"He never got excited and carried away like some of the guys," said
Robinson, who had already started two labels of his own and had long
served as an impromptu consultant to Atlantic Records' Ahmet Ertegun
and Jerry Wexler on their frequent forays into Harlem, "but he kept the
audience with his little gimmicks, which made him attractive as an artist
and as a person." It made him attractive as a potential gold mine, too,
admitted Robinson, who at this point joined the growing throng trying
to persuade Sam to sing pop. "He said, 'What if I fail?' I said, 'Sam, you
can't fail.'" But Robinson could find no assurances to persuade Sam to
set aside his concerns, and they merely continued to bat the subject back
and forth. Apollo owner Frank Schiffman's son Bobby, too, urged Sam to
give some thought to crossing over. He told him, "If the rules are more
important to you than the money, then stay there. If the money is more
important, come this way." But he got no more indication that Sam was
taking the matter seriously than Bobby Robinson had.

Meanwhile, unbeknownst to any of them, including Crume, Crain,
or any of the other Soul Stirrers, Sam had already had his first pop session. Bill Cook had shepherded him into the Nola Recording Studio on
Broadway, between Fifty-first and Fifty-second Street, in an experiment
that Art Rupe had agreed to underwrite. Rupe seemed to have accepted
that the Newark DJ was Sam's de facto manager for a career that was, for
the moment anyway, purely theoretical, and Cook for his part was pressing his case even harder with Sam following the departure of his meal
ticket, Roy Hamilton, in May. Hamilton, just twenty-seven and at the top
of the pop marketplace, had been forced into premature retirement by a
case of "tubercular pneumonia" that doctors told him would prevent
him from ever singing again. Bill Cook, in fact, was booked into the
Apollo the week after the Soul Stirrers closed in what was announced as

the start of a new career as a comedian and singer from which, the *Amsterdam News* reported, he intended to dedicate "a ten per cent commission to his retired client." With his new client, and an accomplished rehearsal pianist, possibly Hamilton's arranger, O.B. Masingill, Cook cut demos on half a dozen of the "little songs" that Sam had been fooling around with on the road as well as a number that he had himself written for Sam, "I'll Come Running Back to You." It's not hard to see why, as Crume said, the girls all went for them. These were beautifully romantic sentiments ("I Don't Want to Cry," "The Love I Lost," "The Time Has Come to Say Goodbye") set off by Sam's gorgeous delivery. There is no pace to the songs; they are steady, stately, and almost uniformly regretful, sung with absolute confidence at the top of the singer's range with his characteristic yodel trailing uncharacteristic clouds of winsomely bittersweet resignation and remorse. The one song that didn't get on tape was a pop translation of "Wonderful," the number with which Sam had by now come to be identified, but it was hardly surprising, given the misgivings that Sam so evidently felt, that he and Bill Cook could not come up with a suitable transposition. Cook dutifully sent off the tapes to Bumps Blackwell and Art Rupe, advising them that this was, of course, in the nature of an experiment and that he was certain they would do better next time.

Art Rupe remained almost as ambiguous as Sam, not about the matter of turning gospel into pop, a process to which he was by now irrevocably committed, but about the harm that Sam's departure would inevitably do to the Soul Stirrers, not to mention the uncertainty of Sam's secular success. For Bumps, though, this was the validation of the moment for which he had been waiting ever since first seeing Sam on the stage of the Shrine Auditorium one year earlier. He had known from that moment that Sam could be "as big as the Platters," and his own education in rhythm and blues and gospel music over the past year had only confirmed that point.

"Gospel songs intrigued me," Bumps told *Sepia* magazine sometime later. "I began to recognize entertainment and cultural value in them beyond their religious interpretations." More important, as he was more than willing to admit in other, less formal settings than a press interview, the music had caused him to abandon *his own* prejudices, his own inclination to "look down my nose at these untrained, undisciplined people." Instead, he came to recognize that "people didn't give a damn what I thought I knew and the technicalities behind the knowledge that I had," that all of his formal training was worth very little in the face of "this abandonment, this honesty, this truth," the raw, unadulterated outpouring of feeling that emanated from the gospel and rhythm and blues music that he was now recording.

With Sam he never gave up pointing out that singing had nothing to do with whether you were religious or not. "A shoemaker doesn't leave religion to make shoes. He attends church on Sunday." So, too, did plumbers, doctors, even people who pursued "decadent professions" — they all had their own covenants with God. So why shouldn't a singer, too? He told Sam, "You don't leave religion to sing." An artist was someone "born and endowed with talent. Character is something you acquire. If you're a singer and that's your living, what's wrong with that?" There was no inherent taint to *any* kind of music, so long as you were not singing degrading material — and he knew Sam would never do that.

He pointed out, too, the success he had had with Little Richard in the past year, the material rewards that both he and Richard had achieved, the bookings and movie offers that were pouring in. And while Sam was playing the Apollo, clearing maybe $400 or $500 for the week, Richard was headlining the twelfth annual Cavalcade of Jazz at Wrigley Field in Los Angeles, where he drew fifteen thousand people, then heading straight into an appearance at L.A.'s plush new Savoy Ballroom and the filming of Alan Freed's *Don't Knock the Rock,* the follow-up to the rock 'n' roll disc jockey's *Rock Around the Clock.*

Bumps *knew* Sam could do the same, or better. He was as certain of it as he had been of anything in his life, and any lingering doubts he might have had on the subject had been altogether dispelled by his experience at the first Soul Stirrers session for which he had had direct responsibility back in February. That was when he finally became convinced that Sam Cook possessed a spark and a talent unparalleled in his musical experience. They were on their way to the studio, and Sam was not prepared — you could call it anything you wanted to, Bumps said, but Sam simply had not come up with the material the group was counting on from him.

"So S.R. Crain was a little upset, but in his little religious way he was sort of nice about it, and he was saying, 'Sam, the folks are waiting for you to sing them a song, and if you don't get yourself together before we get to the studio, what are we going to do?' So Sam said, 'Well, hand me the Bible.' And they handed Sam the Bible, and he was thumbing through it, skipping over it and skimming through it, and he said, 'I got one. Here it is right here.'" At which point Sam put the song together right in front of Bumps' eyes.

"He said, 'Okay, strike the chords.' So the guitar started playing these two little chords, and Sam started singing, quoting right from the Scripture, where Jesus was coming into the marketplace and he met the woman at the well, singing 'There was a woman' — and those chords were coming — 'in the Bible days.' And [then]: 'Whoa-oh-oh, She touched the hem of his garment and was made whole.'" The song was "Touch the Hem of His Garment," one of Sam's most eloquent compositions, and Bumps recognized on the spot, "it was right then that I said, 'Well, I have heard everything.' I said, 'Now this is really, really, really too much.' That song went together so quick you wouldn't believe it!"

From that point on, Sam recalled, with the sense of someone who is merely being persuaded to do something that he already knows he secretly wants to do, Bumps never missed an opportunity to remind him that "I had the voice, the confidence, and the equipment to work as a single and that I ought to give it a try. He was constantly prodding me to make the change whenever he got the chance." Without even being aware of it, Bumps was playing on a lesson that Sam had absorbed from childhood on. "Making a living was good enough, but what's wrong with doing better?"

J.W., too, was more convinced than ever that there was no other way to go. His own experience this past year only bore out this conviction. It had been a terrible year for the Pilgrim Travelers. Total record sales had dropped to a low of 66,000, with just $1,350 in royalty income (compared to 157,000 sales and $3,000 in income five years earlier). In addition to which, J.W.'s lead singer, Kylo Turner, the center of a stable lineup for the past ten years, had left him. And Art Rupe, who he felt had always regarded him more as a trusted colleague than as just another act on the roster, seemed to have grown deaf to his suggestions and entreaties in the face of a market that continued to shrink even as new markets (prompted by the kind of exposure offered by the Apollo's Gospel Caravan and Mahalia Jackson's and Clara Ward's increasing international celebrity) should have been opening up. Even the Soul Stirrers' sales failed to reflect the wave of teenage hysteria that greeted Sam's nightly appearances, and neither "Wonderful" nor "Touch the

Hem of His Garment" managed to sell twenty thousand copies before the year was out.

Herald Attractions bookings for both groups had fallen off, too, as longtime agency head Lil Cumber was forced out in June and the new girl, who was rumored to be a girlfriend of Bumps, appeared incapable of taking well-meant suggestions and in general seemed not up to the job. Alex tried to be loyal ("I have never said you made a mistake in letting Lil Cumber go," he wrote Art some months later, "even though I hear it daily from promoters"), but the treatment that he got in return, he felt, indicated something of the seismic shift that had taken place. In September he wrote to Art from Atlanta, pleading for more support from the company but also informing Rupe as his publisher that "the new number I was telling you about by Ray Charles ["Lonely Avenue"] is really a take off of [the Travelers'] 'I Got a New Home.' I'd certainly like for you [to] give a listen and see about collecting royalties for us." When he heard nothing back from Rupe, he wrote to him again at the end of the month, pointing out that the two tunes were not just similar but the same and that people, as a result "are believing it ['Lonely Avenue'] is us and I feel we should get something out of it." But Art failed to follow up, and J.W. simply took it as one more indication of the extent to which gospel music was being swallowed up by pop.

His solution was to try to do in the new arena what he had always done in the gospel field: scout around for singers with broad appeal and thus prove his value to the company in a fresh way. Unfortunately, he was now dealing with Bumps, not Art, and Bumps rebuffed his efforts with a kind of condescending nonchalance, lecturing him more as if he were an inept amateur than a senior colleague. "It seems," Bumps wrote at the end of the year in response to a tape Alex had sent him, "that you are confusing Blues with Rock 'n Roll (or Pop). We are not interested in Blues at the present time; we would like Pop tunes with a blues chord structure which lend themselves to blues backgrounds. . . . If you have any questions on this I would be most happy to cooperate with you. In writing the lyrics try to write 'white' for the teen-age purchaser rather than 'race' lyrics. It seems the white girls are buying the records these days."

I T WAS IN PURSUIT of that new audience that Bumps took Sam to New Orleans in December. Bumps himself was getting married there on December 16, so the December 12 session date may have been something of a convenience, but the studio, the location, and the rhythm section were not, as they had proved their worth over and over again, with Fats Domino's huge new pop hit, "Blueberry Hill," only the latest commercial manifestation, though perhaps the most spectacular one to date.

Cosimo Matassa's eponymous Cosimo Recording Studios on Governor Nicholls was a recent outgrowth of his old J&M record store and studio on Rampart and Dumaine. Matassa, whose family had long owned a grocery store in the Quarter, had gone into the jukebox business with a friend of his father's at the age of eighteen while he was waiting to be drafted. They sold records as a sideline and then, when the war ended the following year, opened up a brand-new record store, "and my partner, a guy named Joe Mancuso, said it would be a good idea to put a room in the back where people could make personal records."

That was the genesis of the business that had consumed him for the past decade and created an industry with no center (there were no New Orleans record labels, nor did Cosimo appear to have any driving ambition to start one of his own) other than Cos' studio. Matassa, a cheerful, easygoing man with a quick wit and a lifelong passion for reading, seemed perfectly content to record for whatever label (Specialty, Imperial, Aladdin, Atlantic) was putting up the money, and his modest manner, uncommon curiosity and openness to both new ideas and new technology, along with a democratic embrace of people of every stripe and personal background, helped foster an unusually relaxed social and musical atmosphere. From his work with Little Richard, he was impressed after a fashion with Bumps, whom he saw as "a motivated a&r guy, I don't know if 'organized' is the right word, but he was focused, and he was in charge." Cos recognized his deficiencies as well. "Oh, if you're talking about the next level up, I would say that he was maybe his own worst enemy. But that was because he was satisfied that he was good. He wasn't exactly timid."

As far as the great Sam Cook experiment was concerned, from Cos' point of view, it was no big deal. "I had done something like that for Imperial Records with a group called the Spiders." And, musically, it was the most logical thing in the world, "because gospel singers *sang*. It wasn't like taking some fifteen-year-old kid and teaching him." It was, on the contrary, working with someone thoroughly educated in how to sing and sell a song and in possession of a storehouse of musical and vocal knowledge that offered as much depth and sophistication as any musical tradition in the world. As for Sam, "I was aware of him through his gospel singing. He was disciplined. He wasn't egotistical, despite the fact that he sang like an angel. I think he understood it better than any of us."

Sam might very well have questioned this assumption of self-assurance. He was eager, certainly, but not confident by any means that he was ready. He was going into the studio with three songs he had already worked on with Bill Cook, plus several new ones and "Lovable," the adaptation of "Wonderful" that he and Cook had attempted but been unable to successfully complete. The idea of "translating" Sam's gospel hit had appealed to Art Rupe, though, who turned it over to Tony Harris, a twenty-two-year-old gospel singer who had grown up in Los Angeles and recently left his group, the Traveling Four, to move back home with his new wife. In L.A. he had joined another gospel group called the Golden Chords and met a woman named Mabel Weathers, a junior high school counselor who dabbled in the record and talent-management business. Weathers introduced the group to Bumps, who cut a pop demo on them as the Dap Daddies — which was how Tony first came to Specialty. And while nothing came of the demo, Tony continued to assid-uously pursue individual opportunities of his own.

He had been unable to get a recording session, though, because, Bumps told him, Art thought he sounded too much like Sam Cook. So it should have come as no great surprise when Art came downstairs to the little rehearsal studio in the Specialty basement where he was working on a demo with Bumps, "and he asked me, Could I write a song for Sam that was similar to 'Wonderful'? I went home and wrote the lyrics, and then I [demoed] the song myself, and Art loved it."

Harris knew Sam a little. "I had met him after a program in San Diego — we went over some girl's house, and later I saw him in Lufkin, Texas, Crain's hometown, and he was on his way to some other girl's house. I liked him, he was fun, but he was serious about what he did." And though he certainly wasn't aware of it at the time, it didn't surprise Tony Harris to find out later that Sam had already taken a crack at the song or that he might have had trouble with it ("We were all kind of brainwashed about gospel music"). Nor did it bother him in the least to share the writer's credit with Sam.

Sam sang the song to Crume on the road, at the same time that he revealed he was going to New Orleans to make a pop record. "But, Sam, that's just like 'Wonderful,'" Crume protested. And though he was clearly ambivalent about the matter, Sam simply replied, "Yeah, that's why it's going to sell." To Crume's even greater consternation, the recording session was set for the same day that they were scheduled to set out for New York for a return engagement at the Apollo Theater. That was okay, Sam said, he and Crume would simply fly. "How *we* gonna fly?" Crume demanded. And then Sam sprang it on him that he was expecting Crume to accompany him on the session. "No, no, Sam, no way," Crume remonstrated. "I gotta be with the group, man. I can't leave them stranded." So Sam went off to New Orleans alone, revealing his plans to the other Soul Stirrers only at the last minute and telling them not to worry, that he would be in New York in plenty of time.

But in reality he was not all that sanguine about the situation. As much to protect the group as himself, he had agreed to the same plan that Art had proposed to Sister Wynona Carr: to change his name, if not his style, by just enough to sidestep the question of identity should his fans react strongly against his decision. He would be recording his first pop sides under the name of Dale Cook — it could be a brother, possibly a cousin, Sam agreed, if that was what people really wanted to believe. He would be going in, too, he rationalized, not just for himself but for his family. "I had a wonderful time, a wonderful life," he explained just one short year later. "I was doing the thing I liked best and getting paid for it. [But] there were a lot of things I wanted to do. I wanted to do things for my family, and I wanted nice things of my own." Or, as his father had drummed into him from childhood on, "Man looks at dollars. God looks at your heart." And so he took the plunge.

THEY ENDED UP CONCENTRATING on four songs: "Lovable" and a doo-wop ballad called "Forever" by saxophonist Red Tyler (a stalwart on the Little Richard sessions), plus "I Don't Want to Cry" and "That's All I Need to Know" from the New York session. Sam was backed by a small four-piece unit led by drummer Earl Palmer, with pianist Warren Myles taking typical triplet-laden New Orleans leads, and after a good deal of trouble with his phrasing (which may have been exacerbated by the combo's own difficulty with his light, airy tone), Sam finally got "Lovable" right on the sixth take and then delivered an even better version on the seventh at almost exactly the two-minute-and-twenty-seconds length that Art had determined was optimal for pop radio airplay ("Art had been through analysis," Cosimo Matassa remarked with wry amusement, "and he would explain to me why certain records sell"). Sam delivered his new message with the same combination of smooth conviction, precise articulation, and unerring melodic improvisation that was the hallmark of his gospel style, though there is unquestionably something missing. Or, perhaps more to the point, there is an inescapable awkwardness attached to the evolutionary process, somewhat similar to the transformation of a popular song into a television commercial. But once that process got under way, there was no lack of purposefulness, there is, certainly, no lack of intent — and there is no one else directing the show. As Cos observed, "You might argue that he was self-produced from day one. You can't steer that kind of talent."

The other three songs were all completed with varying degrees of dispatch and, like "Lovable," were constructed around the same uncomplicated "ice cream chord" changes that characterized so much of the simple doo-wop-based material of the era. They were, anyone would agree, undistinguished songs elevated only by the sound of Sam's voice — but that made all the difference and set them apart in a way that even the most sophisticated harmonic structure never could. The way that Sam drew out unexpected words ("r-e-e-a-lize" or "te-e-e-ars" or even "tho-o-ought") at unpredictable intervals; his characteristic "Whoa-o-oa-oh," by now an unmistakable trademark; the effortless leap into an almost weightless falsetto; the manner in which he repeats and draws out a phrase like "I know" teasingly until at last he brings it to its inevitable resolution; the endless permutations he lends to the "i" sound of "cry," "why," "my" until the words ring with melismatic grace and it almost seems that sound replaces meaning; above all, the purity and beauty of an instrument in which the singer takes such manifest delight and over which he exerts such striking command remain an abiding source of fascination far beyond the banalities of mere words or the thoroughly conventional I-VI-IV-V chord structure.

Oddly enough, though, the most intriguing material from the session came in a series of five songs that amounted to little more than demos, with an a cappella, almost wordless variation on "I Don't Want to Cry" that far surpassed the finished version (if there were anything needed to prove the compelling beauty of Sam's voice, this would be it), and Edgar Blanchard's bright jazzy guitar chording providing the principal accompaniment on the rest. Two in particular stand out: each conveys that wistful sense of mystery and haunting melancholy that are at the heart of Sam's sound and that nothing in the fully produced sides comes close to achieving. The first is the Bill Cook composition "I'll Come Running Back to You" that Sam had tried at the August session in New York. No more, really, than the most conventional romantic ballad, it achieves a kind of gravitas by the very way Sam's voice skates on the edge of naked revelation. The song begins with that most familiar of lovers' plaints — something along the lines of who's loving you tonight? — and yet a sense of emotional betrayal comes through that would be unimaginable were it not for the delicacy of Sam's delivery. In the bridge the singer compares himself to a lonely king sitting forlornly on his throne. What could be more hackneyed? Once again, though, with Sam's unique manner of delivery, what could be more heartbreaking?

His own composition "You Were Made For Me" was a poem of which he was justifiably proud. "A fish was made to swim in the ocean," he begins. "A boat was made to sail on the sea / As sure as there's a God above / I know you were made for me." It is plain, it is simple, it is deeply felt. "Darling, we'll have our quarrels / And you will upset me / But what can I do?" he declares in the bridge, which he voices not once but twice, just as in the Bill Cook song.

> You've been mine
> Ever since I met you
> And I'll never leave you

Who is he thinking of? Does he have anyone special in mind? There is a quiet note here, there is no showing off. Any girl who heard the song might think he was singing to her, but he is singing from somewhere deep down inside; just as with the greatest of his gospel songs, it is his directness of communication, not the tricks of his style, that are the key to his appeal.

It's hard to say why this and the Bill Cook number were not further explored, even as other, less distinguished material was being focused on. But the three-hour session proved a point, and while the setting might have been more sympathetic ("Forever," with its unbilled sax solo by Red Tyler, could almost have stood in for a Fats Domino number as interpreted by Sam), the approach better thought-out, in the end they had what they had come for, and Sam had finally done what he had known he was meant to do all along.

From there he flew to New York as planned, where the Soul Stirrers were once again headlining a somewhat truncated lineup that included the Davis Sisters, the Gospel Harmonettes, and the Harmonizing Four, featuring the spectacular lead bass voice of Jimmy Jones. With the addition of Alex Bradford, still riding the wave of success that had begun a year earlier with "Too Close," the booking was extended through Christmas, and Dolores and her son, Joey, joined Sam in New York. But the marriage was dying; Dolores showed increasing signs of dissatisfaction and depression; and Sam was about to become a father again, as Connie Bolling, a slender, light-skinned girl he had met in Philadelphia through Crain's girlfriend, Joyce, was due to give birth in early January.

Bill Cook was jubilant as he and Sam talked about the New Orleans session. He couldn't wait to hear the tapes, he said, but from everything Sam had told him, it sounded as if he and Bumps had achieved the objective they had all been talking and dreaming about for so long. Cook agreed they might really have hit pay dirt with "Lovable," which Bumps was referring to as a potential "moneydripper." All he wanted now, as Sam's manager in the pop field, was to have a chance to start doing his job, to begin promoting Sam the same way he had promoted Roy — and, he was certain, with the same results.

Meanwhile, L.C. had just played Memphis with the Magnificents, the group that the Chicago DJ Magnificent Montague had promoted and produced for Vee Jay Records. Their first number, "Up On the Mountain," had been a Top 10 r&b hit that summer, and L.C. had joined when Thurman Ramsey, one of the group's original members, was drafted several months later. They drove down to Memphis in the Spaniels' green 1956 Mercury station wagon (the Spaniels, who now included Sam and L.C.'s boyhood singing partner James "Dimples" Cochran, were still riding high from their 1954 doo-wop standard, "Goodnite Sweetheart, Goodnite") and were somewhat disconcerted by their first trip to the South. But nothing was so strange to them as the show on which they performed, Memphis' all-colored radio station WDIA's *Goodwill Revue*. Ray Charles and B.B. King were the headliners, but that rock 'n' roll singer Elvis Presley, who was getting so much attention, also showed up at the Ellis Auditorium, and the crowd went wild when he was introduced — in fact, that was the end of the show. WDIA announcer Nat D. Williams, the show's organizer and compere and a frequent contributor to the black press, posed the question in his regular column in the *Pittsburgh Courier*: "How come cullud girls would take on so over a Memphis white boy when they hardly let out a squeak over B.B. King, a Memphis cullud boy?" And answered it with another question as to whether "these teenage girls' demonstration over Presley doesn't reflect a basic integration in attitude and aspiration which has been festering in the minds of most of your folks' women-folk all along. Hunh??"

But perhaps even more astonishing to L.C. was what appeared to be Presley's own unexpectedly democratic attitude. As he did with every other colored performer backstage, Elvis treated the Magnificents with considerable respect ("I've got all of your records — 'Up On the Mountain' and the other side," he told leader Johnny Keyes with disarming humor), but once he heard L.C.'s name, "he shook my hand and told me he loved my brother — he knew his gospel music — and he talked to me for about twenty minutes about Sam." It was just one more proof, if proof was needed, of "the basic integration in attitude" that was overtaking them all.

"Dear art," BILL COOK WROTE to the Specialty label head in a handwritten letter dated January 6, 1957, but not mailed until eight days later. "Sam was describing the session to me and it sounded like you might have captured the thing that we were looking for." Sam had told him to expect tapes or acetates sometime after the first, which was why he was writing now, because "I'd like to hear them." He was delighted to learn of "the new version of 'Wonderful' which is something I'd submitted to him here. I'm glad he did it. It should be great. . . . I'd like to know what your opinion of the new songs and versions by Sam are. [Also] please advise me as soon as possible if and when you plan a release date on Sam so I can start some D.J. contacts."

"Hi Bill," Bumps responded in a neatly typed reply that was dictated to a secretary and furnished both his company affiliation, "SPECIALTY RECORDS," and his full name, "Robert A. Blackwell," in the spaces above and below his signature. By now, he wrote, Bill should have the acetate of what Specialty was proposing as Sam's initial release, which, Bumps felt, "will make a good introduction for Sam. Altho I know we can and will do a better job on our next release — with stronger material.

Sam is definitely a modern Morton Downey [the Irish tenor from the thirties who specialized in sentimental songs and was known as "the man with the choirboy's (voice)"] and concentrating commercially with this in mind, and securing OLD DOWNEY HIT MATERIAL etc., with today's POP treatment, should bring Sam to the front — with both the teenagers and housewives.

Sam should also be concentrating on a better and stronger follow-up record, with stronger material. I am also looking and filing away what I feel Sam can do. I would like to know Sam's availability, and will be back in New Orleans (tentatively) around the 1st of February.

The release date has not been set on the record — but it will be soon — within three or four weeks.

Musically yours

There is no record of Bill Cook's reaction, but J.W. by now had lost almost all faith in both Art and the record company. "Dear Mr. Rupe," he wrote from Detroit, on January 22, in a pained lapse into formal expression, "I really hate to make myself a nuisance but things have been going very poor for my group." They had not worked more than 30 percent of their usual schedule, and "it definitely is not because [lead singer Kylo] Turner isn't with us." What they needed, said Alex, was a new release to promote their personal appearances, since in this business "everything is tied together [and] if you miss on one, you'll hit on the other. [In any case] the group would certainly appreciate your consideration and suggestions on how to better our situation very much."

He may have regretted asking the question, because on January 24 Art wrote to him care of Newark gospel promoter Ronnie Williams and unloaded feelings that must have been festering for some time. "Here are the facts of life as they exist and you might as well face up to it," Rupe declared with little regard for the social niceties.

(1) You are not acceptable as the lead singer and should forget about singing lead — particularly on records.

(2) Turner is most definitely missed and many promoters refused to even book you without Turner. As a matter of fact some promoters who have played you without Turner refuse to have you back because they feel they were gypped and you don't draw without him.

The solution, Art concluded, was obvious: "Either get Turner back and make some good records or do it the hard way with a new lead singer like the Stirrers did with Sam Cook when he first joined them. We have released more records on you, Alex, than on any artist and frankly we do not have anything on the shelf at the moment good enough to do you any good. Hoping that you appreciate the honesty of this letter, I am, Yours very sincerely . . . "

"It was very kind of you to take time out to answer my letter," Alex replied with even more strained politeness, rebutting Art's points one by one and suggesting that if Herald Attractions would release him from his booking contract, he could perhaps do better on his own. He pointed out, too, as he had in his last letter, that "I have a very good [young] lead singer and some very good material.

> But if you feel that the group is no longer any service to you, please let me know. . . . Please remember Art that my loyalty and personal feeling for you is definitely the reason that I didn't always operate on the best business principles with you. The fellows would like to know. Please let me know by return mail.

What hurt even more was the knowledge that Bumps, who could have been an effective ally and whose own agenda Alex had always helped to advance, whatever his personal reservations, had stabbed him in the back and was even now trying to lure Turner into signing a solo contract. ("Sam Cook's release in the other field will be going out soon," Bumps wrote to Kylo on January 4. "I am interested in recording you — POP or otherwise — depending on material.") But Bumps, he had long ago concluded, was a lost cause; Bumps looked out only for himself — and even in that regard, Alex felt, he had a limited perspective.

Ironically, Art had no more faith in his number-one employee, who, he was increasingly coming to believe, was not so much malevolent as "just dumb and naive." He had checked up on Bumps' credentials in September and discovered no record of degree credits at either of the schools he had claimed to attend. He had stated emphatically in his notes for Bumps' new contract of five months earlier that Bumps would "personal manage only those I approve — will drop all others [including Little Richard]," and that his 5 percent management fee on Art's pre-approved list would be split fifty-fifty between the two of them. But this was just to protect himself from Bumps' overreaching. For all of his doubts about Bumps, they continued to share a similar vision of the future, and

Bumps, despite his transparent scheming, remained surprisingly malleable to the stringent demands of a boss he continued to call "Pappy."

In fact, if Art mistrusted anyone, it was Sam Cook, who was clearly playing both ends against the middle with Bumps, Bill Cook, Crain, and, for all Art knew, even poor old Alex. He had observed Cook closely from the beginning, and he had never had the feeling for him that he had had for Crain or Alex or even Alex Bradford, whose inventive attempts to take advantage of his employer amused Art as much as they annoyed him. Other artists like Brother Joe May might blow up over one vexed issue or another, but Art, a nonbeliever, had always been able to palliate them with bromides about their all being "creatures of the Creator [with no] barrier of me being the boss or of us being of different shades of skin." Or reassure Brother Joe that since "you know that we are in your corner, and we know that you are in ours," they should both be patient and "wait for the success and rewards that God intended for both of us." Even Alex, who prided himself on his business acumen, always folded when enough patient pressure was applied. But Sam gave away very little of what he was thinking, he was "an intense guy, and he gave the impression of being a little bit cocky, very sure of himself. Prove it! You gotta show him." When you talked to him, "he didn't give an appearance of being nervous . . . he'd really listen and look like he was taking in impressions with his pores as well as with his eyes and ears." He was, Art felt, a genuine "enigma. He had two sides, his talent and his character." And given how little of himself Sam ever revealed in his dealings with more experienced colleagues and mentors, the Specialty Records boss had genuine misgivings about the latter. But "his talent was unique and unusual," and as a businessman with confidence in his own unique and unusual qualities, Art felt he had little choice but to forge ahead.

The Soul Stirrers had misgivings of their own. Crain was concerned about the group's dwindling record sales, and by now he was well aware of Sam's pop session, so when Sam started lobbying for an Imperial LeBaron, the new luxury model with the decorative spare on the back, he was understandably reluctant to jump right on his lead singer's request. "It was the first year they put it out," Crume said. "It was different than any car on the street, and Sam fell in love with that car, he wanted it in eggshell-white."

The other Soul Stirrers were no more sanguine about Sam than Crain at this point. They had all seen him hanging around with Bill

Cook, and Tony Williams of the Platters appeared to be offering him plenty of advice. But they all tiptoed around the subject until R.B. Robinson brought it up in a group meeting. "Now, Sam," he said, "if you're going to stay with us, we can do it. But if you're not going to be here, man, you know those are big-time car notes —" But Sam just said, "Hey, man, I ain't going nowhere. Where am I going?" So they got the car, and many nights Sam got to keep it, and he would come by Crume's house, "and he would say, 'Hey, man, let's go for a ride.' Just to show off. He'd say, 'I'll tell you what. Today you be the chauffeur, man, and tomorrow I'll drive for you.' And we'd drive down State Street, wouldn't talk to anybody, just wanted to be seen."

Even Crume was beginning to feel uncertain about Sam, though. The way Sam was talking, it was difficult for anyone to tell what exactly he was going to do next. Looking at a magazine with Paul Foster, he pointed to a picture of Harry Belafonte, whose calypso-flavored "Banana Boat Song (Day-O)" was currently in the Top 10, and said, "I want to be just like [him]." To Morgan Babb, leader of the Radio Four gospel quartet, he declared, "I just want to make some money." But to others, like Oakland piano and organ player Faidest Wagoner, he seemed to indicate unfeigned ambivalence. It was almost as if he were trying to conduct an external argument with himself. And when he went to his father for advice, Reverend Cook offered the same reassuring encouragement he had always offered his children: "Whatever you strive to be, be the best at it." Which was, really, no answer at all.

"Lovable" (backed with "Forever") was officially released on January 31, with a black male chorus overdubbed clumsily on both sides. It got a lukewarm reception in the trades (the material was weak, *Billboard* wrote in its March 9 issue, though new Specialty artist Dale Cook made a "personable debut [with] the church touches he injects into his style") and sold no better than recent Soul Stirrers' releases, but there was no question that it made a declaration from which it was going to be difficult to retreat. *Everyone* knew it was Sam, and the diverse reaction within the gospel community merely indicated the inevitability of the choice he was going to have to make. To Clarence Fountain of the Five Blind Boys of Alabama, it was just "a little penny-ante" kind of a record but "a big letdown in the gospel field." To fifteen-year-old Aretha Franklin, who had worshipped Sam ever since she had first heard him sing with the Soul Stirrers at her father's New Bethel Baptist Church in Detroit and was now out on the gospel road herself as "the World's Youngest National Gospel Singer," it didn't come in any way as a shock; in fact, it took its place immediately among her girlfriends' and her all-time favorites. And Gatemouth Moore, who had put the QCs on the radio in Memphis in 1949, introduced the song on his gospel program on WEDR in Birmingham. But this would not by any means have been the typical reaction within the gospel world.

Quartet singers and fans up and down the gospel highway tried desperately to dissuade Sam from pursuing this new path. And not just gospel singers. When the Soul Stirrers came to Atlanta on March 24, 1957, pioneering white DJ and r&b station owner Zenas Sears (it was Sears who had set up the recording session in Atlanta for Ray Charles' breakthrough hit, "I Got a Woman") did everything he could to "talk Sam out of it. Preston York [Sears' "valued friend and advisor" and lead singer for the Reliable Jubilee Four] and I spent four hours, all afternoon, trying to persuade him. 'You can go on forever doing what you're doing, you can go on forever. Now you're gonna switch, you're shooting dice, you may not make it.'" Sam seemed to listen politely, Sam was *always* polite, "the nicest guy in the world," but Zenas was not at all sure that what he said had registered. Nor in retrospect was he convinced it should have.

"There was a whispering campaign going on," J.W. Alexander observed. "He was ostracized, and he was hurt. One night in Tuscaloosa I said to him, 'Hold your goddamn head up and go out there and sing.' I said, 'They'll accept you. If anybody says anything, you sing.'"

Next to what Sam himself was going through, it was worst for the Soul Stirrers, who, seemingly in a collective state of denial, tried to reassure the public of something about which they could no longer help but have the gravest doubts themselves. One time, Crume remembered, they were at a radio station to promote their show, and the announcer asked Sam on the air, "Are you going to do 'Lovable' tonight?" Crain and the other Stirrers were beside themselves, they were certain the effect on the program would be devastating, but their audience was as enthusiastic as ever that night. Another time, a promoter said, "Sam, you really, really goofed. Everybody knows it's you." But Sam just said it was his brother, without even batting an eye. At one of the regular stops on their tour, they were riding down the street listening to the radio, when the DJ played "Lovable" and announced, "That was Dale Sam Cook." Shaken,

Crume turned to Sam and said, "Sam, man, everybody knows," and that night at the program, the MC introduced "Dale Sam Cook and the Soul Stirrers." There were "real tears" in the eyes of their fans, Crume said, "grown men and women." And yet Crume still could not believe that Sam was actually going to leave. "I saw no reason for it. We were drawing good crowds, making good money, we really had that magnetic touch. And I just didn't think it could get any better."

Sam continued to have doubts of his own. He indicated to Bumps that he was ready to abandon the whole experiment, but Bumps put him off, saying, "If this [record] doesn't make it, just give me one more chance, and if that doesn't make it, we'll go whole hog for the gospel field." They shook on it, but to Bumps, Sam's state of mind remained "dubious," and Art's state of mind was, if anything, even worse. To Bumps, practically at war now with his employer on a variety of financial and artistic issues, Art was little more than a "frightened businessman, any opposition whatsoever and he would pull in. So when he received various knocks from the gospel disc jockeys, he stopped the push, [and 'Lovable'] died on the vine."

Art, unquestionably cautious, and certainly a businessman, would have described the situation differently. He was dissatisfied not just with the sales but with the quality of the product, and after analyzing the record, "I decided Sam would sell better if instead of a funky band accompaniment [and overdubbed chorus] we used a male quartet similar to his successful Soul Stirrer records." He felt that "the contrapuntal effect of Sam's delicate tenor against the strong male backing would be unique in the pop field." Nor was he going to permit Sam and Bumps to go back to New Orleans. *If* he sanctioned another pop session at all — and he was still not certain of his feelings on the subject — they would record in Los Angeles, and under his direct supervision. Bumps kept talking to him abut Sam being another Morton Downey. "I said, 'Morton Downey has been gone a long time.' I had no idea [if] he would make it in the secular field."

The Stirrers returned to the studio in Chicago on April 19. Originally scheduled for February 21, the session had had to be postponed when the drummer Crain hired to join Chicago gospel keyboard stalwarts Evelyn Gay and Willie Webb turned out to be a union member and threatened to report to the union that his two fellow musicians were not. This time Crain was not taking any chances and got Sam's brother L.C. to keep time ("No, I never did play no drums; Sam just asked me, 'Keep the beat for me, bro' ").

It was, all in all, a highly successful outing, with the achievement of six solid masters in three hours, including two fine leads by Paul Foster and three originals by Sam. Paul's numbers may very well have served as a kind of safeguard against a possibility that no one was willing to openly admit, but Sam's compositions were marked by so much sincerity, and were of so uniformly high a standard, that it would have been hard at the time to concede that such a possibility could even exist. "That's Heaven to Me" proved that gospel could actually *be* pop as Sam sang feelingly of "A little flower that blooms in May / A lovely sunset at the end of the day / Someone helping a stranger along the way / That's heaven to me" in so pure a tenor, and with so romantic a tone, that no one — and everyone — could doubt his intent. "Were You There (When They Crucified My Lord)?" was, obviously, more overtly religious, a variation on the traditional gospel theme, but once again sung with such passion, originality, and intimacy of tone ("A fella said, 'I want you to tell me, If you were there, kindly tell me / I wonder did He really hang there / And never say a mumbling word'") as to turn all concepts of the limitations of the form on their head. And "Mean Old World," which according to Crain had become the Stirrers' new "theme song," while very much a traditional blues *and* gospel plaint, was presented here with so improbable a sense of cheerful uplift as to defy categorization, a classic example in other words of exactly the kind of song that Art and Bumps were looking for, one that, with a change of a word or two, could take its place instantly on the pop charts.

On April 20 Crain wrote to Art, "Hope you like [the] songs. I will be ready to record again in August. We are working on something now."

Barely one week later Sam wrote to Bumps, saluting him either jokingly or inadvertently as "Hi Bumbs," and including a tape. "Enclosed you'll find the songs I was telling you about," he began. "The only music I used was the guitar and I'm playing that. I hope you get a rough idea of what the songs are like."

The songs that he had demoed were "I'll Come Running Back to You," the Bill Cook composition that he had recorded both in New York and New Orleans the previous year; a new approach to "Summertime," the George Gershwin standard; and four originals, "You Were Made For Me," "I Need You Now," and "I Don't Want to Cry" (all three of which he had recorded at Cosimo's studio in New Orleans), plus "You Send Me," a song he had been trying to get L.C. to record for Vee Jay with his group the Magnificents. Of the six, "I'll Come Running Back to You" and "I Don't Want to Cry" (both of which he had recorded at the Nola Studio in New York as well as in New Orleans), were the two "I definitely want to do," and all were accompanied by a guitar that merely hinted at a melody, sometimes failing to do even that, with Sam's voice carrying the entire burden of communication. It is almost as if one were listening to Sam playing his ukelele in the car with Crume, with the guitar tuned to an open chord and Sam sliding into very imperfect barred sixths to sketch in those "ice cream chords."

"I'm going to New York on Saturday May 4," Sam concluded the body of his letter. "If by then you've decided on the songs you want me to do, I could get in touch with this fellow 'Obie Masingill' [Bill Cook's arranger] and go over the songs with him. Anyway I'll call you Friday morning."

Bumps' reply is not recorded, but its import was clear. There was no way he wanted to see Bill Cook back in the picture, even through the agency of O. B. Masingill. "I hit the ceiling, and I ran to Art, and I said, 'All right, let's go all [out].'" And then he must have informed Sam, whether by phone or by letter, that yes, there was going to be a session but that it was going to take place in L.A.

On Friday, May 3, Crain telegrammed Art from the Hotel Cecil in New York.

> MR RUPE SIR THIS IS IN REGARD TO THE RECORDS
> THAT YOU RECORDED OF SAM COOK. THE ONE
> ALREADY RELEASED (LOVEABLE) IS HURTING US
> IN THE SPIRITUAL FIELD. AND ANOTHER RELEASE
> WILL STOP US
> COMPLETELY SO PLEASE DO NOT RELEASE
> ANYMORE
>   THE SOUL STIRRERS S R CRAIN MGR JJ FARLEY
> SECT
> CECIL HOTEL, RM 481

They had arrived a day early, evidently, for the weekend programs in Newark and Philadelphia that promoter Ronnie Williams had set up for the Travelers and themselves. Things clearly must have come to a head for Crain to finally acknowledge the reality he was facing. He had thought the matter resolved several weeks earlier when Sam confronted him over the issue of royalties. Sam didn't think it right to have to split his songwriter's royalties six ways when he wrote most of the songs and he was the most popular member of the group. There had been an ugly scene, as Crain stuck to his guns at first, insisting that was the way the Soul Stirrers did it, share and share alike. That was the way the Soul Stirrers had done it from the start. "Well, do it your way," Sam flung back at him. "But do it with another singer."

At that point Crain put it to a group vote — and to begin with, the group flatly turned Sam down. R.B. Robinson, who had brought Sam to the Stirrers' attention in the first place, was the most adamant on the subject. Sam couldn't be trusted with money. He gave it away when he had it, and he spent other people's money when he didn't. If Sam didn't have a house and a car of his own, R.B. said, it was nobody's fault but Sam's. In the end, Sam got his way, but even Crume saw that the resolution represented an ominous trend. Just like Harris, "Sam wanted certain perks, but with the Soul Stirrers everyone was [supposed to be] equal."

Crain had hoped against hope that that would be the end of it — but clearly it was not, and he didn't know who to turn to. He had believed Art was his friend, but Art, it seemed, was playing a double game. There was no question about his feelings toward Bumps. "I hated Bumps. He was taking my living. The Soul Stirrers was my creation. The Soul Stirrers was all I was thinking about." But he couldn't think how to fight back.

J.W. meanwhile watched from his position on the sidelines, seeing the future more clearly perhaps than any of the direct participants, seeing the end of his own time at Specialty and the end of the quartet era rapidly approaching. He saw, too, how all this endless self-scrutiny was tearing Sam apart — and to no good purpose, either. Anyone with a brain in his head knew the inevitable conclusion. "So I talked to Sam back at the Cecil after our program in Newark. We were having dinner, and Sam said, 'Alex, I want to ask you something. Do you really think I can make it?' I said, 'Sam, you can't stick your head in the sand like an ostrich. You can't be Dale Cook. You got to be Sam Cook as you are.'" If he did that, J.W. said, "I have no doubt you can make it."

Sam never told any of the other Soul Stirrers directly. Just as he had slipped away from the QCs without ever explicitly declaring himself, he approached each of the Stirrers in private conversations that suggested the matter would continue to remain open to further discussion. To Paul Foster he said that he was "thinking about going out for himself. He said, 'I want to create something for myself, and I would like for you to come with me.'" He hadn't made up his mind yet, he reassured Paul, but he was seriously thinking about it. With Crain: "He asked my opinion, and I told him [to] stay." As for Crume, "He never even told me he was leaving. [By the time] I knew anything he was gone, and we were searching for a [new] lead singer. We were getting ready to go out on tour, and he just wasn't there."

Once he made up his mind, he seems to have had few second thoughts. His father told him he owed no loyalty to the Soul Stirrers; just as with the QCs, it was simply a matter of self-interest: "I said, 'Now, listen, that's not your religion. That's your job; you do that for a living. The Lord gave you a voice to sing to make people happy. And if you can make more money singing pop music than you can the church songs that you're singing — don't nobody get saved over singing.'" As far as the church people's disapproval was concerned, "I said, 'If you can make it where people are going to boo you, you made it. When you get out there, put all you got in there, just get in there with all your soul, mind, body, and strength. "A-l-l" spells "all." And never be scared. Nobody can beat you singing.' And he never failed."

He had come to a parting of the ways with Dolores, too. He was leaving Joey and her back in Chicago. He was giving up a life in which it seemed everything had always fallen into place for him, everything had been taken care of, from the time he first joined the Highway QCs at the age of seventeen.

On May 28, 1957, his friend Duck, whom he was helping send through court stenographer's school, drove him to the airport in his '54 Oldsmobile. The family had all said their good-byes. They knew Sam was moving to California for good. At the airport Duck accompanied him to the gate, and they talked excitedly about the new life on which Sam was about to embark. He was twenty-six years old and had never really been on his own before. He was about to take his place in the world.

How He Crossed Over

The expression "rhythm and blues" originally was a musical designation that was synonymous with an important segment of the music market. Today, for almost no rhythm and blues manufacturer, however, is the Negro consumer the prime target. His operation is typically geared economically to anticipated sales to both white and Negro customers, with definite emphasis on the former. . . . Racial identification with either the pop or r&b idiom is gradually but steadily coming to a halt — and this is a great economic boon not only for Negro artists and writers and r&b diskeries. The traditional pop field's horizons have also been broadened.

— "On the Beat" by Gary Kramer, *Billboard*, March 9, 1957

ART RUPE WAS UNCHARACTERISTICALLY LATE for the Saturday afternoon session. Those in the company who had known him longest were well aware that he had been distracted by his pending divorce from his second wife (and former secretary) Leona in order to marry his present secretary, Dorothy. But there were other matters, business matters, having to do with the future of the music, the future of the company, the ever-increasing pressure of payola (paying the disc jockeys to play the records), and the escalating problems he was having with his principal star, Little Richard, who had refused to come into the studio for the last seven and one-half months and was now making increasingly public threats, mixed with demands to renegotiate his contract, that he just might quit the business altogether to become an evangelist.

Bumps in any case had his instructions. Art had gone over the ground with him very carefully, and they were in full agreement that what Sam needed for immediate identification was something more like

Sam and Bumps, fall 1957. *Photograph by William Claxton © William Claxton/ABKCO*

his gospel sound — that was what had been missing from his first pop release, and that was the way they were going to cut him now, along the lines of Ray Charles, with a male quartet that sounded as much as possible like the Soul Stirrers.

Sam had been staying temporarily in a little room over on Avalon ever since his arrival from Chicago four days earlier. Bumps had stopped by to visit him with Clifton ("Clif") White, the Mills Brothers' longtime guitarist, who had landed in L.A. three years before, on quitting the enormously popular singing group (the Mills Brothers were the first black group to appeal widely to whites, and among their earliest hits was a 1931 collaboration with Bing Crosby). In Los Angeles, Clif had renewed his acquaintance with Bumps, whom he had originally met in Seattle, and he started working sessions at Specialty almost from the time

Bumps first arrived there in February of 1955. Bumps was accompanied by his pretty, young wife, Marlene, whom everyone called "Little Mama," and Clif had *his* wife, Judy, with him, too, so by the time they all squeezed into the tiny space, there was barely enough room to breathe. "The girls were nearly sitting out in the hall," Bumps recalled. "I was over the back end of the bed, Sam was near the head, and Clif was sitting on the bed like a Hindu playing the guitar."

White, a big, bluff man of the world, was understandably frustrated. Thirty-five years old, raised in the cosmopolitan cultural setting of Monterey, California (where his mother worked as a domestic, his father as a carpenter and stonemason), he was a devotee of Count Basie and Count Basie's rhythm guitarist par excellence, Freddie Green — and he had never been more baffled in his life. He had always had his reservations about Bumps, whom he viewed on the one hand as "the worst musician in the world" but on the other as someone with "a great sense of what was going on," with a notable ability to "put things together." But for the life of him he couldn't understand what Bumps saw in this kid who, for all of his likeability and brash self-assurance, seemed to be "in tune [only] with himself."

The first song they did, "You Send Me," Sam sang for him at first just to give him the idea, "and I thought it was the most ridiculous song I ever heard in my life. Simply because it wasn't saying anything. I mean, he just kept on singing, 'You send me,' and I thought he was out of his fucking mind. I said, 'When is the song gonna start?' I thought he was lost. I said, 'Hell, I think he forgot the words to his song.' "

Next they tried "Summertime," the Gershwin standard, and Clif played it the way it was supposed to be played, "but Sam said, 'No, man, you're playing the wrong chord.' Well, I don't *play* no wrong chords, you know, particularly to a song like that. He said, 'Lend me your guitar a minute.' So he starts playing, he didn't know a heckuva lot, but he knew enough to fiddle, and he plays this major chord in front [of] this minor chord, and, man, it's like the harmony was entirely reversed, it's like a piece of chalk on the blackboard. [But then] I began to hear what he was doing, because the two chords are basically the same, the major sixth and the minor chord, the notation of them is basically the same. And he said, 'Now that's what I want.' So I started playing it."

Almost in spite of himself, Clif found that he was being drawn in, first by the indisputable beauty of Sam's voice, then by the way he was able, like so many great gospel singers, just to grab the changes out of the air. But it was the power of his personality that got Clif in the end, that peculiar mix of shyness and a self-confidence bordering on arrogance, the sly self-deprecating humor coupled with an awareness of everything that was going on around him. He possessed, Clif observed, the kind of playfulness that a kid could get away with — but this wasn't no kid, and this wasn't, as Clif quickly came to realize, no game.

The next day they laid down the songs in Specialty's basement rehearsal studio, working from approximately a dozen that Sam and Bumps had zeroed in on, some from the New Orleans session, several from Sam's recent demo tape, some still in the process of development. Art came in, monitored the rehearsals, listened to the tapes, and eventually, with Bumps, picked four songs to focus on: "Summertime," Sam's two compositions "You Send Me" and "You Were Made For Me," and "Things You Do to Me" by Bumps' new apprentice a&r man and protégé, Sonny Bono. The small room over at Radio Recorders on Santa Monica was booked for the next day, Saturday, June 1, and Sam signed a new contract as a solo artist which, as Art explained to him, with a 1 percent royalty, would pay him twice as much as what he had been getting with the Soul Stirrers, whose 3 percent royalty was divided six ways.

Sam also got a $400 advance on his artist's contract, plus a $100 advance on a songwriter's agreement, which he signed at the same time. The songwriter's agreement stipulated that he would split his one-penny-per-side mechanical royalty with Venice Music, Specialty's publishing division, which, according to the terms of the 1909 Copyright Act, received a manufacturing fee (the "mechanical") royalty of two cents per side, that was generally collected from the record company (in this case Specialty) by the Harry Fox Agency, a licensing organization. According to custom, the mechanical royalty was then split fifty-fifty between the publisher and songwriter or writers. By accepting a royalty of half a cent, Sam, like Little Richard and most of the other Venice writers, was in effect embracing an unacknowledged partner who was entitled to half his income on all of his own recordings of his songs. This was by no means an uncommon arrangement, but it meant that on a million seller, the songwriter would earn approximately $5,000 in mechanical royalties, the publisher $15,000, with the three-to-one ratio only escalating the gulf in income as sales increased.

Sam readily assented to the new arrangements, and by the day of the session, Rupe was confident that "as per our procedure, the actual recording session would merely be implementation of our well-planned rehearsals."

That isn't the way it turned out. The session was in full swing by the time that Art arrived. Bumps was at his flamboyant best, conducting the small rhythm section and four backup singers with a mixture of extravagant gestures and upbeat advice. The band consisted of Clif and arranger René Hall on guitar; Ted Brinson, a longtime fixture on the Los Angeles r&b scene and a postal carrier who often wore his uniform to sessions, on bass; and Earl Palmer, the driving force behind Cosimo's fabled New Orleans session band and, like Sam, a recent arrival in L.A. himself, on drums. But it was the singers that Art fixed on the moment he walked through the door. They were white, they were singing in a light, poppy style, and, worst of all from Art's point of view, they included two female voices. It was all wrong — it was against everything he and Bumps had agreed upon — and to Art's ears the sound of those female voices clashed with Sam's rich tenor in a way that was both personally offensive and distinctly unmusical.

There was no mistaking Art's reaction on the part of anyone in the room. "I just knew Bumps was in trouble," said Harold Battiste, yet another New Orleans native and a schooled jazz musician, who had been working as Specialty's "talent scout" in New Orleans for the past year and a half. He was present, almost accidentally, to observe the Specialty operation firsthand before setting up a small office (and going on the payroll as a full-time Specialty a&r man) in his own hometown. They had already completed Sam's little number "You Send Me," for which Harold had sketched out a simple "jazzy, sort of hip" vocal arrangement on the spot because nobody else had bothered to address the background singing and, with his own predilection for jazz and no specific direction from Bumps, he just figured, "So what, they don't really care about this tune."

René, forty-six years old and another native New Orleanian, with extensive grounding in every aspect of the business going back to the twenties, had come into the session with a fully developed arrangement for "Summertime," the number that everyone, including Bumps and Sam, clearly thought was going to be the hit. He, too, had only recently arrived in Los Angeles, having just left a longtime position as guitarist and arranger with Billy Ward and His Dominoes. He had, in fact, just done a big-band arrangement of "Stardust" for the Dominoes and, keeping in mind Sam's own idiosyncratic feel for the Gershwin tune, had worked up a somewhat similar small-group approach to "Summertime." They were on the third or fourth take of the song, just closing in on what René felt was really going to be "something new in the creative world (we didn't want to do it in the classical Gershwin style, [it was] pop music with a gospel flavor)," when Art walked in the door.

Art clearly was not concerned with sparing anyone's feelings as he launched without preamble into a tirade that included Sam, Bumps, René, the backup singers, and the whole highfalutin approach that presupposed that there was an audience for this junk. "You're going to try and turn everything into Billy Ward's Dominoes with your ideas," he yelled at René. "This is not a symphony. I don't go for that stuff!"

They all sat there in shocked silence, with singers, musicians, and Sam, too, all seemingly in a state of suspended animation. But no one could have been more shocked than Bumps. From his stunned expression it seemed to everyone present that Bumps had not expected Art to show up at all. And if he did, Bumps had certainly not anticipated this kind of reaction. For Bumps had had a vision. And from his long experience as a bandleader and musical entrepreneur, and more particularly from his growing stature and success at Specialty, Bumps had learned to trust his own instincts, his ability to talk his way out of a jam as easily as he could get himself into it, over the kind of careful rote planning and analytical white-man's bullshit that Art favored in nearly every situation.

It had happened like this at least once before. Bumps was on a plane to New Orleans to record Little Richard in May of 1956 with all of Art's carefully written-out plans and instructions. One of the principal songs they were going to cut was a new number called "Rip It Up," for which Art had worked out a carefully articulated approach, but then Bumps fell asleep on the plane, "and when I woke up, I had a different concept of the song. I fell asleep, dreamed it, woke up, sketched it [out], and when I got into New Orleans I really did it. When I came back, I just knew I had a smash, [but] Art was very unhappy because the piano triplets was gone, I had the hi-hat and a whole different concept behind the song, and he was going to fire me — but I bet him it would be a hit, just put it out. So he did, and I won the bet, and I won a suit from [Hollywood clothier] Sy Devore. The first time in my life I had a suit that cost that much."

In this instance Bumps had had a similar vision: to set Sam's gospel-trained voice against the unmistakably white sound of the Lee Gotch Singers, L.A.'s number-one pop session group — they would be, as he and René saw it, "the classical frosting on the cake," the "refinement" that would make Sam acceptable not just to his old fans (who Bumps was convinced would never desert him) but to the new white audience that he knew was out there just as much for a romantic talent like Sam's as for an outlandish one like Little Richard's. Bumps was so convinced of the correctness of his concept that he never gave any thought to the consequences of countermanding the plan that Art had devised and to which he had so blithely agreed — and he might even have succeeded if, as in the case of the Little Richard session, it had simply been a matter of bringing back a tape from New Orleans and presenting Art with a fait accompli.

What he hadn't counted on was the effect of Art's actual presence in the studio, or the ferocity of Art's indignation. Art was beside himself. He saw what Bumps had done as a direct betrayal, as the kind of disloyalty that went well beyond simple deviation from a plan. And he let him know it, in front of the musicians, the backup singers, the engineer, and the artist himself; in fact, he treated them all with such disrespect that Sam, Bumps recognized with a sudden sense of powerlessness, "just wanted to quit. He was very hurt and very insulted and felt that it was completely unnecessary. Which it was."

But most of all Bumps saw himself being belittled in front of the musicians that he worked with every day and in front of the young man whom he was grooming for stardom and whom he saw as his ticket out of the "nigger heaven" — you can get so far, but no further — that he perceived his present position in life to be. It was a humiliation that he was not prepared to suffer — and yet one for which he had no retort, as they finished the session without the backup singers (after all, Art reasoned, the time had been paid for, and there were still two songs left to do), with all parties silently seething and Art still pushing for a more punched-up r&b approach. At the conclusion of the session harsh words were once again exchanged, and, as Art recalled, "I instructed Bumps and Sam to come to the office for a meeting the following Monday."

Not surprisingly, "the ill feeling that was created by me criticizing the session carried over into [our] talks," and it quickly became apparent to Art that this was simply not going to work. Words had been spoken on both sides that could not be unsaid. But worst of all, he was beginning to

see a kind of conspiracy between Bumps and Sam that he had long suspected and certainly could not tolerate. "I began to feel that Bumps was
functioning [more] as Sam's manager" than as Specialty's employee.

He began to see a Sam Cook, too, that he didn't know that he wanted
to be associated with, no longer the watchful, waiting, somewhat calcu-
lating young man whom he might often have wondered about but had
no grounds for dismissing, but someone who, unlike Bumps, was now
willing to challenge his employer's authority. At their meeting Sam
came right out and demanded a larger royalty, "even though we had
[just] negotiated a new contract for his recording services," and he
refused to back down on the matter of the white backup singers, an
argument, Art felt, that could go nowhere. Most of all, he showed an inso-
lent, arrogant manner, "an egotistical, self-serving" side and an almost
naked, covetous desire "for bread pure and simple" that Art found
insupportable.

Sam for his part could scarcely believe the manner in which he and
Bumps were being treated. He grew angrier and angrier at the way this
humorless white man brushed aside all their objections, ignored their
suggestions, treated them as if they were *children*. It was true he had
signed a new contract just three days before, but he had signed it knowing that contract was bullshit, knowing that 1 percent was not 3 percent,
and knowing from Lloyd Price, who had bought his way out of his Specialty contract the previous November, that Art was going to try to play
on his ignorance and fuck him any way he could. They all talked about it
among themselves. "Art just assumed he was superior in every way,"
said Sonny Knight, Bumps' first signing to the label, who was so fed up
with what he considered to be the prevailing "plantation mentality" that
he had put his sister's name on his own compositions ever since leaving
Specialty rather than honor his onerous songwriter's contract. According to Sonny, Art had offered him yard work while he was waiting
around for his first session, and he had responded, "You must be out of
your fucking mind. I signed a contract to cut records, not cut your fucking lawn." Which definitely shortened his stay on the label.

Sam had heard all the stories. Little Richard wasn't making jackshit, he
knew from Bumps, with an artist's royalty of half a penny a record. But Art
had never done him that way. So he had signed the contract, figuring that
the philosophy he had first learned from his father, then from Alex and
Crain — go along to get along, just yes them to death — would continue to

serve him in good stead. Act nice, be pleasant, always be sure and give Mr. Rupe a nice smile — and then let Bumps and his own success make everything right. Bumps had boasted that he could take care of Art, Bumps had said he would take care of him, that Sam didn't have to say anything, Bumps would do all the talking — and here the white man was just knocking Bumps and everyone else all around. He and J.W. and the others all knew that Art pictured himself as a friend of the colored man, but he wasn't being no friend to anybody here, not even himself.

Art was no less furious. "I just felt, I'm not going to fool with these people." At first he thought maybe if he cut Bumps loose he could bring Sam back into the fold, and the next day, he wrote out a memo to himself proposing the terms for a resolution: he would give Bumps back four of his own unreleased instrumental masters along with $1,500, and Bumps would in turn release Specialty from all future financial obligations, including bonuses and royalties already owed. On Wednesday, June 5, he presented the memorandum to Bumps, formally typed up as a simple one-paragraph release, with one additional condition: "that the songwriter's contracts between the undersigned and VENICE MUSIC, INC. . . . shall remain in full force and effect between the parties."

Bumps rejected it out of hand, even after Art put it in terms he thought Bumps would find difficult to resist. They obviously couldn't continue to work together under these circumstances, Art said. Then he told Bumps, "I know I owe you money, but if you let me be your lawyer — [that is] if you need a lawyer, it's going to cost you a third to fifty percent [contingency fee]. So for twenty-five percent I'll be your lawyer." Which Bumps understood to mean "he'd give me seventy-five cents on every dollar that he owed me."

Bumps didn't see it that way. Fifteen hundred dollars wasn't one-tenth of what he had coming. "I knew I had ten thousand dollars in bonuses coming — we had a deal: every record that I produced that sold over a hundred thousand, I got a thousand dollars, and I had ten records on the charts." Plus he had a $1\frac{1}{4}$ percent royalty against his $550-a-month draw. The way he figured it, Art might owe him closer to $20,000 than $1,500. And who knew what was going to happen with Sam's record?

They went back and forth on the subject for several days, and finally Art came up with a new formulation. "I said, 'Bumps, how much of a gambler are you?' Then I told him that since he was so certain that Sam was going to hit, and that the records were so good, that I'd assign him Sam's recording contract and the four recordings that Sam just made" — in addition to Bumps' four instrumentals — in exchange for a full release from all future financial obligations. From Art's point of view, it was a deal on which he couldn't lose. Sam and Bumps would remain tied to Specialty as songwriters, he would be rid of two troublesome and intransigent characters, and no money would change hands. Even if Bumps managed to place the masters with another record company, "I figured, well, this stuff'll sell maybe a hundred, a hundred fifty thousand," and he was even able to cover himself with an "insurance" clause that obligated Sam to "perform and make eight sides at the option of SPECIALTY RECORDS, INC., during the term of the contract" and specified that Bumps would have "no right, title, or interest in and to said eight sides which will be made by SAM COOK for SPECIALTY."

He was right in his judgment of Bumps' gambler's instinct. Bumps believed in Sam, he just *knew* he was going to be a star, he had been telling that to everyone who would listen for the last two years — and besides, he was tired of Art's feudal system. On June 14 he signed the release — but he never told his wife that they wouldn't be getting the money from the bonus arrangement with Specialty, he figured that would just have to take care of itself.

B UMPS WASN'T IDLE during the thirteen-day interval between the session and his and Sam's formal split with Art. Even before the terms of the separation were fully worked out, he put out word throughout the Los Angeles r&b community that he was looking for a deal. Central Record Sales, the principal independent one-stop distributor in the area, suggested that he put out the record on his own and distribute it through them, and Dick "Huggy Boy" Hugg, the fast-talking white r&b jock who had started broadcasting from the window of Dolphin's of Hollywood in 1953 while still in his teens, would have been more than happy to see the release come out on his brand-new Caddy label. But it soon became evident to everyone that Bumps wanted more than just some little record release. He wanted power and prestige and a title to go with it.

René told him about a businessman named John Siamas, who was thinking of starting up a label with Artie Shaw–style white clarinetist Bob Keane in charge. But he didn't really know how to get in touch with Siamas, or Keane, until he ran into a fellow named Art Foxall, a saxo-

phonist he had worked with when he first arrived in L.A., and then Foxall happened to encounter Keane, whom he knew from jamming around
in various downtown clubs, outside the union hall.

"I think I ran into him on the corner," recalled Keane, thirty-five
years old at the time and something of a small-time entrepreneur, who
had first signed with the MCA talent agency in 1939 as "The World's
Youngest Band Leader." "Foxall was a pretty sharp guy, he knew what
was going on, and he asked me if I was going to have an r&b division. I
said, 'Yeah, what else is there?' 'Cause I had never been in the record
business before. I didn't know what was going to sell. I didn't even know
how to make a record, for Christ's sake. So he gave me a little story about
Sam: [how] he got kicked off the label. He told me about Sam's manager,
too, and he put me in touch with Bumps, and the next thing I know,
Bumps and J.W. Alexander are sitting up in my little home at the top of
the hill on Dillon Street. I remember saying to my wife, Elsa, 'I love that
"Summertime"' — we were sitting on the couch, and we made some
kind of handshake deal."

The deal, which was going to have to be run by John Siamas, the
Greek airplane parts manufacturer who was funding the as-yet-
unnamed label, basically put Bumps in charge not just of the r&b line
but of a division dedicated exclusively to gospel music as well, which
Bumps enthusiastically predicted was going to be the next big trend.
Alexander's world-famous Pilgrim Travelers would be the first signees,
and the other Specialty gospel acts would soon follow, he and J.W. confidently asserted, given both Art Rupe's current state of mind and what
Bob Keane indicated was the new label's ability to pay. There was some
talk of ownership potential, there was some talk of Bumps' previous
bonus and royalty arrangement with Specialty, but clearly the next step
would be for Bumps to meet with John Siamas.

This he did almost immediately in Siamas' Windsor Hills home
overlooking the Crenshaw district. Siamas, a big, square-jawed forty-
two-year-old first-generation Greek-American with an engineering degree
from Northwestern, where he also played football, had worked at
Wright-Patterson Air Force Base in Dayton, Ohio, during the war, married, had a son, and then suffered the sudden loss of his wife to an
aneurysm nine months after their child was born. With his second wife
and son, John Jr., he joined his brother Alex in Southern California,
where most of his immediate family, including his mother and uncles

Andrew and Paul, had moved. He and Alex started their own company, Randall Engineering Corporation, on Higuera Boulevard in Culver City in 1952, which supplied aircraft parts primarily to Boeing and had developed several patented designs, including a widely used thrust reverser. A jazz buff and an audiophile, Siamas had met Bob Keane through his chief engineer, Rex Oberbeck, and they soon became fast friends, with Siamas not only attending Keane's club performances but even offering him a salesman's job with his company. He also invited Keane and his girlfriend, Elsa, who was a singer, out to the Friday-evening dance sessions he held in the spacious living room of his home, where he spun records by everyone from Louis Prima to Bill Doggett and had a professional dance instructor demonstrate how to do all the latest steps. When Keane and Elsa decided to get married that spring, John Siamas stood up as Bob's best man. Not long afterward, John Siamas announced to his family that he was going to be in the record business.

Bumps came out to the house for the first time probably the day after getting his Specialty release and, according to the memory of John Siamas' son, John Jr., nearly twelve at the time and a passionate devotee of rock 'n' roll, it was Bumps who was "the prize" for his father. "I remember my father telling me that Bumps had [produced] Little Richard — I mean, Sam Cooke was a nice aspect of it, but that wasn't going to be the focus of the recording company. They were going to record jazz, they were going to record gospel, there was going to be a diversity, they were going to go into the music business."

They agreed on terms similar to Bumps' arrangement with Specialty but considerably more advantageous in a number of respects. Bumps would continue to get his $1,000 bonus for all singles that sold over one hundred thousand copies; his 1 percent producer's royalty was a decrease by $1/4$ of a percent, but it was on gross, not net, sales; best of all, from Bumps' point of view, there were no restrictions on his management contract with Sam or any other artist. Whereas at Specialty he was limited to a 5 percent fee, which he split with Art, here he assigned himself 10 percent, with no split and no approval of his client list necessary from the label owner.

They made the deal pretty much on the spot, and Bumps went into the studio with the nucleus of the "You Send Me" rhythm section plus some additional musicians for instrumental sessions on June 26 and June 27. The session was billed to Rex Productions, the corporate name

John Siamas had assigned to his new company with a bow to his friend and employee Rex Oberbeck. Not long afterward he came up with a name for the label, Keen, partially in deference to his principal advisor, partly because it was short, snappy, and conveyed an image in keeping with the tenor of the times. The corporation had four principal investors: Siamas, his brother Alex, and his uncles Andy and Paul Karras, who in sum put up $20,000. His lawyer, golfing partner, and best friend, John Gray, contributed legal expertise, just as Bob Keane would provide the musical direction and serve as a recording artist as well, in return for which he fully expected to earn his share in the company. Bumps, too, anticipated a substantial ownership share in exchange for the knowledge, contacts, and other valuable considerations that he brought to the table. This was going to work out great, Bumps told Sam. Siamas had unlimited funds, he was going to give them part of the publishing, Sam just had to sit back and wait because before they knew it, the money was going to be rolling in. They were sitting in the catbird's seat.

WHILE HE WAS WAITING, Sam spent the summer on the sofa in the living room of Bumps' apartment at 3949 ½ South Normandie. He was living good, he told his brother L.C., Bumps always kept some money in his pocket, and he had the free use of Bumps' brand-new gold-trimmed white Chrysler whenever he wanted to go anywhere. Bumps' one-bedroom apartment would have been a little confining, of course, even if it hadn't been stuffed with music charts and acetates and Bumps and Little Mama's extensive collection of ceramic figures. But this was merely temporary. Bumps had a master plan and, he told Sam over and over again, Sam was going to be his number-one boy.

Early in the summer Sam met Sheridan "Rip" Spencer. Rip was still a high school student, finishing up that summer at Jordan High, where he had played football and was president of both the a cappella choir and his senior class. He and his cousin Brice Coefield had a group as well. They had come to Bumps' attention the previous year as the Chevelles, and now as the Valiants (named for Prince Valiant, the Knight of the Round Table–type cartoon hero) were introduced by Bumps to John Siamas at his Windsor Hills home. Bumps told Rip it was a "rehearsal" for a session for Siamas' new label.

"Sam was there," said Rip, "and some of the guys in the band that was going to record with us. Bumps took us over there because he was proud of the artists he was turning on to Rex Productions and so John would spend his money to record [us]. John Siamas was a very nice gentleman and very interested in the music, [but] this was all brand-new to him. I remember he had this nice big den and his little boys [John Jr. and his young stepbrothers] were all excited that we were there. But he didn't know nothing about the recording business, and Bumps had talked him into [it]. Bumps was a well-educated man. He was a helluva talker, and he knew the business and he knew how to make you do things."

Rip never could remember if that was where he met Sam for the first time or if it was over at Bumps' apartment, but he and Sam soon became the best of friends. "He would come by and pick me up at my house at Four-thirty East Eighty-fourth Place after school. I would get off the school bus and walk down there, and there he was, waiting for me in that white Chrysler. I would go in and change, and then we were off and running."

Mostly they visited girls, "different women he had met during his religious tours. Sam was very much of a ladies' man. When he came around, just more and more women came over. They would call their girlfriends, and, you know, we had a good time. Sam used to tell me all the time, 'Rip I'm going to be a big star.' It didn't come across as bragging, just friendly conversation, but he used to tell me that all the time. He used to call me 'Rip 'Em Up,' and he'd say, 'Watch and see, Rip 'Em up,' and I'd say, 'Yeah, Sam, I know, I know.' 'Cause I knew Sam could sing good, but this is a heckuva business, and [I was thinking] maybe you'll get through, and maybe you won't.

"Sam had personality, talent, he stayed clean, dressed well, I guess he learned that through the religious circuit, those guys dressed real good. But Sam didn't know anything about the music business or record labels at that time. None of us did. But we believed in Bumps, because the way that he talked, we believed that he knew. He was our leader. And I believe he convinced Sam to go with Keen Records because it was a new label, and John Siamas was a very rich man and Sam was going to get all the attention. Sam always wanted the attention, you know, because he always had it. I think that's what sold Sam."

When Sam asked him where he could get his hair processed, Rip took him to the Élite Coiffure Men's Salon, just down the street from the Watkins Hotel, which manufactured its own brand of hair straightener, King Conk, and where you could see Nat "King" Cole and all the stars. Sam took Rip to a church in another part of town where they were having a gospel program, and he introduced Rip to the various groups — Rip couldn't remember them all because he wasn't into gospel at the time, but the one quartet that Sam really wanted him to get to know was the Pilgrim Travelers, led by an immaculately dressed, soft-spoken, gray-haired older gentleman with a smooth manner, and featuring a dapper, razor-thin young bass singer named Oopie and a new lead singer, a close friend of Sam's just out of the army named Lou Rawls.

That was a rare foray into Sam's old world, though. Mostly Sam wanted to meet Rip and his cousin Brice's friends on the Los Angeles music scene: twenty-year-old Cornel Gunter, who in 1953 had joined a group called the Flairs at the invitation of his Jefferson High School classmate Richard Berry, whose current group, the Pharaohs, was enjoying a local hit with Berry's Caribbean-flavored composition, "Louie Louie." Gunter, who would go on to join the Coasters, had been one of the founding members of the Platters, too, and both Gunter and Berry had long-standing roots in the burgeoning L.A. r&b community.

Then there was Rip's uncle Marvin Phillips, who with Jesse Belvin (as Jesse and Marvin) had had a number-two r&b hit on Specialty in 1953 with "Dream Girl" and then, as Marvin and Johnny (with various partners, including Jesse, serving as Johnny), had continued to have various hits and misses, including Phillips' notorious signature tune, "Cherry Pie." There were Obediah "Young" Jessie, another original Flair from Jefferson High and Jesse Belvin's singing partner in the Cliques; Eugene Church; Gaynel Hodge, with his brother Alex an original member of both the Platters and the Turks; and countless others, all frequenting the clubs up and down Central Avenue, all haunting the publishing houses that lined a four- or five-block stretch of Selma Avenue in Hollywood (or hanging out at the Nickodell restaurant on Argyle, just around the corner), where the record company a&r men all came looking for songs.

At the center of it all was Jesse Belvin, a young, somewhat Hispanic-looking, extraordinarily talented twenty-four-year-old with a slick process who had cowritten both "Earth Angel," the Penguins' 1955 number-one r&b hit, and "Goodnight My Love," recently adopted by Alan Freed as the sign-off song for his nationally syndicated show. Jesse had had a direct hand, as either writer, performer, or both, in virtually every major development on the L.A. r&b scene over the last five years. It was Jesse whom Bumps had first had in mind for the kind of balladeering stardom for which he was now grooming Sam, and Clif White had made his first

Specialty appearance on guitar on one of Jesse's early records. But Jesse Belvin, as René Hall pointed out, was not exactly a model of focus or responsibility. "Jesse would record for anybody. I don't think he ever had a contract with any one company in those days." Nor was he particular about his songwriting royalties. "Jesse could sit down and write songs on the spot, but he'd always turn around and sell 'em outright for $100 or so." He didn't even seem to care if his name went on the record, cutting demos to which strings and horns could be added and then "teach[ing] the lead to another singer," so that singer could go out on the road and front the group. "That way he could sit there in the studio and crank out records. . . . That cat [just] loved to record." "We worshipped Jesse," said Gaynel Hodge. "He was like a big brother to all of us. We never questioned the things he did, even when it went against our own interests." Sam for his part merely observed. He was in no position to do anything but watch and wait, and he eagerly soaked it all in.

It was a wholesale introduction to a world which, as Rip recognized right away, Sam knew very little about. But it was an education which he picked up very quickly, and a world which he found to have more layers than he could ever have imagined. Rip, and Bumps and J.W., too, introduced him not just to singers like Jesse Belvin who were his own age or younger but to black entrepreneurs of an earlier generation as well. Bumps took him around to meet John Dolphin, a big, burly, cigar-chomping larger-than-life former car salesman, whose record store was one of the principal hangouts for the young singers and songwriters and a key source of education in the record business in one way or another for them all. Dolphin, who had opened his first shop in 1948, when "race records" were still being sold almost exclusively out of barber shops and shoe-shine stands, had named it for what he considered its two star entities, "Dolphin's" for obvious reasons and "of Hollywood" because, for one thing, he considered Central and Vernon, where the store was located, to be as glamorous as any white-folks' neighborhood, but also because, as he boasted, if black folks couldn't go to Hollywood, "then I'll bring Hollywood to the blacks." He started his own record labels, too, Recorded in Hollywood first, then Lucky, Money, and Cash, and his own song publishing operation, which, in keeping with the philosophy of his two most recent label names, was notorious for benefiting its owner far more than the young songwriters he was constantly discovering and signing up.

He could discourse for hours on the business, and for a discriminating listener like Bumps or J.W. Alexander he was an invaluable source of information and advice. What he and his shop were best known for, though, was the all-night radio show that broadcast from the record-store window over KGFJ, L.A.'s most popular black station. It had started with a two-hour purchase of time in 1950 and had now grown to the point where not only was it a highly effective means of advertising the store, it had proved the perfect vehicle for "market research." Distributors were not about to miss the point, said Huggy Boy, the white jock who had the show for a couple of years before going out on his own. "I could break a record — a good record — if I played it enough, and distributors learned that if John Dolphin would get a [free] box of a certain record, he'd want to play that record on the show until the box was sold out. . . . After two o'clock in the morning when the bars let out, Dolphin's was jam-packed, especially on weekends. We'd invite everybody down to the party — I'd say, 'Turn the car around, don't forget we're on the corner of Central and Vernon, Vernon and Central, ten magic paces from the corner of Central and Vernon, meet Lovin' John Dolphin, the man with the big cigar.' Dolphin loved it. He'd tell me, 'Lawdy be, Dolphin's of Hollywood is the greatest record store in the whole United States of America. Now Huggy, baby, all I want you to do, you tell those people, those little white kids, to turn their cars around, get their butts over here, and buy Lovin' John Dolphin's records, and I'll make it right with you.'"

There was Ted Brinson, the bass player on the "Summertime" session, who had arrived in L.A. with the Andy Kirk band in 1939 and, a dozen years later, purchased some recording equipment and built his own home garage studio at 9514 South Central, where "Dootsie" Williams, another longtime fixture on the scene, recorded "Earth Angel" for his DooTone label, by now almost equally well known for Redd Foxx's under-the-counter "blue" comedy routines. Then, too, there was Rafael "Googie" René, a versatile young piano player with a flair for record producing, who oversaw (and was supported as an artist by) his dad Leon's Class Records. Leon René and his brother Otis, Creole songwriters from New Orleans originally, who went back in the business to the 1920s, had been operating their own labels since 1942, and between them had written such pop standards as "When It's Sleepy Time Down South," "When the Swallows Come Back to Capistrano," and "I Sold My Heart to the Junkman."

It was a whole world of music, a homegrown recording scene of such diversity and sophistication that it made Chicago look like a sleepy country town. "The Vernon Avenue–Central Avenue area," local historian Michael Betz remarked in terms that could equally well have applied to Bronzeville when Sam was growing up, "was a self-sufficient community with two black-owned newspapers, banks, insurance companies, churches and civil rights organizations." But nowhere was this sense of self-sufficiency more exemplified than in its music community, nowhere was there a sense of greater excitement and possibilities than in this independent black enclave of musicians and entrepreneurs that Sam was now determined to make his home.

S AM TOOK ACTING LESSONS that summer at the Phil Carey Jones Drama School, both with an eye toward the movies and, as he later told a reporter for the *Chicago Defender,* to improve his "speech, enunciation and poise." And he added a letter to his last name. Bumps thought it would be "classier" to spell Cook with an *e* on the end, and Bob Keane, whose original name was Kuhn, agreed. So Sam got in touch with his friend Duck back in Chicago, who through his court stenographer's training knew the system cold and told Sam how to go about making the change legal.

He observed closely, too, the changes on the current music scene. Harry Belafonte, the lithely handsome young West Indian folk singer, on whose success he had told Soul Stirrer Paul Foster he wanted to model his own, was still near the top of the album charts with his *Calypso* album more than a year after its initial release; in addition, at thirty he was about to star in his second major motion picture, was an outspoken voice in the civil rights movement, had produced his own box-office record-breaking national tour, "An Evening with Belafonte" (the live recording of the show had recently joined *Calypso* at the top of the charts), and was reported to be looking at a $1 million gross in 1957. All with a sexy and sophisticated style and deliberately soft-spoken presentation that went directly against every stereotype that white men like Art Rupe seemed bound and determined to perpetuate. And Johnny Mathis, the living embodiment of the romantic brown-eyed crooner whose arrival Bumps and Alex had insisted was inevitable, was challenging the very premise of rock 'n' roll with one dreamy, color-defying ballad after another. With the Montgomery bus boycott settled and integration generally acknowledged by men and women of good will as the law of the land, there were no limits to be placed on a forward-thinking young man of determination and ambition.

Bumps, meanwhile, was hard at work building up Keen Records for its September launch, doing all he could to help make that ambition a reality. He scheduled sessions and scouted new talent, contacted artists he had worked with in the past, and confidently predicted the demise of his former label. To Sister Wynona Carr, whom he and Art had been encouraging to "cross over" for several years now, he let it drop that not only would Specialty be losing "a lot of [its] spiritual artists" but Little Richard, too, would soon be leaving. He rehearsed the Valiants sometimes at his sister's house at Forty-second and San Pedro, more often at Rip's cousin Brice's house on Twenty-third. He had acetates cut on "Summertime" and "You Send Me" at Radio Recorders at the end of July, and when Sam grew impatient and complained that nothing was happening, he hadn't been in the studio since that fateful day in June, Bumps jollied him along with paternal good humor, addressing him as "Goodfellow" and telling him with that characteristic air of breezy assurance not to worry, there would be plenty happening soon.

But Sam couldn't help but worry as he watched Roy Hamilton come back from his long illness under the continued guidance of Bill Cook. The phone lines of Hamilton's booking agency, the *Los Angeles Sentinel* reported, were swamped with requests for dates, and as a kind of test run for a summer-long tour, he had done $12,000 worth of business for B.B. Beamon in Atlanta alone. It would have been difficult for Sam not to wonder at this point whether he had made the right decision. When he went to J.W. to ask his advice, Alex had urged him to go with Bumps because, he said, Bumps would focus on him, and Bill hadn't really done all that well for Roy. But now Roy and Bill were being talked about all the time in the news, and he had passed up Bill's powerful connections at Atlantic and Roy's own label, Epic, for a record company that did not yet even exist. Clyde McPhatter, with his third Top 10 r&b hit of the year currently climbing the charts, was about to begin an eighty-day tour of one-nighters with Fats Domino, Chuck Berry, LaVern Baker, and half a dozen other acts under the banner of the Biggest Show of 1957, while eighteen-year-old Little Willie John had been out with Arnett Cobb all summer, playing everywhere from Seattle to the tip of Florida. Sam knew everything was being set up for him — but what if it didn't work? He watched the Soul Stirrers struggling with their own problems and, as difficult as he had always known it would be to go back, he was now forced to wonder if there would even be anything to go back to.

The Soul Stirrers themselves were beginning to wonder the same thing. They were so unprepared for Sam's departure that they had had to go out without a lead singer at the beginning of their June tour. They played a few dates with Paul Foster doing the best he could, but they soon found that the promoters didn't want to pay the agreed-upon fee for a group that couldn't adequately perform its own songs, and the people just kept calling out, "Where's Sam?" Then in Augusta they picked up Little Johnny Jones, the lead singer with the Swanee Quintet, who was in many ways the perfect substitute: he knew all of Sam's material, had sung with Sam occasionally, possessed a similar vocal style with a spectacular falsetto and a wider natural range, and, best of all, he had learned from Sam "how to carry myself, [he] gave me a lot of advice about singing [and] was the first to appreciate that I was not trying to sing like him but had my own style." They brought him back to Chicago at the end of the tour, but Johnny got homesick for Augusta, and for his girl, and he left as quickly as he came, on the eve of their upcoming July tour.

Gospel promoter Herman Nash was still advertising the "inimitable Sam Cook" when they played Atlanta on July 14, and the angry reaction that they got from their audience, despite the presence of an exciting new lead singer, led Crain to give an interview to the *Atlanta Daily World* the next day. The Soul Stirrers, "[he] told disappointed Atlanta gospel music lovers . . . would be more 'beloved and respected than ever' . . . despite the loss of star vocalist Sam Cook to the popular music field.

> An audience of some 5000 at the City Auditorium earlier had learned that Cook had quit the group Thursday and was in Los Angeles, Calif., where he will receive coaching and study bookings for a national tour.
> The Soul Stirrers rejected an offer to join the rock 'n' roll ranks along with Cook because "We've always sung gospel music. Our lives are dedicated [to] spreading His word in the highways and byways. It will be impossible to change our style now."

Their new vocalist, the paper pointed out, was "almost a carbon copy of Cook in looks, voice and style [and] performed flawlessly all of the Soul Stirrers recorded hits." He possessed all the talent that Sam did, Crain insisted, "and I think will be even more popular than Sam once the public gets used to him and respects his ability." Sam, Crain said, "has our best wishes. We know the public would not expect us to try to hold on to a man who wanted to do something else. If the people love us then they will not let one man stand in our way." Crain requested all "well-wishers of the organization," the article concluded, "to write the group at 4526 South Woodlawn [his home address] to affirm their confidence in the group."

The newest Soul Stirrer was the same singer who had taken Sam's place in the reconstituted Highway QCs just two years earlier. Johnnie Taylor continued to possess the same uncanny vocal similarity to Sam that he always had, and the other Stirrers for that reason had always viewed the QCs as serious potential competition, but now, they realized, Johnnie's mimetic skills could be turned into a real asset.

Crume had gone to see him at two in the morning, right after Johnny Jones had decamped for Augusta. "I drove over to his house, and we sat out on the steps, and I explained everything. Johnny was temperamental — he was a hard guy to deal with — and I said, 'You got to be one of the guys,' and he agreed that he would cut his little temper. So he says, 'How much time have I got?' I said, 'Till you can put a few things in a bag. I'll be waiting downstairs for you.' He got his clothes, and we went to Atlanta." Johnnie had the whole act down, all of Sam's gestures, yodels, and seemingly spontaneous interpolations, he even said the word "fucker" in casual conversation just like Sam. He was a nice-enough-looking young man, but he didn't have Sam's warmth, he didn't have Sam's charm, and, even though he went over well with the audience, everyone in the group pretty much agreed that Johnnie was a cold-hearted motherfucker.

Still, things really started picking up after he joined them, and they were all looking forward to the Big Gospel Cavalcade, the first all-star gospel revue set up along the lines of the enormously successful rock 'n' roll package tours, which was scheduled to start in Baltimore on August 15 and play nothing but ballparks, auditoriums, and stadiums with seating of at least five thousand over the course of an eight-week national tour. Clara Ward was the headliner, but the Soul Stirrers were at the top of a quartet lineup that included the Caravans, Dorothy Love's Original Gospel Harmonettes, the Swanee Quintet, Julius Cheeks and the Sensational Nightingales, the Harmonizing Four, and the Five Blind Boys of Alabama. Like the rock 'n' roll touring shows, they had their own specially equipped, streamlined tour bus, which was augmented by whatever vehicles individual stars chose to drive (including Clara Ward's $12,000

twelve-passenger, cream-colored, eight-door Chrysler purchased specifically for the occasion). For the first time the popularity of spiritual music
was being tested in head-to-head competition with touring packages like
Roy Hamilton's all-star revue. Which may have been one of the reasons
Sam approached Crume at around this time and asked what he thought the
other fellows' reaction might be to Sam coming back to the Soul Stirrers.

Crume could understand Sam's dilemma, and he was fully sympathetic to it. "It was before he got the record going, and nothing was really
happening for him." Nor would anything have made Crume happier
than to see Sam return. He certainly held no grudges. "That sort of thing
never did bug me. Like I say, we were free spirits." But at the same time,
he didn't want to serve as Sam's emissary either. "I told him, 'Hey, man,
just come on back and talk.'" But Sam evidently was either too embarrassed or too ambivalent to bring himself to do that.

Sam said something else to Crume, too, that didn't really register at
the time. He asked Crume if he could put Crume's name on his new
song. The way Crume understood it, it had something to do with Sam
not wanting to share songwriting income with the Soul Stirrers, and he
wouldn't really be asking very much of Crume except to allow his name
to be listed as songwriter and to turn over the money to Sam when he got
his royalties. "I just want you to give me my money when the checks
start coming in," Sam joked. Then he sang the song to Crume over the
telephone and said he was going to send him a tape of it, too, "so if anybody questioned you about it, you wrote it, right?" Crume said okay, but
he never got the tape or heard anything more about it, so he assumed
Sam had worked out the problem, whatever it was.

B OB KEANE WAS GOING THROUGH vicissitudes of his own. He had
spent much of the summer working the Golden Nugget in Las Vegas with his wife's act (she recorded for Capitol with her twin sister), but
now that he was back in L.A., he couldn't get any answers out of the Greeks
about what was going on with the company. He had started work on his
album, *Solo For Seven,* which was planned as the debut release on Keen's
Andex subsidiary ("And" for John Siamas' uncle Andy, "ex" for his employee Rex Oberbeck), a mix of Dixieland, pop, and Artie Shaw. He had
another session on August 22, but by this time, he could see that his position was beginning to seriously erode. A bright, quick-tempered, some-

what choleric man, Keane had never really put much faith in Bumps, but now he was certain that he lacked brains, talent, trustworthiness, and integrity — everything, in fact, except ambition. The way he saw it, Bumps had usurped his position, and when he took it up with the Greeks, they just pretended not to know what he was talking about, especially when he brought up the whole matter of his share in the company, the ownership inducement he believed he had been promised from the start. His situation was under such severe strain that he went to see Art Rupe somewhere in the midst of all this, with the idea that if things weren't going to work out with that double-dealing prick Siamas, he might have something to offer Rupe, who looked like a man who was up the creek without a paddle. Rupe seemed perfectly happy to meet with him but, as it turned out, more from the standpoint of pumping him for information than to offer him a job. They badmouthed Bumps for a while, and Rupe went on a little about Sam's untrustworthiness, but then Art asked: if a record release by Sam was really imminent, why hadn't Keane's record company requested a publishing license from Venice Music, which held the rights to all Sam's songs? That really took Bob by surprise. He hadn't been aware that Sam was under contract to Venice, but Art showed him the agreement and told him he'd better go back and advise his bosses so they could dot all their *i*'s and cross all their *t*'s properly on this first release.

Bob spoke with Andy Karras, Siamas' uncle, and told him he had seen Sam's songwriting contract with Venice and it looked kosher to him, so they'd better go ahead and apply for a license. When Andy countered that this just sounded like sour grapes on Art's part and that Bumps had assured them they had nothing to worry about, Bob exploded that Bumps didn't know what the fuck he was talking about — but what was new about that? It became almost immediately irrelevant in any case, as the ill will that had been building over Bob's partnership status swiftly came to a head. That was all as it might be, John Siamas patiently explained to him — but when they had first talked about it, the company was going to be set up on a shoestring investment. It had quickly required more capital than anyone had anticipated, and for Bob to take his place as an equal shareholder now, he would have to put up $5,000, too. But he didn't have $5,000, Bob screamed at his erstwhile friend. John *knew* he didn't have $5,000. John was just acting like some kind of Little Caesar, but he wasn't going to get away with it — he would

be hearing from Bob's lawyers. The next day, August 27, he got a registered letter from Siamas, formally stating the nonnegotiable terms of his
participation, and within days after that, he found himself locked out of
his own office. So Bob Keane left the company that he considered he had
started before the "Greek gang" even put out their first release — but
with a plan to start his own label from which no one was going to be able
to evict him.

In the meantime, Sam had finally gone back into the studio on
August 23 and laid down three tunes under Bumps' careful direction.
Once again the emphasis was on ballads, once again the songs were
transformed by Sam's trademark vocal style, with gentle ululations, verbal repetitions, unexpected swoops, and melismatic elongations placing
Sam's unmistakable stamp on Nat "King" Cole's first number-one pop
hit, "(I Love You) For Sentimental Reasons"; a rather jazzy, almost jaunty
number by Eden Ahbez (author of 1948's "Nature Boy," Nat's second
number-one), "Lonely Island"; and "Desire Me," a typical teenage pledge
of eternal love, which might have been better served by the simplicity of
Sam's own songwriting approach and a less awkward hook. The sound
was pure pop, with the same antiseptic chorus to which Art had so vociferously objected, and whatever the pedigree of the material, or its limitations, Sam carried off the performance without a hint of hesitation,
condescension, or awe.

On September 7, with the release of the first two Keen singles
momentarily at hand (his own "Summertime," backed with "You Send
Me," along with a misguided marriage of rockabilly and football by Jack
Rogers called "Hey Team"), Sam finally signed his contract. As Bumps
had promised, it was better than anything Art would ever have offered,
with a 3 $\frac{1}{2}$ percent artist's royalty, though Bumps took his 10 percent
manager's cut off the top.

The single started selling right away. Dolphin's of Hollywood had
been well primed for the release both by Sam's frequent visits to the
store (with and without Bumps and Bob Keane) and by his record company's generous contribution of several hundred free copies of the
record. Lonnie Johnson and Lew "Moondog" Russell, the two DJs who
were on from 10:30 P.M. till seven in the morning, played it over and over
all night long, even as they plugged Sam's upcoming appearance at a
promotional dance for Dolphin's at the Elks Hall just three blocks from
the store. The promotion was intended to spotlight Googie René's new

hit, "Beautiful Weekend," and Sam arrived with a certain degree of trepidation. "Nobody," said René Hall, a disinterested observer who could work with virtually any of the players on the scene without friction or rancor, "realized how big the record was until Sam got up there and sung. People had been brainwashed to hearing this record around the clock, and they just went crazy, they didn't even want to hear Googie [after that]. That was it. Sam was a star."

He played the Los Angeles County Fair in Pomona, too, for Art Laboe, the influential white DJ on KPOP who played rock 'n' roll from Scrivners Drive-In at Sunset and Cahuenga, just down the street from Hollywood High, every afternoon from three till sundown. Laboe, a short, stocky, thirty-two-year-old first-generation Armenian-American named Egnoian who had taken his professional name from the secretary at his first radio job, met Sam and Bumps when they came to Scrivners to promote the record. He wasn't too impressed with Bumps ("He had a little 'star-itis'"), but he found Sam to be "very cordial and congenial, a real gentleman," who walked around, like all the hopefuls, giving away his records and autographing them for the teenagers in their cars. "I interviewed him — the standard interview, you know, what he'd been doing, and then I'd say, 'Well, let's play "You Send Me,"' and I'd play it, and everybody would cheer. I had my own kind of research, where I could tell if a record was any good or not. Six plays would get it started. If it didn't, then it wouldn't." Evidently in Sam's case it did, because Laboe invited him to play a date at the Los Angeles County Fair, a predominantly white venue. He never had any doubt which side was the hit. "You Send Me," he reasoned, was a love song for teenaged girls, black *and* white.

The Prudhomme sisters, Beverly and Betty, identical twins who looked a little bit like the glamorous movie star Elizabeth Taylor, were playing the fair, too. They had a song out on Imperial, but they considered themselves songwriters primarily, and they had met Sam that summer at Bumps' apartment, where they had gone to have Bumps write lead sheets for some of their songs. They were impressed with Sam right away. "We said, 'Oh you've got to do our songs.' He was a real gentleman with us, as sweet as he could be." But onstage, while he conveyed those same qualities, "there was something very different about his style and personality. Women of all races were chasing him, beautiful, gorgeous women" — but he was never crass, never vulgar, there was an intimacy that communicated almost as well from the stage as it did in person.

They were so impressed with him, in fact, that after the show, on their own initiative, they gave John Dolphin another $100 to keep playing his song. For no reason other than that he was "such an uplifting person."

Art Rupe would have painted a very different picture, as he watched the song break with a mixture of frustration and regret. There was no question that it had been an error on his part to let Sam go. He had allowed himself to be misled by emotion, a cardinal sin in his principles of business — but he had at least kept his wits about him by retaining the publishing, and, if the song was a hit, he could hold Sam to his contractual commitment of eight additional sides at no additional cost or obligation. The way Art saw it, he couldn't really lose, no matter what happened. The label credits were little cause for concern (Sam's brother L.C. was listed as songwriter, with publishing assigned to Keen's publishing company, Higuera). Bumps had assured him that this was no more than a simple clerical error, a product, he figured, of equal parts greed and naïveté. It was an oversight, Bumps told him; he didn't know where anyone could have gotten the idea that L.C. had written the song.

THE RECORD JUST KEPT ON CLIMBING. It was touted as a Territorial Tip for Los Angeles in *Billboard* on September 30. In San Francisco, Magnificent Montague, who had masterminded and managed L.C.'s group, the Magnificents, was riding it to a fare-thee-well, introducing each play with the kind of erotically charged romantic poetry that had become his trademark, as he declared, "If I could touch your hand and feel your soul / If I could look into your eyes forever more / Darling, you send me."

That was the one thing Bumps couldn't quite figure. The damned thing had already sold almost a quarter of a million copies, it was taking off everywhere, but to Sam's and Bumps' disbelief, nearly all the jocks were playing the B-side. In Cleveland, Bill Randle, the influential white DJ who had helped break Elvis Presley's career, turned the record over, the same thing happened in Detroit, and in St. Louis, top r&b jock E. Rodney Jones played "Summertime" to a lukewarm response, but when he played the flip, the phones really "exploded."

In the gospel community, word spread like wildfire. To Jimmy "Early" Byrd, the Durham, North Carolina, gospel jock who always partied with Sam when the Soul Stirrers were in town, "I thought it was the worst thing, I admit it. The man was up there singing the blues. Preachers all across the country predicted that he would not be successful. There was a lot of rejection." Brother Joe May vehemently expressed his disapproval, and the Cook family heard that Mahalia Jackson was upset with Sam, too. Marvin Jones and Creadell Copeland, his old colleagues in the Highway QCs, were both devastated. They couldn't imagine how Sam could ever make the change when "he was such a king out in the spiritual world." Thirteen-year-old Bobby Womack and his brothers, with their own stature in the gospel world just beginning to grow, had a slightly different perspective. "We were sad that he had to leave the fold, because we thought it [gospel] was going to go back to the old way — I mean, it's still all right to make people shout, but don't do nothing fancy. Don't do anything that looked like it could be rock 'n' roll!" At the same time, though: "Everybody was afraid. That's just the way we were taught. If you betray God, stop serving Him and start singing the devil's music, then something terrible's going to happen to you. So everybody was just waiting on the day."

There was no such ambivalence in the Cook family. Charles, still in jail but awaiting his release, bet some of his fellow inmates that Sam's record would be number one by the time he got out, while to Agnes "it was just a way for Sam to make more money, we were all happy for him." L.C. figured Sam's growing fame could do nothing but improve his own fortunes. Everywhere he went he had always been the beneficiary of Sam's reputation — with girls, with club owners and DJs, even with Elvis Presley. There was just one time, in Pittsburgh, that it failed to work, when the Magnificents were playing a sit-down gig and "this one girl was there four nights straight. So I told [group leader] Johnny Keyes, 'Man, you see that little girl right there? Tonight she's going back to the hotel with me or I'm going home with her, either one.' [Later that night], after we laid in the bed for a while, she said, 'You know what? You sure remind me of somebody.' I said, "Baby, who is that?' She said, 'You remind me of Sam Cook.' I laughed and said, 'That's my brother.' She looked at me, and then she jumped right up out of that bed and said, 'L.C., get out of my house. Don't you come back to see me no more.' And she put me out, wouldn't give me no more pussy." But that was the only time he could remember that Sam's magic hadn't worked; otherwise Sam had never failed to take care of his brother, and L.C. tried to do the same. As far as L.C. was concerned, Sam's reputation could do nothing but grow and grow.

JOHN SIAMAS WASN'T SURE just how to respond to the overwhelming success of his first record release. He had been as unprepared for it as anyone; according to his just-turned-thirteen-year-old son, "he was stunned." One of the first things he did was to rent offices on Hollywood Boulevard near Gower, so that his little record company, which still occupied a corner of Randall Engineering on Hygereia Boulevard in Culver City, could have its own Hollywood home. Then at Bumps' urging, he turned over $5,000 to his a&r director, promotion genius, and chief cook and bottle washer so that Bumps and Sam could hit the road and promote the record. The idea, as Bumps explained, was to get it to certain key jocks all across the country. Then it would be just like a snowball rolling downhill. Once Bugs Scruggs got on it in Cincinnati, Okey Dokey in New Orleans, King Bee in Houston, and Jockey Jack Gibson in Atlanta, the disc jockeys in the secondary markets would jump all over it, and the record would separate itself out from the rest like wheat from the chaff.

They started out in the Midwest at the end of the month. In Cleveland, Bill Randle, the erudite self-styled hit picker whose instincts were so finely tuned that he boasted, "I can tell my listeners, 'This tune will be number one in four weeks,'" set up some record hops around town while remaining resolutely on the flip side ("Bumps was on the wrong side, but how could you hear the first sixteen bars and not know it was a hit? The public knew instantly"). They visited Casey Kasem, another big rock 'n' roll jock, in Detroit. And in Chicago, Bumps used Marty Faye's show (which generally thrived on controversy) to launch an attack on pop star Teresa Brewer for trying to steal not just their song but Sam's style, right down to his patented "Whoa-oa-ohs." There were two other cover versions out, both in the L.A. r&b mold (one was by Jesse Belvin, the other by Cornel Gunter), with a third, instrumental treatment by transplanted New Orleans sax man Plas Johnson on the way, but none seemed to rouse Sam's and Bumps' ire like Brewer's polished pop version, which was rising fast on the charts, perhaps because of its technical skill, perhaps simply because the singer was white. Teresa Brewer may not have realized it, Bumps declared on the air, but what she was doing was nothing less than stealing. "Because Sam's style, like Billie Holiday's, is so distinct that anyone who copies the song is actually singing Sam Cooke."

They came into Philadelphia on their way to New York and visited with Georgie Woods, "the Guy with the Goods," at WDAS, setting up an appearance with Georgie at the Uptown Theater over Christmas. Woods, who had come out of the Georgia cotton fields, joined the navy at sixteen, and then taken advantage of the GI Bill to attend broadcasting school, had a virtual monopoly on the Uptown, the site of almost every big r&b revue, but they wanted to see his chief rival at the station, Doug "Jocko" Henderson, too. Henderson had already left for his 10:00 P.M. to midnight shift on WOV in New York, so, making allowances for a social hour or two, they calculated his likely return and then showed up at his affluent suburban home at four o'clock in the morning.

Henderson, a rhyming jock with a flair for humor and an entrepreneurial bent (his *Rocket Ship Show* offered endless opportunities for both invention and self-promotion, particularly in an era of space travel), came from a very different background than Georgie Woods. An accomplished athlete and tennis champion whose father was superintendent of the black city schools in Baltimore, he had been studying biology at Tuskegee when he fell under the influence of pioneering rhyming jock Maurice "Hot Rod" Hulbert. Jocko and Georgie had been in competition, each with his own striking style, ever since Woods' arrival in the city in 1953, but Jocko's inability to break Georgie's lock on the live r&b scene had led to his becoming a "rail jockey," commuting nightly to Manhattan, mostly by train. Now, as one of the top three rock 'n' roll jocks in New York (Alan Freed and Harlem's Tommy Smalls were the others), he had a whole new market to exploit as he put on shows at the Apollo Theater in Harlem, went head-to-head with Freed at the Loew's State on Broadway, and was about to have his own teen dance show on television.

Henderson, not surprisingly, was sound asleep when Sam and Bumps arrived. "Somebody's kicking on the front door, and I said to my wife, 'Who in the world is that?' So I put my bathrobe on, put my gun in my pocket, and went down and put the light on and saw two fellows out there, looked like very nice guys. I hollered through the door, said, 'What do you want?' Said, 'Jocko?' I said, 'Yeah.' Said, 'My name is Sam Cooke, and this is Bumps Blackwell, my manager. And we have a record we think is going to be a big smash. And we just wanted to let you hear it. And pardon us for coming out here at four o'clock in the morning.'" What could he do? He listened to the record, pronounced it a smash, and promised to have Sam on his new TV show as soon as it went on the air.

Sam and Bumps had already run into the Soul Stirrers back at the hotel. Crume had no idea that Sam was in town until after the Stirrers finished their program at the Met and found the lobby of the Carlisle across the street jammed. "I'm thinking to myself, 'What the heck, what are all these people doing here?' Then I heard Sam's voice — you could always hear Sam, he talked so loud, you could hear him from practically a block away — he was right in the middle of the crowd. And he looked around and saw me, and he said, 'Hey, Crume, remember what we used to talk about?' And I knew exactly what he was saying. Then he said, 'What room are you in?' And I told him, 'cause I couldn't even get near him, and he came to my room and said, 'I told you, fucker. I told you. I got it, man. I got a hit. I'm on my way.' Just like that."

He asked Crume where the Stirrers were playing next, and when Crume told him they were going to be in D.C. in a few days, he said that he and Bumps would be there. And they were. When he walked into the auditorium, the place went crazy. And when Crume got him up to do a number, he stopped the show. In Bumps' words, "he emaciated the house."

In New York they were running like crazy — DJs, distributors, the Harlem social scene, and, for the first time, agents from national booking agencies who said they wanted to put Sam on the map. A little guy from William Morris had been chasing Bumps around for the last couple of weeks on the telephone, but Bumps kept putting him off, finally agreeing to a 6:30 P.M. appointment that he had no particular intention to keep.

Larry Auerbach had been tipped to the record by Bernie Lowe, an old friend and owner of the Cameo label in Philadelphia. A twelve-year veteran of the business at twenty-seven, Auerbach had graduated from mail room clerk to teenage agent, then gotten drafted during the Korean War. When he returned, he was put in charge of the record division, a job no one much wanted at an agency that thrived on cabaret bookings and one for which Auerbach was singularly unsuited for the simple reason that, as he proclaimed to his superiors in his flat New Yorker's bray, "I'm tone deaf. What do you want me to go in the record business for?"

Nonetheless, he persevered, made some contacts, got Sammy Davis Jr. his deal with Decca, and had a hit with "The Ballad of Davy Crockett." Still, as he saw it, it was pretty much a dead-end street, unless he discovered some new, unaffiliated talent who could really get the agency to sit up and take notice. For all he knew, this kid Sam Cooke might be it.

"I was sitting in my office with a guy named Paul Cantor, who worked for me: six-thirty, seven o'clock, seven-thirty, no Bumps. So I say, okay, I gotta find him, and I start on the natural haunts. So I call Al and Dick's, say, 'Who's around?' you know, to the bar, to whoever answered the phone, and they say, 'Who you looking for?' I don't know. Finally, I say, 'Goldie Goldmark,' a guy who worked for Moe Gale, a publisher who was also an agent. Goldie was an active guy. So I say, 'Goldie, do you know Bumps Blackwell?' And he said, 'Small world. I don't know him, but he's sitting in my boss's office.'"

Right away Auerbach knew he was in trouble. If Bumps was in Moe Gale's office, that probably meant he was on the verge of signing an agency contract with Moe. "So I don't know what to do. I don't want to sit there all night. I want to get him out of there. So, Lord knows where I devised this scheme. I say to Paul Cantor, 'Get me Moe Gale's office on the phone.' I get them on the phone, and now I do this terrible impersonation of Timmie Rodgers, the black comedian: 'This is Timmie Rodgers. Is Bumps there?' And sure enough, the girl puts Bumps on, and I say, 'Get your black ass out of there. This is Larry Auerbach at William Morris, and if you're interested, you better get over here now.' And that's how we met, and ultimately that's how I signed him."

What Auerbach proposed to Bumps was something that, without his having any way of knowing it, was naturally designed to appeal to both manager and client.

All that Larry Auerbach could offer were the club and cabaret bookings that were the focus of William Morris' personal-appearance business. Auerbach didn't know anything about the one-nighter circuit that most of the r&b acts were limited to and that agencies like Universal and Gale specialized in. So the tack he took with Bumps was that his client was too good for the one-nighters — with an across-the-board smash like "You Send Me," the kind of song that could appeal to all ages, all races, he was sure William Morris could come up with a combination of club and television dates that would enable Sam to "make the conversion to the white clubs, and if he makes the conversion well enough, he won't have to depend on hit records."

Never having set eyes on his prospective client, he was at this point talking through his hat, but once he actually met Sam and found him to be not only polite and intelligent but "very good-looking, with this angelic look to him," Auerbach came to believe his own pitch, which was only reinforced when he was able to book him on *The Ed Sullivan Show* on very short notice, and Bumps signed what amounted to a letter of intent on the basis of this one-shot deal.

That was the way it seemed to go everywhere they went, with a combination of charm, luck, and serendipity guiding their fate. In Atlanta they were able to set up a show in advance with B.B. Beamon, who booked Sam into the Magnolia Ballroom on October 10 for a quick $1,000. "Sam Cook, Formerly With Soul Stirrers," announced the ad in the *Atlanta Daily World* on the day of the show beneath a smiling new publicity shot of Sam with a neatly coiffed pompadour. They couldn't get ahead of the record, no matter how fast they drove. It was catching on in every city even before they arrived — it was like being in a time warp in which the experience in every city was exactly the same. But even as musical barriers continued to fall, it was equally impossible not to dwell on the aftermath of the ugly racial drama that had unfolded in Little Rock over the past few weeks, when Arkansas governor Orval Faubus blocked black students from registering at Central High School, and President Eisenhower reluctantly called out federal troops to uphold the law of the land. "The way they are treating my people in the South, the government can go to hell," said Louis Armstrong, America's unofficial "Ambassador of Goodwill" abroad, in a series of increasingly militant public pronouncements that were reported assiduously by the Negro press. The American Negro, said Armstrong, who had not infrequently been accused by more outspoken members of the community of being an Uncle Tom, was no longer going to be pushed around. "We don't take that jive no more," he said, "[and] I'll tell the same thing to anyone I meet." But, as Sam or any other attentive reader of the black press couldn't fail to note, there were more and more calls for white boycotts of Louis' concerts, and even his own longtime road manager suggested that he had spoken "in haste," while a white NAACP lawyer declared that he had "stepped out of line."

By the time they got back to California toward the end of October, the record had sold over half a million copies, and the little record hops they had been doing with Art Laboe just a month before seemed like something left over from another life. Which was exactly how Laboe felt that he was himself treated when he approached Sam and Bumps about doing another KPOP show. He wasn't really all that surprised about Bumps, who had acted like a big shot before he had anything to be a big shot about. But he was disappointed in Sam, who was, "I wouldn't say conceited, but very short, *testy*, you know. He was not as easy to get along with, would be the easiest way to put it. It seemed like he had a lot on his mind."

They had to turn around again almost immediately anyway to fly back to New York for *The Ed Sullivan Show*. Two young white singers, Jimmie Rodgers and sixteen-year-old Paul Anka, both with recent number-one pop hits, were also featured on the program, along with all the acrobats, magicians, and comedians who made up Sullivan's usual Sunday fare. Bumps and Larry Auerbach watched anxiously from the wings as the show ran longer and longer, and Sam, who was scheduled to go on last ("If Sullivan didn't like an act," according to Larry Auerbach, "he put you on last, and you had to be lucky to make the show"), tried hard not to show his nervousness. He was wearing a nicely fitting tailored suit with the top two buttons of the jacket buttoned, his hair was cut short and slicked back, a square-folded handkerchief nestled in his breast pocket — he looked, in other words, every inch the picture of the all-American boy that he wanted to project. Reverend C.L. Franklin's daughter, Aretha, playing a gospel program in Atlanta with her father, watched in the lobby of B.B. Beamon's Savoy Hotel. "We were all crowded around the small set behind the front desk. All of us except my sister Erma. When she finally came through the lobby door, I thought I would never stop laughing: she had on a prom gown! And [there] we were, all poised and waiting. And finally, when the big moment arrived, you know, 'And now, ladies and gentlemen, Sam Cooke,' and he came out, the lobby just erupted with cheers and screams and swoons and what have you — and then they cut him [off]! And we just had a fit. We all but turned the lobby and the hotel out."

What had happened was that after calling actor Rod Steiger out to plug his latest movie, Ed urged him to "listen to young Sam Cooke" as the orchestra struck up a mincing introduction to Sam's song. But then Sam didn't even have a chance to get through the first verse. With his arms held close to his body and gestures so practiced they seemed stiff from overthinking, he was in the middle of the second line ("I know you-oo-oo —") when the CBS eye filled the screen. There's no telling what the reaction was like in the theater, whether Sam and the orchestra finished the song for the live audience, but, once he realized what had taken place, Sam was utterly crestfallen. Nor did it help when Larry

Auerbach reassured him that the William Morris Agency would never stand for this, that he would get Sam back on the show in no time — to Sam it was the end of the world. As it turned out, though, it might have been the best thing that could have happened. There was so much hue and cry from the public that Sam was rebooked almost immediately, and by the time they returned to New York four weeks later, Bumps said, "We had killed [all the] covers, we were way over a million, and there was a chance to build up and cash in on the snafu!"

But for the time being, they were back on the Coast with little to do for the next three weeks other than give Sam the opportunity to bask for the first time in all his newfound glory. Except that now there was a new storm brewing.

Art Rupe had grown tired of waiting for a response from Siamas — or maybe it had finally begun to register with him that the novice label owner might have other plans afoot. So, on October 21, he fired off letters to Higuera Music Publishing Co., Siamas' umbrella corporation Rex, the Harry Fox Agency (which served — and continues to serve — as a one-stop licensor and collector of mechanical songwriters' royalties for any number of publishing companies), and the Library of Congress, instructing the latter to institute a copyright search for "You Send Me" on a rush basis. He also wrote to Bumps, formally reminding him of his obligation, as per the terms of his June 14 release agreement with Specialty and the assignment to him of Sam Cook's contract, to see to it that Sam "perform and record eight sides for our firm," as required upon demand. "This is to give you notice that unless we have performance by Sam Cook within thirty days of this letter that the above-mentioned release agreement . . . is rescinded by us, and we will seek an accounting from you for all loss of profits and damages."

On October 24 the Library of Congress wrote back to him that "You Send Me," with words and music by L.C. Cook, had been registered in the name of Higuera Music Publishing Co. on September 4, 1957.

One week later he heard from John Gray, as attorney for Rex Productions, "to categorically deny [Venice's] allegations of ownership. . . . We have no intention of honoring your bare-faced claim of ownership, which apparently is substantiated by nothing other than your signature." He also heard from Gray, in three additional letters, as attorney for Sam Cook, as attorney for Robert A. Blackwell, and on behalf of Higuera. The letter on Sam's behalf was addressed to Specialty Records and stated that

"Mr. Cook rescinds the contract [requiring him to make any additional records for Specialty] on the ground that his consent to the signing thereof was obtained by fraud on behalf of the President of your company, Mr. Arthur N. Rupe, and also because of the duress, menace, and undue influence practiced upon him by Mr. Rupe." So far as Specialty's claim on Mr. Blackwell was concerned, Gray declared, "Nowhere in [his] release do I find anything which would support the contentions you set forth. . . . We see no obligation on the part of Mr. Blackwell to assist you in your negotiations with Mr. Cook."

Finally, in his letter to Venice Music, he affirmed Higuera's copyright ownership and further informed the company that "We have discussed this matter with Mr. Sam Cook, who has informed us that he did not write this composition and that it was written by his brother, L.C. Cook." In addition, it had been stated (in Art's letter of October 21 to Higuera) that there had been discussion with Mr. Robert A. Blackwell several weeks earlier and that Mr. Blackwell "left you with the impression that he would straighten out this misunderstanding. Mr. Blackwell informs us he at no time informed you that Sam Cook wrote the tune 'You Send Me' and that you, at all times, attempted to obtain the rights to this song through Mr. Blackwell's intervention, by threatening to fail to pay him royalties which had accrued to him by Venice Music, Inc. . . . unless he saw that Venice got that song." Any further attempts "to claim ownership in the composition," Gray admonished Art impersonally, "can only be deemed wilful and malicious, and you will be prosecuted to the fullest extent of the law by my clients."

Art was beside himself. He *knew* that Sam had written the song, there was no question about it in his mind, and he couldn't believe that Sam would lie not only to him but to his new company. But the more he learned of Sam, the more his view of his devious, deceitful, and totally unscrupulous behavior was borne out. Just days before, he had received a letter addressed to Sam care of the Specialty Recording Company and, after getting past the opening salutation ("Hi Sweet"), discovered that it was from some poor schoolgirl from New Orleans whom Sam had made pregnant. "Look Sweet," she concluded, "whenever you get a chance write me back because I still love you very much." But Sam "did not [even] come for this letter," Rupe wrote disgustedly on the envelope, one more proof of the way in which he believed Sam "squandered his intelligence and made unwise moral choices."

On November 1 Art went into the studio with arranger René Hall and overdubbed the demo that Sam had cut on Bill Cook's "I'll Come Running Back to You" at the New Orleans session in December. He got the same mixed singing group that had backgrounded Sam on "You Send Me," and René came as close as possible to replicating the hit record's feel and sound not only on the Bill Cook number but, with new vocal overdubs by the same Lee Gotch Singers, on both "Lovable" and "Forever," "Dale" Cook's debut Specialty release. Art mastered the songs four days later, put "Forever" on the B-side, and had the new record out in two weeks. He took a hurriedly designed three-fifths-of-a-page ad in the November 25 issue of *Billboard* with a small circled head shot of Sam at the center and "New!" the only selling text. By the end of the month, Specialty Records' "I'll Come Running Back to You" was a hit.

Sam didn't really pay much attention to any of it — or at least tried not to. Art wrote to him about his recording obligations care of Rex Productions on November 7. He was evidently hoping to appeal to Sam on a personal basis, but he could barely keep his rage in check. All this talk of fraud, duress, and menace was, as Sam knew, "a bald-faced lie. . . . When you signed the contract with me, it was done of your own free will; and in fact, you were more anxious to enter into this contract than we were. . . .

"You have probably not told your attorney," Art continued, "about the first artist contract which our firm still has with you under date of February 1, 1956." If Sam proposed to throw aside the validity of his present artist contract, then Specialty would hold him to the earlier one, "<u>and then you couldn't record for anyone but us!</u>"

"Before you get involved in a lot of unnecessary lawyer's expense, I suggest that you contact me immediately so that we can set up a schedule for the performance of the *eight* sides which we have coming from you; and, stop this needless bickering."

It was Art, though, who couldn't stop himself. He broached the matter sorrowfully to J.W., who by now was with the new label himself. "He said to me, 'Alex, we've been friends for a long time, and I respect you enough not to ask you [about the authorship of "You Send Me"].' So I never answered." Somehow or other, Art seemed to feel that one of them would see the error of their ways. But if Sam had any second thoughts about it, he never gave any indication. As L.C. saw it, "He just wasn't going to let Art Rupe get his songs." Nor did it surprise L.C. that his brother should outwit the white man at his own game. "Sam was smart. He learned. He watched. He wouldn't let nobody ever tell him nothing, but he'd ask questions. And he never would let you know that it was something that he really needed to know. He just said, 'L.C., you wrote such and such a song.' I said okay, and that was it."

Sam was focused on the future. He spent time at Keen's new offices on Hollywood Boulevard, made a guest appearance on the brand-new ABC-network Guy Mitchell television show on November 11 (for which he received $750, minus his William Morris commission), and two days later went into the studio to begin work on his first album. At Bumps' direction, accompanied by the Bumps Blackwell "Orchestra," which consisted for the most part of Clif, René, drums, and bass, augmented by the same vocal chorus that had played such a prominent part on "You Send Me," he focused on standards like "Ol' Man River," "Danny Boy," "Moonlight in Vermont," "Ain't Misbehavin'," and "That Lucky Old Sun," songs to which he had always been drawn but which had the added advantage, Bumps pointed out, of demonstrating his versatility, expanding his appeal, and helping to further the scenario that the William Morris agent had painted for them so persuasively.

On the strength of Sam's success, Keen Records, too, was rapidly expanding. They had hired a combination promotion man / art director in Don Clark, formerly with Aladdin Records. They had set up foreign distribution through London American, a division of the English conglomerate Decca Records. They announced the upcoming release of the first two albums on their new Andex subsidiary, Bob Keane's jazz outing and the Pilgrim Travelers' *Look Up!*, for which Bumps drafted Sam to sing tenor on one track behind a rare (and haunting) J.W. lead. In mid-November they signed Johnny "Guitar" Watson, a star on the L.A. r&b scene whose talent was exceeded only by his panache and by his ambivalence about whether he wanted to be a singer or a pimp. And not long before that, Keen put out its first release by the Valiants, "Good Golly, Miss Molly," once again landing the label, and Bumps, in hot water with Art Rupe.

Bumps was scarcely a passive agent in this new brouhaha. He had worked with Little Richard on the song (for which he had cowriting credit) at Richard's last New Orleans session, at the end of July 1956, when Richard was already beginning to balk about going into the studio under the terms of his Specialty contract. Art rerecorded the number at

The Keen crew, fall 1957: Paul Karras, John Siamas, Rex Oberbeck, John Gray, Sam Cooke. *Courtesy of John S. Siamas*

Richard's last regular session for the label in October, but in the year that had passed since then, he had never released it, and now that Richard had dramatically announced that he was quitting show business (he had thrown all of his rings into the water at the end of a two-week Australian tour, during which he saw the Soviet satellite *Sputnik* pass over the Sydney stadium like a "fireball" and took it as a sign that the Day of Judgment was near), Bumps doubted that he ever would. In any case, doing the song with the Valiants was one more chance to stick it to Art, the former boss in whom he had once so fervently believed. And he never mentioned any of the possible complications to John Siamas — why should he? He just put the session together, got Don and Dewey, signed to Specialty as an incendiary teenage vocal duo but equally talented multi-instrumentalists, to back them up, along with an expanded rhythm section of Nicaraguan percussionists on congas and bongos whom Bumps had discovered in a Hollywood nightclub.

The entire emphasis was on speed. With their talented lead vocalist, Billy Storm, setting the pace, they started fast and, at Bumps' urging, just kept gathering velocity. "Pick it up, pick it up," he kept yelling at the four Valiants, determined that no white boys would be able to take this song from them. In the end, they carried it off better than any of them would have believed possible, and for the other side, Billy laid down "This Is the Night," a beautiful ballad penned by all four, which just went to show their versatility on top of Billy's Hollywood good looks.

"ANOTHER KEEN HIT, taking off like a rocket" was the way that Keen Records was promoting its new release, and though "This Is the Night" appeared to be the A-side, Art was not the least bit sanguine about what he took to be another stupid provocation coming from an all-too-familiar direction. He suspected, he wrote to "The President" of Rex Productions Incorporated on November 7, the same day he wrote to Sam, that "you do not have all the accurate and honest facts about this whole mess. I'm certain that most of your information [has come] from 'Bumps' Blackwell, our former employee whom I was forced to discharge." The release of "Good Golly, Miss Molly" by Keen, Art informed them, "reflects an out-and-out violation of our property rights" because of the fact that it had not been released to date by its owner, Specialty. "I cite this as an example," Art continued, "to show you that you are making decisions without all the facts." And he then went on to suggest that "if you had all the honest facts, I'm sure that you or any other ethical business man would do the right thing, which in the long run is the most practical and profitable for all concerned."

He proposed a private meeting at which they might iron out their differences, but when he and John Siamas met eleven days later, he found that Siamas, while a perfectly pleasant man, was willing to discuss only the matter of licensing "Good Golly, Miss Molly." When he brought up Sam and the eight sides he owed to Specialty, Siamas was "evasive," said that Sam was "back east" (which Art didn't believe), and told him, somewhat insultingly, that Sam would be happy to take a lie detector test if Art would.

Art was suddenly tired of it all: he was tired of Sam and Bumps, he was tired of Richard, he was tired of the endless wrangling, he was, in fact, tired of the business. The impression that he got of Siamas was that here was a businessman perfectly willing to fight over business issues, a self-made man with the attitude that he had come into this world with nothing, that he would go out with nothing, and that "what happens in between doesn't count." Art wasn't about to give up, but neither was he going to hold a grudge against a man who had been purposely misled, a man in some respects very much like himself. So he agreed to the license, continued to make plans for his upcoming European vacation, and prepared a rush release on Little Richard's "Good Golly, Miss Molly" that would blow the Valiants' version out of the water.

If Sam was affected by any of this, he didn't show it. To thirteen-year-old John Siamas Jr., Sam remained the most thoughtful and down-to-earth person in the world — "and *interested,* in situations where there was nobody around to impress. Sam would shoot baskets in our back-yard. He tried to teach me how to play the guitar, which was his one miserable failure. One of the things I vividly remember was when he came and performed at the junior high school I attended, Audubon Junior High, south of Crenshaw, which was racially diverse at the time — he just sat there with his guitar and sang songs and invited me to come up onstage with him and introduced me as his friend."

The single most dominant impression that John Siamas Jr., a bright, serious young man destined to become a lawyer, took away from his contact with Sam was of his warmth, his kindness, his "love of life." And why not? He was at last in the place he had so long wanted to be. He had gained not just the financial wherewithal but the "legitimacy," the respect, the *identity* that his father said you must always seek (and never settle for anything less) in the white man's world. Following Bumps' lead, he began to cultivate a collegiate look: V-neck sweaters and pleated beltless pants for casual situations, a growing number of modestly elegant business suits for more formal ones. He was wearing his hair more and more close-cropped with less and less straightener, in direct contrast to all the elaborately processed fashions of the day.

For all of the fact that his fame and status were growing so rapidly ("In just three sensational weeks," reported the black wire service, ANP [Associated Negro Press], with some hyperbole at the end of November, "he has become the 'top man' in all popularity departments . . . and has zoomed from a $150 a week performer to one who can ask and get a cool $1500 every seven days"), what stood out most was the easy grace with which he accepted it all, almost as if it were something about which he had had no doubt all along. "He was very conscious of [who] he was, what he looked like, how he was groomed," said Herb Alpert, who had just gone to work at Keen with his friend, twenty-four-year-old Lou Adler, as one of Bumps' three "junior assistant a&r men" (Fred Smith, who had come over with Bumps from Specialty, was the first, and the only, one with any real experience in the business). "He made everyone feel at home, he had lots of charm, was full of smiles, and seemed to be enjoying himself. And yet he was intimidating at the same time. He seemed to suck up all the oxygen in the room — I mean, the focus would go right to him." It wasn't that he sought it out, Herb was convinced. It was just that he had "this larger-than-life quality about him, he had star-dust on him."

Fred Smith, who had met Sam at Johnny Otis' talent show at the Nite Life that summer and whose mother was a well-known blues singer, saw it a little differently. An accomplished songwriter himself, he was unreserved in his admiration for Sam, but at the same time, he recognized in Sam an element that neither of Bumps' two young white assistants was likely to pick up. "Sam was a genius. He's one of those people who when he walks in the room, you almost get cold chills, but he had an attitude: Hey, man, I deserve this. And he did deserve it, because of who he was and how he got there. But in some cases he wouldn't back down."

Sam went on a five-day West Coast tour with Little Richard's band, the Upsetters, second on the bill, and an acquaintance from the Chicago gospel and r&b world, Dee Clark, singing all of Little Richard's hits. Upon his return to L.A., he went back into the studio on November 26, then flew to New York for his second Ed Sullivan appearance with his fee doubled to $2,000, perhaps to make up for past "insult and injury."

"Sam," Ed Sullivan said, introducing him with that discomfiting awkwardness that was his most distinctive characteristic, "here's the time." Sam, looking almost equally awkward, stood with his hands clasped and elbows drawn in. The smile was removed from his face, and his hair stood up in spiky strands, as if it couldn't quite decide between being "natural" and woolly like his father's and J.W.'s, or slick and smoothed back as it had been for his last appearance. The musical accompaniment was different, too. He opened with "You Send Me," but there was none of the cloyingly sweet sax vamp that had accompanied his ill-fated debut, the song was taken slower, with a barebones rhythm section, a vocal chorus, and Clif, who had just agreed to go out on the road with him as "bandleader" and arranger, leading the ensemble on guitar. And Sam just sang his song, weaving endless romantic curlicues around words so simple and repetitive ("You send me" must have been repeated two dozen times) that the mere variation of "You thrill me" carried a disproportionate weight of its own, and when he got to the release

212 | *How He Crossed Over*

that led into the bridge ("Honest, you do"), it was like an ice floe letting go. But it wasn't about the words, as Clif had learned at their first meeting just six months earlier. Sam had a way of turning hypnotic repetition into a kind of musical suspense that, for all of his experience in the business, Clif would never have imagined any singer could sustain. But Sam did — and he had utter confidence in his ability to do so and in his instinct for *when* to do so. Siamas at one of the early sessions had tried to interject his own well-intentioned sense of how to improve the song they were working on by giving it the "Sam Cooke feel," and Sam had blown up at the label owner in his own quiet way, telling him, "You can't just put in a 'whoa-oh' in every song, you got to feel it, man," saying it perfectly politely but not bullshitting around, because for Sam it was a musical trademark, not a gimmick.

He came back out to sing his new Keen single, "(I Love You) For Sentimental Reasons" (there was no way he was going to plug his Specialty single, Bill Cook's "I'll Come Running Back to You," which was by now closing in on nearly half a million sales), and Ed took the opportunity at this point to make further amends. "I did wrong one night here on our stage," he told audience and home viewers alike, then apologized directly to Sam, adding that in the aftermath of the incident, "I never received so much mail in my life!" Sam wore a tux for this number, once again kept his gestures to a minimum, and improvised off the vocal chorus, lagging behind and singing all around the beat. And then at the end, he clasped his hands together and bowed his head as if to receive a benediction.

"You Send Me" officially hit number one in *Billboard* the next day, and Sam and Bumps celebrated in New York. As John Siamas Jr. remembered it, his father had flown in to be with them for *The Ed Sullivan Show,* but they protected him from certain elements of their lives. "Sam and Bumps said they were going to spend the night in Harlem, and my father said, 'Okay, that sounds right.' And Bumps said, 'No, no, I don't think you understand. *You* can't spend the night in Harlem. *We* have to go spend the night in Harlem.' So that was the one night they did not stay in the same place."

Sam knew all kinds of girls in New York by now. He had always known a certain type of girl in New York as a Soul Stirrer, and since Crain had started booking them into the Apollo the previous year, he had had time to get to know more of them. But the girls he was meeting now

were a faster crowd, more knowing, more glamorous, more sophisticated, more to his current taste. "Sam had quite a way with the ladies. I
always stood back and waited my turn," said Lithofayne Pridgon, who
came out of "Dirty Spoon," the black section of Moultrie, Georgia, and
had met Sam the previous year when she arrived in New York at the age
of sixteen. She had taken immediately to the life, started going with
Little Willie John, and first kissed Sam in Willie's bedroom at the Cecil,
looking out the window on 118th Street. "He wasn't the world's greatest
lover — but he was, you know, [because] he was on another page. It
wasn't so much a physical thing [as] a whole social thing. He wasn't the
most dynamic bed partner, but he was so cool it took up the slack. He
was a gentleman, [which was] all the way the other way from what I was
accustomed to."

Sam, Lithofayne said, "could rub elbows with anybody," and that in a
way was as much a part of his charm as his talent, intelligence, or physical beauty. Without it, he might have been insufferable, another one of
those "hincty niggers" who acted like their shit didn't stink like everyone
else's. But Sam was as likely to salute the bum in the alley as the highest
high mucky-muck. He had no intention, he firmly told family and
friends, of leaving anyone, or any part of his life, behind. To that end, he
convinced Crain to join Clif and him on the road. Crain could be his
"road manager," he said, he really needed him — and for all of Crain's
dedication to the Soul Stirrers, it seemed as if he had just been waiting
for Sam to ask. "I'm going with Sammy-o, the greatest lead singer in the
world," he told the group, scarcely giving them time to react and
bequeathing his managerial responsibilities to J.J. Farley, the bass singer
from his home town of Trinity, Texas, who had joined up in 1936. Sam,
Crain, and Clif were perfectly matched, with the two older men well
qualified to offer different kinds of advice but equally amenable to
accepting Sam's decisions as final.

In New York Sam picked up a driver / valet, too, even though he
wasn't convinced that he necessarily needed one. Eddie Cunningham
just started hanging around and running errands — he got Sam's white
leather coat cleaned for him when Sam didn't think it needed cleaning,
and after he brought it back sparkling white, Sam told his brothers,
"This cat is something else." Eddie, who was originally from L.A., was a
sharp dresser who knew his way around, but more important, he knew
everyone in the business. It turned out his sister was Mabel Weathers,

Tony Harris' manager, and Eddie had taken care of Tony when Tony played the Apollo earlier that fall with a little record of his own. The way Eddie saw it, Sam was going places, and he wanted to go there with him. "Sam never really hired me," Eddie admitted to L.C. some months later. "I just started straightening up, getting him food and coffee, and then I told him, 'You need for me to drive for you.'"

Sam remained in the East for most of the next two weeks, with a three-day interlude in Chicago, where he played a show sponsored by popular DJ and television personality Howard Miller at the Civic Opera House on the Friday following his Ed Sullivan appearance. The entire Cook family turned out. "There were so many people there, you could hardly get in," said his twenty-two-year-old sister Agnes, who was accompanied by her husband of five years, Eddie Jamison. "We all had seats right down in the front, and we sat through both shows." It was a rock 'n' roll show for an almost all-white audience. Brash new rockabilly sensation Jerry Lee Lewis was the co-headliner, with the Four Lads, the mixed group the Del Vikings, Howard Miller discovery Bonnie Guitar, and Pat Boone's brother Nick Todd on the bill. As he had on *Ed Sullivan,* Sam performed in his tux, and the Cooks had a family picture taken outside the theater, with girlfriends, neighborhood acquaintances, and Sam and L.C.'s best friend, Duck, all in tow. Everyone looks proud and pleased, with the possible exception of Annie Mae Cook, whose pale, doughy face appears to be worriedly contemplating the future. "I can say this," Annie Mae told a reporter doing a story for *Sepia* magazine. "None of my children have turned out badly. They don't run around with gangs and stay out all night either. . . . God has blessed us with their voices." As to a proposed family move to Sam's new home base of California, Mrs. Cook said, "Maybe we'll stay six months in one place and six months in the other — just so long as Sam is satisfied."

He played the Newark, New Jersey, Armory with Hank Ballard and the Midnighters the following night, opened a one-week engagement on December 12 at the upscale Lotus Club in Washington, D.C., and found time in between to give an extensive interview to one of the country's most prestigious black newspapers, the *Amsterdam News,* which ran a rare in-depth feature on him just before Christmas. In the picture published with the article, you can see Sam leaning forward to engage Women's Editor Margurite Belafonte with what one imagines to be all the charm at his disposal.

The Cook family and friends at the Civic Opera House, December 6, 1957. Left to right: Agnes, Mary, and David Cook (front), with Roosevelt (unknown last name) and Sam Milsap (in hat with dark band) behind; Leroy Hoskins ("Duck") in dark hat, Rev. Cook, Willie Cook in white hat, Sam, L.C.'s girlfriend Barbara Clemons, Annie Mae, Charles, L.C., and Hattie Cook. *Courtesy of ABKCO*

Before the interview's Q and A format begins, several key points are established, including the fact that the "teenage idol" is not married (he had initiated divorce proceedings against Dolores on November 15) and that "unlike most of the Negro stars, all his managers [Bumps and Crain] have been and still are Negroes."

After a brief musical history, in which he describes street-corner singing as a teenager with Johnny Carter and James "Dimples" Cochran (now with the Flamingos and Spaniels respectively), his stint with the QCs, and his discovery by S.R. Crain of the Soul Stirrers, he credits his decision to change over into the pop field to "the man who was my personal manager at the time [who] encouraged me to sing ballads [an unnamed Bill Cook]," and to Bumps Blackwell, "my personal manager now [who] had confidence in me and bought the masters from Specialty and set up 'Keen' Records in Los Angeles to release my discs."

As to his family's feelings about his music:

> My father, Reverend Charles Cooke [*sic*], agrees to my work. We have talked it over, and I enjoy my work, and besides I haven't stopped

singing religious songs. I sing them when I am on tour. I like them better than I do ballads. I have more feeling for them, and they have greater meaning for me, and greater satisfaction.

Likes and dislikes?

I like the Ivy League look in clothes. I am fashion conscious. . . . I'm impressed with New Yorkers. They seem so well polished, well versed and they keep you thinking. . . . I would like to know more about psychology.

He returned to Los Angeles briefly, where Keen Records held a party at the Brown Derby in Hollywood to celebrate the official certification of the record as a million seller and the release of Sam's first album. Sam proved himself "a prince of a guy," the *California Eagle* reported. Everyone present was dressed to the nines: Bumps and his "gorgeous missus"; J.W. proudly avuncular in a sharp patterned suit; René with his wife, Sugar, who is beaming at Sam from underneath a stylish fur hat; a bespectacled Lil Cumber, her hair done up in marcelled waves and wearing a white fur wrap. And Sam himself is practically aglow, the sharpest one of all in his stylish pinstripe suit, wearing, the *Eagle* reported, "his sudden success in fine style [with] no padding, no put-on," as he stands beneath portraits of other recording greats like Dean Martin and Nat "King" Cole, his close-cropped, almost "natural" haircut in sharp contrast to the gleaming, processed look that stares out from the album cover in his hand.

He seems possessed of an almost serene self-confidence, as well he should be. He has just completed his first real tour as a star, he is on the cover of the current *Cash Box* magazine with Bumps and John Siamas, and he will be opening in three days at the Uptown in Philadelphia, from which he will go on to New York for an appearance on *The Steve Allen Show* at a fee of $2,500, his third Sunday-night network appearance in two months. The criticism of the press can scarcely touch him, the criticism of the church seems almost irrelevant when he has friends like Lil Cumber, a columnist now as well as a booking agent, who will defend him against the naysayers. "If church people feel that Sam deserted them," Lil wrote in a widely quoted column, "they alone are to blame. If they would support their own, then the offers from the other side would not seem so appealing." Sam's "charm, modesty, and devoutness" were unexceptionable, she declared, citing her own background in the spiritual field, but "it is this writer's belief that the final decision to change was due to the churchgoers' themselves" and specifically their refusal to support gospel music financially.

Sam opened in Philadelphia on Christmas Day with the Arnett Cobb Orchestra, comedian Redd Foxx, Atlantic Records artist Linda Hopkins, and Sister Rosetta Tharpe's one-time singing partner Marie Knight. He gave an interview to the *Philadelphia Tribune* similar in scope and emphasis to the *Amsterdam News* feature, in which he went even further to credit Crain. Sam described the former Soul Stirrers manager, wrote *Tribune* reporter Malcolm Poindexter, as his " 'guiding force' for the past seven years. Every bit of coaching, stage presence and style are credited to the manager of many talents." Interestingly, Sam recalled that he was a "rather melancholy youngster before escaping the strict atmosphere of home and school," but, the article concluded, "his frank personality and clean-cut physical makeup symbolize the 'dream of tomorrow's entertainer.' . . . Carefree and unassuming, he has little hope of becoming wealthy and seeks only the security and comfort of the average man."

The paper could not have been aware at the time of writing that Sam had practically been pulled offstage at the Uptown and arrested in the middle of his performance. Connie Bolling, whose son, Keith, was now nearly a year old, had been persuaded by her girlfriends that if she let this opportunity go, she would never see any money from the father of her child. He was rich now, he was successful, and, like all men, he wasn't going to do anything for her unless he was forced into it. It was against her nature, but her baby didn't have a father and his first birthday was coming up on January 6.

The sheriff and his deputies showed up backstage but let Sam finish his act before arresting him and taking him to a cell down at the municipal courthouse. Crain followed close behind with a former state senator, whom he had engaged as Sam's lawyer, and $500 to bail Sam out. A continuance was granted, Crain managed to keep the news from leaking out, and Sam completed his engagement without further incident.

But something changed inside of him. He felt nothing but cold rage at this woman who had publicly embarrassed him. What she had done was a clear act of betrayal whatever her motivation, and he was determined to have nothing more to do with her *or* her son. But, more than that, he was determined not to let anything like this happen to him ever again.

The Biggest Show of Stars for 1958

LARRY AUERBACH, the William Morris agent, watched his new client perform for the patrons of Club Elegante, a Brooklyn supper club that didn't entirely live up to its name. It was next door to a cemetery, and the William Morris reps always joked among themselves, "If you die there, you don't have too far to go." On the other hand, it represented a first step toward the kind of broad-based acceptance that Auerbach, Bumps, and Sam had mapped out as their long-term strategy. To Auerbach there was definitely something about the kid. He might be stiff and restrained in his stage movements, he seemed to think he had to play it that way, but "he had such excitement and rhythm," even in a milieu with which he was almost entirely unfamiliar, he had such natural magnetism and charisma that Auerbach felt he couldn't miss.

It was a five-day booking, and Auerbach attended faithfully nearly every night and made suggestions. He felt like if he could just "loosen him up, [get him to] give some of his gospel training in his performance," then Sam would really come across to a white audience that was looking for flash and excitement. But Sam had his own ideas, and in a way, the success that he had already enjoyed, the national exposure that he had gotten on *The Ed Sullivan Show* and, two weeks earlier, on January 5, with Sullivan's Sunday rival, Steve Allen, only confirmed them.

Auerbach was as taken with the kid as anybody else. "I thought he was a sweet, innocent young guy, [not all] that outgoing but personable. He had the best look at that time of any black singer. Adorable. The women were going to love him, obviously." So when Sam pushed him in that nice, unassuming way to go on to the next level, and Crain, the older man who rarely left Sam's side and was generally so taciturn, strongly

Sam with friends, probably 1958. *Michael Ochs Archives.com*

seconded Sam's demands, against his own better judgment the William Morris agent gave in. He spoke to Sam Bramson, the old-time agent in charge of William Morris' "variety" department, who in turn persuaded Jules Podell, the autocratic manager of the Copacabana, the midtown Manhattan nitery, to come out to Brooklyn to catch the kid's act. When Podell, a drinking buddy of Bramson's who almost never left his 10 East Sixtieth Street post, indicated a willingness to book Sam at the beginning of March, Larry Auerbach couldn't very well say no. He knew Sam wasn't ready yet, but he figured there would be time to polish the act, and it was, after all, the number-one prestige booking in the country.

For Sam it was just further proof of the basic soundness of his plan. Clearly this was the time for the new Negro entertainer. While Sam was playing the Elegante, Harry Belafonte was appearing at Brooklyn's genuinely elegant seventeen-hundred-seat Town and Country Club and carving out a leading-man movie career. Johnny Mathis, "the young man with the golden voice," had two albums on the bestselling pop charts, had sung the title song for a major motion picture, *Wild Is the Wind*, and was headlining at the Crescendo in Hollywood. Even Johnny Nash, a clean-cut seventeen-year-old regular on *Arthur Godfrey Time*, was currently enjoying a Top 40 hit with a ballad sound very much in the vein of Sam and Mathis. It was a matter, Sam explained to L.C., of not appearing too threatening. That was why he had cut his hair. If you had all that slick stuff in your hair, he told his brother (who continued to cling to his upswept process), the white man was going to think you were slick, he wouldn't trust you around his daughter. "But when they see me," he said, "I'm the perfect American boy. That's all they can say about me." At a time when fellow performers were naming their process (there was the "Quo Vadis," Dee Clark's was called the "Sugar Ray," and Lloyd Price nicknamed himself "Dark Clark" for the movie star Clark Gable), Sam was wearing his hair in a modified crewcut, close-cropped and "natural," brushed up in front. And he was establishing a new life for himself, along with the new look.

He had gotten a little one-bedroom apartment on St. Andrew's Place off Washington near Normandie for when he was at home in L.A., but he was also enjoying a very active social schedule in New York. He was dating Sallie Blair, "the red-haired vampire," whose torrid act took equal elements from Dorothy Dandridge, Eartha Kitt, and Lena Horne; also, Zola Taylor of the Platters, eighteen-year-old *Ebony* cover model Harlean Harris, Lithofayne Pridgon, and any number of other dark- and somewhat lighter-skinned young ladies. "He was one of the coolest gentlemen I knew, very warm, loving, as smooth as his voice," said interpretive dancer Lee Angel, who had left Savannah, Georgia, two years earlier, at the age of sixteen, had a brief but torrid relationship with Little Richard, and met Sam in Manhattan at just about this time. "He had his choice of any woman he wanted, he didn't have to chase them," she said. And while she herself never had a romantic relationship with him, she, Zola, and Sallie would frequently get together and discuss their boyfriends, who not infrequently turned out to be one and the same. "He's cute as a button," Sallie told a *Time* magazine reporter about one of her beaux, perhaps thinking of Sam. "He's one of those people you want to walk up to and say — 'Okay?'"

Sam *was* one of those people the world seemed prepared to say okay to. He had "a wardrobe full of Ivy League clothes," *Tan* magazine reported, a somewhat fanciful income of $4,000 a week, and, getting a little ahead of himself, a new home in Los Angeles with its own swimming pool. And what was success like? Sam was asked by the *Tan* reporter at the end of January on the set of Patti Page's CBS-network *The Big Record,* while pictures were being taken with Latin dance king Xavier Cugat, choreographer June Taylor, Broadway star Carol Haney, and r&b pioneer Louis Jordan. "It's pretty much as I expected it to be," he said. "It's competitive, it's exciting, it's rewarding and I love it. But you've gotta produce. You can't fool the public with slipshod performances, and you can't hoodwink the people who buy and sell talent. . . . Actually, television has been more helpful to me than records. Bookers, promoters and agencies can see first-hand what my capabilities are on TV, then decide where and when they can use me."

He was, indeed, the all-American success, paying tribute once again to Bumps and in particular to Crain, "my old mentor, [who] helped on the arrangement [of 'You Send Me']. It was he who taught me to use my voice the way I do," he declared, as Larry Auerbach hovered attentively in the background. *Sepia* already had a story in preparation, and *Ebony* was planning one of its own. Sam celebrated his twenty-seventh birthday on January 22, at Harlem's famed Palm Café, and in the weeks following the celebration, a picture ran in Negro newspapers all across the country that showed party-giver Sylvia Robinson (of the hit duo Mickey and Sylvia) feeding him cake.

H E FLEW HOME to cut a new single and do one last show for Art Laboe at the Orpheum Theater downtown. His co-headliner was Ernie Freeman, just coming off a number-one r&b instrumental hit with "Raunchy," with whom he started out on February 17 on a whirlwind seventeen-day package tour put together by superpackager Irvin Feld in association with r&b booking agents Archer Associates. The show included Thurston Harris, the Drifters, the Dubs, and the Silhouettes, all but the Drifters essentially one-hit wonders, though in the case of Harris ("Little Bitty Pretty One") and the Silhouettes ("Get a Job"), they were

Top 10 pop hits. It was not the kind of booking that Larry Auerbach was looking for long term, but it provided two and a half weeks of solid work, and Auerbach was well aware that Sam "needed to support himself, and we weren't prepared at William Morris [to book] the black one-nighters."

The Ernie Freeman Orchestra accompanied all the acts, and Clif White grumbled about having to walk another bunch of new musicians through Sam's arrangements, but the thirty-five-year-old Freeman, an industry veteran originally from Cleveland, had one of the top working bands in L.A., made up of guys who could actually read, and the tour provided Crain with welcome affirmation that Sam was bringing the gospel crowd along with him. "Sam took Sister Flute," said Crain, using his term for the typical female gospel fan of a certain age, "and he carried her over — he made her shout — *in the pop field*. Sister Flute didn't like it, but she came to his shows. And she say, 'Mr. Crain, I ain't got nothing, but I sure want to hear that boy.' I got her a seat. I said, 'Let her go on in and let her hear it.' She come out and say, 'Mr. Crain, I'm going to pay for that boy. I shouted for him in church, and I shouted for him tonight, and I'm going to pay.' I said to myself, I said, 'He got her. He got her.'"

They were back in New York for *The Steve Allen Show* once again on March 2, with the Copa opening just four days away. Sam and Bumps and a white PR man named Jess Rand, with whom Sam had recently begun working, caught Tony Bennett's closing night at the club, and Sam embarrassed both Jess and Bumps by announcing "That fucker never sang one song in tune" in a voice loud enough for everyone to hear. Jess, a thirty-two-year-old Broadway habitué with thinning red hair who had moved out to the Coast six years earlier and whose principal clients were Sammy Davis Jr. and actor Jeff Chandler, thought that Sam was just scared, and from Jess' point of view, he had every reason to be. "I didn't think Sam belonged there [at that point]. I was horrified." But if Sam was nervous, he didn't reveal it, at least not in so many words, not even when rehearsals for the opening proved to be a disaster.

It turned out that Bumps' "song arrangements" for the show, essentially lead sheets for the kind of combo you might encounter on a one-night stand in Kansas City, were totally inadequate for the sixteen-piece Copa orchestra. "Bumps had written rhythm parts, not full orchestrations," said Lou Adler, one of Keen's three young a&r assistants, who had come east for the opening more out of his growing friendship with

Sam than out of any professional obligation. "We were all on the floor copying out parts right up to the last minute, and you knew it still wasn't right!"

"Bumps didn't know what he was doing," observed arranger René Hall, who had helped out on the Coast as much as he could. René had had experience putting together legitimate shows, and his arranging skills were far superior to Bumps', but Bumps seemed to want to do it all by himself. "[He] was trying to create a show for a Broadway audience," René said, "and he went in there doing the same type of thing you'd do at the Elks Club across the tracks, in the black part of town!"

Nonetheless, Sam persevered, showing little of the sense of panic that he must surely have felt ("Bumps was a complete wreck," said Adler, "but I never saw Sam in a frenzy"). He was opening for popular Jewish dialect comedian Myron Cohen, and, despite a few half-hearted attempts to attract the youth crowd ("Well, girls," the *Amsterdam News* announced on March 8 to its sepia readers, "Sam has promised to sponsor a dinner-show date . . . with any girl between 15 and 19 and her chaperone who can write the best letter on 'Why I'd Like to Date Sam Cooke'"), the Copa was definitely not going to draw an audience attuned to r&b or pop radio. That was all right with Sam. The program that he had put together with Bumps was an assortment of the kind of standards that he had featured on his first album. He opened with a Latin-flavored "Begin the Beguine," went on to include "Canadian Sunset," "Ol' Man River" and his own hit version of Nat "King" Cole's "(I Love You) For Sentimental Reasons," and concluded with "Tammy," the syrupy ballad that had been a number-one hit for film actress Debbie Reynolds the previous year. He generally encored with a gospel-inflected treatment of Gene Austin's 1928 standard, "The Lonesome Road," and a brand-new finger-snapping number by Bill Haley, "Mary, Mary Lou."

It was a show almost altogether lacking in either distinction or distinctiveness. But that was because it never really became a *Sam Cooke show.* "It upset everybody," said Clif. "It upset me. I had no feel and confidence in the material. I mean, the tunes were great, [but] he was still a gospel singer singing pop tunes." What surprised Jess Rand, as it had surprised Larry Auerbach at the Elegante, was that he wasn't more of a gospel singer. "What shocked me was that he had no showmanship, he didn't know what to say. I was just the press agent, but I [tried] to tell him, 'You've got to communicate more than just music.'" But when

Sam tried to do just that, when early in the engagement he interjected even the mildest gospel exhortations, "Jules Podell told me to cut that stuff out or get out. So I cut it out." Podell, a bull-necked authoritarian figure whose rumored Mafia connections were more than just rumors, left no doubt about his feelings on the subject of Clif, either. "You don't need no guitar player on the floor with you," Podell said, with little regard for Clif's (or Sam's) sensitivities. "Get that guy back up on the bandstand, where he's supposed to be."

It was, without any question, a thoroughly humiliating experience. "He looked like a fish out of water," said Lou Rawls, in New York on a promotion tour with the Pilgrim Travelers to plug their new gospel album on the Keen subsidiary label Andex. J.W. Alexander's view was considerably less restrained. "Sam was on his own. There was no one who knew [what they were doing enough] to help him. He was just the little colored boy on Myron Cohen's show."

Much of the Negro press was surprisingly open about its disappointment. "We were pulling for him all the way," reported the *Houston Informer*. "We hated to see him not go over, for he's a good kid, talented and shy and with ambition to get ahead without tricks and stepping on others. But . . . his performance at the Copa was lacking." Some of his black critics even seem to have perceived him as getting a deserved come-uppance. Sam Cooke had "laid a golden egg," crowed syndicated columnist A. S. "Doc" Young, whose mixed feelings were further evidenced by his follow-up declaration that "some smart-aleck Broadwayites had predicted that he would goof." More predictable perhaps was *Variety*'s dismissal of the "handsome Negro lad with two hit records [who] may be a teenage idol but he doesn't seem to be ready for the more savvy Copa clientele. . . . His stint," sniffed the showbiz bible, "seemed slightly overlong and there was a feeling that he had overstayed his welcome."

It was a painful three weeks, but he stuck it out, with Crain consoling him that it wasn't his fault, he was just playing to the wrong crowd, and Bumps doing his best to cheerlead him through the mistakes. He was able to distract himself with the attentions of Harlean Harris, "the pretty model with an amazing hair style," according to a syndicated ANP dispatch, who had the prettiest thighs, Sam told his brother L.C. proudly, and then got Harlean to show them to L.C. Harlean's attention began to wander, though, as Sam's star temporarily dimmed, and he was brought face-to-face with the transitory nature of success.

His anger boiled over only once, when a wiseass agent from William Morris came into his dressing room, looked him in the eye, and, as PR man Jess Rand looked on, said, "Boy, did you bomb tonight." This was not, Rand hastened to make clear, either Larry Auerbach or Sam Bramson, the agent who had gotten Sam the Copa date, but it was a senior William Morris agent nonetheless. "Everybody in the room," said Rand, "turned and went, 'Holy shit!' But Sam just looked at him and, I'll never forget, he backed him towards the door and said, 'Did you ever make a quarter of a million dollars singing?' And the guy said, 'No . . . ' Sam said, 'Well, I have. So until you do, keep your fucking mouth shut, and don't tell me how to sing.' And he pushed him out the door."

The trouble was, he told his brother Charles, who had driven Sam's new Cadillac from Chicago for him to take out on the road, he had put his trust in the wrong people. "He told me he got the wrong advice from people who were supposed to be in the know," Charles said, fully recognizing the ominous implications for those unnamed parties from whom his brother might have had reason to expect more.

THERE WAS LITTLE TIME to dwell on it, anyway. Toward the end of his stay at the Copa he went into the studio to record the title track for the new Cary Grant–Sophia Loren movie, *Houseboat,* plus "Mary, Mary Lou," the jaunty Bill Haley number he had adopted as his closer. Three days later, on March 22, he performed on Dick Clark's brand-new *Saturday Night Beech-Nut Show* on the ABC network with Bill Haley as his co-star, and then the following Saturday, with the three-week Copa engagement at last over, he drove down to Washington, D.C., with Charles and his driver/valet Eddie Cunningham, to do *The Jimmy Dean Show* on CBS for $3,000.

Charles didn't think much of Eddie's driving ("He do a hundred miles per hour going nowhere but to the airport") or, for that matter, of Eddie himself, who never removed his sunglasses, even at night. Charles took over the driving chores ("I said, 'Hey, the dude ain't going to kill me out here' "), and he made sure that Sam let Eddie know in no uncertain terms who was in charge of the car when Charles was around. It was a beautiful car, a white convertible with gold trim and red upholstery, the kind of car Sam had always boasted to his Soul Stirrers pal, Leroy Crume, that he was going to have someday. In fact, he had shown up at Crume's house in Chicago in December, "he drove up with the top down, and it was *cold*. And he said, 'All right, fucker, come on down, let's go for a ride.' Really rubbing it in. And we rode all over town with the top down. He was the happiest guy in the world."

He showed his new car off to his brothers and sisters and Duck on that trip, and he ran into Barbara for the first time in a long time, too. He was standing outside the poolroom at Thirty-sixth and Cottage Grove that was operated by a guy named Diddy who had grown up with them all in the Lenox Building across the street. Diddy, like Charles, was involved in a number of dubious enterprises but on a much grander scale ("He wasn't no bug or nothing," said Charles), and Sam was just standing out there on the street talking to some of the fellows from the neighborhood, when Barbara suddenly came out the door. She was looking good, wearing her hair in a blond ponytail, and they started talking about one thing or another, he told her he was dividing his time between New York and California, acting the big shot, and then he asked her where she was living. So she told him she was living right here on the third floor, "and he said, 'You're living with Diddy that owns the pool room?' I said, 'Yeah.' He said, 'Well, where is my daughter?' I said, 'Oh, you mean you're claiming your daughter [now]?' And he said, 'Oh, Barb, you know what I mean.'"

They talked a little longer. She told him she had been living with Diddy for a while, he was crazy about her little girl, and, yeah, as he could see, she was getting by pretty good, she had the food concession at the poolroom so she had her own source of income, even though, in one respect, it was all Diddy's. She asked him about his wife, and he told her what she already knew from Mildred Richard, that they were separated and she had moved back to Fresno. But, he said, he didn't feel like he really wanted to divorce her, she was so low-spirited all the time. He asked if he could see Linda now, but she told him Linda was playing with her cousins over at Barbara's aunt Geraldine's. Maybe next time, he said, and Barbara gladly agreed.

The next time she saw him, she had persuaded Diddy to move the three of them into a one-bedroom apartment on Sixty-third, with a partition for Linda. She wasn't sure what exactly she wanted from Diddy, but she was consolidating her situation with him as best she could. She knew he wasn't going to marry her, since he was already married. But he took good care of her, which was what she was looking for from a man, because she didn't have the patience to learn a trade like her sister, Ella, who was a nurse, or her twin, Beverly, who worked as a bookkeeper. She liked to think of herself as a domestic, *Diddy's* domestic — she took care of his house, and he in turn took care of her. He liked to show her off. They drove all over in his big black Chrysler, and he bought her a beautiful mink coat. There was no question that Diddy was going places, there was always a ready supply of weed, and they made the scene with all the players — they were the talk of the town.

It was ironic: she might never have seen Sam again if Diddy hadn't liked to show her off so much. It was clear to her from their one brief meeting that Sam didn't like the idea of Diddy and her one bit — more than that, she knew how it had to hurt Sam to see his daughter being brought up in that environment. And there was no question Diddy was certainly jealous of her having been with Sam. He was always talking about who the fuck did Sam think he was, coming back into the neighborhood and acting like a big shot, all the women after him just because he was a motherfucking star. But then the fool couldn't resist putting her on display the next time they ran into Sam, boasting loudly that she was his woman now and Sam had better stay away. Which, of course, you didn't say to Sam — ever. Sam just laughed the way he always did, never willing to reveal what he was really thinking. He said he knew it was Diddy's shot now, he had had his chance, all innocence, giving off nothing but smooth talk and smiles. And Diddy *believed* him, the fool even asked Sam out for a drink, even though anyone could plainly see the man was still interested in her and, if the truth be told, she just might still have her eye on him. Diddy was blind to it, though, and Sam acted like they were all old friends, which in a way they were, and then she didn't see Sam for a while. And when he came back to town at the beginning of May, he was headlining a national tour.

T HE SPRING EDITION of the Biggest Show of Stars for 1958 featured Sam Cooke as headliner, with teenage Canadian sensation Paul Anka, rhythm and blues veterans LaVern Baker and Clyde McPhatter, and cleancut rock 'n' rollers Frankie Avalon and the Everly Brothers as co-stars, plus the Silhouettes, the Monotones, the Royal Teens, George Hamilton IV, and, at the bottom of a sixteen-act bill, blues singer Jimmy Reed and explosive new solo act Jackie Wilson. Presented by Irvin Feld, the onetime Washington, D.C., druggist and record store and label owner who with his brother Izzy had been promoting gospel and r&b shows out of the

District under the rubric of Super Enterprises or Super Attractions since the late forties, the Biggest Show of Stars went back as a fully integrated transcontinental rock 'n' roll revue to the spring of 1956 and could trace its ancestry at least to The Giant Rhythm and Blues Show of 1952 for which Irvin Feld had handled regional promotion. Feld had had his eye on Sam ever since "You Send Me" first broke and had even announced an all-star gospel tour including Sam at Christmastime, then promoted the February tour with Ernie Freeman and signed Sam to the Biggest Show in its immediate aftermath. The Felds had had the rock 'n' roll revue field largely to themselves for the first year or so, but more recently had picked up competition and run into serious racial situations in the South. "As though to highlight current segregation upheavals," *Billboard* reported on October 21, 1957, with the Feld Fall Edition in the second week of an eighty-day tour, "the package will operate for five consecutive dates in Chattanooga, Columbus, Georgia, Birmingham, New Orleans and Memphis without [its white acts]. In the cities mentioned, Negro and white performers cannot appear on the same stage in the same show."

The problem had been solved after a fashion in the spring of 1958 by rerouting the tour, but success had bred imitation as Universal Attractions, the booking agency with the largest stable of black acts, mounted its own Rhythm and Blues Cavalcade of '58, and Alan Freed, the biggest DJ in the country, with the ability to make or break stars nationally from his position at New York station WINS, put together a Big Beat package to go head-to-head with Feld's tour. The result of this direct "competition between the Feld and Freed presentations for prime locations as well as attractions . . . [in a severe] economic slowdown" was predictable enough, as *Billboard* reported it. Talent costs were up (Super Attractions' costs were likely to exceed $35,000 a week, Feld announced), and box-office grosses (which could go as high as $10,000 to $15,000 a night, and sometimes double that, if two shows were presented on the same day) were almost certain to be down. And with bland, Brilliantined rock 'n' roll television personality Dick Clark (who was fast overtaking Freed in popularity and influence through his five-afternoons-a-week television dance party, *American Bandstand*) announcing his own tour for later in the year, the future of this brave new world of commercial integration seemed very much in doubt.

The Biggest Show of Stars opened in Norfolk, Virginia, on April 5 ("for the first time in 'package show' history," the city's black weekly proudly announced, "a really big-time unit has elected Norfolk as its kick-off city"), after a couple of days of rehearsal in New York. The troupe was traveling on "buses, Cadillacs, planes, etc.," according to the *Norfolk Journal and Guide,* which quoted a spokesman for the production company as saying, "If the show is a hit in Norfolk, it stands better-than-average chances of being a smasheroo elsewhere."

The news of Sam's settlement with Connie Bolling, the source of the "fornication and bastardy" charge that had landed Sam briefly in jail in Philadelphia, was just being reported in black newspapers all around the country. It was the first time that his arrest the previous December had been publicly revealed or, in fact, that there had been any news of the lawsuit at all. The settlement was for "well over $5000," the *Philadelphia Tribune* reported in a headline story on April 1. His lawyer would concede only that Sam had agreed to the payment to "avoid a long and expensive court battle which might damage his career," but there was no question that the child was his — Sam had had Crain check it out, and at this point he just wanted to put the whole sorry mess behind him.

Feld's regular backup band, Paul Williams and his newly crowned Show of Stars Orchestra (Williams was the originator of the huge 1949 r&b hit "The Hucklebuck," and a New York studio stalwart), provided solid instrumental backing, but Clif grumbled just as much about having to teach them Sam's arrangements as he would have about working with any other group of musicians who did not play exclusively for his employer. "I carried a great big old suitcase full of arrangements, two of them, in fact. There was enough acts on the show to go for almost three hours, and when it was time for Sam to go on [at the end, after Clyde McPhatter and Paul Anka, the two acts that Irvin Feld personally managed], you'd just go out onstage, work your way through the amps, and plug in." It was something of a comedown for someone who had performed with the Mills Brothers on stages around the world, but he believed in Sam, Sam treated him and everyone else around him with the utmost courtesy and financial consideration, and Sam was the star of the show.

In Philadelphia they drew less than one thousand, with Philadelphia's most popular black DJ, Georgie Woods, MCing the show. Without any question the economy was a factor, maybe the bad publicity about the paternity suit contributed, but clearly the single element that cut most directly into box-office receipts was the fact that the Alan Freed package — with Chuck Berry, Jerry Lee Lewis, Buddy Holly, Frankie Lymon, and Ed Townsend, among others — had played Philadelphia just eleven nights earlier, and Ray Charles was coming through with his own self-contained show in nearby Chester two days later.

They did good business and bad business. In New Haven, Frankie Avalon was hailed by *Billboard* reporter June Bundy as the star of the show, and Feld's directive to the performers to "play down suggestive gestures and material" amidst the "powder keg" atmosphere of the crowd was approvingly noted by Bundy. Sam, Clyde McPhatter, and LaVern Baker were hailed as the "most showmanly," and indeed, in city after city the nonstop revue came to be seen as something of a personal contest between Clyde and Sam, two pure stand-up singers who captivated the house each night not with steps, acrobatics, or gyrations but strictly by the intricate arrangement of their art.

Clyde certainly possessed the voice, the background, and to some extent even the temperament closest to Sam's. Born in 1931 in Durham, North Carolina, to a minister father whose ten children all called him "Bishop" and a mother who lived for her children, he had moved to New York with his family at an early age, forming a spiritual group with David and Wilbur Baldwin, whose brother Jimmy was a writer. It was while he was with this group, the Mt. Lebanon Singers, that he first came to the attention of Billy Ward, a musical martinet, who was in the process of putting together a new r&b group, the Dominoes, that would merge the styles of the Ink Spots, the Ravens, the Orioles, and the gospel quartets. Clyde first burst upon the national scene in 1951, in the same year and at the same age — twenty — as Sam, but with a succession of Top 10 r&b hits rather than spiritual numbers. His tremulous natural falsetto was able to tease a phrase in that familiar melismatic manner to the point that music historian Bill Millar would count out the number of notes to which he could draw out a single syllable (twenty-two) in an attempt to quantify McPhatter's astonishing capacity to extend both meaning and emotional depth. Like Sam, he was quick to acknowledge his debt to Bill Kenny of the Ink Spots, but, also like Sam, he brought something of his own, in his case an undisguised vulnerability, the kind of soulful excess that could transform "White Christmas" into a prayerful plea.

He left the Dominoes in 1953 and quickly formed a new group, the Drifters, at the instigation of Ahmet Ertegun, for whose Atlantic label he would enjoy even greater success (and create even more widely known r&b standards) with such songs as "Money Honey," "Such a Night," and "Honey Love" while serving as the same kind of inspiration to the young white singer Elvis Presley that Bill Kenny had been to him. After a two-year stint in the army, he went out on his own, and in the past three years had enjoyed seven Top 10 r&b hits, all but one of which (a duet with Ruth Brown) charted pop. Every night he performed an array of these hits, including, typically, "Have Mercy Baby," "Come What May," and the soaring, gospel-based "Without Love," which "left the audience," as the *Houston Informer* reported, "gasping for more."

It was a spirit of friendly competition, in which Sam, Clyde, and LaVern Baker, the irrepressible twenty-eight-year-old life force who had preceded Sam at Wendell Phillips High School by a year and started out her show-business career at seventeen as Little Miss Sharecropper, frequently sang spirituals in the locker-room dressing rooms of the arenas in which they played. LaVern, an uninhibited, cheerfully bawdy ball of fire both on and offstage, closed the first half of the show with her biggest hit, "Jim Dandy," and was known, according to *Ebony*, for her "sexy gestures and daring body movements," which included sticking her finger provocatively in her mouth and rolling her eyes. She was as likely to cuss out a fellow performer with a string of epithets few of her male co-stars could match as she was to sew a button on the shirt of one of the kids on the show. But she was as dedicated to her gospel roots as either of her co-stars, and, the *Norfolk Journal and Guide* reported in a syndicated story, "If they can get permission from their respective record firms, they want to turn out an album of their favorite gospel songs as a trio." One night, the Everly Brothers, whose specialty was close country harmony and who currently had the number-one pop hit in the country with "All I Have to Do Is Dream," walked into the dressing room while Sam and Clyde were singing. "It was the most spectacular thing," said nineteen-year-old Phil Everly, "the two of them changing off, [they] were about the best I ever heard."

What set Sam and Clyde apart from so many of the others, a quality remarked upon by both reporters and peers, was a sense of restraint, an impression of natural elegance and introspection that manifested itself in both their person and their art. What Sam found so compelling about Clyde, though, were his private views on a whole range of subjects, views that, while not altogether foreign to Sam, he had never heard so forcefully expressed.

Religion, for example. To Clyde, the kind of religion on which he had been raised was a swindle, "based on fear [and] hocus-pocus. You know, 'God don't like this, God don't like that,' so one day I said, 'Goddamn it,' and my father beat the hell out of me." His father, too, the "Bishop," he saw as something of a hypocrite and an oppressor, a man lacking in both sympathy and understanding, where his mother, a woman of little education but much "mother wit . . . never tried to hold me back." He could always communicate with her, he said, because she supported his dreams. "She was a country girl [who] would say, 'You can bring your biddies up, but once they learn to fly, you must let them use their wings.'"

He was a man with an acute sense of injustice, fully committed to the civil rights struggle, with a lifetime membership in the National Association for the Advancement of Colored People (NAACP) and a willingness to make public gestures of support, as he had the previous Christmas when he was pictured in an ANP dispatch, mailing a box of records from his music shop in New Rochelle, New York, to the embattled black students of Little Rock. He was equally indignant at the inequities of the music business, racial and otherwise, and he railed quietly against the mistreatment that he had received at the hands of Atlantic Records.

All of this was so much against his perceived image that only an attentive listener would have picked it up, and many of his contemporaries missed it altogether. Clyde was shy, soft-spoken, polite almost to the point of diffidence, and because he liked his liquor, many of his fellow entertainers tended to dismiss his views or simply not to hear them. But he could have found no more attentive listener than Sam, who soaked it all up in much the same way that he took in all the information and opinions that he gathered from his wide-ranging reading, absorbing it all, trying out new perspectives, reserving judgment for another day.

There were other outstanding acts and personalities on the show. Sam could appreciate the pure pop sensibilities of some of the young white acts, like sixteen-year-old Paul Anka and eighteen-year-old Bobby Rydell, and he and Clyde would sometimes fool around with country tunes, which made perfect sense to the Everly Brothers, who recognized in their ornate vocal embellishments a striking resemblance to the way

Sam, LaVern Baker, Jackie Wilson, 1958. *Courtesy of Reginald Abrams* in which Lefty Frizzell, one of their idols in country music, would wrap his voice around a song. But the talent to which Sam was drawn most of all was twenty-four-year-old Jackie Wilson, who had emerged from a gospel background in Detroit to take Clyde's place as lead singer with the Dominoes, then gone solo the previous fall at almost exactly the same time that Sam had emerged in the pop field. Wilson, a strongly extroverted personality who was crazy about both the Soul Stirrers and comic books, brought the house down every night with his opening set, which consisted entirely of his first two hit releases, "Reet Petite" and "To Be Loved," complete with splits, knee drops, spectacular falsetto flights, and a sense of showmanship that never failed to electrify the audience. Offstage he was equally bold, brazen, and streetwise, with very much of a "player"'s personality, but for all of their differences, and for all of the smooth urbanity that he himself sought to cultivate, Sam was drawn to that, too.

T HEY HIT CHICAGO on May 3. Like the Alan Freed package the previous week, the Biggest Show of Stars was booked into the old Civic Opera House, where Sam had played the previous December. Once again the old neighborhood was out in force, and Jake Richard induced Sam to stop by Creadell Copeland's house for an informal QCs reunion. None of the QCs had seen him perform — they all remained strict in their avoidance of secular music. Which bothered Sam in a way, even though he didn't say anything. It kind of hurt the way the quartets would do him, he told Alabama Five Blind Boys guitarist Johnny Fields, who had come to see him three weeks earlier when the tour played Raleigh. "Sam had been in the gospel field, and he knew there weren't no saints over there, either. He said, 'I'm the same Sam Cook that was singing "Jesus Give Me Water."' He said, 'I haven't changed. I'm still Sam.'"

To the public at large he permitted no such glimpse of vulnerability. "The transition from gospel to pop tunes was easy," he told an ANP wire service reporter backstage at the Civic Opera. "When I first started singing pop tunes, I wondered how my former associates and fans would react. But they accepted me, as I see them all sitting on the front row . . . just like they did when I was with the Soul Stirrers."

That same night the violence that had been predicted by rock 'n' roll critics since the start of both tours exploded at Alan Freed's Big Beat show in Boston, when dancing broke out in the middle of Jerry Lee

Lewis' set and, after being stopped by police, broke out again during Chuck Berry's performance. The show would not continue, the police announced, until everyone returned to their seats, and even then, the houselights would be left on as a security measure. "It looks like the Boston police don't want you to have a good time," Freed announced from the stage. Which was more than enough for the crowd, as the seventy-two-hundred-seat Boston Arena, primarily a hockey arena, erupted. Within a week Freed had been indicted by the Suffolk County D.A. for "inciting to riot" and fired from his job at WINS, as the tour itself came to an abrupt end. Universal Attractions' R&B Cavalcade had already gone on permanent hiatus by this time, and the Dick Clark tour, which had been scheduled to begin at the end of the month, was almost immediately canceled.

Only the Biggest Show of Stars soldiered on, completing a western segment that included Saskatchewan and British Columbia, then swinging back through Texas and Oklahoma until it reached the Southeast once again, where, fifty-six days after its start, the tour returned to Norfolk for what the *Norfolk Journal and Guide* anticipated would be another keen "battle of songs" between Sam, a "newcomer to the million-sales record field, and Clyde McPhatter, an old pro, [who] have clashed in wars of words and music . . . everywhere the show has appeared to date."

In addition to the stories in *Tan* and *Sepia,* there were features on Sam in the teen magazines *Song Hits, Hit Parader,* and *Rhythm and Blues.* There was some concern on Sam's and Bumps' part that they had yet to come up with a suitable follow-up to "You Send Me," which had now sold nearly two million copies and, in something of an historic first, actually managed to launch a label with a number-one hit. But the album was selling well enough to bear out Bumps' strategy of musical diversification, and Sam's signature hit had entered the national consciousness to such an extent that its very paucity of lyrics had become a frequent object of good-natured satire. Prophet John the Conqueror, a Chicago freelance preacher/promoter Sam had known since his QC days, confidently predicted that Sam's next three recordings, "regardless of the type or title, [would] sell a million or more copies." None of it seemed to touch Sam anyway. Irrespective of record sales or the Copa debacle, said Lou Adler, who saw the Biggest Show of '58 on the Coast, "Sam just seemed to be comfortable within himself. I mean, the excitement backstage with all those performers was unbelievable, but it all changed when he walked in. This was a guy that was different from everyone [else] who was in the room."

KEEN RECORDS by all appearances was thriving. Bumps had by now built up a full-fledged roster, with the Valiants, Johnny "Guitar" Watson, and J.W. Alexander's Pilgrim Travelers, who, as the Travelers, had just put out their first two pop releases, including "Teenage Machine Age." Bumps had developed a gospel line, too, with strong new releases by the Gospel Harmonettes and the Five Blind Boys of Alabama as well as the Pilgrim Travelers, all former Specialty artists. There were in addition a host of newcomers, with artists like Marti Barris, Milton Grayson, and a young group from the Greek community, the Salmas Brothers, all showing varying degrees of commercial promise.

John Siamas spent more time at the record company now than at his aircraft parts business, mostly because, as his teenage son oberved, "he enjoyed it more. There were other executives at Randall to run operational matters, but this was his avocation." As a longtime sound buff, he had planned from the start "to develop a high-quality recording studio," and to that end he had recruited a Greek-American engineer, Dino Lappas, who had designed it and was building it for him at the label's new West Third Street location.

Lou Adler and Herb Alpert had long since graduated from their assistants' roles; they were now not only writing and producing for pretty, blond Marti Barris, they had written and produced Sam's latest single, "All of My Life," which unfortunately turned out to be his first not even to chart. They had at this point learned all there was to learn from Bumps, but they were still in the process of seeking an answer to the question that bedeviled everyone who went to work at Keen: "Where's Bumps?!"

"Bumps was a teacher," Lou said, expressing a sentiment on which both he and Herb were in full agreement. "His strength was [as] an educator — and he wanted you to learn. [When we first started], he'd give us a stack of tapes and acetates, and he'd have us break 'em down by verse and by chorus. And then he would grade us, just like school. 'That was good. You picked the right verse. You picked the right song.' He pretty much taught us song structure."

His downfall, unfortunately, was organization. "After he hired us, we spent the next three months trying to find him. He'd say, 'Meet me here.'

We'd go there, and they'd say, 'He just left.' We knew Bumps was scattered, everyone knew that Bumps would make an appointment and not show up, not follow up on something he should have taken care of — that was just Bumps. He never felt professional, even to us. He felt *great,* he felt like he'd do anything for you, stay up twenty-four hours a day, he was always thrilled about [any] event that elevated things and took them to another level, levels he had probably dreamed about. But they were beyond him — the monetary thing for Bumps was secondary, but he always sort of outhustled himself, [he always] reached his level of incompetence."

Follow a&r apprentice Freddy Smith felt much the same way, only more so. Freddy was trying to pitch a song that he and his new songwriting partner, Cliff Goldsmith, had written. It was called "Western Movies," a kind of cowboy comic opera along the lines of a Jerry Leiber and Mike Stoller–produced Coasters record, and every time he sang and played it for Sam on the piano, Fred said, "Sam would roll on the floor, laughing like nobody's business. He says, 'Bumps, you gotta do it, man. You gotta do it.' But Bumps kept procrastinating, and Cliff, my partner, is dying, 'cause I can't get nothing done."

The way Freddy saw it, it was symptomatic of the way Bumps took care of business — or didn't. "Bumps had no organization. *None.* And all these people scattered out everywhere with promises that he's going to do things and stuff. My thoughts of Bumps was, I learned the business by watching his mistakes. As far as I'm concerned, Bumps should have paid [more] attention."

But Bumps was paying attention to something else. He had been cultivating a Latin dance sound ever since discovering a group called Raul Trana and the Nicaraguans in a Hollywood nightclub the previous year. He had even gone so far as to record them for a single release. Now Sam had brought in a song with a Latin feel that Bumps was convinced could be Sam's next big hit, and when they went into the studio again toward the end of June, several weeks after Sam's triumphant homecoming, that was the number that Bumps was determined to concentrate on.

Sam had started writing more and more. He carried a blue spiral notebook with him everywhere he went, filling it up with his lyrics, sometimes even jotting down words while he was talking to you. One time he showed Herb Alpert a song he was working on, "and he asked me what I thought of the lyric, and it really seemed trite to me. [So] I asked him what does the song go like, and he pulled out his guitar and started playing. And all of a sudden this thing that looked so corny on paper just turned into this magical event. 'Cause he had a way of phrasing, a way of presenting his feelings that was uniquely his. I mean, he was talking right to you, he wasn't trying to flower things up with words that didn't connect. He had a very clear way of expressing himself."

"If you listen to his lyrics," echoed Herb's songwriting partner Lou Adler, "they're very conversational. And it's something that he always expressed. He said, 'If you're writing a song that you really want to get to people, you've got to put it into a language that they understand.'" Although he was an avid reader of poetry, his rhymes were more a matter of feel than formality. "It didn't matter if it was a real rhyme or not," said Adler, "[as long as] it felt right. I've seen him pick up a guitar and, you know, almost talk to you in the way that he was writing. And maybe it's a song or a lyric that he'll never use. But it sounded good when he was doing it."

He had his own decided ideas of production as well. With René Hall, who was writing most of Bumps' arrangements by now, whether credited or not, Sam was always insistent on getting it exactly the way he imagined it in his mind's eye. He was "stubborn," said René, "[but] he knew what he wanted to do. He would come in [to my office] with his guitar — or Clif White would play the guitar, because Clif knew more chords — and he would [show] me what line he wanted, he'd hum what he wanted the bass to play, hum what he wanted the strings to play, he would tell you exactly what he wanted every instrument to play." To Herb, a trumpet player with a somewhat formal approach to music, it was Sam's uncanny ability to communicate — as much by gesture as by language — that allowed him "to set up an environment where the musicians felt comfortable enough to express themselves through Sam, and that was the key. He told me something once that's riveted to me, it's like a permanent memory. He said, 'People are just listening to a cold piece of wax, and it either makes it or it don't.' I said, 'What do you mean?' He said, 'You know, you listen to it, you close your eyes, if you like it, great. If you don't, nobody cares if you're black or white, what kind of echo chamber you're using. If it touches you, that's the measure.'"

One time Sam and Herb were listening to a young West Indian singer who was auditioning at the Keen studio. "He even brought his own box to put his foot on for the audition. And I was saying to myself, 'Oh, wow, man, this guy has the whole tool kit. I mean, he's nice to look at, he plays nice guitar, his songs are good, and he'll look great on television!' And Sam looked at me and said, 'What do you think?' So I told him, and he said, 'Well, turn your chair around for a little while and listen to him.' And I did, and, of course, nothing happened. And I said, 'Oh, well, it's not as good when I turn my back.' And he said, 'Yeah, I know.' But, I mean, that was Sam. He wouldn't be intimidated by how you looked, it didn't matter if you were handsome or funny-looking, he was listening for the feel."

As to how Sam picked up the Latin sound (which had been pervasive since the mambo, rhumba, cha cha, and calypso crazes that had periodically swept through the music business over the past five years), it wasn't any more a matter of conscious study, Herb felt, than the way Sam sang. "I don't think he was listening to Tito Puente. Sam had his antennae up at all times, and I would guess that Sam just kind of took the concept [that Bumps had introduced to the Keen studio] and put his own stamp on it."

The song that he and Bumps were planning to focus on, "Win Your Love for Me," was a real departure for Sam. He recorded it at the Capitol studios on the same day that he finally laid down a satisfactory vocal for "Almost in Your Arms," the theme from *Houseboat* that he had originally cut while he was in New York in March. The movie theme had been written by Jay Livingston and Ray Evans, the veteran Hollywood team who had come up with everything from Nat "King" Cole's classic "Mona Lisa" to Debbie Reynolds' "Tammy," and there was no question that it would be the A-side of the single, both because of its cinematic pedigree and because of Bumps' strong belief in upward musical mobility. But, however smoothly Sam delivered it, it remained a conventional romantic ballad, whereas his own composition had the airiness, the space, above all that inimitable sense of "motion" that so strongly marked Sam's feel for a song.

Light, lilting, with a kind of modified calypso beat that fell somewhere in between recent recordings by the Orioles' Sonny Til and Little Willie John, it was also the first new composition by Sam to appear on record since "You Send Me" — and, of course, it was credited to L.C. It opened with bongos on top of drums, with Clif's guitar (played in the most laconic, tuned-down fashion) adding one more percussive element

In the studio, 1958. Above: Bumps Blackwell, Sam, and Herb Alpert.
Top right: Bumps and Sam. Bottom right: S.R. Crain, Sam, Bumps, Clif White
Photographs by Jess Rand, © *Michael Ochs Archives.com*

to a tastefully churning rhythm track. Sam's voice at the outset is accompanied by his own overdubbed high harmony, then the chorus falls in
behind him with the quiet quartet sound that has been otherwise missing from his pop numbers. The lyrics themselves are sung in a modified
patois, and there are plenty of "whoa-oh-ohs" along with other instantly
identifiable vocal byplay, but the strength of the song lies in its very simplicity, in the apparent effortlessness that recalls his most graceful
(though certainly not his most intense) gospel performances. It is as if
he were, finally, freed from all constraints, the kind of singer so at home
with the sound of his own voice that he is, in the words of his one-time
Atlantic Records suitor Jerry Wexler, "a perfect case," the very definition

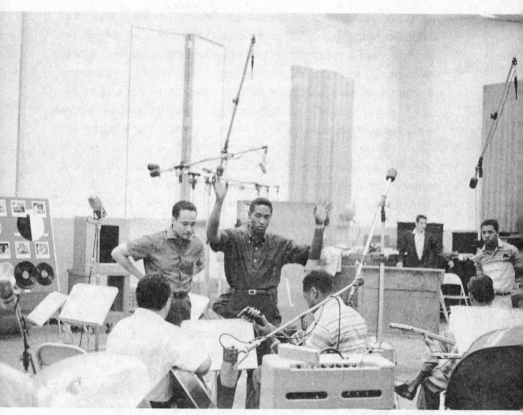

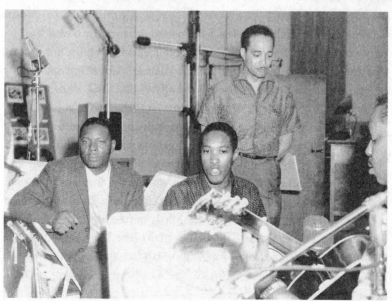

of the indefinability that lies at the heart of classic art. You get the feeling that at this moment he could sing the telephone book — and might very well do so if he were convinced that in so doing he could reach a larger audience.

Sam was thoroughly enjoying his time at home. The apartment house on St. Andrew's was rapidly turning into a kind of extended-family complex. Marlene Blackwell was over all the time visiting her girlfriend, a dancer from Boston, who lived upstairs, and Huggy Boy, the white DJ, and Oopie (George McCurn), the exuberantly eccentric bass singer for the Travelers whom Sam called Oopie Doopie Doo, were living there as well. Lou Adler started going out with Marlene's girlfriend, and soon he, too, was close to a full-fledged resident, staying upstairs or camping out at Sam's apartment most of the time. "There was always a lot of people around," he remembered. "I was half living there and half staying there, I was living the life. We'd get up at two or three in the afternoon and have breakfast, you know, everything was a party. It was gatherings at one apartment or another, all the doors were open to the apartments, and we'd go out to the clubs at night, the 5/4 Ballroom and the California Club, and then to the after-hours places after the clubs closed and back at six in the morning."

One of those nights, they all ended up at the California Club, and Ed Townsend, whose "For Your Love" was a huge pop hit that summer, was onstage. To Adler's surprise "he taunted Sam enough to bring him up, and then he tried to outdo him. And I remember it just going and going, Ed was just doing some of his riffs, and then Sam went into some gospel stuff, and it just tore the place apart. I mean, this was a guy who could literally lift women out of their seats, depending on what he did vocally, and he moved Townsend right off the stage, the women were going [so] crazy."

The July 4 *Larry Finley Show*, a local television program, offered a tribute to Keen Records' success, as Sam got an award from the host for being the "Brightest Young Singing Talent to Grace the Airwaves of KTLA for 1958," and Bumps got his own award "for discovering Cooke, Marti Barris, and other new recording stars." Sam and Bumps wore their elegant Sy Devore suits, while John Siamas beamed proudly at Sam's debut performance of "Win Your Love For Me," backed by the "Bumps Blackwell Rockin' Combo." Jess Rand, the PR agent on whom Sam was increasingly leaning for advice, was there, too, taking pictures to distribute to the trades.

Then he was back on the road, playing the Bolero, a classy fifteen-hundred-seater in Wildwood, New Jersey, a boardwalk resort on the Jersey shore, then going on to Atlanta, where he appeared on the first night of promoter B.B. Beamon's two-day birthday celebration at the Magnolia, with Jackie Wilson and the Drifters booked for the second. Beamon, who, according to the *Atlanta Daily World,* bought over $2 million worth of talent annually, took a dim view of much of the current crop, because, he said, they "hardly know how to get on and off a stage." But that was clearly not the case with Sam or Jackie, or Clyde McPhatter or LaVern Baker, for that matter, whom he booked again and again — and who consistently kept drawing.

Sam stayed out until August 2, when he returned to give a deposition in Art Rupe's continuing legal action against him and to play the fourteenth annual all-star Cavalcade of Jazz, for which Lil Cumber had booked him as headliner the following night. The lawsuit was just one of his ongoing concerns. He had finally settled his divorce action with Dolores. She had sued him in May, alleging that she had not been aware of the import of papers she had signed the previous fall agreeing to an uncontested divorce and seeking that the judgment entered against her in default be set aside. Then in June her motion was granted and the judgment set aside, and, perhaps based on what she had read in the papers about his new house and swimming pool, she sued him for $5,000 in attorneys fees and $5,000 a month alimony. Sam's lawyer got her lawyer and her down to $10,000 in a single lump sum — no alimony, no attorneys fees — and Sam instructed him to get it over with once and for all.

He was concerned enough with his reputation, though, to put together a first-person article for *Sepia,* which, while undoubtedly ghost-written, bore all the earmarks of Sam's present thinking and preoccupations with the perils of success. "As a Soul Stirrer," he declared in a story entitled "The Trouble I've Seen," "I wasn't too familiar with what goes on in show business." The gospel world, of course, had not been without its own snares and delusions, "old ladies crowding around me after we had finished a concert, many of [whom] made passes at me which I naturally ignored." Or introduced him to their daughters with the idea of trapping him in marriage. All of that he had learned to deal with.

As a pop singer, however, he found himself "smack dab in the middle of a sinful world," amidst beautiful women who were not so easily distracted, beautiful women who "have money, know how to dress and talk about things they never mention or think about among the teenage crowd." The only way of avoiding this kind of temptation, given that he was a normal red-blooded young man, was "to really put on the brakes . . . to take each step in stride to avoid making those mistakes that have wrecked the careers of other promising singers." He valued, as he always had, he wrote, his parents' "steadying advice" and spent a great deal of time "in silent prayer."

At the end, he addressed his own domestic situation. "Because so many things have been written and said [about it], I feel I am entitled to speak for myself." He and Dolores, "a swell and lovable person," had simply gotten married too young, during a time when he should have been concentrating exclusively on his career. As for Connie Bolling, "the Philadelphia secretary who brought [the] unfortunate paternity suit against me . . . I am still convinced it was just one of those things that happen to a guy when he is on his way up." He was now, he acknowledged, paying for his mistakes, and it was "most upsetting. I can say seriously that it sure doesn't 'send me' as the song says." But he was not going to make the same mistake again. "For I've learned a lot since I went into show business. I know now that things can come back to haunt you. Like past mistakes of judgment and passion." And, he pledged to his fans, and perhaps more significantly to himself, he would keep those passions tightly reined in, from now on cool reason would remain in control.

He did not, of course, speak of Barbara, though things had finally come to a head with her. She had brought the baby to see him at the Evans Hotel the last time he was in town, and Linda piped up, just as cute as a button, "My mama won't tell me who you are, but I know you are something to me." It had just about killed him. He wanted to claim his daughter right then and there, but Barbara was playing that two-faced game, doing all she could to make him jealous of Diddy, when she knew he knew all about the kind of life she was leading. Finally, against his better judgment, he said that he really hated the idea of her being with Diddy, and she just looked at him as if to say, Well, what the fuck is that to me? And he said, cautiously, "But I could never accept you with a kid of his." Because it was obvious that she was pregnant — her clothes were loose-fitting enough to be maternity clothes. She stared at him like was he really serious, and said, "Well, you don't want me no kind of way, so what difference does it make?" And he didn't say anything else, but he told her girlfriend Mook, Mildred Richard, that he wanted his little girl, that he would take Barbara and the baby both, but not with some other man's child.

So she had an abortion and went to see him again at the Evans Hotel, like she expected him to come through on his promise right there on the spot, and he didn't know what to do. He knew what he had said, but he didn't know what to do. Because the girl he had left was the woman that he wanted, but the girl he had left, the one he had loved when they were both little more than children, was almost unrecognizable within her new hard and polished shell. Then Barbara was completely outdone. She pleaded with Crain, but his heart was adamantine. He said there was nothing he could do for her, there was nothing Sammy could do even if he wanted to, he didn't have any money because, after all, they were just starting out in the business. She stared at him in disbelief. *What was wrong with these people?* Didn't they have any morals? Then, as if to prove how low an opinion of her he actually had, Crain tried to get her to give him some. She just looked at him in utter dismay, like, What did he take her for, was this just something he was going to run back and tell Sam about, or did he really need it that bad? He said, "Well, you a girl that's been around town, you with these drug pushers and all," as if to excuse some little faux pas, and then he backed off in embarrassment. But he was insistent that there was nothing either he or Sammy could do to help.

She might have resigned herself to it, tried to get Diddy to marry her or improve her situation some kind of way, but she had gone too far — she didn't want Diddy anymore, she wanted Sam. And she wasn't willing to leave it like it was, with her thoroughly humiliated and him acting like he was the king of the fucking castle.

So, after they had gone back to California, she went to Sam's sister Mary — she never knew why, because Mary never liked her any better than any of the other Cooks, but she liked Barbara's fur coat, and Barbara offered it to her if she would only get a message to Sam. She had an uncle in Los Angeles, Obie Lee, she told Mary, and Obie Lee had offered to take care of her and the baby and get her started out there, so Sam didn't have to worry about nothing like that, she just needed the money to get out to California. Mary nodded and said she would see what she could do — she surely did like that fur coat, which, even if it wouldn't fit her, she could have a rug made out of it. She was as good as her word. She told Sam what Barbara had told her: that Barbara and Diddy had gotten picked up by the police, and the welfare people were coming around threatening to take Barbara's baby away from her, and the next thing Barbara knew, she had two tickets and a $125 money order for her and the baby to fly out. So she crept away from Diddy, and when he caught her and told her not to take anything but the clothes on her back as she packed the cardboard suitcases that her stepbrother, Don Cornelius, a Chicago policeman, had brought to the house, she turned the full fire of her fury against Sam on him. "I screwed for these clothes," she said. "I'm taking my damn clothes with me." But they lost her suitcases on the American Airlines flight.

S AM REMAINED EMBROILED in Art Rupe's ongoing attempts to prove him a liar. Art had initially begun his lawsuit against Rex, Sam, Bumps, and various other interconnected parties in February, seeking, essentially, restitution for his loss. By his figuring, Keen had earned close to three quarters of a million dollars from Sam's hit, and while that was something to which they were entitled fair and square, he was entitled to something like $45,000 in the way of publishing income on "You Send Me" alone, not to mention his share in Sam's future songwriting royalties.

With Art's own increasingly lucrative investments in oil and real estate, it didn't really amount to all that much in the greater scheme of things, but as he saw it, it was a simple question of justice. He had been trying to find someone — *anyone* — who would testify in a manner that would rectify that injustice. At first he thought he had discovered that person in Leo Price, Lloyd's brother, who declared that he was the author of the song, or one very much like it called "Why You Send Me." But when he tried to pin Leo down and get something out of him that seemed more than just another interested party's attempt to cash in on a confused situation, the whole thing pretty much went away, and, for the time being, he was back where he started, clutching at straws.

He tried to see if anyone had slipped up when the record was first released and it had ever been advertised or announced as an original by Sam. He contacted Bob Keane, who couldn't offer legal proof of Sam's authorship but was convinced that he had written it — and equally convinced, he told Art, that Bumps was ruining Sam as an artist "by removing the Negro quality and making him sing things he doesn't feel." Rupe had given up on his half-assed idea of holding Sam to his 1956 Soul Stir-rers contract, and he started cutting the group in March with its new lead, Johnnie Taylor, who sounded almost identical to Sam but evidently not identical enough to sell any records.

Finally, as depositions continued and he found himself confronted with more and more of Sam's and L.C.'s baldfaced lies, he reached a point where he was ready to dismiss Sam once and for all as one more in a long list of disappointments. The naked avaraciousness of the man, his total lack of business ethics only strengthened Rupe in the determina-tion that had slowly been building to leave the record business and its corrupt practices behind. He may have treated his artists like children, but always, from his perspective, with a concern for their greater good. Their lack of gratitude — Little Richard's, Lloyd Price's, Bumps' and Sam's — saddened him but only confirmed him in his bleak view of human nature. Henceforth he would leave the running of the business for the most part to others — to Sonny Bono in Hollywood, Harold Battiste in New Orleans, and Professor Alex Bradford in the gospel division — but only under the strictest financial controls.

As for Sam, he felt no compunction whatsoever about his role in the affair. As far as he was concerned, Art had long since made his money, what was he complaining about? He and L.C. and J.W. only chortled when L.C. was called upon to claim authorship and, under close examination by Art's lawyer, Dave Pollock, L.C. not only affirmed the compositions to be his own but recited the lyrics verse by verse, note by note. Art's lawyer at this point drew Art aside and, speaking in an urgent undertone according to L.C.'s recollection, declared, "The wise father knows his own children. I would stake my reputation that he wrote these songs."

"You know," said J.W. Alexander to L.C. afterward, "I was almost believing that you actually wrote them!"

DESPITE KEEN'S GROWTH, and Sam's success, things had not been going particularly well for Bumps at the label. He still did not have a written contract spelling out either his partnership agreement or his profit participation, and his relationship with John Siamas grew increas-ingly testy that summer. At the beginning of July, he had asked for a clar-ification of his status and, a month later, demanded an accounting, since he had as yet received no royalties. In response, as he understood it, he was promised formal recognition of his ownership share in the company, but, he was given to understand, this would be in lieu of unpaid royalties, so there was still no hope of money actually changing hands.

Sam, too, was upset with him, Bumps had little doubt it was at Alex's instigation. Bumps had reassured Sam again and again that here at Keen, unlike Specialty, they were going to own their own publishing, that Siamas had promised them at least an equal share in their own songs with Higuera, Keen's publishing arm. But so far not a word had come from the company itself, and Sam kept pressing him for proof. Bumps knew that Alexander was always playing devil's advocate, telling Sam Bumps didn't know what he was talking about, that you needed more than pretty promises to be in business, and Bumps put down Sam's growing impatience to Alexander's interference. One time Sam said to him, "You taking care of all these other people's business instead of taking care of mine — and I'm your bread and butter." Which shocked Bumps in a way, but he thought it was just a little too much ego and would most likely pass.

Then his "assistant," Fred Smith, left over what Bumps might have termed a little "misunderstanding" but to Fred was more a matter of his life's blood: his songs. It all came back to "Western Movies," the novelty number that Fred and Cliff Goldsmith had written for Sam and that Bumps kept stringing them along about. Nothing happened and nothing happened, and finally Fred's mother, Effie Smith, a blues singer who with her husband, John Criner, had various music business enterprises of her own, was taking this group called the Challengers into the studio for the first time, "and she let me hear the stuff [that they were gonna cut], and I said, 'Man, me and Cliff got a song that would make them number one.' So I told Cliff, I said, 'Man, I'm just tired of Bumps. Let's go do it.'" The group changed its name to the Olympics, the song was a hit right out of the chute, and when he got wind of what Fred and Cliff had done, Bumps fired Fred and recorded the song on his wife, Marlene, who no one had even known was a singer up till then.

It was as if Bumps' magic was deserting him. René Hall's description of Bumps in the studio could just as easily have summed up the man: "He would just talk loud and boss everybody around and create the impression that he knew what he was doing. Then he would hire capable people that would straighten it out and do it their way, and he'd say, 'Yes, that's what I want.'" Only now it seemed some of those very problem solvers were instead creating problems of their own.

J.W. had no doubt that "Bumps should have protected Sam better." J.W. was staying temporarily with his lead singer Lou Rawls' mother, Evie, and her husband, Marion Wooten Beal, whom everyone called "Keg" because he had always wanted to be a bartender and, in the absence of achieving his professional ambitions, had set up a bar in his own home. J.W.'s latest marriage had recently broken up mostly because his wife, Shelley, had started working as a manicurist at La Couture and fallen in with a sporting crowd, but also because she disapproved of what she termed his unhealthy professional preoccupation with Sam Cooke. "She thought the only reason I was interested in working with him was because we was friends in the gospel." She accused him of neglecting his own career for a pipe dream, and she dismissed out of hand any claims he might make for Sam Cooke's extraordinary talent, appeal, and artistic potential.

On July 1, 1958, J.W. registered his new publishing company with BMI. It was called Kags after Lou's stepfather, Keg (his second choice, if "Kags" had already been taken, was Evie for Lou's mother), and he had just two songs in it. But he had long since come to recognize the value of publishing. Label and record store owner John Dolphin had told him, "You know, they making thousands of dollars off you. You should have a publishing company of your own." And now he did, and one day that summer, as they were leaving the Keen studio, he told Sam about it. Sam said that was all well and good, but what did it have to do with him? Keen was going to give him publishing on his own songs. "I said, 'Don't you believe that. They won't give you no publishing. You ought to have a company yourself.' I said, 'I ain't got nothing going, but [at least] I got a company.'"

Sam didn't say anything more for a while, but he seemed to give the matter some thought, and then he told Alex to learn all he could on the subject. And while he was at it, Sam said, maybe Alex could supply him with a good ballad from that publishing company of his. So J.W. did. "I wrote a song called 'Little Things You Do,' and I told Sam, '[If you're going to record it], sing it just because of the song, not because of our friendship.'" When Sam said that that was exactly why he was going to record it, because he loved the song, J.W. immediately released the news to the press, including the fact that it came from J.W. Alexander's own newly formed publishing company and that "orchestras and arrangers can get the sheet music through . . . Kags."

Sam sought J.W.'s advice about Barbara, too. Bumps had been warning Sam that bringing her out to California could constitute a violation of the Mann Act, but J.W. told him that was nonsense, Barbara wasn't under age and, anyway, white slavery didn't apply. On the matter of Jess Rand he was more ambivalent. He didn't like Jess, and he could tell the cocky little PR man didn't much care for him, treating him with condescension and dismissing his views as if they were by definition naive and without merit. And yet he knew that Jess had something to add, that Jess provided an unmistakable veneer of respectability by putting a white face on Sam's business — and that he was going to undercut Bumps' standing with Sam, too. So Alex encouraged Sam to continue to solicit Jess' professional counsel while never doubting for a moment that Sam would keep coming to him, J.W., on both personal and professional matters.

The Cavalcade of Jazz took place on August 3 at the Shrine Auditorium in Los Angeles, the scene of Sam's first meeting with Bumps as well as Bumps' formal introduction to gospel music just three short years ago. Past stars of the show included Nat "King" Cole, Billy Eckstine, Louis Jordan, Count Basie, and Little Richard, and Sam's fellow headliners at the Shrine were Little Willie John, Ray Charles, and bandleader Ernie Freeman, with whom he had gone out in February. Four of the city's most prominent r&b jocks — Charles Trammel, Huggy Boy, Jim Randolph, and Hunter Hancock — served as an integrated team of MCs, and Sammy Davis Jr. was drafted to present the crown for the Miss Cavalcade of Jazz beauty contest, whose judges included DooTone label owner Dootsie Williams and *Los Angeles Sentinel* gossip columnist Gertrude Gipson.

Jess Rand was there and saw to it that his two clients had their picture taken together. Sam had a genuine admiration for Sammy, most of all for his sophistication, his savoir faire, and his taste in clothes, and Jess was quick to let him know where Sammy got his tuxedos custom-made in New York. Sam had been flattered, too, when Jess told him that he was one of the few stars that Sammy didn't even try to imitate — because, Sammy said, Sam's style was inimitable. They got along all right, as far as Jess could tell, especially given that they were from such entirely different worlds, but he couldn't fail to notice that Sam was no more above flirting with Sammy's girl than Sammy was above pulling social rank on Sam. To Jess, Sammy was the more complete entertainer by far, not to mention the more "legitimate" act. He was well aware, though, by virtue of both Sammy's ironclad commitment to, and managerial contract with, his "uncle" Will Mastin (Sammy was still billed with his father as part of the same Will Mastin Trio he had joined at the age of three, even though he had long since established himself as a solo act) that he would never officially be Sammy's manager, as frequently as he might have fulfilled that role. At the same time, he *knew* there were places he could take Sam, both through his connections and through Sam's undeniable talent, and he was confident that with a well-versed musical ally like Clif White, who shared Jess' love of Gershwin, Harold Arlen, Irving Berlin, and the classical school of pop songwriting, he could educate Sam and introduce him to whole new worlds, worlds that Bumps could never even imagine.

All of the headliners were advertised with their own bands. Ray Charles had the same incomparable septet with whom he had just played a mix of his own hits, jazz originals, and standards at the Newport Jazz Festival in July, while Little Willie John, whose "Talk to Me, Talk to Me," was still on the pop charts after four months, was backed by a very different kind of group, Little Richard's old backing band, the Upsetters. The Upsetters, with whom Sam had shared a bill just after Richard's retirement the previous fall, were about as hard-rocking as anybody out there, and they put on a show. In combination with the delicate sinuousness of Willie's voice, they couldn't be beat. But Sam felt like the eight-piece band he had put together for his upcoming tour was a step in the right direction, especially after some of the mismatched units he and Clif had had to suffer with in the past. Bumps had insisted once again on putting his name on the package (it was, nominally, the Bumps Blackwell Orchestra), but Sam had hired Johnny Otis' old drummer, Leard "Kansas City" Bell, as his personal bandleader, and Bell had in turn hired twenty-six-year-old Bob Tate, an experienced sax man originally from Phoenix, as musical director and arranger. With your own band, there was no question you could present your music the way *you* heard it — look at Ray, look at Willie — and with Clif as musical liaison, he felt fully confident of his ability to approach the music any way he liked, even on a standard in his own style. Just like Ray.

Barbara arrived with Linda eight days later, on the day after her twenty-third birthday, but by then Sam was already out on tour. Her uncle met them at the airport, and she was going to stay with him, but

Sam had left the keys to his apartment and $2,000 in the bank for her to fix it up real nice. It was the same way she had started with Diddy, telling him she needed a steady job and then working as his housekeeper — which was how they ended up living together. Sam had told her he wasn't going to be home for any length of time for quite a while, but she just hoped for her little girl's sake that if he liked what she did with the apartment, it might work out the same way.

The tour had opened in San Jose on August 8 and worked its way up the Coast. It was a kind of Keen Records Revue, with Bumps' wife, Marlene, opening, the Travelers singing pop songs and backgrounding Sam, plus Marti Barris, the Valiants, and Johnny "Guitar" Watson. The only nonlabel acts were Obediah "Young" Jessie, whose "Mary Lou" was a West Coast r&b staple, and, for one or two dates, a couple of young white guys named Jan and Arnie who had just graduated from high school and were coming off a big pop hit with "Jennie Lee." No one could quite figure out what the white boys were doing there ("They were singing some of that surfer stuff," said Bob Tate, "and it just didn't go over"), and Young Jessie for some reason was given the unenviable task of following Sam, but they tore up the crowd everywhere they went, and even the Travelers got the house once in a while with their corny old routines.

"We had a ball," said Rip Spencer of the Valiants' experience on the tour. "We did 'Good Golly, Miss Molly,' 'This Is the Night,' Roy Hamilton's tune 'Don't Let Go,' and [Bobby Darin's current hit] 'Splish Splash.' It was Billy, Brice, Chester, and myself, and Sam called us 'Rip 'Em Up,' 'Brice 'Em Down,' 'Billy in the Middle,' and 'Chester on the Side.' We were young, handsome guys, and I think Sam might have been a little jealous [even though] we were an opening act, because the girls really went for us. We had a routine, we had these nice red scarves, we'd wear them like ascots, and take them off and wave 'em, and the girls would grab them and like to pull me and Chester off the stage. Oh man, the girls were a dime a dozen. I mean, they would sneak in the hotels, climb up the fire escape, we had one group of girls would follow us from town to town, but if anything else came through, you just gave them the line, 'We got to take care of some business.'"

Johnny "Guitar" Watson grew so tired of the Valiants' adolescent high spirits that he put them out of the car on the way to Sacramento. He just said, "All right, you niggers, get out," and roared off in his rose-colored

Cadillac, leaving them stranded on the side of the road — which is where they might have remained if Kansas City Bell hadn't come along right behind him in his little equipment camper and picked them up.

On their way to Oakland, Sam and Clif stopped off in Monterey to see Clif's mother, who was still working as a domestic for a wealthy white family. She had never shown much interest in her son's career, "she never had been for me being in music, because musicians as far as she was concerned were a bunch of bums." But she was a great gospel singer, and when Clif told her that Sam used to sing with the Soul Stirrers, "from then on, man, he was king."

Bob Tate could appreciate that it was a revue with something for everyone; even the "working girls" turned out for Johnny "Guitar" Watson. But there was no question who was the focal point. "You know, a voice comes along every so many years that just captivates the people, and [Sam] had one of those voices. After Sam got through upsetting the house, there wasn't nothing you could do." Tate was the kind of taskmaster who could piss a lot of people off because he wanted his music right, but, he quickly came to realize, Sam wanted it right, too. That was what made playing Sam's music so satisfying, and there was no question Sam was satisfied with the job *he* was doing, because when the tour was over, Sam told him to hang loose, he had a few weeks' worth of bookings to fulfill, but then they'd be going out again very soon.

S AM BARELY HAD TIME to get acquainted with his five-year-old daughter before he was off again for club dates in Chicago, Detroit, and St. Louis. Linda was enthralled as he drew elaborate pictures for her on long sheets of paper, and they drove around, the three of them, in his wing-tipped Cadillac, while his latest record, "Win Your Love For Me," played on the radio. She loved the sound of the congas, it was as if they were calling to her from some far-off land, and she loved the way her father spoke to her, almost as if she were an adult. He talked to her about his plans. He talked to her about his music. And he told her about himself and her mother, how they had first fallen in love, but then things didn't work out and they hadn't been able to get along. That didn't mean they hadn't always loved her, though, and now that she was finally with him, he was going to take care of her and make sure everything was all right. He would sit with her for what seemed like hours just talking in that calm, soothing voice, animated with love and laughter. There was no question about it, Barbara thought, he had really gotten his daughter's heart.

H E OPENED FOR TWO WEEKS at the swanky Black Orchid on Rush Street in Chicago on August 21 backed by Clif and a sophisticated white jazz combo, the Joe Parnello Trio. The focus of the set was not the hit numbers he had recently been playing for delirious audiences up and down the West Coast but a selection of standards like the ones he had been recording recently for his forthcoming second album (Bing Crosby and the Andrews Sisters' "Ac-cent-tchu-ate the Positive," Billie Holiday's "I Cover the Waterfront," the Ink Spots' "The Gypsy," even the Mills Brothers' "Someday You'll Want Me to Want You"). Johnny Mathis had broken attendance records at the Black Orchid in May, but, *Variety* reported, "Sam Cooke's disk stature is of very uncertain value here, [and] this intime smart spot . . . will have to count largely on external factors . . . per the wide open spaces at the opener."

Variety's reservations, interestingly, had less to do with Cooke's "nice beat," "authoritative piping," or "smart catalogue" than with his "vocal sincerity for outfront focus. As they play now, pipes are a bit too mechanical to really rouse tablers. Talk is minimal, his patter limited to some brief intros, and spoken without a show bizzy flavor." He was, in other words, as *Variety* saw it, still suffering from that same inability to loosen up that Larry Auerbach had first noted in his Elegante and Copa appearances, and that Jess Rand was convinced was holding him back from gaining the acceptance of an upscale white audience.

The *Chicago Defender,* on the other hand, was burdened with no such doubts. They deemed the smart-spot debut of this hometown phenomenon "socksational" and dispatched a reporter and photographer to capture it in a two-part feature that would run the following month. Skipping the jitters of opening night for a weekend crowd of hometown friends and acquaintances, they found a singer who was "completely relaxed, [endeared] himself to his audience by telling them little things about [each] song," and effectively mesmerized that audience by "drawing them into the mood with his soft voice. . . . If he's crooning a ballad, you can hear an audible sigh when he finishes. But if he belts out with something like 'Canadian Sunset' the audience joins him in popping their fingers [and] when he's through cries of 'more, more' follow him off the stage."

It's always hard to adjudicate these kinds of aesthetic, social, and, unquestionably, racial divisions, especially so long after the fact, but the pictures taken by *Defender* photographer Cleo Lyles show a very relaxed Sam, sleekly elegant in his tux and jubilant on a visit to his old neighborhood, where he is shown surrounded by friends and acquaintances and bemused by his brother L.C.'s boldly blond girlfriend Barbara Clemons. The text once again elucidates what he has clearly come to see as the Horatio Alger pattern of his life: his father's faith, the family's history, the triumphs of the Singing Children and the Highway QCs, not to mention the sodality of the Junior Destroyers social club, with each family member and QC, Duck, and even several Junior Destroyers (including Cleo Lyles) duly named. He fully expounds upon the debt he owes to spiritual music and his various mentors, Crain most of all, and L.C. is credited as the prolific songwriter responsible for much of his success. L.C., the story mentions, is "better known in the musical world around Chicago as Larry Lee," but it fails to note that L.C. is about to embark for the first time on a full-fledged career of his own. He has just signed with the Checker label, in fact, where he will soon cut his first sides (not as "Larry Lee" but as L.C. Cook) under the supervision of his longtime manager, Magnificent Montague, recently returned to Chicago after two years of exile on the Coast.

His principal hobby, Sam tells Cleo Lyles, is photography, and he shows Lyles the $600 Hasselblad 500C with which he likes to take candid shots. He has a lot more equipment at home, he says, for with his success, he has been able to afford far more than he could ever have dreamt of. As to what he plans to do with his money in the long term, however, "I'm setting on it and waiting," he wisely declares.

In Detroit he played for the first time at the famous Flame Show Bar, one of the most celebrated "black-and-tan" (white ownership, black locale, mixed clientele) showplaces in the country, where both LaVern Baker and Johnnie Ray were discovered and where Gwen Gordy, the sister of a young songwriter named Berry Gordy who had cowritten Jackie Wilson's first two hits, had the photography concession. It was a gala occasion, and Crain invited Little Willie John's sister Mable, whose family gospel group had appeared on programs with the Soul Stirrers and who now worked for Gwen and Berry Gordy's mother's insurance company. "Everybody went to see him," said Mable, "they never had so many Christians at the Flame! 'Cause, naturally, they loved him as a gospel singer, and they wanted to see the transition. And he was great. He was handsome, well dressed, composed, and he did what Mrs. Gordy taught me [in the insurance business]: if you want to be good at anything and you want a following, don't try to sell your product first, sell yourself. Because once they trust you, people will buy [whatever you're selling]. That's what Sam did, he sold himself, and the church people just crowded the Flame."

In St. Louis he played the Club Riviera, the self-billed "Showplace of America," and stayed at the Atlas Hotel two blocks away, where his Hasselblad was stolen, along with most of his clothes. By the time the story got back to Los Angeles, by way of Chazz Crawford's *California Eagle* gossip column, a "thoughtful thief" had taken the trouble "to pay Sam's hotel bill on the way out," just another example of the way in which celebrity both paid its own way and exacted its dues. The following week the *Eagle* reported with equally poetic license that Sam might get "the Negro lead in Columbia Studio's 'Last Angry Man' film." It was rumored, reported Chazz Crawford on an uncredited tip from Jess Rand, that "Sammy Davis wanted the role but would be too old for the part."

Jess had been getting Sam's name in the papers on a regular basis for the last six months, mostly on the pretext of movie contracts and movie roles that no one had yet considered him for, but he had little doubt that they would. All kinds of new opportunities were opening up. You could read about them in the Negro press every week. It was impossible to miss the great strides that were being made in the entertainment world by Harry Belafonte and Sidney Poitier and Nat "King" Cole. And while there were bound to be disappointments along the way, like the cancellation of Nat's highly regarded network television show the previous December after its failure to attract a single national sponsor, the critical reception of Sidney's bold new film, *The Defiant Ones*, seemed almost like the dawning of a new era of brotherhood and understanding. In every interview, Sam spoke of his acting ambitions, referring to the training he had received the previous summer, and he was confident that Jess, with all of his Hollywood connections and his longtime "in" with the William Morris Agency, which had been affiliated with Sammy Davis Jr. going back to the mid-forties, would help guide him to the achievement of his dream.

So he could weather a little thing like a robbery. It only went to show that now at last he actually had something to lose.

SONG STAR SAM COOKE TO MAKE TOUR OF DEEP SOUTH

NEW YORK. — Sam Cooke, America's newest and most widely ac-
claimed male vocalist, who catapulted [to] fame with his hit recording of "You Send Me," is poised for another record-breaking tour of
the South.

The dynamic song star, who quit the famous Soul Stirrers gospel
unit to climb to musical heights such as achieved by Roy Hamilton,
Billy Eckstine, and Johnny Hartman . . . will return to many familiar
scenes and thousands of admirers [who] have staunchly supported
his appearances as a popular singer. . . .

Cooke's tour of Alabama, Georgia, South Carolina, Florida, Tennessee, and North Carolina is being arranged by B.B. Beamon, the
Atlanta, Ga. promoter.

— *Atlanta Daily World*, Wednesday, September 17, 1958

THE CALIFORNIA TOUR with the Valiants turned out to be little more
than a rehearsal for a considerably more ambitious undertaking: a kind
of self-contained Sam Cooke Show, with Sam's old champion, B.B. Beamon, sponsoring him. To the Valiants' intense disappointment, neither
they, nor any of the other Keen acts that had accompanied Sam on the
West Coast tour, were included on this one. They had certainly expected
to be, and they were even more miffed to discover that their place had
been taken by the Pilgrim Travelers.

"We were hurt," said Rip Spencer. "We thought we had a good relationship with Sam and Bumps, and we thought for sure Sam was going
to take us. The Travelers had no movements. They were good singers,
but it was an old man's sound. But Sam knew them longer than us, and I
guess his friendship with them was more dedicated than [it] was to us.
And after that we kind of lost contact."

Musical director Bob Tate's opinion of the Travelers as a pop act
wasn't any higher. "They had never sung with a band before, and they
had no arrangements. They would just get up there and sing, and we'd
have to find what key they were in and write the music behind that. This
one guy, George McCurn ["Oopie," the bass singer], we'd play the introduction, and he'd back up to the bandstand, and I'd punch him in the
back to let him know that it was time to sing."

They went out in two Cadillacs, a station wagon, and a truck for the equipment. They opened at the Magnolia in Atlanta after playing a warm-up date in Macon. Jackie Wilson was booked with them at the Magnolia for one night only, and, after having failed to show for B.B. Beamon's birthday celebration in July, he promised his fans in the pages of the *Daily World* that this time, "barring an act of Divine providence," he would be there. "It has never been my policy to not fulfill all engagements I've booked," he told the paper but could well understand why the promoter was concerned about "the adverse publicity I've received, and I plan to give him and the public an explanation."

If he did, it didn't impress Bob Tate — in fact, nothing about Jackie impressed Bob very much. Back at the hotel, Jackie asked if anyone had any reefer, and when some was produced, Jackie said that was fine, but he had to have his rolled for him. Bob said, "What do you mean, you have to have it rolled? We're giving you a gift here, you roll it." Then Jackie said, "You don't realize who I am. I'm Jackie Wilson." And Bob said, "Yeah? You don't realize who I am. I'm Bob Tate."

After that, things went from bad to worse. As Tate recalled, Jackie failed to show for rehearsal, and when he did finally appear that night and his road manager produced his music just before he was due to go on, "We were like, 'Well, so? What are we supposed to do with this?'" The result was a predictable shambles. "It was not kind of raggedy, but all the way ragged — I didn't [even] bother to tune him up. He took his tie off, and nobody made any advance to get it. The women [just] weren't reacting. And when he went offstage, he was scratching his head."

Sam's show, on the other hand, was an unmitigated triumph, with women climbing over each other to get to him, and Sam's driver, Eddie Cunningham, implacably kicking them off the stage as they grabbed at his watch, his rings, his tie. "But Sam," Tate observed, "didn't care. I mean, he wouldn't wear anything cheap. Man, chicks would pull their drawers off and throw them on the stage." It was the usual scene of pandemonium. Which only went to show, as Bob Tate pointed out, "Never mess with anybody that has to play your music."

They went on to Chattanooga, Augusta, Charleston, and Asheville, with the excitement growing nightly and Sam gaining confidence with each performance. Even the Travelers acquired more polish and assurance as they showed off their close harmonies and increasingly practiced precision steps. Every night, there was a point in the show that Bob Tate came to expect when "all of a sudden Sam would turn his head all the way back, and it was like something just straight out of his gospel, he'd just tear up the whole house. I mean, you didn't know what he was doing, it was some kind of thing he did with his voice, it wasn't a yell, [but] the women would go nuts. And you'd be playing your horn, and you couldn't concentrate for listening to him."

To Lou Rawls, more familiar with the gospel experience, Sam was just doing what he had always done: opening himself up, *revealing* himself in a way that, for all of his polished craft, could never be calculated or planned. That was what set Sam apart, it was his mark: what made Sam Sam. That, of course, and the way he got to the women, seemingly without even trying. Sam could pick out whoever he wanted, and however many, and the rest would be fallout for everyone else. That was nothing new, either. It was the way it had been since they were kids. What was new, Lou observed, was the recklessness with which Sam now went about it.

This was still the South, after all. In Little Rock they were told they would have to do separate performances for blacks and whites, and Sam refused. In the end the authorities agreed to run a rope down the middle rather than cancel the show. Sam's stubbornness didn't really surprise Lou, though with all the tension they had down there, he knew not everyone would have acted that way. Nor did it surprise him that as often as not, a goodly number of young ladies who just happened to be white showed the same kind of feelings for Sam as their darker sisters. The police even followed Sam into the restroom in Little Rock when some of those young ladies were particularly persistent. But Lou never expected Sam to openly reciprocate, as he did in Florida when he agreed to meet two ardent young white girls out in the woods. "I said, 'Hey, man, don't you know, they kill you for that down here.' He said, 'Oh, man, ain't nothing gonna happen.'" He seemed to think he had it covered by driving out in the band truck, when everyone in town knew he drove a white Cadillac with gold trim. When they arrived at the agreed-upon assignation, he and Lou and the two girls kept hearing these strange noises coming out of the woods, and Lou nudged Sam repeatedly to express his strong reservations. But for all of his characteristically careful manner and cool-as-a-cucumber control, sometimes, Lou realized, Sam just didn't give a fuck. "Every now and then someone or something would come along and perk his interest, and he'd go for it, no fear."

Sam took a break from the tour after the Birmingham date to fly to New York on October 6 to do NBC's *Arthur Murray Party,* his first national television exposure since the Dick Clark *Saturday Night Beech-Nut Show* in March. *The Arthur Murray Party,* which featured sumptuous displays of every kind of ballroom dancing and was hosted by the sixty-three-year-old Murray's wife, Kathryn, served as an advertisement for its namesake's national chain of dancing schools. This particular show featured a celebrity dance contest including Farley Granger, Shelley Winters, Fernando Lamas, Janice Rule, and, as it turned out, Dick Clark, who had grown up next door to the Murrays in Mount Vernon, New York.

It was Kathryn Murray, dressed in an elegant black-and-white ball gown, hands cupped together in front of her, lips pursed in a graciously restrained smile, who performed the introductions. "It's Sam Cooke," she announced. And then all of a sudden, there he is, dashing in from the wings, threading his way through a fairy-tale world of Junior Leaguers in their formal gowns, accompanied by their indolent-looking, tuxedo-clad mates. Sam is wearing his own elegantly fitted tux, along with a smile that conveys his sense of enthusiastic meritocracy, as if to say, 'Yes, I, too, could belong, but I choose not to,' and certainly the way that he delivers his number, "Mary, Mary Lou," the one cut from his upcoming album that could serve as a "bop" stand-in, merely serves to reinforce the point. He is indisputably more relaxed than in any of his previous television appearances, snapping his fingers with practiced ease while surrounded by a vacant-looking cast of extras just itching for a chance to dance. Which they do as soon as he gets to the chorus, jitter-bugging with elbows flying and petticoats swirling in a scene of awkward abandon so at odds with the playful assurance of the singer as to seem to have an almost satiric intent. If there is irony here, though, it is certainly not going to be pointed out by Sam, who, ever the gentleman, stands apart from the crowd and claps his hands in time, throwing in those impossibly graceful vocal interpolations as if merely to egg the kids on. It is a study in contrasts, as black and white as Kathryn Murray's gown, but done with such charm, such natural grace as to never call attention to Sam's indisputable distance from the scene. It is Sam as you imagine him to be, adaptive but not subdued, the kind of Sam that Lou Rawls had come to know, proclaiming his presence by his very act of self-effacement, brashly winsome or winsomely brash, for all the crispness of his enunciation, for all of his deliberate shrugs and gestures and the downy way in which he bites his lower lip, somehow uncompromisingly free.

One can only imagine that he was much the same, only more so (no footage appears to have survived), when he appeared in front of a mixed crowd of six thousand local teenagers on Dick Clark's Saturday-night show broadcast from Atlanta's forty-fourth annual Southeastern Fair five nights later. There was a strong element of racial tension, not so much at the fairgrounds as in the Southern air. To Clark's consternation certain threats had been received, but when he broached the subject to Sam prior to the show, his star had no hesitation about going on. "He said, 'I'm gonna be out there for two and one-half or three minutes. You're gonna be there for the [whole show].' So we did it." It was an everyday occurrence for Sam, but it was, as Clark came to see it "one of the few ballsy things I ever did."

BARBARA WAS BUSY while Sam was away. Things hadn't worked out with her uncle — she had never gotten along with him all that well anyway — so she and Linda moved into Sam's apartment, even though he had never really suggested that as a possibility. She rationalized that living there would enable her to redecorate better. It wasn't that much of a job, with all the furniture supplied and screwed down to the floor, but she could brighten it up, put in some carpeting and new wallpaper, and she made friends with the building super and his wife, a nice colored couple who seemed to really care for Linda. She was able to familiarize herself with Sam's life, too, with all the telephone calls from his girlfriends and from going through his mail. She hadn't known about the other children — the one in Cleveland, the one in Philadelphia, it seemed like he might have gotten another girl pregnant in Oakland — and she filed away the knowledge with the idea that she would need to learn all she could about Sam if she was ever going to come up with a plan to bring the three of them together once and for all, like a real family.

She started going to work with Bumps at Keen, leaving Linda with the building superintendent's wife. That turned out to provide valuable information, too. It didn't take her long to figure out that Bumps was more interested in his wife's career than in Sam's, and she soon concluded from watching the way he operated at Keen that he wasn't much of a manager for either one. She didn't say anything, though.

She was going to save it, like all the other knowledge she had acquired, until it could do her some good. But she noted with more than a little bit of pride that when Sam's new single came out, it would have her name on it.

The new single, "Love You Most of All," a cheerfully catchy up-tempo number, was something of a departure for Sam, without even a hint of the wistful undertone of most of his other compositions. What was most unusual about it, though, was that Barbara Campbell was listed as the songwriter. Which was understandable, given L.C.'s embroilment in the Specialty lawsuit. But it said a lot, Barbara had every reason to believe, about the degree to which Sam was willing to trust her with his business and his money. She was no more than a pass-through, she knew, but still, it made her feel like she was at least getting *somewhere* with him.

T HE TOUR STARTED UP AGAIN on October 13 at the Labor Union Hall in New Orleans, but before long, they had run out of solid dates, and Sam had Crain advance the show and start booking some dates on his own. He and J.W. had had dealings with just about every promoter out there, and, so long as B.B. Beamon could continue to supply them with their linchpin bookings, Sam was beginning to think they could stay out till Christmas.

"Usually we knew the next place we were going to play," said Bob Tate, who was accustomed to a more orderly way of doing things, "but [sometimes] we didn't." There was no advance advertising. "They just put the signs up, put the place, the name [of] the place, you don't know whether this is a ballroom or what, just find out when you get there." Sometimes they played cotton or tobacco warehouses, sometimes well-appointed clubs. A lot of the time, Bob Tate said, they would stay in different people's homes, "me and the guitar player in one house, the saxophone and the trumpet player in another. 'Cause Sam knew all the gospel people, he knew all the women, and some girls went for drummers, some girls went for saxophone players, but you [knew] there was going to be a girl looking out for you."

It was almost as if they had fallen into a kind of no-man's-land which Sam intended to navigate with little more than a crude compass and his own mother wit. He seemed stubbornly determined to prove that he was master of his own destiny in every respect, that he had no real need for

Bumps or William Morris or Art Rupe or even B.B. Beamon if it came right down to it, and, as Bumps and René Hall frequently observed of his music, it seemed sometimes as if he was making it up as he went along.

There is a curious document dating from this period, an amateurishly printed souvenir book that looks like the sort of program that could very well have been sold on this tour. And, indeed, that may be exactly what it is. It is called "Take a Look at the Sensational Sam Cooke," with the first six hand-lettered words scrolled across the bars of two clefs attached to a flying disc, the *S* of "Sensational" a hand-drawn G-clef, and the *o*'s in "Look" transformed into half notes with simpering eyes. There are little drawings throughout the book that look like something Sam might have created for his daughter Linda, and the overall effect is that of a high school yearbook with a "Sam Cooke Story" as sweetly ingenuous ("Sam greatly admired the Soul Stirrers for their professional technique and poise") and as hopeful about the future ("This is only the beginning of the 'Sam Cooke Story.' How far it will go and where it will end, WHO KNOWS?") as any adolescent dream. Next to the biographical text is a drawing of a relaxed collegiate-looking singer, his foot up on a pair of joined eighth notes, and there are photographs and song lyrics scattered throughout. "You Send Me" is illustrated by a set of crudely drawn playing cards with three different-shaped hearts underneath, and "Lonely Island" is set off by a picture of a very small island with an undeniably lonely-looking palm tree occupying its center.

They played a show in Memphis for Brother Theo Wade, the Spirit of Memphis Quartet manager and WDIA gospel jock who had helped bring the QCs to town nine years earlier. Sam was messed up at the beginning of the evening, according to Bob Tate, because he started playing for all these girls in his hotel room on an out-of-tune guitar. "I walked in, and there was Sam with five or six women in all states of undress, and he was entertaining them. I said to Sam, 'Man, why don't you tune that thing up?'" But he didn't want to interrupt his show or give the girls reason to doubt him, and playing out of tune all afternoon affected his ear to the point that he had to cut the first set short before he could get the sound out of his head.

He was on tour when he heard L.C.'s record, "Do You Remember?" on the radio for the first time, and he called him up right away to express his brotherly pride. "He said, 'I just called to tell you something. I heard your song five times, and I only heard my song once!' And then he hung up!" They ran across the Soul Stirrers in Miami and kept crossing paths with a Universal Attractions package starring Jackie Wilson and LaVern Baker that got consistently better billing. Little Willie John, an occasional co-headliner on that tour, was arrested in Atlanta at the beginning of November on charges of "cheating and swindling" local telephone companies with a phony credit card and was said to be suspected of "much more serious charges."

The road unquestionably was a precarious place from any number of points of view — race, money, lodgings, husbands and boyfriends just for a start. Simply keeping the show together took more effort than Sam had imagined. Travelers baritone singer Jesse Whitaker, for one, was sick of the whole business. He had gone out on this second pop tour with more than a little skepticism — Ernest Booker, the Travelers' second lead, had refused even to participate. But Jesse, persuaded by J.W.'s conviction that taking the group pop was the only way to survive, had agreed to give the approach one more try. And now that he had, he didn't like it any better than the first time. It was all right for Lou and Oopie, young guys just looking to make their mark in the world of entertainment. And Alex had always had ambitions of his own. But the Travelers, it was clear, were going nowhere as a group, and at the end of the tour, Jesse figured they would all just go their separate ways. There was no one out there calling for "Katie the Kangaroo," their latest release, and even if there were, Jesse didn't want to be the one singing it.

They played the Riviera in St. Louis on November 8, where Sam had had his camera stolen a couple of months earlier. Sam picked up his little brother, David, in Gary the night before and took him along to St. Louis for a treat. Eddie Cunningham got into a fight with one of the Riviera's patrons, and Oopie, who had learned martial arts in the army, got cut when he interposed himself between Sam and a jealous boyfriend, with nothing but a rolled-up newspaper for protection against the boyfriend's knife. Otherwise it was just another Saturday night in St. Louis, with lots of girls for Sam and plenty left over for everybody else. They had Sunday off, with a Monday-night gig in Greenville, Mississippi, a distance of some four hundred miles, so they spent a leisurely Sunday with the girls, and Eddie put David on a plane back to Chicago the next day around noon. J.W. and Crain sat patiently in J.W.'s '57 Fleetwood while the band waited in the station wagon and truck until Sam finally sent down word that he was just getting up and they should take off for Greenville without him — he and Clif and Lou Rawls would catch up with them at the show. There was a little bit of grumbling, but everyone knew that the way Eddie drove, they could easily make up the time.

The band was onstage playing behind a makeshift Travelers trio, who were running through their limited repertoire with increasing concern. Jesse Whitaker hadn't wanted to go on without their lead singer, but J.W. insisted they had no choice, with Kansas City Bell's Hollywood Band rapidly running out of tunes. The crowd was growing more and more restive, and Jesse said to Alex, not for the first time, "Something's wrong," when a couple of white Highway Patrol officers appeared at the door and confirmed Whitaker's worst fears. There had been an accident outside Marion, Arkansas, and it sounded bad.

The way they all later came to understand it, it happened just like it could have happened any number of times before. Sam was having too good a time with his girl to leave, and he kept putting off and putting off his time of departure until, finally, it was late afternoon before he and Clif and Lou and Eddie got on the road. They ran into heavy traffic on the two-lane highway between St. Louis and Memphis, and Eddie was putting on speed when he came up over a big hill on U.S. 61 a little after 8:00 P.M., with 150 miles still to go. By the time he saw the big cottonseed truck that had stopped to come to the aid of another truck with a load of soybeans, it was too late, he had no room to pull around, and with a sickening screech of metal, he ended up going under the first truck. Sam was asleep in the front passenger seat, with Clif sitting behind him and Lou behind the driver. When Clif woke up, the truck was in the front seat, and Eddie was moaning, practically cut in half by the bullet steering wheel. Lou was out cold, his head flattened by the bar that held the convertible top in place, and Clif was all wracked up inside, with his shoulder and collarbone feeling like they were broke. Fearfully he glanced over at Sam, who by all odds should have been dead, but it looked like all that had happened to Sam were a few minor scratches and some glass slivers in his eye.

They were all taken to the nearest colored hospital, Crittenden Memorial in West Memphis, where Eddie died. Then Lou was transferred to Kennedy Veterans' Hospital in Memphis, still in a coma, after Crain and Alex arrived and loudly insisted that as an ex-paratrooper, the man was eligible for better treatment. At their urging, Sam and Clif were moved to Memphis, to E. H. Crump, another colored hospital but one with better facilities than Crittenden. The band remained out on the road, doing its best to fulfill all its bookings with an acrobatic blues singer named Guitar Shorty that Tate had picked up in New Orleans. J.W., Crain, and the two remaining Travelers, meanwhile camped out at the Lorraine Motel in Memphis, waiting to see how things would turn out.

J.W. went out to Kennedy every day to check on Lou's condition, which remained the same until Sunday, when he awoke but failed to recognize his stepfather, Keg, who had flown in from Los Angeles. Sam was scheduled to be released from the hospital the following day and was feeling good enough to give an interview to the *Memphis World*. He was getting "good service [at Crump]," he told the *World* reporter. "I don't believe it could be better anywhere else." The vision in his left eye was still somewhat impaired, he said, and he was in a fair amount of pain, but he considered himself lucky not to have been killed, and, he said, "I'm going back to work as soon as they release me. . . . I'm going to catch up with the band right away."

As it turned out, he joined Crain and J.W. first at the Lorraine, where they waited for Lou to get better. J.W. continued to go out to the hospital every day, but now it was to prod Lou with song lyrics and melodies, which seemed to be the one way of bringing his memory back. When the doctors saw the salutary effect, they agreed with J.W. that maybe the best thing for him was to get back on the road, big bandage on his head, confused state of mind and all.

The news of the accident traveled throughout the black community. It was carried in virtually every black newspaper in the country and taken as a sign by many of what the preachers had been warning about all along: this was what happened when a man turned his back on God. Some said it out loud, others just thought it, but the sentiment was impossible to avoid in any social stratum.

Charles Cook brought Crain's new Oldsmobile down from Chicago, and Sam asked him if he would stay on at least for the duration of the tour. Charles didn't mind. He wasn't doing much anyway, he was just getting over a bullet wound that he had sustained in a fight over a woman after a party in the old neighborhood. So he agreed to stay out with his brother. He would see how he liked it, and they could go on from there.

One morning, just after he got out of the hospital, Sam and J.W.

were having breakfast at the Lorraine. Sam was getting more and more anxious to catch up with the band. They had a weekend date coming up in Orlando, another show in Fort Lauderdale, and a one-week booking at the Palms of Jacksonville starting on December 1. To anyone else Sam might have seemed unshaken, but Alex could tell the future was very much on his mind. Somehow the subject turned to publishing, and Sam asked once again about Alex's company, Kags. "Man, I keep telling you, you ought to get *you* a publishing company," Alex said. "Well, who's in your company?" asked Sam. Alex just looked at him. Sam knew it wasn't nobody but him, he said. And with that, for no reason other than that he seemed to have finally made up his mind on the subject, Sam said, "How about us being partners?" Alex didn't hesitate for even one second. With a big grin he reached across the table and grasped Sam's hand.

"I said, 'Okay, partner, I'll build us the biggest fucking publishing company in the world.'"

Sam, Barbara, and Linda

LOU RAWLS' MOTHER, Evie, and her husband, Keg, threw a big welcome-home Christmas party at their place on 3011 LaSalle just off Western near the Watkins Hotel. Lou was still recovering from the accident and taking it easy, and Keg was, as usual, busy behind the bar. The whole gang was there, not just René and his wife, Sugar, and Alex and Oopie but all of Evie and Keg's friends and their friends' kids, too, including Sam's little girl, Linda, all dressed up in a brightly colored party dress. At one point in the evening everyone was out on the dance floor doing the cha-cha, even the children, and Sam was standing on the sidelines watching Linda, when all of a sudden at the turnaround, one of the kids called out, "Everybody, cha cha cha!" It just caught his attention, the festive holiday spirit, everybody dancing, his little baby out there on the floor, and almost without thinking the song arrived full-blown in his mind: "Everybody loves to cha cha cha." It took him all of five minutes to write it down — he grabbed a piece of paper and scratched out the lyrics while everyone else continued with their laughing and carrying on — and when he went into the studio the week after New Year's, he laid it down just like that.

Like all of Sam's best songs, it told a simple story in elegantly concise fashion. The singer and his girlfriend go to a dance, and, as they walk in, the band is playing a cha-cha, skillfully invoked by the sprightly combination of congas, bongo drums, and percussion. The singer's girlfriend doesn't know how to do the cha-cha, but the singer tells her not to worry, the band will soon be playing another type of song. Except they don't. For an hour and a half "every song they played was the cha cha cha," emphasized now by the cowbell that enters the instrumental picture. To save the day the singer wisely offers to teach his girl how to cha cha cha, but

Sam and Barbara. *Courtesy of the Estate of Clif White*

then as they keep dancing, "Was I surprised / For, you see / After we practiced for a little while / She was doing it better than me." And so it ends, with Sam first offering instruction and then perhaps being *given* instruction, only to tail off with his characteristically graceful "Whoa-oa-oh," with a "La-ta-ta-ta" thrown in for good measure at the fade.

It is a piece of such pure, irresistible froth that it's easy to overlook the craft: the way in which, as J.W. admiringly noted with all the envy of a fellow craftsman who more often than not created a generic product, Sam always told a particular story, the way that Sam was somehow able to project himself *into* the story and thereby invite every teenage girl or grown woman who heard the song to imagine that she was the one teaching Sam (who really didn't know how to do the cha-cha!).

"It was all I could do to concentrate on the music," recalled Darlene Love, a high school senior at the time who was in the studio with her group, the Blossoms, to sing backup on the song. Sam was eating breakfast in his hotel room when she and the other girls in the group first met him, "wearing only a silk robe and cute little briefs . . . there was no escaping the man's beauty." Even *he* couldn't seem to get around his own beauty, she observed, sneaking frequent and approving looks at himself in the mirror. But that didn't make them like him any less. Here in the studio, she and the other girls were all but mesmerized by his presence. "He had this way of biting his lower lip that made the walls come tumbling down. Gloria [Jones, another member of the group] saw it, too, and we got to the point where we could anticipate the glorious overbite. 'Look, look,' Gloria would whisper, 'he's gonna do it again. Lord save us.'"

Everyone was knocked out by the way the song came together, and they rushed the record out, with "Little Things You Do," the ballad J.W. had written for Sam, on the B-side. Both songs were registered to Kags Music, and, just as Alex had promised, John Siamas agreed to split the publishing with them on the record, with half going to Kags, half to Keen's new publishing arm, Hermosa. Which was more, Sam noted, than Bumps had been able to accomplish in a year and a half, and he began to take more and more seriously what by now nearly everyone was telling him: Bumps was out for Bumps first and foremost, he really didn't have Sam's interests at heart. Alex was even pissed off about the record. He thought Bumps had deliberately left the bottom off his song, and no matter how much he protested that you couldn't hear the fucking bass, the sound never improved. Sam wasn't so sure about that, he didn't think Bumps would deliberately sabotage Alex's number — but he *was* convinced that Bumps, for whatever reason, simply wasn't up to the job.

The week after the "Cha Cha" session, he went back into the studio to begin work on his most ambitious project yet. Together with René Hall he had conceived of an album that would pay tribute to forty-three-year-old jazz legend Billie Holiday, whose sinuous, sophisticated vocal style had served as an inspiration to a generation of singers, from Frank Sinatra to Sarah Vaughan. With her intimate, behind-the-beat conversational approach, hornlike phrasing, and transformational way with a lyric, she was not the first person who would have come to mind as an influence on the composer of "You Send Me" and "Everybody Loves to Cha Cha Cha." For Sam, though, Holiday's strengths — the tart transparency, the unfailing interpretive skills, above all the deep-seated melancholy at the heart of her music, no matter what the actual words might be — clearly served as an inspiration in the development of a style that, like Holiday's, in the words of black novelist Leon Forrest, could itself be seen as "simple on the surface yet rich with colorations, illusions, nuances, and contradictions when you commenced to unveil the layers."

Unfortunately, the arrangements that Sam and René Hall worked out at René's Selma Avenue office reflected neither the spare astringency of Holiday's music nor the underlying subtlety of Sam's. With Sam establishing the basic guidelines, René wrote out the parts for such classic songs as "God Bless the Child," Duke Ellington's "Solitude," and "Lover Come Back to Me" in much the same way that he had arranged the standards at the heart of Sam's nightclub act and his two Keen albums to date. That same insistence on radical reinterpretation that had so shocked both René and Clif White when they first encountered Sam's approach to "Summertime," that same sense of unassailable confidence, even cockiness, with which he had previously tackled work by Billy Eckstine, Bing Crosby, Frank Sinatra, and Nat "King" Cole were still present in abundance. What was missing was a sense of the songs themselves.

The first session, and each of the succeeding three, had an orchestra of no less than fifteen or sixteen musicians, and while the lineup featured a number of prominent L.A. jazz players, the arrangements are stuffed with harps, cellos, violas, clavinets, and overblown vocal choruses. The effect, not infrequently, is disconcerting, as Sam seems unable to subordinate the easy fluency of his voice to the deeper meaning of the song. "This is a sincere album," veteran saxophonist Benny Carter (who had first played and arranged for Holiday twenty years earlier) would write in his liner notes — and indeed it is. And yet, like so many well-intentioned stabs at upward social and musical mobility, it is a mistaken one, a rare instance in which Sam's innate capacity to assess a situation clearly, then bring his skills to bear upon it, is overwhelmed by the impatient need, bred in him since childhood, to take his place at the table.

There appear in any case to have been few dissenters within his immediate circle. To J.W. no less than René, one of the things that gave Sam his distinctive voice was the "audacity" he possessed "to change a standard to his way of thinking. He liked to think of himself as the black counterpart to Irving Berlin or Cole Porter." To John Siamas, still flush with Keen's unexpected initial success and anxious to expand upon it, this was the kind of music that had gotten him into the record business in the first place, and Sam's enthusiasm for it only further solidified his belief in Sam. Perhaps just as important, it proved once and for all that there was no more need for Bumps; the sessions had been supervised start to finish by Sam and René without any of Bumps' boastful and tendentious claims. It was an expensive project but one John Siamas didn't mind spending his money on. Because this was something he believed in, this was music that was really going to last.

Perhaps the lone voice of disagreement would have been Jess Rand. To his mind, Sam simply was not as much of a genius as Sam seemed to believe he was. Jess had *known* Irving Berlin (he had started out in the business at fifteen as a "counter boy" for Berlin's publishing company), he was someone who genuinely appreciated a legitimate pop song and valued Clif White for his wide-ranging frame of musical reference. From his point of view, Sam did not know the songs well enough at this stage, nor did he treat them with sufficient respect. But Jess kept his mouth shut, doing his best to steer Sam toward a humbler, more high-class way of presenting himself while reserving the idea that he might get a chance to offer Sam more of an education along the way.

That opportunity arose much sooner than he expected. One day Roy Crain approached him on the steps of the Keen studio. To Jess, Crain was the single person around Sam other than Clif who was looking out for his employer's interests. "Crain got me in a corner and said, 'I just spoke to Sam. Let me tell you what our plans are. If you'd like to come along, it's with [our] blessings.' I said, 'What about Bumps?' He said, 'Bumps is going to be taken care of.' I said, 'I don't like stealing clients.' He said, 'This is not stealing a client. I trust you, and Sam trusts you. You won't have to say anything to Bumps.' About half an hour later, Sam came out and gave me a hug. That's [how] we got together on a management deal."

Jess Rand was confident that he could deliver just what Sam wanted. Sam, he knew, was desperate for legitimacy. He wanted acceptance by white audiences. He wanted an acting career. He wanted to play the same cabaret circuit that Sammy and Nat and Harry Belafonte were working, he thought he was that good, and, while Jess had his doubts, he was confident that with his connections, he could at least get Sam in to see the right people, something that neither Bumps nor Crain nor Alexander, who, Jess was certain, was scheming to manage Sam himself, could deliver.

That he had no formal background in management was irrelevant. He had practically grown up in the business; he had been Sammy Davis Jr.'s friend, confidant, and publicist for years; and he was in the midst of setting up a film production company with actor Jeff Chandler, another longtime client, who had convinced him to come out to California in the first place. A snappy dresser in an understated eastern kind of a way, Jess had already introduced Sam to some of the best Hollywood and New York shops — Zeigler and Zeigler at Sunset and Crescent for suits, George Unger in New York for jewelry, Sammy's tailor, Cy Martin in New York, for custom-made tuxes — and Sam had soaked it all in, looking and dressing the part as if he were to the manor born. Jess had no doubt that Sam was an apt pupil; what he couldn't get a handle on was the man underneath. If he gave Sam direct advice, Sam generally took it, but not without an argument. He had a habit of framing a question in such a way that you were never sure he didn't already know the answer. And occasionally a kind of smoldering resentment would creep in, just below the surface, but then it was gone so quickly, smoothed over by that effortless charm, that you wondered what it was you had actually glimpsed.

"He was so involved with himself," Jess theorized, "that he always felt like he had to cover his back. I don't know what he got out of it, or if it was meant for you or for himself, but he would never concede a point." Early on, he gave Jess the job of firing his longtime accountant. "He didn't think the guy knew anything. I said, 'Why don't you do it?' He said, 'No, you're my manager, that's your job.' Now this was an awful thing for me because I was good friends with the man, and I kept saying to myself, How do I approach this thing? until finally we're just outside the guy's door and Sam's doing his biting-the-bottom-lip routine, and I realize I've just got to cut through the conversation and get right to the point. So I did, and the man says, 'Well, don't you want to hear my side?' I said, 'No, unfortunately, there are no sides here. Sam just wants out of this thing.' And we get outside, and Sam throws his arms around me and says, 'Man, you really handled that good.' " It was as if, Jess felt, he had finally passed an important test. Now if he could only get rid of J.W. Alexander as easily.

S AM CELEBRATED HIS BIRTHDAY with a party at the Nite Life on Thirty-eighth and Western, with *Los Angeles Sentinel* columnist (and Nite Life operator) Gertrude Gipson hosting an array of friends, guest artists, and the paying public. He kept his hand in, too, with an appearance on KGFJ radio personality Charles Trammel's new show. But mostly he was just enjoying himself, kicking back. He was living now in a suite at the Knickerbocker

Hotel on Hollywood Boulevard, where he had moved not long after getting home. It had become immediately obvious that Barbara wasn't going to move out anytime soon, that she and Linda, for all her talk of finding another place, had nowhere else to go. It was equally obvious that
Barbara had little interest in finding a place that did not include Sam. So
they lived together for a while as a kind of family, with Sam and Linda occupying the twin beds and Barbara sleeping on the floor. No matter what
Barbara had in mind, he was determined to keep a well-defined distance
between them. So, even though he knew from all her hints and overt statements how much she felt she could do for him, and despite how badly
he would have liked to give Linda a real home, he kept everything strictly
on a superficial level, going out every night without telling her his plans,
letting her deal with all the girls who called as if she were his private secretary, not even sleeping with her. And after a little while, without telling
her where he was going, he moved into the Knickerbocker.

Lou Adler was not far behind. "It was one of those things where, you
know, I was living the life with him, and it started out, 'Meet me at the
hotel, and we'll go out.' Then we'd go back to the hotel afterwards with
some girls that we'd met during the night, and pretty soon [I'd start leav-
ing] my clothes, and then I was staying there, I just sort of moved in. He
could have pretty much any girl he wanted. And the ones that he didn't
have, I had. But we spent a lot of time alone, too, just sitting around, I
never saw him really drinking, I never saw him smoke reefer — I did,
but I never smoked around Sam. He was conscious of anything that was
new to him — a film, a book, clothes — and he didn't hesitate to ask,
'Where'd you get that, where does that kind of thing come from?' He
was always opening his mind up to something new, he was always
expanding. Wherever he was, he was always moving out to another
place, and yet he always had that thing about how he was never going to
leave his roots, he was always going to have some place to go home to."

It was a very different view of Sam than Jess Rand's, seemingly free
of any tinge of personal or racial resentment. The Sam that Lou Adler
knew was probably closer to the Sam that Alex or Crain or Lou Rawls
knew, easygoing, relaxed, able to laugh at himself even at his most stubborn. One time at the Knickerbocker, there was a whole bunch of girls
standing outside, and Sam, playing the big star, asked Lou for a pen to
sign autographs with. When Lou said he didn't have a pen, Sam went
back to the gift shop and bought one himself. "So we go out, and we get

to the top step, and the whole group comes running at him, and he looks over at me, and one of them says, 'Can we have your autograph? Can we have your autograph, Mr. Mathis?' He laughed as we were walking away. He said, 'There's a lesson in there somewhere.'"

And yet Lou was well aware there was an elusive quality to Sam, there was a side he didn't want you or anyone else to see: if there were worries, he wasn't going to show them; if there were conflicts, they weren't going to come up. Even when he was uncool, Lou realized, he found a way to be cool. In all of the conversations that they had, Lou never heard him express his feelings about his family, and his feelings about religion were left unspoken. There was no question in that sense of who was directing the conversation, but at the same time there was equally little question that there was no one else even remotely like Sam. "I never met a man like him in my life," Lou mused many years later in a statement he might have found difficult to express at the time but one no less reflective of his deepest feelings. "He was a shining light."

Barbara was a whole other story. Lou got to know her in the two or three months he lived with Sam, and he liked her a lot, but "she was totally different. She never put on any airs, she was more street, whatever her lifestyle was, she hadn't changed." In certain respects Lou was more comfortable with that lifestyle than with Sam's. With Sam, for example, he always felt he had to hide his marijuana smoking, but with Barbara he could just be himself, and the two of them could get high together. Maybe because Sam knew how comfortable Lou was with Barbara, he felt free to express his feelings about her without any element of disguise. He talked about how part of him just wanted to settle down with a wife and daughter of his own, but another, larger part of him told him to hold back. Lou started going out seriously with a girl at around this time, and Sam seemed to seize on that as a way of resolving his own conflict. He urged Lou to get married, as if maybe Lou could do it for him by proxy.

Lou met Sam's brother L.C. for the first time during this period, when L.C. came out belatedly to collect his Christmas present. "I came out for my Cadillac. See, Sam asked me, 'Man, what kind of car would you like?' I said, 'Sam, I ain't got nothing, I'm walking. Anything, man.' He said, 'C., what kind of car you want?' I said, 'I'd like to have me a convertible Cadillac. I'd like to have me a Continental kit on it. As a matter of fact, Sam, I'd like for it to be so long that when I go to turn a corner I need a turntable to make the turn.' He said, 'You so crazy' — he called me a little crazy shit all the time. But I had no idea he was gonna buy me a Cadillac until my mother and father come over my girlfriend's house and said, 'Sam got you a Christmas present.' I said, 'Why didn't he send it to me?' I thought it was a little watch. And my father said, 'Son, you got to go to Los Angeles to get it. He bought you a Cadillac.'"

He didn't arrive until well over a month later, and when he did, he found that everything had been taken care of for him. Sam sent money for a plane ticket, but then Reverend Cook wanted to go out, too, and L.C. invited his running buddy, Herbert Henderson, along, so he cashed in the ticket and the three of them drove out. "We was over at one of my cousin's house, and Bumps brought the car over, and, boy, when he turned the corner, man, I just said, 'Lord have mercy.' It was a 1954 canary yellow Cadillac, like brand-new, just twelve thousand miles on it, with a black nylon top, black upholstery, and a Continental kit. Bumps said, 'Now, L.C., if you like the car, all you got to do is go over to Wilshire Cadillac and pick up the papers.' Said, 'Sam already paid for it, but he wouldn't pick up the papers, he told the man it was on your approval.' I said, 'Man, you better get in right now and show me where to get those papers!'"

Everything about his visit to California was covered first-class, just like he would have expected it to be. Sam arranged for him to stay with Bumps and his wife, Marlene, on Normandie, and every Saturday Bumps gave him enough cash to get through the week, told him if he needed more, just ask for it, because it was Sam's money and Sam said he wanted his brother to be treated royally. He had a charge account in Sam's name at the filling station around the corner from Bumps' house, and Bumps and Marlene really extended themselves for him, with no evidence of any ill feeling toward Sam on Bumps' part. Which, as L.C. saw it, probably went back to the way Sam had always treated the people who mattered in his life. Bumps didn't need to be told how hard it was to get through some of those doors out there, he had to know that a white manager would just make it that much easier. And if Sam told Bumps that he would come back and get Bumps once he had gotten through those doors himself — well, there was no reason for Bumps not to believe him. He probably would.

L.C. and Marlene would go out together at night and have a ball.

"That girl was from New Orleans, we used to call her Little Mama, and she was as nice as she was pretty. You talking about a beautiful person." He hung out with Clif, who told him that the way he was spending Sam's money, his initials should stand for "Long Cash." Sam got L.C. in with his L.A. crowd, too: Jesse Belvin; Eugene Church, whose hit "Pretty Girls Everywhere" was still on the charts; Bobby Day, who had toured with Sam off and on the previous fall behind his own hit "Rock-in' Robin"; Johnny "Guitar" Watson; and Alex Hodge, who with his brother Gaynel had sung at one time or another with all of the others. He met Darlene Love, too, and proved that he could be as "mannerable" as his brother, picking her up at high school, bringing strawberry ice cream for her mama and cigars for her daddy. "You so full of shit, L.C.," Darlene would say to him laughingly — and he didn't put up much of an argument, but she was a very pretty girl.

All the while, Sam was trying to get L.C. to move out to California permanently. But he had his girl, Barbara Clemons, back in Chicago, and he had his own career to think about, and, besides, to L.C. Los Angeles wasn't nothing but a country town. Things were going good for him and his manager, Montague; his first record on the Chess subsidiary label Checker was still getting airplay, and his second was scheduled to come out before long. He had played the Royal Peacock in Atlanta in January, where he was billed with Clyde McPhatter, in a "Big Battle of the Singers," as "L.C. Cook (Sam Cook's brother)."

"Sam said, 'Look, C., I want you to stay out here with me.' I said, 'Sam, you know I don't like L.A.'" Not that he wasn't grateful, but he had his own life to lead. So he drove back after a month or so, not long after it was announced in February that he had won a BMI songwriting award for Sam's hit from the previous summer, "Win Your Love For Me." He was glad he had been able to help Sam out in his long legal dispute with Specialty. But he had done no more for his brother, certainly, than his brother had always done for him.

"WE'D BE SITTING AROUND TALKING," said Lou Rawls, "and maybe something would happen or somebody would say something, and that would trigger an idea. He always wrote with other people in mind. He would say, '[So-and-so] would sound good doing this.'"

"Sometimes," said J.W., laughing, "we'd be sitting on the floor partying with a bunch of girls, creating while we were partying."

The Kags catalogue was growing almost daily, even if for the time being its financial prospectus was not. J.W. really *believed* in their new venture, and his enthusiasm and energy were practically irresistible. He formalized the partnership early in the new year, and, with a canniness that did nothing to belie his smooth charm, he included Crain in the partnership papers, which listed 1845 South St. Andrew's Place #2, Sam's apartment, as the business address. The two of them, Sam and Alex, were writing like crazy, both separately and together, taking the sensible view that good songs were an investment that never diminished, particularly if you wrote the kind of standard that continued to be sung long after the original hit version was forgotten. For all practical purposes the Travelers no longer existed as a working group (Jesse Whitaker was already contemplating a revamped quartet that would be called the New Pilgrim Travelers and devoted exclusively to gospel), but J.W. recorded a couple of Sam's new songs, "I'll Always Be in Love With You" and "I Gopher You," under the group's name. He had Lou Rawls, whom he was undertaking to guide toward a solo career, singing lead, and while he would not have turned down a hit, the primary intent was more to create a glorified demo at Rex Productions expense, a record he could take around to other artists with the idea of their cutting the song and reaching a wider audience than the Travelers at this point were ever going to have.

He was, in fact, buttonholing every potential customer he could at any and every available opportunity. He approached Fats Domino, still at the height of his popular success, while he was getting his hair styled in the barbershop of the Hotel Watkins. But when he tried to tell Fats about publishing, "he looked at me like I had a tail, like, 'Who is this stupid nigger?' I felt embarrassed and cut down. But Sam had faith in me." He went up to Jackie Wilson in the lobby of the same hotel. "I told him, 'Man, I got a song for you ["I'll Always Be in Love With You"].' He said, 'Sing it to me.' So, fuck, I went on in the toilet and sung it to him. And he cut it! Then the Flamingos were in town, and I told one of them, I said, 'Man, Sam wrote a song ["Nobody Loves Me Like You"], I think it would be perfect for you guys.' So I sung it to them. [Some of the] musicians asked Sam, 'What's Alex doing? He's got a hole-in-the-wall type of thing, you know.' But I had confidence. I was operating out of my apartment, and it wasn't even my apartment!"

Alex's confidence seemed to be catching. Without any of the constant touring or major television exposure of the previous year, "Everybody

Loves to Cha Cha Cha" was proving to be Sam's biggest hit since "You Send Me." He had his last session for the Billie Holiday project on February 25, then returned to the studio five days later for an impromptu session designed primarily to lay down three more songs he had recently written. This time, there is no arranger, there is no orchestra, there is only Clif's acoustic guitar, Adolphus Alsbrook on bass, a teenage drummer named Ronnie Selico, and a quartet that sounds suspiciously like the latest trio of Travelers (J.W., Lou, Oopie) for vocal support. The first number was a song Lou Adler and Herb Alpert had been working on that had caught Sam's fancy. The thrust of it was that you didn't need to possess any great degree of knowledge or education to know what your feelings were, and it circled around the idea that love — and love alone — could make the world a wonderful place.

Not even Lou Adler thought it was much of a song, "but Sam kept coming back to it. He'd say, 'What about that song, you know?' And then he'd start on it again. His idea — since it was all about reading and books and what you didn't have to do in order to [find love] — was to take it more towards school, and that's how it evolved. And then when he pretty much finished what he wanted from the song, we were over at the Keen studio one day, and Sam said, 'Let's try "Wonderful World."' I don't know what it would have been if he didn't get involved, but what it became was because of him."

What it became was a perfect pop confection in which, as Sam might have defined it, the simplest elements were allowed to coalesce in such a way as to form a whole much greater (and more memorable) than the sum of its somewhat flimsy parts. "Don't know much about history," Sam declared over a light Latin beat while completing the educational transformation of the song. "Don't know much biology / Don't know much about a science book / Don't know much about the French I took:

> But I do know that I love you
> And I know that if you love me, too
> What a wonderful world this would be.

It had become, as Lou said, a kind of conversation with the listener, "it was light, it wasn't, 'Listen to this song.' Sam always told me, 'You got to be talking to somebody.' Even if the lyric was heavy, his approach to it wasn't that intense." The third song he did that day, "No One Can Take

Your Place," once again with Clif's jangly acoustic lead, bore out this dictum even more strongly, as Sam translated an unadulterated gospel feel into a swinging celebration of life, love, and freedom, propelled by interjections and hand claps from the gospel chorus.

Ironically, the formal gospel session that he had the next day achieved little of that feeling. Bumps had long contended that gospel possessed the greatest unrealized sales potential of any music in the world; in fact, ever since first hearing Sam at the Shrine, he had come to believe in the visceral power of the music and its inherent appeal to a mass audience, to *any* audience, if that audience could only be exposed to it. His intention, from the time that he and Sam had come over from Specialty together, was to cut Sam singing gospel, only classier, with strings and a big chorus, hell, they might even use the Mormon Tabernacle Choir. His recordings with the Five Blind Boys of Alabama and the Gospel Harmonettes for Keen's Andex subsidiary the previous year were only a barebones rehearsal for that session. But Keen's gospel series, as true as it was to the classic quartet sound, had failed to sell, the Blind Boys and the Harmonettes were on the verge of leaving the label, and Bumps himself was to all intents and purposes out of the picture. Nonetheless, Sam's eight-hour session, arranged by René with strings, harp, kettledrum, and a near-operatic "jubilee" chorus, could not have better captured the spirit of Bumps and Sam's plans.

Perhaps the very length of the session, coupled with the fact that they were able to complete only five titles in all that time, is an indication of the vexed nature of the enterprise. On the other hand, the tempo not only on such old-time standards as "Steal Away" but on Sam's own "That's Heaven to Me" was *very* slow, and Sam's singing, however beautiful, was very stately and very somber. So perhaps they were just taking their time. It was in any case a project dear to Sam's heart, something that unquestionably comes through in the sincerity of his singing. And it was, as it turned out, the last time Sam would set foot in the Keen studio for a formal session.

He and Alex continued to set up demo sessions for their songs anywhere and everywhere they could. Sam was writing now at almost fever pitch and would continue all through that spring. "Only Sixteen," which was inspired by Lou Rawls' stepsister Eunice's sixteenth birthday, was intended for a teenage actor and singer named Steve Rowland, a friend of Ricky Nelson's, who hung around the studio sometimes and whose father was a B-movie director. "We just liked him," J.W. said, "and he asked Sam to write this song. Sam used the bridge from 'Little Things You Do,' and we cut a tape and gave it to Steve, but his producer didn't like the song, and it broke Steve's heart. So Sam recorded it himself."

He wrote "I Want You to Know" and tailored it specially for Milton Grayson, a silky baritone and former Domino who had joined Keen as a solo artist the previous summer. Sam and J.W. wrote "Try a Little Love" as their own "sideways" interpretation of "Try a Little Tenderness," the heartfelt ballad that had been recorded by both Bing Crosby and Frank Sinatra in its original crooner's version but then, in 1952, had been reinterpreted by Little Miss Cornshucks in a homegrown Dinah Washington–influenced variation. He wrote the bright and bouncy "Just For You" in addition to "When a Boy Falls in Love," a romantic takeoff on an idea he had picked up from gospel singer Clinton Levert, and "Cupid," which took a corny Hallmark card kind of image and forever italicized it by the manner in which he drew out the signature line. Each of the songs was simple, direct, conversational, and Sam and J.W. demoed them all, just singing into a tape recorder with strummed guitar accompaniment if no studio time was available. They were determined to get their product out any way they could. They had a business to run.

J ESS RAND DIDN'T KNOW anything about their business, and he didn't care. He did know that Sam was worried about this chick he had brought out from Chicago. As Jess understood it, he was afraid she might sue him, or take the songs he had put in her name — but Jess didn't concern himself with the particulars. At this point he hadn't even met the girl or her daughter. What Jess did concern himself with was Sam's career, and he was confounded by how best to advance it with a client who didn't want any advice. One time Sam actually asked how he had liked the show, and Jess said he thought it was a little wooden, Sam could use some more movement onstage. "Sam just looked at me and walked away." He told Sam that Sammy Davis Jr. had suggested he might take either tap or drumming lessons to loosen up his act, and this time Sam wouldn't even look at him — but the next thing Jess knew, he was taking tap from Eddie Foy and putting together an act with Lou Spencer, who worked out of Eddie's studio. To J.W. it was all a lot of bullshit, fomented as much by William Morris as by Jess. "They told him he needed an act. They built it up so all of his failures [stemmed from] the Copa. When he wanted them to book him into some of the other clubs, they'd say, 'Well, Sam, you know you have to get an act.' I went out to Eddie Foy's studio [because] he wanted me to see what he was doing, and he was tapping with the top hat and cane. Sam wasn't any kind of a dancer, and it was clumsy, very clumsy. I mean, I came up tapping, and this wasn't for him. But Lou Spencer says to me, 'He looks like a little doll, doesn't he?' And I [thought to myself], 'Yeah, that's just what he looks like. He don't look like Sam Cooke. He looks like a fucking doll.' " But J.W. knew that Sam was going to have to figure that out for himself.

Sam was out again right after the March 3 session. He played Honolulu, then appeared on Dick Clark's ABC-network *Beech-Nut Show* in New York the following Saturday night, singing "Everybody Loves to Cha Cha Cha" and, of course, "You Send Me." He was booked into the Palms of Hallandale, a converted drive-in just north of Miami with a 106-foot bar and an outdoor barbecue, the week of the twenty-third, with a booking at the Palms' sister club in Jacksonville the following week. Charles was accompanying him on the road now, serving as full-time driver, valet, and muscle, if muscle was needed. Like Crain, like Clif and Alex, he was someone with whom Sam could always be himself, someone on whom he could absolutely rely. "Sam did things exactly the way he wanted to," observed L.C., too independent to ever formally go to work for his brother but an equally loyal member of the team. "He would tell you exactly what he wanted you to do and what he didn't want you to do. Like he told my brother Charles, 'Charles, you are going to have an expense account. I know you are going to spend money, because if I had someone else's money, I would spend it. But there's only one thing: don't kill me while you're spending. Bring me a receipt for everything you spend, but just don't kill me.' Charles said, 'I will never kill you, bro. I am sure going to spend your money, but I am not going to kill you.' And Charles lived up to that."

Sam had just arrived in Hallandale when he got the news that Dolores had died in an automobile accident in Fresno, California, where she was living with her son. She had moved back six or seven months earlier, after the divorce. Sam always stayed in touch with her and was glad when she got herself a job as a cocktail waitress, but she had been depressed and drinking heavily, and the people she was with on Saturday night tried to persuade her to let one of them drive her home from the bar where she had been drinking. She was at the wheel of the 1958

Oldsmobile convertible Sam had given her when she ran off the road at a high rate of speed at 12:40 A.M. on Sunday morning.

Crain watched Sam worriedly for his reaction, but Sam just told Mr. Busker, the Jewish club owner, he would have to curtail the engagement because of the funeral on Thursday, but he would be back in time to honor his booking the following week in Jacksonville. The newspapers and ministers made the most of it. "The Grim Reaper has been shadowing [Sam]," the *Birmingham News* reported, and there were sermons once again on the subject of turning your back on God. But that was nothing more than ignorant superstition, Sam understood, tinged with not a little jealousy. At the funeral he was deluged with autograph requests, and he satisfied them all as best he could.

He stopped off in L.A. briefly on his way back to Florida and told Barbara about Dee Dee. She had never been able to figure out how he really felt about his ex-wife. She got the impression that Dee Dee had taken him for a lot of money, but he never talked much about his private affairs, and mostly she was just thinking about what this could mean for Linda and her. She thought that now that he really was a "free man," he might at last want to be with her. But she was no more able to penetrate his reserve now than she had been at any other time since moving to California, and he rebuffed every attempt she made to bring up the subject. She was thoroughly disheartened. From what she could see, he didn't want to be accountable to anyone.

H E RETURNED TO THE APOLLO on April 10, going through Atlanta on his way to New York in order to see the Soul Stirrers, who had just done a program there. He still felt a little uncomfortable around the fellows — not Crume or Johnnie Taylor so much as Paul Foster and J.J. Farley, the group's manager ever since Crain had left, who still seemed to hold him personally accountable for the group's visible decline in fortunes. He told Farley he had written some new spiritual numbers that he would like for the group to record, and Farley said he'd get in touch with Art Rupe and see what he had to say on the subject.

Then he was off to New York, where he was sharing the bill with the Clovers and "Glamorous Sallie Blair," and he and Sallie worked up a cute little routine that "ran the audience wild," as the *Amsterdam News* reported, "when he 'taught' curvaceous Sallie . . . how to Cha Cha." Three-year-old Charla Mae Story, who went to the show with her aunt, was desperate to meet her idol, according to the newspaper, but back-stage "little Charla had to wait her turn . . . because a few bigger girls had formed a long line seeking autographed pictures."

Nineteen-year-old Lithofayne Pridgon, who had first met Sam with the Soul Stirrers three years earlier, didn't have to wait in line. She was by now "a connoisseur of men" in her friend Etta James' phrase, and she and her gang of "little freaky friends" did what they called their "sets" in various numbers and combinations with all the stars who came to town. "I was very well schooled by now. I was such a little tramp. I was all about having fun and partying and doing all kinds of silly stuff. I didn't care anything about dating or a wonderful white picket fence or one-on-one 'love' — I couldn't handle that. I knew what I was doing, and I knew what to do, and I think one of the reasons Sam and I had a ball was because I wasn't any threat. He knew he could call me any hour of the day or night, I just wanted to hang out. I had no intentions of going to heaven. If anything, I was going to help him go to hell."

Jess joined Sam in New York and promptly found himself in the middle of an embarrassing business dispute with Apollo owner Frank Schiffman. William Morris had negotiated a deal that would have paid Sam $2,000 for the week plus 50 percent of the box-office gross over $19,000, but Sam turned it down. He didn't trust the Schiffmans, he said, and held out for a $2,500 guarantee against $20,000, and then, when he got it, he wanted Jess to question the ticket count. Jess was astonished at the depth of Sam's bitterness as Sam railed against the way that everyone was trying to take advantage of him, but he never said a word to the Schiffmans themselves, nor did Jess. That, he tried to explain to Sam, was just not the way you did business.

Sam was an anomaly to Jess in so many ways he wondered some-times if it was a deliberate strategy on Sam's part to keep him guessing. One night they were standing in the wings, and the comedian Willie Lewis had the audience, and Sam, in stitches. Jess looked over at Sam, "and the tears are coming out of his eyes, and he put his hand on my shoulder and said, 'That's the funniest thing I ever heard in my life. You tell him, don't ever do that again.'" Another time, they were at the Palm Café, just down the street from the Apollo, "and the Palm gave Sam a champagne breakfast and advertised it, so for the price of a drink, you could come in and see Sam Cooke sitting at a table. And some guy comes over to the table and said, 'Sam Cooke?' and Sam looked at him and said, 'Come on, man, you know I'm Sam Cooke.' 'No, no, if you're Sam Cooke, get up and sing something.' Well, Sam stood up, just smiling, and just as fast as that, he put his arm around the guy, threw him over a chair, and had him laying belly down looking at the floor. He said, 'I'm going to break your fucking neck if you don't get out of here when I let you up. Are you ready to go?'" Jess had seen this side of Sam once before, and it remained as frightening now as it was then — and just as inexplicable. But as quickly as it happened, it was over, and Sam was back to his cool, calm, collected self.

They were both staying at the Warwick on Fifty-fourth Street, which Jess had introduced Sam to on an earlier trip. Sam loved the Warwick, the kind of small, dignified business hotel where he took a half suite across from the elevator so a girl who valued her privacy could come and go as she pleased. But he kept a room at the Cecil, too, where Lithofayne and her "tenderoni" girlfriends could always be found, and one night he called Jess up in the middle of the night and told him that it was urgent that he come uptown right away. "I knocked on the door and said, 'It's me — Jess.' And he said, 'Hold on, J., come in.' And, I'll never forget, there was Sam laying in bed with five women, like, 'Look at me-e-e.' That's what he got me up for in the middle of the night!"

Jess wondered sometimes who was fooling who, he felt like he was constantly being tested in a language he didn't speak on a subject he didn't know. He was aware that no matter what he did, he was unlikely to gain Sam's 100 percent trust, that as close as he was personally to Sammy Davis Jr. or Dean Martin and Jerry Lewis, Sam for some unwarranted reason always treated him like a "civilian." "If he said it to me once, he said it to me a thousand times — every time, I'd find out something, he'd say, 'J., there's a lot you don't know about me, man.'" But somehow it was a mantra that was repeated so often, with such casual lack of discrimination, it was as if the repetition alone put Jess on the inside of Sam's secretive world.

Barbara had no more confidence in her reading of the man she had known and loved since childhood. At his invitation she joined Sam on the road when he was playing the Flame in Detroit at the end of May. She didn't know what exactly he had in mind, but she was hoping it might have something to do with finally making things more "permanent" between them. He had started sleeping with her once in a while, she knew it didn't mean anything, but she was thinking if she could just get him to try living with her — they didn't have to get married or anything — then maybe she could prove how useful she could be in his life. But when she got there, his whole family was present, and his mother invited her to go to church with them on Sunday. Sam put his foot down about that, letting his mother know on no uncertain terms that Barbara was with him, she wasn't there to go to church with his family — even though the truth was, they never even had sex while they were in Detroit, he was so busy running around with other women. She knew Sam's reaction was just one more proof to Mrs. Cook of what a bad influence she was on her son, but there wasn't anything she could do about it.

She just didn't understand him. She didn't understand what he wanted. She hinted that if they didn't reach some kind of accommodation, she might have to fall back into her old way of life — she didn't want to, but she had no other skills, no job, no education, not even a place of her own. And she had a child to support. Sam never even nibbled at the bait. She said, if he would only give her a chance — if she couldn't make him happy, well, she would have to accept that. But he acted like she was someone who had just wandered into his life, it wasn't that he had anything against her, it was as if there was no connection between them. She felt like she didn't even know this man, it made her sick inside. But Sam sent her back to Los Angeles with no more than the promise that she could continue to live at St. Andrew's until he got off the road, and then he would help her find an apartment of her own. That was all he could do.

S AM WENT STRAIGHT from the Flame to the start of a new eighteen-day tour. In what amounted to an outright admission of their own inability to supply Sam with enough club and theater dates to fill his schedule, William Morris sold him for $1,000 a night to Universal, the most successful of the r&b booking agencies. Universal, after putting Sam together with Jackie Wilson, their fastest-rising attraction and the opening act on the Biggest Show of Stars tour just one year earlier, sold the dates in turn to a brand-new national production company, Supersonic Attractions, the brainchild of Henry Wynn, the thirty-nine-year-old black Atlanta businessman who was moving in aggressively on B.B. Beamon's territory.

Wynn, a man with big dreams and little sense of his own limitations, had deliberately chosen the name to challenge Irvin Feld, the man behind the Biggest Show of Stars (all of whose ventures came under the heading of Super Attractions), and, with equally little sense of humility, was now taking it directly into Feld's territory. Short, dark-skinned, and easygoing but with an unswerving dedication to the entrepreneurial spirit, Wynn had arrived in Atlanta in the late thirties from Albany, Georgia, where his father owned a filling station and convenience store that had helped provide him with a stake in his new life. In Atlanta he had built up an extensive network of businesses — various club and hotel ventures, a cab company, a chain of shoe-shine stands, a dry-cleaning establishment, a car wash, a liquor store, and Henry's Grill and Lounge, next door to the Royal Peacock on "Sweet Auburn" Avenue, the city's black Broadway. With this portfolio, and backed by the money of Charles Cato, Atlanta's black numbers king, he had decided to challenge Beamon, the former Pullman car porter, who had held a virtual monopoly on Atlanta black music promotion for almost a decade, and with the same canny judgment that had served him in all of his other enterprises, he had formed an alliance with Universal to supply him with the talent.

Twenty-eight-year-old Dick Alen, the Universal booking agent who had set up the deal, drove down from New York for the first show, at Carr's Beach in Annapolis, Maryland, on June 2. He was there to make sure that the tour got off on the right foot and to keep an eye on the ticket window with veteran tour manager Nat Margo, who would be the company's eyes and ears on the road. Unfortunately, there was trouble right from the start.

"I had to leave my house at five A.M. so I could be there by nine, when people started coming in with their families — it was a beach with a band shell, and if you left before the show started, you'd get a refund. But we're watching, making sure they sell a ticket to everybody and the money goes in the box, 'cause we're on a percentage basis. I think there was equal billing, and we [may have] actually split the placards, but the fight was over who was going to close, Sam or Jackie, and I'm running back and forth, until finally Jackie agrees he'll let Sam close but only on condition that he goes directly in front of Sam each night."

Alen viewed it as an equitable solution, and one that shouldn't necessarily work to the advantage of either singer. That wasn't exactly how the other performers saw it, though. Hank Ballard, who had headlined Carr's Beach over the weekend and was now going out on the undercard of the bill with his group, the Midnighters, had first made his mark with the "Annie" songs (starting with "Work With Me Annie" and including "Annie Had a Baby") in 1954. These had had the singular distinction of being banned on both white radio and black radio, but Ballard had been a consistent hitmaker over the years, with three records currently on the r&b charts, including a gospel-inspired novelty number with a country lick called "The Twist."

"They had a little war going. Sam was not going to bend. He wanted exclusive headlining or nothing," Hank said with considerable disbelief at Sam's hardheadedness, if not his pride. Sam insisted that it was all strictly contractual, said Billy Davis, the Midnighters' new guitarist, a twenty-year-old so good-looking, according to Lithofayne Pridgon, that he was known among her and her girlfriends as "The Face." "He said it wasn't him, his management had it that he had to close the show. [At the time] I believed him, too, because who would want to come on behind Jackie Wilson if they didn't have to? Shit, it was crazy."

The result was exactly what Hank Ballard or Billy Davis or any of the other acts on the bill might have predicted. "It was so sad, so pitiful," said Ballard, whose exuberant nature found little in life that was sad or pitiful. "Man, when Jackie left the stage, people just started walking out of the damn joint." To both Hank and Billy it was as much a matter of idiom as of stage presence. Sam may have ruled the gospel world, but in r&b, said Billy, "nobody could follow Jackie at that time. And you could see that Sam didn't really have the confidence [to]. I used to study his face: you could see the nervousness."

And yet he clung tenaciously to his pride. "You know what Sam told me?" said Ballard. "He said, 'Hank, when people leave here tonight, they will know that I was headlining.' That's what he told me. But, man, that's embarrassing — I mean, who would want to go through all that embarrassment?"

Even without Sam and Jackie it would have been an all-star bill. In addition to featuring the Midnighters, a strong draw on their own with their precise harmonies, energetic showmanship, and sharp, synchronized steps, the show consisted of a vocal group out of Detroit called the Falcons, whose lead singer, Joe Stubbs, had some of the same deep-throated gospel sound as fellow Detroiters Ballard and Jackie Wilson; Marv Johnson, another Detroit artist, whose big hit number, "Come to Me," was the debut release on songwriter Berry Gordy's new Tamla label; Sam's Keen labelmate Johnny "Guitar" Watson; the ubiquitous Jesse Belvin, whose major-label deal with RCA had just produced his first pop hit; a haunting-sounding eighteen-year-old soul *chanteuse*, Baby Washington; an exotic pair of "shake dancers," the Spence Twins; and Gladys Knight, a fifteen-year-old ninth-grader out of Atlanta who was billed with (and chaperoned by) a group made up of her brother and three older male cousins called the Pips.

Backing up all the featured artists was the twelve-piece band of Sil Austin, a graduate of the Willis "Gator Tail" Jackson school of honking sax, whose "Slow Walk" had been a big instrumental hit two and one-half years earlier. Different acts got different billing depending upon their popularity in a particular city or region, and, as with every package tour, the program was always subject to change. The one constant was that Sam always had to follow Jackie, who, with his patented splits, spins, slides, breathtakingly sudden knee drops, and slow, impossibly arching re-ascents, created a hothouse atmosphere that almost palpably exuded sex. Jackie was handsome, crude, brash, with a classically jaunty process and a playful curl to his lip that made him look more than a little like a bronze Elvis Presley. He was, in essence, everything that Sam was not: bold, feral, unrestrained, an extravagant showman with an ex-boxer's lithe grace, a Dionysian celebrant so dedicated to a sense of orgiastic frenzy that he presented himself each night at the close of his act as if for sacrifice, flaunting himself at the edge of the stage until his female fans broke through security and clawed at his body, invariably leaving him bloody with their marks.

There was something else going on, though. Sil Austin's band had been touring with Jackie off and on for the last few months — it might as well have been Jackie's band, and, Charles said, "They wouldn't play right for Sam. They deliberately messed him up. I got in a fight with the dude, man. I said, 'I know you all can play better than that shit.' I cursed them out."

Billy Davis, who had known Jackie Wilson from the time he was a kid and would almost certainly have joined Jackie, not Hank, were it not that the Midnighters' regular guitarist had just gone to jail, knew that Charles was right. "It was so obvious. Sil and them used to be talking about it backstage. I mean, I was mad, even though I knew Jackie way longer than I did Sam. It was just wrong, and Jackie didn't [even] have to do it."

But he did, perhaps as payback for Sam's cavalier attitude, perhaps in memory of the way Sam's bandleader, Bob Tate, had done *him* when they played Atlanta together the previous year on the Travelers' tour. Night after night it went on, no matter how fiercely Charles or Clif, as commanding a figure as Charles in his own way, continued to object. Still, there were moments of transcendence, moments when Sam's confidence in his own ability to get the crowd in his own way were borne out by an almost ecstatic result. Sometimes, Billy said, he would simply stand there, at the Houston City Auditorium, for example, "just popping his finger, holding his jacket, he just had that groove, and it looked like the whole building was moving with him, swaying with the rhythm. It was like I was hallucinating or something, 'cause I was standing backstage saying, Man, look at the people, they was just [in a trance] — and he was just standing there, he wasn't doing nothing but straight singing." To the Falcons' Eddie Floyd, no one could beat Jackie, but then, on some nights, "Sam would come out, and Boom! he tops it. Every night on that tour, I would watch from the wings once we had finished our spot. Sit there and just watch."

The tour was not without its lighthearted moments. There were the after-parties, advertised by local club owners and open to the paying public, for which there was frequently a bonus for any member of the troupe who could get Sam or Jackie to attend. Every night, there was gambling backstage and at the hotel, too, fierce games of craps in which even little Gladys Knight participated and Charles generally emerged the winner. Sam, according to Hank Ballard, would just "dip and dab," probably because everybody else was doing it and he didn't want to be left out.

For Gladys Knight, a conscientious student who had never been on a full-scale tour before, it was like a dream summer vacation — even if she *was* closely supervised, she couldn't fail to observe things she would never have seen in school. Jackie was her "teen idol," and she got as excited watching him perform as any of the women in the audience, "but he was always a gentleman to me." It thrilled her when he invited the whole troupe back to his dressing room after one performance, congratulated them on a fine show, and then declared, "And you, little lady, you are really something with that powerful voice you got." She was not as fond of the Spence Twins, the "hard-core" shake dancers on the bill, though, as she indicates in her memoir, she probably learned as much from them. "When they performed, they did the bump and grind until they bumped and grinded off every stitch of clothing on their twin-toned bodies. I swear! Aboard the bus, they were every bit as down and dirty. They could outcurse any of the men. They would sit in the front of the bus with their legs sprawled across the aisle, inviting and offering taunts of the worst kind [and] apologizing to the quiet little [fifteen]-year-old with her face buried in a comic book." For a girl who "hadn't been introduced to sex yet," it was quite an education, and one she wouldn't have given up for the world.

Billy Davis spent as much, or more, time with Sam as any of the other performers on the tour, primarily because he made it his business to. "I used to go to his room a lot, and he'd be sitting up in the bed writing songs. I remember one time in Dallas, at the Peter Lane Motel, I took him a song I wrote. I hadn't really copied it from anything, but he said, 'That's just like such and such,' and I said, 'Oh, you're right,' and after that, I didn't feel like taking him no more. I'll never forget what he said about writing a hit song. He said, 'Billy, all you got to do is look and see what's happening around you. Look and see what's happening every day. Something people know and can identify with. See, that's where you get your hits.'

"He loved to party, but he was kind of shy. I never saw him be really aggressive with a woman. One time we were in a club after the show, and this club was just full of beautiful women. So I'm sitting at a table with him, and he wasn't [doing nothing], and I said, 'Sam what's wrong?' He said, 'What do you mean?' I said, 'Man, look at all these women, you could get any of them you want in here.' And he just smiled, and I said, 'Well, if you're not going to get them, I'll go get them [for you].' So I find a table with the most beautiful women, and I say, 'Would you ladies like to have a drink with me and Sam Cooke?' So this lady says, 'Aw, what you talking about? Sam Cooke wouldn't be in here.' So I took them over to the table, and the ladies went crazy, and Sam just pick whichever one he want."

Sometimes they shared women, sometimes the women were more monogamy-minded for the night, but always the pattern remained the same: Billy made the introductions, Sam made his choice, and with the exception of the time that Billy's girl took off in Knoxville with $400 of his money as he chased her down the street in his underwear, everyone ended up happy. Even then, Billy's plight was at least good for laughs. "Sam had no problem with the girl he had, and he laughed at me for a week."

292 | *Sam, Barbara, and Linda*

A lot of the time, Billy rode with Sam in his new Cadillac limousine, keeping quiet while Sam studied his magazines or worked on his songs. Once, he persuaded Sam to ride on the bus. "Everybody couldn't believe it. Most of the entertainers didn't want to be around just the plain musicians, but me and Sam sat right up in the front of the bus. That's just how he was. He was a gentleman in every respect." Sam drank bourbon, so Billy drank bourbon, too. "At that time I'd drink anything, I'd get blasted in a minute, but [even though] he drank a lot, he always handled it well. He just got more happy, laughing and stuff. We'd sit up sometimes and kill a pint, but I never knew him to mess with marijuana or pills."

They got to Atlanta on June 15, at the end of the second week, and Henry Wynn threw a twenty-fifth-birthday party for Jackie Wilson at his home. Henry's nine-year-old daughter Claudia and her big sister, Henrietta, were enlisted to clean the house from top to bottom by their mother. "Polish the silverware," Claudia recalled. "Wash the chandelier, we had cloth napkins — oh, Mama just spoiled those people!" The show was a spectacular success. Jackie had his chauffeur drive Gladys Knight and the Pips right up to the stage in the middle of the Herndon Stadium ball field so they could make a star's entrance in their own hometown, while Jackie himself just tore the place up. "He fell on the floor with the mike," said Claudia, "and those women attacked him. They pulled everything off him but his underwear!" But Sam, too, according to Lonnie Brooks, a blues singer from Louisiana who had come to town a couple of weeks earlier to open up the two-day fifth-anniversary celebration of Zenas Sears' WAOK radio station, "flatfoot killed them, stood there and sung, and when he got off the bandstand, the ladies just started coming after him." Brooks had driven out to Herndon with a cabdriver friend and watched those same ladies follow Sam as he jumped in his limo but didn't lock the door. "So they got in, too, and he ran out the other side, got in our cab (I had never met him before), and said, 'Do you mind if I share this cab? Drive off!'"

The tour played another four nights, then broke up with the usual mixture of good feelings and bad. They had covered Texas, the Carolinas, the mid-South, and Alabama, all in less than three weeks. Charles was still pissed off at the way his brother had been treated by Jackie, and he and Crain more than suspected that they had been shortchanged, too ("Jackie had some people working for him that wasn't nothing but thieves. We caught them with their hands in the till"), but he was confirmed once again in his view that the straight life no longer held any-thing for him. "There was nothing compared to what was happening out there on that road, you know. I mean, we had a life out there."

They all had a life, and they all got the most out of it. Everyone made fun of Billy because he liked his girls so young, but Billy didn't notice anyone turning down his "tenders" when they became available. Every-one had their own way of doing things. Hank Ballard had an "affinity" for schoolteachers because he believed in bettering himself. Hank's valet, Gorgeous George, so called (by Henry Wynn) because of a flam-boyance in dress and manner that frequently overshadowed the stars around him and might very well have made *him* a star were it not for a discernible lack of vocal talent, had a workable theory about fat girls and the prosperity that they were eager to share with all those within their orbit.

The shows themselves were something like all-out, full-tilt medieval jousts, in which the sheer intensity of the competition was bound to lift the audience from the edge of its seat. It was a world in which experi-ences and emotions were tightly encapsulated, a merry-go-round that never stopped running so long as you kept having hits and one that nobody except Sam seemed to have any thought of ever getting off. If you had studied Sam closely, you might have wondered at the vague look of dissatisfaction in his eye, at the oddly dispassionate manner in which he took in everything going on around him without ever fully taking part. Observation, as Barbara had often noted, was a double-edged sword. Sometimes it seemed like Sam was looking past his immediate surroundings to a place that existed only for him, or one to which, for whatever reason, he was not able to go.

B Y THE TIME SAM GOT BACK TO L.A., Barbara was pretty much run-ning out of patience and ideas. Sam had told her she could stay in the apartment until he returned, but now that he was back, she didn't really know what to do. He told her he just wanted her to be happy, all he wanted was for Linda and her to have a place where they could be com-fortable and secure — but when it came to finding that place, he seemed to feel like he knew what would suit her better than she did herself, and every place she looked at wasn't good enough for him. She didn't know what else she could do. She agreed to whatever he asked of her. She had let him use her name on his songwriter credits without raising any questions about it, and now she signed a paper relinquishing all rights to the songs with equally little fuss. She knew what she wanted, and she even thought she knew what *he* wanted, but she couldn't figure out how to get it. So she got herself a boyfriend, someone who just wanted to take care of her and Linda — it didn't matter that he was married, he was willing to take her just as she was and set her up in a beautiful apartment of her own. She even met him in church, but there wasn't anything surprising about that, because he was one of the biggest preachers in town.

The reason Sam wanted to get his songs back was that he was at last nearing a resolution of his legal problems with Specialty, even as he was reaching a point of crisis in his relationship with Keen. The Siamases' lawyer, John Gray (who had also served as Sam's and J.W.'s lawyer in various personal business of their own), had proposed a settlement to the Specialty dispute in March which Specialty owner Art Rupe seemed on the verge of accepting. In essence, it was predicated on balancing Rupe's formal endorsement of the fiction that L.C., not Sam, had written "You Send Me" (as well as a number of Sam's subsequent hits) with an acknowledgment by Keen that Specialty was due some form of compensation nonetheless. This would come in the form of $10,000 from the escrow account that had been set up almost two years earlier in the aftermath of the initial dispute over authorship and, more pertinently, publishing. Art Rupe forever gave up all claim to Sam's songs but in turn was granted the right to release one last single by Sam (with an upgraded artist's royalty of $3^{1}/_{2}$ percent) from the unreleased tapes from the 1956 New Orleans session. Specialty would get the publishing on the two songs that made up the single, plus two others already released, once a standard songwriter's contract, worth twice what Sam had originally agreed to, had been executed with L.C. Finally, Bumps, who had been brought in as a party to the lawsuit by both sides, was to receive $10,038.70 as the sum total of any and all monies due him through December 31, 1958, and give up "any and all [future] rights which he may have in the copyrights and ownership to any musical selections or compositions" subsequent to that date. It was a well-crafted agreement in which everyone came away with something, and after a rocky beginning, Art's lawyer, Dave Pollock, ended up with a lot of respect for John Gray, who had been instrumental in bringing the parties together. But by the end of July, when the agreement had reached its final stages, Sam had a new lawyer and a new agenda.

The new lawyer was Sam Reisman, Jess Rand's father-in-law's attorney, who had little experience in the music business but was recommended to Jess for that very reason (he would be free of all music-business entanglements) and for his tough-mindedness. The reason Sam needed a new lawyer was that he could no longer stay at Keen.

Not surprisingly, it was not just a matter of money but of the future as well. Like almost every small record company, Keen had run into cash-flow problems after its first flush of success. The essential challenge of a record label, like any independent enterprise, is that creditors and service providers almost always demand cash up front for the manufacture of the product, while customers hold off on payment till the last possible moment. In the record business, the principal service provider was the pressing plant, without whom you had no records, the chief wholesale customers a network of independent distributors who waited indefinitely on returns from retail outlets (in the record business there was an open-ended return policy) before paying for goods that they had, essentially, both bought and sold on consignment. The only solution for a small record company, then and now, was a continuous flow of hits: if the distributors wanted the upcoming product badly enough, then they would pay. But Keen, Sam had increasingly come to realize, had no hit records other than his own; indeed, his records could be said to be financing the label. Bumps by now had left the company with ongoing threats of a lawsuit and the unveiling of "a new idea in entertainment programming," a gospel cabaret musicale called *Portraits in Bronze,* starring gospel singer Bessie Griffin. Herb Alpert and Lou Adler were in the midst of dissociating themselves from the company with a variety of independent projects of their own. And the label owed Sam both record and songwriter's royalties. So it was not much of a leap for Sam to determine that he could do better. As a first step, he simply refused to record anymore for Keen. As a second, J.W. suggested that they start up a "production company" to serve as a kind of outlet for all the song ideas they now had floating around. And as a third, almost inevitable consequence of the second, they decided in the fall to establish a record label of their own.

The production company appears to have begun and pretty much come to an end with a session at the Capitol Records recording studio on July 24 that Sam booked and paid for with his own money. The principal idea was to overdub backing vocals on some of the demos that he and

Alex had been cutting, and the song that he focused on in particular, "Just For You," was set to the same kind of shimmering Latin beat that he had been drawn to since the previous summer. He overdubbed his own voice three successive times to achieve a light layered effect, then turned his attention to his and J.W.'s "sideways" adaptation, "Try a Little Love," to which he applied a similar approach. The two sides would have made a perfect follow-up to his current single, "Only Sixteen," which, perhaps because of all Keen's other difficulties, was not selling as well as expected — but there was no way he was going to throw away good time, money, and effort after bad by giving Keen any more of his material.

In fact, he resisted all attempts by the label to mollify him. They still had not paid him his royalties for the last half of 1958, and as of August 15 he had yet to receive even a statement for the first half of the current year. The way his lawyer, Reisman, figured it, they owed him at least $20,000, and Reisman was looking into a way to void the contract altogether on the basis of this failure, a defect in the option language, or, most likely, both. It wasn't that he had anything against the Siamases, either. It was nothing like the situation with Art. It was just that they didn't know anything about the music business. And he was not going to allow himself to be shortchanged by someone else's ignorance any more than by his own.

It was in this climate that he and Alex first learned that the Soul Stirrers had been dropped by Specialty. Gospel sales were down for all the groups, and, as J.W. knew, "Art just didn't believe in [the Soul Stirrers] anymore. If the figures weren't the same, he wasn't interested." Then the group came out to Los Angeles for a series of programs, and Crume called Sam to say they had an offer to go with Vee Jay, which had put together an all-star roster of gospel acts and was offering them more money than they had ever seen.

Sam and Alex saw it as an opportunity. At first the idea was simply to write some songs for the Stirrers, but it almost instantly evolved into a much grander scheme. "We should talk to them about recording them," Sam said to his partner. Then he told the group, "Me and Alex can write some songs for you, and we can get your records played." When Farley and Paul Foster expressed skepticism, he declared with a confidence born strictly of self-belief that he and Alex might not have the money that Art Rupe and Vee Jay had, but they had the money to record the Soul Stirrers, and the know-how to record them *right*. Plus, they would pay a higher royalty rate than either of the other companies, and the fellows knew they could always count on Alex and him to treat them fairly and to promote them right. In other words, Sam said, there was no way, in the long run, the group couldn't come out ahead. And, after taking a vote, the group agreed. But not before Crume went back to Sam with a long face and said it looked like they would be going with Vee Jay. They couldn't, Sam sputtered. Didn't they understand the advantages they would be missing out on? Didn't they understand — But then he caught on. "You fucker!" he exploded happily. "You'll never regret this."

That was the genesis of the record company. There was, as J.W. said, no "great plan" behind it. With the help of Walter E. Hurst, a white music business lawyer he and Sam had met through René Hall who was instructing J.W. in a wide range of basic business practices and principles, from contract law to office etiquette ("Recipients of letters which are written on good stationery with an executive typewriter," Hurst wrote in a primer on the music industry, "are more impressed by such correspondence than by correspondence on ordinary sheets of paper written with a standard typewriter"), they set up a company simply in order to record the Soul Stirrers. The label was called SAR for Sam, Alex, and Roy, because Sam once again insisted that Crain be included. In fact, he had in mind that his brother Charles and Clif White, too, should be part of the enterprise. Sam said to J.W., "Let's give them all a piece of the action," but J.W. persuaded him to hold off at least until they saw if the business was even going to get off the ground. Their base of operations would be the living room of Alex's apartment at 3710 West Twenty-seventh Street, and Alex began making calls right away to find out how to get SAR recordings pressed and distributed.

They started work on the songs right away, too, booking studio time for when the group would be back in Chicago on September 1. They demoed the songs with Sam singing lead and J.W. background, then sent Farley a tape and flew to Chicago for the session. The song they were pinning their hopes on was loosely suggested by "Stand By Me," the Charles Tindley gospel standard from the turn of the century (Tindley, a freeborn Black Methodist minister who was Thomas A. Dorsey's principal inspiration in the creation of modern "gospel" music, also wrote the song that was the prototype for the civil rights anthem "We Shall Overcome," among many other gospel classics). What Sam and J.W. set out to do with the song, though, was something quite different from

Tindley's somber hymn-inspired approach. They created what was in essence a pop ballad, utilizing concise biblical references (to Daniel, Samson, Nebuchadnezzar's fiery furnace) in the manner at which Sam had always proved himself so adept to convey loss, loneliness, and abandonment. The point was further underscored by an improbable pop bridge into which Sam crammed every sentiment of isolation that he could ever have felt in a tumble of syllables requiring patient elucidation if Soul Stirrers' lead singer Johnnie Taylor was ever going to be able to get it right. "All of my money and my friends are gone / Lord, I'm in a mean world, and I'm so all alone / I need you / Stand by me," Sam sang with feeling on the demo in the very voice that Johnnie had adopted so assiduously that many of their fans could scarcely tell the two of them apart. Then, in the bridge, he declared:

> *Well, sometimes I feel*
> *Like the weight of the world is on my shoulders*
> *And it's all in vain*
> *But when I begin to feel weak along the way*
> *You call, and you give me strength again*

It was a lover's cry for help, an almost heartbroken admission of vulnerability, but, of course, it was not a lover, it was the Lord who was there to provide inspiration and support. None of the other three songs carried the weight, ambiguity, or emotional complexity of "Stand By Me Father": two further collaborations between Sam and J.W. ("Wade in the Water" and "He's Been a Shelter") were vehicles for Paul Foster; the last ("I'm Thankful") was a kind of sentimental recitation for Johnnie of all the things for which to be grateful, written by new Stirrers baritone Richard Gibbs. But, Sam and Alex were agreed, "Stand By Me Father," if done right, had the potential to break both pop *and* gospel.

From the start it was all business — or perhaps it would be better to formulate it as J.W. did: the aim was to have fun but to take care of business, too. Johnnie Taylor, typically, didn't. He was late for the session, and Sam got pissed off, but L.C. went off to fetch him, and when he returned, he reassured his brother that Johnnie was going to " 'sing better than you ever heard him sing.' Sam told me, 'C., [I'm sure] you right.' But he didn't like no playing when it come down to his business."

The whole aim of what they were trying to do, Alex said, was to get the Stirrers to communicate the meaning of the song clearly. He and Sam both felt that "even when the spirit comes, [the listening audience] should be able to understand what is being said." They shared the same philosophy in that respect, and they were equal partners in every other way, but there was no question that Sam was in charge in the studio. He had Crain sing tenor in place of Crume so Crume could concentrate on his guitar playing, and he had Clif playing on the session, along with a studio bass player and drummer. You can hear Sam's enthusiastic voice all over the session tapes, prodding, encouraging, demonstrating a vocal figure, employing the "power of positive thinking," putting all of his charm to work to get the best out of the group. "Hey, Paul, can you turn around and watch me?" the neophyte producer says to his former colleague. "Crume, concentrate on your figure, try to get it as clean as possible. . . . Johnnie, you're sure swingin' for me, baby. . . . Group, you're doing nice. Just a little easier if it's possible." If J.W. is saying anything — and he undoubtedly is — he is saying it to Sam.

The session was every bit as rigorous as any Specialty date, but a lot more easygoing. Sam and Alex were determined to prove they could do it, and they did — with one exception. J.W. really believed that with "Stand By Me" they had a chance at a crossover record, "but Johnnie kept saying 'Oh, Jesus,' and I kept trying to get him to stop. And Sam got kind of pissed off and said, 'Oh, let him go, Alex.' Then I tried to edit it out afterwards, but I couldn't do it, 'cause he was singing 'Jesus' on the beat!"

J.W. in any case had more far-reaching concerns in the immediate aftermath of the session. "I went to see Nate Duroff over at Monarch Record Manufacturing Plant, he was the biggest independent on the West Coast, and I said, 'Sam Cooke and I are partners. We got a little money to make some records.' And he said, 'Save your money.' I said, 'Look, we already cut the record. I'm interested in getting pressings.' So he quoted me prices and said, 'Why do you want to get in the record business?' I said, 'I want to make good records.' Then I told him I needed credit, and Nate Duroff, who was known to cut a guy down, looked at me and said, 'Okay, Alexander, I'll give you credit.' [I guess] he believed my story! His foreman was flabbergasted. He said to me afterwards, 'Nate Duroff never did that for *anyone*.' But Nate was very, very helpful to me."

Whatever goals you set for yourself, wherever you made up your mind to go, J.W. had always believed that straightforwardness, a good appearance, and a polite demeanor would serve you in good stead ("James W. Alexander," wrote Walter Hurst in his 1963 music business advisory, "is a man who thinks . . . a man blessed with the ability to sing, the ability to organize, the ability to write songs, the ability to recognize talent [and] the ability to make friends"), and certainly his manner and his reputation served him well now. He set up a network of independent distributors ("I could tell whether I should go with a distributor just by Nate's answer") and settled on an attractive asymmetrical label design, with two green-and-yellow stripes radiating out from the center of the record and the credits in plain black against a white background. It was strictly functional in keeping with the company's modest financial cir-cumstances, but otherwise no expense was to be spared, no corners cut. Everything, J.W. insisted, was going to be first class all the way, even if the only way that could be accomplished was by the sweat of his brow.

"I think I had something I wanted to prove. I was all fired up. I'd go to the clubs at night, get home at maybe four or five in the morning, and a distributor would call and I would wake up: 'SAR Records!' I had Redi-forms to do my billing, I didn't have any kind of calculator, just sit on the floor with pencil and paper and do everything by hand."

They were beginning to get some cuts on their songs, too. Jackie Wilson's version of "I'll Always Be in Love With You" was scheduled to come out on his next LP; the Hollywood Flames, an L.A. group with clas-sic local r&b antecedents, had already recorded its own version of the song (as "Every Day Every Way") for the Atlantic subsidiary Atco. Plus, they had gotten the A-side of Little Anthony and the Imperials' latest single, "I'm All Right," which Sam had fixed up for the group on a quick visit to New York at the conclusion of his supersonic tour.

J.W.'s only real frustration was Sam's impulsive generosity toward his friends. He didn't mind so much about Crain, even if Crain showed little interest in Alex's plan for him to promote the record on the road — Crain at least was looking after Sam's interests. He took great exception, though, to Sam's attempt to foist Bumps on the partnership. "When we got back from Chicago, Sam said, 'Alex, let's call Bumps. We'll give him a piece of the action.' Because he thought Bumps knew something about the record business. But Bumps didn't really know anything." His only advice, in fact, was to cut the price to the distributor by two cents. But J.W. was not about to give up two cents on every record; as he well knew, it was a "penny business." So other than a fruitless discussion or two, in which Bumps made it plain that in his view they would never be able to get along without him, nothing ever came of Sam's suggestion, and J.W. let the matter drop.

Sam left the details of the business to Alex. None of it was of any great concern to him: pressing plants, distribution deals, discounts, accounting practices. He had full faith in his partner. Besides, he had other, more important business to take care of. He was getting married.

H E HAD COME HOME from Chicago to find Barbara getting ready to move out. Her minister had turned out to be a goldmine, and very little trouble besides. He liked to take her to a nice hotel and then read her his sermons while she was getting stoned. He didn't care if she smoked reefer, his sexual demands were brief and few, he was a fat, ugly, little stubby man who was good to her daughter, happy to have Linda come to his house and play with his two children, and desperate to set Barbara up in the style that she deserved. She had finally decided to accept his offer — he wasn't any different from any of the other players she had known; if she couldn't have Sam, she could at least have a life of her own — when Sam showed up unexpectedly at the door. All her things were packed, and Linda was playing upstairs. Barbara assumed Sam was there for his daughter, so she offered to go get her, but Sam took in the scene and started quizzing her about her plans. She wouldn't say anything at first, but she finally told him about her new "sponsor," and for the first time since she had come to California a year before, she felt that she had actually captured his interest. It was Diddy all over again, the man was jealous, and, seizing her opportunity, she asked him what he had expected her to do after the way he had treated her. He seemed genuinely stung, just sat there with his head in his hands until he finally got out, "Well, Barb, what do *you* want to do?" She stared at him. What did *she* want to do? She had never wanted anything other than to marry him. She felt certain she could help him, she said, she knew she could add something to his career.

"So he said, 'Well, okay, then, when do you want to get married?' I said, 'Today!' Just like that."

He seemed to mull it over briefly. And then he said that wasn't right, they ought to get married in her grandmother's house, where they had first courted — he was going out of town in a couple of days, and he had a solid month's worth of bookings, but she could meet him in Chicago after he finished at the Flame, and then his father could marry them there, with all their friends and family present.

She felt a momentary twinge — maybe he was just trying to put her off once again. But she didn't think it was going to be like that this time. Sam seemed to have at last made up his mind. They stayed up all night talking. Sam told her he had been in Reno with Sammy Davis Jr., and Sammy's father had started asking questions about Barbara and told him, if he had a good woman in his corner, he should marry her. "Well, I was thoroughly shocked. Here I'd been trying to get the man to marry me for over a year. . . . But I thank God for Sammy Davis Jr.'s father!" Before he left, he gave her $2,000 to look for a new apartment and furnish it. She knew for sure Sam wasn't going to back out now. So she told her preacher it was all over, and even though he cried and pleaded and made her all kinds of pledges and promises, she told him she was in love: he ought to be able to understand that.

S AM STARTED A TWO-WEEK ENGAGEMENT at the Bellevue Casino in Montreal a few days later, finally debuting his tap routine. He had showcased enough of his new act at the Casino Royal in Washington, D.C., in June for *Variety*'s reviewer to comment on his "pleasing and relaxed manner" and to predict that he "should be around the fancier cabarets for a long time." Evidently he needed to go out of the country, though, before he was willing to test his terpsichorean skills on the public at large.

"You have to be more than just a straight singer to hold a crowd in the lofty Bellevue Casino," *Variety* once again opined, "and that is just what Sam Cooke, young sepia performer, managed during his two-week stint there." He could stand to straighten out his presentation, the reviewer went on, there were "too many bits and pieces of other singers apparent in his act," and since he seemed "most at ease [with] the monotonous beat of rock 'n' roll . . . his progress and polishing should start from this point. [But] a pleasant song-and-tap arrangement near end of session made a neat diversion and backing by guitarist-arranger Cliff White boosted act nicely."

He carried much of the same act to the Apollo the following week (minus tap, top hat, and cane), as yet another reviewer from *Variety* attested. The show, which also featured tap dancer Bunny Briggs, "blue" comedian Redd Foxx, and r&b ingenue Barbara McNair, was "one of the brightest and best-paced reviews the Harlem vaudery has had in a long time," while Sam, "a sort of hip and modern [very much middle-of-the-road singer] Billy Daniels, has a lot of relaxed charm and some swinging special full band arrangements behind his agile and pleasing vocals," of which both "Ol' Man River" and "Summertime" were "outstanding." At the end of the set, taking his cue from relaxed television personality Perry Como and going to what one might think unnecessary extremes to distinguish himself from an extroverted showman like Jackie Wilson, Sam sang a medley of his hits while "draped casually over [a] stool."

From there it was on to the Flame in Detroit, where, despite the absence of any written record, it can be assumed that Sam did much the same show to very much the same response.

Then he flew in to Chicago, on Friday, October 9, to get married.

B ARBARA APPEARED COMPLETELY CALM when she met him at the airport on Friday. Which was understandable because, as so often in her highly charged moments with Sam, she was stoned. She and Linda had arrived the day before and were staying at a hotel on Fiftieth overlooking the lake. Sam expressed his usual surprise at how well she was able to maintain her cool. For all of his so-called sophistication, he didn't have a clue. He was so damned naive about certain things, she thought — but that was *his* problem. It was her secret, and she was going to keep it. They got their license at the county courthouse, and then Sam had her drive him downtown so he could pick up some presents for her: a mink stole, some jewelry, a wristwatch. He told her to circle the block while he collected his purchases, but this was one time her cool betrayed her, and she had been driving around aimlessly for nearly half an hour when Sam finally spotted her and whistled her down. Where had she been? he demanded. But she answered — still calmly — that she had just been following his directions and driving around.

The wedding on Sunday was everything she could ever have imagined. They all gathered at her grandmother's house on Ellis Park: her sisters and their husbands, her mother and stepfather, Crain, Sam's friends Duck and Sonny Vincent, their photographer friend from the *Defender*, Cleo Lyles, and all of Sam's family. Her grandmother's living room was filled with gladioli, Linda was practically jumping out of her skin with excitement, and Barbara felt good about herself for once. She was wearing a simple, fitted beige dress with a scoop-neck lace top to set off her beautiful new diamond choker, and her hair was done up in a neat bob with bangs that framed a pretty, oval face which was, at least today, wreathed in smiles.

Sam's father gravely presided, and Sonny and Duck both stood up for him while Barbara's twin sister, Beverly, was her best girl. Sam had had her diamond band specially made by Jess Rand's jeweler in New York, and there was a lot of kidding among the men about how Sam wasn't going to be able to tell the twins apart. But Sam told L.C. later that if this marriage didn't work out, he would never marry again, he would just get seven women, give them all Cadillacs, "and be with whoever I want to be with" — and L.C. wasn't sure that he was joking.

That night, they went to see Al Hibbler at one of the clubs on Sixty-third, and Hibbler introduced them from the stage as man and wife. Al got Sam to come up and sing with him, and then he had Sam bring Barbara up. "Man, she's pretty," the blind singer said as he felt the contours of her face. "Man, she's real cute." The next day, they flew back to California so that Barbara could continue fixing up the airy two-bedroom duplex she had found for them at 2704 West Forty-third Place, a few blocks from Leimert Park, just down from Baldwin Hills. It was the beginning of their new life together.

But if Barbara was expecting things to change in any fundamental way, she was immediately disappointed. Sam was at home for less than a week, and he was running around town attending to all kinds of business even then. His protracted struggle with Keen was about to come to a head. On September 23 the lawyer Jess Rand had recommended, Sam Reisman, had demanded a full accounting from Keen, and, in the absence of any meaningful response, he was about to sue to have Sam's contract voided. Sam and Alex had already attempted to confront the company about songwriting and publishing royalties on their own. They went into John Siamas' office to ask for their money, and Siamas told them he couldn't pay. J.W. understood the company's dilemma — once it became known that Sam was refusing to record for the label and that there were legal issues involved, there was no way to keep the distributors from concluding that, without any more Sam Cooke hits coming from Keen, there was no real incentive to pay. Nevertheless, as Alex saw it, the situation was not altogether lost until John Siamas treated Sam with the kind of disrespect that Art might have shown when, instead of dealing with the situation directly, he tried to put it off on his lawyer. "Sam just said, 'Come on, Alex, let's go.' He said [to John Siamas], 'You got an unhappy boy on your hands.'"

Before leaving town, Sam had told Barbara that if she needed anything, she should just get in touch with his manager. He spoke excitedly about plans for their future together, but mostly, it seemed to Barbara, he was talking either about their daughter or about her improving herself by going to college — which she just could not see. And then he was gone, just like he always was, playing "Achievement Day" (another redneck word for "Nigger Day") at the Dallas State Fair on Monday, October 19, the same date that his lawyer formally brought the lawsuit against Keen.

B*ILLBOARD* GAVE THE SOUL STIRRERS' new SAR release a four-star review ("Fervent . . . moving"), and to the astonishment of nearly everyone except Sam and Alex, Alan Freed even played "Stand By Me Father" in the last days before the gathering rock 'n' roll payola scandals forced him off the New York airwaves once and for all. A Top 40 station in Pittsburgh picked up on it, too. "Everybody thought it was Sam singing," said J.W. "Johnnie sounded so close, and we [did nothing to] discourage the rumor, 'cause it could only help."

Meanwhile, Jess seemed to have finally gotten Sam's movie career off the ground. Earlier in the year, he had obtained an interview for Sam at Paramount. He was counting on Sam's charm to win over the studio executive, and, before going in, suggested to Sam that he might cite "repertory work" in Chicago if he was quizzed about prior experience. Things were going fine until the guy started asking Sam questions about some of the roles he had played, and Sam just kept getting in deeper and deeper until finally, Jess said, "the man just looked at Sam and said, 'You've never acted a day in your life, have you?' And Sam looked back at him and said, 'I'm doing it right now.' We walked out of that place screaming and laughing!"

This time, there was a more satisfying dénouement, as Jess got Sam a supporting role in a Sammy Davis Jr. half-hour drama, "The Patsy," which was scheduled to be broadcast on CBS' Sunday-night *General Electric Theater,* hosted by Ronald Reagan, the following February. Sammy, who had gotten his first dramatic role on the same series just the year before, vouched for Sam. It was a role that offered few lines but a good deal of on-screen exposure in an ensemble piece set in an army barracks that had previously been done with an all-white cast. Sam never hesitated, though the fee came to only $500 and he knew there would be plenty of hard work involved. In fact, he was so enthusiastic that he leapt at Jess' suggestion that they drive to Las Vegas so he could rehearse with Sammy, who was headlining at the Copa Room at the Sands for most of November.

Sammy, it turned out, didn't have the same enthusiasm for rehearsal, and Sam was forced to chase him around in almost humiliating fashion, carrying his script in an otherwise empty briefcase and grabbing whatever time he could. Finally, in desperation, he suggested a breakfast meeting, but Sammy just gave him that big grin and said, "I don't get up for breakfast, baby." He was also brought face-to-face with the harsh realities of show-business segregation once again. On their first night in Vegas, he and Jess were relegated to the worst table in the house, and only grudgingly at that. Sam did his best to hide his disappointment, but Jess could see that for all of his sophistication and all of his extensive experience in the business, he was deeply hurt to discover that even at the pinnacle of show-business success, the only way you were going to be treated well was when you were the show. Sammy went to bat for him, and Jess practically made a scene, and after that, they always got a good table, no matter how the other patrons might stare. "But he knew," said Jess, "if he wasn't standing next to Sammy Davis Jr., he wouldn't be standing there [at all]."

Jess was busy on a number of other fronts as well. Through Larry Auerbach he had made contact with Hugo and Luigi, two colorful first cousins who operated as a production team and had been hired by RCA earlier in the year (at the unheard-of sum of a million dollars over five years) to rejuvenate the company's pop music department. Despite contractual guarantees of independence, they had trouble at first with RCA's traditionally stodgy attitudes, but just within the last couple of months, they had had their first big hit on the label with Della Reese's "Don't You Know," which not only reached number one on the r&b charts but eventually went to number two pop. It exemplified, said Luigi, the kind of hybrid sound typical of the Hugo and Luigi approach, an operatic adaptation of a Puccini waltz set to an r&b sensibility.

Hugo and Luigi (their last names were Peretti and Creatore, but everyone knew them by the more familiar appellation, which served as

their production handle) were unashamed hitmakers and practical jok-
ers for whom Jess had less than total respect because of what he took to
be their somewhat crass view of both their business and their craft. On
the other hand, Sam hadn't really left him with a lot of alternatives. It
would have been his personal preference to go to Atlantic. The label had
a sterling reputation in the business, it was set up to do the kind of
music Sam was best at, and, after losing Clyde McPhatter to MGM earlier in the year and having recently become aware that they were about to
lose Ray Charles, their biggest star, to ABC, Atlantic's owners, Jerry
Wexler and Ahmet Ertegun, made Jess aware that there was almost
nothing they wouldn't do to get his client. But Sam wasn't interested.
Sam had heard from Clyde McPhatter that he had been treated with
racial condescension and disrespect at Atlantic, and no matter how
much Jess argued the point and reminded Sam that this was the music
business, after all ("I said, 'Maybe they'll steal, but you'll sell more
records with them than with anybody else"), and that Ahmet and Jerry
were liberals in good standing, Sam clung to his own view of the matter
and flatly ruled the label out.

Jess would have approached Capitol, too, except that Capitol already
had Nat "King" Cole, they would not go above a 3 percent ceiling on royalties, and they were adamant that Sam would have to split his publishing, something Jess understood was completely out of the question. So
he was left with RCA, which was offering a 5 percent artist's royalty, the
same as Presley got, and would leave Sam's publishing alone. Plus,
Hugo and Luigi had agreed to include Sam's guitarist, Clif White, on all
his sessions, a nonnegotiable item from Sam's point of view. So Jess
moved from discussions with Hugo and Luigi into more formal business negotiations with newly promoted RCA vice president Bob Yorke, a
straight shooter he had known for some time and always liked, and even
though he would have preferred to have had more options, he made his
points and listened to what Yorke had to say, following the principle that
had guided him ever since he had first entered show business at the age
of fifteen: make deals, don't blow them.

On November 9 *Billboard* ran an item disingenuously headlined
"Hugo-Luigi Want Cooke" that reported on "the hottest rumor around
the trade last week," namely that "the hit-making a&r men at RCA . . .
had made a fabulous offer to Sam Cooke to join the label after his Keen
pact expires." Even the size of the offer seemed designed to discourage

308 | Sam, Barbara, and Linda

literal interpretation, as a relatively modest proposal of $30,000 for a single year (with $20,000 of that against royalties), and another $30,000 (all against royalties) for a second-year option, was inflated to "a guarantee of $100,000, a rather sizable sum."

With that, the fate of Keen Records as an ongoing label was to all intents and purposes sealed. Sam's lawsuit up until this point had been proceeding in deliberate fashion, with motions and countermotions and moves for dismissal, but, as John Siamas now read the situation, with the RCA rumor out in the open, the distributors would simply stop paying, the money would dry up, and whatever chance there might have been for an amicable settlement, even a new start with Sam, was gone for good. The label had an album out on Sam called Hit Kit, a greatest-hits package that had been put together, as Cash Box presciently remarked, "for quick commercial consumption," but even it stopped selling, and, while it would take another month before John Siamas threw in the towel, there was no question now, as John Siamas Jr. later observed, that his father simply "wanted to go back to the kind of thing that he had done professionally for twenty years [his aircraft parts business] and looked forward to doing again — and in an atmosphere that he, frankly, considered to be more ethical." Siamas agreed to pay Sam a lump sum of $10,000 and transfer all song copyrights to him in exchange for Sam's acknowledgment that this would stand in full payment of all artist royalties owed through June 30, 1959, as well as all songwriter's royalties through the end of the year (in sum, close to $35,000). There were no bad feelings on either side, John Siamas Jr. felt certain. Keen, as his father saw it, simply "did not survive the record industry," and while it continued as a catalogue label for the next couple of years (almost entirely Sam's catalogue), John Siamas Sr. was not going to invest any more of his money in what he now saw as an essentially failed venture.

Sam was no less disillusioned in many respects with the business. Out on tour once again, he had decided to do without the services of William Morris, who he was convinced were no better than Bumps, just better educated and better able to get away with it. What had they ever done for him, he railed to Jess and his brother Charles, except sit on their ass and collect his money, money that he earned by the sweat of his brow? He was still pissed off about the Jackie Wilson tour. It would never have come about — and he would never have had to suffer the kind of humiliation that he did — if they had supplied him with the proper kind of bookings. And he was pissed off at what he took to be their dismissive attitude toward his pay: they sold him *like a slave* to Universal, they sold him for a pittance — $1,000 a night — and then they didn't even concern themselves with how much more Universal was actually getting for his services. They told him they had talked Universal into splitting the commission — fuck that. They were all just making money off his back.

So he told Charles and Crain to go out and look for dates on their own. "Me and Crain got in the car, and we just drove. Stopped in places that looked like they could use a show. Then we find out who the promoter was in that town or whoever owned the biggest club — Crain knew most of them anyway, he had worked with them before, and he knew who to trust. We'd approach them, say, 'We got Sam Cooke, and we want to come to you with a show.' All down in Florida and Alabama and North Carolina and South Carolina. We never had no problem, man. Sam was trying to prove a point."

Sam put it out in *Jet* magazine that he would be touring with L.C. "to help promote [his] career," and that, in partial payment of the debt he owed his brother for "You Send Me" and all the other hits L.C. had written for him, he had now written a tune for his brother, which L.C. was scheduled to record. "Sam do what he want to do," observed L.C., "and they be glad to get them dates, 'cause they knew they was going to make some money. Sam was different from everybody [else]. He didn't care who he cussed out. He said, 'I ain't got to wait on nobody.' "

All of his loyalty, as Charles and L.C. saw it, was to the tight circle of family and friends around him. As far as Jess Rand went, "I didn't know too much about Jess Rand," said Charles. "Jess Rand wasn't around us too much," according to L.C. Crain was the only one functioning as any kind of manager. As much as Sam needed a manager. And Alex could call himself Sam's *partner* all he wanted — he worked for Sam just like they did. Only they had known Sam longer. Sam didn't trouble himself with such petty distinctions. He knew how everyone fit into his world — Bumps, the Soul Stirrers, the QCs, the Junior Destroyers, Duck, his brothers, even Rebert Harris, who was always going around boasting that he had taught Sam everything he knew. None of it affected Sam's unwavering plan to move ahead with his life, to improve himself and his situation in every way that he could — but at the same time, it seemed like he felt responsible for them all somehow. Or maybe he saw them as responsible for him. It was as if he were determined to leave no part of himself behind — unlike Sammy Davis Jr., he would always mark a clear path to find his way home. And he was no less determined to make his marriage work. No matter how he had arrived at it, or how long it had taken him to get there, he felt as if his identity was as bound up now in the success of his little family as his father's had been in his family of ten. He and Barbara had loved each other once — their little girl was the tangible expression of that love — and now, almost as if he could will it, they would love each other again.

The Soul Stirrers' single continued to sell, and Sam gladly lent his name to a concert promotion in Atlanta on December 6 ("Star vocalist Sam Cooke" would serve as "honored guest, MC," the *Daily World* announced, "pay[ing] special tribute to his old group"). When he joined them onstage, the crowd went wild, and it was just like the old days, only more so. With their prospects looking up, the fellows all welcomed his participation, even Paul and Farley, who had been resistant for so long, and he appeared on several more programs over the next week or two, careful not to steal too much of the glory but pleased nonetheless to be back on the gospel road.

He had carved out Christmas to be at home with his wife and daughter. Jess and his wife, Bonnie, had been helping Barbara to decorate the apartment. The first time Sam brought Barbara out to their house on Stuart Lane, Jess said, "he saw these lamps we had, they were about five feet tall, shaped like vases, and he fell in love with them. Bonnie said, 'Well, I know someone down at the Furniture Mart who can get them for you at cost.' Sam said, 'Could you do that for me?' So they ended up with lamps like we had." Barbara purchased couches like the Rands', too, and Sam had always loved the way Jess and Bonnie had one wall covered with nothing but paintings, so Jess gave him a Frank Interlandi work called *Suffragettes,* a bold posterlike composition combining whimsy and determination in its portrayal of the extravagantly behatted women marchers. He and Bonnie had a couple of paintings by Z. Charlotte Sherman, whose work appealed to Sam for its "illusionary [effect] because as you look at it, you realize there's more than one painting in the picture." So Sam went out and bought one of her pictures, too. "He really loved the intrigue about it," said Jess, who imagined it appealed to the secretive part of Sam's nature.

It was a beautiful apartment, as nice, Barbara thought, as any place she had ever lived, with a kitchen/dinette, a patio, a formal living room for the pictures, a den that functioned as a dining room, and a guest room in addition to their own two bedrooms. Barbara put a plastic pool in the backyard for Linda to splash around in. The park was handy, and Sam gave her a cute little black-and-white Nash Rambler to drive around town, while he mostly drove his new white Corvette. It seemed like she had everything she had ever wanted — except for Sam.

She had thought this time it was going to be different, but even when he was at home, it seemed like he was there for Linda, he was there for his books, his paintings, his *things* — but not for her. She thought she knew what it was: for all of her efforts, she still wasn't anywhere near the center of his world. So she resolved to make it even more of her business to learn his business, to be in a position to offer advice whenever it was called for — but she still felt an absence of any real intimacy, and it hurt.

L.C. came out for a visit and at Sam's invitation took a suite at the Knickerbocker, driving Barbara's little car all over town. Sam's oldest sister, Mary, always a formidable presence and even more so now to Barbara because of her role in Barbara's escape from Chicago, came out at Sam's expense with her children, Gwendolyn and Don. She stayed with them for a week, and they all went to Disneyland together. For Linda, who was already an avid reader like her father, it was a little bit like discovering that she really was the fairy-tale princess after all. When her daddy was home, every day was like Christmas. "My most vivid memories are of him planning what we were going to do. He was always talking to me about his plans." He read to her at night ("He was a wonderful reader"), and, of course, he was always drawing pictures for her — but he talked to her about his expectations, too. "My father was very strict about what he believed. He wanted me to go to college and learn the wider aspects of life. He had a certain way that he liked to see things done." And, just as her grandfather Cook's word was law in *his* home, that was the way their household was run.

On December 15, Sam got a draft of his RCA contract from the William Morris office, since by California law personal managers were not allowed to negotiate contracts. Jess made sure that William Morris wouldn't collect any commission on the contract ("I told them, 'I got him the deal, not you'"), and Sam in turn informed Jess that the agency was no more his manager's friend than Sam's. According to Sam, Larry

Sam and Barbara at home: Leimert Park, 1960. *Photographs by Jess Rand,* ©
Michael Ochs Archives.com

Auerbach had asked him what he needed a manager for when William
Morris could take care of all of his needs. Jess just shrugged it off; that
was the way all agencies were — of course they'd like to eliminate the
middle man. But he felt that he and Sam now had a special understanding. He had stood up for Sam, and he had delivered. And as he knew by
now, that was Sam's only measure.

For Sam there was no question of the distance he had traveled in the
two years since "You Send Me" had been released. He had only to look in
the mirror to measure the difference, he had only to look around him to
see all that he had gained. He drove around in the Corvette and stopped
by the Specialty office in Hollywood to see Art Rupe. Art asked him how
he was doing, and he just reached in his pocket and took out a big roll of
bills. He could tell Art got the message, and he could see the way Art

looked down his nose at him — but what the fuck was Art looking down his nose about? What made him think he was better than anybody else? Sam knew he was just after the same thing that Sam was.

For Christmas that year, he sent out a card that he designed himself. The front showed a crooner of indeterminate race, with a bow tie, formal striped pants, and a microphone that looked like a vertical arrow, from which emanated, as though wafting on a breeze, a general-purpose "Season's Greetings," along with the song titles "You Send Me," "Summertime," and "Tammy." Then on the left inside the card, a somewhat comical-looking crown sits atop an escutcheon bearing the initials "SC," while, on the right, a tiny white tuxedo-jacketed figure, arms extended, darker, and more proportionally drawn, offers an eighth-note-dotted rendition of the single line, "You Send Me," with the seasonal greeting conveyed in a carefully practiced but distinctly amateur calligraphic hand.

> May the
> Coming year
> Be your greatest
> One that
> REALLY SENDS YOU

And signed at the bottom: "Sam, Barbara & Linda Cooke."

Having Fun in the Record Business

S AM MET HUGO AND LUIGI for the first time shortly after the start of the new year. He was playing a series of East Coast dates prior to his initial RCA session and stopped by on instructions from Jess to meet the men who would now be guiding his fate in the studio.

The two cousins sat facing each other across large matching desks, with visitors (who were placed in the middle) reduced to turning their heads back and forth, like spectators at a tennis match. Luigi at thirty-eight was the younger by five years and the more outgoing of the two. Hugo, with his pencil-thin mustache and pronounced resemblance to the British actor David Niven, had more of a continental air, but the two of them were not above changing the nameplates on their desks to the confusion of the unwary visitor or, strictly for their own amusement, switching off on the telephone without the caller ever becoming any the wiser. And occasionally they greeted visitors while standing on their heads, an outgrowth of the yoga study they had begun several years earlier.

Although they were first cousins and had known each other since childhood from big family gatherings, they only met as adults at a piano recital given by Luigi's oldest brother, Ezio, in 1948. Hugo, a veteran of the Charlie Barnet and Guy Lombardo bands, was playing trumpet in the pit orchestra of the Broadway show *Hellzapoppin'*, while Luigi, an aspiring writer (his war novel, *This World Is Mine*, had been published the year before to good reviews but poor sales by Rinehart, the same publisher who, despite misgivings about the market for another war novel, was about to bring out Norman Mailer's *The Naked and the Dead*), had been working as a speechwriter for the fledgling United Nations and doing independent publicity work. They went out for coffee after the concert, and Hugo proposed that since Luigi was a writer, maybe he

Sam with Hugo (left) and Luigi. *Courtesy of ABKCO*

could write some lyrics for the children's records that Hugo and his wife, the singer June Winters, were just beginning to put out.

That was the start of their partnership. It was ironic that Luigi should not have been at least an equal musical contributor, since his father, Giuseppe, known as "The Great Creatore," was a contemporary and rival of John Philip Sousa who had come over from Naples in 1902 at the age of thirty-one to play the recently opened Steel Pier in Atlantic City. He had subsequently gone on to record for RCA with great success and traveled the country with a fifty-piece band he brought over from Italy and his own personal barber. Alone among his siblings, though, Luigi had shown no gift for formal musical training, and, in fact, for his eleventh birthday, in 1932, when the family had fallen into impoverished circumstances, his father gave him a present of inestimable value: "He said to me, 'From now on you don't have to take any music lessons. That's your birthday present.' I don't remember what I got for my tenth birthday, but I remember what I got for my eleventh!"

He and Hugo quickly learned to operate independently, writing, producing, and selling their children's records on their own ("If we wanted to do something, we did it," said Luigi, "because if you ask people to let you do it, it doesn't happen"), and Luigi soon discovered that while he possessed no formal musical talent per se, he did have an ear for what worked. He and Hugo were able to support their families through their freelance endeavors, but then they came to the attention of Mercury Records in Chicago, and, after a brief stint in the children's division, in 1954 they were offered the opportunity to run Mercury's pop department in New York. The salary was only $75 a week, but they jumped at the chance.

They had hits with Georgia Gibbs and Sarah Vaughan right off the bat, then in 1955 topped the charts with two cleaned-up covers by Georgia Gibbs of r&b hits by LaVern Baker ("Tweedle Dee") and Etta James ("The Wallflower," otherwise known as "Dance With Me Henry"). From their point of view a hit was a hit, they were as proud of taking Sarah Vaughan pop ("Nobody ever heard her sing like that," said Luigi. "That's what we did. We did pop") as they were of mining the r&b field for Georgia Gibbs. "In those days if anything stirred, you covered it — bam! We weren't making art. We weren't doing anything like that. We were making records to sell." And they were having fun doing it. They had the perfect partnership. They had the perfect perspective. If a record failed, it was only a record. "Sometimes," Luigi said, "Hugo and I used to close the door to our office and get hysterical laughing, we were having so much fun."

In early 1957 they went into the newly formed Roulette record company in partnership with twenty-nine-year-old Morris Levy, a ubiquitous figure in the music world, known for his extensive Mafia associations, his explicit strong-arm tactics, and his ownership of the legendary Times Square jazz club Birdland, the home of bebop. For an investment of $1,000 they acquired 50 percent of the label and a free hand in running it, and although they were aware that Morris was "connected," they took the view that his "connections" had nothing to do with them and, furthermore, that Morris, who for all his crudeness could charm, as well as threaten, the birds out of the trees, was a "diamond in the rough." When two years later RCA made them an offer they couldn't very well turn down ($100,000 salary apiece for the next five years; their own floor in the RCA building; their own promotion staff), they had no hesitation in going to Morris and telling him of their good fortune. He said, "Okay, give me back my stock." Which, for their original investment of $1,000, they did, wisely choosing not to calculate any appreciation in its value and going with his blessing.

They liked Sam from the start. He was polite and personable, well aware of their track record, and, though he seemed a little shy at first, affable enough that they were confident he had what it took. But they had to find him a hit. As Luigi saw it: "We knew he was talented. We knew he had one pop hit, 'You Send Me.' But the others didn't seem [like] such hits to us, because they were within the r&b field. They were not pop hits, which is what we made."

They had gotten some songs together in preparation for the session, and Hugo sat down at the piano to play them for Sam. Sam started humming along, but his voice cracked. "He said, 'I got a little kind of cold.' We said, 'Okay,' and Hugo said, 'Why don't you look at this?' Then he started to sing the other thing, and he cracked again. I said, 'Shit, they sent us the wrong guy!' So that kind of broke the ice, and I don't know whether we picked anything out that night or we met again, but [at some point] he said, 'You know, I write.' We said, 'Yeah? Have you got anything?' So he sang a couple of songs that we were not impressed with. They didn't sound like hits." Then, perhaps stung by their indifference and driven by his own pride, he sang part of a song he had put together with Charles while they were out on tour the previous year. He had just about persuaded Charles to record the song for SAR and was dismayed when Hugo said right away, "Let's do that one." Sam protested weakly that the song wasn't finished yet, but the two cousins just said, "Well, go finish it, then. Because that's a sound."

But the january 25 session did not go as smoothly as everyone had hoped. Hugo and Luigi had hired Johnny Mathis' new musical director, Glenn Osser, one of their favorite string arrangers and someone with whom they had worked since the Roulette days, to conduct and do the orchestrations. With their careful approach to preproduction ("We were not the kind of producers who left things to chance"), they had gone over each of the five songs they had okayed for the session (including three standards and Sam's original composition) with both Sam and the musicians. Sam had picked out the other original, "Teenage Sonata," at an audition by the songwriter himself in Hugo and Luigi's office.

"He loved the song," said Jeff Barry, twenty-one at the time and just breaking into the music business both as a writer for E.B. Marks Music and as a singer recently signed to RCA by Hugo and Luigi. "I had never done anything like that before, played a song for a real live artist, and especially one like Sam Cooke. I sat at the piano and played this real slow ballad, and when I was finished, I turned around on the piano stool, and the publisher said, 'Anybody want to hear it again?' And, you know, the silence in the room was deafening, [but] Sam Cooke said, 'Yeah, I want to hear it again.' It wasn't like I was some big established writer. He just loved the song. It had a certain charm and innocence, I guess."

In the studio, though, it turned out to be hard to get that charm and innocence across, whether because of the arrangement (the strings sounded shrill, never blending in with Sam's voice) or the vocal itself, which, however practiced, precise and professional, failed to achieve the warmth of a Sam Cooke original on Keen. Or maybe it was just the transparent attempt to cash in on two markets. "Teenage Sonata" was, as the title suggests, a direct appeal to the teen demographic while at the same time an attempt to elevate the subject much in the same way that Hugo and Luigi recently had with Della Reese's "Don't You Know" (derived from Puccini's *La Bohème*) and Jackie Wilson would three weeks later with an operatic rendering of a melody from Saint-Saëns' *Samson and Delilah* called, in its English adaptation, "Night."

In any case, they quit on it after five takes (it was, after all, a very simple song, and there was no point, they reasoned, in beating a dead horse into the ground) and went on to Sam's song, which was as odd in every way, including provenance, as "Teenage Sonata" was conventional. "Chain Gang" stemmed from a very specific scene that Sam and Charles had witnessed in the Carolinas several months earlier. "We was driving along the highway, man," said Charles, "and we saw these people working on a chain gang on the side of the road. They asked us, 'You got any cigarettes?' So we gave them the cigarettes we had. Then we got down the road about three or four miles, and we saw a store. Sam said, 'Go in there and get some cigarettes for them fellows' — you understand? To take back to them. So I went in the store and bought five or six cartons, and we carried them back to the dudes that was working on the gang, it wasn't but a few miles — and I asked the guard if it was all right to give them the cigarettes, and they thanked us, and that was it. And Sam said, 'Man, that's a good song. Right there.' And just started singing, and then we went to the hotel and I put in a few words, and Sam said, 'Why don't you do it, man?' But he was so good singing it I never did."

The song was nothing like the experience itself, emerging from Sam's imagination utterly transformed. Despite its grim subject matter, it was, as Atlantic Records vice president Jerry Wexler would observe, an almost "happy-sounding song," in which the prisoner's imagined home-coming ("Mmm-hmmm, I'm going home / One of these days I'm going home / See my woman / Whom I love so dear / But meanwhile I've got to work right here") overrides the cruel realities of the situation. Musi-cally, you might have thought that Sam would choose a blues form, but instead, he sets the song to a jaunty Caribbean beat punctuated by the kind of grunts that just a year before had gotten Ray Charles' "What'd I Say" banned by many of the more squeamish radio stations. Here the grunts are presumably sex-free, stemming from the efforts of men at hard labor and punctuated by the hammering sound of a piece of pipe against a metal mike stand, with Sam's voice incongruously riding over the melody as though he were crooning a love song.

All the elements were present ("We tried so many different things," said Luigi, "[to get] that anvil sound"), but somehow it still didn't work. They went through twelve takes with slight adjustments of lyrics and phras-ing; once again the arrangement may not have been altogether right, but Sam's enunciation was precise, each take possesses the same lilting charm, the same confident, conversational tone — and, indeed, it would be diffi-cult for the casual listener to distinguish among them. What is missing is that indefinable sense of grace which Sam is ordinarily able to convey with the slightest inflection, what is missing is the sense that he is at home in his surroundings. So, after three and one-half hours, Hugo and Luigi called a halt to the session without a single song completed. They took a philosoph-ical view: it had certainly happened before. "You know, many times we started with an artist," said Luigi, "and the first session didn't happen, [because] you have to know what would be good for them, you have to feel what is peculiar about their voice that if you put it with this song, it would make it. And you have to understand that as an artist they have their feel-ings, so you develop [those] feelings. You don't tell them, 'Don't do that. Do this.' You don't give them orders, because it doesn't work."

Above all, they tried to avoid any suggestion of failure, not really all that difficult given the upbeat nature of their personalities and partnership. They had gotten the feel down, they told Sam. There was no point in wearing it out. They could just pick it up again in three days' time.

And so they did. They ran through two new numbers, an English-language adaptation of a Jacques Brel ballad and an old Perry Como chestnut, before returning to "Teenage Sonata," which Sam now polished off with a couple of vocal overdubs. Tellingly, the principal difference between the master take and the previous day's efforts lies almost entirely in the outro (Sam's instantly recognizable yodel occupies most of the soaring fade of the final version, which in earlier takes was filled primarily with clumsy verbal protestations). They finished with yet another undistinguished ballad, but at this point it didn't matter. Hugo and Luigi had their single. There was still lots of work to do, with the record release date just weeks away, and the producers' next immediate priority was to cut an album on Sam for the adult record-buying audience. There was no great hurry about getting back to that peculiar original of his.

S AM WAS IN THE STUDIO AGAIN just three weeks later, back in Los Angeles, but this time as producer, not artist. "The Patsy," the *General Electric Theater* drama he had filmed with Sammy Davis Jr., had aired the night before and gotten him plenty of attention in the black press but no critical raves. It was a small part, and Sam could not have failed to be aware of the awkwardness of a performance whose chief virtue, and chief defect, was his own winsome charm (Sammy, by way of contrast, played a kind of holy fool with impassioned belief) — but Jess was confident it was bound to lead to bigger things, and so far everything Jess had told him had come true. With Sammy having just completed a movie in Las Vegas called *Ocean's 11* with Frank Sinatra and Dean Martin, and Jess' new production company with Jeff Chandler about to get under way, who knew what the future might hold in store?

The February 22 session was Alex's idea. They had had no additional SAR sessions since cutting the Soul Stirrers in September, and Alex had long contended that Kylo Turner, his old lead singer for the Pilgrim Travelers, was a prime candidate for crossover success. So they wrote some new songs for a pop session, contacted René to do the arrangements, and put together a rhythm section consisting of Clif, premier studio

322 | *Having Fun in the Record Business*

bassist Red Callender, and drummer Earl Palmer, along with a chorus made up of Alex and Gaynel Hodge and fellow Turks alumnus Tommy "Buster" Williams, and a full string section. But then Kylo showed up in a state of such insobriety that even J.W. had to admit defeat. And all they were left with were some instrumental tracks with a vocal chorus, a couple of barely usable vocals by Kylo, and scratch vocals on two songs that would have to be replaced.

Then Sam ran into Johnnie Morisette.

Johnnie Morisette, known professionally as Johnnie "Two Voice" for his propensity for establishing a dialogue between his natural voice and a throaty falsetto register, had started out with the Bells of Heaven in Mobile, Alabama. He had first met Sam at the Twilight Café on Davis Avenue, a regular hangout for every entertainer who passed through Mobile and every jitterbug in town. Sam had just joined the Soul Stirrers. He was twenty, and Johnnie some four years younger but already an impressive street personality with a powerful imagination of his own (one of his more fruitful imaginative exercises was the composition of his own biography, which placed his birth sometimes on "Montu Island" in the South Pacific, sometimes in American Samoa). Sam was immediately taken with him, and continued to be upon Johnnie's arrival in L.A., where he combined a singing career (for the Specialty label, among others) with a street life, leading to the logical sobriquet "The Singing Pimp." He had, as J.W. observed, a genuine aptitude for pimping. He was handsome, free-wheeling, and bold. But he was a talented singer, too, and it was only natural that Sam would think of him in that regard when he ran into Johnnie coming out of a breakfast club called Master's.

They hadn't seen each other in a while, and they had some catching up to do. Johnnie brought Sam up to date about his string of girls, while Sam told Johnnie about his new record label. As a matter of fact, Sam said, he had a couple of songs he thought might be just right for Johnnie. So they went over to René's office on Selma, and Sam played him the two instrumental dubs from Kylo's session, with voices and full string section — which definitely impressed Johnnie that Sam and J.W. meant business.

Then Sam picked up a guitar and started singing the words to one of the dubs, an "answer song" that he and J.W. had written to his own Specialty hit "I'll Come Running Back to You." Johnnie said, "Yeah, I like that," and they decided right then and there that Johnnie Morisette was going to be SAR's newest star. Within days they were at Radio Recorders to put Johnnie's voice on the two tracks. Sam had to explain to Johnnie about overdubbing, because "I had never heard of that. I'm looking at this big studio, and he said he didn't want nobody there but us. Damn, I'm used to singing in front of a crowd!" But he nailed the "answer song," "I'll *Never* Come Running Back to You," fitting his energetically bluesy voice into its peculiar combination of a childlike New Orleans melody, a cha-cha beat, marching band–style drums, vocal chorus, and percussive strings. It was the kind of big pop sound that Hugo and Luigi had spoken about putting behind Sam — but with none of the awkward concessions to bland emulsification that you hear on Sam's session. On the second number, J.W.'s secular adaptation of the old spiritual "Every Time I Feel the Spirit," it is just gospel with strings, as Johnnie sings in his theatrical second voice, and Sam lets him adlib an outro that feels so good it ends in a laugh. All in all, it was the kind of record that Sam and Alex hoped they could keep on putting out, one on which they could proudly emblazon the assurance that it had been made "Under the Personal Supervision of Sam Cooke and J.W. Alexander." "We felt like we could do things ourselves that were taboo to a company like RCA. It was all about people, really," said J.W. "We just recorded people that we more or less liked."

S AM WAS BACK ON THE ROAD in March but still able to fit in recording sessions for the two "theme"-oriented albums that Hugo and Luigi had conceived for him. *Cooke's Tour,* with songs like "London By Night," "Under Paris Skies," and "Arrivederci, Roma," was a standard variation on Frank Sinatra's 1958 *Come Fly With Me,* while *Hits of the '50s* could just as easily have been called *Hits From Your Father's '50s.* It was the time-honored strategy for broadening an r&b singer's appeal by reaching out to a mainstream white audience ("Albums weren't really a factor in the black market," said Shelby Singleton, soon to become Clyde McPhatter's producer at Mercury), though with the exception of Ray Charles, who was just beginning to sell albums on a consistent basis to his white fans, the crossover-album approach had never really worked for any major r&b star.

"Where is the good new music?" was the question on the lips of every "sensitive citizen," according to Hugo and Luigi's liner notes for the second record. "Where are the good young singers? Well, this album gives the answer." And, indeed, in the liner notes to each LP, they tried to point sensitive ears toward a genuine appreciation of "a new style of singing [which] might be described as playing with a melody or a series of notes (but always coming back to the original melodic strain) in order to heighten an effect." But whatever their good intentions, artistic or commercial, nothing could mask the sessions' uninspired point of origin, and Sam's "simplicity and directness" were almost drowned in the sludge of Glenn Osser's arrangements. It might be argued that Sam's voice occasionally rose above the tawdriness of its surroundings, but the tawdriness was the single inescapable factor.

"Teenage Sonata" came out in early February, supported by a full-page ad in *Billboard* saluting Sam Cooke's "Glorious Golden 60's Debut on RCA Victor." A month later it had barely cracked the charts and never got any higher than number fifty pop while lingering only two weeks on the r&b charts. "You Understand Me," the throwaway final ballad from the second session, was released as the follow-up single in the first week of April and never made the charts at all. Meanwhile the "demo" version of "Wonderful World," the collaboration with Lou Adler and Herb Alpert that Sam had recorded at Keen more than a year earlier, had just been discovered by label owner John Siamas among the tracks that Sam had left behind. It came out on Keen the same week as the second RCA single and quickly rose to number twelve pop and number two r&b, his best overall showing since "You Send Me" and one that easily outsold both RCA singles combined.

This couldn't help but add to the pressure Hugo and Luigi were already feeling from the RCA executive committee downstairs ("They met once a week in a boardroom and played the records that were going to be released," said Luigi, whose general opinion of the RCA higher-ups was that they were "unhelpful, unimaginative, and uncooperative, a lot of 'uns'"). And it could only exacerbate the resentment that Sam and J.W. were feeling toward Keen, who, in the same way that Specialty Records had once ridden Sam's Keen success, were now riding, not to mention threatening, Sam's good fortune in signing with RCA — and still not paying him. Sam and Alex had already initiated another lawsuit against the Siamases a few weeks earlier, this time for $8,000 in publishing money that was owed to Kags and close to $5,000 in artist royalties that had accrued to Sam since the December settlement. But now the matter seemed to be taking on an even greater urgency of its own.

*　　*　　*

S AM HAD A TWO-WEEK Supersonic Attractions tour for Henry Wynn coming up in mid-April, then a month of theater and club bookings, and various other dates that would keep him busy through mid-August. Before setting off on his four months of touring, though, he went back into the studio for a singles session with Hugo and Luigi on April 13.

It was a different kind of session. To begin with, instead of an orchestra, the producers had assembled a rhythm section made up of New York session stalwarts, with Clif, as always, supplying the solid underpinning, and Hugo pitching in on organ. Perhaps because of the absence of strings and horns, they used a different arranger, and, more significantly, Sam brought all the songs to the session. One in particular, "Sad Mood," sounded to Hugo and Luigi like it could be a smash, but after four takes, they recognized that the feel wasn't right and set it aside. For all of its differences, the session would have been counted no more of a success than its predecessors had it not been for one central element: they completed "Chain Gang."

They used the twelfth take from the January session as the instrumental master, and Sam ran through three vocal overdubs, each gaining in mastery and assurance ("Oh wow," Sam declares as he breaks off the second with an easy peal of laughter) until he sails through the last as if there could never have been any doubt. Once again much of the difference appears in the fade, where Sam's improvisational skills are fully engaged and the length of the song is increased by a full nine seconds, but the subtle alterations he has made to the lyrics (no longer are these prisoners at hard labor "thinking of their women at home / In their silken gowns"; instead, they are "working on the highways and byways / And wearing a frown") further add to a recalibration of sound and meaning that can neither be precisely defined nor denied.

With this session, too, Hugo and Luigi seem to have come to a new appreciation of their artist. Part of that appreciation may have been a result of their seeing him work the Town Hill Club in Brooklyn the week before. It was, said Luigi, "an experience to live through, to see Sam singing to a black audience. He just stood there, he hardly moved, a little bit of sweat on his forehead, but it seemed like it was effortless, the audience just loved every nuance, they fed on every little thing, they were enwrapt." That, said Luigi with a certain degree of self-amusement, was what finally convinced them they had the right guy. "We went backstage afterward and said, 'You were singing real good.' And he said, 'Oh, man,

Clyde McPhatter, Hank Ballard, Lloyd Price, Freddie Pride, Sam, Dee Clark, ca. 1960. *Courtesy of Billy Davis*

I was just shuckin'.' You know, he threw it off. But we were just floored by what he could do with an audience."

The Henry Wynn Southern swing started the weekend after the session, playing Birmingham on Easter Sunday. The featured acts in addition to Sam were Dee Clark, Hank Ballard and the Midnighters, the Drifters, blues singer Big Maybelle, Motown Records founder Berry Gordy's latest success story, Barrett Strong (Gordy had also cowritten Strong's current hit, "Money"), along with the Hank Moore Orchestra. There were lots of girls, lots of parties, and Sam enjoyed hanging out once again with Midnighters' guitarist Billy Davis and various individual Drifters. But inevitably much of the talk was of Jesse Belvin's death three months earlier in an automobile crash that had taken the lives of his guitarist, his driver, and his wife as well and directly raised the question: just how dangerous was this new racial climate getting to be?

Belvin had been killed when the tires on his 1959 Cadillac blew out following a show with Jackie Wilson and Arthur Prysock in Little Rock, Arkansas. It was the same old ugly peckerwood story. The show was booked to play a segregated dance, and when Jackie refused to do a second show for whites, after a "hot dispute with [the] dance managers," the *Los Angeles Sentinel* reported, "Wilson and his group were allegedly ordered out of town at gunpoint.

"Investigators believed," the story went on, "that . . . disgruntled [white] dance fans were responsible" for slashing Belvin's tires, a conclusion bolstered by the rumor that both Jackie and Prysock also suffered tire problems as they drove to the next date in Dallas. Although nothing was ever conclusively proved, there was little doubt about culpability among Belvin's fellow performers ("Did Racism Kill Jesse?" was the headline in the *Norfolk Journal and Guide*), and it could only have served as a sobering reminder of the dangers that each of them faced almost daily. Like it or not, they were being drawn into a conflict they could scarcely avoid. As they headed through the Carolinas, they saw the spreading sit-in movement and the implacable white resistance to it. Increasingly there was no hiding place, and even entertainers who in less perilous times might simply have clung to their conventional role as good-will ambassadors for the music were induced to speak out. "They try to knock us down," said the normally phlegmatic Count Basie of the sit-ins, "but we get right up again." It was, he said, a "beautiful" movement.

By the time they got to New Orleans on April 27, Sam and Clif were thoroughly dissatisfied with the drummer for the Hank Moore Orchestra. Sam was eating at Dookey Chase's Restaurant on Orleans Street and freely expressing his unhappiness when local bandleader Joe Jones overheard the conversation and suggested to nineteen-year-old drummer Leo Morris that he introduce himself to Sam. Morris, who came from a family of drummers and had grown up playing percussion for his "play-cousins," the Neville brothers, did just as Jones suggested. "So I introduce myself, and he's talking and eating, and he said, 'Man, do you know any of my songs?' I said, 'Yeah,' and he started singing, and I started playing on his dinner table, and he hired me! I knew all his songs, and that night, I just walked on, asked the drummer to get up, put my snare drum down, and played the show. The next day I left town with him."

They went straight from there into the Apollo. Leo Morris had never been to New York before, and, according to Charles, he spent most of his time looking up. "Charlie was my mentor. He was showing me the ropes, man. I didn't drink, and I didn't gamble, but he showed me all the ropes.

He used to call me Little Brother, said, 'Little Brother, now look, when you get there, this is what you do.' And he would tell me different things. He said, 'We're going to New York, New York. The town is so hip they named it twice!' He would take care of Sam, and then him and I would go hang out. It just was Clif [I had problems with]. I think Clif was kind of disappointed that Sam had hired this guy and I could walk right up and play Sam's show without any rehearsal. He would try to tell me about, 'The arrangement go like this,' and this and that. And Sam would say, 'Oh, fuck it, man, whatever he doing is good, man.' I think that was kind of a shock for Clif, that I was that good and Sam liked me that much."

For Leo it was a lesson in music and in life. "Sam was so soulful, you could follow him [musically] wherever he went. He had a way of singing, it was like Mahalia Jackson, she could sing a Christmas carol, and people would cry. And Sam had that same communication line. He could sing to an audience, and he would have their complete [attention] — I would look down the rows from the stage, and everybody would be looking at him, man, they couldn't take their eyes off him."

They played weeklong runs at the Howard in Washington, the Royal in Baltimore, the Tivoli in Chicago, "and everywhere we went, they had to pull him offstage, because the people [wouldn't let him go] until he'd come out and just sing a few more notes. In those theaters they show a movie and a newsreel and a cartoon, but they usually had to cut some of the newsreel or the cartoon because the show was always running over. He was a wonderful guy to be on the road with, because everything went so smooth. I had a daughter — I got married at eighteen when my girlfriend got pregnant and I didn't really know too much about how to maintain a family, but Sam would always tell me, 'Man, you're lucky you're married. You got a daughter, and you got a family.'" Leo's impression was that Sam would like to have a family, too. Sam talked to him all the time about how much he would like to have a son. But Leo was unaware that Sam was even married ("Because, you know, the ladies was there every night, you had to beat them off of him"), let alone that his wife was pregnant with their second child.

Barbara was, in fact, almost five months pregnant but not anywhere near as far along in her marriage as she had believed she would be by now. Some of Sam's friends, she knew, thought that with another child she was just trying to tie him up in a trick bag, and it had certainly occurred to her that if she could provide him with the son and heir he so desperately wanted, he was unlikely to ever leave her again. But she had other plans to make herself indispensable in his life. At Sam's suggestion she was familiarizing herself with his business, she had read books and articles that he and Alex recommended and learned some of the language that the attorneys spoke. She spent time with his manager and his manager's wife, too. She knew they looked down on her for her lack of education, and perhaps for that reason, she didn't always present herself to them in the best way. Sometimes she got a little too "relaxed" in preparation for going to see them and their highfalutin friends, and she was well aware that, lacking Sam's gift for bullshit and charm even when he didn't know what the fuck he was talking about, she could get lost in the conversation and make a fool of herself. But she was determined to stay close to Jess, because Jess was taking Sam places, and this time she was not going to get left behind.

So far as his so-called friends and family were concerned, she generally kept her distance. She knew they would cut her out in a minute — they were all out for themselves, Sam seemed to attract hangers-on like flies. But if she wanted to be able to give Sam the advice he needed, she had to maintain her objectivity, she couldn't get all caught up in the gossip and infighting that was bound to go on with all these weak-minded motherfuckers. Sam didn't seem to understand that he had to get rid of the deadwood, he needed to learn to take care of business, and if their marriage was going to have any kind of meaning, he needed to understand that she was the one person who could help him to achieve that goal.

S AM ARRIVED IN CHICAGO on May 20 for a weeklong engagement at the Tivoli Theater, and, as usual, it was nothing but a party. Sam's whole family, and most of the old neighborhood, showed up, the liquor was flowing backstage, and women were practically falling out of his dressing room. The Flamingos, a Chicago-based quintet founded by four Black Jews whose harmonies were distinctly influenced by the Jewish minor-key tradition, were the second act on the bill. Their latest record was Sam's song, "Nobody Loves Me Like You," the number J.W. had pitched to them the previous spring and Kags' first big independent hit. Jess came to town, too, and once again felt challenged by his client for reasons he didn't altogether understand.

"I thought Sam would be staying with his parents or at some decent hotel, so I made reservations for myself at the Congress, but Sam said,

'Cancel that. I got a room for you where I'm staying.' So we get in a cab to the South Side and get to this four-story hotel with a big lobby and just a couple of chairs and a television set in it and — 'Hey, Sam, how are you?' He knew the guy behind the desk, and it seemed like here's his whole neighborhood waiting for him. Sam says to me, 'Get your key.' No one took your luggage, no one showed you to your room. So I go over to the desk and say, 'Can I register?' and the guy says, 'What's your name?' I told him and said, 'Cooke says I have a reservation.' He says, 'Yeah, we got a room for you, let me have a dollar deposit.' I said, 'Deposit?' And now I'm watching other people check in who are with us, and they're not asking them for a dollar. The beds upstairs were these old spring-type beds, but [Sam's] attitude was, 'I stay here, you stay here.'"

It was, Jess felt, as if Sam were constantly testing him, racially, politically, financially ("He made me sweat out my commission check sometimes; he let me know he was out there working, and I was back in L.A.") — but he tried to shrug it off, recognizing that Sam had legitimate reasons for his anger and willing, for the time being at least, to bear some of the brunt.

What he wasn't willing to do was to indulge Sam in extended conversations about his so-called business interests. From his perspective, the business was a joke, and Alexander was just draining off the money that Sam made from his writing and performing to build up his half-ass label. J.W. for his part saw Jess as an ill-tempered snob, someone who could get Sam through doors that he and Sam could never go through on their own but to whom you never revealed your true thinking because he always had some smart-ass white man's logic to dismiss it with.

Johnnie Morisette's first SAR single came out at the beginning of May and was immediately designated a *Billboard* pick. L.C.'s manager, the disc jockey Magnificent Montague, jumped on the record in Chicago, and it was a turntable hit in several other cities, where good will was able to generate significant airplay. So, even if it didn't sell that many copies, it definitely put SAR on the map. And it encouraged J.W. to take professional office space in the Warner Building at 6425 Hollywood Boulevard, just ten feet by fifteen feet with barely enough room for two desks, a file cabinet, a phonograph, and a tape recorder but directly across the hall from Lew Chudd's Imperial Records, home of Fats

Doing business at SAR: Sam and Alex. *Courtesy of Carol Ann Woods*

Domino, Ricky Nelson, and Slim Whitman. ("Being on a major boulevard," wrote Sam and J.W.'s idiosyncratic consigliere Walter Hurst,
"made this a good address, and the building had sufficient turnover [so
that should the company want to expand] they would be able to find
appropriate offices in the same building.") On the door a sign grandly
announced KAGS MUSIC CORP, SAR RECORDS INC, MALLOY
MUSIC CORP (a secondary publishing arm of the business), but inside,
it was just J.W. working the phone — unless he was on the road personally promoting a record.

It was purely a matter of belief on Alex's part — in himself *and* in
Sam. They talked a little about trying to sign Aretha Franklin, who, with
her father Reverend C.L. Franklin's permission, had announced that she
was going pop just after her eighteenth birthday. J.W. had no doubt
about her talent, and equally little doubt that she would go with them if
asked, she was so crazy about Sam. But neither he nor Sam wanted to
mess with her daddy, who had made it clear that he was going to put his
daughter on a major label. So they focused on the artists they had already
signed: the Soul Stirrers, Johnnie "Two Voice," and a white boy named
Joel Pauley with a resonant r&b sound, who sold even fewer records than
Kylo Turner.

It was strictly a one-man operation, as Barbara kept pointing out to
Sam. She made the argument vociferously, J.W. said, that "she didn't
think that was right. We had some BMI money in a little drawer. I must
have been living off $40 a week, and I couldn't even get Crain to take a
record to a radio station." So in the end, with Barbara's approval, they
kicked Crain out. "Crain lived in Chicago," was Walter Hurst's diplo-
matic observation, and long-distance calls were expensive. "Sometimes
founders of empires change their minds." Then SAR, an acronym to
begin with for Sam, Alex and Roy, became, according to the understanding of the first two, Sam and Alex Records.

ONE TOUR ENDED, and another began. Sam started on a new Henry
Wynn package in June, this one with Roy Hamilton and Little Willie
John. There couldn't have been two more opposite personalities. Hamilton, still working with Bill Cook, Sam's original manager, was the big star
to whom Sam, with Bill Cook's encouragement, had first submitted
his "little songs," and who had provided much of Sam's inspiration to
switch over. He was, as Willie's twenty-nine-year-old sister Mable ob-

served, "very reserved, very dignified, a very private person." Mable, who had only recently started opening the show for her younger brother, was banned by Willie from any of the racier aspects of the tour (and thus largely from any offstage contact with Willie), so she found herself frequently in conversation with Roy. Although a staunch member of the African Methodist Episcopal (AME) church, he was very much interested in race, politics, and the Black Muslim doctrine of economic and social self-determination, "and he would talk to me for hours about that." He also disapproved of her habit of eating pork. "He would look at my plate and say, 'I don't eat swine.' And I'd laugh and say, 'Well, I'll eat enough for both of us.'" With his clean-cut appearance, near-operatic voice, and dignified stage presence, Hamilton frequently drew as many whites as blacks, and in some areas he became the show's headliner, "but everybody," Mable John was quick to point out, "watched everybody else's show. And rooted for them." Even if at the same time they did everything they could to take the show for themselves. As Mable saw it, if you had one bad performer on the show, the show was bad. But with all of Roy Hamilton's musical and philosophical distinction, he was as competitive as the rest.

Little Willie John, by contrast, was a character, a twenty-one-year-old juvenile delinquent. "Few people," as even his sister observed, "were more mischievous than Willie. He cared very little about anything except his music." Others were less charitable: he was a thief in the assessment of many, "a spoiled little brat" who would, said Etta James, "pour lemonade over your head, pick your dress up over your head, [and] stick his finger up your booty." And, of course, he would con everyone in sight, including the promoter, seemingly assuming that they would be as quick to forgive and forget as he was to forget and forgive himself. He was what his fellow musicians called a "CPA," or constant pain in the ass. But he could sing; there was no question about that. Just five foot three, a natty dresser in his sharp little hats and ever-present pipe, he looked, said James Brown, "like a little kid playing grown-up." Brown, still struggling to break through nearly four years after he had first started opening shows for Willie, admiringly described the unique properties of Willie's voice to music writer Gerri Hirshey. He and Willie both sang songs about "knowing and missing," he said, "[but] where missing makes me scream, Willie did not scream it." Like Sam, like Roy Hamilton, he could sometimes plumb almost unbearable emotional depths with his restraint, and no matter how infuriating his offstage behavior might be, you couldn't go up against Little Willie John onstage and not expect to work.

Sam, who had known him since the early days with the Soul Stirrers, when Willie and Mable's family gospel group, the United Five, often appeared on the program in Detroit, was unwavering in his appreciation not only of Willie's talent but of the "chain of devilment" that Willie's actions were likely to set off. He just *enjoyed* Willie, much as he enjoyed Johnnie Morisette — it was as if he got a kick out of their very irresponsibility. It was a strange contrast: Sam so buttoned-down and under control, Willie a walking advertisement for chaos theory. But Sam never acted like he was above Willie, and that was probably why, as Mable John pointed out, there was no one who could calm her brother down better than Sam. "Willie could be in a rage sometimes, and Sam would just walk up to him and basically not say too much, but just Sam's presence [would settle him down]. They had a lot of respect for each other. And he and Sam had fun."

Sam had a lot of respect for the way Willie presented his music, too. Because unlike anyone else on the tour, and unlike most other r&b acts at the time, with the notable exception of Ray Charles and Lloyd Price, Willie always toured with his own band, the Upsetters — and had for the last two years. The Upsetters, Little Richard's original backing group, were one of the premier r&b show bands, with lots of steps, lots of musical versatility, and a strong lead vocalist of their own. They had met Willie through the same West Coast promoter who had paired them with Dee Clark when Richard quit show business in late 1957 and, recognizing Willie as the stronger commercial talent, had transferred their allegiance to him by the spring of 1958. With members primarily out of Houston and New Orleans, they maintained a stable rhythm section plus three tenors and a baritone sax and gave Willie a *sound* that he could always count on, a manner of presenting himself that Sam couldn't help but envy.

To Mable, Sam and her brother had a similar knack for the improvisational life of the road. They both knew where all the good restaurants were, "and they knew where all the good sisters were, 'cause they'd sung gospel everywhere, and some of the greatest cooks in the world were these Christian women. They'd bring us all the food we could eat, or we'd go to their homes, because we couldn't eat in the restaurants, and they'd prepare as much of everything as they could, and we'd [take it with us] to the next town."

Willie was as concerned about his sister's reputation as he was indifferent to his own. "He would lock me in my room at night. Take my key and say, 'I'll bring you whatever you want back.' I knew everything he was doing. It wasn't that. He was just trying to keep anyone from saying anything about me." But when it came to gambling, Willie made sure his sister was there to hold his money. Henry Wynn, who was related to the Johns on their mother's side, accommodated the musicians by setting up places in different towns where they could get together after the show and have an uninterrupted game. Roy Hamilton didn't gamble. And Sam just played at it. But Little Willie John was a gambling fool. And Charles took it as an opportunity that was heaven-sent. Leo Morris just looked on wide-eyed as Charles beat Willie out of all his money, till Willie had to go to Nat Margo, the white tour manager, and get some more. And then Charles and Clif would beat him out of *that*. They would play all night sometimes, said Mable, until it was time to get back on the bus and go on to the next town.

SAM TOURED THE WEST INDIES for the first time during the last two weeks of July. Rhythm and blues was all the rage, New Orleans music in particular, with Fats Domino's recent hit, "Be My Guest," the one song you heard on every radio station and in the repertoire of every local group. Sam and his entourage were scarcely prepared for the airport reception that greeted them when they landed in Nassau, as thousands of Bahamians surged against police lines to get a glimpse of Sam, and even the customs inspectors waved him through as "the man from the Wonderful World." He played Kingston, Trinidad, Montego Bay — Leo Morris was amazed, everywhere they went, traffic came to a standstill, and at the clubs, hundreds of people would be turned away. "Everybody knew [all his songs]. They would sing along. And the women, oh God, man, you had to whip them with a stick. Charlie used to have to just literally pull them away from Sam. I mean, Charlie was a good-spirit person, and his heart was great. But we enjoyed ourselves, because we were working hard. I mean, Sam wouldn't come down unless the people was satisfied. He wouldn't come off the stage."

"I BURN WITH AMBITION to achieve the kind of showbusiness stature that Harry Belafonte and Nat 'King' Cole have achieved," Sam declared in a guest column ghosted by Jess that ran in the *New York Journal-American* within days of his return. "Or the kind of stature Jackie Robinson and Dr. Ralph Bunche have achieved in their fields. With it I can achieve material gain — and more than that, I believe that the aforementioned distinguished Americans have been able to do so much for the Negro people and for the human race because they first achieved great stature in their fields, then utilized their stature to impart to the world a better understanding of what is right and what is wrong.

"I have always detested," Sam went on with surprising vehemence, "people, of any color, religion, or nationality, who have lacked courage to stand up and be counted. As a Negro I have — even in the days before I began to achieve some sort of recognition as a performer — refused jobs which I considered debasing or degrading."

Show business success, he pointed out, stemmed as much from dedication to "the practical business end as to the 'show' end, although they are related," and, he concluded, in words that his father must certainly have approved of: "I have the natural desire to be recognized as being 'the best there is' in my chosen field, and for obtaining the material things that such recognition brings. But in my case it goes even deeper than just that."

It was a carefully worded distillation of Sam's thinking, all cleared with Sam before Jess submitted it to Dorothy Kilgallen, the self-proclaimed "Voice of Broadway," whose notably liberal views on race ensured its place in her column. But three days before it was published, immediately following his triumph in the West Indies, Sam started off on yet another Southern tour that — with its segregated bookings, run-down motels, and demeaning racial treatment — could only test the very basis of his belief in American democracy.

The tour had been organized for promoter Rip Roberts by trumpet player Dave Bartholomew, Fats Domino's discoverer, bandleader, and producer, and a ubiquitous figure on the New Orleans music scene since the late 1940s. They would be going out with Bartholomew's band, a stellar aggregation featuring twenty-two-year-old Allen Toussaint on piano, along with a host of other handpicked New Orleans talent (Ernie K-Doe, Earl King, Snooks Eaglin, the Spiders), plus co-headliner Dakota Staton, something of an anomaly in this company with her jazz-oriented supper-club act. The first show was scheduled to take place at New Orleans' Municipal Auditorium on August 3, but when it did, there was a security force of fifty policemen on hand and the threat that if anything

took place even remotely resembling the violence "that gave Negro concerts black eyes several days ago," as Elgin Hychew put it in his "dig me!"
column in the black *Louisiana Weekly*, it "might in the future make it difficult for promoters of Negro shows to obtain the facility" at all.

What had occurred at the earlier concert was just another, more
mundane variation on the Jesse Belvin story. The Jackie Wilson Show,
which continued to inflame audiences all across the South (it had
already led to a direct ban on all rock 'n' roll revues in Birmingham), had
hit New Orleans on July 17, with Larry Williams and Arthur Prysock (the
co-headliner in Little Rock in February) on the bill. "The commotion
started," the *Louisiana Weekly* reported, "when Larry Williams attempted
to sing from a sitting position on the edge of the stage." A black policeman informed him that it was against auditorium policy to sing from
the floor, "and then a white officer allegedly pushed [him]." Williams, the
man who wrote and recorded "Bad Boy" for Specialty Records in 1958
(he was a follower of the Johnny "Guitar" Watson/Johnnie Morisette
school of thinking, in which music frequently fought a losing battle with
pimping), was never one to avoid a confrontation, but it was Jackie Wilson, a former boxer, who at this point jumped from the stage and pushed
the policeman, followed by five members of the band. There was no
question in the mind of anyone in the crowd as to who provoked the confrontation, and bottles and bricks began to fly, as "patrons [scrambled]
for the exits . . . auditorium officials got the fire hoses ready [and] ten
patrol wagons came blasting their sirens to the scene." Jackie, who never
even got to perform, was bailed out at three in the morning and
promptly left town, thereby avoiding charges (if the defendant couldn't
be found, the judge pragmatically ruled, there was no choice other than
to dismiss), but the bitterness lingered on all sides, as some of the performers grumbled that none of this would be happening if the white
man would leave them alone, others that Jackie and Larry were so
damned hotheaded they just helped bring it on themselves.

What they were all agreed upon was that the situation was getting
worse. As Clyde McPhatter, probably the most outspoken of them all,
had said just weeks earlier while addressing student "Freedom Fighters"
at the fifty-first annual NAACP Convention in St. Paul, Minnesota, there
could be nothing but a sense of solidarity and pride in these "young
people who, rather than continue to endure the humiliation of Jim Crow,
are willing to risk verbal abuse, physical assault, expulsion from school

and imprisonment in Dixie dungeons . . . in this irresistible crusade." And even in the absence of such stirring sentiments, or when such stirring sentiments were not so readily expressed, there was still a choice to be made night after night, day after day: whether you were going to continue the way the old folks had always taught, go along to get along, or stand on your own two feet like a man. Even Fats Domino, the most mild-mannered of performers, who sought to avoid controversy at all costs and like Roy Hamilton had as big a white following as a black, was dragged into it when he canceled an August dance in Virginia Beach, Virginia, after learning that "plans had been made to run a rope or fence the length of the building" to divide his fans from each other. "The New Orleans–born entertainer declined," the *Norfolk Journal* reported, "to be a party to such obvious segregation."

Sam's New Orleans show went off without a hitch, and columnist Elgin Hychew congratulated his fellow citizens on their restraint while chiding them for their failure to acknowledge the superiority of Dakota Staton's singing style. "The SAM COOKE crowd," Hychew wrote, "did not fully dig the delightful set of tunes from her night club repertoire," and some of the city's "more serious-minded jazz lovers" stayed away. But the audience response to Sam was one of unqualified approval at every stop on the tour, and it soon became clear to his fellow performers, New Orleanians all, that this was a response he had come to both expect and exploit.

"Some people said he was kind of snobbish," said Ernie K-Doe, an extravagantly extroverted young entertainer who had yet to have a hit of his own. To K-Doe, though, Sam was not so much snobbish as "picky. Everything had to be exact with him. He pick the places he want to go in. If it didn't look [just] so, he didn't go in. If you couldn't play his music right, Sam didn't sing." To Allen Toussaint, on the other hand, the elegant young pianist and arranger who chose his words as carefully as his notes, Sam was "hip but not rowdy. Extremely hip but not the kind of guttural hip that carries a knife. Hip that carries a comb or a handkerchief." Which may have been a different way of saying the same thing.

"Chain Gang" hit while they were in Texas, and it hit with a force matched by nothing since "You Send Me," eclipsing even "Wonderful World" and eventually reaching number two on the pop charts. Sam sang it in the car, with Leo beating out the rhythm on the back of the seat, and in Texas, Florida, and Alabama, it rapidly became everyone's number-one request. People sang along, just like they did on his old songs — they knew it from the first time they heard it because, as Luigi pointed out, it was nothing more than one long conversational sentence, "it was just a story," and that was what people fastened on to.

All the musicians headed back to New Orleans after the tour wound up in Dothan, Alabama, and Sam told his new drummer they'd be going out again in about a month. Leo Morris was glad for the time off, but he couldn't wait for the touring and good times to start up again. Sam had told him repeatedly how pleased he was with his work, he had even given him a cash tip. All in one-dollar bills. "One hundred one-dollar bills. It was too big to fold in your pocket. He said, 'Here, little brother, this is for you.'"

THERE WAS ANOTHER Johnnie Morisette session scheduled just a few days after Sam got home. Johnnie contributed a couple of the songs himself this time, including "Dorothy On My Mind," a gospel rewrite that, with Alex, L.C., and Crain all singing the background, vividly evoked the spirit of the Paramount Gospel Singers' 1949 "I've Got Heaven On My Mind." He did a song of J.W.'s, too, that Sam had been thinking about recording, an innocuous triplet-laden ballad called "You're Always On My Mind" that in typical "Two Voice" fashion he just ripped into.

Sam seemed, as always, to take inspiration from Johnnie's unquench-able spirit, and he ran the session in a manner that served that spirit. He appeared to believe that if he could only translate Johnnie's appetite for life into the grooves of a record, they would have a surefire hit. J.W. was a little more skeptical. He had no doubt about Johnnie's talent, just his commitment. He could see right through Johnnie. Johnnie was a big bullshitter, and he was always hustling Sam with one story or another for money that was just going to go to his girls. But as J.W. saw it, he was a likeable enough fellow as far as that went, and Sam wasn't some naive mark off the street; if he enjoyed Johnnie's line of jive and didn't mind laying out something for it, there was no reason not to keep working with Johnnie in the studio. He had the talent, and, J.W. would have been the first to concede, with his unusual vocal propensity he even had the commercial potential.

The Soul Stirrers, meanwhile, were long overdue for a return to the recording studio, but Sam and J.W. were in a quandary as to what to do about it because in the year since their first session, they had lost their lead singer. This had come about after Johnnie Taylor got into an automobile accident in which he hit a little girl who ran out into the street in front of his car. The girl wasn't seriously injured, but the police suspected Johnnie of driving under the influence, and on closer investigation, the influence turned out to be marijuana. "I been smoking weed since I was twelve or thirteen," Johnnie unrepentantly told the other Stirrers when they bailed him out, but before they got a chance to fully register their disapproval, he announced that he was quitting the group for the ministry. Almost without missing a beat, he preached his first sermon at Fellowship Baptist and then hit the road as "The Reverend Johnnie Taylor (Formerly with the Soul Stirrers)."

They tried carrying on without him. Paul Foster took over the lead once again for a brief time, but it was a strain for him, and the audience missed Johnnie's "Sam Cooke" sound and the unique vocal interplay it had come to expect from the Stirrers. So they picked up a little Holiness guy in New Orleans. J.J. Farley, who had been managing the group since Crain left, liked the way the guy sang, but no one else in the group did. Then Sam called Crume and told him he had a guy out in L.A. "Sam said, 'He's a mix between me and June Cheeks.' And I was so glad to hear that, because Sam and June was about the baddest dudes on the road, and I just didn't like this Holiness guy — his singing, not him personally. Well, we get to Newark, and the promoter, Ronnie Williams, tells us, 'I know a guy that would really fit you guys good. I'll have him come to the auditorium in Philadelphia, and you can listen to him.' So after the concert, Ronnie introduces us to Jimmie Outler, and right away we went to my room in the Carlisle and rehearsed with him, and he didn't sound like anybody we had ever had, didn't sound like Sam, didn't sound like Paul, he had a different sound and he had soul. Then he left out of the room so we could talk, and I said, 'Guys, this is the fellow we need right here.' He had kind of a raspy voice, he talked like he was hoarse all the time, and J.J. Farley said, 'How long do you think he'll last at the Apollo?' I said, 'How many times do we [play] the Apollo? Maybe once a year?' And J.J. said, 'No, we better wait till we get to California. Sam said he had a guy out there.' I said, 'Jesse, this is the guy we need right here.'"

The upshot was that they carried Jimmie Outler to California, where Sam had an audition set up for his singer, seventeen-year-old Willie Joe Ligon, of the Los Angeles–based Mighty Clouds of Joy, who were just on the verge of their own breakthrough. Crume tried to cancel the audition. "I told Sam, 'I got a guy, he's *dangerous.*' Sam said, 'Yeah, but he can't be as bad as this guy I got for you.'"

Sam arranged to meet Crume and the other Stirrers at the hotel to go out to the Mighty Clouds program together, but as usual he was late, so they went out with J.W. alone. Sam's singer did just one song, "and I said to J.W., 'Let's get out of here.' He said, 'Crume, you haven't even heard him yet.' I said, 'My guy can chew him up and spit him out. Let's go.' By the time we got back to the Dunbar, Sam was there, and he was all excited, because he knew [we'd] gone to see Joe. He said, 'Did you hear him?' I said, 'Yeah, I heard him.' He said, 'Didn't I tell you? Isn't he bad?' I said, 'Hell, no.' Well, that disappointed Sam, and he said, 'You're a damn fool.' Well, we was at the Shrine the next day, and Sam said, 'I'm going to be there tomorrow, and I'm going to be there on time.' He said, 'I want to hear this guy [of yours].' I said, 'You be there. I'll show you something.'"

The next day Crume was as nervous as a cat. "Because I had done all this talk. I was in the dressing room, and Jimmie Outler's new on the road, so he didn't have no friends, and he was a low-key type guy. So I was trying to get him excited. I said, 'Jimmie, there's going to be some important people coming to hear us.' I said, 'How do you feel?' I was used to doing him like I did Sam. 'How do you feel?' And he's picking at his fingers, looking down. He said, 'I feel okay.' I said, 'But Jimmie, we got to have this one today.' He said, 'Okay.' Just like that. No excitement or anything. Now I'm worried: he might be off today. And we went out there, Sam hadn't shown up till we were doing 'Nearer to Thee,' and the people was really excited, the crowd was yelling and screaming, and all of a sudden, the crowd went up another decibel or two, they *really* started yelling now. And I'm looking around to see what Jimmie's doing, and I look down the aisle, and there's Sam waving his hands and saying, 'Yeah, Crume, you're right.' And he come up onstage and put his arm around my shoulder, yelling in my ear, 'He's bad.' And I said, 'I told you, fucker.' And afterward in the dressing room, Sam said, 'All right, the fucker can do it one time, but it could be luck.' He said, 'When is your next date?' I told him, and he said, 'I'll meet your ass at the hotel.' I said, 'Now, Sam, I can't wait on you.' 'I'll be there, fucker. I'll be on time.' And he was."

Sam was so impressed, according to J.W., that he went home and wrote a song for Outler that very night. Before Jimmie got to record it, though, they cut a session on L.C., whose career had never ignited on Checker, and for whom Sam had written three new songs (two with J.W) to add to the number L.C. had brought in himself. The first song they tried was L.C.'s own "Sufferin'," and it took fifteen takes to get it down, with Sam cheerfully spelling out tempo, instrumental voicing, and phrasing every step of the way. His enthusiasm never faltered, though, even as he declared, "Yeah, we sufferin' with this song. Sufferin' through it all!"

"Sam tell you what he wanted," said his brother, "and that was it. Sam knew everything he wanted before he got to the studio. He had it all in his head. He told me, 'C., now the only thing wrong with your singing, you're holding your words too long.' He said, 'Don't hold your words as long as you do. Say your words quick.' Said, 'I wouldn't tell nobody else that.' I said, 'Thank you, brother.'"

"Sufferin'" sounded very much like a Sam Cooke song, with that patented vocal delivery, a bright Latin beat, Clif's ringing guitar chords, and René delivering a burbling bass lead on his Danelectro. The other three songs mixed blues, gospel, and pop in equal measure, with Sam's "The Lover" offering up a sly blues boast that Sam might have let slip in a club but never for his record-buying audience. Throughout it all Sam is wheedling, cajoling, trying to bring something out in L.C. that L.C. doesn't always seem prepared to offer. "We gonna do this in one take," he announces, before going on to any number of additional efforts. "You feel like doing one more for me?" he asks L.C., always positive, always encouraging, but unwavering in his determination to help his brother reach the goal.

Four days later, on September 6, Barbara gave birth by caesarean section to their second child, another daughter, whom they named Tracey Samia. Sam scarcely had time to acknowledge her arrival, caught up as he was in the whirl of business to be taken care of before his departure for another New York album session in three days and the tour that would be starting up two days after that. Hugo and Luigi had sent out a new conductor/arranger, Sammy Lowe, a former Erskine Hawkins sideman and old friend of René's, to work with Sam on the Coast. They had little choice in their selection of location for this presession conference, the producers wrote in the liner notes for the resulting album, because "the recording schedule we had set up for Sam did not allow for such personal interruptions [as having a baby]. Both Sams paced the hospital corridor firming up arrangement ideas until Mrs. Cooke presented Sam with a fine baby girl."

That night, Sam was in the studio for the Stirrers session. They started out with a couple of beautifully modulated Paul Foster leads, and then Sam guided the new arrival through a relaxed version of Crume's latest composition, which mixed a convincing invocation of Jehovah with an equally convincing cha-cha beat. It wasn't until the end of the evening that they finally got around to the song Sam had written for Jimmie, "Jesus Be a Fence Around Me."

Like all of Sam's best compositions, it was both simple and profound, and Jimmie sings it from the start with the kind of conviction that Sam had heard in his voice that first night at the Shrine. There are just two verses, and they mix, like so many of Sam's gospel numbers, an overt message of faith with an almost inadvertent revelation of despair. "I wonder / Is there anybody here / Who late at midnight sheds briny tears / All because you didn't have no one to help you along the way?" the song opens with that same note of confessional urgency that elevates "Nearer to Thee," for example, to the status of some of Thomas A. Dorsey's greatest gospel compositions. One wishes the Stirrers had had the same opportunity that Sam seized in live performance to expand on the premise of the earlier song, but "Jesus Be a Fence Around Me" is as perfect a cameo as any of his pop hits, and while you can easily imagine Sam taking the lead (the articulation, the phrasing, the emphasis are all Sam's), the voice is Jimmie's, "raggedier" than Sam's, as J.W. observed, more declamatory, full of the kind of individual fervor that they both took as the only gauge of a true gospel performance.

It is as if Sam has found a new way to express himself, and, like a film director or writer who has discovered his subject, he is determined to explore it however he can. The Soul Stirrers in any case provide impeccable support. And when they swing into the chorus (augmented by Crain, and probably Sam, too), an underlying sense of salvation comes through, as much in the gathering of the voices as in the simple prayer that the song enunciates: "Jesus, be a fence all around me every day / Jesus, I want you to protect me as I travel on my way."

At the end of the evening, they overdubbed background vocals on a couple of the songs from L.C.'s session, and the next day the Soul Stirrers came back into the studio and cut four more songs, evenly split between Paul and Jimmie, with Paul seemingly challenged to rise to greater heights by the presence of this dynamic new lead. But "Jesus Be a Fence Around Me" was clearly the number on which Sam and J.W. were pinning their hopes.

My goal is to someday be in the same singing league with Harry Belafonte, Dean Martin and Frank Sinatra. But whether I achieve my goal or not, I have organized my career on a business-like basis and I know there will be well-paying jobs waiting for me, even if my records stop selling. . . . If, in the future, I can't find anyone who will pay me to sing, I'll still be in a position of getting paid when others sing.

— "Sam Cooke . . . Man With a Goal," by Sam Cooke, *Pittsburgh Courier*, October 8, 1960

THE NEW YORK recording session seems to have had only the vaguest point of focus, save for the somewhat rhetorical question posed to Sam by Hugo and Luigi: "How would you do 'Swing Low, Sweet Chariot,' if it came in as a new song today?" They formulated that question, they wrote in their liner notes, "as we were looking over material for his new album. We had been going over new songs, old songs, standard songs, and then drifted into the early American songs of the Stephen Foster era." As far as "Swing Low, Sweet Chariot" went, Sam thought about it in their account, then suggested an arrangement that would retain the spiritual quality of the song but pick up the tempo and add brass. "Sort of a swingin' 'Swing Low,'" he declared. "And so," they wrote, "the theme of this album was decided. We would lean heavily on songs from another era [but] in addition we sprinkled in songs of a later period that fit the mood we were developing [including] Sam's own hit of last year, 'Chain Gang,' which seemed to belong."

They crammed in two four-hour sessions on Friday, September 9, and an afternoon session on the tenth, but despite the presence of Sammy Lowe's more idiomatic arrangements, two originals by Sam and J.W., a beautifully polished version of Harry Belafonte's faux folk song "I'm Just a Country Boy," and "Pray," a jubilee number that Johnnie Taylor had done with the Highway QCs, the tone was no less confused than Sam's purported response to Hugo and Luigi — or than their original question.

A look at "Pray," which Sam had originally attempted when he was with the Soul Stirrers, is instructive. In the QCs' and Stirrers' versions, it is a bright, finger-popping number, somewhere between the "Negro spiritual" presentations of the Golden Gate Quartet and modern-jazz vocal harmonies. In Sam's new version, it is as if Perry Como has met the Negro spiritual with a peppy choral group from *Oklahoma!* thrown in for good measure. All of Sam's most prominent vocal characteristics — his easy, relaxed manner and precise articulation (we hear, twice, of awakening to "a beauty-ful morning"), his elongation of syllables, even the free-ranging adlib with which he customarily stamps a song as his own — work against him here to produce an almost soporific effect. If someone else were singing, it might be taken as a painfully exaggerated parody, but when Sam himself concludes the song with the kind of self-parody that no producer has ever been able to get out of him before ("Pray, la da da da da da da / Pray, la da da da da da da"), with that big chorus chugging along behind him, arms figuratively outstretched, faces grinning, one can only speculate as to whose misreading of both the public and Sam has created such an all-out disaster. It is worse by far than Sam's straightforwardly romantic "Jeanie With the Light Brown Hair" or even "My Grandfather's Clock," the sentimental children's song that Jess had induced him to record, and the experience could only be made more painful not simply by a familiarity with Sam's own past work but by an awareness of the session Sam has just produced on the Soul Stirrers. One might almost imagine that in Jimmie Outler he has, for the moment, found a truer voice than his own.

Whatever inner misgivings any of them may have had, Hugo and Luigi, and Sam, too, for that matter, never maintained anything less than a cheerfully positive demeanor. The atmosphere was at once "relaxed and hectic," the *Michigan Chronicle* reported of the Saturday session. "Relaxed, in that all concerned had foregone their weekday business suits for slacks and Italian-style sports shirts, and Luigi had brought his wife and two young sons along; hectic, because Sam Cooke is capable of doing a good many things at once, which most other people are not." Sam, according to the *Chronicle*, was engaged in complicated business discussions about his upcoming tour, carried on an interview with "a representative of RCA Victor's press department, [and] besides all this several friends had come over to hear him sing. . . . One of the friends kept starting sentences that began, 'You know, Sam, I think for this number you should —' and never getting to finish them. Hugo and Luigi . . . just smiled and went on with their work [while] in the midst of it all Sam Cooke sang and sang — without the slightest indication of nervousness or irritation, [making] it seem as natural and as inevitable as breathing."

The two cousins even rented striped prisoners' jerseys and caps from a costume shop and took a picture with Sam to publicize the success of the current single, as though they were members of an integrated chain gang who had hung on to their expensive slacks. Sam was a good sport about it, though he looks decidedly less amused than the others as the three stand stiffly against a blank backdrop, each dapper and distant in his own way.

A NEW DRUMMER JOINED THE GROUP at the start of the new tour. Twenty-nine-year-old Albert "Gentleman June" Gardner, like Leo Morris, was from New Orleans and, in fact, had been recommended to Sam by the same Joe Jones who had promoted Leo in the first place. June got a call from Joe Jones out of the blue and was simply told that Leo hadn't worked out: was he interested? Everyone knew that June was primarily a jazz musician, he had a regular gig with Harold Battiste and Red Tyler at Joy Tavern, but Joe Jones suggested that if he went with Sam, he and Leo could merely switch places. Then June got a call from Sam, whom he knew a little from Soul Stirrer days. Sam asked him if he could meet the tour in Richmond on the eleventh. "I said, 'Just wire me the money. I'll be there.'"

Leo, for his part, was crushed. The first he heard of it was when June called offering him his weekend gig. He never heard from Sam, he never heard from anyone in the organization — but he took the gig. He knew he was young and still finding his way, he knew Clif had never much liked him, but he couldn't stop wondering where he had fucked up.

June fit in right away. Mild-mannered, easygoing, somewhat jug-eared in appearance, with a receding hairline, a mustache and soul patch, and a warm, inviting smile, he had been on the road with Lil Green, Roy Brown, and Lionel Hampton and was a keen observer of the scene. He got along well with Charles and Crain, and he and Clif could talk for hours about music, but perhaps most important, he was both experienced and patient enough to wait his turn. The band members were all riding together in Sam's new red Buick station wagon with their equipment and clothes, and June wondered at first where everyone was going to sit — "but then Big Clif say, 'I'm gonna sit here,' and that ended that!"

It was Sam, though, whom he recognized from the first as the unquestioned boss. You didn't necessarily have to agree with him on everything, but on certain issues, like the music, there was no room for dispute. He was concerned with "the diction, the feel, the flow of a song. But he could get right away from there and get on the floor. He knew people everywhere we went. All walks of life. He wasn't one of those stars who [act like], 'I pee Falstaff and shit ice cream.' That was never his thing. He touched all bases. The police, the ushers, the stagehands. He was good [to] the people who worked for him, but he was a downfront person, say what he had to say and bam!"

June's first tour was an abbreviated two-week edition of Irvin Feld's Biggest Show of Stars. Eighteen-year-old teen idol Bobby Rydell, with three Top 10 pop hits since the beginning of the year, was the headliner, and twang guitarist Duane Eddy and Dion (late of Dion and the Belmonts, and out for the first time on his own) were the two other white teen-oriented acts who made this a "rock 'n' roll" show. But Sam, Chubby Checker (whose version of Hank Ballard's "The Twist" would that week hit the top of the pop and r&b charts), and Bo Diddley more often than not took the show. They played Louisville on the next-to-last night of the tour, and eighteen-year-old Louisville native Cassius Clay, just back from the Rome Olympics, where he had won a gold medal in the light-heavyweight boxing division, jumped up onstage and, with his inherent sense of theater, joined the singing Olympics in "Western Movies," their original Fred Smith and Cliff Goldsmith–authored hit. He was a well-mannered, good-looking kid, and he came around afterward to the guesthouse where all the black performers were staying, his eyes big for the girls. He talked happily about Lloyd Price and some of the other stars he'd met, and Charles could see Sam was really getting a kick out of him, so he didn't run him off. He was a big overgrown kid who wanted to be in show business just like everyone else. The rest of them were all drinking, but he was content to hang around and watch. He had the kind of personality, Charles thought, where people were just plain going to like him.

Sam was scheduled to begin another Henry Wynn Supersonic Attractions package show within a couple of weeks, but he managed to sandwich in an RCA session on the afternoon of a one-nighter in Bridgeport, Connecticut. He recut "Try a Little Love" (now retitled "Tenderness"), the ballad he and J.W. had written the previous year, along with a version of forties bandleader Buddy Johnson's beautiful blues ballad, "Since I Fell For You." The song with which he began the three-hour session was "Sad Mood," the number he had attempted with Hugo on organ back in April, but even with strings, an all-star rhythm section, an assured vocal, and a Sammy Lowe arrangement that was not all that different from many of René's, the song did not come alive. Perhaps sensing that the feel still was not right, Sam picked up the tempo a little, but that only went to undercut the reflectiveness of the mood and lyrics. "Sam was in and out of the booth," wrote Washington, D.C., *Sunday Star* reporter Harry Bacas. "You just sing, and we do everything else," Hugo told him, and then, perhaps to take the sting out of it, kidded, "If we could sing, who would need you? We'd do it all ourselves." Sam's response was not recorded, but, even though his producers pronounced themselves satisfied, announcing their intention to mix the track the next day and put it out as the follow-up to "Chain Gang," it seemed evident that neither the song nor Sam was fully satisfied. "Sad Mood" simply did not lift off in the manner of so many of the gospel sides, it did not say *Sam Cooke* in the same way that "Chain Gang" or "Wonderful World," or even "Everybody Loves to Cha Cha Cha" or "Win Your Love For Me" so clearly did; it was not stamped through and through with his indelible and impermeable presence.

G ORGEOUS GEORGE, Hank Ballard's colorful valet, entertained everyone on the Henry Wynn show with his stories about Castro's visit to Harlem the previous week. The stars of the show were all familiar to Sam: Little Willie John and the Upsetters, LaVern Baker, Motown artist Marv Johnson, pioneering vocal group the "5" Royales, whose guitarist, Lowman Pauling (author of "Think," "Dedicated to the One I Love," and "Tell the Truth") was one of the most influential r&b songwriters around, Jerry Butler, and Hank Ballard and the Midnighters, with Sam's protégé Billy Davis on guitar. The way that Gorgeous George told it, Castro had spotted George "and these three fine chicks I had" while peering out the window of his ninth-floor suite at the Hotel Theresa across from the

Apollo. He was in town to deliver a speech to the UN and had moved uptown from his luxury midtown hotel with the explicit intention of showing his solidarity with some of the chief victims of American oppression
("All people are alike to us in Cuba," he declared in a joint interview with
Black Muslim spokesman Malcolm X). The reason the Cuban leader happened to be looking out his hotel window, according to George, was that
"there were thousands of folks lined up on the streets shouting, 'We want
Castro,' and we was hollering, too, me and Billy Davis, and the fine chicks
with us. I told him, 'Come on down.' Told him our room number. And
twelve minutes later he shows up, thick black beard, green dress fatigue
suit with the big pockets and big flap, about six cats had on black suits,
and his brother, I think, came in with him. Then Billy started playing,
and we sung to him, and he gave us an invitation to come to Cuba."

According to Billy, Lithofayne Pridgon was there, too, although
Lithofayne said, "By the time I found out about it, it was something that
was [already] fully in motion." Her girlfriends definitely got in on the
action, though, and there were more than three of them. "He came
down because of the girls," Billy agreed. "In fact, he invited one girl to
Cuba, and she asked me, 'You think I should go?' I said, 'Yeah.' She said,
'I'm scared. They might get me down there and [not] let me come back.'
I said, 'Well, you're missing a hell of an opportunity.' But he told us he
would come to the show at the Apollo Theater, and he did. Hank Ballard
should remember that."

"Man, we had a ball," was Hank's typically irreverent memory of the
experience. "I remember all those goddamn women Castro had. Had
them lined up three deep. Beautiful girls, goddamn, you could smell
dope [all over] the goddamn hotel. If I went to Cuba, I bet Castro would
recall being at the Theresa Hotel and going to the Apollo Theater to see
Hank Ballard and the Midnighters. Those were the good old fucking
days!"

It made for great conversation anyway, as the bus rolled down the
highway, through the South and the West and then back into the Northeast. In Denver Billy met a sixteen-year-old girl through Gorgeous
George. She had a little lounge area in her house that her parents gave
her all for herself, and George had sex with her there, and then Billy did,
too. Eventually they all did. "She was the most beautiful young lady,"
said Billy, "but she loved to have sex with entertainers. There was certain
girls I saw, that's just the way they was. She wanted me to be her regular

boyfriend, but she wanted me to give her permission to have sex with other stars. She said, 'If I do, will you still like me?' I said, 'Yeah, baby,' 'cause it's what she wanted. Sam loved partying with us and partying in general. He'd always get what he wanted, [then] I'd get what I wanted. He always had the cream of the crop."

Barbara joined the tour for a few days with Linda and the baby. It was all part of her plan to get next to Sam, and she brought plenty of weed for the musicians. The guys all loved it, especially June and Clif; they appreciated her presence, and even Crain started to see her as an asset. Little Willie John went around boasting to everyone that he had forced his tongue in her mouth when she went to give him a friendly kiss in greeting. "He would mess with people," June observed. "I've seen big men cry, honest to god, rather than hit him, just say, 'If I hit your little ass, I'll — I'll kill you.'" Marv Johnson and Willie got into a fight, and Willie said, "Come on outside, and I'll kick your ass." Marv was provoked enough to say, "All right, come on, you motherfucker," but as he took off his coat, Willie pulled out a .38 and shot it in the air. Marv, said Billy Davis, almost died, "but Willie just fell out laughing. Marv was real dark, but he turned green. It was days before he got himself back together."

Barbara didn't have time for foolishness like that. She was determined to tighten up her game. Sam was crazy about the new baby, whom he called "Fats," and, of course, he couldn't get enough of "Lindalena." Barbara was the one who still had to play it cool. But she miscalculated. Sam got pissed off at the way the guys all responded to her, even his brother Charles. It wasn't the reefer, though Sam did not smoke reefer, he was square as a brick. But he was just plain outright jealous. Finally he told her he was sending her home. "I'm the leader of this here," he said. "Damnit, *you* are not the leader." She talked back to him for once. She didn't get in his business, she said, but what was the matter with him that he needed to control everything so much, he got rid of everyone and everything he couldn't control? And then give you the shirt off his back if you approached him all humble with your hat in your hand. It was like he was a whore for the spotlight, she said, and no one was ever going to satisfy his insatiable need for approval, not these chicks with their skirts up over their heads or her or nobody. That seemed to bring him up short, and he quietened down and said she was the only one who understood him, she was the one person who had known him from the start. But that didn't change the fact that she had to go home. Crain even tried to intervene. "Aw, Sammy, Sammy, Barbie does everything, son," he said. "You don't have to go up and tell her, she just get the whole thing done." "Yeah, my wife is kind of smart," Sam conceded, "but she's my wife, and I want you to butt out." For a man that smart, Barbara thought, he was so damn stubborn it was a crying shame.

THE SHOW CAME to the Rockland Palace at 155th Street and Eighth Avenue in Harlem on October 21, where a young French jazz critic, François Postif, described with wonder the scene that he happened upon. It was midnight when he arrived, and the 2,211-capacity arena was jammed with what Postif estimated had to be twice that number. Sam was onstage, "so popular that everyone is singing along with him. His latest hit, 'Chain Gang,' speaks of the sound that the workers on the chain gang make, and its rhythm is so hypnotic that everyone dances — I really wonder how, since everyone is so pressed in. But everyone dances."

Sam stretched "Chain Gang" out, Postif wrote, for "a good quarter of an hour," and then Hank Ballard and the Midnighters came on with a very different kind of act. They did an extended treatment of Hank's original version of "The Twist," and the crowd, Postif observed, seemed to go into a posthypnotic trance, with ecstasy replacing language or logic. The ecstasy took a different turn as the Midnighters started to disrobe, getting down to their underwear and miming sexual release in a manner that was assisted by a spray of milky water. At this point a number of black patrolmen arrived on the scene and put an end not only to the Midnighters' self-display but to the Midnighters' act.

"The crowd howls and yells," Postif continued, "but right away Sam Cooke returns to get the audience back under control, and I must admit that it is the handiwork of a master." Once Sam got the crowd primed, he made way for LaVern Baker, who left them limp with an intense and varied program, including a very bawdy "Jim Dandy," during which LaVern danced with her own touring Jim Dandy, a small, "very well-dressed" man with a derby and cane, who comported himself with LaVern in a manner that incited a "savage delirium." The show was still going on when M. Postif reluctantly made his departure at 2:00 A.M., to go see pianist Les McCann at Small's Paradise. For him it was a moment never to be forgotten.

For the performers it was one more night on the chitlin circuit — and, in the case of Little Willie John, one that would end an hour later with a female fan emerging from the crowd to punch him savagely ("I never saw the woman before in my life," said Willie. "She told me she was going to stick a knife in my back as soon as I left the Rockland") and six policeman escorting him to his automobile.

S AM DID NOT RETURN HOME for any extended length of time until just before Christmas. While he was still out on the road, a former gospel singer named Theola Kilgore, whom J.W. had discovered, recorded an "answer song" called "Chain Gang (The Sound of My Man)," with Kags getting the publishing on both sides of the record; Jess put out a press release announcing that Sam would soon be interviewed on network TV by hard-hitting newsman Mike Wallace; and John F. Kennedy was elected president. Kennedy's election on November 1 had the support of Nat "King" Cole, Harry Belafonte, Sammy Davis Jr., and Mahalia Jackson, among others, and encouraged Barbara to cast her first vote, but Sam was in Canada, playing Chautiers, an elegant Quebec supper club. He was reading more and more, books on race, politics, and history, many of which had been borrowed from Jess' library, all of which whetted his appetite for more. The reading only reinforced his indignation at the social injustice he saw all around him and the need to address it in the manner he had advocated in his Dorothy Kilgallen guest column. But as he went from the Crossing Inn in Trenton to Sciolla's in Philadelphia, from the Evans Grille in Forestville, Maryland, to the Twin Coaches in Belle Vernon, Pennyslvania, he wasn't sure if he was ever going to get his chance.

Clyde McPhatter evidently had no such misgivings. While playing the Royal Peacock, the crown jewel of Atlanta's black nightlife, which Henry Wynn had taken over in October (Wynn conferred upon it what the *Atlanta Daily World* described as "eye-popping splendor," with a decor "as captivating as a lover's kiss"), Clyde had taken his place on a downtown picket line with Martin Luther King Jr.'s father and brother. The picket line was made up primarily of Atlanta college students, to whom McPhatter declared, "Until we attain freedom for everybody, [none of us can] be free to breathe the fresh air of liberty." When he was unable to attend an NAACP fund-raising dinner in New York, he bought half a dozen $100 tickets to the event and urged everyone to follow his example by giving NAACP memberships instead of expensive gifts for Christmas.

Meanwhile *Jet* magazine reported that many big-name stars were bypassing the Deep South altogether due to the endemic prejudice of its racial practices, while lucrative rock 'n' roll packages such as the Biggest Show of Stars were in danger of extinction because of the "prejudiced parents of white southern teenagers. . . . The territories of Alabama, Louisiana and South Carolina, where mixed units of performers were [recently] accepted, are now shunned by booking agents lining up cities to display their supermarket-type revues, which feature 15 or more singers and quartets of both races." With the latest edition of the Biggest Show of Stars (featuring such white performers as Fabian, Brenda Lee, and Duane Eddy), Chubby Checker had received a not-so-subtle lesson in prejudice when "after the show played in Houston and set out for towns in Louisiana, Mississippi, and Alabama, Checker and another sepia act on the bill, Jimmy Charles, were given a week's 'vacation' and told to rejoin the revue when it got 'up North' — which happened to be the 'liberal' . . . State of North Carolina."

Sam had issues of his own with respect to both race and restraint of trade. He was furious once again with William Morris, this time, he told his brothers, because they had taken an idea he had brought them, a sing-along television show, and given it to Mitch Miller. Larry Auerbach, in fact, was the agent for the show, *Sing Along With Mitch*, which had been introduced on *Ford Startime* the previous May and was scheduled to begin as a regular NBC series in January. Sam demanded a meeting with William Morris, and Jess dutifully set one up with Harry Kalcheim, head of the New York office. "You think I'm your little fair-haired nigger," Sam railed at Kalcheim, in his brothers' account. "You think I'm stupid. I come to you with an idea, and you told me it wouldn't work. And then you take my fucking idea and give it to Mitch Miller. I made eighty fucking thousand dollars for y'all last year, but you won't make it this year off Sam Cooke. I'm through."

Jess' recollection of the meeting did not include the singalong idea, which, as William Morris might have pointed out to Sam, had already reaped Mitch Miller enormous rewards in the recording field, with eight Top 10–selling *Sing Along With Mitch* albums since 1958 (and a total of 997 weeks on the charts). To Jess, the issue continued to be about the more down-to-earth matter of booking, but it was no less deeply felt. "Sam said, 'What the fuck do you know about one-nighters? You have no black agents. You don't know what it's like on the road. And you get twice as much for your white artists as you do for me.' When he was finished, Kalcheim said, 'Mr. Cooke, are you asking for your release?' Sam said yes. And Kalcheim said, very gentlemanly-like, 'Well, why didn't you say so in the first place. And by the way, the answer is no.' Sam said, 'You know, I think you mean that.' And we walked out."

Mostly, though, his problems were the problems related to his profession and craft. It was the music, as June Gardner, the new drummer, soon realized, that was his principal concern. Unlike June's other experiences, with Roy Brown and His Mighty Men or the Lionel Hampton band, with Sam it could be a different backup band every night if they were playing a schedule of one-nighters. "Sometimes the bands could be so bad. Big bands, small bands. Sometimes Sam would say, 'Let the fuckers stay out,' and it would just be the three of us. 'Cause Clif could fill in so many things on the guitar, and the song would [still] go over. Clif was the glue that held it together — musically, and saying what was on his mind. He'd [always] get the band's attention. His opening statement was, 'If you don't play my music, I'm going to snatch your arm off and beat you with the bloody end.' He was a big guy, you know, big actor, had a great sense of humor. I learned a lot from him."

Loyalty meant everything to Sam. But he still wasn't where he wanted to be. To get there, to present his music properly, he knew he needed a band of his own. And to make good records, he knew he had to persuade Hugo and Luigi to record him in California, where he would once again be working with René and musicians who understood his music. Sam sometimes wondered if for Jess playing the Copa, a table at Ciro's, headlining in Vegas like Sammy were not the sum total of show-business success. That was not the limit of his own ambition. One of the faceless RCA vice presidents tried to compliment him by declaring that Sam Cooke didn't belong at the Apollo, Sam Cooke should be playing the Waldorf-Astoria. Sam just stared him down, refusing even to address him in the "proper" English he had spent so much time acquiring. "I ain't never gonna sing at the Waldorf," he declared angrily. "They're not my people." The truth was, he wanted to sing for everyone. But to do so, he had first to be true to himself.

Another Country

You know how it feels — you understand
What it is to be a stranger
In this unfriendly land

— Bobby "Blue" Bland, "Lead Me On," 1960

NOBODY WAS SURPRISED when Jackie Wilson got shot. He had a reputation for smacking women around, and everyone knew he maintained two households — one in Detroit, one in New York. The shooting took place at his $500-a-month luxury apartment on West Fifty-seventh Street in the early morning hours of February 15, 1961. The way the papers reported it, a "love-crazed fan" showed up at his door, threatening to kill herself if he rejected her. "When the handsome singer tried to disarm her," according to the *Philadelphia Tribune*, "she shot him twice, once in the [upper] thigh and once in his lower abdomen."

What the papers failed to report was that, far from being a "love-crazed fan," the shooter had been involved in an off-and-on affair with Jackie for years, and rather than herself, it was the girl entering the apartment with him, Harlean Harris, whom she was trying to kill. Harris was the teenage model "with the amazing hair style" who had dated Sam when he first came to New York in 1958 and then taken up with Jackie. Now twenty-one, she had been living with Jackie for the past year or so, but she disappeared from the picture altogether when Wilson's wife, Freda, the mother of his four children, left their home in Highland Park, Michigan, to be at his side as he lay in the hospital clinging to life.

Sam had seen him just three weeks earlier at the BMI awards dinner in New York. Sam had gotten a pop songwriting award for "Chain Gang"; Jackie had received one, too, for "You Were Made For All My Love"; and, ironically, Barbara had been recognized as well — For her writer's credit on "Wonderful World." Jackie brought Harlean to the dinner, and everyone was having a good time until Jackie started mouthing off at Sam's manager, Jess Rand. He had been drinking and was obviously feeling no pain, and Sam let it go at first, but after giving Jackie's manager, a slick young mobbed-up white guy named Nat Tarnopol, a chance to settle his client down, he stepped in and defused the crisis. Afterward, Jackie asked Sam out for a drink with Harlean and him, but Sam went back to the Warwick instead. He had nothing against Jackie, they had long since patched up their differences over the 1959 Supersonic tour, and he always got a kick out of Jackie's street swagger, but sometimes hanging out with Jackie just wasn't that cool.

Sam and Jess had their own differences to iron out. Jess had just issued a press release announcing the formation of Cooke-Rand Productions, whose avowed aim was to present "touring musicals and gospel shows." Their first show, according to the press release, would be "a gospel caravan [with] a score by Cooke," Jess as producer, and L.C. as musical director. But Sam knew it wasn't going to happen. They were talking about two different things: what Jess wanted was to put gospel on the college circuit, while Sam's only interest was to help more people of his own race appreciate the music. Sam wasn't sure why he objected so vehemently to the idea, except that it seemed like Jess felt like he was doing gospel a favor. And the music didn't need any favors from white people — and neither did Sam.

He was still pissed off at Jess over the whole BMI debacle. Now that it was over, and he was officially registered as a BMI writer, it seemed almost funny, but Jess' condescending attitude toward his publishing company — and the growing rift between Jess and Alex — continued to rankle. The cause of the original problem was Sam's own failure to sign up as a writer with BMI, one of the two major performing rights societies charged with collecting songwriter's royalties (ASCAP was the other). The reason for the oversight was Sam's inability to put his own name on any of his songs until the resolution of his legal difficulties with Art Rupe. As long as those difficulties were ongoing, L.C., and then Barbara, had been assigned songwriting credits, and while Kags was a BMI company, and both L.C. and

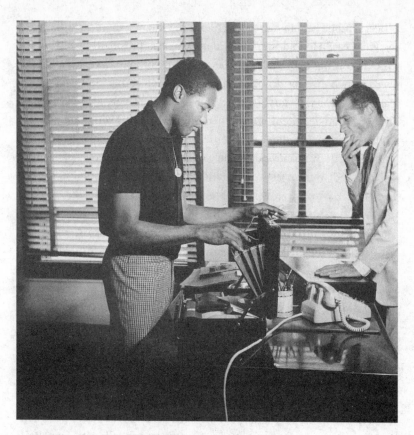

Sam and Jess Rand, ca. 1961. *Courtesy of Jess Rand*

Barbara had duly signed up as BMI writers, it was only after "Chain Gang" became a hit in the fall of 1960 that any real BMI money for Sam came due. That was when he and J.W. discovered, much to their consternation, that Sam was not an affiliated writer and, due to that lack of affiliation, had already lost almost $10,000 in performance royalties (money collected by BMI from radio, television, and any other public performance of his songs, which went into a common pool from which it could not be recovered if the songwriter was not already registered).

J.W.'s reaction was to simply go in and pick up the pieces. He had no interest in scapegoating or trying to assess blame. Jess, on the other hand, kept telling Sam, "We'll go in there and sue. Can you imagine all the writers that haven't gotten their money? We'll start a [class-action] suit." But J.W. had become friends with Dick Kirk, who ran BMI's West Coast office, "and he said to me, 'Look, Alexander, there's more ways than one to skin a cat.' He told me, 'Bob Sour (who was president of BMI at the time) is coming out in a few weeks, and I'm going to have a few friends over to my house for drinks, and I'd like you to come.' So I went, and I was telling Bob the story; I said, 'I'm Sam Cooke's partner, not his manager. It's been his intention to join all along. All of his songs are in BMI.' And he said, 'Why don't you come to New York? I'd like to see him [join].' So I drew money out of the company and bought myself a couple of suits and went to New York, and Bob Sour had George Marlo and Theodora Zavin [two veteran BMI executives] come into his office to meet me, and they worked out a fantastic deal."

What they offered, in a three-year agreement dated November 21, 1960, and taking effect on January 1, 1961, was what was termed a three-for-one deal. BMI offered to guarantee as an advance against royalties for 1961 150 percent of what Sam *would* have earned in 1960 if he had been a BMI-affiliated writer, including in their calculation of the theoretical base all sums earned by Barbara and L.C. as well. The minimum guarantees for 1962 and 1963 would similarly be figured on 150 percent of Sam's actual earnings in the preceding year.

J.W. brought the deal back to the Coast with understandable elation. "I was really thrilled, and I went over to Sam's house and was telling him about it, and he called Jess and said, 'Man, Alex has really got a good contract.' And Jess' answer was, 'I don't know, let me talk with Sam Reisman about it.' That was his lawyer, you know. I said, 'Sam, don't you make no fool out of me.' I said, 'I went and got you a good deal. I'm not your manager, but I'm your partner.' So he said, 'Give me those fucking papers.' Just like that. And he signed them. And that was the start of Jess Rand being out."

To Jess it wasn't that simple. He was used to Sam's secretive ways, and this was certainly not the first time Sam had gone behind his back. He had seen the way Sam had dealt with Art Rupe and outmaneuvered the Siamases, and he hadn't really been surprised when Bill Cook turned up in the fall of 1960 with a management contract that he said rendered Jess' invalid. Jess told him to take it up with Sam, and evidently he must have, because *Jet* magazine reported in its February 18, 1961, issue that the claim had been settled out of court for $1,500. But this whole publishing business, as Jess saw it, represented fundamental differences in philosophy and direction.

For Jess, who had started off in the business at fifteen out of a deep love for the popular songwriting tradition, ASCAP, which represented all the classic composers from Gershwin and Cole Porter to Harold Arlen and his first employer, Irving Berlin, was the one legitimate performing rights society. BMI, which had been in operation only since 1940 and had been founded as much as anything else to take up the spillover of "race" and "hillbilly" music, which ASCAP declined to license, was a kind of unregulated marketplace — and Sam's choice of what Jess deemed BMI's "fast money" over ASCAP's "more astute" long-term approach was a direct slap in the face to Jess' business judgment. There was a brief, bristling confrontation that appeared to be over almost as soon as it started, except that, knowing what he knew about Sam's brooding nature and Alexander's antagonism toward him, Jess was not altogether optimistic about the outcome. Still, there was nothing he could do about it, and if there was one thing he had learned from his long association with Sammy Davis Jr. and its bitter dénouement the previous summer, it was that "a contract with a client is only as good as your relationship with a client." So he gritted his teeth and simply accepted the fact that there were certain areas of Sam's life in which by definition — *Sam's* definition — he did not belong.

Sam and Alex for their part saw Jess as increasingly out of touch and out of step, like someone who was all too proud of his mastery of the fine points of a subject whose fundamental premise he did not understand. But J.W. counseled patience. "Sam realized he was selling, he wasn't buying," J.W. said. They both recognized the duality with which they had long since learned to live. "Sam's attitude," said J.W., "was give them what they're buying." But always keep something for yourself.

SAR was for Sam and Alex. By April they had put out four new singles and conducted a pop session with Johnnie Taylor, who had grown tired of the ministerial life. They put out their first album, too, *Jesus Be a Fence Around Me* by the Soul Stirrers, with a beautiful four-color cover shot by celebrated jazz photographer William Claxton. Shortly after the LP came out, J.W. got a call from Leonard Chess, whose Checker label had an extensive gospel line. He told Alex SAR was going to ruin the market for everyone else if they insisted on giving gospel music that kind of high-class treatment. "He bawled me out! But I told him, 'Look, Leonard, I was a gospel singer and Sam was a gospel singer, and everything we do is going to be treated with the same respect.'" It was an album of which they were both very proud. As J.W. quoted his partner in the album's liner notes: "Although I wrote 'Chain Gang' (one of the country's top hits), I thank GOD for the inspiration to write . . . 'JESUS BE A FENCE AROUND ME.'" Or, as Sam put it in another context, assigning at least as much credit to purposeful intent, "I am aware that owning a record company is a losing deal much too often for comfort. But this company of mine is concentrating on recording Negro artists I feel have the ingredients to become as successful as I have. [And if I] lose a few dollars along the way, in the end it'll be worth it to me. Morally, it's a worthwhile project."

"It was fun. It was family," said Zelda Sands (née Samuels), SAR's newest — and so far only — employee, who had come to work at $85 a week just after the start of the new year. She had arrived in Los Angeles not long before Christmas, looking for a music-industry job. A strikingly attractive, combative woman with the kind of figure that provoked both comments and stares ("I used to like to go over to her house and watch her tan," reflected one musician wistfully), she was a veteran of the music business in New York, where she had first met Sam when he was playing the Copa and she was trying to pitch him a song. Ed Townsend steered her to SAR's tiny office when she arrived on the West Coast, and she started making job calls from there, since the motel where she was staying didn't have a phone. J.W. was in and out, but she only saw Sam once, when he came in off the road and, recognizing her, asked if she had gotten married yet. "I said no, and he said, 'Good.' He said, 'You shouldn't be married.' 'Ever?' He said, 'No, you've got too pretty a smile!' I mean, he was always that way — with everybody.

"Then Christmas came, and I saw Sam again at the California Club. He asked how things were going, and I said I still hadn't found anything, and I was all alone 'cause I didn't know anyone in town, and I started to cry — I didn't expect to, but I did. And he said, 'Let me ask you something. How much would it take for you to pay your bills?' He said, 'Figure it out to the dollar.' And I did. I told him it would be $85 a week. And he said, 'Okay, you've got a job.'"

She went to work the following Monday, but the building superintendent had to let her in, because Sam and J.W. were both on the road. She quickly picked up the business, wrote label copy, did the paperwork for copyrights and clearances, dealt with pressing plants and distributors, and started writing songs with J.W. It wasn't about work as much as it was about being part of a team, working for two guys she loved and admired. "I had to teach them how to be bosses. I watched over them. I protected them." As far as she was concerned, Jess Rand wasn't even in the picture. "Other than Lou [Adler] and Herbie [Alpert] at social events, I was the only white person in their lives. I'd always yell at Alex, I'd try to teach him. Not about the business. He made sure he was knowledgeable in that. What he wasn't good at was people. He was nice to everybody, he believed everybody, I never heard him talk against anybody, and he [got] such a kick out of himself when he had all the right answers, he would just get tickled. But he didn't really want to make waves in a white man's world." She conceived of herself, she said, almost as a watchdog over their interests, and Alex for his part got a kick out of *that*. "She would call up the distributors when I was out of town," he chuckled, "and yell at them. 'You take advantage of Alexander,' she'd say. 'He's such a *good* person!'"

Sam she found a thornier problem, as much for personal as professional reasons — but her feelings about him were no less admiring. "He was very pretty to look at, he was charming, he was warm, he was handsome. He had a very good heart, always had his hand in his pocket to give people a few bucks if they were in need. He took you at face value — as long as you didn't hurt him. I know he would discuss everything with Alex. [But] there was a part of Sam — he could hold the final cards and not tell anybody anything. And if he caught you at something he didn't like, that he felt was dishonest, instead of talking it out [with you], he walked away from you forever."

To Sam and Alex both, SAR Records was clearly something more than just another business venture. As J.W. said, "We wanted to give young black artists the benefit of as good a production as they could get with a major company. We used the top studios. We didn't short-cut. We never thought of it as a training ground. We thought of it as an opportunity to contribute something back to the community."

LUIGI WAS FINALLY PERSUADED to come out to the Coast and record Sam, with René Hall writing the arrangements, in April. They had had another New York session when Sam was in town for the BMI awards, and the resulting single, like "Sad Mood" before it, sold no more than 150,000 copies, or one-quarter the sales of "Chain Gang." So, despite the fact that Hugo wouldn't be accompanying him (he didn't fly), Luigi cheerfully embraced the new arrangement, arriving several days early for what

362 | *Another Country*

he considered to be the most important part of any session, the pre-production planning.

They met at René's office, just around the corner from SAR, Sam, J.W., Luigi, and René. Luigi had never met René before, but he immediately felt comfortable with him, and he felt comfortable with the arranging ideas René sketched out for the two songs on which they were all agreed — which didn't seem substantially different from the arrangements that Sammy Lowe might have come up with if they had conducted the session in New York. What made them different was the input Sam had already provided prior to Luigi's arrival. It was the same input he had had on every session he had ever done with René — he would come in with a rough voice-and-guitar demo that he and Clif had put together, then dictate his arranging instructions as René played the song back on one tape recorder while recording both it and Sam's instructions on another. It always astonished René how "with no formal musical training whatsoever, Sam could hear the entire orchestra, the string lines, the bass lines, the horn lines and hum [the parts] in perfect harmony." Then René would bring the instructional tape to the studio — mainly so Sam couldn't give him a hard time about his blueprint not being followed.

Like Jess, Luigi discounted J.W.'s role, despite his business partnership, his presence, and his numerous songwriting credits. "He was very nice, very affable — but he didn't say anything. He stayed in the background." From J.W.'s point of view, he was simply glad to have gotten Luigi out to California. "[He] gave us respect. He was smart enough to know a good song and just stay out of the way."

The song that Luigi had picked for the hit this time was "Cupid," a number that Sam had first demoed for Kags in the Capitol studio in the summer of 1959. He had brought it to New York with him when he was playing the Apollo at the end of February, not to record it himself but because he and Alex both thought it might be good for Sandy Stewart, the girl singer on the television series hosted by Perry Como, another RCA artist produced by Hugo and Luigi. They were sitting in Hugo and Luigi's office with the demo still in J.W.'s briefcase when the two cousins played them some songs they had already cut on the girl. Sam and Alex didn't even have to look at each other to know that this was not the right singer for Sam's song. So Alex just handed Hugo and Luigi the demo and said, "Here's one you can cut on Sam."

The song was not all that different from "That's It, I Quit, I'm Movin' On," the last, non-Cooke-authored single Hugo and Luigi had picked for Sam — it was in a sense no less formulaic, it was, with its invocation of the urchin greeting-card god, certainly no less sugary and no less oriented to the white pop market. But it was written *by* Sam, it was accented *for* Sam, it fit his phrasing and intonation as precisely as "Chain Gang" and any number of his earlier hits, it was the perfect representation of a pop sensibility in its own way as keenly developed as Hugo and Luigi's but with a broader ambition, a greater sense of the way in which even the most inoffensive pop sounds can sometimes soar.

Luigi got ready to go into the studio on the morning of Friday, April 21, with "an old yogi trick" he had learned: "You lie down, and you think of nothing, and then you imagine the session and how well it's going, and how everybody's enjoying it a lot. Then I got up and I showered and I got dressed in black pants and a black shirt and a red Eisenhower jacket, and I walked into the studio and introduced myself to everybody. I said, 'I know you. I've heard you. I'm glad you're on the session.' So that kind of broke the ice, and then Sam came in and said, 'I got the best-dressed producer in the world.' [So] it worked!"

The session itself had an easy, relaxed feel — Luigi was happy with the atmosphere, and Sam seemed utterly at home and utterly unembarrassed about indulging the perfectionism that attended the apparent simplicity of even his most transparent compositions. The song opened with the mournful sound of a French horn set against the steady chording of Clif's rhythm guitar, an unusual voicing for an r&b number made even more unusual when the strings entered on the second chorus, and violins and French horn played a kind of muted call-and-response duet. The message of the song couldn't have been plainer as Sam sang in his sweetest voice, "C-u-upid, draw back your bow / And let / Your arrow go / Straight to my lover's heart / For me-e-e-e," with the verses set off from the chorus not just by their more clipped conversational style ("Now, Cupid, I don't mean to bother you, but I'm in distress . . .") but by the cantering calypso beat that Earl Palmer introduced with his drumming.

The first four takes were fairly straightforward, but on the fifth, Sam came up with an idea to dramatically underscore the lyrics. He had run into Bobbie and Kenneth Sims at the California Club the night before and asked them if they would be willing to sing backup on his session. The Sims twins were a gospel duo Alex had discovered singing pop (as

the Silver Twins) at a local club around Christmastime. Then he had gotten Sam to come out and listen to them singing in church, and they had
signed the brothers right after that to a SAR contract. Four months later,
though, he and Sam still hadn't figured out what to do with them, and
the twins were a little hesitant about going into the studio as backup
singers on a pop session without rehearsal or preparation. Sam told
them they wouldn't have anything to worry about, on one song all he
wanted them to do was to come in on a couple of lines of the chorus, and,
for the first few takes of "Cupid," that was all they did.

Then he asked if they thought they could imitate the sound of an
arrow in flight, and when they said they could, he had them duet on that.
Kenneth mimicked the sound of the arrow as it left the bow, Bobbie as it
reached its target, and when they did it each time at the conclusion of the
phrase "And let your arrow go," their harmony was so perfect in the
whoosh-and-thwack they created by pressing their lips to the microphone (it sounded a little bit like the air going out of a balloon), it might
just as well have been one person creating a single effect.

Sam went back to the control room, lit a cigarette, and turned his
attention to the playback, bending his head down and rocking back and
forth as he listened for something that engineer Al Schmitt was convinced nobody else could hear. Then he laughed, and they wrapped the
song in two more takes: the unexpected juxtapositions, the melancholy
sound of the French horn set against the jaunty Caribbean rhythms, the
almost ethereal loneliness of the vocal in stark contrast to the deliberate
plainspokenness of the words, the cartoonish sound effect from the
Sims Twins all creating a richness of texture that went almost unnoticed
but that represented exactly the *feel* that Sam was looking for.

Luigi was certainly pleased. He knew in his bones that this time they
had themselves a hit. There would be discussions down the line as to
how Sam thought the actual record should *sound*, Sam would suggest
that it might have more of a contemporary r&b flavor if Luigi placed
Sam's voice further back in the mix. Some of his friends had suggested
the idea to him, was the way he phrased it in a phone call several weeks
later. As Luigi recalled, "I said to him, 'Sam, do any of these friends of
yours make hit records?' And he said, 'No.' I said, 'Well, I do.' And that
was that."

The rest of the session was taken up with yet another version of
"Tenderness," Sam and J.W.'s 1959 adaptation of "Try a Little Tender-

ness," to which the Sims Twins contributed a harmonizing chorus. Sam and J.W. evidently continued to think that the song could be a hit given the right treatment, but Luigi didn't care. Sam could do whatever he wanted at this point as far as he was concerned. Luigi had what he had come for. At some point, Sam started fooling with "Soothe Me," a new song he had written that took off from the familiar folk melody "(Run Along Home) Cindy, Cindy." As he worked on it with the twins, though, he was so taken not only with their upbeat approach but with the super-charged energy of their vocals ("Just the two of them," said J.W., "had a sound like a whole group because of [their] overtones"), that he let them take over and, after they had turned the song inside out, asked how they would like to record it on their own as their SAR Records debut. Not surprisingly, Kenneth and Bobbie expressed unreserved enthusiasm for the prospect, and Sam promised them a session in June, as soon as some time opened up in his schedule.

TWO WEEKS LATER, after a brief series of engagements in Nassau and the Bahamas, he started on another Henry Wynn Supersonic tour, accompanied once again by such familiar performers as Clyde McPhatter and Hank Ballard and the Midnighters but with the addition this time of nineteen-year-old Aretha Franklin as well. Aretha, who had ended up signing with Columbia Records the previous summer, had already had two Top 10 r&b hits but was experiencing some of the same difficulties in making the transition from gospel to pop that Sam initially had. After a number of polite supper-club bookings, two consecutive one-week engagements with Sam at Baltimore's Royal and Washington's Howard Theater in March had provided her with her first extended exposure to the chitlin circuit. She was awkward and self-conscious onstage, and Sam did his best to help her, offering useful tips on where to stand, how to phrase, how to get across, while, on her own, she studied his show with unswerving dedication every night. It was plain to anyone who observed this gawky, almost coltish young mother of two, with her spectacular three-octave range and deep-set sorrowful eyes, that she was hopelessly in love with Sam — and had been ever since they first met at a Soul Stirrers' program at her father's church in Detroit. She gave up Kools for Kents, she liked to say, because Sam smoked Kents; she kept a scrapbook of clippings about him, going back to his earliest pop days, and even saved a crumpled cigarette package of his from the first time he had played the

Flame. She knew that if Sam had twenty girls in a room, each one would leave feeling that she was the only one — "he just made you feel like it was all about you." But she knew, deep down, it wasn't all about her. And so she asked L.C. to accompany her on the road.

She told him her father wouldn't allow her to take his '61 Lincoln out on the tour if L.C. didn't drive it for her. L.C. wouldn't have hesitated to accept, "but Sam didn't want me to. He said, 'Man, you're a star. I don't want you driving nobody.' He said, 'You got a career to think of. That's why I got Charles to drive me instead of you.' He fussed at me for a while, but then [after] I calmed him down, he said, 'Well, if that's what you want to do, go ahead and do it with your crazy self. You're going to do what you want anyway.' I said, 'Yeah, I am, Sam.' And he laughed. And I had fun on that tour, I had a good time with both my brothers and Aretha, too."

It was heavy competition onstage. Hank Ballard never failed to get the crowd going. And Clyde, who had started drinking more and more and was sometimes preoccupied with matters he shared with no one else, could still bring the audience to its feet with his delicate falsetto. But for Aretha "it was Sam's tour as far as I was concerned. He followed me, and he just wore people out, he wrecked every place that we went. He could stand on one leg and wipe you out. When he would come on, the building would just erupt."

There was a not dissimilar element of competition offstage as well. Sam, of course, always got his first choice of girls, but L.C. and Charles were not far behind, and L.C. saw it in many ways as a kind of family enterprise. One night Charles spotted a girl in the front row, "and he came backstage and said, 'C., boy, I saw a fine broad out there. I'm taking her home with me.' I said, 'Where she at?' And Charles pointed her out to me. Well, I went right up and stole her, fine as she was. You see, Charlie, once he whispered [into a girl's ear], you couldn't do nothing. But I didn't give him a chance to whisper. Another time on that same tour, I had a little dark girl, she was bow-legged, built, and had hair on her legs sticking all out of her stockings — she was *bad,* man, that little girl had everything. Well, Sam saw her and said, 'C., I like that girl.' You know what I did? I just took her hand and put it in Sam's hand and said, 'You got her, Sam.'"

Maybe that was what led Aretha to seek romance elsewhere after being out with the Cooke brothers for a little while. Even with the most "forgiving" attitude, it would have been impossible not to become aware that L.C. was no more likely to be faithful to her than his brother and, perhaps hoping to get the attention of both, she took up with Hank Ballard, who had made his feelings known from the start. "I fell in love with her when she had her first crossover, 'Today I Sing the Blues' — she sung the shit out of that song. Then, when I saw a picture of her in *Jet* magazine, I mean, she was superfine, I said, I got to have her. And, you know, I got her." But he was soon disillusioned not just by her obvious preoccupation with the entire Cooke family but with her drinking ("I found out she loved her I. W. Harper") and the burden of sadness that she bore. Like many people, he put that down to her father, the Reverend C.L. Franklin, who, despite his prominence in both the church and the civil rights movement, was widely perceived as a hustler, a "slick," who exerted undue influence on his daughter. The effect on Aretha, as Hank saw it, was that due to her "low self-esteem she was really into a lot of pain and shit, and I couldn't handle it." So he invited his wife, Helen, a candidate for her masters in education, to join him on the tour.

For all of her pain, Aretha's devotion to Sam never wavered. It wasn't as if he had promised her anything, and he always treated her with consideration and respect, throwing up a partition for her to dress behind when they played some of the field houses and gymnasiums where the entire troupe might share a single dressing room, never failing to address her particular fears and concerns. She continued to study the way he was able to hold a crowd, "the polish and the savoir faire [and] immeasurable charm onstage [that had] people just falling by the wayside." But she studied other aspects of his personality as well. "He was reading a book called *The Rise and Fall of the Third Reich* [a twelve-hundred-page history of Nazi Germany], so I went out and bought *The Rise and Fall of the Third Reich*, too. I never read it. I couldn't tell you today what was on page one or two. But because he had it, I wanted to have it."

His brothers were no less befuddled by Sam's reading habits. He was going to ruin his eyes, Charles told him, when Sam ordered a swivel light, like the kind they had on airplanes, so he could read in the car. It seemed as if he was determined to absorb everything all at once, magazines, newspapers, a book on slavery by the black historian John Hope Franklin, Tolstoy's *War and Peace, The New Yorker, Playboy,* and

Aristotle's *Poetics*. "We'd go into a drugstore," said Charles, "and Sam would come up to the counter with so many books people would be laughing. He'd get every magazine that was in there and then say, 'Take care of it,' and I'd have to stand there and take care of it." "He was," said the drummer June Gardner admiringly, "well versed on many subjects. He was aware of what was going on. He could sit down and explain himself." His thirst for knowledge had been with him since earliest childhood. It had always been something of a mystery to L.C., but it was one of the many things that made Sam different, that L.C. felt placed Sam on a higher plane not just from Charles and him but from almost anyone else out there. "Sam was more than me. Sam was a thinker. He could see the whole picture. He didn't go by anyone else. He did things exactly the way he wanted. He had the looks, the personality, the education — Sam had it all."

THEY ARRIVED IN MEMPHIS on the evening of Friday, May 12, at about 6:00 P.M., a couple of hours before the show was scheduled to start. There was a telegram waiting when they checked into the Lorraine Motel, just a few blocks from the auditorium. It was addressed to Clyde and had been sent by Jesse Turner, the president of the local NAACP, who would have been there himself, he explained, except that he was attending a testimonial dinner in his honor. The purpose of the telegram was to inform the entire troupe that in spite of all of the NAACP's efforts, seating for the show that night would be even more heavily segregated than usual, with Negroes restricted to the left side of the first, second, and third balconies, thus limiting not only sight lines and participation (there would be no coloreds dancing on the floor) but keeping their numbers to less than a thousand in a crowd of four thousand.

There was no doubt about where Clyde stood on the issue. He and Sam had had any number of discussions on the subject, both as it applied to the Movement and as it applied to what Clyde saw as their own status of indentured servitude in a business that was dominated by whites and governed by greed. But refusing to play a show to which you were contractually committed had any number of potential consequences, from the obvious legal and financial pitfalls to the one result no entertainer ever wants to contemplate, the alienation of a substantial portion of his audience.

Sam didn't hesitate in his reaction. If what the telegram said was true, the fuckers could do whatever they wanted, he said, he wasn't going to play. Shit like this was always happening to him in Memphis. The last time he had been in town, they had run out of gas, and he had sent Charlie to get some. While he was waiting for Charles to come back, a white policeman pulled up and told him to move the car. Sam explained the situation, but the policeman had no interest. "Well, push it, then," he said. Sam drew himself up to his full height. He was a singer, he told the policeman. His name was Sam Cooke, and he didn't push cars. If Frank Sinatra was there, he said, "you wouldn't ask him to push no car." Charles was back by now, trying to get his brother's attention, but Sam just shook him off. If it was all that important, he suggested to the policeman, "You push the fucking car. You may not know who I am," he said, "but your wife does. Go home and ask your wife about me."

Just like his father had taught him, he didn't ever take a backseat in his personal affairs; if he felt that he had been injured or wronged, you might just as well wait for hell to freeze over before he would back down from a direct confrontation. But public stands, his brothers were well aware, were another matter. Ordinarily Sam knew "just how far to push the buttons," said L.C. "And he knew what buttons not to push because it might hinder his career." This time he didn't give a fuck about his career, because, as Charles said, "we was right in the middle of it. Sam told me to go check it out, and when I came back and told him yes, [the auditorium] was segregated and all the blacks was up in the balcony, Sam said, 'Shit, forget it. Cancel it.'"

L. C. Bates, the publisher of the *Arkansas State Gazette*, who with his wife, Daisy, had bought the black weekly in 1941 "to carry on the fight for Negro rights" and had helped organize the 1957 school integration drive in Little Rock, arrived at just about this time to confer with Sam and Clyde in his official capacity as NAACP regional field secretary, which only solidified their resolve. Sam called Henry Wynn in Atlanta to let him know they would not be going on, then spoke to the local promoter, popular WHBQ DJ Ray Brown, "the Round Mound of Sound," who explained that the show had been advertised as part of Memphis' annual Cotton Carnival week, which by definition made it a predominantly white event. That was the reason for the seating policy, Brown said; it wasn't his personal decision. Sam had to be aware that there had never been a fully

L. C. Bates, Aretha Franklin, and Sam, Lorraine Motel, May 12, 1961. © *Ernest Withers. Courtesy of Panopticon Gallery, Waltham, Mass.*

integrated concert at Ellis Auditorium. Sam was unmoved by the argument. If there hadn't been one before, there ought to be one now.

Then he and Clyde hastily convened a meeting of as many of the other acts as they could assemble on short notice and tried to persuade them not to go on, either. "Sam asked everybody to come back to his room," said Midnighters guitarist Billy Davis. "He was explaining the seating, he said everyone was paying the same money and should have equal seats. Even if they wasn't together, even if one side was white and one side was black. But he said they wouldn't do it. So he [wasn't going to] go." Everyone listened politely, and Billy even hung around afterward to have a drink with Sam, but in the end no one else joined the two-man boycott, and Bill Murray, the show's MC, announced from the stage that Sam and Clyde had missed their flight connections. Meanwhile, at Jesse

Turner's testimonial dinner in the recreation room of the Universal Life Insurance Company, the local NAACP president let the room know "that Sam Cooke, singer and idol of thousands of teenagers, had just refused to fill an engagement before a segregated audience," the *Memphis World* reported, "[an announcement that] brought thunderous applause."

There was one more attempt at persuasion on the part of a by now infuriated white establishment. The police showed up at the motel. "Man, they locked us all in," said Charles indignantly, "because Sam wouldn't go on. They told Sam they was gonna confiscate his cars — we had the limousine and the station wagon. He said, 'Shit, you may lock me up, but you ain't gonna touch my goddamn cars.' He said, 'You let everybody enjoy the concert, and I'll gladly sing.' But he didn't back down. And they didn't take the cars, either."

The city's two white newspapers reported on the news with some bewilderment. "2 Negro Singers Fail to Appear," declared the *Press-Scimitar*, while the *Commercial Appeal*, describing the contretemps with somewhat more accuracy, ran a sub-headline that conceded, "Segregation Issues Cited by Performers." The show lost money, the *Press-Scimitar* was told, with only eleven hundred in the four-thousand-seat hall, "includ[ing] about 300 negroes."

Sam released his own statement to the Negro press, declaring that it was "against his policy and the policy of his promoter to play to a forced segregated audience. He added, 'This is the first time that I have refused to perform at show time simply because I have not been faced with a situation similar to this one.' He went on to say to a representative of the NAACP, 'I hope by refusing to play to a segregated audience it will help to break down racial segregation here and if I am ever booked here again it won't be necessary to do a similar thing.'"

THE NEWS FROM MEMPHIS was all over the Negro press as they finished the tour. "Singers Say No to Jim Crow Seats," was the headline in the *Amsterdam News.* "Top Singers Spurn Segregated Audience," "Singing Stars Balk at Memphis Jim Crow," "Clyde McPhatter, Sam Cooke Clip Memphis Bias" were some of the other headlines, as Sam submitted himself one last time, in a recording session in New York on May 19 and 20, to Hugo and Luigi's vision of crossover success.

The session was prompted by Ray Charles' first number-one pop hit the previous fall with a heavily orchestrated version of the 1931 Hoagy

Carmichael standard, "Georgia on My Mind." This was a far cry from Charles' own groundbreaking "I Got a Woman," and it gave Hugo and Luigi a new sense of a pop marketplace they had originally exploited by covering black records with a white sound. "You listen to ['Georgia']," said Luigi, "they're playing eggs in the background, everything is very vanilla, very white, and Charles is doing a soul thing [over it]. He captured the country with that, because he's doing their stuff his way. I thought, if we could get Sam accepted doing that, it would [add] another dimension to his career."

There was just one "little, knotty problem," though, as even Luigi recognized, and that was Sam's style, "which was so distinctive that you couldn't easily do [a standard like] 'Stardust' nice and plain, 'cause if you did, it wasn't Sam Cooke, and if he put his yodel into it, it interfered with what you thought 'Stardust' was." The further complication was that if you pushed Sam in a direction that went in any way against the tack that he had selected, you were faced with a quiet but insurmountable core of resistance. "One song he was singing — it was a legit song, with the strings and all that, and he very prettily sang, 'And I axe you.' I said, 'Hold it.' He said, 'What's the matter?' I said: 'I *ask* you.' He said, 'What did I say?' 'You said "axe."' And he was very obliging, and we came to the same part, and, 'I axe you.' I said, 'Hold it.' I went out and said, 'Sam, you said it again.' He says, 'You're taking away my heritage.' I said, 'Bullshit. This record is going out with your name *and* our name on it, and it's not going out with "axe".' And the third time he did it." But even Luigi knew it was a Pyrrhic victory.

The result in any case was not satisfactory from anybody's point of view, with the album that emerged, *My Kind of Blues,* no more Sam's kind of blues than the previous albums had been Sam's kind of folk, spirituals, or even travel songs. The paradox was not so much in the choice of material ("Sam Cooke has found the blues in the most unexpected of places," wrote Hugo and Luigi in the liner notes, explaining that it was Sam who had insisted on drawing from the songbooks of Gershwin, Ellington, and Irving Berlin) as in the happy-beat treatment that was given them. It was as if every song ended with a big smile, a flourish of horns, and an underlying message of accommodation, the opposite of Sam's own compositions, which, for all of their seemingly innocent charm, conveyed more of a sense of melancholy and regret than anything recorded under the catch-all of "blues" at this New York session.

The failure seemed predicated on the same misunderstanding that had plagued every other session that had taken place in RCA's New York studios, that Sam was like Hugo and Luigi's other artists, that the moving parts of a Sam Cooke hit were somehow or other interchangeable. Even the cousins were now willing to concede the point. "I guess we started listening closer," said Luigi, "and we came to the conclusion, This is what he feels. That's going to be the best direction. Not to impose a song that may or may not be a pop song but to know enough to smile and shut up."

Two WEEKS LATER, Sam was producing a Sims Twins session in the United Recording Studio in Hollywood. He and Alex had decided to take "Soothe Me" at a brisker clip after playing a demo for Imperial Records owner Lew Chudd, whose offices were across the hall from SAR's. Chudd, who artificially speeded up many of Fats Domino's releases as a matter of course, felt the song needed more of a push, and Sam and Alex agreed — though, as it turned out, Kenny and Bobbie Sims didn't need a push so much as a restraining hand, so great was their enthusiasm at finally being in the studio on their own. Sam coached them on their articulation, phrasing, harmony, dynamics, and pronunciation. He was in and out of the control booth, on the floor more often than not, coaxing, wheedling, correcting, guiding the singers and rhythm section to a performance that reflected the laid-back deliberate feel he was looking for and the perhaps not-so-deliberate echo of its author's own style. The twins didn't object. Twenty-three years old, the youngest of eleven children who had moved from Elba, Louisiana, to Los Angeles with their family when they were eleven, they were so attuned to each other's moods that they frequently finished each other's sentences, but their talent was not accompanied by a strong personal vision or direction. "That's a good job, a very good job, Kenny," said Sam enthusiastically as they neared the master take. "Do it just like that. Soothe me, baby!"

They had more trouble with the second number, "(Don't Fight It) Feel It," another of Sam's "situational" story songs with a repeated punch line, which he had been thinking of recording himself. Bobbie and Kenny kept messing up both phrasing and emphasis, and Sam's impatience becomes all too evident. "They won't understand you," he says in frustration as he coaches them on line scansion ("Don't fight it, *feel* it, you understand, Twins?"), and he kept after them about their artic-ulation ("Fellas, give me those words plain, don't give me those slurs") until they finally got a master take. Sam could console himself that this was only the B-side anyway. "Soothe Me" was the hit.

Sam and Alex threw a release party for Johnnie Taylor and all their other SAR artists at the California Club that same week. It was, accord-ing to reports in the Negro press, "one continuous floor show, featuring many top-flight performers," but it was Sam who brought the party to a climax when he "loosened his tie . . . and gave the crowd a show they will talk about for a long time to come. From the time Cooke took up the mike until the employees had to literally sweep the customers out at closing time, the entire audience was swept up in tune with the beat set by the dynamic singer." He sang the Brook Benton–Dinah Washington hit "A Rockin' Good Way" with the "exotic," light-skinned (and very blond) Mickey Lynn, performed an impromptu duet with Beverly and Betty Prudhomme, the white singing and songwriting team he had first met in the summer of 1957 (he sang "Exactly Like You," and first one glamorous twin, then the other, posed the question, "Exactly like me?," leaving Sam in an enviable quandary), and finished out the show with a medley of his biggest hits. There was a sense of almost palpable expecta-tion as Sam crooned "Wonderful World" to an audience made up of his closest musical protégés and friends. RCA had a full-page ad for "Cupid" in *Cash Box* that week, it seemed clear from the assembled collection of talent alone that SAR Records was on its way, and Sam was going to be the focus of a brand-new television show scheduled to debut on the Westinghouse network in a few days.

PM East/PM West was the brainchild of Jess' crazy friend Mike Sant-angelo. Jess had jumped the gun on announcing the appearance twice already, first when he planted the item about an upcoming interview with Mike Wallace back in October, then when the *Hollywood Reporter* ran a similarly unsourced note in December that Westinghouse television was "putting together an hourlong spec to star Sam Cooke with Mahalia Jackson." This time, though, it was for real, after Santangelo, an award-winning producer barely thirty years old ("Mike was a baby," said Jess, who had known him for almost a decade, "when he started as head of PR for Westinghouse, brilliant, unbelievably good-looking, always in the right place at the right time, crazy but a fucking genius"), finally hit on the right format for Sam, an offbeat, late-night show focusing on popular music and the arts hosted for its first hour by Wallace and Joyce Davidson in New York, then by *San Francisco Examiner* television columnist Terence O'Flaherty for its concluding thirty minutes. Santangelo had met Sam a year or two earlier through Jess and was sold on him from the start, but he couldn't figure out an angle until Jess, on impulse, took a glass from his desk and threw it on the floor. "What the hell was that?" said Santangelo. "That's the sound of broken glass," Jess replied, not quite sure where this was going. Santangelo stared at him quizzically. "That's the opening of your show," said Jess, with a PR man's flair for instantaneous invention, declaiming in a television announcer's voice, "Put on a Sam Cooke record, you're going to hear a one-million-dollar sound." And that, with some modifications, was the genesis of the show.

They spent a couple of days in New York rehearsing at the ABC studios on Sixty-seventh Street. The only other guests on Sam's segment of the program, now entitled "Sam Cooke: Phenomenon," were Hugo and Luigi and Jess himself, with Clif White leading a backup trio consisting of an upright bass player and top New York session man Panama Francis on drums. Sam showcased his new single and, including medleys, performed another ten or twelve numbers while easily fielding the puffballs that Wallace, ordinarily a combative interviewer, lobbed at him. Mike Santangelo had warned Sam in advance not to just sit there waiting for the next question, so Sam never let the conversation lag. He talked about some of the artists he had recorded recently — the Sims Twins, the Soul Stirrers, his brother L.C., and Johnnie Morisette — and spoke of the ambitious plans he had for his record company, laughing comfortably as Wallace asked for a thumbnail sketch of his life, and then providing it. He even jumped in when the interviewer was quizzing Hugo and Luigi about their role in the process. "I write some of the songs, too!" he said in that winsome way of his, and everyone laughed. All the men were dressed in business suits except for Sam, who was wearing a distinctively chic ribbed cardigan sweater. In the few stills that survive from the show, he appears attentive, alert, unquestionably *engaged* — but most of all he appears to be enjoying himself, as if somehow he can't quite believe that he and Jess are actually pulling this off.

For Jess it was a rare point of stillness in a relationship more often fraught with conflict and mistrust. One time late at night, he and Sam had been in the studio, each puffing silently on a cigarette, and they both caught their reflection in the window of the control-room glass. "Looks like an old black-and-white picture," Sam said to him in a moment of profound solemnity and profound casting off. That was a little bit the way it felt to Jess now, as though time hung suspended, all suspicion was erased, and he had momentarily earned Sam's full and unqualified trust. They went out to P.J. Clarke's after the show. Sam was carrying his guitar case, and as they walked in, some guy said to him, "What are you, a Freedom Rider?" Sam just looked at him and said, "That's funny, man." He said, "You're funny." And the way he said it, Jess knew if the guy opened his mouth again, Sam would gladly wrap the guitar around his head.

The reviews were uniformly glowing. This was "one of the few instances where a top Negro entertainer has been so honored by a network," the *Hollywood Reporter* observed, while *Billboard* pointed out that "for Sam Cooke, without doubt, the show was an unalloyed smash which should pay off where it counts most — at the record counter." Sam's manager and producers were among the contributors, the reviewer wrote, but "taking nothing away from [them], the show was best when Cooke was on camera. He proved a relaxed, likable, intelligent performer, with genuine magnetism," and the show itself was "apt to become a most sought-after promotional avenue for recording talent," based upon Sam's success. It was a great triumph for both manager and singer, a vindication in many ways for them both. With Jess in the midst of new contract negotiations with RCA, it seemed like it could only be a harbinger of things to come.

S AM OPENED AT THE FLAME in Detroit on June 16 for an extended ten-day run. The Cook family and Sam's friend Duck all came in from Chicago and took over the top floor of Sunnie Wilson's Mark Twain Hotel. No one missed Barbara. There remained a distinctly chilly feeling toward her among all the Cooks, along with deep suspicion of her motivation. Sam didn't even bother to tell them that his wife was three months pregnant, with the baby, Tracey, just nine months old. He had told Barbara she could come out on the road with him anytime she liked, but it wasn't easy for her now, obviously, since he had sent her Grandmother Beck home to Chicago. Maudie Beck, her mother's mother, had come out to Los Angeles around Christmastime to help with the children, but Sam found out that she was a drinker and told her he couldn't trust her with them. "Don't make no difference to me, son," she said. "You sent for me, I didn't send for you." Which gave Barbara a big laugh but left her stranded when it came to joining her husband on the road. Because packing up the kids was tough, and she knew she couldn't expect any help from him.

On the weekend of June 23, the Womack Brothers, a teenage gospel group from Cleveland, arrived in Detroit in a 1957 Dodge driven by their father, Friendly, a steelworker and sometime barber who served as their manager. They had come to town to talk with Sam about the possibility of a recording contract. The group was made up of nineteen-year-old Friendly Jr. and Curtis, Bobby, Harry, and Cecil, ranging in descending order from age seventeen to thirteen. They had originally met Sam when the Soul Stirrers played Temple Baptist Church in Cleveland nine years earlier and Sam had insisted that they be included in the program over the objections not just of the Temple Baptist minister but of Soul Stirrers manager S.R. Crain as well. He had even taken up a collection for them at the conclusion of their performance, and, after the congregation came up with $72, he had thrown in $28 of his own to make it an even $100. The Womack Brothers had played on other Cleveland programs with the Soul Stirrers and Pilgrim Travelers over the years, but it was Sam's old friend Roscoe Robinson, whom he had known ever since the Highway QCs' first program in Gary, Indiana, in 1948, who tipped Sam to the idea of recording them.

Roscoe had taken over the lead for the Five Blind Boys of Mississippi when Archie Brownlee died the previous year. "The Blind Boys were like members of our family," said Bobby Womack, the middle brother. "They used to stay with us. My mother would cook for them, and they would just lay around until it was time to do the gig. We were saying, 'Roscoe, we trying to get a record. We been singing all these years, but we ain't never gonna be established unless we start recording.' So Roscoe says, 'You remember Sam Cooke?' And we say, 'Remember Sam Cooke? Yeah.' And he said, 'He's my partner. I should call him and see if he remembers you.' We all thought he was jiving and we were listening in when he called. First thing he says, 'Sport, this is Sco. I think I got some-thing for you.'"

Sam told Roscoe he remembered the group well. "He said, 'They was bad, them little boys. Can they still sing?' I said, 'Can they still sing? They worse than that, man. Now they want to holler at you!'" So he told

The Womack Brothers and their father. Left to right: Bobby, Friendly Sr. (father), Curtis, Friendly Jr., Harry, Cecil. *Michael Ochs Archives.com*

Roscoe to put together a tape, and, after he heard it, he called Roscoe from the road. " 'You right,' he said. 'They really *can* sing. Just help them get some material together and meet me in Detroit. We gonna *discuss* this.' "

The Womacks caught up with Sam in his suite at the Mark Twain on Saturday afternoon. They had been in town since the previous evening but didn't know how to get in touch with him. They ran into Sensational

Nightingales lead singer June Cheeks in the lobby of the shabby hotel where they were staying six to a room for $3, but he wouldn't give them any information about Sam because, they concluded, he was looking to score some money for himself and was afraid they might get there first. Then, when they finally got a call from Sam, they had to sit around his hotel room for a while before he emerged with a friend named Duck and his brother L.C. He was friendly, but he kept writing down things in a spiral notepad as they sang the three songs that they had prepared with their father and one that Roscoe had given them. L.C. sidled up to Bobby while they anxiously awaited Sam's verdict. "Y'all bad, man," he said. "My brother gonna do you right." They didn't believe him, though, until Sam himself said he wanted to cut them: could they meet him in Chicago in four days?

It was a thrill, said Bobby, but at the same time, it was something of a disappointment, too. "We said, 'Oh, man, we thought you was gonna bring us to California.' He said, 'Yeah, but it'll be closer for me to cut you in Chicago. And it'll be cheaper, too.'" Their father, who had seen Sam's departure from the gospel world as betrayal, had reservations of his own, but there wasn't much he could say. "Sam was just a likeable person," said Bobby. "I mean, he made you like him without even trying. Because as big as he was, he made you feel like, Damn, he don't seem standoffish. I feel like I been knowing this guy all my life." And no matter what the preachers might say about how God was going to cut him down, you only had to look at him to see, "This guy ain't going nowhere. He looks healthy to me!"

Sam gave them a contract on the spot. He told them to look it over if they wanted, but it was a fair deal, as good as anyone starting out in the business would ever get. They were hardly about to go out and hire themselves a lawyer, but Bobby and his brothers agreed they shouldn't look too eager, so they took the contract back to Cleveland with them "and put marks on it to get it real dirty and funky" so it would appear to have been carefully reviewed. "Then our dad called Alex, because they was both high up in the Masons, and I remember, they made some secret signs, and he told Alex, 'I don't know about Sam, but I'm looking for you to be responsible for my boys.' And we signed."

Meanwhile, Sam quizzed his brother and Duck about the group they had just listened to. Which was the better singer, he asked them: Curtis, who took the majority of the leads, or his rougher-voiced younger brother Bobby? "Sam said, 'Which brother do you like, C.?' I said, 'Shit, man, no contest. Curtis.' And Duck said the same thing. Sam laughed, and he said, 'You like Curtis, because he sings pretty, like me.' I said, 'You're damn right.' But Sam said, 'Now let me show you something about Bobby. It's different when you close your eyes and listen. When Bobby sings, he demands attention — whether you like him or not, you're going to listen to him.' He said, 'Bobby is the star of the group, you just watch.'"

THE WOMACKS SHOWED UP in Chicago on Wednesday, June 28. Sam put them up at the Roberts Motel, where he stayed whenever he was in town. The session was booked at the Universal recording studio in the evening, after Sam had finished a full day of promotion work for "Cupid," which had already outsold any of his previous RCA releases except for "Chain Gang." They started off with "Couldn't Hear Nobody Pray," a showcase for Bobby's throaty, almost pinched lead vocal, then took up "Somewhere There's a God," the number Roscoe had written for them, which featured Curtis singing lead and sounding as close to Sam as an eighteen-year-old not fully in control of his voice could do. Sam coached him a little on his phrasing and diction, but after five takes, he pronounced himself satisfied and then asked if they would background him while he altered one word in the song. Clif chorded discreetly behind him, and the Womacks sang the same exact backup that they had for Curtis on "Somewhere There's a God," but the song was wholly transformed as Sam sang a romantic ballad called "Somewhere There's a Girl."

It was more than just a single word — but not much. There was a sense of yearning altogether different from the feeling of the gospel number, and the Womack brothers stood almost transfixed at the change. What gave it its special feel, Bobby thought, was that Sam was singing not about some real-life girl but about the *perfect* girl, an idealized girl. "You know, 'Somewhere there's a girl, and she'll know everything about me.' And he was talking about, 'She knows when I'm right, she knows when I'm wrong' — this perfect girl, the one that's gonna be the one." He did just one take but appeared to be very moved by it, and when he got back in the booth, he announced excitedly to L.C., "I don't have to hear that back. I'm gonna do it. I'm gonna release that." Whether or not he was entirely serious, it was an object lesson to the Womack brothers, a simple demonstration of how easy it would be to switch over.

Whatever his vision of a perfect girl and a cloudless future, Sam got in trouble again when he played Dayton four days later. There had been a "bastardy" warrant out for his arrest in Cleveland since January 27, 1958. It was over the little girl, Denise, whom he had fathered in 1953 just two days before Linda was born, and for one reason or another, it had never been served. Now it was, when he played Wampler's Arena on July 2 — and, after pleading guilty through counsel and making a motion for a blood test to prove paternity, he was forced to put up a $1,000 appearance bond before he could move on to the next show.

They worked hard all through the summer, one-nighters mostly in the Northeast and Southeast but in the Midwest, too, stopping off in New York long enough for him to record "Feel It," the song he had put out on the Sims Twins, once it became clear that their version, the B-side of the 45, was not going to get any airplay. "Soothe Me," the A-side, was just beginning to break into the charts, so he set up a session for the twins to record "I'll Never Come Running Back to You," the Sam-and-Alex collaboration that had served as Johnnie Morisette's debut on the label, as the substitute B-side on a reconstituted single.

Barbara had joined him on the road by now. She was almost five months pregnant and determined to give him a boy. She knew how much that would mean to Sam, and she thought maybe that could solidify her position with her husband once and for all. But she really didn't know. He had been acting more and more strangely toward her since he had seen her leaving June Gardner's room by herself on the last tour. She liked June, he was dear to her heart, but she and June and Sam's brother Charles had only gotten together to smoke some good weed, and then Charles had to go and take care of something about the cars, and when she emerged from June's room, Sam happened to be coming down the hall just at that moment. He blew up and as much as accused her of cheating right then and there. She drew herself up to her full height and said he was judging her by his own standards, did he think she was *crazy*, did he really think she was that low and immoral — but he sent her home on the spot and would probably have fired June, too, had it not been for Crain's intervention. Ever since, he had muttered dark accusations about the paternity of her unborn child and made her feel like she was on some kind of damn twenty-four-hour watch on those rare occasions when she traveled with him.

Lithofayne Pridgon came to see him when he played Newark on

August 12, because she had heard Barbara was out with the show. Never one to subscribe to the picture-postcard view of life, she was curious as to just what kind of woman a footloose man like Sam could be married to, but she didn't get much of a chance to find out because she spent most of the evening running back and forth between the dressing rooms of the two stars. The show had been advertised as the "Big Rhythm Show of '61," and at the top of the bill, it pitted an elegantly tuxedoed, neatly afroed Sam against a drape-suited James Brown with his customary and spectacular processed pompadour. Brown was very much on the rise in the world of rhythm and blues (he was about to have his third straight Top 10 r&b hit in 1961), but it was his explosive stage show, his breathtaking dance routines and unmatchable theatrics, along with his tireless dedication to the road, that had long since earned him the sobriquet of "The Hardest-Working Man in Show Business." There couldn't have been a greater disparity of styles between the two performers, and there was real resentment on James' part, not so much due to any overt action of Sam's as to the combative view of someone who had come up the hard way and could only imagine that Sam, with his looks, education, and infuriating air of sophistication, must be looking down on him. He was not in any case going to surrender top billing — to *anyone* — and he made a big fuss about who was going to close the show, getting right up in Sam's face and seemingly almost disappointed when Sam, who had evidently learned his lesson on the 1959 Jackie Wilson tour, said he'd be glad to go on first.

Lithofayne, who knew both men well ("James was a good friend, that's all"), was drafted by Brown toward the end of the show after people started calling for Sam and he still hadn't gone on. "James asked me to go over and feel the situation out, and when I hit the door, Sam said, 'Hey, Chinese-y' — that was what he called me sometimes — but it didn't seem like he was in any big hurry. So I played it off and went back and told James what was going on, and eventually Sam ambled out — but then he wouldn't get off, he just kept singing and singing and tore that stadium up, and James could [hardly] go on." She was neither shocked nor wholly unsurprised by Sam's actions, but she did get her look at Barbara, and she got a big laugh out of the way Sam had outwitted James and landed, like Bre'r Rabbit, right in the briar patch.

This was how he earned his living, he told the *New York Sunday News.* He was gone two months out of every three, maybe more, but this wasn't the way it was always going to be. He didn't speak of civil rights or racial issues, though they were never far from his mind. He couched his ambition in business terms that anyone could understand. "I want to sing," he told reporter Don Nelsen, "until I have enough money to invest in something else. I own two music publishing companies now. When I get a little older, I'd like to leave the singing to the younger fellows."

For now, though, he was doing his best to improve his own situation. Jess Rand had been negotiating with his friend Bob Yorke, RCA's new a&r head, for months now, but the tone had turned increasingly bitter. "I feel that we left our discussions in New York somewhat unresolved," Yorke wrote in June, "[but] I cannot help but feel that you prefer it this way. . . . I have tried, Jess, to be fair, honest, and direct with you. I have to confess my uneasiness about the future; but I am virtually out of suggestions on how to proceed."

What Sam wanted, Jess worried, was more than the market in which he found himself could bear. Sam wanted quarterly royalty statements, a greater amount of money upfront, higher monthly payments, a higher royalty rate, and a lump sum that would allow him to buy a house, since with the new baby the apartment was going to be too small. "Bob Yorke knew I wasn't [necessarily] for the way Sam wanted to proceed. But Sam was my client, and I said, 'Bob, I'm just doing what my client wants me to do. Bottom line, it's Sam's decision. That's the way it has to be.'"

In the end, they came up against favored-nations clauses in other RCA recording artists' contracts, particularly Elvis Presley's: for that reason, Jess convinced Sam, there was no way they were going to get a royalty rate higher than 5 percent — and neither Capitol nor Atlantic, the only other companies even considered, were going to give them that. After a while, Jess began to worry that it was starting to feel like liar's poker. "So finally I called Bob and said, 'Let's make a deal. We can trim some if you want, [but let's] get it done.' And I got a lot of things for Sam."

What he got as of the middle of September was a cash advance of $30,000 (nonreturnable but recoupable against artist's royalties) and monthly payments of $1,875, adding up to a recoupable sum of $22,500 a year for the two-year duration of the contract, with that amount doubled for the third year if the option was picked up. Sam's songwriter's royalty was increased from $.015 to $.02 per side, unless RCA opted to advertise the single with a color sleeve. And only LP recording session costs — not singles sessions — would be charged against Sam's account. Plus Jess got an off-the-books commitment on RCA's part to help with Sam's house if and when he located one — if only with some of the furnishings, a color television and sound equipment that could come from the RCA line of products. Sam felt he should have gotten more, and Luigi agreed that despite his track record as a consistent hitmaker, Sam was being taken for granted. Still, it was a reasonable resolution for both parties, and Sam directed RCA to send the $30,000 advance to his manager, because, Jess assumed, Sam didn't want Barbara to know his business.

At the same time, unbeknownst to Jess, Sam and Alex were preparing once again to go to court. The lawsuit that they had filed against Keen eighteen months earlier for all royalties accrued (artist, songwriter, and publishing) since the settlement in December of 1959 had so far done little but prompt more filings and counterfilings. With the failure by Keen to pay anything toward the $13,000 cited in the March 1960 filing, Sam's continued catalogue sales, and the enormous success of "Wonderful World," there was now a good deal of money at stake, but Sam and Alex were no longer looking for money; their aim was nothing less than ownership of Sam's Keen masters. Like the protracted battle with Specialty, it had to do with issues of fairness and artistic control, but equally important, J.W. felt, was that they be taken seriously as *businessmen*, that the music world understand that, nice guys or not, he and Sam were going to assert their rights, just like RCA or any other music manufacturer.

"Soothe Me," by the Sims Twins, continued to build momentum. It hit first in New Orleans, and *Cash Box* reported that the record was breaking nationally in the same September 9 issue that included a full-page ad for Sam's new RCA release, "Feel It." Two weeks later, SAR Records ran its own tiny ad for the Sims Twins, with the single word "Tremendous" festooned with nine exclamation marks, while the record itself was listed at number twenty-eight on the "Looking Ahead" chart and was inching ahead of Sam's single in actual sales. Alex put the twins with Sam's agent, Dick Alen, at Universal Attractions, who took them on strictly as a favor and promptly booked them into the Regal with LaVern Baker. Bobbie and Kenny Sims took it all in stride. "Being on the road wasn't about nothing but singing and making money," they concluded. "That's it."

In the wake of the Sims Twins' success, SAR Records scheduled a flurry of sessions and moved into new quarters just down the hall from the cramped space they had inhabited up until now. Sam and Alex would each have his own office, and Zelda was given a free hand in decorating the entire four-room suite, picking out a coral-and-white desk for herself against a coral wall, while Sam's office provided a stark study in contrasts, with one black wall and one white and plush black-and-white drapes. She was determined, she said, to let her natural antipathy to bureaucratic decor run wild.

Sam asked Bumps to produce a session on their one female artist, Patience Valentine, in Los Angeles on September 20, over J.W.'s strenuous objections. Bumps was still busy trying to break the gospel sound on the nightclub circuit. His show, *Portraits in Bronze,* with New Orleans gospel singer Bessie Griffin, had become something of a cabaret hit in Hollywood, and this past spring he had even taken it to Vegas. He cut three sides on Patience, one of them cowritten by J.W. and Zelda, but his attitude, J.W. felt, was insufferably condescending, as he lectured Alex with a convert's zeal on the commercial promise of the gospel sound — all the while acting as if he were the one doing *them* a favor. "Sam was always trying to do something to help Bumps," J.W. reflected philosophically, "and Bumps read it the wrong way. He figured that we needed him, that we were coming to him in trouble, you know," and, the way J.W. saw it, Bumps fully expected eternal gratitude as his reward for a record that wasn't going to sell two copies.

One reason Sam had given the producer's job to Bumps was that he was in Chicago with Alex, supervising a Soul Stirrers session on the same day. He had persuaded Leroy Crume that writing gospel lyrics to the melody of "Soothe Me" could provide them with the follow-up they had been looking for to "Jesus Be a Fence Around Me." Crume wrote the song, it was a catchy melody, but with "Soothe Me" rapidly rising in the charts, now he wasn't so sure. Sam waved aside his objections, they'd wait until "Soothe Me" had had its run — did Crume think that Sam lacked all common sense? — but three weeks later, "Lead Me Jesus" was the A-side of the Stirrers' new single, and one month after that, Crume was facing a very angry Herman Nash, the longtime Atlanta promoter, at the Municipal Auditorium. "When we got there, he was just standing out on the steps, didn't say hello or nothing, just said, 'Crume, why in the world did you guys do that?' I said, 'Do what?' He said, 'You all recorded a rock 'n' roll song.' I said, 'No, man, we didn't record a rock 'n' roll song.' He said, 'Well, it's just *like* a rock 'n' roll song. It's not gonna work, man. You guys used to be number one around here, but you can forget it, you might get booed off the stage.'

"Well, I put on my little happy face and told Nash, 'Don't worry, everything's going to be all right,' but, man, I was so scared. I took Jimmie Outler, our lead singer, in the dressing room and said, 'Jimmie, let's don't even touch that song. Just sing one line and let's walk.' And that's just what we did, and, man, the crowd went crazy, and Nash came up to me and said, 'Damn, you guys can do anything.' I said, 'I told you not to worry.' But we didn't go back out onstage. I didn't want to press our luck." And in the back of his mind, Crume could hear Sam saying, "I told you, fucker. Didn't I tell you?" And, as always, he had no reply.

The business with Keen, too, came to a fortuitous conclusion of its own while Sam was still on the road. On October 16, judgment was delivered in California Superior Court that the plaintiffs were owed $11,000 and that according to a compromise agreed to by all parties, "this judgment is granted and is expressly conditioned upon the condition that plaintiff will satisfy the judgment by levying on and causing the sale of [Sam Cooke's] master recordings [in] Full Satisfaction of Judgment regardless of the price realized on such sale." In other words, Sam and Alex could reasonably expect to be able to purchase the masters for the money that they were owed. Three days later seven cartons of Keen master tapes were taken away by the sheriff's office in preparation for the stipulated sale.

In the meantime, Sam had found a new home. Through his friend Lowell Jordan, a sometime songwriter, assistant engineer, and "technical advisor" on SAR sessions, J.W. discovered that the house of renowned Hollywood soundman Glen Glenn, who had died in an automobile accident the previous August, was being sold at probate. Through another of Lowell's connections at the court, Alex had been able to determine the high bid submitted to date, and on October 27, Sam and Barbara's higher bid of $58,250, offered through Sam Reisman's law office with a $6,000 down payment, was accepted.

It was exactly the kind of house both Sam and Barbara had always dreamt of, the "mansion" they had fantasized about as teenagers and the "Hollywood home" Sam had described with such vividness in his earliest interviews that reporters for the black press could not help but believe that he already lived in one. It was a sprawling, vine-covered, cedar-shingled Cape with a swimming pool in the front, a four-car garage, a children's playhouse, a small living room with a fireplace and a much larger one with floor-to-ceiling speakers that Glen Glenn had used for his movie work. There was a little house out back that Barbara thought they could turn into a guesthouse but that Sam was determined to have as his own rehearsal room and studio. It sat on close to three-quarters of an acre of land and was located at 2048 Ames in the exclusive, virtually all-white section of Los Feliz below Griffith Park. To Linda, just eight years old but with a precociously adult view of life, it was both a fairy-tale castle and a frighteningly austere setting, separated from the world she had always inhabited by figurative moats and all-too-real obstructions. "I think for him and the time and the stature of what he was building to, it was something that was very important. But, you know, [for me] we went from this warm, sweet little neighborhood, where you know the people next door and you have friends down the street, to this very isolated, insulated home, with everything closed off. You just don't see people walking past anymore or holler at your friends. When you're young, you know, it's different."

Alex got the Keen master tapes at the sheriff's auction on November 1. Sam was in Puerto Rico, booked for two weeks into the exclusive El San Juan Hotel right after Nat "King" Cole had played there, when Alex called with the news. As it turned out, he had had to pay $13,000, $2,000 beyond the stipulated judgment, because for some reason Imperial Records owner Lew Chudd had decided to bid against him. But he was confident they could get the $2,000 back, and, in fact, recover the full $13,000, from RCA or some other interested party.

There was no love lost at this point between Keen Records owner John Siamas and Sam Reisman, the lawyer who had taken up Sam and Alex's cause. Siamas bore no ill will toward Sam and Alex themselves, but he and his lawyer John Gray (who was also a principal in the record company and John Siamas' best friend) both felt Reisman had treated them with disdain from the start, as if they were small-time crooks, not well-intentioned businessmen, with neither recognition nor sympathy for their plight. They took consolation, though, from the fact that Reisman, who had insisted on the sheriff's sale, the bureaucratic equivalent of having them led away in handcuffs, didn't seem to fully comprehend the limitations of this kind of forced auction — which John Gray and

John Siamas definitely did. All that Sam and the Kags Music Corporation were acquiring was the physical property, the seven cartons of master tapes offered at the sale, along with the right to manufacture and sell records made from those tapes. The sale could not affect the licensing agreements that Keen Records already had with EMI in Great Britain, France, Germany, and numerous other territories, nor would it necessarily prohibit John Siamas or his corporate entity, Rex Productions, from licensing reference copies of the master tapes that he had retained — and that were never mentioned in the judge's order — to unnamed other parties in future. "They bought what they bought," John Siamas declared with some measure of satisfaction to his son. "And what they didn't buy they didn't buy."

J.W. wasn't thinking about any of this. What he was thinking about was how to get RCA to purchase the masters from them. He and Sam gave some thought to putting out the records on SAR, but they quickly decided that their own company wasn't big enough to fully exploit the value of Sam's old masters. They couldn't get RCA to show any interest, though, and Jess Rand didn't seem able to get his friend Bob Yorke to make them an offer, advising J.W. that he should just approach the record company himself, hat in hand, as Alex saw it, and more or less beg the label to take the masters off his hands.

So J.W. suggested that they release one record on SAR, and they settled on "Just For You," the Latin-flavored number they had cut at their own expense in the summer of '59, backed with "Made For Me," one of Sam's favorites. J.W. was sure "Just For You" would get lots of attention. He was equally sure RCA would never realize that much of the attention would stem from the fact that it had never been released before and, since it was not a Keen master, was not even one of the titles RCA would be acquiring.

By three o'clock on the afternoon that he had a batch of DJ promo copies pressed up, J.W. said, "I had a dub on KFWB. Then I sent one airmail special delivery to San Francisco and one to Minneapolis — they had a sister station to KFWB there." Despite the fact that there were no copies for sale to the general public, the record was reviewed in both *Billboard* and *Cash Box*, and *Cash Box* ran an item informing the trade that Sam and J.W. had bought back all of Sam's Keen masters, including an unspecified number of previously unissued sides, for release on their own label. It was then, J.W. said with a laugh, that RCA finally called, and at that point, after eliciting his price of $13,000, he pulled the record off the air.

S AM AND BARBARA PREPARED to move into their new house at the beginning of December. Barbara was due in a couple of weeks, and they didn't have anywhere near enough furniture, so Jess put them in touch with a pair of interior decorators, and his wife, Bonnie, once again helped Barbara out. Jess and Bonnie's little boy was nearly a year old now, and Jess was managing a new white vocal group, the Lettermen, who had a big hit with "The Way You Look Tonight," even as his latest signing, a veteran "girl group" called the Paris Sisters, had an even bigger one, the Phil Spector–produced "I Love How You Love Me." Jess' movie-production company had fallen apart with the sudden death of his partner, actor Jeff Chandler, earlier in the year, but as Sam saw it, his manager still had plenty to offer not just in the way of show-business connections like Michael Santangelo, who kept trying to get Sam interested in a new gospel-based show called *Black Nativity* he was putting together, but in the kind of solid new booking opportunities that were bound to open up through his clean-cut young white groups.

Sam was in and out as the house took shape. "It was really a project," his daughter Linda recalled. "The house was just completely torn apart and renovated. He was on tour a lot, and he would have to come back and deal with the decorators. His favorite spot that he did was his bar [decorated] in silver dollars and black formica and mirrors, with all of his special glasses and martini stirrers and things. He taught me to make special drinks. Crème de cocoa and milk — *that* was my drink!"

The Denise Somerville paternity suit was finally resolved in an out-of-court settlement on December 4. With the blood test he had taken providing inarguable evidence that he was indeed the father, Sam agreed to pay $5,000 for all maternity and child care expenses to date plus court costs and $15 a week until his daughter reached the age of eighteen.

Barbara gave birth to a son fifteen days later, on December 19. They named him Vincent Lance Cooke, and Sam told everyone how happy he was, but Barbara thought it would have been nicer if he could have taken her to the hospital himself or spent a little more time with her before and after their son was born. Instead, he was in the RCA studio with that little Italian producer of his both the night before and eight hours after Vincent's noon delivery at University Hospital. And then he was back in the studio with J.W. the following afternoon to try to get those goofy Sims Twins a follow-up hit. She saw more of her sister Beverly (who had recently moved out to Los Angeles with her two boys) than she did of her husband, and when she saw him, he just looked at the baby like he couldn't believe it was his. It was true, Vincent was a pretty little boy — he was very light and very plump with big ears and a full head of brown fuzzy hair — but he didn't look like either of the girls; if she was honest, she would have had to admit he didn't look like he belonged. And Sam's eyes bored into her with an accusation that didn't have to be spoken for her to know what was in his mind.

L UIGI HAD FLOWN out to the Coast to record the new song Sam had played for him over the phone. The Twist had been all the rage among the kids for well over a year now, but it had suddenly taken off with the "society crowd" at the Peppermint Lounge in New York City, and Chubby Checker's version of the Hank Ballard original was well on its way toward achieving the number-one pop position for the second time in sixteen months, while Joey Dee's "Peppermint Twist" was also heading toward the top of the charts. Sam happened to catch a television show one day featuring scenes from the Peppermint Lounge. "Look at those old ladies dressed in diamonds, twisting away," he said in amusement to J.W., then took out his notepad and wrote a song.

"Let me tell you about a place / Somewhere up in New York way / Where the people are so gay / Twistin' the night away," it began, moving on to a description of the scene itself:

> Here's a fellow in blue jeans
> Dancing with an older queen
> Who's dolled up in her diamond rings
> Twistin' the night away
> Man, you ought to see her go
> Twisting to the rock 'n' roll
> Here you find the young and old
> Twistin' the night away

Like nearly every one of Sam's songs, it was so simple, both lyrically and melodically, as to defy analysis — but so carefully put together at the same time, so perfectly matched in meter, melody, and rhyme as to be instantly memorable and, once heard, virtually unforgettable. For all of the self-evident silliness of its subject, Sam probably put more of himself into this number, to which all of the first night's session was devoted, than into any of his previous RCA efforts. To the casual observer, there was little evidence of any unnecessary expenditure of energy. Indeed, in Walter Hurst's eccentric account it was all about "getting the musicians used to the song arrangement and sound. . . . Sam Cooke's knowledge of music makes it easy for him to tell René Hall what he wants, and Mr. Hall, whose hobby is electronics, can easily communicate with the A&R man [Luigi]." Sam himself got an obvious boot out of the usual hand-picked band, which included the masterful Earl Palmer on drums, Jewell Grant anchoring the rhythm section on baritone sax, and Jackie Kelso taking the tenor solos. But the real push came from Sam, whose vocal strained against the beat and gained in emphasis and enthusiasm with each successive take.

No one would have compared it to gospel in either subject matter or format, but it harkened back to some of Sam's most spirited moments with the Soul Stirrers in two essential ways: the skillfulness of its story-telling and the fervor with which the story was told. Sam purposefully roughened his voice at times to convey an excitement that seems almost at odds with his reportorial technique. "We're gonna do one more right away," Luigi announced over the PA after the sixth take, "'cause you got the spirit about the second half." "All right. Got the spirit, huh?" said Sam sardonically. But he threw himself into a seventh take, which did, indeed, turn out to be the master — after Sam directed an overdub of hand claps and a chorus calling out what sounds like a cross between football signals and dance commands that was built into his original conception of the song.

Most of the same musicians were back in the United Studio at three o'clock the next afternoon for the Sims Twins session. Sam and Alex had brought in three strong originals, the Simses had been working steadily and were booked into the Tivoli in Chicago as headliners the following week — everything was right, in other words, for a repetition of their previous success, but the session just didn't catch fire. There was no lack of electricity in the air, everyone was up, and Zelda (who had a cowrite with Alex on one of the songs) lent an air of expectation simply by her presence. But somehow it all came out sounding like a roughened-up Sam. "I think Sam just heard the music in his head, and he couldn't hear it any other way," said session engineer Bones Howe. "He'd go out in the studio and sing it for them, and I'd hear him come through the microphone, and I'd go, 'That's the way it should be.'" "If you took their voices out, and then you put Sam on the track," said Bobby Womack, "there wouldn't be any change."

It seemed like everybody stopped by the house to see the new baby in the last days of the year. Lou Rawls, whom J.W. continued to advise in the same way that he had once advised Sam, had recently signed a recording contract with Capitol Records. Lou Adler, after producing Rawls, the Valiants, and Jan and Dean for the independent production company he and Herb Alpert had formed after the dissolution of Keen, had gone off on his own now, while Herb was pursuing a performing career. René Hall's wife, Sugar, was almost like a surrogate mother to Barbara, and Jess Rand and his wife brought a housewarming present, while Sam's buddy, Oopie, who, without Sam's knowledge, always brought Barbara a little weed, was constantly in and out. There still wasn't enough furniture for any kind of a crowd, so everybody sat on the floor with the lights turned down and the music playing, drinking just enough to feel good. Maybe it was Sam's voice drifting out from the giant speakers, singing his brand-new song about "Twistin' the Night Away" that got them up and dancing. "Here they have a lot of fun," he sang, "Putting trouble on the run." *Los Angeles Sentinel* columnist Gertrude Gipson, a friend of Sam's and something of a mentor to Barbara, reported to her readers that she had heard that "Barbara Cooke, whose new heir is 2½ weeks old, is already down to a size (7) and was twisting a while with hubby Sam Cooke." Barbara just wished she could engrave this moment in memory — because before long, all their friends would leave and she would be left with a man who did not even seem to want to look at her or his new son.

Boogie-Woogie Rumble

H E WAS IN ATLANTA on April 12, 1962, playing the Rhythm Rink on yet another Henry Wynn Supersonic tour, when the idea for the song came to him. The billing for this "Spring Spectacular" was different from most of Henry's previous shows, taking its cue from a thirty-day Supersonic tour the previous fall that had pitted Jackie Wilson against white rock 'n' roll singer Jerry Lee Lewis (amidst a solid slate of r&b stars) in what was advertised as the "Battle of the Century." This time it was Dion (formerly of Dion and the Belmonts) who was the lone white star in a sea of r&b talent that included twenty-two-year-old Atlantic recording artist Solomon Burke, a warm, charismatic singer just beginning to make a name for himself, the Drifters, Dee Clark, and B.B. King. For Dion, who had embarked upon a solo career in the fall of 1960 with his appearance on the Biggest Show of Stars tour that briefly included Sam, "it was kind of tense at times," stemming not just from the situation in the South but from the racial attitudes that a number of the r&b musicians had by now, understandably, developed on their own. "Sam was a kind of champion for . . . cooling everybody out," said Dion, and, as on the earlier tour, some of Dion's most treasured memories were of singing with Sam backstage — "he was full of music."

The idea for the song had been simmering for some time. Its original inspiration had come from hearing blues stylist Charles Brown sing his original composition "I Want to Go Home" every time Sam played syndicate boss Screw Andrews' Copa Club in Newport, Kentucky, a wide-open town across the river from Cincinnati. Charles, perhaps the most influential blues singer of the late forties and early fifties, with a delicate but distinctive piano style and the soft confidential vocal approach that had stamped such numbers as "Drifting Blues," "Black

Night," and the perennial "Merry Christmas Baby" as instant blues classics, was an individual of considerable charm, prodigious intelligence,
and an equally prodigious attraction to gambling — which was what had
landed him in Newport, "a no-man's land," as Charles described it,
where they *killed* people who didn't live up to their end of the bargain.
Whenever at one time or another he tried to leave, Screw Andrews (né
Frank Andriola), to whom his debt kept on accruing, would raise the question of who loved Charles best, tip the singer $100, express his apprecia-
tion for all that Charles had done for business, and point out, "You know,
I bought you that limousine Cadillac with the gold wheels." To which
Charles could only gratefully assent. Then Screw would say, "You wouldn't
want to find a bullet in your head down the road, would you?" and
Charles, who viewed Screw as a kind of second father, would declare,
"Oh no, Papa, I don't want to go. I'm not going." And he didn't. At least
not until the Kennedy administration Justice Department came in and
closed down the town in mid-1961, Screw got sick with cancer, and
Charles took off for Los Angeles, where his grandfather had fallen ill.

Sam told Charles he was going to record his song from the moment
he first heard it. It was based on the old spiritual "Thank God It's Real,"
and, like the "sorrow songs" of the slaves, had its own secret and subver-
sive message. "I want to go home, I want to go home, 'cause I feel so all
alone," Charles sang, and he really *meant* it — but Screw Andrews, obliv-
ious to the underlying text, pronounced it his favorite song and asked
Charles to sing it over and over again. Charles even recorded it, first for
Johnny Vincent's Ace label, then for King Records in Cincinnati, both
times with one of his most popular disciples, fellow Texan Amos Milburn, who had had number-one r&b hits himself with "Chicken Shack
Boogie" and "Bad, Bad Whiskey." In fact, when Charles came out to Los
Angeles and played the Club Intime all through January and February,
Sam went to see him and talked to him about playing piano on a session
that would include his song. When Charles' grandfather died, Sam
offered to help with the funeral expenses. But Charles told him, "No,
Sam, my papa was insured good. He was a Mason and everything." And
rather than pursue the idea of playing on Sam's session, Charles maintained his own priorities. "I went to the races [instead]."

Sam and Luigi. *Michael Ochs Archives.com*

Sam and Johnnie Morisette.
Courtesy of ABKCO

Sam and L.C. with SAR recording artist
Jackie Ross, Chicago, March 2, 1962.
Courtesy of ABKCO

Sam stayed busy at home. He focused primarily on SAR business, with time for an album session of his own with Luigi in mid-February to capitalize on the success of "Twistin' the Night Away," which was rapidly closing in on number one on the r&b charts. Sam contributed such unlikely originals as "Twistin' in the Kitchen with Dinah" and "Camptown Twist," along with a sprightly duet with Lou Rawls on "Soothe Me," now that the Sims Twins hit had run its course. He produced sessions on Patience Valentine and Clif White, but mostly he was concentrating on trying to get Johnnie "Two Voice" Morisette and Johnnie Taylor the kind of hit the Sims Twins had already enjoyed.

He cut Johnnie "Two Voice" in early January with a song Alex thought he should have kept for himself. It was called "Meet Me at the Twistin' Place," and what made the record was the audible party atmosphere created by studio visitors like Ricky Nelson, local chanteuse Toni Harper, and René Hall's wife, Sugar, all of whom contributed to the chorus, and Johnnie's typically manic falsetto ad lib at the fade. "Oh meet

me, meet me, baby," he screamed in that strangled half cry that fell
somewhere in between gospel intensity and unintentional parody:

> *I'll be looking for you, and I know you can't miss me*
> *'Cause I'll have my red suit on*
> *And Caldonia will be there*
> *And Paul will be there*
> *You know, Della will be there*
> *And Uncle Remus will be there*
> *And don't forget Ol' Man Mose*
> *He'll be there*
> *Oh, come on, you better meet me*
> *(Meet me at the twistin' place)*

Alex remained dubious about Johnnie ("He's got to make up his
mind whether he's a singer or a pimp," he told Sam, "they're both full-
time jobs"), but he loved the song. He thought it was better produced
than "Twistin' the Night Away," and it got plenty of airplay when it was
released two months later, even if the distributors laid down on it after it
entered the pop and r&b charts in April.

The record that he and Sam both had their hopes set on, though, was
Johnnie Taylor's "Rome Wasn't Built in a Day." It was a song, like "Wonderful World," with a history. This time it was the Prudhomme twins,
Betty and Beverly, the ones with the striking (and not entirely unintentional) resemblance to Elizabeth Taylor, who had written the original,
not long after meeting Sam in the summer of 1957. They took it to producer Fabor Robinson, who wanted them to record it themselves on his
Malibu-based Radio label, but when Beverly told him she was pregnant,
he gave it to country singer Johnny Russell, an eighteen-year-old Missis-
sippian whose family had recently moved to Fresno and who recorded it
as the B-side of his first single. In Russell's version it was little more
than a dour ballad in B-minor whose chorus, repeated three times with
minimal variation and no discrete, individual verses, was the centerpiece of the song: "It takes time / Give me time / And the world will be
yours and mine," it went, "Rome wasn't built in a day."

The Prudhommes were always pitching songs to Sam with little
encouragement from Alex ("J.W. told us, 'I can hardly get him to do my
tunes — how can you expect him to do yours?'"). They maintained a flir-

tatious relationship with Sam, which they knew Barbara didn't like and Zelda clearly resented, too, but "we loved him as a friend, we loved music together, he was a really cute guy with a beautiful personality, he was always a gentleman with us, and if you went somewhere with him, he'd have you laughing half the evening."

Sam heard something in their song that they didn't and asked if he could fool with it. They told him he would have to deal with Fabor Robinson on the publishing, but it was certainly okay with them, so he added two verses, recast it as a more up-tempo number, flavored it with his characteristic sixth chords and a hint of a Latin beat, and changed the message from one of dogged persistence to a more adroit tone of his own. "Give me time, give me time," the singer now urges his reluctant lover, "And I'll make your love as strong as mine." Betty and Beverly loved what he had done to their song. But then, without telling them, he brought it to Johnnie Taylor.

Johnnie was still debating whether or not he had made the right decision in signing with SAR in the first place. A tight, suspicious man by nature, Johnnie had listened to friends tell him over and over that Sam had only added him to the SAR roster to ward off direct competition, that he would never promote a rival who sounded so much like him — and the sales of his one SAR release to date only went to prove those friends right.

This was a better session from the start. It was better prepared, Sam had brought in better material, René had assembled a solid ten-piece ensemble anchored by Clif on guitar and Earl Palmer on drums, and Lou Rawls was available for background singing — it was just like one of Sam's own sessions. Sam worked everybody hard, but no one harder than Johnnie. He stayed on Johnnie about his pronunciation, his emphasis, and his meaning. He was very particular with the backup singers on how to swing the chorus without holding on to their notes and getting in the way of the lead vocal. And he kept checking with Johnnie to make sure he understood, showing him exactly how he wanted it done but urging everyone, always, to keep it funky.

Johnnie got his vocal down on the Prudhommes' song almost immediately. His voice broke in a couple of places, but that wasn't really a problem — he got the phrasing and the feeling right, nearly identical, in fact, to Sam's, down to the humming that Sam would so often interpolate into his vocals. The band, too, helped convey the world-weary sense of determi-

Beverly and Betty Prudhomme, with Art Lebow, Los Angeles County Fair, September 1957 (note Sam in booth). *Courtesy of Betty and Beverly Prudhomme*

nation that Sam had written into the song ("Don't, honey, don't go away / Do you hear, do you hear / what I say?"), that peculiar combination of hope and despair that provided the underpinning for so many of his songs. Earl Palmer's drumming was impeccable, the horns extended Johnnie's clipped phrasing, and poor Clif just about wore his wrist out as they went through take after take ("You had that roll effect rather than chunka-chunka-chunka — it went on forever, and, man, I was damn near dead!") but getting it right every time with his unfailing gift for metronomic precision. In the end, only the background singing left Sam less than completely satisfied — he had a precise idea of how he wanted it to sound, concluding each "ha cha ra" with a "huh!" so that it rolled off the singers' tongues in a way that even Lou Rawls at first couldn't quite grasp. Eventually they got it with Sam and Alex, too, pitching in, and the song came together without losing any of its freshness or originality. To Alex, who had gotten a little frustrated trying to clear the publishing on a composition he wasn't sure was worth the effort, it was further proof of his partner's vision. Johnnie felt for the first time like he really had a hit. And Lou Rawls, who just enjoyed being around Sam ("Sometimes he'd call and say, 'Hey, Lou Lou, what you doing?' and we'd ride around, maybe even go to the beach"), soaked up an atmosphere that he felt for every one of them represented a rare break from the day-to-day rounds. It wasn't a matter of how much you got paid — though generally every-one did get paid. But there was a sense of progress, of pride, of limits being challenged and ambition being achieved, there was a positive energy that infused the situation in a way that transcended the mere cir-cumstances of a session. "Everybody just wanted to be there to see what was happening."

Only the Prudhomme sisters were upset. They felt as if a trick had been played on them. When Sam first let them hear a dub, they thought it was him, and when he told them it wasn't, they felt hurt and even put up some halfhearted resistance to the record coming out. They couldn't understand why he would record another singer who sounded just like him doing their song. But after he promised them that he would do the song himself someday, after Johnnie's version had played itself out, they abandoned all opposition. With all of his bubbling enthusiasm, all of the manifest delight he so evidently took in every aspect of his life, how could anyone, they wondered, stay mad at him for long?

To Barbara it sometimes seemed that the whole world saw a differ-ent Sam than the one she knew. She could dress up to go out with him and still feel like his "sophisticated doll" — but it was an image, not a reality, and no one was more aware of the gulf between the two than her. She had never seen a man take more pride in his new home — he seemed so consumed with every detail of its furnishing, answering the questions of her two lady decorators as to his vision for each room with voluble pleasure. He got a grand piano for the music room, leather-bound volumes for the library, a new Jaguar XKE sports car, and he brought home paintings from his frequent forays to the Beverly Hills galleries. He hired a gardener, a pool attendant, and two maids for Barbara to supervise in one full-time position — at first she thought he was putting her in a position of genuine responsibility because she had finally earned his trust. But then she realized it was all strictly superficial; there was little room for her, or anyone else, in the picture.

He was a different person at home than he was out in the world, brooding, solitary, lounging around in the silk pajamas she bought him, smoking cigarettes and drinking his Scotch. He might be reading one of his books or listening to his music, something might capture his attention and he would pick up his guitar and start working out a song, but as far as he was concerned, she might as well not have been there. He could be stubborn over the smallest things. She begged him to put a fence around the pool, or at least to get a pool cover, but he adamantly refused, despite the advice of his friends, because, he said, with the pool in front, it would disfigure the appearance of the property. She didn't think it was a question of money; Sam wasn't like that. But one time early in the new year, she tried to get him to give her sister Beverly $300 for a down payment on a little Renault, and he blew up and started yelling at her and saying that he wasn't going to take care of her whole damn family, and then he actually hit her and disappeared for days. The next time she heard from him, it was as if nothing had happened. He called and told her to cook him up a steak, and when he came home, there was nothing more said. It was like they were playacting, and the only way she could get through her role was to stay stoned.

He didn't like her to invite her friends over, and when he had *his* friends over, it was as if he were ashamed of her, staying with them in the bar or the music room, limiting any contact they might have had with her. He was indulgent with Tracey, who at sixteen months showed no signs of speaking, but Linda was the only one who could really get his attention. He could sit and talk with her by the hour, read to her and make up songs in a way that both warmed and broke Barbara's heart. He had relented a little with Vincent, especially after his mother had pronounced that the little boy looked just like Sammy as a baby, but there remained that obstinate withholding of himself, he never accepted or gave his heart to the chubby little boy. She didn't have anyone to talk to except her sister, and she didn't know who to trust. The presence of any other woman in the room put her on immediate alert, it was like a switch got turned on in Sam and she could watch him go to work, practically making an assignation right then and there under her very nose. He was out every night with his friends, he and Alex were always talking "business" — they kept plotting how they were going to break this or that SAR artist, and they were just as involved with Lou Rawls' career as they were with their own. It seemed sometimes like there was no division between work and play, and she didn't fit into either.

H E HAD BEEN HOME for the better part of three months when he flew to Chicago at the end of February for a series of SAR sessions. Alex stayed in Los Angeles to promote the new Johnnie Morisette release (they had decided to hold back Johnnie Taylor's single until the beginning of May to give "Meet Me at the Twistin' Place" some breathing space), so Sam was on his own, focusing his attention on the first day on R.H. Harris, his one-time mentor, now forty-five years old but still in possession of one of the most thrilling voices in gospel. The former Soul Stirrers lead had formed his new group, the Gospel Paraders, a couple of years earlier, with the explicit idea of developing the most advanced contemporary harmonies in gospel or any other kind of music, but Sam and Crain appear to be in the thick of the background singing on this session, and Sam worked Harris with no evident trace of self-consciousness for up to thirty or forty takes of each song. The result was a masterpiece of "gospel blues" expression, and though neither Sam nor Alex had signed Harris with any expectation of commercial success (it was as much as anything, J.W. said, a matter of keeping faith), they believed in Harris, they believed in the music, and they were determined to use their label, at least in part, as a vehicle for expressing that belief. It was the session on the day after Harris', though, that was the real reason for the trip.

Sam had finally persuaded the Womack Brothers to switch over to pop. He and Alex had put out a second gospel single on the group at the start of the year. It was probably the best song from their June session, "Couldn't Hear Nobody Pray," with the seventeen-year-old middle brother Bobby's rasping, buzz-saw lead, but neither Sam nor Alex had any hopes for the record's prospects. Mostly they wanted to prove to the Womacks that there was no commercial future for them in gospel music.

The Womack Brothers had certainly enjoyed their brief moment in the gospel spotlight. Their first release had put them out on tour with the Staple Singers and the Dixie Hummingbirds, but, as Sam kept telling them, it wasn't going to do a thing for their pocketbooks or prestige. Even the girls in their high school, Bobby said, still liked "the basketball players, the football players, the baseball players, they said, 'That's the Womack Brothers, but they be singing something about "Thank you,

Jesus,"' It was embarrassing!" And once they saw Sam perform at a rock 'n' roll show at the Pla-Mor Ballroom in Cleveland in August, the first rock 'n' roll show they had ever attended, it was all over. "My father told me, 'You might as well kill me if you go to that show,'" Bobby said, "but, you know, I *had* to go, and it was all different. The people screamed, the women were going crazy — we didn't get a chance to talk to him, they just ushered him out, but I was saying, 'Shit, man, you know, we want to do that.' You know, *this* is what I wanted to do."

It led to a family crisis. J.W. worked on his fellow Mason, Friendly Sr., while Sam continued to stand as the primary role model for the boys. In the end, despite the continued vehemence of his opposition, Mr. Womack relented enough to let their mother drive them to the session but told them in a family meeting that if they went, they were on their own, they were not going to pursue a rock 'n' roll career while living in his house. "We all cried," said the oldest, Friendly Jr., who had his own misgivings on the subject, "[but] we said, 'We're gonna do it anyway.'"

Zelda and J.W. had prepared a song for them based on their second single, Bobby's showpiece "Couldn't Hear Nobody Pray." The new number was called "Lookin' For a Love," and Sam was sold on it from the first, he loved the *energy* of the song — "but we felt strange," said Bobby, "almost like we were making a mockery of God. Sam was saying, 'Man, [now] just don't be tense. I know you feel tense.' He was laughing. He said, 'Ain't no [Holy Ghost] coming in here after you,' 'cause he had been through all that and he knew we were tripping hard, 'cause this was God's song."

Sam told Bobby, "You gotta stop chewing your words if you want to reach over. If they don't understand what you're saying, they can't relate." But, he said, on the other hand, he didn't want Bobby sounding *too* proper. "'Cause then you'll start to sound like me!" He spent a good deal of time positioning them so their hand claps would sound just right. "He'd run from the board back out to where we were," said Bobby, "he was on me about my phrasing and getting the message across, but he'd be like, 'Damn, I wish I could be in this, too!'"

The only other song they attempted that day was "Somewhere There's a Girl," the lyric that Sam had improvised over "Somewhere There's a God" at their first session. They didn't quite achieve the ethereal quality that Sam had imparted to the song, but with Curtis singing lead they came close. "Wail it for me, huh, Curt?" Sam implored good-naturedly, and when, after seven takes, he felt that they were nearly there, he declared, "This is for the Womacks," as if to make the distinction that now they were singing the song for themselves.

Everyone was happy at the conclusion of the evening. Sam pronounced that they had cut themselves a hit, and he told them that he and Alex had come up with a new name for the group, too. It was a name they had first hit upon when things started to go bad at Keen and J.W. thought he and Sam might record as a duo for another label. They had never actually used it, but now they had the perfect recipients for the title: five young boys with a different sound who, as J.W. said, were all "slim, long-haired, all but Friendly played left-handed, we were going to take them to Sy Devore and dress them up like lovers." And that was how they signed their new contract — as the Valentinos.

Sam was home for another month after returning from Chicago. J.W. concluded the deal with RCA for the Keen masters, thus paving the way for a Sam Cooke Greatest Hits LP. Liberty brought out the single that Sam had produced with Herb Alpert and Lou Adler on their mutual friend, George McCurn, the former Pilgrim Travelers bass singer better known as Oopie Doopie Doo ("Baby, put your hand on top of my head," Oopie told Herb as an explanation for some of his lapses from orthodox phrasing. "You feel all that motion there?"). The song they had recorded was an update of "The Time Has Come," one of Sam's earliest compositions, given an eccentric romantic twist by the resonant agility of Oopie's voice. Sam swam in the pool almost every day, and J.W. had just about persuaded him to take up the game of tennis. Every night, Johnnie Morisette or Johnny "Guitar" Watson or Johnnie Taylor was playing somewhere around town. There was no question that Sam had enjoyed this unaccustomed interlude, but with the Henry Wynn tour scheduled to start on April 6, he was ready to go back on the road.

H E HAD BEEN OUT for just under a week when the idea for a radical reworking of Charles Brown's song first came to him. He was in the limo on his way to Atlanta, the car's headlights sweeping the highway as he sat in the backseat with the little pinprick of light from his reading lamp illuminating the lyrics he was writing down. The song would retain its gospel flavor and the call-and-response format that made it in essence a vocal duet, and some of the words would even continue to suggest its spiritual origins — but its refrain ("Bring it to me, bring your sweet lovin', bring it on home to me") would leave little doubt as to its secular intent.

He pitched the song excitedly to Dee Clark in the dressing room after the show. Dee hadn't had a hit since "Raindrops," number two on the pop charts the previous summer, and Sam felt like the new tune was perfectly suited to him. But Dee, who had covered a couple of Sam's songs already, couldn't hear it no matter how many times Sam played it for him — he said it just wasn't for him. So Sam called Luigi and sang the song for him over the phone along with "Having a Party," another new number he had just written. Luigi was instantly sold and set up an L.A. recording session in two weeks, once Sam told Henry Wynn that he was going to have to take a brief break from the tour.

The atmosphere at the April 26 session matched the title of Sam's second song. The Sims Twins were there at Sam's invitation to sing backup. So was Lou Rawls. Sam and Alex's lawyer/advisor Walter Hurst, was present, along with Sugar Hall and Fred Smith, the former Keen assistant a&r man who with his songwriting partner, Cliff Goldsmith, had had one hit after another from "Western Movies" on. Zelda wouldn't have missed it for the world, and Alex remained constantly by Sam's side, but it was a surprise to RCA engineer Al Schmitt to see Barbara, too, an occasional visitor at best and one who did not always contribute an upbeat note. Tonight, though, she was just one more part of an uninhibitedly festive mood. "It was a very happy session," said Schmitt, a twenty-seven-year-old New Yorker who had grown up in his uncle's recording studio. "Everybody was just having a ball. We were getting people out there [on the floor], and some of the outtakes were hilarious, there was so much ad lib that went on."

They started with "Having a Party," the "lighter" of the two songs, written in the reportorial manner of "Everybody Loves to Cha Cha Cha" and "Twistin' the Night Away," except that this one injected a more personal note. René had assembled an eighteen-piece backing group composed of six violins, two violas, two cellos, and a sax, plus a seven-piece rhythm section that included two percussionists, two bassists, two guitars, and a piano.

It opens with Cliff's countryish guitar brightly echoed by the violins, then, as Sam's voice comes in, the cellos and violas supply a mournful counterpoint to the vocal. "We're having a party," Sam declares in a deliberate, almost wistful way:

Dancing to the music
Played by the DJ
On the radio
The Cokes are in the icebox
Popcorn's on the table
Me and my baby
We're out here on the floor.

The tempo picks up a little as they run through a dozen takes, with Lou's voice joining in on the chorus, just out of synch enough to suggest spontaneity but totally attuned to Sam's lead. "So, Mister, Mister DJ," the two of them sing together, as though recalling times that would be no more, "Keep those records playing / 'Cause I'm having such a good time / Dancing with my baby." The sax takes its second solo on the outro, while the strings, almost unnoticed, keep up their stately threnody and Sam and Lou go out over the instrumental with a recapitulation of the song's original message.

It was, as engineer Al Schmitt said, a happy, feel-good kind of session, and as they listened to the playback of the twelfth take, Barbara and Sugar Hall started to do a slow twist, and J.W. and some of the musicians joined in. Then they overdubbed the additional voices and hand claps of just about everyone in the room, and the music swelled and took on an almost anthemic quality — it had all the uncalculated fervor that defines a group of people who have lived through good times and bad times together and cherish the good times despite the near-certain knowledge that they are not going to last. Except that this was calculated, and calibrated, down to the last rough harmony. "These were easy, natural things," Luigi said, but it's doubtful that Sam would have agreed.

The bittersweet mood of "Having a Party" seemed to merely set the stage for the second song, the Charles Brown–inspired "Bring It On Home to Me." The song opened with piano and drums taking the lead and Lou dueting with Sam in the foreground as Sam declares in full gospel mode:

If you ever
Change your mind
About leaving, leaving me behind

Ohh, bring it to me
Bring your sweet lovin'
Bring it on home to me.

Then the strings come in with their by now familiar undercurrent of melancholy, and Sam goes into the call-and-response that is the heart of the song (this was something notably absent from the much smoother Charles Brown original) as he emphasizes his message with a forceful "Yeah," and a chorus that now includes J.W., Fred Smith, and probably the Sims Twins in addition to Lou, delivers an equally forceful response. "We were after the Soul Stirrers–type thing," said René Hall, "trying to create that flavor in a rhythm and blues recording." It was, said J.W., an entirely conscious decision. "We felt that light shit wouldn't sustain him. We felt he needed more weight."

They nearly got it all in one take. This was the closest Sam had come to the classic gospel give-and-take he had once created with Paul Foster, and the only adjustment that he chose to make on the second, and final, take was the decision to use Lou alone as the echoing voice and dispense altogether with the background chorus. What comes through is a rare moment of undisguised emotion, an unambiguous embrace not just of a cultural heritage but of an adult experience far removed from white teenage fantasy. There was nothing to add or subtract. There was no thought on Luigi's part of trying to fit in another song or extend the session. He was convinced by now that Sam knew his own talent best. And he was equally convinced that they had a pair of hits on their hands.

Sam rejoined the Supersonic tour two days later in Birmingham, where, for the first time, the *Birmingham World* reported, Rickwood Field employed "Negro citizens [as] ticket-takers, handlers, and sellers" after it had been suggested that, without such measures, the show "could possibly prove a financial flop." There was a new kind of pride in the air and a new kind of proclamation. Sam's "natural" hairstyle was finally beginning to catch on ("People used to say to him, 'Why don't you get a haircut?'" said June Gardner, who had wondered the same thing himself when he first joined in 1960. "All this was virgin territory at the time"), and a few months later, the *Philadelphia Tribune* defined "soul," a term confined for the most part at this point to the downhome instrumental sounds of jazz musicians Bobby Timmons, Horace Silver, and

Cannonball Adderly, as "the word of the hour . . . a spiritual return to the sources, [an] emotional intensity and rhythmic drive [that] comes from childhood saturation in Negro gospel music." "Oh, we all heard it," said onetime "Wonder Boy Preacher" Solomon Burke, a lifelong Soul Stirrers devotee who had positioned himself somewhere between Sam and Brother Joe May in his own persuasive style, of Sam's new soul sound. "Pop audiences heard that yodel . . . like it was a shiny new thing. But if you knew Sam from gospel, it was him saying, 'Hey, it's me.'"

And when he left for the West Indies with Barbara and Linda just five days later for the start of a two-week tour, he finally had a band of his own.

THE TOUR WAS BILLED as Sam Cooke's *Twistin' the Night Away Revue*, Featuring the Upsetters, who had been teamed with Little Willie John until just a few months earlier. Sam had had his eye on them ever since first touring with Willie in October of 1960, but he hadn't made a move until Willie, never a model of professional or personal responsibility, proved no longer capable of maintaining a band and the Upsetters had gone out on their own. The band was built around a core of two or three saxophones, a trumpet, keyboards, and a rhythm section whose bass player, Olsie Robinson (known as "Bassy"), Sam would put to work with Clif and June. They were a show band who could do a strong set of their own with unison steps, costume changes, and instrument twirls, and, more important, once Clif schooled them, they should be able to deliver the rhythmic kick and tonal variety he was looking for to put the music across. Crain objected strongly to their addition, it would only add an unnecessary expense, he said, for something that would not translate into either greater ticket sales or higher ticket prices, but Sam was not about to be deterred by anything as immaterial as money. He was prepared to pay anything it took, he told his brother Charles, to get that sound behind him.

The show was as big a hit as ever at The Cat 'n' the Fiddle in Montego Bay. Sam was hailed as "Sweet Man" everywhere he went, and drummer June Gardner was once again led to wonder at Sam's uncanny ability to mix with beggars and kings, as he proved himself equally at home with stagehands, bellboys, and the aristocracy of island life. But, as Barbara was well aware by now, Sam set his own limits. She was having a good

Sam, Barbara, and Linda arrive in the West Indies, May 1962. *Courtesy of ABKCO*

time on her second Bahamian trip. The worst problem she had encountered so far was that Linda got so covered with mosquito bites that they wanted to quarantine the child until they could be sure it wasn't anything contagious. Then one night after the show, a nice-looking man offered to take Sam and her to the club where he was singing, and he made the mistake of trying to pay her a compliment. "You have a lovely wife," was all the man said to her husband, but that was it. Sam grabbed her by the arm, took her back to the hotel, and beat the living hell out of her because, he said, she had been flirting with the guy. She couldn't understand it coming from a whorehopper like him. All that poor man was trying to do was to compliment *you,* she told Sam. But the fool wouldn't listen, the only thing that stopped him was that Linda woke up and started crying. He stormed out then, and she was left to console her daughter until Crain arrived and looked at her and just shook his head. She knew Sam had sent him, she knew Sam felt bad. He alternately tried to comfort her and dissuade her from leaving. Sammy had had too much to drink, he hadn't meant to do this, Crain said, he was sure Sam was sorry. Barbara had stopped crying by now. She knew she wasn't perfect, she didn't doubt that she had given her husband reason to be disappointed in her, and she recognized, finally, that she could never be all that he wanted her to be — but that freed her, too. Because there was nothing more he could do to her. He was only educating her to hurt him as much as he had hurt her.

For Sam it was an encounter with an identity that he would never willingly have chosen to reveal, even to himself. He was deeply embarrassed, and deeply ashamed, but there was nothing to do about it other than to pretend that it had never happened. Crain was loyal, the people around him were loyal, and he believed deep down that Barbara was loyal, too. But he no longer knew if he could make this marriage work. He had believed so strongly that he could. He had believed that, with the right approach, he could turn Barbara into just what he wanted her to be, the girl who knew everything about him and understood — *the one.* He didn't know anything to do but to go on. It was a situation he no longer knew how to control.

SAM TOOK JOHNNIE MORISETTE out on tour with him in Florida, Texas, and Louisiana when he got back. Johnnie's single, released in late January, had just crested at number eighteen on the r&b charts and number sixty-three pop, and Alex had finally put out Johnnie Taylor's "Rome Wasn't Built in a Day." The Sims Twins joined Sam, Johnnie Morisette, and the Upsetters on a few dates. They were always a hit in person, "Soothe Me" invariably got the crowd, but it was proving difficult to get them a follow-up, and Sam was beginning to suspect that they might be too hardheaded, and insufficiently disciplined, to adapt to the rigors of studio recording. The Valentinos' record was the one he and Alex were counting on, anyway. Sam was convinced that with their youthful good looks, high-energy stage act, and eager educability, they could be stars of a magnitude that none of his other artists could even imagine.

The road was a little too much of the straight-and-narrow for Johnnie Morisette, especially with a string of whores back home to worry about. "I was living in California, used to all that good shit, [and] back in them days, they'd give a nigger ten years for a roach, you dig? You'd go through Mississippi in one of them new cars, they pull you out and beat you damn near to death. Stay in fleaboxes, eat out of little stores on the highway, be onstage singing, and you'd be funky as a motherfucker, 'cause you had to ride all day to make the job. I couldn't cut that shit." Still, Sam didn't stint on anything, and Sam was not above having a good time himself. "Everything he did, he did first class. But he was a businessman, business come before pleasure with Sam." When they played the Howard in D.C. in mid-May, Sam furnished Johnnie with all of his arrangements for a ten-piece band, and when they played Baltimore's Royal Theater the following week, Sam surprised him with a red-and-gold Cadillac for his upcoming birthday. Which gave Johnnie such a kick he missed one of the scheduled shows just driving around.

The Upsetters were not on that date (the theaters had their own house bands), but they played with Sam on one-nighters all through the South — with their presence specified on the Universal contract either as an advertised act whose fee the club covered or as a $250 add-on for which Sam picked up the tab.

On July 7 they opened for three days in Atlanta, where the NAACP was holding its annual weeklong gathering for the first time since 1951. "Welcome NAACP Convention," read the ad for the show at the Royal Peacock, which also included Lotsa Poppa, a good-natured three-hundred-pound Atlanta native who featured the songs of two-hundred-fifty-pound Solomon Burke in his act. There was a gospel program at the Auditorium with the Highway QCs the weekend before Sam's appearance, and Martin Luther King addressed the convention on July 5, declaring that "true peace is not merely the absence of tension. . . . The tension which we see in the South today is the necessary tension that comes when the oppressed rise up and start to move forward toward a permanent, positive peace." At the conclusion of his speech, historian Taylor Branch wrote, "he rushed feverishly to a closing, four-word slogan: 'All. Here. And now.'" And between what Branch described as "rhythmic applause [that] allowed him to speak only one sentence between bursts of mass emotion," he declared, "We want *all* of our rights. . . . We want our freedom *here*. . . . We want freedom *now!*" The crowd, inspired not just by the sense of the speech but by the stirring manner of its delivery, burst into a response that, Branch wrote, "King stilled only with a solemn reprise on the likelihood of persecution and death, and . . . a flourish of inspiration from the prophets. . . . [But] his NAACP speech did not register with the white world. As with many sensational scenes from his life, it remained a matter of journalistic whimsy whether interest crossed the racial line, and the only kind of event almost guaranteed to command an audience on both sides was the drama of white force seizing personally on King's body." Which happened when he was jailed in Albany, Georgia, five days later, a matter that was reported extensively, as Sam went on to play a self-booked date in New Orleans that got equally little attention outside the black community.

Barbara and all three children joined him on July 11 in Savannah, where he spent the afternoon bowling at the invitation of the manager of the Hi Hat Lanes. Over three hundred people showed up to watch, and Sam finished off the afternoon signing autographs, talking bowling, and giving an interview to a local reporter. "I have always had a rather bright insight on business," the reporter quoted him as saying, while detailing some of the ventures that Sam described to him, including the record company, "vast realty holdings, and a new beer company slated to get started sometime in August." From there, the whole family was off to Miami for the weekend, where Sam was playing three nights at the Knight Beat Club at the Sir John Hotel. Barbara spent most of her time in the room with the kids, and Sam got annoyed with her for that, but from what she could see, he had girls stashed all over the hotel. At the end of the weekend, she and the children flew to Chicago, and Sam was off for another ten days to places like the Evans Grille in Forestville, Maryland, the Harding Street Rec Center in Petersburg, Virginia, and Midway Park outside Portsmouth, Virginia, before he would have a chance to catch up with his family again in Chicago, where he was booked for a week at the Regal Theater.

It was a grueling schedule, as Johnnie Morisette had learned, but for tenor sax and de facto Upsetters leader Grady Gaines, it was like being at a party that never ended, on or offstage. As far as Grady was concerned, the road just provided you with the kind of extended family that you had no reason to want to leave, and of all the people he had ever worked with — Little Willie John, Dee Clark, Little Richard, all the big acts he had backed at the Club Matinee in Houston before that — Sam was the best. "He was the nicest, you couldn't get no smoother than him, always a big smile — but he was real business." As far as Grady was concerned, Sam put more of himself into the new single, "Bring It On Home to Me," than any other song he did ("and he sang his heart out on everything he sung"). Sometimes, when he was feeling good, Charles would sing the Lou Rawls part, frequently Crain chimed in, too, and the song drew an ecstatic audience response everywhere they went. But it was "Having a Party" that was, invariably, the climax of the evening, as the other acts came out onstage, just like at a gospel program, and band and performers and audience alike all joined in. It was, as Grady described it, emblematic of the spirit of good fellowship and fun that Sam established for everyone within their little world. "People would come and say, 'Sam, I need a hundred dollars, two hundred, whatever, and he let them have it. But good advice [can] be help. And he would take the time out and do that, too. We were like brothers, all of us was like one. We had lucked in, and that's just the way it was."

There was another new face on the scene, a brash young booking agent who had just come over to William Morris from GAC (General Artists Corporation) and was so taken with both the music and the life that, after wresting the account from Sam's longtime agent, Paul Cantor, he almost immediately started flying in for gigs. Jerry Brandt had first seen Sam while working as a waiter at the Town Hill Club in Brooklyn. He was the only white waiter in the place, he claimed, and was intrigued by the atmosphere, knocked out by the music of all the big names — Roy Hamilton, Jackie Wilson, Dinah Washington — but he was *"mesmerized"* by Sam from the moment he first saw him. "I was standing there with a tray, and people were yelling for their drinks, and I just couldn't move. To me, Sam was the most real thing around. No tricks, couldn't move his two feet — [he just had] that fervor that makes you believe in Jesus, but since I didn't believe in Jesus, it was him. Him."

Brandt was twenty-four years old, and, however he may have justified it to his superiors at the talent agency, "I was out for an experience. Are you crazy? I was getting laid twice a day." Perhaps just as important, he was getting a chance to hang around someone he truly revered. He saw Sam's temper flare up on occasion, but mostly he admired his cool. "He was on top of everything attitude-wise. I loved going on the road with him, I loved going *anywhere* with him. They made fun of me, they used to call me the light-skinned fellow, but I never heard Sam speak of [race]. There was them and us, but that's just the way the world is."

S ALES OF THE NEW SINGLE had at last gained Sam new status at RCA. With three Top 20 pop hits in the past year ("Cupid," "Twistin' the Night Away," and now the double-sided success of "Bring It On Home to Me" and "Having a Party") in addition to the appearance of *Twistin' the Night Away* on the LP charts, Hugo and Luigi had started referring to him good-naturedly as "The Consistent One," but now even top RCA executives like Record Division president George Marek were waking up to his financial value to the company. "Do you know that Sam Cooke is the second-biggest moneymaker at RCA [with singles sales] after Elvis Presley?" Marek asked Luigi one day. "I said, 'Of course we know that. We make the records.' But they were just discovering it." At an RCA Records convention at around this time, Sam had the industry crowd wrapped around his little finger just as surely as if it were a packed house on a steamy night at the Palms of Hallandale or the Flame Show Bar in Detroit. "It was like a party," said RCA engineer Al Schmitt, who had yet to see him perform for a black audience. "He would get people up to dance and sing along, always [with] this great smile on his face. [It was] like having Sam in your house, or you being in his."

Sam was the only one who remained unsatisfied. "Bring It On Home to Me" never quite sold a million copies, and while Ray Charles' country crossover "I Can't Stop Loving You" topped the pop and r&b charts all through June and July, Sam had to be satisfied with an unqualified r&b smash, whose A- and B-sides reached numbers thirteen and seventeen respectively on the pop charts. "We're not getting number ones," he said to Luigi. "That's right," his producer replied, trying to mollify him with humor. "We're getting number four, number six on the *Billboard* charts, and as long as we get that, nobody's gonna bother you. But if you get two or three number ones in a row, then you got no place to go but down. Then you're competition, and they're just going to do everything they can to knock you off."

It was cold comfort to someone who could mask everything but his ambition, but Sam still had to laugh at the funny way Luigi was always able to put things. It did not fully assuage his impatience, but he had long since proved his staying power as an artist, and he and Alex had long-term business plans of their own. They were confident that the Valentinos' debut single, which was poised to enter both the pop and r&b charts at the end of July, was going to usher in a whole new era at SAR. They were going to expand the company. They were going to add to their roster, start putting out albums on more of their artists. And Sam was going to start taking advantage of some of the business opportunities that were coming his way.

That was how he got involved with the beer company he had told the reporter in Savannah about. Alex was not too clear on all of the details, but he knew better than to question his partner's business acumen. From what he understood, Sam had met a gentleman named Herbert G. Cook while playing the Royal in Baltimore in June. Cook, a "popular and dynamic nationally known promoter," according to the *Philadelphia Tribune,* "who [had] made a name for himself [with] the Revolutionary Coffee Distribution Company, which made sensational inroads in the Negro coffee trade," established the first Negro firm "for the distribution of beer under his own label" in Philadelphia in 1960. Two years later, he appears to have moved his operation to Baltimore and as of mid-July announced that his company, Cook's Beer, would add an *e* to its name, that Sam had become its new president, and that "entertainer Johnnie Morisette [would] be affiliated with the firm." J.W. didn't like the smell of it — he could only imagine what it had cost Sam to become president, and he had heard rumors that Herbert Cook was mixed up in the numbers racket. But he didn't say anything until Sam invited him to a board meeting in Baltimore sometime later. All it would take for J.W. to participate, Sam told him, was an investment of $1,000. "He said, 'Alex, I want you to get in on this damn thing. Why don't you take a check out of SAR, and you can [attend].' So okay, I got a certified check, caught a plane, and went to Baltimore." And after he heard exactly how much more it was going to cost them just to be able to continue to participate, "I unveiled those shysters. I tore up the check, and lowered the fucking boom." It was one of the few times Alex had ever seen Sam taken in by someone else's line of talk, but evidently he was ready at this point for reeducation. He just laughed at his own foolishness and said, "Well, partner, let's go to New York and have some fun." Which is precisely what they did, grabbing a flight to New York and riding off into the sunset like Butch Cassidy and the Sundance Kid and all those other western heroes Sam had watched on the screen and read about so avidly as a kid.

Another Saturday Night

SAM OPENED AT THE REGAL THEATER in Chicago on July 27. Although he wouldn't be staying at home (he had reserved his customary suite at the Roberts Motel on Sixty-third Street), his mother cooked for a week in preparation for his arrival. She made chicken and dressing, her famous dinner rolls, red beans and rice, and ham hocks and greens for the family and friends she and her husband would be entertaining during their son's annual weeklong homecoming. All of the nieces and nephews would be there — Sam called them the Gas House Gang, after the daffy 1930s St. Louis Cardinals baseball team — and sometimes, with their friends, there could be as many as fifty of them, but Sam just plunged into their midst, like another kid, and would take them all out to Riverview Amusement Park for the rides. It was a weeklong party for everybody, said Sam's youngest sister, Agnes, now twenty-seven and a mother of two. "We would be up all night long, talking, singing, doing whatever — we just enjoyed each other."

Nobody wanted to miss a single show. The whole family would gather backstage with Duck and his wife, and Sam would keep up a furious game of checkers with Hattie's son Maurice right up until the moment he had to go onstage. Maurice could easily have won, his mother insisted, except that Sam always distracted him with his animated chatter. The other kids would all be saying, "Don't listen to him, Maurice, don't listen to him," but Sam just kept talking at him, talking him right into defeat. Then he really did have to go on, but not before he made sure that the kids all got their seats in the front row, or sometimes right onstage, where one time they even got their picture in the paper.

He'd organize singing contests, the boys against the girls — his twenty-year-old brother, David, coached the boys and Mary's oldest,

Twistin' the night away: Sam with his niece Ophelia Woods, Regal Theater, Chicago, end of July/beginning of August 1962. *Courtesy of ABKCO*

Gwen, coached the girls, as Sam went back and forth between the two until he determined that they were ready for the competition. Then he'd bring them all out in front of his brothers and sisters to judge, but the girls always had their dance steps down, laughed Hattie, and they would always win. "And Sam would say, 'I got to work with you over here, you can't be letting them girls win all the time!'"

Linda watched with a somewhat jaundiced eye. She and her sister, Tracey, had spent much of the summer in Chicago, shuttling back and forth between their paternal grandparents, various Cook uncles and aunts, and their mother's older sister, Ella. The Gas House Gang was for her cousins, she sniffed, "they didn't see him as much as we did, we had a different thing." What Linda prized was the time she spent with Papa and Mama Cook, and the way her grandmother and her father would be when they got together sometimes. "My grandmother was very quiet, she never talked, [but] she and my father used to laugh. She was very Indian-looking, and one time I remember him putting a blanket around her, and he made up this song [about] a papoose, and she just laughed and laughed. She used to grab me and hug me — she was a big woman, real loving — and I remember [thinking] she was going to smother me in her breasts!"

Everybody laughed when second-billed Chuck Jackson split his pants onstage, but Linda didn't think it was funny when Sam invited her cousin Ophelia to come out and twist with him as the Upsetters kicked off "Twistin' the Night Away." She said she hated him, and when Barbara tried to soothe her ruffled feelings, she announced that she was never going to speak to her father again. She got over it, Sam made it right with her just like he was able to make it right with everybody else, she adored her daddy. But she was just like him, too, Barbara thought. He could try to safeguard her from this world all he wanted, he could insist that his daughter was going to get an education and do something different, something better, with her life, but in the end she was going to do just as she pleased. Because she was stubborn, Barbara thought. Just like her daddy.

"When Sam come to town," said L.C., "it was like a holiday. If you had to go to work, you wouldn't go, because you wouldn't want to miss the party. When Sam come here, he wouldn't buy no bottle of gin, he would buy a case. Every kind of whiskey, man, Charles would have it in his dressing room — by the case. Sam told Charles, 'Charles, don't never let me get out of whiskey.' Charles said, 'Brother, you don't have to worry about it. I can spend your money.' Sam used to spend so much money when he came here — he didn't care. 'Just be sure and get the receipt.' And then when we leave the Regal, we would go to Crain's house at Forty-fifth and Woodlawn and continue to party. Like I said, it was always a party."

Marvin Jones, the peppery little baritone singer from the original Highway QCs, hadn't seen Sam in a long time. He and his wife, Helen, went backstage after the show, and "the room was full of people, all of Sam's sisters was there, and when he saw my wife, Sam come out from behind a screen in his shorts and said, 'Lord, that's Sookie.'" Then he asked them to come back to the hotel, "and he took me in the bathroom, left fifteen or twenty people just sitting there, and we had a drink and talked about old times — he was sitting on the bathtub, and I was sitting on the toilet — and finally when we started to singing, that's when they come banging on the door!"

The leukemia rumor first cropped up around this time. "Uncon-firmed rumors swept the Eastern Seaboard," reported the *Philadelphia Tribune,* along with nearly every other Negro newspaper in the country, "that popular singer Sam Cooke is suffering from leukemia, a dread blood disease which is incurable and always fatal." J.W., who could only postulate that it might have stemmed from the inclusion of "Somebody Have Mercy" (with its lyric "Tell me what is wrong with me") on Sam's *Twistin' the Night Away* LP, denounced it repeatedly as "one of the mean-est and lowest canards I've witnessed during many years in show busi-ness and public life." Nevertheless, the story persisted and grew to the point that much of the black community believed that Sam had willed his eyes to Ray Charles, and William Morris agent Jerry Brandt was still vehemently denying the rumor when Sam appeared at the National Association of Radio Announcers (NARA) convention in St. Louis the weekend of August 17.

The National Association of Radio Announcers was a professional organization that had been founded by thirteen prominent black DJs in the mid-1950s (as the National Jazz, Rhythm & Blues Disc Jockey Asso-ciation) and by 1962 had gained a membership of over three hundred, including a few whites, like all-night r&b DJ "Hoss" Allen, who was deemed an honorary "ace boon coon" by his fellow jocks. The organiza-tion's original impetus had been to combat some of the fundamental inequities of the job: what black-radio historian William Barlow described as everything from "low salaries to lack of employment oppor-tunities in mainstream radio to the uneven distribution of payola along racial lines." The record industry's response to these complaints had been, essentially, to bankroll the conventions, which, as Barlow wrote, were transformed by this cash infusion "into a weekend of around-the-clock revelry and highjinks." In the words of one of its founding mem-bers, "Jockey" Jack Gibson: "We partied until it was time to go to church."

With the growth of the civil rights movement, however, NARA was beginning to see itself as occupying if not higher at least more socially significant ground. It was still a trade association, according to promi-nent New Orleans jock Larry McKinley, in which the idea of self-help predominated. "It was just an idea of camaraderie. All of us had some interest maybe in a song, maybe in publishing, or in the act itself, the artist, and as we got older, we started to learn how to network. I mean, I could call Houston, get Boogaloo, get Hot Rod [Hulbert] in Baltimore, Al

[Jefferson] up in Detroit, and Rodney [Jones], of course, in Chicago —
Jockey at that time was in Cincinnati, and, of course, Hoss Allen and [fel-
low white r&b jock] John R. were crisscrossing all over [on Nashville's
"clear-channel" WLAC]. There was never any money exchanged, we just
did favors for each other that no outsider could do."

And as the Movement gained a foothold, those favors extended
almost necessarily to the entire community. "You have to understand,"
said Jockey Jack, "that we were the voice that the people listened to, and
if you gave us a message to say, 'There will be a meeting tonight of SCLC
[Martin Luther King's Southern Christian Leadership Conference] at the
First Baptist Church,' we would go ahead and elaborate all around it,
[saying], 'Now, Dr. King says to be there at seven sharp, no CP [colored
people's] time, and you know what I mean . . . 'cause this is important
for you and me and our children.' . . . And it worked. People came out on
time." It was, said Philadelphia DJ Georgie Woods, like having a "freedom mike" over which a secret message was being sent out directly to
the people, with little or no interference from white ownership or the
white world, which was for the most part either ignorant or indifferent.

Harold Battiste, who had gone to work for Specialty in 1957, written
the vocal arrangement for "You Send Me," and returned to his native
New Orleans to run Specialty's office there for the next three years,
attended the St. Louis convention with trumpeter Melvin Lastie. Together
with three other fellow New Orleanians, they had formed a musicians'
cooperative, a production company called AFO, or All For One, whose
avowed aim, in Harold Battiste's 1959 Manifesto, was for the "laborers,"
or musicians, to take back the means of production and distribute the
profits equally among themselves. This the AFO label had done with its
second release, Barbara George's "I Know," which had gone to the top of
the r&b *and* pop charts earlier in the year, and Melvin and Harold
attended the St. Louis convention in the belief that its stated theme, "A
Time to Speak," meant just what it said. "We thought they had the same
kind of motives that we had about utilizing [their] strength as a group to
make inroads into ownership." In the event, they may have been disappointed, but, like Sam, they were not about to give up. There was room,
Harold Battiste felt strongly, for practical black idealism in the world of
business, and he felt that AFO, along with established pioneers like Sam
and Alex and Berry Gordy in Detroit, could show the way.

Sam entertained at the RCA reception on Saturday night, and Crain had his money and briefcase stolen. He had had a party with another couple and a woman named Peaches in his room at the Sheraton-Jefferson, the convention site, and "early the next morning," the *St. Louis Argus* reported, "he discovered that more than $250 in cash and an expensive camera were missing." Sam was barely able to contain himself as he gave the older man a stern lecture about responsibility and Crain complained bitterly about how this chick had ripped him off. "That chick just wore you out," the others all ragged at him. "She knew right where the money was at. What did you do when you were finished? Just close your eyes and go to sleep?"

Sam spent five days at home after the convention, and Luigi flew in for a session the night before he was scheduled to go back out on the road. They couldn't get into the RCA studio until midnight, but Sam was determined to record "Nothing Can Change This Love," a recent composition that he had first attempted in February with Oopie singing bass behind a bouncy doo-wop beat. This time he took an entirely different approach, sketching out a lushly orchestrated string-laden arrangement for René that transformed the song. It opened with a piano introduction by Eddie Beal, then unfolded with a sorrowful deliberation so at odds with the cheeriness of the earlier version that it almost seemed as if some life-changing event must have intervened.

"If I go / A million miles away / I'd write a letter / Each and every day / 'Cause nothing can ever change the love I have for you," Sam sings as a swirl of violins, cellos, and violas washes over his voice. It sounds for all the world like the most clichéd version of romantic love, but then as the song develops, you realize that what you are hearing is not the embrace but the denial of illusion, set forth in a tone of deeply ambiguous regret. "You're the apple of my eye / You're cherry pie / And, oh, you're cake and ice cream," is the explicit message of the bridge, even as the singer's world-weary mood, the unspoken layers of irony, yearning, and knowledge that accompany his heartfelt declarations, work to undercut any suggestion of belief. It ends with as straightforward an admission of the lover's plight as you're ever likely to get from Sam ("Mmmm, make me weep / And you can make me cry / See me coming / And you can pass on by / But nothing can ever change this love I have for you"), followed by the whisper of strings, a muted clash of cymbals, and trailing notes from the piano that recapitulate the opening passage of the song. Eight takes merely refined the message, and RCA put the record out on the street two and one-half weeks later, where its sales swiftly rivaled "Bring It On Home to Me."

With the Valentinos' "Lookin' For a Love" really beginning to take off, Alex got the group booked on a James Brown theater-circuit tour starting at the Apollo in October, and he was already planning an all-out promotion campaign for the Sims Twins' next single in the weeks following that. Sam pointed a reporter for the Raleigh-Durham area black weekly, *The Carolinian,* toward the Valentinos' hit while playing a September 17 Supersonic date with Clyde McPhatter in Raleigh. "I was also informed by Sam that [his] brother L.C. Cooke . . . will have a release very soon called 'You're Workin' Out Your Bag on Me,'" wrote *Carolinian* reporter Oscar Alexander in his "Diggin' Daddy-Oh!" column. But what Sam really appeared to be excited about was his upcoming European tour. He would be going, he said, for "both business and pleasure" and spoke of visiting the French Riviera, though, in fact, his month abroad would be confined to a week of one-nighters at American military bases in Germany, followed by a three-week tour of England October 8–28. What, asked the *Carolinian* columnist with a verbal wink, would he do about the exotic fare he was likely to encounter over there? "Man," said Sam, replying in kind, "I'll stow away as much as I possibly can, and when I get [back] to the States, I'll find the first real home cooking restaurant and order some real 'soul food.'" But there was no disguising his genuine excitement about the trip, Riviera or no Riviera.

BRITISH PROMOTER DON ARDEN had been courting Sam for some time. Arden, born Harry Levy, was a thirty-six-year-old show-business veteran who had originally made his mark as Europe's best-known folk singer in the newly revived Hebrew language. He had started producing shows in 1954 and had come over to Los Angeles at the beginning of the summer specifically to sign Little Richard for a tour. Richard had not sung rock 'n' roll in almost five years, and Arden, the only promoter in England seriously committed to importing authentic American rock 'n' roll, felt he could make a killing if he could just persuade the star to return to his former field of glory.

"I made a couple of journeys to L.A. to get hold of him, and eventually he said, 'Very well, I'll sing rock 'n' roll again for you. But,' he said, 'the Lord will punish you, because I've always believed it's somebody evil that's going to bring me back.' And I loved that. I thought it was great." Arden's view of promotion was, quite simply, to create a stir. Controversy was nothing new to him, and he knew the British press would become aroused at the first sign of conflict. But he didn't trust his star — "I didn't dislike him, I *distrusted* him" — and right up until opening night he was uncertain what exactly he would do.

With Sam he harbored no such doubts. He had posed the terms of the engagement straightforwardly to Jerry Brandt, explaining that there would be two shows a night at venues seating between two thousand and twenty-five hundred and that Sam would be the co-star, closing out the first half of the bill, but Richard would unquestionably be the star. Then he met with Sam. "A perfect gentleman, exceptionally good-looking and [well-spoken], I'm sure he was highly educated, and he had confidence in the people he was working with." J.W. accompanied Sam to Arden's hotel, and Don found him to be a perfect gentleman as well. "I felt he knew all about Sam's talent and was capable of telling people what his artist needed without being a heavy." To Arden, Sam "probably had the best voice I'd heard in over twenty years, artistically I was jealous of him," but the delightful surprise was his sophistication and curiosity. "He said, 'I want you to tell me about England. I think we must have spent three or four hours together.'"

Arden's fears about Little Richard turned out to be well founded. None of the legitimate theaters would book a rock 'n' roll show, so Arden was forced to slot the revue into movie theaters for the most part, with the Granada chain (which had more than half the dates) more or less "sponsoring" the tour. He had assembled a program that included "Gag Slinger" Bob Bain as comedy act and compere; twenty-three-year-old Jet Harris, who had recently left Cliff Richard's band, the Shadows, as co-star of the second half; a saxophone-heavy instrumental group called Sounds Incorporated to back the various acts; and American expatriate rocker Gene Vincent serving as impromptu audience "plant," since, with the expiration of his British working papers, he could only sing his seminal 1956 hit, "Be Bop a Lu La," from the same seat in the orchestra from which he would then introduce the two stars.

Opening night, October 8, was scheduled for the Gaumont in Doncaster, a small, out-of-the-way northern venue that Arden had picked for its very obscurity ("It was a shocking place — I don't think anybody'd ever heard of it"), because, he calculated, any kinks in the show or in his star's attitude could safely be ironed out there. He had left little to chance, but he could scarcely have anticipated Sam's plane from Germany being so late that he would miss the first show of the evening altogether. Nor could he have been fully prepared for the strange turn that Little Richard's stubbornly recalcitrant piety would now take.

He was not surprised when Richard showed up with a huge Family Bible, nor when he started quoting Scripture at him. He would not have been taken off-guard if Richard had demanded more money, and he had already planned his own response, which would have been to threaten to send his reluctant star home with no money for his return fare — which Arden was perfectly prepared to do. There was little at this stage that could have shocked him. But he was genuinely taken aback, and *helpless*, at the performance that Richard put on at the early-evening 6:15 show.

"As soon as he walked out, I knew we were in for trouble," said Arden. Richard was wearing what looked to the promoter like religious robes, and he started off singing gospel songs exclusively — "Joy Joy Joy"; his own brilliant original "He Got What He Wanted (But He Lost What He Had)"; and the inspirational number "I Believe" — as his accompanist, sixteen-year-old Billy Preston (making his first appearance on the secular stage more than ten years after his debut on piano as a gospel child prodigy) took a featured turn on organ. It was only at the end of a very abbreviated set that Little Richard allowed the band to play what they had been rehearsing for most of the day, presenting a rapid-fire medley of his hits that ended with "Jenny, Jenny" and got a somewhat sparse house on its feet. "But even at this point," wrote Chris Hutchins in the *New Musical Express*, "it seemed we were something short of the great artist who once rocked the world with his records."

Don Arden was fit to be tied. He pleaded, he cajoled, he threatened Little Richard to no effect ("I said, 'Now look, don't double-cross me. That's a naughty thing to do.' He said, 'You're the devil'") — and then he rushed outside to reassure the queue for the second show that, despite what they may have heard from the departing crowd, they were not going to be shortchanged. But he held out little hope until Sam and J.W. finally arrived. He asked if there wasn't *something* they could say to Richard. He begged Sam to intercede, even after J.W. pointed out that Little Richard would most likely just respond to the competition that

Sam had to offer. So in the end Sam agreed, as a favor to the promoter, to speak with Richard in his dressing room.

Sam reasoned with Richard. He said they had both come a long way to do this tour, that this was his first trip to England, and that maybe Richard thought Don Arden had used some kind of trickery to get them over here, but that as far as he knew, they had both signed contracts and he was certainly going to honor his. Arden simply watched in astonishment. "Sam said, 'You're a man. Why didn't you say, "No, I can't," if you didn't want to do it?' And, you know, Little Richard melted. He said, 'I'm only doing this because I respect you as an artist.' And they both shook hands, and Richard decided to shake hands with me. But even after all [that], he still opened up the second show by saying, 'I am here by courtesy of the devil, Don Arden!'"

J.W. was not convinced it wasn't Little Richard's competitive instinct as much as Sam's persuasive powers that prompted him to put on what Chris Hutchins described as a "roof-raising act that began and ended with rock." Sam, according to both Alex and Hutchins, killed the house, but then Richard came out at the end of the show, just as J.W. had said he would, "he came out with a damn chair in his mouth, and he pulled off that robe, and he literally slayed them." He sang all of his hits, ran screaming up and down the aisle, and whatever peak Sam had been able to achieve, Richard was able to overcome with what J.W. called his "energizing approach." It was a lesson in humility for Sam, but one that J.W. felt was not about to be lost on him.

The rest of the tour had its own internal dramas, though none quite so electrifying as the first. Little Richard continued to put on an arresting performance night after night, and Sam and J.W. continued to have the same lesson drilled into them. "No matter how Sam killed the house," said Alex, "Richard could always come back with that energizing approach." Most of the audiences were there for Richard, who was far better known in England than Sam and who continued to introduce new and exciting elements into his act. Perhaps the climax came when, in the midst of a piano-pounding "Lucille," he keeled over at the piano and fell to the stage as though struck dead. Amid cries of "Is there a doctor in the house?" Richard lay prostrate on the stage, while the audience fell silent, and band members, stagehands, and a bewildered security crew anxiously gathered around the fallen star. Then suddenly a sound emanated from him. "A wop bop a lu bop, a lop bam boom," screamed the resur-

Jet Harris, Little Richard, Gene Vincent, Sam: England, October 1962. *Courtesy of Trevor Cajiao,* Now Dig This!

rected Little Richard, and the audience greeted his revival with a fervor that generally brought the show to a close. It was, said Bill Millar, seventeen years old when he attended the show at the Maidstone Granada, "the most exciting thing I'd ever seen, a never-forgotten moment." Forty years later, a passionate and perceptive chronicler of rock history, he could scarcely even recall Sam.

For Jet Harris, on the other hand, who studied both headliners closely from the wings each night, Sam's act was a lesson in polish and sophistication. Harris, a rocker with peroxide-blond hair, had come on the tour as a kind of protégé of Gene Vincent, with a nod to James Dean, and was absolutely fascinated with Little Richard. "Richard used to watch my show, and when I'd come off, he'd say, 'Now, look, you've got to make love to the guitar, treat it like a woman.' He gave me loads of advice. But some of the things he wanted me to do, in my mind, were outrageous. So I didn't bother."

Sam, by way of contrast, was quiet, polite, almost unapproachable because of the way in which he marked off the boundaries of his world both by his manner and by the coterie that surrounded him. Crain and Alex, his brother Charles, his musicians Clif White and June Gardner, all silently served his needs and responded to his direction without his ever having to raise his voice or make a single untoward suggestion. "I was quite in awe of what a sort of gentleman he was. But when he went [onstage], he was a man in his own complete and utter style — he couldn't go wrong. Most of the audience were waiting for Little Richard, but Sam just captured them — you know, 'Here I am, get hold of this, I'm on.' He really just hypnotized — with his hands, his voice, I can't stop using that word, he *hypnotized* the audience."

To Don Arden, too, Sam was unquestionably the class act. "He walked out as easy as anything, like somebody preparing to tell those people his life story. That was his attitude." From Arden's point of view, there was no real comparison with Little Richard. "Richard was a different type of actor. He went out hoping that he was going to make people laugh. And he succeeded in that — and he succeded in making them appreciate his songs. [But] there was nobody to touch Sam."

Of course Arden may have been prejudiced. In addition to the trauma of simply setting up the tour, he had encountered more than a small amount of private trauma of his own. Arden believed in involving his family in his business — contrary to the thuggish public image that he had always cultivated ("In those days, if I lost my temper, you know [there'd] be headlines about it, and I kind of took advantage of that"), he often had his wife and children with him backstage, and on this tour he had his ten-year-old daughter, Sharon, and nine-year-old son, David, accompanying him. Little Richard's oversized Bible had been a subject of abiding fascination to everyone on the show ("It was never away from him," Jet Harris observed. "He carried it everywhere"), not so much what he was reading as what he was writing in it all the time. He kept it under lock and key whenever he was onstage, and, Arden said, it had become a kind of contest as to who was going to get a look at the book first. It turned out to be Arden's nine-year-old son, when one of his long-time employees got a key to the star's dressing room and, as a joke, gave it to the little boy. David brought the Bible back and was present for the revelation of a very graphic sex diary, with male lovers rated for their specific skills, names and dates included.

Arden was mortified that his son should have been exposed to something so salacious, primarily through the irresponsibility of one of his own employees. He was taken aback as well by what he viewed as Richard's blatant hypocrisy, even though "when you start in show business at thirteen, there's very little that you miss." But most of all he relished the opportunity that this gave him for the perfect conversational comeback, and the next time that Richard started in on his familiar sermon that it was Don Arden who was responsible for all the sin in the world, since he was the Devil incarnate, "I said, 'Yes, and I know about another little devil [who] writes rude things in Bibles.' Well, he went hysterical, but — and I must say, that's what I admire about him — he finished off laughing about it. He knew that he'd been caught out, you see."

It was sex that was the inspiration for Sam's latest song, too — or, rather, the comical deprivation of it. He and Alex had been staying at the aristocratic Mayfair Hotel, but the first time they brought back some girls ("Sam was a guy in great demand," said a bemused Don Arden of Sam's many social conquests), they were informed by the management that they were prohibited by hotel policy from entertaining female guests in Sam's suite. Alex immediately went out and booked another, smaller hotel where they could do whatever they liked, but the incident lingered, and one night in the dressing room, Sam picked up his guitar, said J.W., "and he started strumming. 'It's another Saturday night, and I ain't got nobody / I got some money 'cause I just got paid / How I wish I had someone to talk to / I'm in an awful way' — you know, it was like a joke!" Which was perhaps just another way of expressing what Sam told a *New Musical Express* reporter, who informed his readers that Sam had simply "dreamed up" another hit out of a sleepless night at his hotel.

Sam also spoke to *Melody Maker* about his writing methods and success, pointing out that Jackie Wilson had already recorded one of his songs ("I'll Always Be in Love With You") and that Pat Boone was planning to record another, "When a Boy Falls in Love," in the very near future. In response to a question about *Black Nativity*, the gospel musical drama that Mike Santangelo had recently brought to London for a triumphant West End run (with the same note of thanks to Sam and Jess Rand that had appeared in the original American program book), he said, "I started as a gospel singer, you know. Doesn't [that] music just swing?" All rock, Sam declared, sprang from gospel music, but, no, he didn't include any gospel songs in his act, just his pop hits. So far as his first British tour was concerned, "Honestly, I have never come across audiences like the British ones. They give you so much rapt attention. . . . [But] I don't get time to see as much of England as I want to. . . . I can see myself going back home and people asking, 'What's London like?' And I'll have to say, 'I don't know — we didn't stop long enough!' "

With Maureen Cleave of the *Evening Standard,* he was somewhat more revealing. Dressed in "red-patterned pyjamas, a black dressing gown, and a beaten gold ring, which he wears," Cleave wrote, "because he doesn't like diamonds — or any precious stones for that matter — he lounged about on his bed and when something amused him, which was often, he threw his head back and roared like a bull."

Spotting John Braine's latest novel, *Life at the Top,* on Sam's bedside table, " 'You read books?' I gasped, for Mr. Cooke is a pop singer."

"Excessively," was Sam's response. He read all the time, he said, history mostly, because he "wanted to know how to appeal to people, and books teach you that." He read Winston Churchill and Arthur Schlesinger Jr. (presumably on the Second World War and Franklin Delano Roosevelt respectively), but his current favorite was James Baldwin. He spoke a little about business, about the fact that "his recording label think highly enough of him to put him on the same royalty basis as Elvis Presley and Harry Belafonte, which is high thinking indeed." He spoke of SAR, too, and his brother L.C.'s latest release. Why the initials? the reporter asked. What was his Christian name? "He never did have a name, and I'll tell you why," said Sam in a tone the reporter does not choose to characterize. "Ignorance. You see, my great-grandmother was a slave in Mississippi. She had no education. Neither did my father. He was a self-made man. But he saw the disadvantages to the Negro child in the South, so he . . . went north to Chicago. In many ways I'm very like my father. He has this intense drive that I've got, and I think it's this drive that makes stars out of people. You want to stay at the top."

He designed all his own clothes, he said, because he always wanted to differentiate himself from the current fad. The reporter had to take his word for that, because, as she wrote, "I had only seen the dressing gown." And what of his music? Rock 'n' roll was a highly emotional kind of music, which suited him fine, he said, "because I am a bundle of emotions. I write songs that start slowly and then work in little by little to this pounding beat. That is where the excitement is. But I still have my religious beliefs. Our forebears thought you couldn't sing [both] pops and spirituals, but I have rationalized this. I can do anything I want and still have my religious beliefs. My philosophy of life is: Do whatever is best for Sam Cooke."

The last week of the tour was marked by the turmoil of the Cuban missile crisis. Little Richard reacted in much the same way that he had to *Sputnik* five years earlier: he saw the end of the world approaching largely due to his own embrace, once again, of secular music. "He was praying all day, six or seven hours a day," said June Gardner, "because he figured he was supposed to be preaching — but Sam was cool. It was kind of like Come what may [with] all of us. Come what may."

On Sunday, October 28, with the weeklong crisis finally resolved and the tour proper over, Sam played a stand-alone date in Manchester with Sophie Tucker, the seventy-eight-year-old "Last of the Red Hot Mamas," who was a special favorite of Don Arden's for her unabashed, often bawdy, showmanship. Arden had never seen anyone able to follow the American vaudeville star, and he asked Sam to do so as a special favor only after her original supporting act had dropped out. "Sam said, 'I want you to know, my mother's not Jewish, so I won't be singing "My Yiddishe Mama," but she's a great artist — does she know that I'm on?' I said, 'No, she doesn't care who's on the bill with her, in actual fact,' and he said, 'I think I like it better that way.' But he closed the first half to a Jewish audience at the Palace Theater in Manchester, the top theater in the north of England, and he just slaughtered them. When Sophie came on, she was stunned; in all the years I [booked] Miss Tucker and foolishly idolized her, that was the very first time she failed to follow another artist. She couldn't do it. He had her audience in his grasp, and he didn't let go."

Little Richard, meanwhile, was playing the Empire Theater in Liverpool, where the second act on the bill was the Beatles, whose debut single, "Love Me Do," had just entered the British Top 30. Richard had played one previous date with the Beatles, and, despite all of his conflicts with Don Arden and the emotional turmoil of the past week, he called the promoter after the show. "He told me, 'You've got to grab them. There's nothing to touch them.'" But Arden couldn't do it. He was friendly with the group's manager, Brian Epstein, he explained, though he was very appreciative to Richard and well aware that this might be the only time he would ever see humility from a man who proclaimed himself loudly and repeatedly to be more explosive than the atom bomb.

After the Manchester date, Little Richard went on to Hamburg, Germany, with the Beatles, and Sam and his party flew to New York, where he was scheduled to open at the Apollo in five days. Everyone else stayed in Harlem, but Sam and Alex continued on to Los Angeles so that René could write Sam a new act. Alex had been advancing the argument for some time that Sam needed to develop a set that reflected the gospel *fervor* of his music. "In England Sam could [finally] see the truth of that, and we started reworking his act [with] that gospel approach, and then we came back to California and had René write it into the show."

S AM OPENED AT THE APOLLO on November 2, and the difference in his entire aspect and presentation was immediately apparent. He was backed once again by the Upsetters — with the Coasters, a teen girl group from Brooklyn called the Crystals, and saxophonist King Curtis, who had defined not just the Coasters' yakkety-sax style but the heart of the Atlantic label's "rock 'n' soul" sound, also on the bill. Whereas Sam had been criticized in the not-too-distant past for sitting on a stool on the Apollo stage and adopting the casual approach of a Perry Como, this time, said J.W., who was actively cheerleading from the wings, "he really turned the Apollo out." At the heart of the new act was a medley of his hits presented not in their familiar format but, in some cases, turned almost upside down. It was introduced by a teasing gospelized version of "It's All Right," the B-side of 1961's "Feel It," followed by raucous, good-time renditions of "Twistin' the Night Away" and "Somebody Have Mercy." It is at this point that the show really changes direction, as Sam cries out over and over, "Oh, yeah, oh yeah," egging the crowd on, egging the crowd to respond, with just the punctuation of a fanfare from Clif's guitar, the clatter of the cymbals, a drumroll that accentuates the unrestrained urgency of his tone. "I said I believe we're gonna have a good time," Sam calls out as he launches into the carefully crafted climax of the act. "I feel like you in the mood for me to tell you about my baby," he chants in the kind of loose, free-flowing imprecation that can be cut off or extended at will and suggests a degree of spontaneity that is entirely dependent on the feeling that is put into it. He is singing in an almost pinched tone, with a hoarseness that suggests the intensity that few audiences have heard from him since he left the gospel field. "Well, you know sometimes my baby, we fuss and fight . . .

And my baby leave home
'Cause things ain't right
Oh, but I get to feeling — ha ha — so all alone
And I dial my baby on the telephone
I finally get the operator on the telephone
And I tell her, "Listen here, operator,
I want my b-a-a — aby,
Ohhhh, operator, I want my baby."
Finally the operator get my baby on the telephone
And I tell her, "I got something to tell you, honey."
The minute I hear my baby say hello
S-s-s-s-something start to move deep down inside of me
And I tell her, "Listen to me, baby,
I know I didn't treat you right sometimes
And I want you to know one thing"

He has them now. There's no doubt about it. With all the tried-and-true methods of his gospel training, he has drawn out the tension until it is almost unbearable, people are screaming, they are crying out for release, the level of emotion almost visibly rises, the audience becomes his congregation.

"I just want you to know one thing
And that's . . .
Darling,
You-u-u-u-uuuu, ohhhhhhh . . . you SEND ME
Oh-ohhhhhh, you send me
Ha ha, that's what I want to tell you, baby,
Oh, oh-oh you-ou, awww, you send me
Aw, let me tell you one more time
Oh, yo-u-u-u-u-u
Oh, baby . . . you send me
Oh-whoa-oh-ohohhhhhwowohhhh — Ha ha —
Ohhhhwhoawhoaoh
Honest you do"

It is a version of the song that has never been heard before, a version that denies all prior mood or meaning that Sam's most readily identifiable hit has ever had. It is an ecstatic moment in and of itself, and then pandemonium breaks loose as he hits the familiar opening notes of his biggest crowd-pleaser, "Bring It On Home to Me." Night after night it builds into a mass sing-along in which there is no need to mention church, everyone knows they are *having* it, and the only way to top this communal feeling is to extend it, first with the romantic sway of "Nothing Can Change This Love," then with the ultimate existential statement of what is going on right here, right now, in this theater as seventeen hundred people join in on the chorus of Sam's most universal song: "We're having a party / Dancing to the music / Played by the DJ / ON THE RA-DI-O." There is no one, it seems, who isn't singing or cannot picture themselves in the scene. "The Cokes are in the icebox / Popcorn's on the table." And with that, Sam delivers his masterfully open-ended final line:

> *Me and my baby,*
> *We're out here on the floor*

"Keep on having that party," he calls out over and over as the curtain comes down, "no matter where you're at, remember, I told you, keep on having that party." Through his music, he declares, he will continue to be with them — it's as close to eternity, in their unvoiced understanding, as any of them are ever likely to come.

H E CONTINUED TO EXPERIMENT with it night after night, raising the level of audience response, inviting women up onstage to do the Twist, but most of all inciting the kind of mass hysteria that James Brown and Jackie Wilson customarily got from their audiences, that June Cheeks had brought to the Soul Stirrers' show nine years earlier and Little Richard had reminded him of with an English audience that couldn't even clap on the beat. It was in many ways the kind of devotional response he had always gotten, even as he insisted to Jess Rand or Hugo and Luigi that he was "just shuckin'," but it was accentuated now by a return to the riveting intensity of the gospel approach that had led Lloyd Price to muse on how "he just stood there flat-footed and *rocked* them. He didn't have to do nothing but sing." A lot of people were going to be surprised by Sam's new act, reported the *Philadelphia Tribune,* even as *Variety* described "his rapport with the femmes, letting them hug him as he belts 'Bring It to Me,' tossing out his tie for a bit of localized femme fisticuffs . . . and the like."

L.C. and his girlfriend had driven in from Chicago with Duck and his wife in Duck's new Chevrolet convertible. They were staying at the Cecil, where Lithofayne Pridgon had first met Sam when he was still with the Stirrers and just thinking about going pop. L.C.'s new SAR single was doing no better than his previous ones, but L.C. gave the same impression of success that he always did — he might not be worth a million bucks, but he *looked* like a million bucks, and you always knew he was somebody because of what he himself termed the "likeability factor." He still wore his hair processed, like Charles, and he was not as slender as Sam, but his voice and manner were almost identical to his brother's, and the impish delight he took in all of life's manifold pleasures was even more pronounced. Sam reminded his brother of how Lithofayne had taken a liking to L.C. way back when he had first accompanied Sam to the Apollo and told L.C. then that she was going to get him someday. "Oh no, you ain't," L.C. had laughingly replied. "Oh yes, I am," said Lithofayne with her little smile, but nothing had come of it so far.

This time Sam came knocking on L.C.'s hotel door. "He said, 'Come on, C., I want you to go with me.' He told my girlfriend, 'Me and C. will be right back.' I had no idea that Sam's got Faye and three more girls in the room. We go to the room, and there are the girls, naked, waiting on me and Sam. Faye said, 'I *told* you I was gonna get you.' And, look, me and Sam didn't have to do nothing, just lay back, two ladies apiece working on us, one sucking our titties, one sucking our dicks, I swear to God, we just lay there in the bed with our hands behind our backs." It may well have been on that same trip that L.C. took the opportunity to remind Sam, as he frequently did, of what his brother had told him when they were little boys. "I said, 'Sam, you know you told me you were never going to work.' He laughed and said, 'Man, you remember that?' I said, 'Yeah, I remember that.' He said, 'Did I ever have a job?' And I said, 'Not that I know of, Sam.' And we both cracked up."

Hugo and Luigi came to see him at the Apollo and were knocked out by the new show. They planned for a singles session in Hollywood at the end of the month, with a new friend of Sam's, busy New York arranger Horace Ott (whom Sam had met through Ott's "cousin," the up-and-coming young r&b singer and songwriter Don Covay) handling the orchestrations. They talked about an album of standards along the lines of Ray Charles' recent efforts, and Sam thought he might like to use Ott

Lithofayne Pridgon with
James Brown, ca. 1962.
*Courtesy of Lithofayne
Pridgon*

for that, too — get himself a new studio sound, even as he was changing his whole stage act around. The only real fly in the ointment was the performance of the Upsetters, whose insistence on reinforcing their reputation as a premier "show band" was more and more in conflict with Sam's vision of their role. "One of the fellows wanted to sing all the time," said Charles, "and Sam said, 'I don't need no singer.'" The trumpet player never stopped talking, the bass player wasn't picking up on Sam's cues, and the way June saw it, the group was more concerned with its own act than they were with Sam's. This was the first time Sam had had a chance to directly observe King Curtis' band, the Kingpins, and they were a tight little unit — but, just as important, the way Sam figured it, they could not have become the number-one session band in New York City if they didn't have the willingness, and the musical versatility, to deliver exactly what was asked of them. So he started talking with Curtis, an articulate, outgoing twenty-eight-year-old Texan with a passion for gambling, he asked him if he might not like to come out with them, playing behind Sam and with a featured spot in the show. At first Curtis said there was no way he could *afford* to go on the road with all the session work he had coming in — but, he said, it sounded like fun. He liked Sam, and he hit it off with Sam's brother, Charlie, too, they played dice and cards backstage every night, as Charles told him about the good times they could have together out on the road.

S AM HAD BEEN TOURING for almost six months now, but he continued to take additional bookings. He appeared on *The Tonight Show*, with its brand-new host, Johnny Carson, a week after finishing at the Apollo, and he played a WAOK benefit in Atlanta with L.C., which station owner Zenas Sears recorded and tried to sell to RCA. It was a wonderful performance, said Sears, who had recorded the classic Atlantic album *Ray Charles Live* under similar circumstances in 1959 at Herndon Stadium, but what made it special was the way that Sam addressed the kids, "just talking to [them] and doing these gospel changes, it was the nicest thing." He had a new driver, Clarence Watley, who had been driving for the Five Blind Boys of Alabama for years and was put in charge of the band station wagon while Charles continued to drive the Cadillac. Watley knew the road. "He didn't need no map," said Charles. "He was the best road man I ever run into."

The Valentinos joined the tour after completing their stint with James Brown. Their initial week with James at the Apollo, while Sam was still in England, had provided all the educational opportunities Sam had said it would, in terms of both life and music. Bobby Womack and his brothers had arrived in New York City looking like country cousins, Bobby said, "we done just drove all the way, and we ain't got but about a hundred dollars in our pocket, and we see this big old white chick standing out in front of the hotel. I paid the woman for me and all my brothers, but I was the last one that wanted to fuck with it, to be honest, 'cause I didn't even know where to put it. I think she washed up [two of my] brothers, and they was just gone. So I told her, 'I don't want to be washed. I want the real thing.' But two days later, man, we thought we were dying, we couldn't piss. Solomon Burke was on that show — he used to cook chicken backstage, charge you a dollar for a sandwich, man, he could turn out the house, but he'd always be late getting onstage, because he was, 'I can't come now. The chicken is gonna burn!' — and we went to him, told him it was somebody else that was sick, and instead of helping us, man, he scared the living daylights out of us. He said, 'Aw, man, tell that boy it ain't that bad. The first two days just all your teeth start to fall out. But on the *fourth* day, when your eyes start to decay, that's key — 'cause then you can't see!' He finally let us off the hook and said, 'Y'all have the claps. Go to the clinic, and they'll get you straightened out. But I'll tell you one thing, you got to learn to keep your dick in your pants.'"

They didn't know they could draw on their salary, so when they ran out of money, they stole bread and bologna from the store around the corner. "I mean, we didn't know anything, we were getting burned left and right."

But their greatest education came in the field of music. They arrived in New York, thrilled that the Apollo band, with its full eight-piece horn section, would be playing behind them. Bobby found a guy in Cleveland, "he said, 'I write music,' and I had him write me the chord changes on the song and then [make] about thirteen copies, and we passed them all out to everybody onstage. And the horn player said, 'I got a guitar part.' Somebody else say, '*I* got a guitar part.' *Everybody* got a guitar part. And James come out and say, 'Who did the arrangements?' I said, 'I did. I didn't want to pay a lot of money, so I decided to [have it] copied just one time.' And James said, 'Aw, man, these guys ain't never been out of Cleveland.' So he rearranged it, wrote the parts out."

James didn't seem all that impressed that their first pop single had reached number eight on the r&b charts. He didn't seem impressed with much of anything about them, in fact. "James was up on us every day. I mean, he was an evil man, *everything* made him mad — and he dwelled on perfection. He said, 'You guys, y'all got to learn how to dance, you got to learn how to take your bows, didn't you never hear of an encore in Cleveland?' I said, 'What is that, like a choir?' And he take a drumstick and hit me on the head with it: 'Listen to me when I'm talking to you.'"

He watched them every night from the wings, every show, four shows a day. "Something was always wrong, and when you came off, he was right there telling you. I hated it. I hated him. He had an attitude about us wearing our hair real long — you know, things like that. He was always talking about *his* show." It was obvious from remarks that he made that he had his reservations about Sam, too, but Bobby and his brothers never had any doubt about why Sam had put them with him. "I heard Sam telling Alex, 'I want them to go with James [because] I can't be as hard on them as I need to be.' Sam would try to be different. He was just intelligent. He was like, 'Speaking from a psychological point of view, your virtuosity has dominated the ethereal spectrum.' James Brown says, 'Man, fuck that. Fuck all that shit. Just tell me I'm good, you know.' Sam would laugh and say [about him], 'You see that fucker right there? He'll outlive us all.' "

It was like boot camp, Bobby said, but when they were done, the group was capable of near-military precision. They had also gotten to witness one of the greatest live shows ever put together, pop or gospel, as Brown went out night after night and, rain or shine, good audience or bad, killed the crowd. It was a show so carefully calculated that Brown's band could turn on a dime (and draw fines on the spot if they didn't), but so spontaneous that in the midst of Brown's spectacular dance moves, his splits and twirls and bone-crunching knee drops, he could extend a song like his 1961 ballad hit, "Lost Someone," to ten, fifteen, twenty minutes, drawing the audience in, teasing them with every gospel trick in the book, using moments of stillness to emphasize the astonishing subtlety of his stage movements, using moments of silence to show off the almost unearthly power of his June Cheeks–inspired screams. Just what they witnessed is still available in audio form, as, on October 24, the next-to-last night of the Apollo booking, armed only with his own money and his unassailable belief in himself, James brought in mobile recording equipment and, in a conscious attempt to capture history, recorded an r&b show as it actually was presented night after night all across the country, in the call-and-response fashion that made the audience as much a part of the show as the performer. "Don't go to strangers," James pleads in the "adlib" section of "Lost Someone," the centerpiece of his show, "Come on home to me. . . . Gee whiz, I love you. . . . I'm so weak . . . " The incantation is repeated over and over until it becomes almost hypnotic, and James knows he's got the audience, he could point out to the Womack brothers just where he hooked them, he could analyze it, but he would never repeat it in exactly the same way, and then he tests the limits once again, declaring, "I feel so good I want to scream." "Scream!" cries a voice in the crowd. And it goes on and on until at last he unleashes one last apocalyptic scream, and the music comes crashing down all around.

The Valentinos went on to play the Royal and the Howard with James, and by the time they finally joined Sam's show, they were sea-

soned performers. Sam watched proudly as they executed their synchronized steps, dressed in their fire-engine red suits, and got the crowd. He
had told them it would be different, it wasn't like playing to a roomful of
people who were already sold on salvation and all you had to do was
quote the Bible and sing to those sisters and you had them. In the pop
field, he told Bobby, "You got to give them a show, you got to perform.
When you go out there singing boogie-woogie, you got to come with it."
Which is exactly what the Valentinos did, to Sam's undisguised delight.

He took them all under his wing, but there was no way anyone could
miss that Bobby was his favorite, least of all his brothers. When the
Upsetters' bass player, Olsie Robinson ("Bassy"), walked out of a sound
check after a series of disagreements in which he felt he was being
goaded by Sam for what Sam termed his refusal to play what was being
asked of him, Bobby leapt unhesitatingly into the breach. "I said, 'Well, I
know all your songs, and I can play bass. I know every song that you ain't
never did onstage, 'cause I know everything that you cut.' He said, 'You
going to play for me? You a star now.' I said, 'Yeah, I don't care about
that. Shit, man, I'm with you.' So when I hooked up and started playing
that bass and didn't miss a note, oh, man, it floored him. I knew his
whole show. He said, 'That fucker, he thought he had me in a position.'
He said, 'Bobby, you want to keep playing with me?' "

His brothers were understandably jealous, and the Upsetters were
definitely pissed off. Tenor player Grady Gaines had heard enough about
Bassy's shortcomings and the group's deficiencies, and he didn't miss the
undercurrent of conversation about how tight King Curtis' group was and
how somehow things were going to have to change. Grady had known
Curtis (as Curtis Ousley) since they had first played in competing high
school bands in Houston and Fort Worth, and they had continued to run
into each other over the years. He was playing Alan Freed's Labor Day
show at the Brooklyn Paramount in 1957 with Little Richard when Curtis
was still in r&b saxophone legend Sam "The Man" Taylor's band. "We
talked a whole lot then, that was just when 'Keep A Knockin' came out,
and I taught him that little pop in the back of his sax, tonguing them
notes [that was] all over the Coasters [sound], everybody thinking it was
me. See, I thought of that stuff, but I didn't finish it." Nor was it finished
on this tour, which ended for the Valentinos with a Birmingham date that
featured Johnnie Taylor, the Sims Twins, and Johnnie Morisette. They
sold out two shows at the Birmingham Auditorium, and, as Friendly

Womack, the oldest brother, recalled it, the Valentinos were the stars of the show, but, when they returned to Cleveland, they had less than $100 among them. That was the end of the line for Friendly. He hadn't really envisioned show business being like this. He had just gotten married, he was angry at Bobby for taking over the group, and he agreed with Johnnie Taylor's view that they were being taken advantage of, they were *all* being taken advantage of, by Sam. "We got a number-one record," he told his brothers, "and we ain't got enough money to check into a hotel." Sam was steady talking to the group about moving out to California, he and Alex described it as the land of opportunity, but Friendly had made up his mind: his brothers could do whatever they wanted, they could go chasing after their fool's gold, but he wasn't no fool and he wasn't going to go.

Fame and fortune have a tendency to create, within those [they] strike, the urge to run away from home, family and people who formerly made their world an enjoyable place in which to live.

— Sam Cooke quoted in the *Chicago Defender*, February 27, 1963

S AM WAS HOME in time for Vincent's first birthday on December 19, which arrived in the midst of a frantic burst of recording activity. He cut the standards album, with Luigi supervising and Horace Ott arranging, over the weekend of the fourteenth. Ott was the first outside arranger Sam had used since inducing Luigi to come out to California for his sessions, but he liked Horace's sophisticated "uptown" orchestrations with strings and woodwinds, particularly his work for Scepter Records, and he had come up with a brainstorm for just how he wanted the new album (which was to be called *Mr. Soul*) to sound. The idea, he explained to his new arranger after Ott had flown to Richmond, Virginia, to meet him on tour, was to stitch together a kind of concept album from these traditional romantic tunes. "He said to me, 'Hey, Horace, listen, let's think of this guy that met this chick that he fell head over heels in love with, and we'll do our album in such a way that [the two of them] are listening to the album, they love all the tracks, and it will help the guy get over!'" Horace was intrigued, and Luigi, who for his part was always trying to take Sam "another step up the ladder," found a song called "I Wish You Love" that he felt could be Sam's all-audience breakthrough ("It was a very pretty

song, we were the first ones to do it, and we did it with a straight background, with Sam giving it the soul") — but somehow the experiment
didn't work, the album came out sounding sterile and overproduced, and
even Sam's remake of his early Keen hit, "(I Love You) For Sentimental
Reasons," ended up in a no-man's-land somewhere between bland and
overblown. RCA engineer Al Schmitt chalked it up to Sam's restless musical spirit, his almost insatiable curiosity about new concepts and new
sounds. As Al saw it, it was just something he had to get out of his system. Even Luigi had to admit that overall it was a failure; nothing against
Horace Ott, who was a fine arranger, it just wasn't a good fit.

But this was a rare misstep in an otherwise uninterrupted period of
growth, exploration, and measurable success. Sam and Alex were *fired
up* now not so much over what they had accomplished as with the distance they still had to go. They talked to Crain about an idea they had
come up with in England: Crain could take over the booking agency they
had recently established to book SAR acts. They would fund him for a
year while he was getting the business off the ground, and then they
would turn the company over to him. Crain turned them down flat. He
seemed to take the offer almost as an insult, as though they no longer
considered him competent to handle Sam's affairs on the road. So they
simply expanded Malloy Artists Management on their own. Alex was in
the midst of starting up another label, too, to which he assigned the
name Derby ("It sounded like an establishment name," said J.W., who
believed strongly in the importance of image), which would, naturally,
be the outlet for all their pop-oriented releases. And finally, in the
absence of any evident effort on Jess Rand's part to bring Sam further
film or TV drama roles, Alex announced to the trades earlier in the year
that SAR Pictures had acquired the film rights to an unpublished novel
called *Johnny Canyon* for Sam to star in.

They had given up on Jess at this point. On October 3 Sam had written to RCA on Kags stationery, directing that "all monies now and hereafter due me . . . be sent to my wife, Mrs. Barbara Cooke," and when Paul
Cantor, his old William Morris agent, approached him about becoming
his manager, it was with the assumption that Jess was out of the picture.
Sam turned him down, "but I would never have made that proposal if [I
thought] Jess was his manager because Jess and I were really friends."
Cantor didn't question Sam's decision and eventually ended up going to
work for Scepter Records. "I would have loved to have managed him, but

Sam was on top of everything as far as his career was concerned. I'm sure he was looking out for his own best interests."

Sam produced sessions on virtually the entire SAR roster in the week before Christmas. He practically lived at the United Recording Studio for the five days between the eighteenth and the twenty-second, starting out with the Sims Twins, then bringing in Johnnie Taylor, the Valentinos, Patience Valentine, Johnnie Morisette, and the Sims Twins again for a return session. Nearly half the songs were written by Sam; a good number (like "Ernestine," a song Sam had cut unsuccessfully on Patience Valentine earlier in the year but was still convinced could be her breakthrough hit) were remakes; and the feeling in the studio was, as usual, overwhelmingly positive, though Sam did hear some grumbling from the Valentinos, who felt that as SAR's biggest current hitmakers, they should be treated with greater respect. They had broken down driving out to California, had to get a new set of brakes, and were disappointed upon arriving at the studio that Sam had not seen fit to hire a horn section to complement their sound. Other SAR artists got an orchestra, but they got a drunken Johnnie Morisette singing a very shaky bass on "Tired of Living in the Country," the New Orleans–styled blues Sam had written for Curtis to sing. "Sam thought it was funny," said Bobby. "He thought it was great. 'It's great for the atmosphere.' But he wouldn't [have] let us mess up *his* record like that." Still, it didn't shake them for a moment from their firm resolve to move to California. Nor did it shake their fundamental faith in Sam.

Christmas was coming, and everyone was in a good mood. Barbara was in and out of the studio in the midst of her Christmas shopping, with Linda frequently in tow. Aretha Franklin was playing the Alexandria Hotel; Lou Rawls was at the Memory Lane on Santa Barbara at Twenty-third; and Johnnie Morisette was appearing at *Los Angeles Sentinel* columnist Gert Gipson's Nite Life. On December 19, word started to get out, in an orchestrated wave of publicity picked up by both the trades and the Negro press and clearly directed by Kags Music Corp., that "Sam (Mr. Feeling) Cooke, who left the gospel field when he was its number one star, will return to that form of entertainment as guest star of a star-studded gospel show in Newark, New Jersey, New Year's Eve." It would be, the *Los Angeles Sentinel* reported, "an entirely new program of song [for which] Cooke has composed several modern gospel songs" as well as such "generation-old heart touchers" as "Wonderful," "Touch the

Hem of His Garment," "Nearer to Thee," and "Were You There [When They Crucified My Lord]?" It would be, promised the *St. Louis Argus,* "undoubtedly the most sensational gospel show ever to hit the Newark Armory."

On the final day of sessions, Sam scheduled Johnnie Morisette in the afternoon and the Sims Twins at night. For Morisette he got his old Keen label-mate Johnny "Guitar" Watson to play lead on a pair of blues, while the Sims Twins came back to redo two songs they had cut at their earlier session, plus a new one that Sam had written especially for them.

"That's Where It's At" was one of Sam's prettiest songs, its chorus built almost entirely around the catchphrase that he and J.W. had come up with, the verses registering a broader mix of wistfulness, celebration, and specificity of observation. Bobbie and Kenny attacked it with whole-hearted verve, while Sam seemed only halfheartedly to be trying to restrain the irrepressible *bounciness* of their enthusiasm. He focused instead on the lyric, which was supposed to start off "Lights turned way down low / Music soft and slow / With someone you love so," except that the twins always left out the preposition. "Don't forget that 'with,'" Sam reminded them gently, "'cause it's very, very important." And when, by dint of much repetition, they finally got it, "Oh, that's good," he genuinely enthused. "Oh, that was cookin'. That's cookin', Kenny, Bob, that's it!"

The musicians were packing up to leave when Barbara gave Zelda her birthday gift, an elaborate perfume set with a mirror and tray. Zelda was surprised, because Barbara had already given her a gift several days earlier, a hair dryer from Sam and her that she doubted Sam even knew about, but he picked up on it now, raising an eyebrow and saying, "Oh, it's your birthday, ZZ?" When she indicated that it was, he pushed the call button and told the rhythm section, Earl Palmer and Ray Johnson, the piano player, and bassist Ray Pohlman, to stay out there. "Then he walked in the studio," said Zelda, "we could hear it, because Bones kept the [pots] open, and he says, 'Guys, give me this,' you know, just snapping his fingers and singing 'Happy Birthday,' and [the musicians] just followed." It was undoubtedly the musical high point of the evening, proving once and for all what anyone who had ever listened to Sam should have known all along: that Sam could enthrall an audience by the sound of his voice alone. "I wish a lot of joy to you," he bubbles with the rhythm section swinging along behind him, "Ohh, a whole lotta joy to you / I wish you no sadness / A lot of joy to you." And when, after declaring, "Happy birthday once again, dear ZZ," he draws out the ending with a magnificently melismatic effect, you feel as if you are caught up in a happy family drama in which Sam for once feels at home, beset by neither doubt nor conflict about his role.

Then he and Alex were in New York for an assortment of business between Christmas and the New Year. The gospel program, with an all-star lineup that included the Dixie Hummingbirds, the Swanees, the Caravans, and, of course, the Soul Stirrers, was coming up in a few days, but in the meantime, the two of them put together a song for the Shirelles session they were about to produce for the Scepter label. The session had come about through an improbable set of circumstances, which began with Florence Greenberg, the middle-aged New Jersey housewife who had started Scepter in 1958 in order to record four of her daughter Mary Jane's classmates at Passaic High School, a black girl group who won the school talent contest as the Shirelles. Mrs. Greenberg had in the past four years assembled a stellar r&b roster that included Chuck Jackson, ex-Flamingo Tommy Hunt, the Isley Brothers, and a newcomer named Dionne Warwick, but she had had her eye on Sam for some time. Several months earlier her longtime partner and a&r head, Luther Dixon, left the label in what amounted to both a personal and professional split, and she offered Sam the job of producing her "top disk team," the Shirelles, who had had two number-one pop hits in the last two years. He would start, *Billboard* reported on December 1, "on a sort of freelance basis, and if things work out will become a regular a&r man for the firm. He will continue, however, for RCA Victor as an artist." What she really intended, though, said J.W., was apparent even before they entered the studio. "She had in mind that she could get Sam to come on Scepter." The success of the session ("Sam took us to a different area [with] that gospel vein," said Shirelle Beverly Lee, "and it was brilliant, that song he [wrote], 'Only Time Will Tell,' using our song titles [for lyrics]") only reinforced her resolve, and when Sam balked, that was the end of the deal — before it ever had a chance to get off the ground.

Sam saw King Curtis, too, whom he had finally persuaded to come out on the upcoming tour. It was going to take more money than the bookings — clubs and auditoriums in Texas, Louisiana, and Florida — could sustain, but once Sam made up his mind that the Kingpins had the sound he was looking for, he was no more to be deterred from his goal than he had been with the Upsetters six months earlier. In the end, money wasn't the determining factor anyway. There wasn't money enough to pay him what he could make at home, King Curtis told Sam, but he had one rule of thumb: "I only ever travel with those I like. I never work with them I don't." And after the way Sam had tipped his hat to him in "Having a Party" ("Play that song called 'Soul Twist,'" he had sung, plugging King Curtis' first big hit) — well, he didn't see how he could do anything but return the favor. They were in certain respects kindred spirits. Each was dedicated in his own way to professionalism, organization, and self-advancement (what he tried to do with his studio work, Curtis said, was to negotiate a business arrangement that allowed him to "completely fit the vernacular of the record," thereby ensuring not only financial and musical growth but an increased share of the market as well). What seemed to have brought them together in this instance, however, was a particular delight in seizing the moment, their willingness to trust to instinct (bred of well-earned experience) that they were going to have a good time together — and make good music, besides.

Sam felt similarly drawn to the prominent r&b DJ Magnificent Montague — but in a more conventional personal and business alliance. Montague, born Nathaniel Montague in Elizabeth, New Jersey, in 1928, had helped break "You Send Me" and championed L.C.'s career from the start. He had moved to the New York area just two and one-half months earlier, where he was broadcasting from Woodside, Long Island, on WWRL. Well known as a rhyming jock, he had taken his cue initially from romantic poetry and then from the poets of the Harlem Renaissance, distinguishing himself from his peers not just by his verbal dexterity but by the formal introduction of black history lessons into his programs (he had a regular segment called "Can I Get a Witness?" dedicated to that purpose). A determinedly free spirit who refused to be categorized in any way (he had converted to Judaism in 1960 and considered himself a "landsman"), he alternated his own seemingly extemporaneous verse with lines from poets like Countee Cullen and Langston Hughes and took great pride in "swooning" his predominantly female audience whom he addressed as "My darlings" and for whom he created introductions to some of the more romantic songs that often exceeded the passion and seductiveness of the songs themselves.

But Montague had a secret that few of his listeners (and few of the stars whose records he played) were aware of. A bristling little cockatoo of a man ("He was one of the most pure hustlers I've ever seen," said a fellow black jock, no mean hustler himself), Montague was a collector, a pursuit he had stumbled upon by accident when he wandered into a secondhand bookstore in 1956 and discovered a book of pioneering black writer Paul Laurence Dunbar's dialect poems. "Never had I read words that sounded so real, so raw, so different," Montague declared, particularly struck by Dunbar's seminal statement of the plight of the Negro in the twentieth century, "We Wear the Mask." He was hooked and started his collection of Africana almost immediately thereafter. That was when he was working in Chicago and put together the Magnificents, the group that L.C. joined after their hit "Up On the Mountain" was already on the charts. That was how he had met the Cook family, and that was how he first met Sam.

Over the years, his collection had grown, as he moved from city to city with his wife and son; he had added sheet music and old 78s and cylinder recordings by historic black "minstrel" entertainers like Bert Williams to his search for manuscripts as rare as a first edition by eighteenth-century poet Phyllis Wheatley, but he kept his passion secret from virtually all of the black r&b singers he helped make into stars. "I wanted to be a businessman. I didn't go to the nightclubs [except for business]. I didn't hang out. I was busy with another career as a collector." Of all the artists with whom he interacted Sam was virtually the only one who exhibited a strong independent interest in black history. "He read. He wanted to read. He would come over to my place, and I'd have to hide my books! I couldn't get him away from Dunbar's [1895 collection], *Majors and Minors*. He'd sit there and read about [how Dunbar] was an elevator operator and put out his first book himself. That fascinated him." Sometimes Sam would set Dunbar's poems to music, singing the words from memory to the accompaniment of his guitar.

Montague was busy promoting himself and his first big show in the area, "Magnificent Montague's Down Home Soul Show & Dance Featuring Ben E. King, Jimmy Reed, Gene McDaniel, the Shirelles," and a host of at least twenty other advertised stars, including Dionne Warwick and Otis Redding, whose debut Stax single, "These Arms of Mine," the disc jockey was doing his best to break. He was calling in favors from all the record companies, putting every name he could plausibly suggest on posters and handbills that in many cases he was distributing himself (some of the advertised stars, like Ben E. King, seemed unlikely to show due to previously advertised bookings in other parts of the country) — and in general doing all in his power to promote the January 4 date. Conducting an on-air interview with Sam at this point could do nothing to hurt the show, and if his listeners came away with the impression that Sam might make an unscheduled appearance at Rockland Palace (despite the unadvertised fact that he would be on tour with King Curtis in Texas at the time), well, then, *caveat emptor,* as Montague himself might impressively intone.

The interview took on the aspect of a refined version of the Dozens, as Sam and Montague traded lighthearted barbs in the form of elaborate repartée. "Good afternoon, darling," Montague began, "here in the studio we have a man who calls himself Mister Soul. He claims he is a singer, and he claims he has a background that makes him eligible to be a part of your show." "Well, that's very simple to do," replied Sam laughingly. "Believe me, *very* easy to do. I want to say that knowing you as long as I have, I've had a chance to even sit back and observe you, you understand?" "Mmm, I see. In other words, you've been trying to gather some material for *your* soul through mine." To which Sam could only respond, amid much laughter, "I have no retort, no retort."

They went on from there, touching briefly on topics from Sam's origins in gospel music to the changes that take place in all of us over the years. "You look a little older," said Montague. "A little thinner." "Well, no, I haven't changed that much, Montague," Sam hastened to reply. "[But] I would say as a singer grows older, his conception grows a little deeper, and . . . it gives him a better insight on telling the story of the song he's trying to sing." All of it was only prelude, though, to the poetry contest that Montague clearly had in mind from the start.

Which of his records was his favorite? Montague asked his guest, and Sam picked out one of his very earliest compositions, "You Were Made for Me." "Now, what is the first line, Sam?" says Montague, upon which Sam delivers the opening stanza of the song with feeling.

A fish was made to swim in the ocean
A boat was made to sail on the sea
But sure as there are stars above
You were made for me.

"And I can recap that," Montague jumps in, reciting his own elaboration on the song, which once you get past the initial fish-and-ocean part, enters into neo-Shakespearean waters. "We must get together and collaborate at least once on a song," declares Sam good-humoredly. To which Montague suggests a second improvisation, this time on Sam's "second-best record."

"My second-best record? My current one — I love this very, very much — called 'Nothing Can Change This Love.'" He then recites the opening lines: "If I go / A million miles away / I'd write a letter each and every day / 'Cause nothing can change the love I have for you."

"If I should go beyond the clouds," Montague comes back:

Beyond the world renown
If I should in my sleep stumble out loud
Darling, I am not afraid to write your name a thousand times
For nothing in this crazy world can change my love
I know, thank God, that nothing can change my love for you.

There is, once again, much laughter, and Sam says, "You know, I can't cap that." "No, no, no," says Montague, "I wasn't trying to get you to cap that. I was merely looking at you, trying to observe. And I think that to close the show up very nicely, Sam, I would like for you to hum something for my darlings. In other words, every day I try to describe 'soul.' Maybe you could hum eight bars of what soul represents." And indeed Sam does. "And when the humming's over," Montague declares, with a sincerity that does indeed cap the interview, "and time finds its soul / All I can say to you, darling, is: 'Sam Cooke's yours, he'll never grow old.'"

On a more explicitly political note, Sam gave an interview to a reporter for the ANP (the Associated Negro Press, the black newspapers' wire service) in which "he urged all tan performers to pay more attention to the Negro press. 'This is the bridge over which 99% of us must cross,' he said. . . . In New York for a concert at the turn of the year, he told this writer that wherein the liberal 'white press' will write a Negro up, it will not tell his story. 'All of us would be in grave danger if through lack of interest we let "our papers" down. More advertising dollars should be spent by both the artists and the promoters throughout the country.' He further pointed out that [most Negro] performers . . . make the bulk of their money off Negro fans. Only a handful of them can balance their books by working the plush supper clubs in Hollywood, Las Vegas, Miami, and New York. Even those few must look to the followers of the Negro press for that extra profit dollar." And, the story concluded, "he pledged himself to greater recognition of such papers."

It was a time, as Montague might have pointed out in one of his more apocalyptic moods, in which everything seemed to be coming to a head. James Baldwin had just published a book-length essay in the *New Yorker* a month before that led with a quote from the old spiritual, "God gave Noah the rainbow sign / No more water / The fire next time," and Sam undoubtedly pored over Baldwin's message, couched in language no less ornate than Montague's but richer, more ironic, and suggestive of deeper meanings by far. "This innocent country set you down in a ghetto in which, in fact, it intended you to perish," Baldwin wrote in the portion of the essay that was couched as a letter to his namesake nephew "on the one hundredth anniversary of the Emancipation.

> Let me spell out precisely what I mean by that, for the heart of the matter is here, and the root of my dispute with my country. You were born where you were born and faced the future that you faced because you were black and *for no other reason*. . . . You were born into a society which spelled out with brutal clarity, and in as many ways as possible, that you were a worthless human being. You were not expected to aspire to excellence: you were expected to make peace with mediocrity. Wherever you have turned, James, in your short time on this earth, you have been told where you could go and what you could do (and *how* you could do it) and where you could live and whom you could marry. I know your countrymen do not agree with me about this . . . [but] please try to remember that what they believe, as well as what they do and cause you to endure, does not testify to your inferiority but to their inhumanity and fear. Please try to be clear, dear James, through the storm which rages about your youthful head today, about the reality which lies behind the words *acceptance* and *integration*. There is no reason for you to try to become like white people, and there is no basis whatever for their impertinent assumption that *they* must accept *you*. The really terrible thing, old buddy, is that *you* must accept *them*. . . . You must accept them and accept them with love. For these innocent people have no other hope. They are,

in effect, still trapped in a history which they do not understand; and until they understand it, they cannot be released from it.

T HE GOSPEL CONCERT lived up to its billing in every respect but one. The below-zero weather kept attendance to advance ticket sales (it was the "coldest New Year's Eve in history," reported the *St. Louis Argus*), but the audience of six thousand was rewarded with a show in which each group seemed to go to extra lengths to get the house. Sam couldn't have been happier, not just to be singing once again for a gospel crowd but to be reunited for the first time in a long time with the Soul Stirrers. It seemed almost as if he had been neglecting them, with recent sessions by nearly every other SAR act and a second album from the Stirrers long overdue. He had never given up on the idea of breaking them in the pop market, though, and Jerry Brandt, whom Sam had invited to the program with his fiancée at the last minute ("He calls me and says, 'I want to show you something you never saw before in your life'"), couldn't get over what a powerful singer Jimmie Outler was. His voice was rougher than Sam's, but he possessed that same uncommon gift of communication, and Brandt had visions of signing him to a pop contract.

Onstage, said Brandt, it was like hand-to-hand combat, but in the end the real battle was not with the other groups but within the Soul Stirrers themselves, as Jimmie Outler matched Sam note for note, verse for verse, pushing him to ever greater heights. "Sam gets three lines, Outler gets three lines, they're fighting it out, and then all of a sudden all hell breaks loose, all these women are throwing their arms up in the air, shivering and passing out. There must have been about fifty [women] in white nurse's uniforms, stretchers were coming, people were fainting, the show in the audience was the most amazing thing I ever saw in my life. And I thought, 'Holy shit, they're actually having orgasms, thinking they've been touched by the hand of God!'"

Brandt had never seen Sam put on a better show, he had never seen him work so hard, if only because in a conventional secular setting he wouldn't have had to deal with that kind of competition. In the end, said Crume, still the Stirrers' principal songwriter and guitarist, whom Sam had recently taken to addressing as Crumé because, he said, that was the way the French would pronounce his name, Sam simply had nothing left to give. "He was singing his heart out, and I kept urging him on, but he said, 'Crumé, I've given them all I got. I haven't got any more.'" And so, as the *Chicago Defender* reported, Sam declared, in the well-known words of General MacArthur, "I shall return."

T HE KING CURTIS TOUR began three days later in Texas, and from the start there was no question that it would be a memorable time. L.C. was out for almost the entire month ("Sam just told Crain, 'Whatever money L.C. needs, you give it to him'"), and J.W., in keeping with his new intention to have more hands-on involvement on the road, was committed for the duration — but no one enjoyed himself more than Charles Cook. "King Curtis and I, you understand, we loved to gamble. King Curtis had a lot of money, and I had a lot of money — because I had *Sam's* money — and anytime he's offstage, like for intermission, we'd get to gambling. Sam knew I could gamble. And, boy, I used to win a lot of money off of old King Curtis, I used to beat him out of his money!" One time, according to Charles, "I left him so bad he had to borrow money to pay his band." They played dice, cards, everything. "A lot of times," said guitarist Cornell Dupree, whom Curtis had brought up from Fort Worth to join the band the previous year, "we'd be driving [to the next town after the show], get to the hotel, and instead of going to bed, they'd get on the floor and start shooting craps. I can remember one incident when Curtis had won a lot of money and handed the money to me [to] hold, and I nodded off to sleep, and Charlie was sneaking the money out of my hand while I was sleeping and shooting that with Curtis!"

At one point in the tour, in Norfolk, Virginia, Sam, who was an indifferent gambler at best, broke the game and, to Charles' disgust, gave the money back. "I said, 'Man, you've got to be crazy. You don't give nobody their money back. They wouldn't give it back to you.'" But Sam insisted. "Those people have families, man," he told his brother. "With as much money as I make, man, I'm not going to take their little money." And in the face of L.C.'s and Charles' vigorous protests, he quizzed each player about how much he had lost, even as L.C. pointed out that the man Sam had just given $100 to hadn't come into the game with $5.

The Harlem Square Club in Miami was one week into the tour. That was where Hugo and Luigi had agreed to record Sam's live show. No one was ever sure after the fact exactly how this came about. J.W. thought it might have been the effect of the cousins seeing Sam at the Apollo in

November, but Luigi had no such specific recollection and thought the idea probably came from Sam. It might have been the tape that Atlanta station owner Zenas Sears had sent to RCA. It may even have been that Sam heard from the Womack brothers how James Brown had recorded his own show at the Apollo and it struck a competitive note. Or it may simply have been Sam's pride in his new act. But in any event, the two RCA engineers who had recorded *Belafonte Live at Carnegie Hall* (which, after three years, was still on the charts) were flown down with mobile recording equipment, and both Hugo and Luigi showed up (though Hugo disappeared to visit another of their acts, Perry Como, in Jupiter Beach) to record an album tentatively titled *One Night Stand.*

The Harlem Square Club was a big barn of a building owned by a local operator named Joe Marcus that, like the Royal Peacock in Atlanta and the Palms of Hallandale, was an obligatory stop on every high-profile r&b star's tour. Sam got a guarantee of something like $1,500 plus a percentage of the door, and the club owner agreed to pay $250 toward the Kingpins' salary. There was a poolroom and a long bar at the front of the building where you could buy setups, along with a kind of package store whose cashier sat impassively behind a steel grille. Upstairs, there was a balcony with tables for the patrons, and a small office in which the recording engineers, Bob Simpson and Tony Salvatore, set up their equipment. They monitored the sound at a fairly desultory teenage matinee, then adjusted the microphone placement for the first evening show, starting at 10:00 P.M. Sam gave them a cheery greeting before going on, and then the place erupted in a manner that Salvatore, like his partner a neophyte in the world of rhythm and blues, was simply not prepared for. "There weren't any brawls or anything like that, but I'll tell you, it was like a scene out of a movie, the whole building was rocking, and I remarked to Bob, I said, 'Oh Jesus, I hope this place don't fall down.'" His colleague, who was on the board, sent him downstairs to try to balance the sound, but he could barely make his way to the stage and once he got back, the two engineers decided that, whatever the sonic shortcomings, they would just have to make the best of it, there was no point in risking life and limb for a microphone adjustment.

"Right now, ladies and gentlemen," King Curtis announced in time-honored M.C. fashion at the start of the 1:00 A.M. to 4:00 A.M. late show,

Sam and King Curtis, ca. early 1963. *Michael Ochs Archives.com*

"we'd like to get ready to introduce the star of our show, the young man you've all been waiting for, Mister Soul. So what d'you say, let's all get together and welcome him to the stand with a great big hand — how about it for Sam Cooke?"

Sam was, not surprisingly, a little hoarse, his voice somewhat frayed, but more to the point, he was singing in a guttural style that, as Jerry Brandt had immediately recognized at the New Year's Eve gospel show, few white people had ever heard from him, not even those who had purchased Sam's gospel records. Because the gospel records were tame in comparison with their live performance, and there was no way to get any measure of the ecstatic nature of the experience without being present at the event itself. There was nothing soft, measured, or polite about the Sam Cooke you saw at the Harlem Square Club; there was none of the self-effacing, mannerable, "fair-haired little colored boy" that the white man was always looking for. This was Sam Cooke undisguised, charmingly self-assured, "he had his crowd," said Clif White approvingly — he was as proud as he had been raised to be, not about to take any scraps from the white man's table.

Jerry and his fiancée, L.C., and Barbara all watched from the balcony. It was the same show that he had introduced at the Apollo, but, said J.W., observing from the wings and even coming out to twist for a while onstage, "Sam was really in his bag, you know. When he was really having fun, he could drive the women into a frenzy, it was almost like he was beating up on them to get an orgasm."

Barbara viewed it with a somewhat different eye. Watching the whole scene with L.C., she joked with her brother-in-law about the good taste, and discretion, he had always shown. "She said to me, 'L.C., you know one thing that's different about you from your brothers?' I said, 'What?' She said, 'You don't want to be with no ugly woman.' She said, 'Now your brother Charles and Sam [will] mess with ugly women, but you won't.' I said, 'That's right, baby, you sure know me.' She said, 'Hey, you know I know you. You and me, we go way back.' And we laughed."

With the opening notes of "Bring It On Home to Me," the crowd erupted in fevered shouts, as Sam led them in a sing-along that gained in urgency until he declared, in time-honored r&b fashion, "I better leave that one alone," then entered into an even more transcendent "Nothing Can Change This Love." "Let me sing that middle part again," he cries out, as the crowd roars its approbation, and in the booth Bob

Simpson and Tony Salvatore try desperately to get a balance that will convey some of the sheer commonality of the moment. They couldn't quite get it right, the audience feel wasn't anywhere near as clean as on *Belafonte at Carnegie Hall,* but they stayed with it right up to the end, which finally achieved the climax everyone had been working for all night long, as Sam kept urging them to go on having their party. "Sam Cooke, ladies and gentlemen, how about it, Sam Cooke," declares the MC, taking the mike back from Sam even as the moment begins to fade into eternity. For that is what it is, and that is all it is, a moment that has been captured, like a snapshot from a photograph album: it was, Sam might have argued, not his art but his life.

THE TOUR CONTINUED for another three weeks. Sam got into a show-down with Watley over keeping the station wagon clean ("As much goddamn money as I pay you, the next time my car look like that when we go to a gig, you ain't got a job — 'cause that's a reflection on me"), but Watley straightened out. The game between Charles and King Curtis went on day and night, the party never stopped. Curtis' guitarist, Cornell Dupree, observed it all with admiration and appreciation, both for the music and the life. "Simplicity is the most complicated thing you can get. It was pretty much the same rundown [of songs every night], but every time Sam would do it, it would be another feeling to it — everything would just somehow lock in to make the moment special. Clif told me what to play, I would do the little lines within the song, and he would do the rhythm to support it, but Curtis took the solos — it was a good marriage, you might say. Sam would capture the audience, have them crying and laughing, they loved all the songs he sang, and half the people would sing along, whether he asked them to or not. J.W. would come out at the finale and dance along and participate, and [because of his white hair] everyone thought he was Sam's father. Crain was always there, and Charlie, and Sam was very generous, I just admired him and how he got through."

Sam and Alex surprised Zelda by flying into New York for the BMI Awards dinner on an off-date in the middle of the tour. Sam had sent her to New York to pick up his songwriting awards for "Bring It On Home to Me" and "Twistin' the Night Away," and when he and J.W. showed up in their tuxes, Sam's double-breasted and custom-made with prominent buttons of mother-of-pearl, it shocked the hell out of her. Sam was one of six writers to get two "Citations of Achievement" in the pop field (Carole

J.W. Alexander, Lou Adler, Sam, Zelda Sands, BMI Awards dinner, January 23, 1963. *Courtesy of BMI*

King got five), and he mingled with old friends and new, looking suavely resplendent and entirely at ease. Twenty-eight-year-old country songwriter Merle Kilgore was thrilled to meet Sam, but he was even more thrilled when Sam offered up not just a passing version of Kilgore's own award song, "Wolverton Mountain," but a whole host of country hits. Lou Adler flew in for the ceremony, Zelda wore a tight tan sheath that showed off her figure, and in the photos everyone is raising a glass and grinning to beat the band.

Then they rejoined the tour, playing Jacksonville, Florida, on the twenty-fifth and Atlanta's Royal Peacock the next night, this time with Gorgeous George, the spectacular dresser who had started out as Hank Ballard's valet, as MC. Lotsa Poppa, the affable three-hundred-pound Solomon Burke disciple, opened the show, and Sam got an even bigger kick out of him than he had in July, telling club owner and promoter Henry Wynn that he thought Lotsa would be great for their next Supersonic tour. Watley got into more hot water, this time with Clif, who picked him up and flung him out the door like a limp rag doll in a disagreement over a craps game at the Forrest Hotel. L.C., meanwhile, had a visitor at the Forrest. Aretha Franklin was passing through town, "and I just come out of the shower and was singing this new song I had written, 'Please Answer Me,' and I walked out, and she said, 'Whoo, that's a pretty song.' I said, 'I know. It's one of the things I'm getting ready to record right now.' She said, 'L.C., give me that song.' I said, 'No, girl, you crazy. I can't give you my song.' But she just kept on: 'L.C., please give me that song. Just let me sing it.' And she kept beating on me so that I finally gave in."

L.C. DIDN'T GET TO SING his new song at his February 15 session in L.A., but Sam did give him a new number, "Put Me Down Easy," with Sam and Crain joining in on the backup. Sam had been working on the song in the limo while L.C. was asleep, and when L.C. woke up, he said, "That's mine," and Sam just gave it to him. He did another song of Sam's called "Take Me for What I Am" and one called "The Wobble," after a new dance craze that some said was going to take over from the Twist. He had a full chorus behind him on this one, and J.W. taught him the dance in the studio. When it came to "Little Red Rooster," though, a raw blues that Howlin' Wolf had put out the previous year, L.C. drew the line. "I said, 'I'm not a blues singer.' So Sam said, 'Well, I'm gonna do it, then.'" It was as overt a disagreement as the two brothers had yet had over the direction of L.C.'s recording career, and certainly it was overshadowed by the scrupulous attention that Sam gave to every aspect of L.C.'s sessions, but each was dissatisfied in his own fashion: Sam by what appeared to be L.C.'s manifest lack of ambition, L.C. by the fact that he hadn't had anything resembling a hit since signing with SAR, or anywhere near as good a record as "Do You Remember?," his debut release on Checker in 1958, when Montague was still guiding his career. The principal, unspoken point of contention, though, was how much L.C. felt he was being forced into Sam's mold ("[L.C.] didn't want to sing like him," said René Hall, "[but] strange as it may seem, Sam made all his artists sound like him"), and recently he had started thinking about going back to Montague, with whom he could simply be himself.

Sam secured an $8,000 advance from RCA two days before his brother's session. He had six other SAR artists either in the midst of recording or about to go into the studio, and that may well have been the reason he needed the money. Barbara in any case was furious at him for continuing to finance the record company out of his own pocket. She argued that it made no economic sense and that this was starting to be a hobby that he could no longer afford. She felt a certain resentment of Alex and Zelda, of Johnnie Taylor and Johnnie Morisette and the Womack brothers and all the rest, for leeching off of her husband. But she knew there was nothing she could say to keep him from putting even more of his money into what he had made very clear to her was his own private domain. Sam for his part blamed RCA for placing him in this position — here he was, their most consistent seller behind Presley, and they were still just nickel-and-diming him to death.

He went into the studio himself the following week to cut a new album, despite the fact that *Mr. Soul,* the LP he had cut with Horace Ott in December, had just been released. It was almost as though he had had second thoughts about the previous enterprise, as if he wanted to erase anybody else's definition of soul (" 'Soul,' Hugo and Luigi wrote in their liner notes, "you know it when you hear it. It's about abandoning the formalities . . . and going to the *truth* as the performer feels it") and substitute his own.

This session bore very little resemblance to the previous one. René was once again back in charge, the accompaniment was nothing more than a rhythm section with two keyboard players (New Orleans–born Ray Johnson on piano, and Billy Preston, the sixteen-year-old organist who had accompanied Little Richard in England and just begun work on his debut album for SAR's new Derby label) and a guitar chair occupied, as always, by Clif, but augmented by jazz great Barney Kessel. They started off with three old Charles Brown numbers that set the tone; each was relaxed and mellow in the manner that was almost unique to Brown, but each was infused at the same time with the kind of effortless vocal flights unique to Sam. You could read it, in a sense, as a musical debt repaid: if Brown couldn't find the time to make the session at which Sam had recorded "Bring It On Home to Me," then Sam would pay homage in this fashion to a musician who had educated everyone from Ray Charles to Sam himself in a more refined style of the blues.

The feeling was unmistakable, it came through with no need for explicit testimony, and when Sam returned to the studio the next night to record "Little Red Rooster," his own "Laughin' and Clownin'," and two beautifully realized adaptations of gospel material, the traditional

"Nobody Knows the Trouble I've Seen" (introduced by a bowed bass) and "Mean Old World," which he had recorded with the Stirrers just six years earlier, that feeling was only extended. "Laughin' and Clownin'," in particular, served to define the album as a moment of genuine introspection, with Sam recasting Montague's favorite poem, Paul Laurence Dunbar's "We Wear the Mask," in the form of a love song. "Laughin' and clownin'," Sam sang, "Just to keep from cryin' . . .

> *I'm laughin' and clownin'*
> *Just to keep from cryin'*
> *I keep on trying to hide the fact*
> *I've got a worried mind*
>
> *Being the life of the party*
> *Seemed to be my role*
> *(Since you left me, baby) being the life of the party*
> *Seemed to be my role*
> *I keep on tryin' to hide my feelings*
> *Tryin' to hide my soul*

On the final day of album sessions, he recorded two more Charles Brown numbers, a sing-along version of Big Joe Turner's "Shake, Rattle and Roll," and yet another gospel transposition. The song that seemed to sum up the mood of the entire album, though, and the one with which he concluded the evening's session, was Alex's "Lost and Lookin'." It was a minor-key, gospel-based number, as spare in its lyrics as it was rich in inspiration, with Sam's voice set against nothing more than Clifford Hils' stand-up bass and drummer Hal Blaine's delicate striking of the cymbals. It showed off every one of Sam's characteristic vocal effects — his delicate falsetto, the way he would ride a syllable, elongate a vowel to suggest dimensions of meaning scarcely hinted at in the lyrics, the slight roughening that he could use to suggest intensity of feeling without raising his voice; he employed all of these effects without in any way suggesting, either to the listener or himself, that they were effects, so intrinsic were they to his feeling for the music, to the feelings he wanted to express. "I'm lost and I'm callin' for my baby," he sang, "Baby won't you please come home / I'm lost and I'm callin' for my baby / I need you 'cause I'm so alone." It was in many respects the exact opposite of the show he had put on at the Harlem Square Club, but, like the humming he had done for Montague, it served to summarize his definition of soul.

Meanwhile, the SAR sessions continued, even as Sam remained occupied with his own recording efforts, because, for the first time, he and J.W. had delegated responsibility to someone else. Their new full-time employee, Fred Smith, was no stranger to them; he went back to Keen Records days and had carved out a good deal of success of his own with his songwriting partner, Cliff Goldsmith, starting with the Olympics' "Western Movies." He and Goldsmith, however, had had a recent falling-out, and he had gone to work for SAR at the start of the year as songwriter, producer, and promo man.

He and Alex had just started on the Billy Preston album on February 8. The two of them were also working with Mel Carter, a former gospel singer J.W. had heard at a jazz club in downtown L.A. Mel was a crooner who had taken his example from the highly influential Robert Anderson, a fixture on the Chicago gospel scene. The song on which they were pinning their hopes was "When a Boy Falls in Love," the number Sam had told an English reporter so proudly back in October that Pat Boone would soon be recording. Evidently Pat Boone couldn't get it right, and neither could Johnny Nash or Lou Rawls. But working from a demo by Sam, and with a full-scale orchestration by arranger Joe Hooven, Fred and Alex got a stellar performance out of Mel on the same night that Sam recorded "Lost and Lookin'."

Two nights later, J.W. and Clif were working on the Soul Stirrers' long-delayed second album in Chicago while Sam embarked on a two-day singles session in L.A., working without Clif for the first time since he had started recording pop under his own name. He cut an easygoing bluesy number the Prudhomme twins had originally written for Fats Domino, "I Ain't Gonna Cheat On You No More," along with "She's Wonderful," an almost note-for-note (and swiftly abandoned) transliteration of "Wonderful," the gospel song that had provided him with the springboard for "Lovable," his first secular release. The next night, Clif was back, and, with Barney Kessel, a full horn section, and a mixed male-and-female chorus all in tow, Sam finally cut "Another Saturday Night," the lighthearted take on life, loneliness, and sexual frustration he had written in England, now set to a Latin beat. It was something very much aimed at the pop market, a novelty song with a universal theme ("I got in town a month ago / I saw a lot of girls since then / If I could meet 'em / I could get 'em / But as yet I haven't met 'em / That's why I'm in the shape I'm in") that white audiences and black audiences alike could identify with. "It had what we were selling," said Luigi, perfectly willing to indulge Sam in tributes to Charles Brown and explorations of his gospel roots so long as Sam continued to deliver the kind of good, solid, commercial material he was capable of. The night before, after finishing up his own session in the RCA studio at 11:30, Sam had prevailed on his producer to stay on for the session he had scheduled in the same room at midnight with Johnnie Morisette. Luigi went out for something to eat, and when he came back, the session was in full swing, with Johnnie in typically raucous good humor. "We're going to Smashville," announced Johnnie at one point, while at another, he addressed his song to Patience Valentine, interspersing bloodcurdling screams with a wicked laugh he had been practicing.

"I don't know how you do it," Sam said wryly to Luigi, shaking his head. "I'm not getting anything, and I got the same musicians, same studio, same engineer." Luigi, who had always seen Sam's label efforts as something of a harmless eccentricity, just looked at him and responded in kind. "I said, 'Schmuck, I use the same people — but I got Sam Cooke!'"

Scenes from Life

1 | JOCKO'S PARTNER

SAM OPENED A WEEKLONG RUN at the newly refurbished State
Theater in Philadelphia on March 8. He did it as a favor to "Jocko"
Henderson, the celebrated r&b disc jockey, and against the strong
advice of Roz Ross, Jerry Brandt's boss at William Morris. Ross didn't
think the theater would be ready in time, but, more important, she considered it unwise to go up against Jocko's rival, Georgie Woods, "the Guy
with the Goods," who had had the Philadelphia rhythm and blues scene
locked up for years with his monthly all-star revues at the Uptown Theater.

Sam hadn't played for either Jocko or Georgie Woods since the early
days of his career (the financial terms were too onerous, the intangible
rewards too few, and the DJ was the star of the show), but he was grateful
to both, and particularly to Jocko, for giving him a helping hand when he
needed it most. Jocko, the man who had elevated rhyming patter to a
high art since his arrival from Baltimore eleven years earlier, had been
successful first in his adopted hometown, then in New York a couple of
years later, as he simultaneously established hugely popular afternoon
and evening shows in both cities. A masterful radio personality with a
flair for invention and self-promotion, he had started doing shows at the
Apollo Theater in New York in early 1957 as WOV's Ace from Outer
Space (this, like the rhyming patter, was a direct crib from his chief mentor and influence, Maurice "Hot Rod" Hulbert, who had begun his own
Rocket Ship show in Memphis in 1949 before moving to Baltimore the
following year), and he even made a direct, head-to-head challenge to

Barbara and Vincent, ca. 1963. *Courtesy of Barbara Cooke and ABKCO*

Alan Freed that same year. But he had never been able to break Georgie Woods' hold on the lucrative field of live promotion in his own hometown, and it was only after losing both radio jobs a few months earlier (after an adulatory three-page spread in *Ebony* celebrating the Hendersons' new $110,000 home and luxurious lifestyle had inadvertently raised questions as to where all this money might be coming from) that he began to seriously consider other sources of income.

He went to a friend of his, a thirty-one-year-old accountant named Allen Klein, who had helped him find money he didn't know how to get from various publishing interests he had developed over the years. Jocko, who believed strongly in self-sufficiency and individual initiative, had not been slow to take the hint from his radio station employers that the public exposure they were affording him was not an end in and of itself (in other words, the minimal salary they were providing was not going to furnish him with the wherewithal for the sharp upward mobility he envisioned) but, rather, an invitation to explore alternative methods of remuneration. This he did, in the manner of nearly every other black — and white — jock (for some it came down to simply embracing a kind of "pay-for-play" system, which in its crudest form became known as payola), but as he would have been the first to admit, he was ignorant in the *business* of music. It was not until he met Allen Klein at a show he was promoting at the Apollo that he was able to establish his publishing interests in certain songs to which he had devoted particular attention in a manner that would ensure that henceforth he would be paid in full. To Jocko, Allen Klein was a right kind of guy, a sort of Robin Hood figure with a slide rule who simply by virtue of his disconcerting ability to shut out everything but the problem at hand could make powerful record industry figures knuckle under — he was the kind of person you definitely wanted on your side, a ferocious opponent but a man fiercely loyal to friends and family, his word, Jocko had learned from experience, incontrovertibly his bond. "He couldn't lie if he wanted to," Jocko said of this strange, seemingly humorless man whose emotions appeared to come out only in his work.

Klein, who might have been described in other terms by those in the industry with whom he had done battle, had reason not to value loyalty lightly. A famously focused man, he had spent much of his early childhood in an orphanage after losing his mother at nine months and then, at his father's direction, being taken away from his grandmother, his mother's mother, at the age of three and a half and placed with two older sisters in Newark's Hebrew Orphanage and Sheltering Home. He would never forget his grandmother dressing him with tears streaming down her cheeks, as the station wagon arrived to take him to the Home. Nor would he forget his father, a butcher who had emigrated from Hungary at the turn of the century, coming to retrieve him six years later and presenting him with his new "mother." Perhaps that was what accounted for the oddity of his manner, which could be read either as a brusque challenge or a defensive cover-up — but there was little doubt that he carried his wounds with him, though he rarely shared them with others. He waited till his bar mitzvah to ask his father the one question he had never been able to put out of his mind: Why, after placing his children in the Home, had he never come to visit them in all those years? His father was a blunt man, and the boy believed him when he said, "You have no idea how many times I came, but it broke my heart, so I drove away." But what did that mean? asked the boy, in what amounted, for him, to almost an emotional outburst. He was the child, he told his father. "You were supposed to be the adult. You were supposed to look out for me."

Except for two years in the army, he had lived in his father and stepmother's house in Newark until he graduated from college at twenty-five, but he had always considered himself to be on his own. He had gotten into the music business almost by accident after working his way through Upsala College in three years and graduating with an accounting degree. His first job was with a firm that had the Harry Fox Agency account. The Harry Fox Agency then, as now, served as a licensing organization and collection agency for mechanical royalties for the majority of U.S. music publishers, and Klein took his first commercial plane ride — to Hollywood — to pinpoint the publishing liabilities of the independent Dot label in preparation for its acquisition by ABC Records. That was how he discovered the intricacies of the accounting system specifically developed for a music industry that had been fundamentally converted, sometimes with a good degree of opportunistic obfuscation, from sheet music to record sales over the previous half century.

Then one day he ran into a college classmate, Donnie Kirshner, on his way home from work, and Kirshner, who was just entering the publishing business himself, introduced him to two young rock 'n' rollers from Texas, Buddy Knox and Jimmy Bowen, who shared a band, the Rhythm Orchids. Each had had an individual hit in 1957 that had started with the same small-label single and then been picked up (and reissued on separate records) by Morris Levy's Roulette label. Knox's "Party Doll," the A-side of the original 45, had gone to number one pop, while Bowen's "I'm Stickin' With You" reached number fourteen, but both had come to believe they had not been dealt with fairly by their label. Allen Klein by this time had gotten married and set up his own accounting firm with a loan from his father-in-law, who, unlike his own father, seemed to have no trouble lavishing love on his only daughter or showing faith in her new husband ("I had nothing, it was like — he never expected to get it back, but my father-in-law was a saint of a man"). He offered to help out Knox and Bowen for no fee, simply in exchange for 25 percent of whatever money he was able to find, and he promptly set about auditing Roulette.

When he had completed his audit, he presented Levy with a bill, and Levy, whose reputation as a gangster seemed to intimidate everyone but his then-partners, Hugo and Luigi, and this upstart young accountant, acknowledged that he did indeed owe the money but he was not going to pay it, at least not all at once and not without lawsuits that could eat up every penny — and while they were at it, what was Klein going to do about it? Eventually they worked out an accommodation by which Levy agreed to pay $70 a week for a period of three or four years, and Allen Klein learned his first lesson in the business: you make the best deal you can.

From there, again through Kirshner, he met pop star Bobby Darin and audited Darin's label, Atlantic, which led both to a financial windfall and, indirectly, to Darin's leaving Atlantic for Capitol. It also led to a break with both Kirshner and Darin, as Klein, after getting Darin his publishing back, sought the job of administering it for a 10 percent fee and was turned down — but only after a serious disagreement with Kirshner over the way Kirshner, Darin's new publishing partner, wanted to set up the foreign publishing, in a series of splits that Klein felt was inherently unfair to his client. It was, he said, a heartbreaking lesson in human frailty, and also in learning to deal with people not on the basis of how much you liked them but on your judgment of how you think they will act.

He became known in the business and went on to do audits for a number of other clients. Through Jocko he met Lloyd Price, for whom he audited ABC in the wake of number-one pop hits like "Stagger Lee" and "Personality," but he had greater ambitions than to find other people's money, something he was beginning to feel was almost too easy to do, and in 1961, through a series of coincidences as improbable as his entrance into the music business, he went into the business of making movies ("I just wanted to learn, and I saw an opportunity to get in").

He took his first full-scale production, *Without Each Other*, to Cannes in the spring of 1962, after enlisting Oscar-winning composer Dimitri Tiomkin as musical director. He then screened the film at his own expense a day in advance of the festival opening and got a quote from a connection he had made at *Film Daily* about this "underdog" independent getting the honor of "opening" Cannes. Next he took out an ad in *Variety* expressing the "deep honor" he and his fellow producer, Peter Gayle, felt at being selected the "Best American Film at Cannes." None of this, of course, was true, and none of it made the slightest difference in his finding a studio to distribute the film ("Ben Melniker at MGM said, 'Listen, you've done a great job of promoting the film, but you got to have something to promote'").

That was his third, and perhaps most important, lesson in business, and though he almost immediately began work with the same team (Gayle, writer/star Tony Anthony, and director Saul Swimmer) on another picture, it was never actually filmed, and he returned to the accounting business (which his two loyal associates had been carrying on in his absence) with no money, a vague sense of dissatisfaction, and a renewed determination to do something of significance. When Jocko came to him with the idea of leasing the State, a cavernous five-thousand-seat house in the Goldman movie chain that had fallen into disrepair, he seized on the idea with enthusiasm. It would be a better way to meet new clients than Jocko's occasional shows at the Apollo, but more than that, it would satisfy the need he had to do something more.

He had barely heard of Sam Cooke when Jocko first mentioned him, though, as a keen student of songs, he recognized the titles of Sam's hits as soon as Jocko brought them up. Jocko was in complete charge of the booking ("He said, 'Don't worry, they all owe me favors, I'll book the shows'"), and he installed a lineup composed mostly of acts from Florence Greenberg's Scepter label (Chuck Jackson, the Shirelles, newcomer Dionne Warwick), along with the Crystals, a young singer from Florida named Johnny Thunder with a current Top 10 hit, and — in Sam Cooke — a headliner virtually guaranteed to draw. King Curtis, another sometime Scepter act (Jocko had had a long, and mutually profitable, relationship with Scepter), was providing the backup band, and the headliner was bringing along a young group of his own, the Valentinos, to round out the bill. Allen was well aware of the Scepter acts from his own association with the label (his accounting firm had done a considerable amount of work for Florence Greenberg over the years), but it scarcely mattered, he was prepared to place his full faith in Jocko, who had Lloyd Price lined up for the second week, the Four Seasons for the third, comedian "Moms" Mabley for Easter, and then an improbable (and highly unlikely) wish list of stars from Nat "King" Cole to Johnny Mathis and Ray Charles.

Klein *did* get involved in every other aspect of the business, though, from the water tower that had to be installed on the roof of the building to the new carpeting that was to be laid on the floor. A tireless worker, he showed up at the theater nearly every day and was in constant contact with his partner, and while his ferocious concentration did not fail to take in some of the potential pitfalls of the enterprise (even Jocko started referring to the building as "Big Mouth," because, he said, it would swallow them all), just as with the movies, he was caught up as much in his vision of what it could be as in the way it actually was. But it was only with his first glimpse of Sam Cooke, at rehearsal the day before opening, that Allen Klein saw something that pointed toward a different kind of future.

He was sitting in the balcony with his four-year-old daughter, Robin, and his wife, Betty, just pregnant with their second child. "I had no idea who Sam Cooke was, I don't ever remember seeing a picture. And I sat up there and heard him sing, and he was fucking magic." Jocko introduced him to Sam afterward in their office, and Allen was as enthralled by the man as he had been by his music. "I was just smitten. He wasn't distant. He didn't say, 'My man,' the way Jocko did. There wasn't really any time to sit down and talk, there were people constantly around, but he had a personality that was really captivating and he just charmed the hell out of me. He made you think you were the only person in the world. In one night."

Opening night was a gala affair. "Politicians and Dogs Nearly Steal State Theatre Show," announced the headline on the front page of the *Philadelphia Tribune*. The politicians, the newspaper explained, were unavoidable, and not necessarily a bad concomitant to any such significant public event, with the presidents of both the NAACP and the Congress of Racial Equality (CORE) "us[ing] the opening as their opportunity to get in plugs for their organizations." The police dogs, on the other hand, were "an unexpected added attraction" that brought to mind images of police brutality and aroused protests from the patrons and sarcasm from the stage. Sam in any case got a rave review from the *Tribune* critic, as he presented his recent hits in a format almost identical to the one he had employed at the Harlem Square, sang "Bring It On Home to Me" with a bluesy feeling and "a sense of phrasing and style that puts him miles ahead of the loud pack that comprises most rhythm and blues vocalists," and concluded with a celebratory "Having a Party" that brought a boss-talking Jocko, all of the performers, and probably some of the politicians, too, out onstage to join in.

Some of the earlier acts didn't fare as well. Dionne Warwick, nervous and in poor voice, was "unequal to the demands" of "Don't Make Me Over," her one hit single and, according to one audience member, was laughed at when she tried Ray Charles' "What'd I Say." Chuck Jackson, reported the skeptical *Tribune* critic, got more of a response from tossing his clothes into the crowd than for his music, and the Crystals were "disappointing [for] their hasty, almost sloppy treatment of their own specialties." In fact, several of the young ladies whom Jocko invited onstage midway through the show to dance to King Curtis' music "showed more poise and theatrical ingenuity [in their movement] than any of the paid performers." The Valentinos, with no current hit on the charts, were not even mentioned in the write-up.

Allen Klein, for his part, had eyes for no one but Sam. As far as he was concerned, Sam could have been alone onstage with no supporting acts and no musicians to accompany him. He paid little attention to the audience. "I didn't walk around and watch how they were reacting in the orchestra seats. I was just impressed with Sam, with his voice and personality. I was just listening for myself."

Every night, he went to the show and sat in his balcony seat. He didn't miss a single performance. He saw Sam backstage surrounded by well-wishers, mobbed by his female fans, and rarely ventured to say anything, deferring instead to Jocko, who was not shy about pitching him to Sam. "Jocko said, 'I don't normally recommend anyone, but I recommend Allen.' Of course, I was his accountant." He talked to Sam's road manager, Crain, who complained about the way they were being treated

by their record company and spoke of his associate Mr. Alexander's difficulties in getting paid by RCA on their song publishing. But mostly
Allen just bided his time. Generally considered to be the most aggressive
kind of music industry hustler (he had, after all, acquired his biggest
client to date, Bobby Darin, at a friend's wedding), he held back now
because he honestly "didn't want to appear to be overbearing or pushy."
He wasn't all that sure that Crain knew what he was talking about, but he
continued to find Sam utterly beguiling with that incredible smile, great
sense of humor, and a depth that he had not expected.

Then one night, as the run was coming to a close, Sam approached
him directly, unleashing a controlled tirade of resentment about the
manner of his mistreatment, both as an artist and as a man. Allen was
well aware that, while it was far from unusual for artists to be unhappy,
"he was *visibly* unhappy. And he asked my advice. I said, 'Well, why don't
you call the people you're dealing with at RCA, just tell them and see
what they say?'" He said he had tried that and never got any response to
his calls, but Allen simply said, "Try again." There was no point in
attempting to advance his own case too soon, because, he knew, "to talk
to someone about what they might need and what you [can] do for them,
you have to find out about them. And I didn't know anything about him.
I had to find out."

When Sam left at the end of the week, he asked Allen to stay in
touch. "I asked him where he was going, and he told me, and I said,
okay, I'd give him a call."

SAM PLAYED THE GALAXY SUPPER CLUB in St. Alban's, New York, the
following week, then the Royal and the Howard theaters in Baltimore
and Washington, D.C. He took the Valentinos on the theater dates, and
Bobby continued to play bass for him after the Valentinos finished their
act. "I was always asking questions, and Clif would say, 'Man, why don't
you shut the fuck up?' All the rest of the guys would be laughing, and
Sam would be cracking up" — but his brothers didn't find it so amusing.
They had all, except for Friendly Jr., moved out to California earlier in the
year, staking their faith on the promises that Sam and J.W. had made and
leaving their father's censorious judgments behind. To some extent, that
faith was in the process of being borne out, as this tour plainly showed.
But Sam taking Bobby and putting him onstage with him like his own
fucking son raised real questions of family loyalty. The way they all saw

it, Bobby was out for himself, always had been, sneaking around and complaining to Sam that Curt had the lead vocal on the A-side of their last two singles, then acting like butter wouldn't melt in his mouth.

It had taken them long enough just to get to California in the first place. They had gotten money from Sam and Alex with specific instructions to buy a Chevy station wagon, then gone out and paid $600 for a motherfucking broke-down old Cadillac, because that was what all the pimps and gospel singers drove. They were on Route 66 for what seemed like weeks — first the wipers, then the headlights, then the tires went out, and in New Mexico they ended up in the hospital with carbon monoxide poisoning from the exhaust. Upon finally reaching Los Angeles, they promptly ran out of gas and ended up pushing the car down Hollywood Boulevard.

Sam and Alex were out of town when they arrived, but Ed Townsend looked out for them, and soon they were installed in a basement room at the Dunbar Hotel on Central, where Johnnie Morisette lived, and where they were given three square meals a day on Sam's account. Johnnie showed them the sights of Hollywood, driving them around in his red-and-gold Cadillac, with the windows rolled up as if he had air and talking away on a car phone that wasn't even connected. He pointed out all the big stars copping blow and all the chicks running after them — the biggest stars in every field — it was an eye-opening experience.

Then, when Sam came back to town, he took them around, but to different places: to the California Club, where he pushed them up onstage on Monday night "talent night" with a dozen other acts in the house ("We said, 'But we already famous,'" laughed Bobby, "Sam said, 'You famous in *Cleveland*'"), and to Martoni's restaurant, the high-class Hollywood hangout on Cahuenga that Sammy Davis Jr. had introduced him to, where he presented them to the head waiter and ordered them charred steaks. They went to the SAR offices nearly every day, and Sam and Alex had Sy Devore shirts made up for them with open necks and puffy sleeves so they would look like romantic buccaneers, like *Valentinos*. Sam brought them out to his house, too, in a wealthy white section of town, where a very self-possessed Linda, just nine years old but clearly the apple of her father's eye and at ease with both adults and adult conversation, brought them Cokes and had crème de cocoa and milk for herself. But their new single wasn't doing anything, the session work that Sam had promised them wasn't happening yet, and they continued to feel that they had been cheated somehow on "Lookin' For a Love," which had originated with their own gospel number, even if they hadn't written it. And now with Bobby showing more loyalty to Sam than he did to his brothers, Curtis, Harry, and fifteen-year-old Cecil were beginning to wonder what exactly the future held in store.

CHARLES GOT STABBED at the Howard. It was a typical altercation for Charles, and it certainly wasn't the first time. "In Brandywine [a black amusement park in the Maryland countryside] five dudes jumped me over some kind of misunderstanding and they cut me here and there and kicked out all my teeth before Clif could get down from the stage." Clif had busted his guitar over one of the guys' heads that time, and he and Sam had taken Charles to the hospital to get fixed up, but, as he viewed it, it was all in the game.

This time it was more serious. "I was at Cecilia's Bar across the street, eating, and somebody come over to tell me that the doorman at the Howard wouldn't let this business associate of Sam's and his friends backstage. Now me and the doorman got along well, so I go back and tell him, 'Look, man, these aren't fans. These people have business to take care of with my brother.'"

For some reason, though, on this particular occasion, the doorman wasn't receptive to Charles' way of thinking, maybe it was due to what Hank Ballard termed his truculent manner, "that old ghetto gangster" in him.

"I said, 'Wait a minute, let's get this shit straight. He going backstage.' He said, 'There ain't no goddamn body going back there.' So me and him got into it, and somebody stepped between us and pulled a knife, which I didn't see, and I knocked him down, but then I felt this blood just oozing out. They had to operate on me for about twelve hours, give me a fifty-fifty chance. But I know damn well I got a fifty-one–forty-nine."

The whole family came down to Washington and prayed over him. When the band went to the hospital to visit him, said Bobby, "he was like a dead man, with all these tubes in him, and that shook me up, because [the night before] Charlie was working that motherfucker over." He was still in the hospital when Sam closed out his D.C. run. But he swore he would catch up with them before they even knew it, sometime early in the fifty-one-day Henry Wynn Supersonic tour that was starting up at the end of the week.

Sam's new single, "Another Saturday Night," the number he had written in England and recorded at the end of February, had just come out and looked like it was going to be as big a hit as "Bring It On Home to Me." Sam was about to embark on his biggest tour ever, in what amounted to a partnership with Henry Wynn. And his record label was having its most successful year. But while he was appearing at the State Theater with Jocko, Jackie Wilson was playing the Copa. And while Jackie was making his seventh appearance in two years on *The Ed Sullivan Show, Sepia* magazine published a letter from one of its readers asking the question "Why doesn't Sam Cooke appear on television?" He *knew* why it was. It was because he wouldn't play their fucking game. Jackie had his Mafia management, but Sam had his pride. SAR Records, he announced to the black press in an April 13 press release that might have served as one of Magnificent Montague's history lessons, was going to "resurrect much of the excellent song material written" by Negro songwriters like Shelton Brooks, Andy Razaf, Fats Waller, and Leon and Otis René. "It amazes me," Sam declared bravely if quixotically, "to see music written by [presumably white] mediocres and neophytes" given precedence over such great black music. And he intended to do something about it. But he was aware that he needed some additional muscle of his own. Jess had not been able to deliver the way he and Alex had hoped. He just folded in the face of opposition. When they ran up against the conventional excuses for lowered expectations the white establishment was so adept at handing out, Jess told Sam he was going to have to learn to do business with people who didn't share his enlightened views. Fuck that! He was not about to sacrifice his hard-won independence to gain a hearing at this late stage. But neither was he prepared to give up any of the money and respect he felt were his unquestionable due.

He talked to Alex about Jocko's friend, the accountant, and Alex agreed: it couldn't do them any harm to let the man look into their situation. If he could come up with some money from BMI or RCA, it would be money they would never otherwise see. With Jess no longer in the picture, Jess' friend at RCA, Bob Yorke, was never going to return their calls. Alex's idea was, let this new guy do an audit, and if he found anything, he could take his percentage.

Allen called not long after they had gone out on tour, and Sam told him to meet them in Tampa. "I flew down and asked, 'Did you call

RCA?' He said he had, but he hadn't heard back, and would I please call them. I said, 'Why don't you try one more time? Give them another chance. I mean, they should call you back.'" Once again it was the same story. Bob Yorke wasn't there, no one returned the call. "Sam said, 'Well, what do you think?' I said, 'I think they're treating you like a nigger, and that's terrible, and you shouldn't let them do it.' Sometimes, you know, you just say things — I didn't plan that, I just spit it out."

But it obviously struck a resonant chord.

"He said, 'You're right. I want you to go after them.' I said, 'I'll need all your documents and contracts.'" Sam said that wouldn't be any problem, Mr. Alexander could supply all the documents. And that was that. Except for two brief letters that Allen produced for Sam to sign, one addressed to RCA, the other to BMI, each dated May 1 and each stipulating in identical language that Messrs. Allen Klein & Company were his legitimate representatives and to "please make available to [Klein] all statements regarding myself that he may request. Please give him your utmost cooperation," the thirty-seven-word document concluded, and with Sam's signature neatly affixed, Allen got back on a plane and returned to New York.

2 | LESSONS OF THE ROAD

BOBBY COULDN'T BELIEVE HIS LUCK, playing behind Sam every night while his brothers sat stewing at home. The tour was scheduled to cover twenty-four states plus Montreal and Toronto in just over seven weeks, with the Upsetters back behind Sam, and Jerry Butler closing the first half of the show. Sam had three cars out on the road: the Cadillac, the Buick station wagon, and a new custom-made Checker (a cross between a station wagon and a limo that could hold nine people and all their luggage) which he had had specially built at the Checker taxi plant in Michigan. Charles was still recovering from his stab wounds ("I was hurting when I went back, but I just wanted to be out there on that road"), but Sam hired another driver to fill in, and Crain and Alex were always available in a pinch.

Sam no longer had any need for a middleman in his new "joint venture" with Henry Wynn ("Henry," said William Morris agent Jerry Brandt, "was a man of honor. His word was the Rock of Gibraltar"). The

Sam and Henry Wynn. *Courtesy of the Estate of Clif White*

lineup included several acts Bobby had first met at the State Theater —
Johnny Thunder, affable and easygoing, with his rock 'n' roll adaptation
of a nursery rhyme ("Here we go loop-de-loop"); the Crystals, "bad-girl"
teenage temptresses, the fantasy objects of nearly everybody on the tour;
and a touchingly amateurish Dionne Warwick, whom Sam had first met
as a little girl at Soul Stirrers programs in Newark and Philadelphia that
her mother's group, the Drinkard Singers, frequently opened.

Rounding out the bill were baby-faced two-hundred-fifty-pound Solomon Burke, the self-proclaimed "King of Rock 'n' Soul" ("Onstage
there's nobody who can touch him," Sam told Memphis' *Tri-State
Defender*); Sam's old pal Dee Clark, who, after rejecting "Bring It On
Home to Me" the previous year, had recently recorded a new Prudhomme twins–authored, Kags Music–published song; and the Drifters,
solid staples on any Supersonic tour. The MC was, once again, Gorgeous

George, who fascinated Bobby ("He was such a good-looking guy, the girls would just drag him around like a rag doll. Sam said, 'He can dress a guy into bad health'"). Sam picked him up in Atlanta, along with Lotsa Poppa, whose deft appropriation of Solomon Burke's music delighted not just audiences but the free-spirited King of Rock 'n' Soul himself. "I always liked him," said Solomon, "'cause he made me look small. I was crazy about him." According to Lotsa, billed for some reason on this tour not under his better-known stage name but under his real one of "Little" Julius High: "Sam said, 'First thing, I want to put you on the tour 'cause you make me laugh. Next thing, I want to beat your butt in craps!'" It was, said Lotsa, "like a family. It wasn't about money. It was about everybody enjoying their work and going out every night and just destroying the audience. The people got their money's worth."

Henry Wynn regularly checked in with the tour, flying in and out occasionally, driving to whatever dates he could. Henry by now was in charge of a loose confederation of black promoters covering both the Northeast and Southeast and reaching into Texas, Louisiana, and Oklahoma. He still booked most of his big acts through the Universal agency but more and more was developing a stable and style of his own, which led to his being regarded as the kind of "race man" whose down-to-earth manner ("Don't steal it all," he would tell his employees, "or there won't be any job left") and entrepreneurial ambitions were matched only by his commitment to the community. The secondary acts and the musicians traveled for the most part in a big forty-six-passenger Greyhound bus, but all the headliners had their own cars. For Bobby, who had rarely traveled in the South except as a member of a family gospel group that never left the black community, playing for a mixed audience was a real revelation. "I guess the things I remember most is sitting on the bus, one guy get off and everybody be cool, see if we can get some food. And staying in them dumps. Sam said, 'You know, it's okay for me. I can live like I live, hang out here, and then I can go back home. But [black] people that come to hear me sing can't even [do] that.' He'd say, 'You can hang with them [white folks], they'll let you hang with them — as long as they ain't got to worry about you.'" But at the same time, he told Bobby, if it seemed like you were looking to move up in their world, not only would those white motherfuckers throw you out on your ass, your own people would begin to wonder if maybe you weren't walking away from them. "He said, 'It's a hard spot to be in, knowing what the situation is and pretending everything is great.' He just didn't feel comfortable making music under those circumstances. But if you're a true actor, you're gonna play the role."

Gorgeous George always opened the show with a flourish. In addition to pimping, tailoring, and delivering the stars to the aftershow party at the local promoter's club for a fee, he had developed the role of MC to a high art. "He was the world's greatest MC," said New Orleans DJ Larry McKinley. "He just couldn't sing." Gorgeous George might have demurred about the singing part, but he was in full agreement about his sense of *style:*

> If there was twelve acts on the show, I would change twelve times. I had about forty-some outfits, shoes, socks, rings, everything matched to a T. I had artists pay me $40, $50 not to wear certain suits [so he wouldn't outshine them], and my hair — you ain't never seen no hair like I had, like them Spanish cats, [except] I used to spray it blond, I could walk in, and it would bounce on my head.
>
> I was MC on every tour because Henry Wynn was my manager. Henry named me. My real name is Theophilus Odell George — Theophilus means "God's best friend." My mother and grandmother named me out of the Bible, it's Greek. Henry started calling me Gorgeous George [because] I was sharp. But the way I spelled it — my manager didn't pay any attention — G-E-O-R-G-E-O-U-S. You understand?
>
> I stayed sharp. That was the thing to get you over, man. You had to be sharp to be in show business. We all had a thing going, man, and then the little money we had, half the time you'd be borrowed up, but I was more fortunate 'cause Mr. Wynn would keep most of my money, so I wouldn't be broke. And when I'd come back to town, I'd have a pocketful from shooting dice and swindling at the clubs and performing — and the chicks I met would buy me anything. I found out in show business, the fine chicks with the long, lanky hair, they stayed broke. But the fat chicks with the big hips and three or four pieces of wig on their head, they had the prettiest houses, they drove the best cars, they got the highest positions, they have more finesse — and they *loved* entertainers. I wasn't trying to be no hound, but they would buy me anything. And I didn't care who [else on the

tour] hit on my chick, because I would always make them give me
some loot.

Gorgeous George, who, in addition to all his other income sources,
made good money from costume repairs and nonstop gambling as well,
approved Sam's own sense of style in every respect. "He always dressed
nice, with custom-tailored shirts with the wide sleeves and three buttons
open like Roy Hamilton and Harry Belafonte — they were *like* calypso
shirts, even though they actually weren't. He was a size thirty-eight suit,
had German-cut coats, and wore the neatest Afro. Sam was so smooth,
man, that whatever he did, he wasn't going to get caught."

The only person on the tour who exhibited as much faith in the free-
enterprise system as George was Solomon Burke. Solomon, too, recognized the realities of segregation, but as heir apparent to the House of
God For All People, the church that his grandmother had founded in
anticipation of his birth (with one hundred fifty branches all around the
country), father of nearly a dozen children, and occasional proprietor of
drugstores, candy stores, and funeral homes in his native Philadelphia,
Solomon had long ago applied his resourcefulness to areas well beyond
the scope of his indisputable musical talent.

> I had a cooler, and it would be full of sodas and orange juice and
> tomato juice, and I would make sandwiches and stuff. It was funny,
> man. I never will forget, one time I was back there saying, "Get your
> sandwiches from me, get your soda and potato chips free," and no-
> body want those bologna sandwiches, they all say, "We gonna eat
> down the road here." We got about halfway down the road [with no
> other place to buy food], and there I was, selling those dollar sand-
> wiches for seven dollars and fifty cents!

Lotsa Poppa and some of the others got a big kick out of Solomon's
confidence in his system. "One time," said Lotsa, "he went to get some
sodas, and me and Dee Clark and [Upsetter front man] Gene Burks stole
all of Solomon's food. I was giving it out, and they was keeping a look-
out, and Gene holler, 'Here he come.' We ran and got in our [places],
everybody cool, everybody chewing, and Solomon looked in the bag —
he had one sandwich, one doughnut, and he threatened to get a gun! He

say, 'Who got my stuff? I know you won't tell no lie, Poppa, who got my sandwiches?' I said, 'I don't know' — but I was chewing, too!"

Solomon didn't drink, and he didn't gamble, which put him in a unique position on the tour. At first "if they were all gambling, they'd say, 'Oh, Doc's coming, Bishop's coming,' and everybody'd stop, 'Yeah,' 'Hey,' 'Yeah, how's it going?' and I began to catch on — you know, *I'm holding up the game.* Which made me feel good, because it said, Hey, they're giving you the respect." But it made him feel better when they started giving him their money to hold:

> One time Lotsa walked away with a ring of Jerry Butler's, a diamond stickpin of Dee Clark's, and six thousand dollars that he won from that crap game. "Now," I say, "Lotsa, you had a successful night." He said, "What should I do with it, Doc?" I said, "What you should do is send some money home, buy yourself a house." He say, "I'm gonna get me a Cadillac." I say, "Get you a nice house. Call your wife and let her buy a nice house." You could get a nice house down in Georgia for three or four thousand dollars then. Well, Lotsa wouldn't listen. Lotsa went out the next day and bought this and that. That night we were someplace else, another city, and he wanted to start the crap game again. I said, "Lotsa, don't get into that crap game again, forget it, you got lucky." Well, that night they wiped poor Lotsa out. Sam was throwing, he got on a streak, he made, I want to say, eleven straight passes — before he went onstage he must have gotten those guys for twelve grand. And he comes to me and says, "Doc, you hold it." And I said, you know, "Where's J.W.?"

That, of course, was not the way Lotsa Poppa remembered it. Lotsa, who generally followed Gorgeous George's opening with a blues set consisting mostly of Chuck Willis and Bobby "Blue" Bland hits as well as Solomon Burke tunes, saw Sam as something of an amateur at dice — "he just shoot for luck, he wasn't no compulsive gambler like me." But he admired Sam in every other respect. "He had so much class, and he sang so relaxed." Every night except Thursday, payday, when everybody was shooting dice in the dressing room right up till the moment they were called to go onstage, Lotsa would study Sam from the wings and sing along, providing the familiar gospel response to "Bring It On

Home" himself, even as the audience shouted it back at Sam. As far as his winnings were concerned: "I was always carefree, I was real lucky, and I had plenty of nerve. I had Solomon keep my money, and then, when we got back to Atlanta [a month into the tour], I bought a new Cadillac and had a friend of mine drive me out onto the field, Ponce de Leon, where the [Southern Baseball Association] Atlanta white Crackers played. I was the only one on the show from Atlanta [except for Gorgeous George], and everybody was there. It was a real good feeling."

Lotsa tried to help out Dionne Warwick, the gawky twenty-two-year-old Scepter artist with the odd, almost antiseptically classical voice, who, even with her mother chaperoning her, seemed ill at ease both on- and offstage. Dionne, according to Sam's drummer, June Gardner, would be singing her one hit, "Don't Make Me Over," and suddenly, inexplicably, start to cry. She adopted a kind of standoffish attitude with the rest of the troupe, maybe just to cover her discomfiture, but Lotsa felt sorry for her and broke the ice by complimenting her on her sweaters. That seemed to do the trick. "She couldn't help but like me — and Solomon told her jokes." But she still felt as if she was missing out on most of the fun. One night she ventured out to the party she knew was taking place in Sam's room, and Sam, whom she had known since the age of eleven, met her at the door "and promptly escorted me back to my room. That was the gist of my being involved in any of the activities. The one thing that stands out vividly in my brain was an auditorium we played, I believe it was in South Carolina, and the stage was in the middle, black on one side, whites on the other, and I asked Sam, 'Well, what do you do?' He says, 'You do what you gotta do, that's what you do.' "

Everybody remembered something different about that date, including the location. As Johnny Thunder recalled it, there was more applause from the white side than the black, a fact as puzzling as it was disconcerting. Jerry Butler, perhaps thinking of Jackie Wilson's arrest in New Orleans a couple of years earlier, painted a picture of Sam defiantly jumping into the crowd. June recalled the music bringing everyone in the audience together, black and white. But Sam, who showed none of his anger to his fellow performers, always displaying that cheerfully cool facade by which he was determined to be known, recalled only the police dogs roaming the aisles on the black side of the auditorium, a clear signal on the part of the authorities that they were not going to let their nigras get out of hand.

"Our people are not allowed to do nothing but applaud," he told Bobby when they were alone in the car afterward. "If they stand up and scream, the dogs are gonna get 'em. People don't know how to react, and then they can't even leave until all the white people are gone." "That's some fucked-up shit," Bobby agreed, without fully recognizing the dimensions of the problem — it was, he said in retrospect, "like waiting for war to break out. And Sam said, 'We the gladiators out here. I can't do this no more.' He wasn't talking to me, just saying, 'I can't do this no more.'"

Much more characteristic of his public stance was his reaction to the reception that Johnny Thunder got in Montreal. Johnny, born Gil Hamilton in Leesburg, Florida, and recently rechristened by his manager, had left Florida three years earlier, at nineteen, to join the Drifters, then, after a brief stay in New York, had signed on with one of the several touring groups of Ink Spots, spending weeks at a time in the French-speaking province of Quebec. "I'm a person who adapts, I love languages and I learned to speak French fairly fluently. I was so into the French Canadians, when someone would say, 'What are you doing, Johnny?' I would say, 'Well, you go up there — eh?'

"Anyway, we played this huge stadium in Montreal, and when Gorgeous George announced me, the audience went absolutely apeshit. I thought, Oh no — because he had mentioned something about Sam [coming up later in the show]. I said, 'George, I'm not going out there.' He said, 'Man, they're waiting for you.' I said, 'They think you announced Sam Cooke. You got to go out there and say it again.' So he [did], and they did the same thing, and that's when I realized we had a predominantly French audience. And I played it for everything it was worth!"

Sam, who had almost as many pieces of good advice for Johnny as he did for Bobby (when Johnny came to him, stung by his dismissal in certain quarters as "the nursery-rhyme man," Sam told him, in words that echoed his father's, "Just get out there and be yourself. Don't try to be anybody else. Be the best you that you can be on any given night"), was absolutely fit to be tied. "The *Montreal Matin*," said Johnny, laughing, "had five columns about the show, and three of the columns were about Johnny Thunder!" "Where'd that fucker learn to speak like that?" Sam demanded of everyone who would listen. "Man, I thought I'd learned all the tricks. I'm going to have to learn to speak four or five different languages now." He was, everyone realized, both joking and absolutely serious at the same time.

Sam was the one measure of success for them all. He was the coolest. He was the sharpest. You never saw his down side. He would show Johnny Thunder his books while sipping on his little cups of Beefeater gin, and while the rest of them were driving Cadillacs and Lincolns, he had his hip little Jaguar XKE sports car delivered to him on the road. "Some people are intimidated by people who have a smile all the time," said Johnny Thunder. "They think they are covering [up] something. But [with Sam] the warmth of his presence just came through."

The proof, in any case, was onstage. None of the rest of it would have made any difference if Sam hadn't been able to deliver. "He had a wonderful way with an audience," said Dionne, who was just finding her way to her own. "You felt sometimes as if he was almost a part of the audience, he enjoyed doing what he did so very much. And that translated to the reception he got." His new single, "Another Saturday Night," was by now a smash, pop *and* r&b, and, even though Bobby dismissed it as a concession to the white side of the aisle, June saw the reaction it got night after night from Sam's black audience. "It's just a backbeat, the wood blocks give it the Latin flavor, but it was a very big song with the public, I guess, because everybody can relate. He would always start [the night] very smooth, you know, but then at the end, with 'Bring It On Home to Me,' or 'Having a Party,' the finale, he would have church, everybody would be singing along."

Barbara came out at various points in the tour, sometimes with Linda and Tracey, more often by herself, and Bobby watched in fascinated incomprehension as she continually gravitated toward June's room, where all the weed smokers congregated. "They say, 'Man, you get out of here' — Charles and them. They say, 'Go to your room.' Man, it pissed me off. I didn't want them motherfuckers telling me what to do. But they knew Sam would have a fit if he found out, [so they] wet a towel and put it under the door. Sam always thought something was going on, but they be hiding everywhere — you know, one weed smoker see another, oh man, they as tight as the bark on a tree."

Bobby watched Sam's own clandestine operations with at least equal fascination. For someone who was himself just trying to get laid, it was a frustrating experience to see Sam with all of his different women. "One time there [must have been] twelve of them standing at the bathroom door, each of them go in and spend five minutes and come out. Like they got their blessing or something. And I'm sitting there mad, because I couldn't get none. One chick say, 'I got a nice daughter for him.' I said, 'Yeah? I'm a man when I'm up there playing with y'all.' But the only time I could shine was when I was onstage. Sam knew how bad it both-ered me. He said, 'Bobby, listen, there's gonna be a lot of chicks tonight. Now you don't smoke, and you don't drink, but I'll tell you what, get you a cigarette, you'll look a lot older. And order a martini. That's a nice little drink. You just sip on it. You don't need but one for the night. And grow your mustache.' So I'm sitting there, I'm standing up against the wall, doing exactly what he told me to do [except] I'm drinking this martini too fast. And Sam has this chick, and he says, 'Bobby, why don't you take her? Baby, why don't you go with him to his room?' Shit, I was so fucked up, I couldn't get up off that wall. The woman had to practically carry me to my room. She said, 'It's a shame letting this little boy to drink.' I mean, I almost killed myself trying to be old."

Bobby saw Sam with white chicks, with black chicks, with two beau-tiful blond twins, but the assignation that registered most strongly in his memory was one fueled by rage, not desire. Somewhere down in Texas, the program director for a local white station came by the motel with his wife. It was hot, and the men were drinking, and the program director started feeling woozy, so Sam suggested he lay down on the bed for a little while. Then Sam took his wife in the bathroom and turned on the shower, and they fucked without even taking off all their clothes. And when the man woke up, said Bobby, "that woman was fully dressed, like nothing had ever happened. She said, 'Come on, baby, we got to go.' I said, 'Damn, that's crazy.' But Sam resented the fact that 'these mother-fuckers come down with their women and shit, and their women look-ing at me — yet I can't stay [on their side of town], I gotta stay in this motel.'"

J.W. WAS AN AMELIORATING FACTOR on Sam's moods. The two of them, Bobby noted, were always conferring in muted tones, Alex with his little briefcase, his gray head bent over and nodding mirthfully, like they were shutting out the rest of the world from their private confabula-tions. "J. had been around. He knew the old show business before Sam came along, and he was very dedicated to seeing things go right for Sam and himself, too. A lot of people would come to Alex for advice, because they always said, 'Shit, J.W. knows, and J.W. will tell you the truth, just pass on the information and keep on doing what he doing.' [It] was inspiring for Sam, because they could relate. You know, for a guy as young as Sam, [it was like], 'This motherfucker here, J., been around. I walk into certain places, and he already know. He know how to set up a show, and he know how to help you with it.' In other words, Sam didn't have no dummy sitting there. 'What you think about this, J.?' 'Oh man, whatever you say.' If anything, they would have heated arguments, to the point where Sam would say, 'That gray fucker don't know everything, Bobby, he's on his way out.' Sam be saying, 'J.W.'s exaggerating about that shit,' but J.W. could remember everything precisely, and if you ask somebody, well, J. was on it."

Sam loved Crain, too, but it was more the indulgent love of a child for a parent whose platitudinous wisdom he had outgrown. Crain was always trying to impress young girls who didn't have the slightest idea who he or the Stirrers were. "I can get you in the show," was the line Bobby kept hearing him use. "Now, what you gonna do for Daddy Crain?" Crain's weaknesses became all the more apparent as Alex's strengths emerged, and Bobby watched wide-eyed as their long-dormant rivalry came out into the open. "They had their little war, but, you know, Crain was fighting it by himself. I don't think Alex was paying any attention, but he would laugh about it, and that would make Crain even more mad."

Crain for the most part kept his own counsel, not anxious to test either his power or his prestige with other members of the group. Charles, on the other hand, showed no such restraint. He didn't like Alexander's attempts to rein in his spending, he didn't like Alexander himself, and he didn't care who knew it. "Alexander come out," said L.C., who clearly shared his brother's views, "and he say, 'Charles, you spending too much of Sam's money.' Charles said, 'Wait a minute, Alexander. That's my brother.' Said, 'You work for him, and I work for him.' He took him right to Sam, and Sam set him straight. He said, 'Charles, if *I* tell you it's too much, that's when you worry about it. You don't work for Alexander, you work for me.' He said, 'As a matter of fact, Alexander work for me.'" After that, Charles refused to drive Alex unless Sam was in the car. He said, "I drive for Sam, Alexander. I don't drive for you." But Alex dealt with this, too, with the same easygoing manner that infuriated Charles even more. He saw Charles not as a freeloader but as someone who took advantage of Sam's good nature by *encouraging* free-loaders. But if Sam wanted to tolerate that kind of attitude, that was all right with him — so long as Charles and L.C. had nothing to do with the business. Which they did not — and which was probably the original source of their resentment.

Charles didn't have much use for Bobby, either, as Bobby was well aware. "Charlie was always saying, 'He a slick little fucker, telling you all these little stories. Why he have to ride with you in the limousine all the time?' But Sam just said, 'Bobby? He's green as a cucumber. If there's anything he do, it's not that he's trying to be slick, he just don't know no better.'"

There was hardly anyone on the tour, as Bobby saw it, who didn't get mad at him at one time or another for his favored position. "Everybody would say, 'Man, he gets under Sam.' But Sam knowed I would be straight up with him about anything. Even if it meant somebody else getting busted, I would just tell him, you know, 'That's what happened.' Plus, I always had my guitar, and we'd be kicking it. Now, you ride down the highway, just watching, hearing the sound, you got to get bored. But with me, it was always playing, plus he was always talking, we would always talk."

They talked about anything and everything, just the two of them riding along in the limo. Bobby would have Sam in stitches with stories about growing up in the Womack household in Cleveland, where "you weren't allowed to do nothing but sing gospel. My father, man, you ask him about the facts of life — when you wake up from being knocked out, he say, '*That's* the facts of life.' We had a TV, but my father called it 'the one-eyed monster,' he say, 'Why you watching that TV, the white man invented that, he stealing everything around you while you're watching.'" Bobby would come up with the most naive questions, like: why did they always stay in "motels," not "hotels"? And Sam would patiently explain, carrying him through the etymology of the word, pointing out that "mo-tel" was coded language for "mo' tail," until Bobby started nodding sagely and Sam just cracked up. He had fun with Bobby, maybe, because in Bobby he saw his younger self — that's what Bobby thought some of the time. But above all Sam seemed to want to give him advice, to offer the kind of advice that he himself might have liked to have had when he was starting out.

Bobby still wore his hair in an upswept process, and Sam told him he was showing his ignorance. "You know, we'll never be those people. We black, and we'll stay black," he said. "I'll never straighten my hair again." Bobby said he wanted a big Cadillac, just like Johnnie Morisette, and Sam and Alex both laughed at him — they told him to keep that pencil in his hand, his writing could get him whatever he wanted. "Sam always have a flask, he always sip on it. He start [to] reading black history, and you couldn't get him out of it.

He never got above people. He be driving down the street, and some cats gambling in an alley. He get out and say, "Hey, man, what the fuck is that shit? Let me shoot out." I'm saying, Sam is going to get killed in that motherfucking alley. That's no class. What's he doing in there with the winos. But he say, "Man, I had uncles, I had people that ended up like that, 'cause they couldn't ever get their niche, they didn't go to school, or whatever. They ain't gonna do nothing to you, 'cause they know they can ask you for it. It ain't like you gonna lock all the windows and roll by them. This is where I come from, and if I get scared to come down here, then I'm in trouble."

He would always tell me the position he would be in. He would say, "You be in this position one day, and you'll understand. You know. Mom fix you that favorite bread pudding you like. You know how much you like that bread pudding?" He said, "That bread pudding will cost me ten thousand dollars." He say, "I want to go [visit them] so bad, but, see, they don't see me as Sammy no more, I'm the one that save the world." I was saying, "Yeah, but that's your family." He said, "Man, you'll understand once you get there."

I said, "Sam, I never see you mad, I never see you bothered." He said, "Bobby, I don't come out of my room when I'm in a mood. I don't share it with nobody else. 'Cause when I'm uptight and down, why would I depress everybody else? When people believe in you and you give them such a lift, why show your attitude? You know, it can almost stop a person's world."

He always had this way of making you feel like you were the one; I don't care how you were feeling, before you know it, you was laughing and feeling up. That was the thing that was so special about him. He had the charisma, but he knew [how] to use it. He would say, "Bobby, always have your bad guy. You be telling [people], 'Oh, I want to do it,' and [your] guy say, 'No, he can't do that. I'm not going to let him do that.'" Sam was always a good guy — see, the good guys, they'll wear you out. But then Alex or Crain would be talking about, "Naw, you ain't gonna do nothing. Just shut up." And Sam would say, "Come on, man" — he would fuck around like that, and they'd get back in the car and laugh about it.

You couldn't get him out of his books. We'd go to a motel, and Charles and them would be wanting to get chicks, and they'd be saying, "We have to get all these goddamn books for Sam." When he wasn't chasing, he was reading. And the more history he read, the more [he would talk about it]. "Do you know about this? Do you know about that?" He said, "Bobby, if you read — the way you write now, you writing songs you ain't even lived. You ain't even been with a woman, so how you gonna write about a woman?" I said, "I know people that have, and I see what they go through." But he said, "Bobby, if you read, your vocabulary, the way you view things in a song — it'll be like an abstract painting, every time you look back, you'll see something you didn't see before."

He say, "You have to be universal. You have to be all the way around. You just work every day at your craft." It wasn't like he was trying to sell nothing, he was out having a good time. He kept saying, "Bobby, a star, that's the one you can touch." He would just sit up and listen to people, listen to people talk. He said, "That's where you get your hooks." He said, "It's easy to write the truth, it's hard to tell a story. You've only got three minutes. You gotta hit 'em, it's gotta be strong, and you've got to stick to the script. It's got to be about feeling, but if you're telling a story, you've got to make a believer out of the person that's listening."

Bobby was always playing for Sam in the car, just fooling around on guitar, coming up with little riffs and melodies that sprang into his head. He never thought of them as songs — they went right out of his head almost as fast as he played them. But often the next day Sam would ask, "What was that you were playing?" And if Bobby didn't exactly recall, Sam made him keep playing until he did. "He could remember it so well [for] not being a guitar player. And he'd say, 'I know what I'll do. I'll tape the fucker next time.'"

Gradually it dawned on Bobby that he was supplying Sam with song ideas, and he got into it one time with Sam directly, how he had let Zelda and Alex steal songwriters' credits from the Womacks on "Lookin' For a Love." At first Sam denied it. "He said, 'You took that song [from someone else]. You took a few [others], too.'" But Sam could never take a hard line with Bobby for long, and after a while, he owned up with an impish grin. "He said, 'Okay, I'm taking your shit, but I'm doing you better than James Brown [would].' He said, 'At least I'll fuck you with grease. James'll fuck you with sand.'" Bobby had been on the verge of telling him off once and for all. "I was like, I'm gonna tell this motherfucker, 'If it's good for you, [how come] it ain't good for me?'" But when Sam put it to him like that, he found himself totally disarmed and came to see it as part of his education, part of the same growing-up process that Sam, and all the others, had had to go through. And now that it had at last been openly acknowledged, he assumed that Sam wouldn't be fucking him any more, grease or no grease.

It all got spelled out over the incident with Jerry Butler. "I was in Jerry's room just playing stuff, all these cats going, 'Whoo, this motherfucker's bad,' and Sam said, 'Bobby come on out of there.' He said, 'You never go around playing with these people and just give it to them.'" When Bobby acted innocent — all he was doing was playing for Jerry, just like he did for Sam — Sam really ripped into him. "He said, 'Bobby, you're a writer. That fucker ain't got no melody, he can't sing nothing. That's the reason they want you in the room.' He says, 'They're ripping you off, they're taking your shit. You know what I mean.' I said, 'I could do this all day long.' He said, 'But I don't want you to do it all day long — okay, I'm taking your shit [too], but I'll tell you what, anything we do together [from now on], we're partners on it fifty-fifty.'" Which may not have been exactly the way it worked out, but Bobby took it in the spirit in which it was offered, as evidence of Sam's implicit faith in him. He would tell Bobby, "As you grow, you'll write. It'll come out. You've got things to write about." And Bobby had no doubt that this was true.

Jerry Butler's presence on the tour led to Sam reconnecting with Leo Morris for the first time in years. Leo, the New Orleans drummer who had worked with Sam in the summer of 1960 just before June joined, had been playing with Jerry for the last couple of years but had successfully avoided Sam for the first week or two of the tour. His feelings were still hurt about the callous way he believed he had been let go, "but then one night as I came offstage, Sam was standing there in his robe, and he said, 'Come here, I want to talk to you.' He said, 'Why did you leave me?' I said, 'I didn't leave you, you fired me.' He said, 'I didn't fire you, you quit.'"

As they talked, Leo for the first time was able to pour his heart out about an incident that had wounded not just his pride but his sense of self-worth, and Sam was able to persuade him that he had known nothing about it, that it must have been Clif who had let Leo go — for whatever reason — and then told Sam that his drummer had quit. "So we became good friends — I was kind of [devastated] to find out that he didn't fire me, but [what] was already done couldn't be reversed."

Leo had more pressing problems at this point, anyway. He had brought his wife out on tour at the invitation of his employer, and now he had concerns about both his wife and his employer. He sent his wife home but fell into bad habits and started entertaining fantasies of revenge. It was not-yet-sixteen-year-old La La Brooks, the youngest Crystal, who saved him. "My crazy mind was saying, 'Shoot him, shoot him tonight.' So I drown myself in drugs, trying to get away from it. And La La would sit by me and talk to me about this shit. She'd say, 'Why are you doing this? You going to kill yourself over a woman. It doesn't make any sense.'" The rest of the girls in the group were all fooling with someone on the tour, but La La didn't have a boyfriend, and all the guys were after her. "She said, 'Just pretend that me and you are tight' — you know, to kick these guys off of her — and we got to talking [all the time]. She was fifteen years old, but she was telling me stuff I had never even thought about." And so Leo fell in love, and while it took him a while to straighten out his life, he made a pledge to himself that he would never compromise La La and that he would marry her one day. And, two years later, that is just what he did.

M EANWHILE THE CIVIL RIGHTS REVOLUTION was erupting all around them. Even as the troupe was facing what Bobby called "K-9 dogs" patrolling the aisles to prevent race mixing or overdemonstrativeness on the part of the colored population, in Birmingham, Alabama, the vicious police dogs and fire hoses of Public Safety Commissioner Eugene "Bull" Connor were thown up against whatever forces Martin Luther King was able to rally in opposition to the most intransigent resistance to integration in any form in the South. King's campaign had begun in early April, just before the start of the tour, with Harry Belafonte raising well over $100,000 for bail-bond funds and forty-seven-year-old blind jazz and blues singer Al Hibbler standing side by side with Dr. King and going to jail with him early in the demonstrations. Comedian Dick Gregory had just gotten back from Greenwood, Mississippi, where he was a leading participant in the Student Non-Violent Coordinating Committee [SNCC]'s increasingly confrontational voter registration campaign ("Well, now, Mr. Mayor," he challenged Greenwood's race-baiting Mayor Sampson at a public press conference, "you really took your nigger pills last night, didn't you?").

"Are Show Biz Folk Sincere in Going Down South to Protest Racial Ills?" asked the Negro weekly the *Norfolk Journal and Guide.* "We certainly are," said Clyde McPhatter, who had recently refused to play an exclusive nightclub in Atlanta unless it rescinded its whites-only policy. He had cast his lot with the student protesters, McPhatter said, because he believed in "the right to be treated like an American. If we're ever going to be free, now is the time," he declared once again, as similar views by such notable figures as Louis Armstrong, Lena Horne, folksinger Leon Bibb, organist Jimmy Smith, and Sammy Davis Jr. were all cited, and, it was pointed out, popular entertainers like "Sam Cooke, Chubby Checker and others canceled engagements scheduled before racially segregated audiences. . . . 'We travel all over the country, and sometimes the world, having opportunity to observe — first-hand — the plight of the minority peoples,' [McPhatter] said. 'There is hardly one major entertainer who hasn't at some time felt the sting of prejudice or the stick of jimcrow, and there is not one who wouldn't give his all to erase these things from the face of the globe.' "

Not everyone agreed. Nat "King" Cole, who had been physically attacked and beaten onstage by local White Citizens Council members in Birmingham in 1956, defended "stars who shun[ned] Dixie picket lines." Obviously defensive, Cole, who under ordinary circumstances showed exemplary civility in public discourse, suggested that Dick Gregory and Al Hibbler needed the publicity and that Harry Belafonte was a "professional integrationist." It was an "idiotic idea," he said, that "Negro entertainers should lead the way," even though he could scarcely comprehend that so many of his white fans could love him as a performer, like his songs, even like him personally, "but still dislike Negroes as Negroes. This is baffling to me."

Fats Domino, who, like Cole, had always had a strong white fan base, announced his own break with NAACP thinking by declaring earlier in the year that "henceforth he [would] play in any nightclub or theater which pays him, regardless of whether Negro patrons are permitted." He was doing so, he said, because his band had to feed their families, his own family had to eat, and "I've lost thousands and thousands of dollars in the past because I've gone along with the NAACP, and it has hurt my reputation as a performer. I won't do it anymore." Within days, after a firestorm of criticism from the black community, he rescinded his new policy, declaring in a prepared statement that he had been misquoted and that "I know from my heart that the NAACP is the greatest friend of the minorities" — although, as the syndicated ANP story pointed out, he "did not say whether he was booking for any segregated performances."

Even the black newspapers were not by any means uniformly convinced of the need for further demonstrations, worriedly suggesting to their readers that the militant actions of a few could threaten the gains of all and that this might be the time for patience and consolidation. The *Birmingham World,* along with the *Atlanta Daily World* owned by the Scott family of Atlanta, refused to even cover the Birmingham demonstrations at first, wrote civil rights historian Taylor Branch, "treat[ing] King's campaign as a disturbing rumor," a ragtag movement undertaken solely for reasons of political opportunism that those of good taste and judgment might safely ignore. When King was jailed and placed in solitary confinement on Good Friday, April 12, he began what came to be known as his "Letter from Birmingham Jail," in which he laid out, on scraps of paper at first and in the margins of a discarded newspaper, the moral imperative of civil disobedience, the heroism of those who simply refused to capitulate to oppression. "One day," he wrote, "the South will recognize its real heroes. They will be ... old, oppressed, battered Negro women. ... They will be the young high school and college student ... sitting in at lunch counters and willingly going to jail for conscience's sake. One day the South will know that when these disinherited children of God sat down at lunch counters, they were in reality standing up for what is best in the American dream." It was a document written with the kind of moral clarity that is born of desperation, and it might well have sparked a renewed sense of dedication in both the black and white communities, but, as Taylor Branch tartly observed, "reporters saw no news in what appeared to be an especially long-winded King sermon. Not a single mention of the letter reached white or Negro news media for a month." And the *Birmingham World* saw no reason to rescind its judgment that this type of approach was "both wasteful and worthless."

Then, on May 2, backed into a corner by the white establishment, virtually abandoned by both the Kennedy administration and other civil rights organizations, and desperately in need of some sort of victory, King ignored the well-meant advice of family and friends, not to mention the entire Birmingham black establishment, and, along with SCLC lieutenant and local leader Fred Shuttlesworth, launched what amounted to a latter-day Children's Crusade. On the first day by some accounts, 959 children were arrested out of six thousand marchers between the ages of six and sixteen. On the second day, the police dogs and fire hoses were set loose on the marchers, and the world saw images of children being bitten, of a little girl being rolled down the street by the pressure from the fire hoses, of children singing just the single word, "freedom," to the tune of the old hymn "Amen" as they were brutalized by the civil authorities.

Within days, the Kennedy administration became involved; within a week, the city government had essentially capitulated to the movement's four basic demands, establishing a ninety-day timetable for citywide public desegregation. The settlement was announced on May 10 amid euphoria in the black community ("Do not underestimate the power of this movement," King declared to a packed congregation), only to have riots break out in the wake of the bombing of King's brother's Birmingham home and the Gaston Motel, where King and all the other Movement leaders had plotted their strategy over the last month. It was only when President Kennedy announced his unequivocal support for the settlement, and the federal government's refusal to see it "sabotaged by a few extremists on either side," that the precarious truce was saved. It was, as Martin Luther King remarked just before the bombings, "the nonviolent movement coming of age." But it raised new questions, and new challenges, within the black community at large, and within the community of black entertainers as well.

Brook Benton, who, like Sam, wrote almost all his own hits, had only recently played Clemson College in South Carolina in support of its new policy of student desegregation. "Before it's through," he declared to a *Chicago Defender* reporter in the immediate aftermath of Birmingham, "no one's going to be unaffected. I hate to say this, but I'm pretty sure that before it's over there's going to be bloodshed.

> We're waking up. We're tired of being pushed around. What are we — dogs? The man tells you, "Here's a uniform. Take 13 weeks of basic training . . . and go fight for your country." So you fight, and you get out and you can't even vote. . . .
>
> I'm not a non-violent Negro. If a dog or an Alabama or Missis-sippi cop comes on me, I'm gonna have something to protect myself with. . . . If I'm going to go downtown to try to speak to the officials to explain the rights of my people, and they have dogs there — well, it's hard to fight off a dog with bare hands. So I figure I'm probably gonna have to get me a gun, or a knife, or a few bombs. . . .
>
> Somebody's gonna slip up somewhere, and it won't be Negroes. These Negroes in Alabama have right on their side. Nothing they're doing is wrong; they're simply marching in to demand what's been due them for years. . . . They're not citizens, no matter what it says in the book. They're not free, they're slaves — they're in something even worse than slavery. . . . When a man knows he may die, you'd be surprised how many people he's ready to carry out with him.

Sam might very well have expressed the same feelings — and the same emotional ambivalence. As he declared to another reporter not long afterward, "We're in the middle of a social revolution, and some vio-lence is a part of it. There was violence in the American Revolution and in the French Revolution." But for the time being, all he could do was fol-low the news with avidity as they played Raleigh, Richmond, Augusta, Memphis, and Atlanta. He knew most of the players to one extent or another, he was acquainted with Martin and his father and brother, and, like everyone else, he had stayed at the Gaston Motel, probably in the very rooms that Martin had occupied, the Gaston's only suite. In describ-ing his feelings to one and all, he found himself caught between anger and a sense of proprietary responsibility, joking with Dionne Warwick and Johnny Thunder in some measure to ease the pain of humiliation but telling Bobby about the time when he was with the QCs in Memphis, no older than Bobby now, "and they come and slap me in the park, 'cause I was black and I wasn't supposed to be there." His father had taught him: when you're in the right, don't never back down. But when

Bobby said, "Man, if all black people would just [get guns and] fight back," he told Bobby, "We got to buy the guns from *them*." Part of him felt like he and Alex had figured out a way of operating in the white man's world, they were gaining respect in the manner that mattered most, *as businessmen*, climbing the success ladder in the one way that permitted them to escape both detection and self-analysis. "I don't care what the fuck you doing," he told Bobby, "you can be oversold to your commitment to what you believe. Bottom line, if that fucker ain't making no money with you, you gone." But then sometimes his heart took over, and his commitment to what he believed overwhelmed his long-range plan, just as it had in Memphis when he and Clyde had simply refused to go on, and as it did not infrequently on this tour when he read fresh accounts of racial injustice throughout the country or simply listened to local news reports on black radio stations as he traveled from town to town. He never doubted that with SAR Records he and Alex were making a difference, but whether it was enough of a difference he was not at all sure.

IN THE MEANTIME, Allen Klein was doing his best to put Sam's business affairs in order. With the accounting records that J.W. had supplied and Sam's tax returns for the last couple of years, the problem became clear almost immediately: all of Sam's money was going into SAR Records. His house might be worth $135,000, and he was owed a considerable amount of publishing money by Kags. "But," Allen concluded, "he never took his songwriter's royalties, and J.W. wasn't getting any money, either. They were using the money to run the company." For much the same reason, he had gone into debt with RCA, too, and Allen suspected the record company was using this as an unstated justification for holding back on its payment of mechanical royalties to Kags (mechanical royalties, as opposed to performance royalties, are paid not to the songwriter but to the song publisher for the right to manufacture records containing copyrighted material from that publisher's catalogue; the publisher then splits the money with the writer). And while there could be no justification for cross-collaterization between Sam's income as a recording artist and the money that was owed to a publishing company in which he happened to be a partner, it would not be the first time in Allen's experience that a record company saw this as a way to quietly recoup its losses. It was hard to see where the rest of his income was going, but life on the road was much the same as any cash business, and Sam was clearly not averse to spending money. In the end, as far as Allen could tell, despite all of his record sales and all of his valuable copyrights, Sam's entire net worth amounted to his house.

As soon as he had Sam's signature on the May 1 letter of introduction, he entered into a dialogue with BMI, the performing rights organization that paid performance royalties directly to both songwriter and publisher. He met initially on May 8 with BMI president Bob Sour (who with Theodora Zavin had worked out Sam's original songwriter arrangement with J.W. two years earlier), negotiating a deal over the next few days whereby Sam would get a $15,000 guarantee against his songwriting royalties for the present year, and an additional $14,000 in 1964, while Kags would receive an advance of $50,000 over the next two years, with various upgrades and bonuses attached.

As far as J.W. was concerned, that was more than enough to prove Allen's value to them.

But there was still no word from RCA.

JACKIE WILSON WAS SHADOWING THEM up and down the road. He played Florida just behind them, headlined a Georgie Woods–produced benefit for the NAACP in Philadelphia, and hit number one with "Baby Workout" at the beginning of May. James Brown, whose touring schedule of 330 to 340 dates a year never let up, was crisscrossing the East and Midwest with his own self-contained show, while Ray Charles, probably the most celebrated of all rhythm and blues performers and the one with by far the greatest crossover success, played Carnegie Hall before taking off for Europe on a monthlong tour. Henry Wynn even promoted a few competing dates with the Motown label's *Motortown Revue,* starring Mary Wells, Smokey Robinson and the Miracles, Marvin Gaye, and Little Stevie Wonder, hopscotching much of the same territory as *The Sam Cooke Show.*

They ran into the Five Blind Boys of Alabama in North Carolina, and Sam asked if they needed anything, reaching into his pocket and pulling out a big roll of bills. "No, man, we okay," said lead singer Clarence Fountain, who had been so entranced when Sam read westerns to them when he was still a Stirrer. Sam, Clif grumbled to L.C., would feed every gospel singer on the road if he had the chance. "Every time I look around," Clif told L.C., "some gospel singer got their hand in Sam's pocket, every one, I don't care who it is, they all [get] some money from Sam." Clif and June saw it as one more example of Sam's trusting nature. Clarence Fountain took it another way. To Clarence, it went to show how Sam had succumbed to the sin of pride when he crossed over, how he had come to put his faith not in God but in the almighty dollar.

For William Morris agent Jerry Brandt, who joined the tour from time to time for no other reason than his own fascination with Sam, the truth was somewhere in between. "He was charming. Totally [dis]arming. He would make you defenseless — [but] *you could not charm him.*

> You could never get what you wanted from him. You know, it's that elusive thing you fell in love with [but] could never touch. He'd let you see it, it's there — but it's not yours. Endearing and heartbreaking at the same time. He didn't reveal anything to anybody.
>
> He had the ability to call out your name in a roomful of fifty people and make you feel like you were the only one. It was amazing. He was a woman's man, but he could totally capture men, sometimes in a sexual way — but the men didn't know why. He could make the audience do anything he wanted, stand up, sit down, fall down, they would follow. He was a man about town, wherever that was. And if he was fixed on something to do, he was going to do it, no matter what you said. [Any problem with jealous husbands?] I didn't see it. If there was, I should have been one of them.

The tour ended on June 2 in Kansas City. For the last few days, Sam left the women alone and sent Charles to get fresh oysters in Baltimore so Barbara wouldn't know what he had been up to. "You got to have the oysters, Bob, to keep your pencil hard," he told Bobby Womack. But not even Bobby was so credulous as to believe Sam could fool Barbara in that way.

Within ten days, Henry Wynn had yet another revue back out on the road. It was now *The Jackie Wilson Show* presenting Ben E. King, the Orlons, the Cookies, Ed Townsend–produced act Theola Kilgore, and, as a special favor to Sam, the Sims Twins, with the Upsetters Band once again backing all the performers and Gorgeous George featured as MC. The marquee might change, the headliner and supporting acts might vary from tour to tour, but within the world of Supersonic Attractions, the show always went on.

3 | VINCENT

H E WAS SCHEDULED TO BE AT HOME for almost the entire month of June. He and Linda played with the little racing-car track he had set up on the floor, laughing and betting quarters on the outcome of each race as Tracey and the baby looked on. He told them stories and drew pictures for them. Linda's favorite place was the library, with books up to the ceiling, "all kinds of books, *War and Peace* and *Hawaii* and the beautiful leather-bound classics you find in real estate-home libraries. We had a full black history library before black history was even talked about or known, all the way back to Egyptian history, and we found the one and only black history [bookstore] in L.A., way out Exposition — we probably got every book in the world that [they] had, and my father used to read all that to us."

Linda would talk to him about his music, too. At ten she knew just what she wanted to do when she grew up, whatever her father might think. It had nothing to do with being a "star" — "I didn't look on [it] like that, I knew the depths of what he was trying to do, and I knew the purpose in it, and [I wanted] to carry it on. He said, 'No, no, you not gonna —' He wanted me to go to college and learn the wider aspects of life that he felt were maybe further progressed than the pitfalls that I [might] find in this business. And I respected that, [but] I didn't deal with it."

Whatever his ambitions for her, he valued her musical opinions. "My part was as the bounce-off person. He would test out the songs on me, make sure that the dance groove was right and that I thought the stories were good. He was always writing in his notebook, and he had a small reel-to-reel tape recorder, which he put a lot of stuff on. When I saw him onstage, it was more like something for outside people, but he could see I was really excited about seeing him work at home, that was a different and deeper emotional exchange. I guess he was in the time when he was trying to weigh: Should it be commercial? Should it have the hook that people will dig? Or should it be just what I feel? So a lot of times, he would be bouncing things like that off me. He would tell me, 'Well, people need to come here,' he wanted to reach *everybody,* but as a child, I just knew what I saw him love to do, and I always wanted him to feel free in expressing that, and that's what we used to talk about all the time. He was always intent on growing to be able to reach people, and at the same time to say something that would be a mark in their life."

Barbara continued to try to please him. At Sam's urging she read James Baldwin, and she did her best to represent him in public in a way that would make him proud, but somehow it was never enough. She was a member of Gertrude Gipson's gang of glamorous gals, the Regalettes (which also included Mrs. Ray Charles and Mrs. Earl Bostic), whose doings Gipson chronicled in her *Sentinel* column, and she attended social and charity functions both with and without her husband, but always, Gipson noted approvingly, under Sam's watchful eye. One time, Gipson wrote, Barbara "had a custom outfit made [of] gold brocade trimmed with dark mink . . . it had cost a pretty penny [and] she was real excited waiting for Sam to approve. He came home from the engagement, took a look at the outfit and said, 'I don't like it, Barbie. It just isn't you.'" And went out and bought her another.

She withdrew more and more into her own world. Her behavior became increasingly erratic, her distance as much a product of incalculable need as of any domestic disagreement that could be talked out. She watched Sam and Alex run up and down Hollywood and all over town — there wasn't anyone who didn't know her husband was a player — and she couldn't understand how the man could go through life like that, keeping her and everyone else at a distance. Only Linda could get inside the barriers. She was strictly an outsider. So close but no closer: that was his rule. And it broke her heart.

Jess Rand had his own reasons to mistrust Sam. He had known since the previous fall that something was wrong, and he had more recently heard from his friend, Bob Yorke, at RCA that someone named Allen Klein was nosing around in Sam's business. But every time he approached Sam about signing their management renewal contract, Sam just said "J., what do we need a piece of paper for?" and acted like everything would go on as before. Jess made some inquiries about Klein and decided the guy wasn't much of a threat. Just another small-time *grubber* in the music business, not right for Sam, very likely no more than a passing fancy. Sam, Jess had finally come to believe, was never going to be happy with the way he was treated — by anyone. So if this guy found him some money, more power to him. And if Sam didn't choose to say anything about it to Jess, just kept the money for himself, that was all right, too. It was all part and parcel of Sam's furtive nature.

Luigi flew out for a singles session on June 15, the second Saturday that Sam was home. Once again Sam decided to do without the services of René Hall, working with Gerald Wilson, one of L.A.'s best-known, and most respected, big-band leaders and arrangers, who had played on the Billie Holiday tribute album for Keen. It was a curiously desultory session. The one original Sam brought in, "Cool Train," was a conventional blues, similar in some respects to "Little Red Rooster" from the *Night Beat* album, but with a languid, Gershwin-like tonal arrangement that presented him as a kind of swinging blues sophisticate, a role for which he did not seem altogether suited. The only other number they attempted was a third pass at "My Grandfather's Clock," the children's parlor song that Jess had originally induced him to record, and it came out no better than the first two times. Then he was off into the night with Alex — to check out Patience Valentine at the California Club, or Lowell Fulson at Gert Gipson's Nite Life, maybe stop by Johnny Otis' new Ben Hur club and catch Johnny "Guitar" Watson's act or look in on the 5/4 to see if they might run across Oopie or Johnnie Morisette or Lou Rawls in the course of their pleasant peregrinations around town.

The following night, according to the *Sentinel*'s "Theatricals" column, Sam and Barbara, J.W. "Jack" Alexander, and Lil Cumber, who had been in charge of Specialty's Herald Attractions while Sam was with the Stirrers and had long had an agency of her own, all met up at the official opening of the "posh, posh" Small's Paradise West, where singer-organist Earl Grant was beginning a five-day engagement. Barbara was wearing a brand-new "high-fashion wig" and one of the two mink stoles Sam had just given her, and "their party rivaled that of PR woman Marilyn Green's, who had a crush on vodka gimlets." Sam cut his usual elegant figure, perhaps wearing the same pale blue suit and white silk shirt that r&b singer Etta James remembered him going clubbing in, giving you the feeling, as Etta wrote, that "he was very glad and blessed to be Sam Cooke."

He went for a swim late the next morning, then rushed off to an appointment without thinking to put back the electric pool cover that he had recently had installed for the clover-shaped pool. Barbara went shopping not long afterward, and Blanche, the maid who had charge of the children, wouldn't let them play outside because the cover was off the pool. When Barbara came home a little after four, the kids were going crazy, and she told Blanche it would be all right for them to go out now — Tracey, who was almost three, could watch the baby for a little while. She was hanging up the new clothes she had just bought when she became aware of an ominous silence, and then Tracey was in the bedroom, by herself, without Vincent, and Barbara stared at her as a growing sense of dread overcame her and Tracey said in her babyish way, "Mommy, Vincent's in the pool." She reacted without even thinking, rushed out of the house and dove in the water with all her clothes on, but it was too late. The little boy had blood, or some kind of pinkish mucus, coming out of his mouth, and even as she dried him off and tried to give him artificial respiration while Tracey explained that he had just been trying to get his rubber duck, she knew it was hopeless, and she picked him up and started walking around with him in her arms, her beautiful, plump, happy little boy. She was sitting on the ground just rocking him when the emergency rescue squad arrived.

Barbara's twin, Beverly, called Sam at the office. She reached Zelda just as Sam and Alex were getting ready to go out. Sam got on the phone, said, "I'll come on," then told Alex, "Vincent just fell in the pool," as he rushed out the door. By the time that Alex arrived at the house, Sam had shoved the rescue workers aside and was making one last hopeless attempt to revive his little boy, trying in vain to bring Vincent back. He accompanied the body to the morgue. Then he went to the bedroom to be alone.

THERE WAS NO TALK BETWEEN THEM. There was no consolation to be had. Everyone could see how devastated both parents were, but there was no talk. Lou Rawls could sense Sam's anger and despair, "but he never opened up." As long as Lou had known him, Sam had always projected an unshakeable air of confidence that whatever problem might come up, he could find a solution. But now there was no solution. He never discussed it with Crain or J.W. Crain came out from Chicago as soon as he heard, and Sam asked him to stay at the house — but they didn't talk about it. Alex saw his role as a friend not to intrude. If Sam wanted his help, he would say so; otherwise, you just offered whatever support you could.

The funeral was held three days later at Forest Lawn cemetery. Sam's mother and father had flown out the day before, and Sam was surrounded by family and friends, but he sought — and found — no relief. Barbara hated Sam, and she hated herself. "You never cared about him, you never wanted him," she berated her husband, even as she berated herself. One time, *one time*, she saw him cry — but the rest was all a blur.

Bobby Womack's most vivid memory of Vincent was of him dressed in a little white robe, picking up an ashtray full of ashes and mischievously blowing them all over his parents' guests. "You see," Sam had said, laughing, "I know that can't be my son." But he picked him up and hugged him anyway. Maybe, Bobby thought, it was simply a case of how, "when you play around a lot, you always have negative thoughts." But now there was no way to let go of those thoughts, it was too late for Sam at this point, and "he just didn't know how to say, 'I wish I could have given him more love.'"

Jess Rand could scarcely bear to watch Sam at the funeral, bending over the little white casket and straightening the boy's bowtie, murmuring to his son the whole time. "I thought it was going to destroy him. I thought he [might] kill Barbara." But when Jess tried to offer consolation and advice, suggesting that maybe Sam could cancel some of his upcoming engagements, take a little time off, Sam brushed him aside and said he needed to get back to work.

He was in the studio the following evening for the second night of a Mel Carter album session. Mel's single, "When a Boy Falls in Love," was just beginning to hit — and, perhaps not surprisingly, more on the pop charts than in the r&b field. Zelda had insisted all along that Mel was that rare kind of singer, like Mathis, who could cross categories — if they would only hire a white promotion man. At first Sam and Alex were reluctant, but after the disaster with Fred Smith, they were more willing to listen. They had given Fred $1,500 to take the record around the country, present it to the top disc jockey in ten key cities. Fred was emphatic that this was not enough money to convince even a single jock to play Mel's record, and to prove his point, without informing anyone, he took the money to the track. This was a stratagem that, as an inveterate devotee of the horses, he had employed with some success on one or two previous occasions, but this time it failed him, and he lost half the money. He was almost too embarrassed to go back to the office to return the little that was left, and he announced then and there that he was quitting the business. That was when they finally hired Ernie Farrell, the independent promo man Zelda had been pushing for, who had worked for Frank Sinatra and Dean Martin for years.

With only two titles in the can, these new sessions were intended to provide material for an LP to cash in on the single's success. J.W. had gotten five tracks the night before, and now, with Sam present, they once again buckled down to work. The songs that they had assembled were a lighthearted assortment of romantic ballads, lushly arranged, with pizzicato strings and an opportunity for Mel (who sounded a little like the way Roy Hamilton might have sounded if he were a high tenor with a falsetto that floated effortlessly above his fully rounded tones) to take off on one of his virtuoso vocal flights. Sam coached Mel on his words, but he was not as audibly present as usual. Alex remained at his elbow, just trying to keep Sam focused on the work.

Allen Klein arrived the next day with his four-year-old daughter, Robin, and insisted that they all go out to Disneyland. He never saw Barbara, but in his blunt way, he overcame Sam's objections to the outing. "He didn't want to go, but I told him, 'You always had your mother and father, but I lost my mother when I was nine months old. You've got two other children. Those two girls need you even more now. You're their only father, and you've got to take care of them.'"

At Disneyland Sam carried Tracey around on his shoulders, and the two men watched as Linda and Robin rode the bumper cars, and Allen took home movies. They didn't talk much, Tracey was pulling at both their noses, and Sam did his best to smile. "I never saw him cry, but I know he didn't want to live. He just didn't understand it. I think he was starting to lose faith, not in God but in himself. He didn't know where his son was going, he was doubting what happens after death. There's nothing you can say that's going to soothe someone's soul or heart about having lost a kid. I just said, 'You gotta live for your two other children.'"

Independence Day

S AM AND BARBARA AVOIDED EACH OTHER as much as possible in the one additional week that he stayed at home. Barbara felt as though all the love had gone out of her life. Sam was like a zombie, and she was, too. She had nightmares in which she saw her son at the bottom of the pool, and Sam was consumed with guilt and rage in a way she had never witnessed before. They lived their lives in silence, and every time he tried to talk to her, she started to cry and he would leave the house. It was just a mess.

An then, once again, he was gone. He played the Apollo with King Curtis, the Crystals, and SAR artist Patience Valentine, whose second single had just come out. Patience, a dancer and personality as much as a pure singer, studied every one of his shows, and Sam continued to give her encouragement and support, but she couldn't help but notice how much he was drinking and the uncharacteristic bleakness of his moods when he did. Lithofayne Pridgon saw the change, too. "I don't know, maybe I had just put him on a pedestal. I was just shocked to see a couple of people that had never been on his scene before. It was a quick thing — they were there, and they weren't there. I didn't think anything was necessarily wrong with it. I guess I just thought I knew him better than I did."

He played various dates in Philadelphia, New Jersey, and Carr's Beach, Maryland. Then he was booked for the first time into the elegant Club Harlem in Atlantic City, where LaVern Baker's ex-husband, comedian Slappy White, was the seasonlong MC, and Sammy Davis Jr. was scheduled for two weeks in August. The Club Harlem, which went back in its present Kentucky Avenue location to 1933 and had been called by Ed Sullivan "the best sepian night club show I've ever seen," was

Sam, Oopie, René Hall, J.W., Lou Rawls. *Courtesy of the Estate of Clif White*

renowned for "tall, cool, cigarette holder–carrying" Larry "Good Deal" Steele's spectacular *Smart Affairs Revue,* deemed by one observer to be as important to Atlantic City as the Miss America pageant. It stood in sharp contrast to most of Sam's usual bookings, with leggy, light-skinned chorus girls and a mixed audience dressed to the nines. "It was beautiful," said June Gardner, who had been with Sam for almost three years now and could not recall a comparable gig. "Very, very warm feeling." Less satisfying was a visit from an RCA executive seeking to dissuade Sam from the collision course with the company that his new representative, Allen Klein, seemed set on. The man said his piece, like he was talking to some *little boy,* as Sam's brother Charles observed from the doorway. "Then Sam said, 'Don't send me no flunkies, I don't even want to talk to you, man.' He said, 'Put him out of here, Charlie,' and I [did]. He said, 'If you want to talk to me, send the president [next time].'"

Meanwhile, Allen Klein was still trying to make something happen, still working without a contract, perfectly aware that Sam could just walk off and make a deal for himself at any time. Everything in life was a gamble in his view. Whatever you did, you did, ultimately, on the basis of belief. "I don't know how you get someone to agree to something [when] they just met you and they don't know what you're going to be able to do. Sam had no idea what he wanted, really, and *I* didn't know what I was going to be able to do. So you have to take a chance. You have to deliver."

J.W. watched with some bemusement as Allen "kept pushing himself to get in." The guy was like a gale force, but something about him just tickled Alex, even though there was no question that Allen had no idea sometimes of the effect his single-mindedness had on others. Alex didn't think he was trying to put anything over on Sam or him; his mind just focused on one thing at a time. But Alex believed to his core that the guy was really going to do something for them.

There was still nothing going on with RCA, so Allen approached Columbia — through Jerry Brandt. In order to draw RCA into negotiations, he needed someone else to show interest, so he had Jerry introduce him to Dave Kapralik, Columbia's East Coast head of a&r, who had recently signed Jerry's new client, Cassius Clay, to do a comedy album for the label, centered around his poetic fight predictions and boasts. Brandt had himself met Clay through Sam — he had been with Sam in Atlanta, and Sam was reading a story on the twenty-one-year-old boxing sensation in the *Police Gazette*. "I said, 'Sam, this is a big guy,' and he says, 'You gotta get him,' and tells his driver, 'Take Jerry to the airport.' So I get on a plane and go to Louisville, Kentucky. I don't know where Clay lives, I just go to a cab driver and say, 'Cassius Clay's house.' I knock on the door, and his brother, Rudy, answers, and I say, 'Hi, I'm Jerry Brandt from William Morris.' That means nothing. I said, 'No, Sam Cooke sent me.' And then Cassius Clay comes out. He says, 'Where's Sam? Is Sam out there? Sam Cooke, the greatest singer in the world. Come on. Sit down. What's happening?'"

The Columbia executive, Dave Kapralik, an effusive, diminutive man, was as taken with Sam as the Clay family had been. "It was a heart-to-heart connection. Sam would come into my office and kick his feet up on the coffee table, and we'd talk stories, as they say. He was warm, warm, warm, that's the overriding description I would have of him — you wouldn't want to fuck with him, but that was not the nature of our relationship." J.W. was frequently with him — it was a "father-son relationship" from Kapralik's point of view — and Jerry Brandt was always by his side, "brash, hyperactive, but I was hyperactive, too." The one person who didn't fit into the picture was Allen Klein, who possessed not a hint of Sam's natural urbanity and "Cary Grant" charm and who, Kapralik suspected, was most likely using Columbia as a stalking horse. But he turned Allen over to Walter Dean, the head of Business Affairs, and sat in on some meetings where Allen pushed for such unrealistic goals as a 10 percent royalty (Dean explained they couldn't even consider the figure, given that 5 percent was the label's top rate, and they had favored-nations agreements with many of their top-selling artists) and something Allen vaguely described as "total control."

Control was the key from Allen's perspective. Sam wanted control of his records, and Allen wanted control of the business. But how exactly to get there he didn't have a clue. "I really wanted to go with Columbia. They didn't have the old baggage, and in my judgment Columbia Records was the best record company in the business at that time. They sold more albums than anyone else. And when I was negotiating with them, I remember saying we would take a five percent royalty on the albums but we didn't need them [to sell] singles, so we wanted ten percent on singles. Dave Kapralik was a charming guy, and he really loved Sam Cooke's music. But what RCA had that Columbia didn't have was all of Sam Cooke's old catalogue." And without that back catalogue, Allen quickly came to realize, "we would [not] be able to control the manner in which his records [albums and packages, primarily] were put together and sold."

At Dave Kapralik's invitation, Sam met Dave and Cassius Clay in Las Vegas for the Floyd Patterson–Sonny Liston rematch on July 22. Floyd, who was both Sam's and Kapralik's favorite (the menacing Liston, an ex-con who was virtually nobody's favorite, held that "a prizefight is like a cowboy movie . . . only in my cowboy movie the bad guy always wins"), had lost his heavyweight championship to Liston ten months earlier in just two minutes and six seconds of the first round and was destined to fare little better in this fight (he lasted four seconds longer). Within moments, Cassius was in the ring, shouting into the microphone, "The fight was a disgrace. Liston is a tramp, I'm the champ. I want that big ugly bear," as Sam and the Columbia a&r man looked on with a combination of shock and amusement. Later in the evening, the three of them were standing at the back of the lounge, watching one of Dave's acts, when Sonny Liston crossed the floor behind them. "All of a sudden," Kapralik said, "we turn around and there's no Cassius — but simultaneously we're hearing this voice in the middle of the casino: 'Let me at him, let me at him,' you know, and he was making such a ruckus that all the tables and games stopped. The room is in chaos now, Cassius is banging at the doors to the ballroom where the victory party is being held, and Sam and I are standing there, half laughing, half stunned. Then the doors to the ballroom open, and out walks Joe Louis, who walks over and says something to Cassius that cooled him down very fast. But Sam and I were in convulsions."

All in all they had a great three days in Vegas. "It wasn't business, it wasn't deep philosophy, it was just fun," said Kapralik. "One night we went to see this girl singer I had just signed make her Las Vegas debut [as Liberace's opening act] at the Riviera. That was Barbra Streisand, and I had a party with Sam and Cassius, and Reverend C.L. Franklin was in town with a couple of ladies, and they joined our party. Sam got a big kick out of it, and Cassius was deferential to him, you know, not obsequious [but] deferential, because Sam was a big star. They liked each other a lot." And while Dave was aware of all the complications, and the warning signs that Allen's byzantine business negotiations were raising, he firmly believed that in the end Sam would sign with him, if for no other reason than personal affinity. But then Allen learned that the man who had been his and Sam's principal nemesis at RCA, a&r head Bob Yorke, had lost his position of independence at the company.

Joe D'Imperio was the new man in charge. Smooth and urbane, he was, proudly, the son of an Ocean City, New Jersey, barber, who had attended the University of Pennsylvania on the GI Bill. He started out as a trademark attorney at RCA, graduated to General Counsel, and then on July 1 had been promoted to management status with the title of Division Vice President and Operations Manager of Business Affairs. This might have meant little had he simply acquired the normal responsibilities of Business Affairs and overseen the a&r department's budget, but, in a highly unorthodox lateral move, he was put in charge of a&r, with Bob Yorke now required to report to him, and George Marek, the president of the company, his only direct overseer. Which undoubtedly would have set off more waves (it amounted to business superseding creative) if Yorke had been more popular within the company or if D'Imperio had not been so personally magnetic. But he was the kind of guy, RCA engineer Al Schmitt said, who was so likeable "that people just enjoyed being around him. He had a way of making you feel — he did this to me — he had so much confidence in you that you wound up having confidence in yourself. And he thought Sam could be a major, major talent, [maybe] the biggest talent RCA had. And he wanted to do everything he could to make that happen."

Sam came into New York after a week at the Regal and was playing the Town Hill Club in Brooklyn when he and J.W. met with Allen at his new offices in the Time-Life Building on August 13. They had finally worked out the formal mechanism by which Allen would be involved with the company, as exclusive administrator for Kags Music Corporation, SAR Records, and their affiliated companies. For a fee of 10 percent of the companies' gross receipts, he would handle all bookkeeping, accounting, sales, deal making, and administrative chores for a period of five years, with his term, and fees, backdated to March 1 of the current year (approximately the time that he first met Sam) and all expenses to be paid by the company off the top. In addition, Allen's lawyer, Marty Machat, would become Kags' lawyer for a $500 monthly retainer, and J.W., who up till now had been at best on a very informal salary draw, would, as president of the corporation, be guaranteed $300 a week, with two weeks' vacation, for a period of five years. It was a modest, if necessary, financial arrangement for Allen, unlikely at the outset to yield more than an $8,000 or $10,000 annual commission, but it enabled him to get his foot in the door. And it enabled Kags for the first time to be set up on a businesslike basis, with tax returns that properly reflected assets and liabilities rather than the loose reassignment of publishing funds to record company expenses that had been the well-intentioned norm over the years. Allen noticed that Crain's name, which was in the original incorporation papers, never came up, but it wasn't his business to raise the issue, and he assumed that if there was any problem, Sam would take care of it. He was well aware by now that Sam kept his worlds separate and that if he wanted you to know something, he would let you know. So he just brought Sam and Alex up to date on the latest developments at RCA and the next day produced a contract in the form of a letter to him from Kags Music Corporation that J.W., as president of all three divisions of the corporation, signed.

That weekend Joe D'Imperio came down to see Sam at the Hurricane Room in Wildwood, New Jersey, a beach resort that had showcased Fats Domino, LaVern Baker, and Dinah Washington at different clubs the week before. Sam's genial supper-club version of "Frankie and

Johnny" had just entered the Top 20 pop charts, and D'Imperio was knocked out by the show. There was no trouble this time about getting backstage, and when D'Imperio asked Sam if Allen was really authorized to negotiate for him, Sam just flashed that brilliant smile that could disarm both knaves and kings and said, "He's the guy I want." Allen heard from D'Imperio at the beginning of the following week, and with that, the real negotiations finally began.

A LL SUMMER, preparations for the massive civil rights March on Washington had been under way. It represented the fruition of a dream first envisioned in 1941 by A. Philip Randolph, president of the Brotherhood of Sleeping Car Porters, a coming together of all the voices of peaceful protest against the forces of racial prejudice and economic oppression that had denied true emancipation to the Negro at that point for three quarters of a century. When the idea of a massive demonstration was first revived in the winter of 1962–1963, by Randolph and longtime peace activist Bayard Rustin, it was originally conceived as a "March on Washington for Jobs and Freedom," but with the entry of Martin Luther King and the rise in racial tension in Birmingham and throughout the South, the emphasis shifted to civil rights legislation, and for the first time, all six of the major civil rights leaders (Randolph, the Urban League's Whitney Young, NAACP executive secretary Roy Wilkins, John Lewis of the upstart Student Non-Violent Coordinating Committee, the Congress of Racial Equality's James Farmer, and King) were united under a single national banner. There was a profusion of public events preceding the March, and, as usual, such stalwarts as Harry Belafonte, Sammy Davis Jr., Sidney Poitier, and Lena Horne had been in the forefront of fund-raising and publicity drives, but by the summer, Nat "King" Cole and Johnny Mathis, too, had pledged the proceeds of Hollywood and Chicago concerts to the Movement, and on August 5, Mathis, who had previously avoided any identification with the cause, participated in a Birmingham benefit for the March, stating, "These are not the days for anonymous and quiet approval. . . . The time has come to take a stand." The benefit, which took place while Sam was playing the Regal, also included Ray Charles, Clyde McPhatter, Nina Simone, the Shirelles, boxing champion Joe Louis, and author James Baldwin and was transferred at the last minute from Birmingham's Municipal Auditorium to the football stadium of all-black

Miles College when civic authorities suddenly discovered that the auditorium urgently needed painting.

There was another benefit, at the Apollo on August 23, that raised $30,000 with a lineup that included Tony Bennett, comedian Red Buttons, actors Sidney Poitier, Ossie Davis, Paul Newman and Joanne Woodward, and jazz headliners Thelonious Monk and Ahmad Jamal. That same weekend, Sam and Barbara threw a party for NARA, the organization of black radio announcers, which was holding its annual convention in Los Angeles. It was a catered affair, and "[Sam's] Los Feliz area manse buzzed with a multitude of show folks and those in related businesses," the *Los Angeles Sentinel* reported. "It was like old home week when guests began to loosen up and swing — from the gaily colored umbrella tables in the patio to the exquisitely furnished music room. J.W. Alexander flew in for the bash." It was, said Carol Ann Crawford, the young woman Alex had been seeing for the last few months, a sophisticated, glittery affair. "I was terrified!" said Crawford, just twenty-one years old and a recent graduate of the Patricia Stevens modeling school in Hollywood after having been turned down by the segregated franchise in her home town of Houston. "I was just practicing being comfortable in a world I had never entered before." But Sam and Barbara couldn't have been nicer to her. "They thought I was this cute little girl that Alex should hold on to. And I looked at them as a couple. I didn't see no evil. I didn't know nothing. I was just looking at the picture." There were colored lights, and there was barbecue, and Sam, as always, picked up his guitar at some point in the evening and started singing little story songs about different friends and party guests, just plucking the guitar and making up words as he went along.

The March took place four days later, on August 28. Close to half a million people converged on Washington and rallied at the Lincoln Memorial in what was widely referred to as the largest political demonstration to date in American history. The Brooklyn chapter of CORE walked 230 miles, and three teenage members of the Gadsden, Alabama, Student Movement walked and hitchhiked all the way. Marlon Brando, Charlton Heston, Burt Lancaster, Paul Newman, and director Billy Wilder were all a prominent part of the Hollywood contingent, with SNCC's Freedom Singers, Josh White, Odetta, Joan Baez, Bob Dylan, and Peter, Paul and Mary (singing Dylan's new civil rights song, "Blowin' in the Wind," currently number two on the pop charts) providing entertainment in a free morning concert at the Washington Monument emceed by Sammy Davis Jr. Introduced at the rally itself later in the day by A. Philip Randolph, Mahalia Jackson was the last "entertainer" scheduled to perform before Martin Luther King's climactic speech, and, at Dr. King's request, she began with the old spiritual "I've Been 'Buked and I've Been Scorned."

"The button-down men in front and the old women in back came to their feet screaming and shouting," wrote journalist Lerone Bennett of the reaction to Mahalia's performance. "They had not known that this thing was in them, and that they wanted it touched. From different places, in different ways, with different dreams, they had come and now, hearing this sung, they were one." With the crowd's response ringing in her ears, Mahalia delivered perhaps her most enduring and uplifting "hit," W.H. Brewster's classic composition "How I Got Over," and then Rabbi Joachim Prinz, a German refugee, briefly took the stage before, at twenty minutes to four, A. Philip Randolph introduced Martin Luther King as "the moral leader of our nation."

King spoke of freedom and justice. He delivered, as historian Taylor Branch wrote, "a formal speech, as demanded by the occasion and the nature of the audience," not just the several hundred thousand who had brought all their hopes and dreams to Washington but a national television audience that could watch his speech "live" on any of the three major networks. They had come to the nation's capital, they had come to this historic site, King declared, to collect on a promise, a promise made one hundred years earlier with the Emancipation Proclamation. They had also come "to remind America of the fierce urgency of *now*." This was no time for empty rhetoric. This was no time for delay. Now was the time "to make justice a reality for all of God's children."

It would be a terrible mistake, he said, for the country to ignore that imperative. There could at this point be no turning back, he insisted, enumerating the everyday brutalities and indiscriminate burdens of discrimination. "We can never be satisfied as long as our bodies, heavy with the fatigue of travel, cannot gain lodging in the motels of the highways and the hotels of the cities . . . as long as our children are stripped of their selfhood and robbed of their dignity by signs stating 'For Whites Only.'"

It was a moving speech, it was a speech that touched every base and raised the crowd to a height of emotion that "carried every ear and every heart," wrote William Robert Miller, a pacifist colleague of Bayard Rustin, "along that rise of intensity and into the emotional heights as well." But then as he got to the end of his allotted seven minutes and the conclusion of the prepared text, King seemed to be lifted up by the crowd, and, rather than stick to his prosaic written summation, he began to preach.

"Tell them about the dream, Martin," Mahalia Jackson was heard to call out, recollecting the speech he had given at a massive civil rights rally organized by the Reverend C.L. Franklin in Detroit just two months earlier. "I have a dream," he declared, "that one day on the red hills of Georgia the sons of former slaves and the sons of former slaveowners will be able to sit down together at the table of brotherhood." He had a dream, he said, that his children would come to see a world in which men and women were measured by their character, not their color. He went on to detail every aspect of his dream, morally, thematically, spiritually, geographically, with each segment ending "I have a dream today." It was, wrote King biographer David Levering Lewis, "rhetoric almost without content, but this was, after all, a day of heroic fantasy. And so it continued with increasing effect [until] the antiphonal response of the multitude was almost deafening."

If America was ever to fulfill its promise and become a truly great nation, King declared, quoting and echoing the song "My Country 'Tis of Thee," then freedom must ring all across America, from every hill and valley, from every city and town, from every mountainside. When that day came, then *all* of God's children, black and white, could come together "and sing in the words of the old Negro spiritual 'Free at last! Free at last! Thank God almighty, we are free at last!' "

IT IS IMPOSSIBLE TO CALCULATE the full effect that watching this on television, listening on the radio must have had on Sam. These were people that he knew. This was the world from which he came. Mahalia had called the Highway QCs "her boys" when Sam was just starting out, at the age of seventeen, and the Soul Stirrers had cut a new version of "Free At Last" for SAR no more than six months ago. He and Alex had been talking with student sit-in leaders in North Carolina on the spring tour. And when he first heard "Blowin' in the Wind" on the new *Freewheelin' Bob Dylan* album J.W. had just given him, he was so carried away with the message, and the fact that a white boy had written it, that, he told Alex, he was almost ashamed not to have written something like that himself. It wasn't the way Dylan sang, he told Bobby Womack. It was *what he had to say.* His daughter was always telling him he should be less worried about pleasing everyone else and more concerned with pleasing himself — and maybe she was right. But like any black entertainer with a substantial white constituency, he couldn't help but worry about bringing his audience along.

It was a dilemma for them all. Julian Bond, the young SNCC Communications Director, was one of the few black activists who had made the connection between the music and the Movement explicit. "I, too, hear America singing," Bond had written in the June 1960 edition of *The Student Voice*, the first issue of the SNCC newsletter.

> *But from where I stand*
> *I can only hear Little Richard*
> *And Fats Domino.*
> *But sometimes,*
> *I hear Ray Charles*
> *Drowning in his own tears*
> *or Bird*
> *Relaxing at Camarillo*
> *or Horace Silver doodling,*
> *Then I don't mind standing a little longer.*

Roy Hamilton had attended the March on his own and was so inspired by it that he wrote to CORE national director James Farmer, "I still feel that there is something more that I can personally contribute. . . . Don't hesitate to call on me." But he didn't hear back for almost five months, and then it was from an assistant community relations director, who suggested that he give her a ring so they could discuss just what he might have in mind. "We didn't count," was the matter-of-fact assessment of Lloyd Price, like Sam, an independent businessman and solid Movement supporter. "They wanted high-profile artists like Sammy, Harry Belafonte, Louis Armstrong, artists [who appealed to whites and the black middle class] like Nat 'King' Cole — but what could have been more high-profile than rock 'n' roll singers selling millions of records and playing interracial music, interracial dances?"

"I'm going to write something," Sam told J.W. But he didn't know what it was.

*   *   *

ALLEN AND J.W. HAD A LUNCH MEETING with Joe D'Imperio and RCA's hulking Division Vice President and Operations Manager Norm Racusin at D'Imperio's invitation. It started off with an exchange of pleasantries, as D'Imperio reiterated how impressed he was with Sam and what great potential he had with the label. Allen readily agreed but then returned to the subject that had preoccupied him from the start: money. After carefully scrutinizing Sam's financial records, he had come to the conclusion that if RCA owed Sam any artist's royalties, they were negligible and offset in any case by the fact that Sam was in essence overdrawn on his account. But at the same time, it had not escaped his attention that, as both author and publisher of his own songs, Sam (and Kags Music) had supplied the lion's share of Sam's hits. A conservative estimate put that share at eight million sales of individual titles (whether as a single side of a 45 or a double-sided hit), not to mention album sales, including the previous year's *Best of Sam Cooke* (with ten original titles), which, after nine months, had only recently gone off the charts. This should have generated at least $200,000 for Kags in mechanical royalties. But, so far as Allen could tell, Sam's song publishing firm had received very little in the way of compensation. If RCA was somehow thinking that this was an acceptable way to balance their accounts, Allen was sure that they must be aware that they were supported by neither contractual nor statutory law. So unless they were willing to open up their books and pay Sam every penny he was owed, maybe they should all just pack up and go home.

But Sam's record sales were disappointing, the RCA executives suggested conciliatorily. None of his singles had sold a million copies, his last few singles had not even hit the half-million mark. What they were talking about was *potential*. "They said to me, 'Let's make a new deal.' I said, 'Listen, you don't want him, because he didn't sell a million? [We'll just] leave.'" D'Imperio tried to smooth things over but remained resistant to the idea of an audit — it simply wasn't necessary, he said. Surely they could come to some kind of agreement without it. Allen didn't back off one bit in his demands, brought up again the necessity for a self-contained artist like Sam to be able to "control" his catalogue, and the meeting ended on an inconclusive note. But Allen could tell, they were nervous.

Allen and Alex were in the lobby afterward having their shoes shined, when the federal marshal served the papers in the RCA offices upstairs. The first that they became aware of it, Norm Racusin, a former football player, came storming out of the elevator, waving the court order at them as if, J.W. thought, he was going to take their heads off. "How could you do this?" he was shouting. What kind of bullshit was it to come in for a so-called legitimate meeting and then follow it up with this kind of grandstanding crap? They could stuff their audit up their ass if this was the way they were going to conduct business. As far as Racusin was concerned, discussions were at an end.

J.W. chuckled to himself as Allen professed total surprise. There must be some kind of mistake, he said, let him just call his lawyer, and then, with Racusin looking on, he coolly upbraided Marty Machat on the phone. "I said, 'Marty, how could you do this?' He said, 'What are you talking about? You told me to do it.' I said, 'It's so embarrassing. I [come] here to have lunch, and you serve RCA with a federal marshal.' I said, 'Call it off.' He said, 'Well, I can't.' I said, 'Yes, I know.' And we went on [from there]."

It was all part of his strategy of bringing people down to size. Hardly the most socially confident man himself, Klein was determined to eliminate class, convention, or social status as any advantage in negotiations. He might not be able to compete in the corporate boardroom or the country club, but if these people wanted to deal with him they were going to have to learn to operate on a level playing field. J.W. couldn't get over Allen's nerve; he laughed out loud later in recounting the scene to Sam. But there was no question in Allen's mind that he had gotten the record company's attention. D'Imperio, a down-to-earth man himself, informed Allen in no uncertain terms that he would brook no further stunts like this one, that if they were going to do business, they would have to learn to work together. But as Allen saw it, "When they got served, they saw I wasn't fooling around. I hit them and woke them up. And they turned over and gave us the information."

S AM ENJOYED HIS BRIEF RESPITE at home. He recorded an L&M cigarette commercial (and shot an accompanying photo spread with the band) that he got through the J. Walter Thompson advertising agency. "When a cigarette means a lot," he crooned to a fully orchestrated background that could have been used on one of his own hits, "More body in the blend / More flavor in the smoke / Get lots more from L&M." He drove around town in the Maserati he had just purchased from Eddie

Fisher for $14,000. And he invited Jess Rand to lunch at the Brown Derby for a very belated reckoning. "Sam said, 'You did a lot for me. But maybe you took me as far as [you thought] I could go.' I said, 'Where do you want to go?' I could see he was very uncomfortable. He was tap-dancing all over the place. He said, 'I want to give you something. We'll straighten it out.' I was terribly hurt. I kept looking at the picture of him on the wall of the Brown Derby with the gold record for 'You Send Me,' saying, My God, what am I listening to here?" But Sam kept after him, almost desperately exerting all of his charm, because, said Jess, "he still wanted me as a friend. And, you know, it was very strange: we *stayed* friends."

New SAR business was at a standstill, as all efforts were focused on Mel Carter's "When a Boy Falls in Love," which continued to sell in the pop market. Mel was playing the top nightspots around town and was prominently featured in a big rock 'n' roll show at the Sports Arena on August 31 with the Beach Boys, the Righteous Brothers, and Marvin Gaye. Zelda Sands, who was taking an increasingly active role in Mel's career, teased Sam that this was the direction in which Sam's career could be going, if he would only adopt more of her advice. "I said, 'I'll show you [by] putting him where you should be.' 'Cause I always felt that Sam should be with the pop crowd."

The Sims Twins and Johnnie Morisette weren't selling any records. L.C.'s latest single, "The Wobble," had sunk without a trace. And Johnnie Taylor, the *Sentinel* reported, was cruising around town in the new Buick Riviera he had gotten as a gift from one of his female "admirers," still unable to choose between the life of a singer and the life of a pimp. The Soul Stirrers, meanwhile, were in a limbo of their own with the arrest of their lead singer, Jimmie Outler, for kidnapping, robbery, and rape, and their indispensable second lead, Paul Foster, forced to miss an increasing number of recent dates due to illness. J.W. announced to the press that Jimmie, whose troubles stemmed from a Stirrers party at the Dunbar Hotel, was not the lead singer on the group's best-known coupling, "Stand By Me Father" and "He's Been a Shelter," though he didn't bother pointing out that that particular record had been released in 1959. Still, he and Sam were not about to give up on the Stirrers. Nor were they about to give up on Jimmie, whose last name was transliterated not entirely inappropriately to "Outlaw" in print and popular pronunciation. Sam liked Jimmie, just as he liked Oopie, the former Pilgrim Travelers bass singer, and Johnnie Morisette. There was something about the rough life they led that he was clearly drawn to; denying them would have been like denying an ineluctable part of himself.

He had his first session under the aegis of Allen's new company, Tracey, on September 11. The idea behind Tracey, Allen explained to him, was to provide a kind of holding company for his income, which would allow him to pay taxes only as he drew money from the Tracey account. Allen would own Tracey (otherwise it would be regarded as Sam's *personal* holding company, which would be taxed no differently than an individual), but J.W. would be president and Sam's daughter's name would stamp it as his own. Allen was working out the details with Joe D'Imperio — if all went as planned, this would give Sam full control of his masters, in addition to a substantial improvement in his financial situation. But even if it didn't work out, it gave them a model for independence; it established a kind of prototype for future negotiations. And by doing the session under the umbrella of Tracey, without any input from Hugo and Luigi or RCA, they let the record company know they really did mean business.

Sam went in with a new arranger, Jimmie Haskell, who had done most of Ricky Nelson's hit sessions, along with a sixteen-piece string section and a big pop chorus. The result was not particularly scintillating, a florid remake of Harry Belafonte's "I'm Just a Country Boy," which Sam had cut three years before (and with which Oopie had recently had a hit under his real name of George McCurn, on Herb Alpert's new A&M label), and a cheerful retrieval of his own "Sugar Dumpling," which he had originally recorded for his *Twistin' the Night Away* LP. Three days later, he was back on the road, with nothing officially resolved but two songs in the new Tracey catalogue.

Allen was by now fully settled on his plan. Despite the little misunderstanding over the process server, there was no longer any question in his mind that Joe D'Imperio was a Sam Cooke fan, so there was no further thought of going to Columbia, even if he was not yet prepared to admit that to RCA. The template for the deal was based on a simple manufacturing and distribution agreement but was dissimilar in most other respects from any of the normal ways in which a record company did business. The idea had evolved from bits and pieces of his own accounting experience, but it was based on something in between a misconception and a blinding flash of illumination. From the time that he had first moved into the former Hecht-Hill-Lancaster offices in the

United Artists building on Seventh Avenue in 1960, he had been fascinated by the concept of independent production. To make a movie, you
needed a director, an editor, a writer, and a star, and if you had all of those
in one package, as Burt Lancaster and his partners in Hecht-Hill-
Lancaster had proved, what did you need a studio for? Solely to distribute your product.

Then he recalled what he had heard about Frank Sinatra's Essex Productions, which Sinatra announced boldly to the trades in 1957 would be
his own "full-fledged independent record company," with Capitol merely
serving as its distributor. In reality, Capitol owned Sinatra's records outright and rejected any modification of that arrangement, because, as
Capitol vice president Alan Livingston observed, it would have been
"totally contrary to everything going on in the record business then," but
Sinatra continued to trumpet Essex not just as a holding company but as
a record manufacturer. Allen also knew of a partnership between Harry
Belafonte and Nat "King" Cole, which was actually intended for extra-
musical ventures and which turned out in any case to be extremely
short-lived, but which Allen for some reason took to be an arrangement
by which each manufactured the other's records, thereby escaping IRS
classification as a personal tax dodge.

That was the genesis of his idea for Sam, cobbled together, as Allen
himself would have been the first to admit, from nothing more conclu-
sive than imprecise scholarship, his own instincts on the subject, and a
willingness, actually a *desire*, to try something that had never been tried
before.

Here was how it would work, he explained to Joe D'Imperio, something of a maverick thinker himself within the music world. Tracey
would be neither a production company nor a personal holding company, since Sam would not own, hold stock in, or serve as a controlling
officer of the corporation. It would, in fact, function as a full-fledged
record company, assuming the burdens and responsibilities of Sam's
artist contract with RCA, taking on the status of record manufacturer,
and, of course, owning the masters of the records that it manufactured.
But it would assign to RCA exclusive distribution of those records for some
indeterminate period of time — Allen suggested five years, D'Imperio
came back with a nonnegotiable thirty — and RCA would in turn provide Tracey with free studio time and, in addition to purchasing the
records from Tracey at a price that allowed Allen's company a reasonable

rate of profit, reimburse Tracey for its recording costs at a fixed rate of $2,000 for a single, $6,000 for an album.

There was one additional catch. Allen recognized that RCA could not raise its 5 percent artist's royalty because of favored-nations agreements with other artists, but it would not have a contract with Sam, it would have a contract with Tracey Ltd., for which, since there was no record-business parallel, there could be no favored-nations concerns. Allen wanted a 6 percent royalty for Tracey, and he wanted it paid on 100 percent of all sales. Sam's royalties, like every recording artist's, were calculated on the basis of list price minus excise tax (on a single listing for ninety-eight cents, the excise tax came to approximately four cents) and were paid on 90 percent of all sales, the assumption being that 10 percent represented "promotional" distribution and breakage. Sam's royalty of 5 percent was thus, in reality, no more than 4.23 percent, and it was to be set against a substantial, still-to-be-agreed-upon advance (in other words, Sam would see no royalties until the advance was earned out), but under Allen's proposal, Tracey's 1.77 percent share (the difference between Sam's actual royalty and Tracey's 6 percent) would come off the top. So, if, for the sake of argument, Sam sold a million singles and three hundred thousand albums, Tracey's royalty would amount to approximately $35,000. And Allen wanted to be paid not quarterly or biannually, as was customary in the business, but monthly, on the basis of verifiable sales reports.

To Allen's surprise, not only did D'Imperio not blink, he seemed intrigued by the idea. What about Sam? Did Sam understand the full implications of the deal — they would need to have a piece of paper from him in which he assigned his RCA contract to Tracey and indicated his full knowledge that henceforth all monies that would have been paid to him by RCA would instead be paid to Tracey and that all past sums owed to Sam or to his publishing companies, Kags and Malloy, would go to Tracey as well. That, Allen said, would represent no problem. Sam's partner, J.W. Alexander, would be president of Tracey (though he, too, would have no financial stake in the corporation), and both Mr. Cooke and his partner, Mr. Alexander, were sophisticated businessmen who, as Joe was well aware, owned their own publishing and record labels.

There remained, however, the continuing problem of back royalties. Allen was not in the least interested in putting the company through a lengthy auditing process, it would be a needless expenditure of time and effort (and, in the long run, money) for them both, why couldn't RCA simply concede that there was a sizeable amount due and then work out a reasonable formula by which it could be calculated and paid out? Again to his surprise, D'Imperio agreed. It appeared as if RCA owed Sam and his publishing company back royalties of at least $125,000, D'Imperio conceded, and if Allen would be satisfied to allow RCA to make a good-faith final determination based upon the internal audit it was currently conducting, he thought that a good portion of that sum could soon be released. That was all very well, Allen said, but if they were going to make a deal, he needed a deal memo right away, because Tracey's fiscal year had already begun, and if he didn't have something by the end of the month that could be backdated to September 1, RCA could just forget about the whole thing.

This was pure bluff. There was no fiscal year, there was no need for anything but a quick close ("I wanted to get it done fast so that they couldn't change their mind, I just wanted to make sure I had it"), but in this, as in everything else, D'Imperio proved the soul of gentlemanliness. Whether or not he believed in the literal truth of Allen's fiscal year was no longer the point. They both wanted to make a deal. He overruled his sales force, which argued that blacks didn't buy LPs, by insisting vehemently that it was up to the record company, then, to change that. Sam, he declared, was a major talent on the order of Harry Belafonte, who had undeniably sold a lot of albums for the RCA Victor label — and with the proper exposure, on television and in showcase bookings, Sam would, too. D'Imperio's interests coincided even further with Allen's in that by being prepared to make so substantial an investment — an investment that could never be recouped in singles sales — he was virtually guaranteeing a label commitment that no r&b artist other than Ray Charles had ever received. By endorsing this kind of deal, Allen recognized, there was no way D'Imperio could survive if Sam didn't succeed. The whole idea was to make Sam Cooke into a major star.

Jerry Brandt, in the meantime, watched from the sidelines with a mixture of skepticism and resentment. He hadn't liked Allen on first acquaintance. More to the point, like nearly everyone else in the record business in a position to offer Sam advice, he didn't trust him. "I tried to talk Sam out of it. I thought Allen was not up to it, and Sam would get hurt. Prior to that, Sam wanted to open an agency with me for his acts. I said, 'No, let's open up a management company,' [but] he didn't want me to manage him. [At first] I didn't see Allen moving in. I think he just overwhelmed Sam. His whole ploy was, 'You're broke.' But then he smoothed me, too."

Jerry's plan for bringing Sam into the money, not surprisingly, had its own element of self-interest. He and his boss, Roz Ross, had gotten involved in the Sweet Chariot, a brand-new gospel nightclub on Broadway owned by Crystals manager Joe Scandore (who had previously owned the Club Elegante in Brooklyn), which was bolstered by an exclusive deal with Columbia for on-site recordings that Jerry had set up with Dave Kapralik. Gospel nightclubs, with waitresses dressed like Playboy bunnies with wings, were the latest rage, and Jerry's idea was that this would be a safe way to introduce Sam into a mainstream Manhattan showroom without risking the kind of public humiliation that failure at the Copa or Basin Street East could entail. With Sam's unimpeachable gospel roots and appeal, Jerry was confident of Sam's success at the Sweet Chariot, and the attention he would surely attract there would pave the way for a return to the supper-club circuit from which in recent years he had been largely absent. Sam and Alex thought it was the most ridiculous thing they had ever heard. It was against everything they had been working for, no competition, certainly, for the money Allen was talking about but, more important, a scrimped vision compared to the grand schemes that Allen had advanced. Jerry finally just gave up the fight. Sam, he decided, was simply not manageable, and Allen was another overbearing hustler who thought he could roll over everybody. "He was bright, aggressive, he pulled the wool over my eyes and everybody else's. He's a charming asshole, you know. But he was just a homo to Sam. We all were. Straight guys who became homos. No question about it."

S AM HAD BEGUN HIS NEW TOUR, with Bobby "Blue" Bland, Little Willie John, Baby Washington, Freddie Scott, and the white rock 'n' roll star Dion, on September 14. They played Nashville the following day, just after getting word of the Birmingham church bombing in which four little girls had been killed. It was like a constant assault, an almost stupefying catalogue of mindless racial insult and injury. "What murdered these four girls?" declared Martin Luther King in an uncharacteristically angry public outburst. "The apathy and complacency of many Negroes

Onstage. *Courtesy of the Estate of Clif White*

who will sit down on their stools and do nothing and not engage in creative protest to get rid of this evil." It hung like a shroud over the whole
tour — the cops in Louisville who stopped the show because two white
girls in front got up and started dancing, the teenage white boy in Charlotte, North Carolina, they chased up the aisle simply because he was having a good time. "It was not only against Sam or the black acts," said J.W.,
"it was against the music. Period." And, of course, it was against the mixing of the races that the music inevitably provoked.

But the music always offered some reprieve. Bobby "Blue" Bland, a
stand-up singer, stolid in appearance but much like Sam in the way he
could turn an audience out just by the sound of his voice, was riding the
crest of a remarkable wave of gospel-inflected hits ("He knows consciously what he's going to do in advance," Sam said to a white interviewer, suggesting that Bobby's music was perhaps a little too
"premeditated . . . but it comes across effectively"). One night Bobby and
his opening act, singer Al "TNT" Braggs, teamed up with Little Willie
John to — as J.W. put it — "gang up" on Sam onstage. "They really
planned to cut Sam up on the finale," J.W. said, which was, as usual,
"Having a Party." They all got out and did everything they could to take

the song away from Sam, and Sam acted like he was simply going to quit and leave the stage to them, when, by prearrangement, J.W. came in from the side, and, "you know, I could always dance, and a lot of the girls thought, 'This must be Sam's dad,' and I just brought the house down." It was so successful, in fact, that it became part of Sam's nightly act, and it broke the crowd up every time.

Little Willie John, who hadn't had a big hit in three years, was as irrepressible as ever, and Baby Washington invited Linda onstage for the finale, when she and her mother joined the tour briefly one weekend. A teenage white girl who saw the show with a friend in Columbus, Ohio, remembered Little Willie John's childlike charm and the thrill she felt when Sam spotted her girlfriend and her doing the twist in their fourth-row seats. "Sam pointed at us and said, 'Those girls are doing some twisting,' and we just went out of our minds." But when Bobby "Blue" Bland did "Stormy Monday," and his guitarist, Wayne Bennett, played the liquid notes of the solo, "I just slid down into my seat and felt like I was dying."

THE RACIAL CLIMATE IN NEW ORLEANS was tense when they came into town on Thursday, September 26. There had been a series of marches protesting discriminatory voter registration procedures, which had culminated in the arrest of ninety members of the Youth Crusaders' Corps the previous week. In Shreveport a scheduled Sunday march in memory of the four little girls killed in Birmingham was blocked by the police, and more than five hundred black churchgoers were attacked by armed riot squads, deputies, and a mounted posse as they left a memorial service, with the Reverend Harry Blake, president of the local NAACP "dragged out of [his] church, clubbed to the ground" and taken to Dallas for treatment, the *Louisiana Weekly* reported, due to "fear of foul play at Shreveport hospitals."

On the other hand, *Weekly* writer Elgin Hychew noted in his "dig me!" column: "We congratulate the mixed crowd which turned out at the Auditorium the other night for the James Brown Show. . . . Our hearts really throbbed at seeing the people of this community enjoying themselves without incident. [The police contingent of fifty] did not harass the rock and roll fans who just could not sit in their seats during the four-hour show. We saw white girls and Negro girls, white boys and Negro boys seated side by side and together whooping it up. . . . We were proud because this was the New Orleans we love . . . the city which for so long enjoyed the reputation of being so cosmopolitan until the hate factories started working overtime. [The upcoming Sam Cooke/Bobby 'Blue' Bland double bill] promises to be the biggest rock and rollarama presented in the Municipal Auditorium in many years. Both sides of the auditorium are expected to be filled to overflowing [for this] 'battle of hits.'"

Allen Klein arrived the night of the show. He flew in with his lawyer, Marty Machat, and a check for $110,000. RCA had issued the check accompanied by a four-page document which stipulated that the $110,000 was "the approximate aggregate of all and any amounts due and owing to Sam Cooke, Kags, and Malloy [Publishing] up to and including August 31, 1963," that the sum could be modified upward or downward by further forensic accounting, all parties would be bound by such final determination, and that in the event that the anticipated agreement "is not formally executed on or before October 31, 1963, Tracey agrees to return forthwith the said sum of $110,000."

"I didn't go to the auditorium," said Allen, "because I flew in late. I met Sam at my hotel after the show. It was the day before *erev* Yom Kippur, and I could only stay overnight, I had to get a flight back to New York early the next morning. I remember Alex sang me a song they had written together, 'Memory Lane.' I showed Sam the check, and he was thrilled. I had gone out there and done this, we were going to get the contract done soon, and he was going to get $100,000 for his first-year guarantee. He said, 'What do you want?' — and it was awkward for me, but I told him, because I needed the money. He wrote out a check for twenty-five percent [Allen's one-time "finder's fee"] without any question. It was more money than I had ever seen [at one time], and we had done it without a piece of paper. Then he took me into the bedroom, I remember Machat was out on the balcony overlooking Bourbon Street, and there was a living room, but we were in the bedroom just by ourselves, and he said, 'Hey, listen, Allen, why don't you manage me?' I said, 'Look, I never managed anyone before.' I wasn't being clever. I just felt awkward about it. But he looked at me and said, 'Well, before I wrote my first song, I'd never written a song before.'"

Allen was, quite simply, overwhelmed. It was, for him, a truly "tender moment" and released a flood of emotion, the kind of feeling he had learned from early rejection to steel himself against. His inclination was to hang back, just to keep from getting hurt, but Sam had put his finger on Allen's vulnerability, a need to be loved that he disguised from nearly everyone outside his immediate family. He agreed to represent Sam almost without thinking about it and, once again, without a piece of paper being signed — there was no "deal" involved, because, Allen made clear from the outset, he wasn't going to take any part of the nearly half a million dollars in advance payments D'Imperio had in principle agreed to, nor was he going to get involved in Sam's personal appearances. He was just going to take his five-year 10 percent administrative fee for the publishing, whatever he could make as the record manufacturer, and his ownership of the Tracey masters, which, while it would not pay off in full for thirty years, assigned to him the equivalent of something like 30 percent of the 6 percent royalty rate for at least the next five. A cynical observer might have suggested that in taking on additional managerial responsibilities he was only protecting his investment, but for Allen it was about something much more important: it was about trust.

"I got back the next morning and called the office. I told my secretary — her name was Nancy Mays, but I called her Nancy Nurse — 'Get all the bills on my desk. I'm going to pay off everything that I owe.' So that's what I did. Then I went home and went to sleep."

It marked, as Allen would always acknowledge, his real beginnings in the business. Sam Cooke was not just a client; he represented Allen's professional legitimacy and his musical "heritage." And, as he would later reflect in a rare moment of introspection, "Sometimes I don't know how I was able to get certain things done. I certainly am persistent. And I don't give up. I try to have all of the facts, so that when I make a decision, it's with the inclusion of everything that I know. And there is no short-term thing. I'm not going to make a deal that is based on just one day or one record. Can't do it. It has to be based on belief. I mean, I hate the word, everybody uses it, but it's a vision."

SAM AND J.W. WERE JUBILANT. Allen had come through, just as he had said he would. Others, like Scepter Records head Florence Greenberg, former William Morris agent Paul Cantor, and Jerry Brandt, might warn them against Allen, but each of them had his own motivations, and Alex wasn't worried. He and Sam were perfectly capable of looking out for themselves. They had outfoxed Art Rupe and the Siamases, outlasted Bob Yorke, J.W. had watched Bumps and Jess Rand

selves, and through it all, he and Sam had maintained a steady course. The deal they were making with Allen put real money in their pockets for the first time, and if it didn't work out, it had a five-year expiration date. There was no question in either Sam's or Alex's mind that Allen could open doors for them. He had already proved it. He had told them the money was there, and then he went in and got it.

Twelve days later, the traveling show arrived in Shreveport at 7:30 in the morning after an all-night drive. Sam had called ahead to make reservations for Barbara and himself at the brand-new Holiday Inn North just outside of town, but when they pulled up in the Maserati, with Charles and Crain trailing in the packed Cadillac limo, the man at the desk glanced nervously at the group and said he was sorry, there were no vacancies. Charles protested vehemently, but it was Sam who refused to back down. He set his jaw in the way that Barbara knew always meant trouble, and, long after the clerk had simply gone silent, Sam kept yelling at him, asking, Did they think he was some kind of ignorant fool? He had just as much right to be there as any other damn body. He wanted to see the manager. He wasn't going to leave until he got some kind of damn satisfaction. Barbara kept nudging him, trying to get him to calm down. They'll kill you, she told him, when the desk clerk's attention was distracted. "They ain't gonna kill me," he told her, "because I'm Sam Cooke." Honey, she said, down here they'd just as soon lynch you as look at you, they don't care who you are. Finally the others got him out the door, but he sat in the car fuming, staring at the desk clerk who just stared coldly back, and when he drove off, it was with the horn of the Maserati blaring and all four occupants of both cars calling out insults and imprecations.

The police were waiting for them when they arrived at the Castle Hotel on Sprague Street, the colored guesthouse downtown where the rest of the group was staying. They were taken to the police station, where they were charged not with attempting to register at the Holiday Inn but with creating a public disturbance. They were held for several hours and finally let go, but not before the contents of Crain's small suitcase had been carefully scrutinized and counted: it amounted to $9,989.72 in coins and wrinkled bills and represented, Crain told a skeptical police captain, "the receipts collected from recent performances." The Maserati's horn had stuck, Crain explained to even greater skepticism, because there was a short in the electrical system that caused it to go off whenever the automobile turned sharply to the left. Crain posted a cash bond of $102.50 apiece shortly before 1:30 P.M., and they returned to the Castle Hotel.

That night, a bomb threat was called in to the Municipal Auditorium, and the building had to be thoroughly searched before the show could go on. Tensions were rife all through the performance, and the police presence was very much in evidence. Early in the evening, Charles went out to a package store to pick up the liquor for the after-party. Still smarting from his treatment earlier in the day, he carelessly asked the white woman behind the counter, "Baby, how much is that V-O-five?"

"So this white man come up to me and say, 'You call that woman "baby"?' I say, 'Man, get out of my face before I knock you down' — because I was mad already. When I went to walk out of the store, they called the police on me." The police arrested him for DWI after finding an open cooler of champagne in the backseat of the car. When he told them he wanted to call his brother, "they put a gun to my head and told me, 'You say another word, nigger, and I'll blow your brains out.'" He wasn't scared. Like Sam, "I just couldn't stand for people to treat me any old way. You didn't belittle me." But when Sam found out about it, he just laughed. He might have been tempted, he told Barbara, to let his brother's ass sit in jail for another few hours, but he wanted to get out of town as fast as he could.

They finished out the tour without incident, while newspapers across the country picked up the story. The *New York Times* ran an AP report the following day headlined "Negro Band Leader Held in Shreveport," but the black weeklies told a tale of racial outrage, and over the succeeding weeks, months, and years, a kind of myth grew up around the incident in which nearly every major r&b singer imagined himself to have been with Sam and presented variations of the story that in their more extreme versions had Sam (and sometimes others) forced by the police to disrobe and sing their hits or, conversely, allowed the larger stakes of integration to be confronted, with Crain holding enough money in his briefcase "to buy the damn motel." It was a measure of Sam Cooke's standing not just in the world of rhythm and blues but in the black community at large, with the indignity that had been inflicted on him felt in a manner that reflected how much Sam was admired and loved. But for Sam it was one more reminder of just how fragile was the black man's place in the white man's world, just how tenuous were the bonds of status, safety, and human dignity in a fundamentally racist society.

H E GOT THE FIRST $100,000 of his RCA advance on October 24, with a full-page ad for his new single and the Charles Brown–inspired *Night Beat* album running in *Cash Box* two days later. The deal had worked out almost exactly as Allen had said it would, only better. He was to receive a total of $450,000 over the next four years ($100,000 on or about October 15 for each of the next two years, additional payments of $75,000 on October 15, 1966, and October 15, 1967), amounting to substantial prepayment by the record company on a six-year, $75,000-a-year deal that, with the two-year option picked up, extended through August 31, 1969). The money was nonreturnable but applicable against future artist's royalties, so that Sam would not see any further income from record sales until the advance-to-date earned out. The agreed-upon sum of publishing and artist's royalties owed by RCA was $119,259.88 (subject to record returns), with Sam, Kags, and Malloy each signing off on that as the full amount of all past monies owed. All of the other provisions that Allen had outlined to Joe D'Imperio would remain in place, fleshed out by legal language supplied by Marty Machat. Future publishing royalties would be paid monthly along with full accounting to support payment, and the contract was backdated to September 1, as Allen had insisted all along that it must be. Most important, D'Imperio accepted the premise that Sam would have control not only of his sessions (with the sole provision that RCA could have "one or more persons present" for consultational purposes) but, with Tracey designated as the sole manufacturer and given approval of all elements of manufacture and fabrication, including art work and liner notes, in effect of his entire back catalogue as well.

At Allen's suggestion, Sam put the $100,000 into General Motors 5 percent preferred stock issued in the form of bearer bonds, which Sam placed in a safe deposit box at the Wilshire-Robertson Bank of America, with the rest of his money deposited in a Tracey account at the same bank, to which he and Alex alone had signatory access. It was, just as Allen had said, a direct pass-through, with taxes to be paid only as Sam made use of the money.

It did not come without a price. For Allen, there was the loss of his longtime Scepter account when Florence Greenberg, who had courted Sam for nearly a year and was furious that Allen, who was, after all, merely an accountant, had not delivered Sam to her, accused him of double-dealing.

Closer to home, in a development that would have been unthinkable to anyone in the SAR family until it happened, Zelda Sands left the company and took Mel Carter, the label's most successful artist, with her. It was not entirely a business dispute, though Zelda had taken violent exception to Allen from the moment she first laid eyes on him. An old friend of Florence's, she told Sam from the start that she didn't trust the man. "It was the only argument I ever had with Sam. I just knew [Klein] was a con. The first thing he did was he ordered me to send the copyrights to New York, and I said to J.W., 'Is this our office or what?' He said, 'Yes.' I said, 'Well, this is where the copyrights are staying. You don't even know the man.'" It was, of course, a losing argument, since that was Allen's deal with Sam and Alex. And it only escalated when Allen questioned whether Zelda could serve as both an employee of SAR and de facto manager of one of its principal artists. Zelda thought she had worked that out with Sam and that they would form a management company together. But then something happened that threw all of the other issues into pale relief.

Outside observers, and just about everyone within Sam's immediate circle, had long assumed that Zelda and Sam were having an affair, though Zelda insisted that the entire reason she could be direct with Sam on a business basis was that she was one female who had never gotten sexually involved with him. Then one day, while Sam was still out on tour, she got a call from Sam and Barbara together, they must have been having "one of those heartfelt things that they seldom had," she said, "where they talked things out, I suppose." They told her they wanted her to meet them on the road, just lock up the office and come to Chicago for a couple of days. She protested that she couldn't just shut down the business, but they were both so insistent that she couldn't say no — it sounded almost like they had some special cause for celebration that they wanted to share with her. When she got to their hotel room, though, she was met not with celebration but with angry confrontation. Her husband, Barbara said, had always found Zelda "tantalizing," and she knew that something was going on. So, she suggested, as Sam sat there stonily, maybe there was a way all three of them could do something about it together.

Zelda caught the first plane back to L.A., but that wasn't the end of it. A few days later, while Sam was still out of town, Barbara showed up at work with a gun and marched her out to her car in the Warner Building parking lot. She never went back, except to collect her things, and then she ran into Sam on the corner of Wilcox and Hollywood. It was obvious he felt bad about the way things had gone down, even if he didn't want to acknowledge what Barbara had done or, for that matter, what had taken place in Chicago. But, Zelda said, he was the same old Sam, "he always smiled when he talked to me, Sam and I were dear to one another. I said to him, 'Listen, I want to take Mel with me. I've had offers, you know, from other labels.' And he said, 'Okay, you can have him, I'll let you have him, ZZ.' Smiling the whole time. He was just as sweet as he could be. There was nothing in writing to let [Mel] out or anything. He just let us go free." Three weeks later, *Cash Box* ran an item that announced: " 'Zelda' — Sam Cooke's gal Friday for the past three years and his right arm in the Sar and Derby diskery and Kags pubbery has recently signed Mel Carter to a personal management pact." It followed with a detailed biography and pointed out that "this busy gal . . . can even be seen on a few album covers."

Crain, too, found himself unexpectedly on the outside. He seemed to keep waiting for an invitation from Sam and Alex to join in the business deliberations, but by the time the deal was done, it was clear he had no place in it. His two erstwhile partners, evidently feeling guilty, renewed talk of setting him up with an agency, but he was no more interested now than he had been before, so they put him on the Kags payroll as of December 4 at $200 a week. Sam approached Allen about Crain working for Tracey, he said Crain wanted to be involved, and Allen went so far as to set up a meeting with Crain at his office. "I said, 'Well, what can you do, Roy? Just tell me.' He said, 'I can give advice.' And he said it genuinely. I told Sam, 'If you want to give him money, give him money.' I could see him being pissed off about Kags. He didn't want to be out on the road anymore."

SAM OPENED AT THE APOLLO on November 22, the day that President Kennedy was shot. He was just finishing his first show of the afternoon, with the whole cast (including the Valentinos) joining him in a reprise of "Having a Party" and throwing confetti into the crowd, when Apollo owner Frank Schiffman came out onstage to make the announcement. "Several women in the audience became hysterical," the *Amsterdam News* reported. "There was noticeable sobbing throughout the theater — from men and women alike." Frank Schiffman wanted to close the theater for the day, but before he did, "I had to consult Sam. He was working on a percentage, and I wouldn't have been able to do it without his consent. I went up to his dressing room, sort of framing words to say to him about it. Before I could open my mouth, he said to me, 'Honest, I don't feel like working today,' [and] we closed the theater."

There was widespread sorrow throughout the black community, the sense, as Mahalia Jackson put it, that "Negroes will mourn doubly the loss of the man who was their great friend." Only Black Muslim leader Malcolm X, who maintained silence on the president's death for ten days on orders from Muslim founder and leader Elijah Muhammad, violated the tone of decorous respect, when, in impromptu remarks to reporters following a carefully scripted public address, he suggested that, after all the violence America had unleashed on the world, after the assassination of Lumumba in the Congo, the killings in Vietnam, the ongoing attempts to kill Castro, the assassination of an American president was no more than a case of "the chickens coming home to roost." He was immediately, and publicly, suspended from all Nation of Islam activities for ninety days by Elijah Muhammad, and *Muhammad Speaks,* the official Muslim newspaper, paid tribute to Kennedy, even as the Honorable Elijah Muhammad, whose imaginatively worked-out evolutionary theory painted all white men as devils, privately snickered, "He wasn't so bad for a devil."

At the Apollo, business gradually returned to normal. As Frank Schiffman noted in his booking diary, had it not been for Kennedy's assassination, "this could have been the strongest show yet for Sam. He and the show were superb." Over the course of the week, Sam renewed his acquaintance with Cassius Clay, who had just signed for a title fight with Sonny Liston and was in town to promote *I Am the Greatest,* his Columbia LP, with an appearance on *The Jack Paar Show.* Clay was staying at the Theresa, where he spent much of his time with Malcolm X, whom he had come to know well over the last couple of years in his pursuit of Muslim teachings. He looked up to Malcolm almost like a big brother, and Malcolm for his part saw in Clay a "likeable, friendly, clean-cut, down-to-earth youngster . . . alert . . . even in little details."

Sam had known Malcolm for years, ever since the first time he had come to the Apollo as a headliner, and he had always appreciated him as an accomplished street-corner speaker — he had known people like Malcolm all his life, caught up in the grip of a hustle they needed for their own personal salvation. He had never much cared for his Muslim beliefs, but now, with Cassius Clay serving as a kind of catalyst, Sam finally began to recognize the greater truth of Malcolm's message. Black pride and self-determination, the principle of *ownership,* the need, above all, to control your own destiny — these were lessons he had learned at his father's knee. Never be satisfied with scraps from the white man's table; it was better to die on your feet than live on your knees — this was the essence of Sam's personal philosophy. And Malcolm wasn't one of these one-dimensional cats whose sum and substance were his lessons, either. Behind his steely gaze, Sam could discern a bright glint of humor, from talking to him he could tell that this was a man who could think on his feet. And, like Sam, he clearly saw some indefinable potential, independent of religious instruction, in young Cassius Clay. "He saw greatness," said Malcolm's daughter Attallah Shabazz, "and wanted to offer a focus for motivation."

Sam saw Lithofayne Pridgon, too, who was in the middle of a "set," or orgy, with a famous gospel singer, his girlfriend, and one of her "young tenders" when the news of President Kennedy's assassination came on the radio. The famous gospel singer immediately grabbed all of their hands and intoned, "Let us fall down on our knees and pray." It was ironic, laughed Lithofayne, how he could switch horses in the middle of the stream.

As she recalled, it was on this trip, too, that she introduced Sam to another of her friends, who, as it happened, she had met in the midst of an earlier "set." This was a young guitarist named Jimmy Hendrix, who, as Lithofayne understood it, had been brought to New York from Nashville by a gay promoter who Jimmy had only recently begun to suspect might be more interested in his person than in his talent. Jimmy was desperately looking for work, and Lithofayne got him backstage and introduced him to Jerry Cuffee, a little man with a raggedy process and bad skin, who took care of Sam whenever he was in New York. Jerry got him into Sam's dressing room, but Jimmy didn't last long, "and he didn't want to talk about it afterwards — he obviously didn't get the gig."

That sent him home to Nashville, but he quickly turned around and was back in New York not long after Christmas, and he and Faye soon became the best of friends and starting hanging out together at Small's Paradise and the Palm Café.

With Sam, Faye noticed even more of a change than the last time he had come to town. He seemed sadder, more distant, but coarser, too. "I started to hear little things that started to raise my eyebrows, like, oh my goodness. I knew plenty of whores and pimps, because they were all over the place, they're human beings, like anybody else. I just didn't want to believe he had to go there."

At the end of the week, Allen told him, "Listen, I want you to go home. You got the money. You don't have to worry about money. Go home. Spend time with your wife and kids. You don't have to do this shit anymore."

BUT THERE WAS NO REAL HOME to return to. Barbara no longer even bothered to hide a lifestyle that was as far removed from Sam's as his had always been from hers. She defied his carefully constructed image of domesticity, the pains he had taken to separate their home life from life outside the home, by plunging into her own chaotic maelstrom, by disappearing without explanation and jettisoning any pretense of personal control. When she returned, she brought the street unmistakably back with her, as her mood became darker and darker and more and more openly hostile toward a husband she both blamed and desperately missed.

Sam restlessly made the round of the clubs. He saw old friends, stopped by Gertrude Gipson's Nite Life for an evening of poetry and entertainment with Cassius Clay, checked out Dinah Washington's closing at Basin Street West. But, said Lou Adler, "for the first time, you could detect that he was carrying something other than the person that he was. There was a [sorrowfulness], a leveling out." He was drinking more, and his smile seemed forced at times; without his ever explicitly acknowledging it, the change was evident to every one of his friends.

For Jess' birthday on December 2 he gave his former manager a fourteen-karat solid gold Dunhill lighter with the masks of Comedy and Tragedy overlaid on the front and the inscription "You're TOPS. Sam." He did *The Jerry Lewis Show* ("Starring The Nut Himself," the printed program announced) with Cassius Clay on December 7, introducing

Linda to Cassius at the afternoon rehearsal and inviting him out to the house. Jerry Brandt had gotten Sam the booking on the strength of Clay's current celebrity. With the title fight coming up and his album on the charts, Cassius, said the William Morris agent, "had the fucking world in his palm," and Brandt simply insisted to the show's booker, "You want this guy, you take this guy." Sam talked to Cassius about maybe doing a record together someday, and the kid's eyes lit up. Jerry Brandt was not surprised. Sam was the kind of guy who never took his eye off the main chance — and, while it was perfectly evident that Sam got a tremendous kick out of him, Cassius Clay was the main chance right then. "I mean, we never discussed it. He just thought this is something to attach yourself to."

Sam came out at the front of the show after a perfunctory introduction by Jerry Lewis, looking a little puffy in an abbreviated dark continental suit jacket and pants. He opened with an elegantly exuberant version of "Twistin' the Night Away," undeterred by audience apathy or the orchestra's Dixieland groove. Then he performed a starkly theatrical reading of "The Riddle Song," an Appalachian ballad recently revived in folk circles, while sitting on a stool and caught in dramatic profile by an overhead spot. Someone who knew Sam's recent history might very well have supplied a deeper emotional subtext as his voice wrapped itself around the lyric's paradoxical simplicity ("I gave my love a chicken that has no bone / I gave my love a ring that has no end / I gave my love a baby with no cryin'"), then supplied the answer to the riddle's ultimate contradiction: "A baby when it's sleeping has no cryin'." For the casual viewer, though, there was only supreme confidence and supreme control, an actor's sublimation of personal experience to express universal feeling. It was, like the refined version of the Twist that he and J.W. had worked out for presentation to this national television audience, a Twist that emerged from the subtlest of gestures and the most carefully choreographed little steps, a declaration on the one hand that he could command any stage, and, on the other, an act of secret complicity with himself.

That same day, a picture of him appeared on the cover of *Cash Box*, seated behind an expansive executive desk and leaning over impishly toward RCA president George Marek beneath a portrait of Giuseppe Verdi. "The two are discussing the continuance of Cooke's highly successful relationship with RCA," reads the caption, "which the artist has just sealed with the pen he is holding." Currently "fire-hot . . . Cooke [is] one of the record industry's most consistent hit-makers, riding an unbroken chain of eight smash singles." A bright future for record company and artist was clearly in the works.

Barbara took the kids to Chicago for a visit not long afterward. Crume and the Stirrers were out on the Coast for a series of programs, and Sam and Crume got together with a pair of cousins they had met at a club earlier in the year. Sam had had to borrow Stirrers baritone singer Richard Gibbs' room at the Dunbar for the earlier date, but this time they went back to the house to fool around. Sam was in a funny mood, he seemed as eager to talk with Crume as to spend time with his girl, and he called Crume on the intercom early the next morning and said, "Let's take the girls home." When they got back to the house, he played Crume three or four numbers that he had been working on for his upcoming session: a song called "Good Times" that was based on an old Louis Jordan hit; a variation on a gospel number, "Ain't That Good News," that they had all grown up singing; plus one or two others that didn't make as much of an impression.

Then Sam told him about his new RCA deal, and how much money he now had in the bank. "He said, 'I don't want you to tell nobody about this. Even Barbara don't know what kind of money I got. If I hear it [from her], I'll know where it came from.'" He was going to take some time off, he said, "because what he wanted to do he couldn't do as long as he was doing one-nighters. He said, 'I'm just another rock 'n' roll singer if I keep doing that.'" But, he said, he was going to keep on paying Clif and June and Bobby, just as if they were working every night.

And he wanted Crume to write him some new songs. What he wanted were r&b numbers that sounded like gospel. "He said, 'Crumé, this is what I want you to do. Put everybody out of your room for two weeks and write me some fuckin' songs.' I said, 'You've got to be out of your mind, man. You mean to tell me you just want me to sit in a room by myself for two weeks and write songs?' He said, 'But this is important. This is your fucking career.' I said, 'Yeah, but Sam, it don't take no fucker that long to write a song.' He said, 'Well, just write me some fuckin' songs, man.'" Crume said he'd give the matter some serious thought. But by the time he got around to it, Sam had already put together all the songs he needed.

Long Time Coming

For people fighting for their freedom there is no such thing as a bad device.

— Malcolm X

T HE FIRST TWO SONGS he recorded at his December 20–21 album session were the ones that had most impressed Crume earlier in the month. "Ain't That Good News" had, in all of its earlier incarnations (including a 1949 version by J.W.'s group, the Pilgrim Travelers), hinged on a variation on the familiar line "Jesus said he's coming again / Ain't that news, ain't that good news." Sam substituted his own secular introduction ("Well, my baby's coming home tomorrow") as the occasion for rejoicing and added a jangling banjo lead, congas, and a horn chart that pushed hard against the banjo's country twang to change both song and message, while his vocal subtly undercut the song's cheerful flavor and upbeat lyrics. He polished off the tune in three takes, then spent the rest of the evening experimenting with "Good Times," the Louis Jordan–inspired number that took up the chorus of Jordan's enormously popular 1946 hit, "Let the Good Times Roll," which had served as an inspiration to a whole generation of singers, from Sam and James Brown to B.B. King and Ray Charles, with its anthemic call. Sam's version, once again, suggested an elegiac tone absent in the original, but his approach was less strictly defined than the one he and René Hall ordinarily took, experimenting with a variety of tempos and instrumentations, bringing banjo back in along with

"Hey, Hey, the Gang's All Here," March 3, 1964. *Courtesy of Sony Legacy*

marimba only with take seven, and breaking off the three-hour session without achieving a master take.

To Luigi it was business as usual. He and his partner and cousin, Hugo Peretti, were nearing the end of their run at RCA — their contract was about to expire in March, and they were increasingly frustrated by what they considered the label's refusal to move on their a&r recommendations ("We said to [RCA president] Marek once, 'You ruin everybody you buy'"). But Sam seemed exactly the same, cheerful, focused, full of ideas. Luigi knew all about the drowning death of the son, but he didn't say anything about it, and Sam didn't say anything, either. That was just the way he was. It was Barbara who was the problem. She sat in the back of the control room, sullen and distracted, visibly out of it in a way that no one could miss. Sam seemed to ignore her for the most part. There were moments, Luigi noticed, when he appeared lost in thought, but then he'd come right out of it — he was, as always, in perfect control of himself and his surroundings.

He could, of course, have been thinking of a lot of things. He might have been frustrated at his inability to get "Good Times" just the way he wanted it. Barbara's presence could well have unsettled him, for all of his studiedly calm demeanor. But mostly he relished the idea of finally being in control — what would make this session different, Allen had told him over and over, was that now he was finally working for himself. He could do whatever he wanted, and contractually he could take any length of time to do it. Which perhaps explained his and René's slight departure from their usual working methods. At the end of the evening, he was no more discouraged than if he had been working out a song at home: he was simply focused on the two sessions coming up the following evening.

He kicked off the six o'clock session with a number he had begun in the car with Bobby Womack while they were out on tour the previous fall. He still hadn't fully worked it out and did only one complete take, a kind of glorified demo, with flute, banjo, and marimba supplying a gentle, clippity-clop sound. "When I go to sleep at night," he sang:

I add up my day
Trying to recall the things I've done
And debts I have to pay
For that is one thing

That I know
What you reap is what you sow

And then in a chorus that seemed to reflect almost unintentionally the challenge of applying Old Testament lessons in an existential age, he offered the only hope he could summon up:

Keep movin' on, keep movin' on
Life is this way
Keep movin' on, keep movin' on
E-v-e-ry day.

The same wistful mood, and same flute obbligato ("That's another Italian!" Luigi volunteered in response to Sam's use of the term), were carried over into the next number, "Memory Lane," the song J.W. had sung to Allen in New Orleans. "One-take Cooke," Sam called out cheerfully after a few takes, and then he returned to "Good Times," continuing to experiment with different approaches until he finally got the sound he wanted on the twenty-fifth take.

The ten o'clock session might just as well have been planned for another artist. Against Clif and Alex's advice, Sam had hired Joe Hooven, the arranger they had used for Mel Carter's lavishly orchestrated SAR sessions, to write the charts for the four songs he had left to do. From Clif's point of view, Hooven's arrangements "just kind of overpowered Sam," but it was almost as if Sam was insistent on making the point "Look at me. I can do anything. Don't corner me off."

He started with "Basin Street Blues," a number virtually defined by Louis Armstrong, sailing through it with all the confidence of someone who, he once told a disbelieving Bobby Womack, had modeled his vocal style on the gravel-voiced trumpet player. ("Listen to us both," he had said. "Don't listen to his voice, listen to his phrasing. It's like a conversation, it's real.") He showed equal confidence in his approach to both "Home," an Irving Berlin composition made popular by Armstrong and Nat "King" Cole, and "No Second Time," a melancholy new composition by Clif, then finished off the session with a beautifully articulated, carefully precise, and somewhat stilted recitation of "The Riddle Song," in which, for all of the pathos of the lyrics, just as little was revealed as in his television performance of the same song two weeks earlier.

But the evening was still not over. It was one o'clock in the morning, and Sam's voice was getting frayed, but he returned once more to "Good Times," overdubbing a couple of deliberately unsynchronized harmony parts as a sketch for one final pass at the song. Allen had told him, "Take your time for once. Don't do another shitty album," and it had really pissed him off at the time. What the fuck did Allen know about making a record? But with these sessions he had done just what Allen said.

H E AND BARBARA threw a small Christmas get-together for their friends. Alex's girl, Carol, was back from Hawaii, where she had been working on the start-up of a new magazine called *Elegant,* and Sam and Barbara teased Alex that he had better make his move soon. You know, they said, he was nearly fifty, and as cool and hip as he might think he was, not every beautiful, young twenty-one-year-old chick with striking Asiatic features was going to be all that impressed with his gray-haired eminence. He had better just start thinking about the future — before she turned around and went back to the islands to marry some wealthy young businessman. Alex just smiled and kept his own counsel, but Sam could see his partner was smitten, and he took every opportunity to let Carol know that he and Barbara were on her side. It seemed like one of the few things the two of them could still agree upon.

He called Alex right after Christmas and invited him out to the house. He told him that he had a song that he wanted Alex to hear. He didn't know where it had come from. It was different, he said, from any other song he had ever written.

He played it through once, singing the lyrics softly to his own guitar accompaniment. After a moment's silence, Alex was about to respond — but before he could, Sam started playing the song again, going through it this time line by line, as if somehow his partner might have missed the point, as if, uncharacteristically, he needed to remind himself of it as well.

It was a song at once both more personal and more political than anything for which Alex might have been prepared, a song that vividly brought to mind a gospel melody but that didn't come from any spiritual number in particular, one that was suggested both by the civil rights movement and by the circumstances of Sam's own life — J.W. knew exactly where it came from, but Sam persisted in explaining it nonetheless. It was almost, he said wonderingly, as if it had come to him in a dream. The statement in its title and chorus, "A Change Is Gonna Come" ("It's been a long time comin' / But I know / A change gonna come"), was the faith on which it was predicated, but faith was qualified in each successive verse in ways that any black man or woman living in the twentieth century would immediately understand. When he sang, "It's been too hard living / But I'm afraid to die / I don't know what's up there / Beyond the sky," he was expressing the doubt, he told Alex, that he had begun to feel in the absence of any evidence of justice on earth. "I go to the movies / And I go downtown / Somebody keep telling me / Don't hang around" was simply his way of describing their life — Memphis, Shreveport, Birmingham — and the lives of all Afro-Americans. "Or, you know," said J.W., "in the verse where he says, 'I go to my brother and I say, "Brother, help me, please,"' — you know, he was talking about the establishment — and then he says, 'That motherfucker winds up knocking me back down on my knees.'

"He was very excited — very excited. And I was, too. I said, 'We might not make as much money off this as some of the other things, but I think this is one of the best things you've written.' 'I think my daddy will be proud,' he said. I said, 'I think so, Sam.'"

H E SCARCELY WORKED the first few weeks of January, just a couple of West Coast dates with Bobby Bland and putting together material for an upcoming Johnnie Morisette session. He was for the most part getting ready for his own follow-up album session at the end of the month. He had a whole new backup band and a whole new approach that he wanted to try.

Harold Battiste, the New Orleans–based multi-instrumentalist who had founded the musicians' cooperative AFO (All For One), a production company and band that fought for ownership and control of its music, had come out to Los Angeles with his four fellow AFO Executives for the NARA convention in August. They were beginning to think that their idealism might have been misplaced after first losing their one and only hit, Barbara George's 1962 smash "I Know," to the rapacity of the music business and then, far from experiencing a wave of fraternal concern from fellow musicians, sensing that they were regarded as interlopers and rivals by both the union and NARA, the association of black radio announcers. With New Orleans a dead end, all five decided to make a new start in Los Angeles after the convention: saxophonist Red

Tyler, trumpet player Melvin Lastie, bassist Chuck Badie, and drummer John Boudreaux, along with Battiste, the former teacher, social communard, and lapsed Black Muslim who had helped with the background vocal arrangements on Sam's "You Send Me" session.

Unfortunately, Los Angeles proved even more daunting than New Orleans in terms of making a living. There was a six-month union residency requirement, they discovered, before you could get steady club work, and they were living pretty much of a hand-to-mouth existence when Harold and Melvin Lastie hit the streets in early fall, looking for any kind of work they could get.

Somehow they found their way to SAR. Sam and Alex were out of town at the time, but Zelda was in the office with Ernie Farrell, the white promo man she had hired to sell Mel Carter's record, and after hearing them out, she said she could use someone to write lead sheets for their copyright applications. Harold, by his own account, stood there like a dummy, "but Melvin said, 'My man can write you some lead sheets.' Talking about me! So that's what I started out doing, just to generate some income. And by the time we hooked up with Sam, we had a good connection going."

Sam certainly remembered Harold from the "You Send Me" session, and he knew Red Tyler, too, from his first pop session in New Orleans (Tyler had played sax and written "Forever," the B-side of the single that had come out under the name of Dale Cook). He hadn't gotten to know either one of them well at the time, but now he and Harold hit it off like long-lost brothers, as they started talking about race, justice, and other matters far removed from the realm of commercial music.

"It was obvious," said Harold, "that he wanted to be more than just a popular singer, that he wanted to be involved in social things." They would go out to the house and talk in the office that Sam kept in the little building out back by the carport, away from Barbara, who didn't really seem to Battiste to be part of Sam's evolving world. J.W. was. Battiste, in fact, recognized in Alex a fellow teacher, something like a tribal elder, "a smooth cat who was always trying to teach someone about the music business, or white folks, or something like that."

Eventually Harold worked up the nerve to approach Sam about something that had always been part of his greater plan, setting up a series of storefront headquarters in the heart of the black community that could serve as both rehearsal space and audition centers for some of the talented but disaffected black youth who would never otherwise find their way to SAR's offices or, for that matter, anywhere else in Hollywood. He had done the same thing to a limited extent in New Orleans, he explained to Sam. "It was part of my little civic thing, we would let the people come in and audition them and help them prepare their material to take it to the next level." They could call each of these storefront locations Soul Stations, and they would be useful for SAR's young artists like the Valentinos to work up material, too. He wasn't sure at first if Sam was fully tuned in to the idea, but then, to his amazement, Sam just went for it. "Go on and find a place," he told Harold without hesitation. "I'll pick up the tab."

By then Sam had made up his mind to use the band not just on his own upcoming session but as a kind of house band for future SAR projects as well. They would give his music a new sound, a different sound, one that would provide a distinctive mix of sophisticated polyrhythms, jazz voicings (Harold had started out playing with Ornette Coleman, and all of the AFO musicians were modernists to one degree or another), and the kind of melodic simplicity that Sam's songs had always shared with the New Orleans tradition. It was the idea of music as a collective experience, Harold felt, that excited Sam most, the AFO sound "wasn't slick, it was sort of raw, [it was] the way that New Orleans people played, and the spirit that happened with that feeling. I hate to seem mysterious, but to me that's what it is, a spiritual thing, the whole atmosphere that's created — I think that's [why] Sam was attracted to us."

The Johnnie Morisette session on which the AFO Executives made their official SAR debut on January 21 may not have altogether exemplified that spiritual atmosphere, but it did nothing to discourage Sam's faith in the band, either. They proved their adaptability and versatility in addition to their unquestionable musicality, as Johnnie displayed his usual mix of natural boisterousness and inebriated good spirits on a variety of songs, including an out-of-tune but supercharged remake of "You Send Me." "Brother Bat!" said Johnnie to Harold. "I see you're slick." "Lord have mercy," said Sam, as the room echoed with Hallelujahs and good-natured soul screams.

Although he wasn't making any personal appearances, Sam kept not only Clif, June, and Bobby on salary but his brother Charles and Charles' fellow driver, Watley, as well. He himself reveled in the unaccustomed role of gentleman of leisure. The Thursday before the Johnnie Morisette session, he and Barbara attended Johnny Mathis' opening at the Cocoanut Grove and the after-party hosted by the high-flying young Hollywood couple Bobby Darin and Sandra Dee. Nat and Maria Cole were there, Liberace, jazz critic Leonard Feather, and film stars Rock Hudson and Connie Stevens. The following night Sam was at blues balladeer Arthur Prysock's celebrity-packed opening at the California Club and, after being called up to sing "Little Red Rooster," couldn't get offstage again without performing two encores. He caught the Soul Stirrers that weekend in a "Gospel Hootenanny" with the Consolers and June Cheeks at Olympic Auditorium, and he spoke to Crume about the Stirrers' and his own upcoming sessions the following week. He wanted to give the Stirrers a real pop sound this time, he said, and to that end he was going to use the same New Orleans backup band for them that he was planning to use on his own session. They could pay him back in kind, he told Crume, by singing background for him on a couple of numbers that he wanted to infuse with the real gospel sound.

"Sam said, 'You know, I try to get those other background people to sound like the Soul Stirrers, [but] I got the real deal here!' He said, 'Now you gotta talk to J.J. [Jesse J. Farley, the group's oldest member and nominal leader]' — because J.J. really didn't want to do it. He thought it would spoil the Soul Stirrers' image. I said, 'Jesse, they won't put our name on the record. Nobody'll know.' But they knew it was us [even though] we denied it for a long time."

Lou Rawls was at the Purple Onion in Hollywood promoting his brand-new Capitol single, "Tobacco Road," with *A Night on Tobacco Road*. Little Willie John was playing the 5/4. Johnnie Morisette was at the Club House on Western, opening for Bobby "Blue" Bland. Sam and Barbara were out almost every night, sometimes together, more often than not on their own. Things were still not right between them. Barbara doubted they ever would be. Sometimes, after a long night of drinking, they might make love, and he would ask her if he still made her feel like she used to — and she would restrain her incredulity and tell him what she knew he wanted to hear. She didn't care. She had found a little boy, just about Vincent's age, he was a sweet round-faced little boy, light-skinned, with a fuzzy head of sandy hair just like Vincent had. His mother was a hooker friend of Barbara's who had lots of kids, and she said, "Well, you can have any one you want." So she took Eric home and dressed him up

Tracey and Linda Cooke
with Eric, with Beverly
Campbell's sons Michael
Halley and Don Coles (left
to right) on the right.
*Courtesy of Barbara Cooke
and ABKCO*

in Vincent's clothes, bought him some new outfits, and told the girls he
was their new baby brother. Sam objected at first, but he saw how happy
Eric made her, and she said, "Sam, you're not here that much anyway."
Then the house was a jovial place again, filled with kids, her sister Beverly's and her own. Until her girlfriend got greedy and Sam balked at
paying a king's ransom for this child who was not his own. So she lost
Eric, too, and she was left with a husband who was more like a little boy,
in her view, than a man. Sometimes he would take the Maserati and
drive until he ran out of gas and then call her to come bring him money
so he could go on and drive some more. She always did it, she told him
she would do anything he asked, she said, "I'm your mate. But that's all I
am." It was like a long-standing business partnership that couldn't be
broken, one friend of theirs observed. It seemed obvious why Barbara
would stay. And Sam? "He made her a promise," said the friend, "and
that was it. He did it for the baby [that they first had together] and for the
promises he didn't keep. He said he would never leave her." But Barbara

had her tubes tied anyway so she couldn't have any more babies with Sam.

S AM HAD CRAIN SING TENOR with the Soul Stirrers at their session at United on the afternoon of January 28. He had worked up a special arangement of the old spiritual "Oh Mary, Don't You Weep," but it was Brook Benton's "Looking Back," a huge hit for Nat "King" Cole in 1958, that was the centerpiece. A heartfelt ballad with a thoughtful philosophical message, it was just the kind of number that Sam had been looking for to break the group pop, and he patiently instructed Stirrers' lead singer Jimmie Outler on the meaning of the words (" 'Looking back over the *slate*,' " he explained. "Like a chalk slate, you know? Like you done chalked everything down. It's in your memory"). With Clif, Crume, Stirrers bass player Sonny Mitchell, the core of the AFO band, plus flautist William Green, the Soul Stirrers finally achieved the kind of "crossover" sound that Sam and Alex had been aiming at for so long. "Clif, play with all your fervor," Sam exhorted at one point, and while there may have been an element of self-mockery in his tone, he was absolutely serious about the feeling and effect he was striving for.

Three hours later, in the RCA studio at Sunset and Vine, he had Crume and Sonny Mitchell playing on his own session for exactly that reason. He instructed the Stirrers and Crain in the precise vocal arrangements and harmonies he wanted them to employ on each song, and he made it clear that what he was looking for was that same gospel fervor. The first number was "Rome Wasn't Built in a Day," the Prudhomme twins' collaboration that he had unexpectedly bestowed upon Johnnie Taylor a year and a half earlier. It had a nice easygoing feel to it, as Luigi kidded the Soul Stirrers about their off-the-beat hand claps and the full AFO band churned along behind Sam with that infectious New Orleans sound. The second number, "Meet Me at Mary's Place," was a reworking of Johnnie Morisette's "Meet Me at the Twistin' Place," another original by Sam, transformed this time into a vivid evocation of the past. The Mary in question was Mary Trapp, a gospel fan and promoter whose big house in Charlotte, North Carolina, was a kind of hangout and guesthouse for all the traveling quartets (she loved both the singer and the song, according to one prominent gospel lead). At Sam's direction, the Stirrers backgrounded him with a cheery "Over at Mary's place — ho!" while the song, like so many of his celebratory compositions, was bathed in an almost indelible atmosphere of regret. "Rome" took almost no time to get a satisfactory master take; "Mary's Place" took even less (just two takes, with the tempo picking up briskly on the second, as if to deny the intrinsic tone). And with that, Sam was off on a gospelized double-time version of "Tennessee Waltz," the country standard, on which the horns replaced the Soul Stirrers with a driving, off-rhythm response, and Sam's achievement of the high note called for in the chorus ("I never thought he was going to make it," said Crume, who was standing right beside him, "he let out a little laugh when he did") provided an ironic counterpoint of triumphant emotionalism for a sad song originally written in three-quarter time.

All three songs were effortless exercises in transformation, all three (unlike several recorded at the December sessions) were clearly intended for inclusion in the album — but it was the session two nights later on which Sam was really pinning his hopes.

He had given René Hall the "civil rights" song he had played for J.W., with no specific instructions other than to provide it with the kind of instrumentation and orchestration that it demanded. René was in no doubt as to the momentousness of the charge. "I wanted it to be the greatest thing in my [life] — I spent a lot of time, put out a lot of ideas, and then changed them and rearranged them, because here was an artist for whom I'd never done anything with my own concepts [exclusively], and this was the only tune that I can ever recall where he said, 'I'm going to leave that up to you.'" René wrote the arrangement as if he were composing a big movie score, with a symphonic overture for strings, kettledrum, and French horn, separate movements for each of the first three verses (the rhythm section predominates in the first, then the strings, then the horns), a dramatic combination of strings and kettledrum for the bridge ("I go to my brother and I say, 'Brother, help me, please'"), and a concluding crescendo worthy of the most patriotic anthem, as Sam extends his final repetition of the chorus ("I know a change is gonna come") with a fervent "Oh, yes it is" and the strings offer a shimmering sustain, while the kettledrum rumbles and the horns quietly punctuate the underlying message of hope and faith.

It was all carefully considered. The French horn, René explained to J.W., who was as surprised as René himself by Sam's singular abdication of control, would give it a mournful sound. The orchestral arrangement would match the dignity of the song. As Harold Battiste, who played keyboards on the session, observed, "All of us have a vision of what we think we are. Sometimes we have an idea about something that we think we need to try to reach. We may overshoot, but I guess we all trying to get that acceptance where Mama and Daddy say, 'Okay, yeah, it's good.'"

Everybody executed his role flawlessly with the exception of AFO drummer John Boudreaux, who was evidently so intimidated by the orchestral makeup of the session that he simply announced, "Man, I can't go out there and play," and refused to leave the control room, impervious to the pleas of his fellow musicians. Fortunately Earl Palmer was working next door, and he came and filled in. But otherwise the recording process went as smoothly as it might have for any of Sam's little "story songs." Then Luigi, as though acknowledging the momentousness of the occasion, asked Sam to give him one more, and after a couple of false starts, the eighth take was nearly perfect. Luigi told Sam how much he liked the song, and Sam, who knew this was going to be their last session together, acted almost surprised, as if, Luigi said, he might think that his "New York producer," the consummate hitmaker, wouldn't approve of a song that sought to make a social statement. "But I *did* like it. It was a serious piece, but still it was him. Some of the other stuff was throwaway, but this was very deep. He was really digging into himself for this one."

WITHIN DAYS Harold told Sam he thought he had found a location for the first Soul Station, but when they all went to the real-estate office, as Chuck Badie recalled, saxophonist Red Tyler wandered behind the counter to get a look at some of the pictures on the wall, "and the man said, 'Hey, you can't come back here.'" Sam, whom the outspoken bass player liked to refer to as "Little Caesar," was carrying an attaché case full of money and visibly bristled at the remark. "He said, 'What did you say, brother? He can't go back there? Well, then we ain't got no business in here.' He said, 'Come on, fellows, let's get the fuck out of here.' That's exactly what he said. And he walked out the door."

That was how they found themselves on the corner of Thirty-seventh and Vermont, where they spotted a little storefront with a "For Rent" sign in the window that seemed like it had been just waiting for them to come along. "It was a cool neighborhood, kind of on the wild side but no problems," said Chuck. They took out a lease on the spot, then went back to Sam's house, where Sam showed them around and, on a whim, gave them the run of his extensive clothes closet. Chuck picked out a blue serge suit for himself and, when Sam said, "Is that all you want?" took a couple of Saks Fifth Avenue sweaters to boot. As they were leaving, Boudreaux, the drummer, said, "Man, you sure is lucky," but Harold, who was not unaware of Chuck's bold proclivities, laughed and said, "He ain't lucky. He's cheeky." It was all in good fun, and Sam had proved himself to them not only as a man of his word but as a good fellow. Now they could get down to the business of fixing up their new headquarters.

Sam told Bobby all about the Soul Station right away. He said it would offer the Valentinos an opportunity to rehearse whenever they felt like it, they could go try out song ideas, put them down on tape, and have the benefit of Harold and the other fellows to critique and help them out with their music. He told Bobby about the new song he had just recorded, too, and played it for him in the darkened music room, with René's swelling arrangement booming out of the giant movie speakers. He explained it all to Bobby like he had explained it to Alex. But there was a note in his voice other than just pride of authorship. It was almost, Bobby thought, as if he were feeling some kind of premonition. He said, "The song just came to me. I never scuffled with the words or anything. It was like it was somebody else's song. What do you think of it, Bob? Just tell me whatever comes to your mind." "It feels like death," said Bobby, never overly troubled with the need for reflection and seemingly sensing the same premonition himself. "He asked me, 'What do you mean?' I said, 'No, I'm gonna take that back. It don't feel like death, but it feels eerie, like something's going to happen.' He said, 'Yeah, but that's the same thing.' I said, 'It's just the way it feel to me. The strings and everything is creepy, something's going on, it sounds like somebody died.'" Sam nodded gloomily. That was why he was never going to sing that fucker in public, he said. But as it turned out, he had very little choice.

He and Alex brought the dubs from the previous week's sessions to New York, where Allen heard the material for the first time. Sam arrived in town on February 4 to promote the new single, "Ain't That Good News" and "Basin Street" from the December sessions, and to appear on Johnny Carson's *Tonight Show* at the end of the week. Allen was delighted with everything that Sam played for him; the range of material, Sam's willingness to take chances were exactly what he had been hoping might result from this new artistic freedom. But when he heard "A Change Is Gonna Come," he asked to hear it again. And again. "It was just my favorite record. It was chilling. And he was telling a story. A personal story. It wasn't complicated, and it wasn't repetitious. Simple words. [But] it was a great piece of poetry."

Sam took in the praise without comment. Despite any reservations he might have expressed to Bobby, he knew the song was probably the best thing he had ever written, and it was, of course, an integral part of the album. But when Allen said that he wanted Sam to sing it on *The Tonight Show* — the hell with the single, this was the statement that he needed to make — Sam raised every objection he could think of. The album wasn't going to be out for another two months. *The Tonight Show* was only three days away. He didn't have an arrangement with him. And besides, he couldn't present the song the way it needed to be presented without exactly the same instrumentation that he had on the record; the *Tonight Show* band, as good as it was, wasn't going to be able to give him a French horn, three trombones, and a thirteen-piece string section.

Allen met every one of his arguments with a forceful counterargument. René could send the arrangement. He would get RCA to pay for a full string section and all the extra musicians Sam needed, and if Joe D'Imperio wouldn't spring for it, Allen would pay for it out of his own pocket. Sam could sing "Basin Street" to promote the single. But he had to remember one thing: he was promoting *himself* at this point, Sam Cooke, not RCA. Joe and the record label were behind him all the way: look at the full-page ad in *Billboard* the previous week. Big things were in the offing. They were going to get LP sales. They were going to get the supper clubs and Vegas, just like Sam wanted. But to get all those things, Sam had to believe in himself. And, not entirely coincidentally, he had to do the song on Johnny Carson.

They all went to the Copa to see Nat "King" Cole — Sam and Alex and Allen and Joe D'Imperio. They lingered upstairs in the lounge, where there was generally a younger crowd and a more contemporary up-and-coming act. Sam hadn't been back to the club since his failure there in 1958, and, he said, he was surprised, seeing it now, how small it was. But he was clearly nervous — for all of his self-conscious bravado, for all of his confident talk about being ready, both Allen and Alex could sense his almost visible hesitancy. They watched the young girls doing the Twist, "all them chicks just shaking their butts," said J.W., "and I said to him, 'What makes you think the people downstairs are gonna be any different?'" That seemed to break the ice a little, and they went down to catch Nat's act, easy, relaxed, full of the universal-emotion ballads and sophisticated banter that made it as accessible to a white audience as to a black. Sam turned to Allen and nodded. Allen took it as a signal. "He saw how easy it was. It was no big deal." But to Alex he leaned over and said, "I can stand this fucker on its ear," and they both burst out laughing.

He did an interview with the *New York World-Telegram* the next day that focused almost entirely on his ambition to return to the Copa. Sam was RCA's second-biggest singles artist after Elvis Presley, the story pointed out, "but on the night club and TV circuit he is virtually unknown. How come?" It all stemmed from his failure at the Copa six years (the *World-Telegram* had it four years) earlier. "I only had a couple of little record arrangements," Sam said. He was amateurish and had gotten scared. "At the end of three weeks, I was a pretty good entertainer, but I wasn't a smash." For the last four years, he had been quietly perfecting his act — this time he wanted to be sure "they're ready for me!"

On Thursday, RCA threw a press luncheon at Danny's Hideaway for nearly fifty DJs and radio reps, plus reporters from *Billboard, Cash Box, Seventeen, Look, Ebony,* and *Jet.* Sam charmed them all. He was planning a different direction for his career, he told the trades. He wanted to cut down his in-person activities to two or three months of selective show dates and concentrate more on his creative role. "[He] said he would rather be the creative producer in the control room than be the worn-out singer in a bistro spotlight," reported *Billboard.* He spoke extensively of SAR, his partner, J.W. Alexander, also present at the luncheon, and his extensive ambitions for all of the artists on their roster. He wanted each of them to "try for a different sound or approach. . . . 'I want my artists to evolve something different, based on their own philosophies,'" he said, providing a convincing display of the scope of his own philosophy and ambition.

Joe D'Imperio was certainly convinced. Against all his better instincts, he had given in to Allen's relentless lobbying for the song — it seemed crazy to throw away an opportunity to promote both sides of the single, and he had serious reservations about the impact of Sam's "social statement" on the Southern market, but how could you argue with the conviction expressed in the lyrics or with the almost equally passionate conviction of Allen's advocacy? He agreed to put up the money for the extra musicians. He agreed to take responsibility for the decision at RCA. He believed in Sam.

S AM DID *THE TONIGHT SHOW* on Friday, immaculate in a dark suit and skinny tie, with a neatly coiffed Afro very much at odds with the conventional image of the Negro entertainer on national TV. He performed "Basin Street" on an economical "New Orleans" stage set, relaxed and confident at the start but letting loose as the song built to its big finger-snapping climax, until at the end he was practically strutting — but in a distinctly Sam Cooke way. It was a masterful performance, and a clearly appreciative Johnny Carson acknowledged it not only with verbal praise but by shaking his shoulders in imitation of Sam's showmanship. "You're going to stand there for the rest of the show," he called out to Sam from his desk, before announcing to the audience that, of course, Sam Cooke would be back in the second half.

Joe D'Imperio was so nervous that he walked out into the hall before Sam took the stage to sing what an NBC timekeeper marked down in the logbook as "It's a Long Time Coming." Allen and J.W. remained in the audience, each convinced in his own mind that this was a moment that would surely go down in history as well as serving as a milestone in Sam's career. Unfortunately, the tape appears to have been lost, so one can only imagine the way in which Sam must have transformed the number in live performance, caught in a single spotlight perhaps, his face alight not just with the inspirational fervor of the song's final declaration of belief but with the fierce determination and unrelenting anger embodied in each of its verses. "It almost scared the shit out of me," he told his drummer June Gardner afterward. But for Allen Klein, there were no such ambiguities. To Allen, this was the reason he had ventured into the entertainment business in the first place; it offered an opportunity for self-expression, certainly, but more than that, it provided vindication not just for his belief in Sam (though that was a big part of it) but for his own involvement in the process. It was his business acumen, his own unflagging zeal for the creative business solution, that had freed Sam to do this. And when Sam sang the line about "my brother," Allen didn't hear the note of rejection in the following line, all Allen heard was Sam's plea ("I go to my brother and I say, 'Brother, help me, please'"), and he identified with the situation, he believed that Sam meant him to be that brother, but unlike the brother in the song, he would never turn his back on Sam, he would never knock him to his knees.

Sam flew to Cleveland the next day to appear on the nationally syndicated *Mike Douglas Show*. Douglas, who had first met Sam in Chicago in 1958, was not simply gracious but unfailingly appreciative of his guest, both musically and personally. "It's good news!" Sam announced after an utterly relaxed performance of the song, as he met guests Howard Keel, the Broadway basso profundo, and comedienne Eleanor Harris. "Let's do a little capsule version of the Sam Cooke story," said Douglas, and Sam jumped right in.

"The capsule version," he said. "Born. My father was a minister. I started singing in the church, naturally, because I was exposed to gospel singing first. Hmmm. Came out of school, went with a professional gospel group called the Soul Stirrers, sang around the country with them for about five years. Decided to go on my own. Made a song called 'You Send Me.' It sold about a million and a half copies for me, luckily enough. Went into the Copa, bombed —"

"You bombed?" said Douglas in disbelief, as the others murmured equal incredulity. But Sam was insistent. "Unless you give it a real adult approach, you'll bomb."

"Why do you think you bombed?" Eleanor Harris persisted.

"I know why I bombed," Sam said. "'Cause I wasn't ready."

He stayed out on the road with Alex, promoting the single with a series of Midwest appearances as Barbara joined them in Chicago. RCA was putting more into the promotion of this record, it seemed, than the sum total of all their previous efforts, and Allen left no stone unturned in his determination to get Sam a number-one hit. At the suggestion of *Cash Box* editor Ira Howard, he hired independent promo man Pete Bennett, who had broken "Lazy Crazy Hazy Days of Summer" pop for Nat "King" Cole the previous year. Pete told his new employer that the only way they could really get Sam into the pop market was with free goods for the DJs and the stores that reported their sales figures to the trades. That way, he explained to Allen, who had never been on this end of the business before, the DJs had something to sell, and the stores had an incentive to push a record for which they had paid absolutely nothing. Allen immediately went to RCA and told them he needed five thousand records to give away, but, whether because he was too explicit or too naive, they told him he would have to pay the same price as any other wholesaler. So he purchased the records and gave them away. "I said, 'Okay.' I did it." But from then on, he made sure to put a free-goods allotment in all his contracts.

In Allen's world, there was little room for any deviation in course. Now that Sam had made up his mind that he was ready for the Copa, Allen's sights were set on the Copa and the Copa alone. But then, to his astonishment, Jules Podell, the Copa's brusque manager, turned him down. Podell's memory of the original engagement was, evidently, just as vivid as Sam's, and he told Allen and William Morris head club agent Lee Solomon bluntly that Sam Cooke was not a Copa act. Allen looked to Solomon for support, but it became immediately apparent that the William Morris agent, a Broadway habitué with a sharp tongue who Allen thought might have been better suited to be a comedian, was no more on his and Sam's side than Jules Podell. He felt sandbagged, he told Jerry Brandt, with whom he had recently forged an improbable business alliance. They had even talked of the possibility of a partnership, and Brandt was steadily steering William Morris clients his way, most notably Bobby Vinton, for whom Allen had just completed a renegotiation with Columbia that would net Vinton, the hottest young singles artist of the moment, a new $553,000 contract. But Jerry and his boss, Roz Ross, couldn't do anything about the Copa, and Jerry still wasn't sold on the idea anyway. His new thought was to book Sam into Basin Street East as an opening act for Sophie Tucker. Which Sam took as a personal insult, and Allen did, too. Allen didn't want Basin Street, he wasn't interested in Basin Street, what he wanted for Sam was the Copa. So he made up his mind that, regardless of personal friendships or business connections, he was going to change agencies.

JERRY BRANDT GOT THEM ALL TICKETS for the Clay-Liston fight in Miami on February 25. Allen brought his wife, Betty, Sam took Barbara, and J.W. came by himself, with Allen arranging for accommodations at Miami's resplendent Fountainebleau Hotel. Allen had already registered and was in his room when Sam arrived, only to be told that there had been a mix-up about the reservations. It was not as blatant as Shreveport, but Sam had no reason to take it any more lightly. Miami Beach, like Las Vegas, had never made a habit of accommodating Negro guests. It might present the best in colored entertainers, but until very recently those entertainers had always come in through the back door. Sam called Allen, and Allen came down to the lobby and made a scene. "I just lost it. I screamed at them, 'Don't you know what prejudice is? How can you people, after all the discrimination we've been through, do the same thing?' It was an embarrassment to me — Jewish place, Jewish people, and they didn't want to give him a room?" Allen threatened to camp out in the lobby until they sorted this thing out. And in the end, the hotel came up with a nice suite on the second floor.

Malcolm X, too, was in Miami, as Cassius Clay's personal guest. He was staying across the bay, at the Hampton House Motel, in a black section of town. Malcolm had arrived with his wife and three little girls over a month earlier for a brief family vacation (the first one they had ever had, Malcolm wrote in his autobiography), a gift from the challenger. Clay had then broken training and flown back to New York with Malcolm for a Muslim rally, where, speaking for the silenced minister (Malcolm was still under the interdiction imposed by the Honorable Elijah Muhammad in the wake of his remarks about President Kennedy's assassination), Clay told "cheering Muslim members," the *Amsterdam News* reported, "that 'Every time I go to a Muslim meeting I get inspired,' [then] predicted to the audience that he would win the fight because 'I'm training on lamb chops and that big ugly bear [Liston] is training on pork chops,' in reference to the fact that Muslims don't eat pork." "Cassius Clay Almost Says He's a Muslim," was the disapproving headline in the *News*, a story that was picked up in newspapers all across the country and brought ticket sales to a grinding halt. The promoter threatened to cancel the fight unless Clay agreed to eliminate any further public reference to Islam or visible contact with his mentor, and Malcolm did not return to Miami until February 23, two days before the fight.

It was the same old story, Sam thought. Everyone wanted Cassius Clay to remain the "All-American boy" — and if he didn't, the same black bourgeoisie that had opposed Martin and the Movement didn't want the white world to find out about it. Fuck the white world. This was a young man who couldn't be contained, who had embraced a despised doctrine of black separatism and self-determination out of religious conviction but who still retained an irrepressible gift for showmanship and abundant intellectual curiosity. Nor did it escape Sam's attention that when the new British group, the Beatles, arrived in Miami for the second in a trio of phenomenally successful appearances on *The Ed Sullivan Show* (their major-label U.S. debut, "I Want to Hold Your Hand," had been dominating the pop charts for the last month), who should they seek out at his dingy Miami training quarters but Cassius Clay? Whatever the outcome of the fight, there was no doubt in Sam's mind that Cassius *was* going to shake up the world, with his wit, his ingenuity, his sheer force of will. As Malcolm X said of his protégé, "Though a clown never imitates a wise man, the wise man can imitate a clown." Like Sam, Clay possessed "that instinct of seeing a tricky situation shaping up . . . and resolving how to sidestep it."

Sonny Liston, on the other hand, was a study in menace, the kind of plodding, surly gangster mentality that Sam had spent a lifetime seeking to sidestep. Liston had always been held up as the devil incarnate, the original bogeyman, by boxing commentators both black and white. "Sonny Liston: 'King of the Beasts'" was the title of a *Look* magazine story on the upcoming fight, and the NAACP had disowned Liston two years earlier. James Brown almost alone among entertainers and sports figures had urged the black community to give Sonny a chance. "Sonny Liston isn't the worst person in the . . . world and should not be treated like he's the world's first public figure to have a record of being in trouble," James had declared, with an empathy born of his own troubled past. But there had been few concurring voices until now, when, faced with Clay's baffling mixture of unpardonable braggadocio and inappropriate religious preference, the white sports establishment found itself forced almost by default to pick Liston as its choice. "An aura of artificiality surrounds Tuesday's heavyweight championship fight," declared the *New York Times*. "On that evening, the loud mouth from Louisville is likely to have a lot of vainglorious boasts jammed down his throat by a ham-like fist," a well-deserved comeuppance, suggested columnist Arthur Daley, even if that fist belonged to a "malefic destroyer." The vast majority of black commentators, wishing perhaps that this embarrassing young upstart would just shut up and go away, reluctantly embraced Liston as well. It was the modern equivalent of the Cross and the Crescent, Malcolm told Cassius Clay upon his return to Miami. "This fight is the *truth*," he said.

It was probably that same night that a number of the Muslims from Clay's camp, including his younger brother Rudy (Rudolph Valentino Clay), who was fighting in one of the preliminary bouts, gathered in Allen Klein's suite. To Jerry Brandt, who was now courting Rudy, too, as a potential William Morris client, the subject under discussion was purely pragmatic. He and Allen were advancing the proposition that the Muslims should keep their distance from Clay for the time being if only to allow him to continue to be able to make a living. Allen, who never ran away from a good argument ("I minored in Christian ethics in college. I had never been with Muslims before, but I heard Malcolm X on [talk show host] Barry Gray very early in his career, and I didn't have to agree with what he said, I just liked to listen to him"), took it one step further. "I hope he loses," he said to the disbelief of the Clay camp. "He'll get more sympathy that way, and then you can really make a lot of money." They were up till four o'clock in the morning, heatedly discussing a wide range of issues. "We were feeding them," said Allen good-humoredly, "and they were just tearing the Jews apart, arguing about which religion came first." At one point in the evening, J.W., who was there without Sam, got into a conversation with Clay's road manager, Osman Karriem, whom he and Sam had both known as Archie Robinson when he was working for the Platters. Karriem was concerned that the growing enmity between Malcolm and the Honorable Elijah Muhammad was developing into a life-and-death struggle for leadership that Malcolm was unlikely to win. J.W., who admired Malcolm for both his intellectual discernment and his oratorical skills, saw few viable alternatives. "I said there were two things he could do. He could either go to Adam Clayton Powell's Abyssinian Baptist Church on Sunday morning and get up and say, 'I have seen the light!'" Which was not exactly a realistic prospect. Or he could make a pilgrimage to Mecca, where, Alex felt, he would discover that the mumbo-jumbo mythology of the Black Muslim religion, with its equation of white people with "human devils" and its elaborate devolutionary theory of genetic "tricknology," was far removed from true Mohammedanism. But Alex was uncomfortable with talking to someone about their religion, and he didn't expect Karriem to go along with his thinking any more than Karriem would expect the older man to go along with his. So they continued their discussions late into the night, and eventually all talk returned to the fight.

T HE FIGHT ITSELF was as strange and unpredictable in its own way as the events leading up to it. The auditorium was only half full, even with all the comps the promoters had given out, when Sam, Barbara, J.W., Allen, and Betty Klein all took their places in the seventh row, with Malcolm just a few seats away. Cassius watched his brother win his first professional bout from the rear of the arena, wearing a black tuxedo. Then he retreated to his dressing room with Malcolm, where they joined together in silent prayer. After all the uproar surrounding the promotion, there was no need for words, and Cassius, who had created such a scene at the weigh-in that morning that the medical examiner nearly canceled the fight, exhibited a calm that appeared to reflect Malcolm's argument that for the true believer in Black Muslim doctrine, there was no such thing as fear, that while "the Mohammedan abroad believes in a heaven and a hell, a hereafter, here we believe that heaven and hell are on this earth and that we are in the hell and must strive to escape it."

Cassius entered the ring, armed with that belief. He was nervous, he admitted afterward ("It frightened me, just knowing how hard he hit"), and he began by furiously backpedaling, ducking and dodging and moving from side to side. But then he dropped his hands to his sides, and, with a look of serene self-confidence, in a manner that could be compared with that of no other heavyweight in history (though it was certainly inspired by his idol, the great welter- and middleweight champion Sugar Ray Robinson), he *danced*. Watched today, it remains a thing of grace and beauty, but it is the expression on Sonny Liston's face that is most revealing — a look of puzzlement that suggested, Sam said later, that Cassius Clay won the fight right then and there.

As Clay continued to dance and Liston continued to lumber after him, there was a slow dawning of recognition on the part of the crowd. Allen had taken Clay in the second against J.W.'s $500 on Liston, and when the fight was over, with Liston refusing to answer the bell for the seventh, J.W. sat in stunned amazement, not only due to the unexpected loss of his $500 but because Sam was making his way to the ring.

Cassius was in the middle of an interview with television announcer Steve Ellis and former champ Joe Louis when he spotted Sam, almost disheveled with excitement, his tie removed, shirt open. "Sam Cooke!" the new champion called out with unabashed enthusiasm. "Hey, let that man up here." Ellis did his best to ignore yet another in a string of uncontrollable developments ("I want justice! I want justice!" the new champ had just been calling out). "This is Sam Cooke!" Cassius shouts. "We see him. We see him," says the announcer, looking utterly bewildered. "Joe, ask Cassius another question." But Cassius is not to be deterred.

"Let Sam in," he insists with all the fervor he has put into the fight.

"This is the world's greatest rock 'n' roll singer." And Sam is almost cata-pulted into the ring as Cassius ruffles his hair and throws an arm around him. "Sam Cooke. Very good friend. Good vocalist," says the announcer, while Sam and Cassius face off, much in the manner that Cassius and the "clown prince" of his entourage, Drew "Bundini" Brown, have been trading lines ("Float like a butterfly, sting like a bee," was the mantra Brown had given Clay) all through training camp. "We gonna shake up the world!" the champ calls out one more time. "You're beautiful," says Sam, his face wreathed in smiles, his expression one of innocent mirth. "Thank you, Sam, thank you," says the announcer, finally able to hustle Sam off camera.

Dee Dee Sharp, who was performing at the Sir John Hotel and had been seeing Cassius on and off for the last few months, had been plan-ning a post-fight party for him, and there was a big victory celebration at the Fountainebleau, but Cassius chose to go back to the Hampton House with Malcolm, Sam, and Jim Brown, the football great, who had provided radio commentary for the fight. They sat in Malcolm's room with Osman Karriem and various Muslim ministers and supporters, eat-ing vanilla ice cream and offering up thanks to Allah for Cassius' victory, as an undercover FBI informant took note of this apparent nexus between the Nation of Islam and prominent members of the sports and entertainment industries. Sam was uncharacteristically quiet, taking in the magnificent multiplicity of the moment. To him, Cassius was not just a great entertainer but a kindred soul. He had made beating Liston look easy, and Sam was convinced he would beat him again. Because, armed with an analytic intelligence, he had made him afraid. Jim Brown, an outspoken militant himself, though not a member of the Nation, appeared to veteran black sports reporter Brad Pye Jr. to be more elated over Clay's achievement than any of his own. "Well, Brown," said Malcolm with a mixture of seriousness and jocularity, "don't you think it's time for this young man to stop spouting off and get serious?"

T HAT IS EXACTLY what Cassius did at a pair of press conferences he held in the two days following the fight. He was a Muslim, he said. "There are seven hundred fifty million people all over the world who be-lieve in it, and I'm one of them." He wasn't a Christian. How could he be, "when I see all the colored people fighting for forced integration get blowed up. . . . I'm the heavyweight champion, but right now, there are some neighborhoods I can't move into.

> I'm a good boy. I never done anything wrong. I have never been in jail. I have never been in court. . . . I don't pay any attention to all those white women who wink at me. If I go in somebody's house where I'm not welcome, I'm uncomfortable, so I stay away. I like white people. I like my own people. They can live together without infringing on each other. You can't condemn a man for wanting peace. If you do, you condemn peace itself. A rooster crows only when it sees the light. Put him in the dark, and he'll never crow. I have seen the light and I'm crowing.

Then he returned to the little bungalow in the North Miami ghetto that he and his entourage had occupied dormitory-style, two or three to a room, for the last two months. He was greeted, as always, by neighborhood children hanging around to see what was happening, the same ones who had faithfully attended the movies he showed every night with colorful commentary in the backyard. "Who shook up the world?" he demanded, and they responded, "Cassius Clay!" "Who's the prettiest?" he called out, leading them in an orchestrated chant, while Malcolm X looked on benignly. Clay and the kids could keep it up for a full hour if they felt like it. "Sometimes," wrote George Plimpton in a story for *Harper's,* "a bright girl, just for a change, would reply *'me,'* pointing a finger at herself when everyone else was shouting, *'Cassius Clay,'* or she might shout, *'Ray Charles,'* and the giggling would start around her . . . until Clay, with a big grin, would have to hold up a hand to reorganize the claque and get things straightened out. Neither he nor the children tired of the litany. . . . The noise carried for blocks."

CLAY ARRIVED IN NEW YORK three days later, checking into the Hotel Theresa on Sunday afternoon after making the trip in his smart new chartered bus. On Monday, March 2, he gave an interview to the *Amsterdam News,* with Malcolm accompanying him to the newspaper's offices. He was henceforth to be identified as Cassius X, he told his interviewer; he would no longer recognize his slave name. He was thinking of going on a boxing exhibition tour that might include Mecca, the Holy City, as well as

Cairo, Rome, London, Germany, Malaysia, Pakistan, and Turkey. Elijah Muhammad was "the sweetest man in the world. Malcolm X? I fell in love with him after watching him on television, discussing Islam with those educators — leaving them with their mouths wide open. . . . The whole world recognizes me now that they know my religion is Islam. The religion is the truth, and I am ready to die for the truth. I am the greatest."

The following evening, he and Sam made the record they had started talking about the previous fall. Sam got Horace Ott to write the arrangements, with a&r man Dave Kapralik, who had courted Sam so assiduously for Columbia and signed Clay to the label, proudly on hand for the occasion. The song Sam had put together to showcase the champion's limited singing skills was called "Hey Hey, The Gang's All Here" and was little more than a variation on the age-old party chant. The one departure was a litany of place-names that evoked the classic r&b instrumental "Night Train," with the singer calling out "Is Memphis with me? Is Louisville with me? Is Houston with me?" and the large backup chorus responding loudly and enthusiastically each time. They worked hard at it, with Sam supplying the energy and direction and keeping everybody's spirits up while Cassius recited poetry and played the drums in between takes. And in the end, everyone walked out of the studio convinced that they had participated in something memorable if not musically significant ("It was a great thing," said Horace Ott. "I said to my wife, 'I don't know what's going on, but I like the mix.' The *New York Times* came in and covered it"), somehow carried along by the champion's indomitable self-belief and Sam's invincible charm. Dave Kapralik alone was left to wonder if it might not be all over before it had even started as a result of Clay's impolitic announcement that he was indeed a Black Muslim.

Cassius and Malcolm went to the UN the next day, where they were given a two-hour tour and Clay announced his plans to accompany Malcolm to Asia and Africa ("I'm champion of the *whole* world, and I want to meet the people I am champion of"), while signing autographs for UN workers and African delegates as "Cassius X Clay."

Very likely that same day, Sam accompanied him to a New York television studio for a transatlantic interview with Harry Carpenter, the dean of British boxing commentators, who seemed to thoroughly enjoy the repartée. After a five-minute analysis of the fight, punctuated by jokes, poetry, and Sam's off-camera chuckles, Carpenter asked, "Cass, who's that you've got there with you in the New York studio?" "Well, here with me," Cassius responded affably, "I have one of the greatest singers in America, and I would say all over the world, Mr. Sam Cooke. Come here, Sam, I've got the British press here. This is Sam Cooke. As you can see, like me, he's awful pretty."

Sam is all smiles, dressed to the nines in a sharp, shiny suit and a radiant smile, as he perches on the edge of the microphone table with his arm around Cassius. They've been working on a record, which they expect to have out in another week, Clay says. "Would you like to give us a preview?" asks the host, and Cassius starts to explain how much better it would sound with the chorus behind him and the party atmosphere they created in the studio, until Sam, relaxed but clearly attentive to every nuance not just of Clay's speech but of his physiognomy as well, starts beating out a rhythm on the table. "Come on," he says, "let's give them —" And then, tentatively at first, Clay starts singing the first verse, his eyes glued on Sam, as Sam guides the vocal with a softly voiced vocal of his own.

> *Hey, hey, the gang's all here, join in the fun*
> *Hey, hey, the gang's all here, we gonna swing as one*

When they come to the chorus ("Is New York with me? Is Chicago with me? Is London with me?"), it is Sam who adds his full-throated "Yeah," to indicate, as Cassius has already explained to Carpenter, the high regard in which he is held throughout the world. It is a thoroughly charming performance, both for its artlessness and for the obvious affection that exists between the two men, and at the end, when Cassius asks his interviewer, "How'd you like that?," the response is instantaneous and sincere. "I like that very much."

"Well, Cassius, it's been really great fun talking to you," Carpenter says after Sam has gracefully excused himself. "It seems to me that you are to some extent a changed man. I detect a little quieting down, a little more dignity behind you. Is this right?"

"Well, I have changed a little," replies the champ. "I don't have to talk like I used to. I've been campaigning. Take politicians, for an example. They walk the streets, talk to people, meet people, shake hands, pass out pickets, talk about how great they are, 'Vote for me' — and then after they're in office, they quieten down." In the background is the sound of Sam (and maybe Alex, too) chuckling to himself. Once the politicians have gotten where they want to be, said Cassius, they don't have to campaign anymore.

What he didn't say, but what he had been saying to the New York press, was that in just a few days, when Malcolm's suspension from public speaking would be ended by the Honorable Elijah Muhammad, he wouldn't have to talk anymore, at least not about his faith, because Malcolm's words would be so much more eloquent than his own. But Malcolm's suspension was not ended. In fact, the Honorable Elijah Muhammad, inflamed by Malcolm's growing identification with the most celebrated public convert in the Nation's forty-year history, as well as Malcolm's all-too-evident disillusionment with his leadership, called up Cassius Clay two days later, on the evening of March 6, and told him that he must permanently sever his relationship with Malcolm. He told Cassius that he must also embrace the new name, Muhammad Ali, that Elijah had given him. Clay had been resistant when Elijah first broached the subject. "Muhammad Ali" was an "original" (that is, Arabic) name, the kind of honorific that Elijah had publicly declared would not be bestowed until the Second Coming of the Founder, Wallace Fard. Not only that, it incorporated a portion of Fard's own Islamic name. But with an official announcement of the name change that night on Elijah's radio broadcast, Cassius Clay no longer had any choice in the matter.

That Sunday, March 8, Malcolm announced his break with the Nation of Islam, making it clear that the break was not of his own volition and referring to Elijah Muhammad on national television as "morally bankrupt." He made numerous attempts to contact Muhammad Ali, but none of his calls were taken. A little over a month later, he set off on the pilgrimage to Mecca that he had discussed many times with his onetime protégé, from which he would return a spiritually changed man. In Ghana, Malcolm ran into Muhammad Ali, on his own pilgrimage to Africa, at the Hotel Ambassador, but Ali would not speak to him. "Did you get a look at Malcolm?" he declared sarcastically to reporters. "Dressed in that funny white robe and wearing a beard and walking with that cane that looked like a prophet's stick? Man, he's gone . . . so far out, he's out completely. No one listens to Malcolm anymore." "That hurt Malcolm more than any other [rejection]," said Malcolm X confidant and biographer Alex Haley. But they never spoke again, and Malcolm was assassinated by Muslims loyal to Elijah some eight months later.

*   *   *

A LLEN KLEIN, MEANWHILE, had flown to England on March 16 as an emissary for RCA. Joe D'Imperio empowered him to offer $1 million plus a 10 percent royalty to the Beatles, but when he met with their manager, Brian Epstein, in his suite at the Dorchester, on his own initiative he doubled the cash offer. Epstein, according to Allen, turned down the RCA bid out of hand, citing loyalty to EMI, their British label, but he did express interest in Sam opening for the group on their next American tour. This, Allen said, he would have to take under advisement — there were too many things up in the air right now. One of which was his own unanticipated signing of the Dave Clark Five, the number-two British band behind the Beatles, whose manager, Harold Davidson, came to see him at his hotel and, based on the success Allen had recently enjoyed with his renegotiation of Sam Cooke's and Bobby Vinton's contracts, asked if he could do the same for the Dave Clark Five. Allen took on the task with alacrity, eventually working out a complicated long-term payout of a quarter of a million dollars that would save the band money in taxes and net Allen $80,000 clear. He was full of fire, it was as if he had finally found his true vocation, and he was already looking around for more business and contemplating a return trip to England in the next month or two. But none of it could hold a candle to his unqualified dedication to Sam.

He renewed his suit for the Copa upon his return to New York, but not before approaching Buddy Howe, vice president of the General Artists Corporation (GAC), at Joe D'Imperio's suggestion. Buddy Howe was, in Joe D'Imperio's view, the best club agent in the business, with the most powerful agency at his disposal. (GAC was the agency with which Irvin Feld, who had created the original rock 'n' roll package tour, had affiliated himself some six years earlier. GAC was also the agency that Jerry Brandt had left with his boss, Roz Ross, to join William Morris.)

"Buddy Howe went in and pulled every string," Allen said admiringly. "He took me around [when] I didn't know what the hell to fucking do. Buddy was a former song-and-dance man. He said, 'Just watch my feet!'"

At Buddy's urging, Allen got Joe to make a substantial commitment on behalf of RCA. "I told him he had to tell Podell exactly what he was going to do. That he was going to buy up the house every night. That we were going for the kids. That we would bring in blacks." D'Imperio also told Podell how much he, personally, believed in Sam, that he saw in

Sam the potential for a whole new kind of crossover success, and what could be more appropriate than that the Copa — faced with box-office challenges in changing times — should be in at the start? Allen, for his part, promised a billboard on Broadway, one that would be bigger than any opening at the Copa had ever seen. In the end, it was, as he saw it, a combination of Buddy's credibility, Joe's commitment, and his own bull-shit that won the day, with Podell finally agreeing to two weeks at prom time. Allen still hadn't signed with GAC. He was going to let Buddy continue to prove himself, just like he had had to do with Sam.

S AM HEADLINED a couple of big East Coast gigs, including Georgie Woods' "Freedom Show of '64" at Philadelphia's fourteen-thousand-seat Convention Hall on March 17, with more than a dozen other acts on the bill (including his brother L.C.) and all proceeds earmarked for the NAACP Legal Defense Fund and three local charities. He appeared on Dick Clark's Saturday-night show on April 4, newly relocated on the West Coast, and, after a lip-synched version of "Ain't That Good News," sat down for a nearly two-and-one-half-minute interview with Clark, an extended sequence within the rapid-fire framework of the show. Why had he turned to pop music in the first place? Clark asked at the outset.

"My economic situation," Sam said with a laugh.

And was there any secret that Sam could point to as the key to his remarkable string of hit songs?

"I think the secret is really observation, Dick," Sam responded. By which he meant? "Well, if you observe what is going on and try to figure out how people are thinking and determine the times of your day, I think you can always write something that people will understand."

What of the future? Was he traveling like he used to? "No, I'm not, Dick. I'm mostly staying home now."

"Will you produce and write and so forth?"

"I'm producing and writing, as I said, for other people."

"What could be the greatest thing in the world that would happen to you, if you had your choice?"

"The greatest thing that [could] happen to me? If all the singers I'm connected with had hits."

To that end he was focused more and more on the future of SAR. Despite all of Zelda's dire predictions, Allen had organized things back in New York to reach a broader market. He had hired former Scepter a&r

head Luther Dixon's brother Barney Williams to do independent promotion in the r&b field, and he was planning to put Pete Bennett, the slick operator he had found to promote Sam's singles, on the Valentinos' new record when it came out. Cash flow had increased, Alex was enjoying being on a regular salary, and SAR's informal new headquarters and rehearsal space at Thirty-seventh and Vermont was fully operational by now, with an old piano, carpet for soundproofing tacked up on the ceiling and walls, a couple of inexpensive tape recorders and mikes, and, as a finishing touch, the sign that bass player Chuck Badie had ceremoniously scrawled in chalk across the plate-glass window: Soul Station #1.

Harold Battiste and the AFO Executives were in charge, but Sam came down from time to time to check out what was going on. The AFO band might be rehearsing, Johnnie Morisette liked to use the storefront location as a kind of clubhouse, and, except for Johnnie Taylor, any of the other SAR artists was likely to stop by. You never knew who was going to show up. Local kids, well-known jazz musicians, even Sonny Bono, who went back with Harold to the glory days of Specialty. Sonny was working up an act with his new girlfriend, seventeen-year-old Cherilyn Sarkisian, as Caesar and Cleo, and Harold was supplying the song arrangements. Mostly, though, it was a hangout, a combination practice room and retreat, where Harold, newly named head of SAR Productions, scouted for fresh talent, sought to develop more exciting (and more commercial) musical settings for each artist already on the label, and mapped out plans for expansion into other neighborhoods with additional Soul Stations.

Sam's principal expectations for the moment were centered on the Valentinos. Their March 24 session had ended up focusing primarily on a song Bobby had written with his sister-in-law, Friendly's wife, Shirley. It was called "It's All Over Now," and it had a different sound, a kind of loose-jointed country flavor that Sam found odd at first but soon came to see as an exciting new direction for their music. Bobby thought one of the reasons Sam was so knocked out by it was that it sounded like none of his own songs, and they ran through twelve high-spirited takes as Johnnie Morisette screamed encouragement and beat on a newspaper while generally annoying the hell out of Bobby and his brothers.

They had another song, "If I Got My Ticket," something which they had been working on at Soul Station #1 and believed in almost as strongly as "It's All Over Now," but after a couple of rehearsals, Sam pronounced it "too churchy" and told Bobby it needed more work, they ought to just set it aside until the Womacks had a chance to polish it and turn it into more of a finished song. It could not have come as a greater surprise, then, when Bobby and his brothers showed up at the studio to play on Sam's session the following day, only to find him exploring the same groove, the same riff they had worked out for "If I Got My Ticket" as the centerpiece of a new number of his own.

"Yeah Man" was a song he had first come up with in England, a dance number along the lines of the call-and-response vehicle he had devised for Cassius Clay, with a large chorus responding to a series of rhetorical questions ("Do you like good music?" "Do you like all the dances?") with a rousing "Yeah, yeah." What made it different was the vocal charm, the rhythmic complexity, the agile horns, and booming bass. In an odd twist, Sam mixed in sports metaphors, too, and concluded with a situation far removed from the dance floor: "You in the middle of an ocean," Sam sings out cheerfully. "Come on, baby," someone in the chorus calls out, as Sam introduces an even more unexpected picture: "Ship going down now ["Yeah, yeah"] / Swim for your life now ["Yeah, yeah"] . . . Swim . . . Swim . . . I'm going home."

Sam was clearly delighted with the song's evolution, but Bobby felt sick about it, and his brothers weren't about to let him forget his turncoat role. "You always talking about Sam, he can't do no wrong with you," they said, and all Bobby could think to offer in response was that since Sam hadn't used any of their lyrics, just a groove that could have fit into any song, you couldn't really call it stealing. But that just inflamed them all the more. "Yeah, he's got your ticket, Bob," Cecil, the youngest brother, said sarcastically, and Bobby didn't even bother to reply. There was no point in arguing. Maybe Sam and Alex really would turn the Valentinos' next record, "It's All Over Now," into a big pop hit. But then, almost before he knew it, Bobby was caught up in rehearsals for the Copa.

They started out in the half studio Sam had crammed into the little house that he used as a retreat back by the carport. Sam had hired a new bass player, Harper Cosby, to replace Chuck, because Chuck wouldn't fly anymore after a rocky plane ride into New York for an all-star show at the Paramount Theater at the end of March. Otherwise, the nucleus remained the same, with Clif the unquestioned leader, Bobby installed as second guitarist on a permanent basis with the band's bass slot finally filled, and June flying in from New Orleans for the start of what would soon become five- or six-days-a-week all-day sessions.

There was just about enough room in the little outbuilding for a couple of amps, a drum set, and five people breathing each other's air. Sam's attitude was clearly different than at the start of any other tour. They tried one number after another, going over each one until they were locked in so tight they could practically play the song backward. Gradually a repertoire began to emerge. To Clif's surprise, "When I Fall in Love," Nat "King" Cole's 1957 hit, which Sam had originally recorded for his second Keen album, was one of the centerpieces of the set. Clif had first seen it as "a complete one-eighty from [Sam's] style," but he had proven that he had a feeling for the song, and now, with that feeling deepened, Clif was finally convinced it wasn't "a copy of anybody, it [was] strictly an original."

They worked on familiar showbiz standards like "Bill Bailey" and "Nobody Knows You When You're Down and Out," experimented with current folk and country favorites like "All My Trials" and "500 Miles," and generally woodshedded as Clif guided the band and provided Bobby with firm direction behind Sam's vocals. "He really knew Sam, and he knew how to keep control of the whole thing. I mean, I could play that cute shit, if Sam hit a note I would hit it right behind him, but Clif held the whole group together so you could have that little cuteness in there. He used to always say, 'All that little cute-ass shit you playing, just watch me.' Because I was ad-lib, ad-lib, ad-lib, and he came up from another era."

The new bass player, whom Bobby dubbed "Hoppergrass" both as a play on his name and because he reminded everybody of a grasshopper with his nervous ways, was working out fine. He played strictly stand-up, but that was Sam's preference. Nobody got to know him all that well. He never really seemed to relax, and he constantly muttered to himself as he played, but everybody liked the way he spaced his notes, and Sam put an end to all speculation with the pronouncement: "This fucker can play."

Linda wandered out sometimes to listen to them rehearse. Her daddy would wink at her as he cued the musicians with a snap of his fingers or a shake of his head, and she knew without his ever saying a word how much the Copa meant to him. "It was very, very important. He had in mind how it was gonna go, but he had to make sure it went that way. So he was very, very focused and very, very intense."

Sam said he was going to get Sammy Davis Jr.'s arranger, Morty Stevens, to write the arrangements for the Copa orchestra. Not René? Bobby asked with some surprise. No, Sam said, Morty had the experience, Morty had *Copa* experience — if Sammy used him, he had to be the best. The only arrangement of René's that they would keep was "A Change Is Gonna Come," and Sam doubted they would use that. In fact, he told Bobby, he was planning to include very few of his hit songs — not "Bring It On Home to Me" or "Having a Party" or "Ain't That Good News" or even "Nothing Can Change This Love." When Bobby protested that these were the songs that always got the best audience response, Sam gave him a lesson in geography as well as demographics. "He said, 'I want to be black. I'm not going to desert my people. But to cross over, you must appeal to that market.' I said, 'What's so important about that fucking market?' He said, 'Bobby, you listen to the [r&b] radio station. When you turn the corner, that station will go off the air, and you go right to a pop station. That's how powerful it is. And white people are not gonna come to the black side of town.'" "Twistin' the Night Away," with its little cute story, was the kind of song that always went over with white audiences; "Chain Gang" could work in a medley; and "You Send Me" was the one song that everybody remembered. But he was insistent: "You have to be all around, you have to be universal."

As they got closer to the opening, they moved into a little studio to rehearse, with Gerald Wilson's band playing Morty Stevens' arrangements. Nobody liked the new sound. It was loud and brassy, and it felt like there just wasn't enough room for Sam. None of them said anything, though, because Sam acted so confident, and nobody wanted to disturb his mood. "I'm gonna kill them fuckers," he said over and over again, and there seemed no reason to disbelieve him. One day he and June were standing out under the carport having a smoke, and he told June about the billboard Allen was putting up in Times Square. "I said, 'Man you're bullshitting me.' He said, 'I'm going to have my picture right up there on the building.' I said, 'Bullshit.' He said, 'Wait'll you fuckers all see.'"

It seemed strange to still be at home when normally he would be out making money, while the weather was good and people had money in their pockets. But he stuck to his rigid daily schedule of rehearsals, and at night he rambled. The Upsetters were at the California Club off and on for close to a month, staying at the Hacienda Motel on Figueroa, out by the airport. The Sims Twins had a regular gig at Bill Goin's Newly Decorated Sands Cocktail Lounge and Steak House just a few blocks from the motel, and Johnnie Morisette, too, played the Sands on occasion. Sam and former Pilgrim Travelers bass singer George McCurn ("Oopie") frequently finished an evening of club-hopping out at the Sands before going on to the Hacienda to party with the band. Earl Palmer, the drummer and L.A. session mainstay who had played behind Sam from his first pop session on, viewed Sam's attraction to the street with increasing concern. He himself had grown up in the New Orleans demimonde, and he knew all the players in the game, but he wasn't convinced that Sam did. And he was beginning to feel like Sam was drifting more and more toward the kind of people that could do him no good. He didn't say anything because, for one thing, he didn't know Sam that well outside the studio. And even if he had, you didn't ever try to tell Sam anything. Not even J.W. confronted Sam directly, though Earl would have been the first to concede he possessed greater powers of persuasion than most.

Sam was still seeing the girl he had met with Crume; there was never any shortage of girls within the easy radius of his smile, and he continued to relish the excitement that came from being always on the prowl, the sense of anticipation that never failed to kick in at the thought of meeting someone new. Barbara no longer even bothered to hide her contempt. She had acquired a "friend guy" she had begun to see with increasing indiscretion, a bartender at the Flying Fox and a well-known player. She was even brazen enough to invite him out to the house on occasion when Sam was out of town, sitting around the pool with him, kissing and holding hands with the kids right there. It was a nice arrangement, she liked to say, but it was strictly an arrangement. She told her husband she was going out with her sister, just like he told her he was going out with the guys. There was nothing Sam could say to her. He understood what she was doing, but he couldn't stop her any more than he could stop himself. Everyone looked at him like he was their fucking savior, everywhere he went he was an object of admiration and adoration — and yet he couldn't muffle the growing discontent, the helplessness he felt at his inability to control not so much the world around him as his private world, the inner world that was revealed to no one but him.

*   *   *

I T WAS A TIME OF MARRIAGES. J.W. unexpectedly got married to Carol
Ann Crawford, the young woman with whom he had been keeping
company for over a year. She had realized she was pregnant only after
returning to Hawaii in February, and she and Alex slipped away to Vegas
on May 18, a week before her twenty-second birthday, for a quiet ceremony
that not even Sam and Barbara attended. They showered the newlyweds
with gifts, though, and congratulated Alex on his good fortune — imagine
a silver-haired old man who had just celebrated his fiftieth birthday getting such a combination of youth, charm, and beauty — and everyone
agreed he had never seemed happier.

Lou Adler married the actress and singer Shelley Fabares three
weeks later, in a fancy ceremony at the Bel Air Hotel. Herbie Alpert was
there, along with Lou Rawls, Oopie, Alex, recording engineer Bones
Howe, and many of their friends going back to the early days at Keen.
The bride's party was dressed in cool mint green, and Sam fronted an
all-star group of Johnny Rivers on guitar, Phil Everly on bass, and Jerry
Allison, an original member of Buddy Holly's Crickets, on drums for a
brief but memorable guest set.

Sam sold the Maserati and bought a tomato-red Ferrari to replace it.
He consistently lost to J.W. in chess and took up archery, while desulto-
rily continuing to pursue Alex's favorite hobby, tennis. It was golf,
though, he told Bobby, that was the key to business success. "Do you
know how many deals are made on the golf course?" Sammy Davis Jr.
had said to him. So he went out and bought shoes and clubs, a whole
golfing outfit, though he never got very far in learning the rudiments of
the game.

W ITH THE COPA OPENING just three weeks away, Allen finally formalized his arrangement with GAC. He extended the new deal
with BMI, too, by which Kags would be credited with 38 percent beyond
the prevailing royalty rate from the first dollar. Despite his rapidly expanding business interests in England, his principal focus remained on
Sam. RCA had kept up its end of the bargain with a big push on for Sam's
new album, *Ain't That Good News,* and his latest single release, "Good
Times" and "Tennessee Waltz," which, with close to half a million orders,
was easily outpacing the disappointing sales of the last. The twenty-by-
one-hundred-foot billboard that Allen had commissioned was scheduled

to go up over Schrafft's, on the corner of Broadway and Forty-third Street, on June 15, posing the teaser, "WHO'S THE BIGGEST COOK IN TOWN?" Three days later, the question would be answered, as Sam flew into the city for a noon press conference to mark the raising of the second stage of the sign: a forty-foot, fifteen-hundred-pound cutout of Sam in five sections, which with its pedestal raised the billboard to a height of seventy feet ("the tallest figure of an entertainment personality ever to be erected in the Times Square area," read the publicity release) and would be illuminated with "sufficient lamps to produce 20,000 watts, or enough current to keep a household refrigerator operating continuously for four years." "SAM'S THE BIGGEST COOKE IN TOWN," read the accompanying message.

All of the trades, and most of the dailies, were present to cover the event. "Technical difficulties kept the figure from being raised on . . . schedule," reported *Record World*, "but that didn't keep the conference from getting off the ground. Sam took the opportunity to talk about himself, his interests and his plans for the future." He spoke of his songwriting, SAR's young artists, and his own ambitions to travel abroad and create a one-man show. "Closing the meeting with a glance out the window to see how the sign painters were progressing, Sam said, 'I want to be good.'"

He was somewhat less delphic in a late-night meeting with a British reporter at the bar of the Warwick Hotel, where, according to *Melody Maker* correspondent Ray Coleman, he was drinking Bloody Marys and the bartenders all knew him. He was in New York, he said, lighting a menthol-tipped cigarette, "to fix everything up for my two weeks at the Copacabana. . . . I want to envelop another area of entertainment which I haven't exploited to its fullest capacity." In his seven years in the business, he had so far appealed primarily to the young, but now that his fans had grown up, he said, he wanted to "mix the old materials with the new — a very careful blend of songs which I'm working on." He started talking about how he was going to begin introducing "more sophisticated things," but then, before Coleman knew it, "Sam was talking of the British pop invasion of the States.

Times Square, June 18, 1964. *Courtesy of ABKCO*

I asked if he resented it, particularly as he has not had a big hit for some time. . . .

"Resent it? No. The British acts who have made it here have injected that fervour into their music that makes people want to dance. . . . Ever see anybody who digs a record? Bet your life he's tapping his feet.

"I like the Beatles. . . . Know why? Because the things they sing rock. And they're melodic too. You can take the songs they write and sing them solo, as ballads."

Did Sam do that?

"No, but it's an idea," he replied. He prodded my lapel with one hand, gulped his Bloody Mary with the other, and muttered something about making a Beatles song, solo. . . .

"I'm emotional myself," he continued. "You have got to move some emotions to get to know music. If you can move emotions, you're home free. This is where the Beatles are clever. They sell emotion."

At this point the bartender made it clear that he was not interested in selling emotion OR any more drinks. He switched off the lights, and the end of our talk was in total darkness. According to my notebook, which has a Bloody Mary spilled over it to prove it, Sam Cooke wandered out of the darkness saying something like: "Real gospel music has GOT to make a comeback."

He never mentioned to the reporter one of the principal reasons he was in town a full week ahead of his Copa opening. Allen had set up a couple of weekend bookings for him in the Catskills. Sam didn't understand the point of it. Allen kept asking him how the show was going, and he kept telling Allen the show was going great. He had Sammy Davis Jr.'s arranger. Did Allen think Sammy Davis Jr.'s arranger didn't know how to stage a Copa show? He had even gotten Sammy to tape an introduction that they could play every night before he went onstage. But Allen wouldn't leave him alone. And Sam knew Allen well enough by now to realize that he wasn't *going to* leave him alone. So, eventually, he gave in.

Allen, for his part, had no idea, really, what you were supposed to do to prepare for a big club opening. He had never been involved in anything remotely like this before, and he was adamant that he had no inter-

est in interfering with Sam's music. But at the same time he was as concerned as in every other aspect of his life to make sure that everything
was done right. And he was not reassured in the least by Sam's bland
platitudes. So he talked to Buddy Howe, and Buddy said it sounded like
Sam was nervous. Anyway, you always had an out-of-town tryout for a
new act. It was usually just a matter of ironing out a few kinks, and it
would give Sam greater confidence at the opening. So he said, "All right,
where do you do that?" "Well, you go up to the Catskills," Buddy Howe
said.

If Sam was nervous, he certainly didn't show it at the sign-raising
ceremony. And Bobby could detect nothing but eagerness on Sam's part
to get the preliminaries out of the way. They sat around listening to
records on a little portable record player in Sam's suite at the Warwick.
The album that they kept listening to over and over again was
Getz/Gilberto, with the smash bossa nova hit single, "The Girl From
Ipanema" by jazz saxophonist Stan Getz and vocalist Astrud Gilberto.
Bobby had heard the album many times before — Sam and Barbara
were all over it in California. But now all of a sudden Sam asked him
what did he think of the song, just out of the blue. "And I said, 'Oh, that's
nice.' He said, 'Ain't she bad? Listen to this chick. Can you imagine me
doing that? I could dance all around that feel.'" Bobby nodded. He was
only half-listening. Yeah, yeah, he could hear Sam doing that — but what
would be the point? He was just glad Sam was relaxed and feeling good.
There was no doubt they were going to turn the Copa out.

The Piper

BOBBY WOMACK COULD SCARCELY BELIEVE his eyes and ears. He had heard Sam talk about "The Girl From Ipanema" often enough, he had listened to the girl sing it on the record, with Sam singing along behind — but when Sam called it out as their opening number at the Laurels on Sackett Lake, their first Catskills show, he had to turn around and look at Sam twice before he was convinced that the man was serious.

They had rehearsed the show till they knew it backwards and forwards, the new arranger that Sam had gotten from Sammy Davis Jr. left little room for guesswork; in fact, Bobby felt, he hadn't left much room for *Sam,* every time he tried to yodel or do one of his little trademark tricks, he found himself in the middle of some complicated horn part or rhythm arrangement. But now it was as if Sam had just decided to throw all that rehearsing out the window, calling for a song they hadn't even fooled with, let alone worked out an arrangement for. They did the best they could under the circumstances — Clif knew the chords at least, Bobby played off Clif, and June and the new bass player could lock in on almost anything — but it was a disaster by any standard. And things just went downhill from there.

Allen and Jerry Brandt and GAC vice president Buddy Howe, sitting at a front-row table, were equally aghast. "I couldn't believe he did it," said Brandt, Sam's recently deposed William Morris agent, still unoffi-

Allen Klein gives Sam a Rolls-Royce, with J.W. Alexander looking on, June 24, 1964.
Courtesy of ABKCO

cially in business with Allen on any number of other projects but present tonight purely as a fervent fan. "You know, none of us understood what he had in mind, and Sam could never tell you why. It was the strangest thing I've ever seen; he went back to why he bombed at the Copa in the first place, and we were scared to death."

The audience, too, a convention of firemen from the city, grew increasingly restive. There was a buffet outside, and more and more of them started drifting toward the exit with their wives, but Sam refused to break or back down, he just went on with his show. For the first time since Bobby had known him, he failed to connect with his audience. Instead, he just got tighter and tighter, almost openly defiant of the chaos that was erupting all around him, and by the time the set was over, there was almost no one left in the room.

Allen didn't know what to do. He knew how much this meant to Sam — he was scarcely able to acknowledge how much it meant to *him* — and he couldn't figure out where it had all gone wrong. This had been Buddy Howe's idea, but it was *his* act and Sam was embarrassing not just Allen but himself. When Sam came offstage, Allen was waiting for him with a towel, like a fight manager, and like a fight manager, he wiped Sam down as they went back to the dressing room. But then he couldn't restrain himself any longer. "What the fuck were you doing?" he blurted out in that brusque, almost reckless manner that seemed so out of place in a business that was generally carried out with bullshit, bravado, and smooth self-assurance. "You were fucking terrible."

Sam didn't even blink, he just stared at him like ice water. It didn't matter, he said coldly. This wasn't the Copa. Everything would be fine at the Copa. The fuck it would, said Allen, wild-eyed. It was like the Three Stooges, Bobby thought, the silent observer. It would have been funny except that "it was so scary, because Sam was desperate and very scared and I [thought], If he blows the Copa again, he'll commit suicide."

Still, Sam continued to put up a good front. It was the musicians, he said. There was no point in even playing the Raleigh the next night. Allen could see for himself: if tonight had proved one thing, it had proved that without the proper musicians, he couldn't do his show. All right, Allen said, what did he need? Sam just glared at him. Obviously he needed a full horn section to play the arrangements. Fine, Allen said, exasperated now, he would get a full horn section — but Sam was *going to* play the Raleigh. And while they were talking about arrangements, the new arrangements were horrible! All this fancy bullshit only succeeded in making Sam sound like someone else. Who the fuck's idea was it to get Sammy Davis Jr.'s arranger? Why didn't he use his own arranger? Sam just shrugged. Allen could call René Hall if it was so goddamn important, he said. René would probably come if the price was right. The set didn't work, either, Allen said. The material was fine except for that fucking bossa nova, but Sam was losing the audience with the order he was presenting it in. Well, why don't you just make up a set list, then? said Sam with more than a hint of sarcasm. And with that, their colloquy was over. At least, Bobby thought, they hadn't killed each other. But for Allen the issue was more serious than that. They had come this far together. He couldn't let Sam fail.

He and Jerry Brandt stayed up half the night redoing the act but mostly — since there wasn't much to it other than moving songs around on the set list — stewing over the way things had turned out. There was a tense moment early on when Buddy Howe, Jerry's employer at GAC until his defection to William Morris two years earlier, told Allen he didn't want anyone from a rival agency working with his act. But Allen said Jerry was there strictly as a friend, something Buddy, an easygoing guy under most circumstances, could see for himself, and Allen and Jerry scribbled their notes on the back of a menu once Allen had called René and arranged for him to fly in from California on the red-eye that night.

René worked all the next day on revamping the show. The airline had lost his luggage, but he had his arrangements in his briefcase, and he knew what Sam needed anyway. His philosophy of orchestration was simple. "A lot of cats try to show off their arrangements. They think *they're* singing lead. But there's only one lead guy. What you put around him is what makes it really happen." When Allen presented him with the new set list, "I didn't argue [because Allen was paying the bills]. He said, 'I want you to create a first-class show.' So I rewrote everything. *Everything.*" But then he faced the real challenge. Which, as he had recognized all along, was inevitably going to be Sam.

There was no problem with the show itself, Sam protested. The reason it hadn't worked the night before was simply that he had had his gaze set on the Copa, he wasn't thinking about any fucking Laurels. René was polite but firm. "I said, 'If it doesn't make it here, it's going to flop in the Copa, take my word for it.'" Then Sam started complaining that this fucker who called himself his manager was trying to tell him how to sing, and René responded, as calmly as Alex would have in the same situation, that at least the guy wasn't afraid to spend his money, look at the publicity buildup he had given Sam. In the end Sam gave in, as René knew he would, and by the evening, everyone was confident they had a show.

It went off at the Raleigh without a hitch. "The Girl From Ipanema" was gone — they opened with the showbiz staple "The Best Things in Life Are Free," just like they had rehearsed it, and the performance built, as Sam had taught Bobby a performance should always build, "till we started getting it in closer, bringing it all closer to home, and then he started doing [the civil rights folk favorites] 'If I Had a Hammer' and ['This Little Light of Mine'], and everybody was going crazy, and I just kind of [tried to] keep the enthusiasm going." But Bobby was still wide-eyed at the near-mayhem he had witnessed.

Sam and Allen very nearly staged a reenactment on the afternoon of the Copa opening. The musicians were all in the dressing room in the hotel above the club after completing their sound check when Allen barged in and started spouting off about the way Sam was dressed. "I made the mistake of criticizing him in front of the others. I told him I didn't like him in light gray. I wanted him to wear a red jacket — I got the idea from a Harry Belafonte album cover, the way it brought out the skin tones. He said, 'What the fuck do you know in your seersucker suit? My fucking shirt cost more than everything you've got on.'" Bobby watched in disbelief as Charles put Allen out of the dressing room in much the same way that he had evicted the RCA flunky in Atlantic City the year before. Allen didn't see it as a forcible expulsion exactly; in his view, he had assessed the situation early enough to leave under his own steam. But as Jerry Brandt, another witness to the scene, observed, it certainly made Allen uncomfortable, and, given his generally insecure nature, it had to make him uncertain of where he really stood with Sam.

But it didn't stop him from coming back just before the first show. Under other circumstances, he might have chosen to delay his surprise until after the performance, but as things stood, he had no choice but to reveal it now, if only to try to get Sam out of his funky mood. Sam had little interest in talking to him, he didn't even want to *see* him, but Allen let J.W. in on the secret, and Alex helped smooth things over. Allen had a very important guy downstairs that he wanted Sam to meet, J.W. said, and after grumbling about the poor timing of the whole thing, Sam accompanied Alex and Allen down the narrow staircase. When he got to the bottom, he looked around. Where was this guy? he asked Allen. Well, actually, Allen said, he was outside. Sam looked at him skeptically. Outside? Was he fucking crazy? In all this rain?

"I said, 'Do me a favor. It's very important. Do this for me.'" And with that, Allen flung open the door and revealed the Rolls-Royce that he had bought for Sam, with the big red bow that his wife, Betty, had tied around it.

Sam just stood there for a moment, stunned. He had been talking with Allen for months about getting exactly this model Rolls. He knew Allen didn't give a fuck about cars — this was just for him. Allen handed him the keys, and someone snapped a picture, and the smile on Sam's face was all the payoff that Allen needed for the $15,000 he had spent. Afterward, back in the dressing room, Sam took him into the bathroom and said, "You know, you're better than Colonel Parker," and when Allen looked dubious, Sam said, "No, I mean it. Because Elvis is white." Allen didn't say anything; he just gave Sam a hug. It was the kind of emotional moment that he rarely permitted himself, but when they emerged from the bathroom, it was time for Sam to go to work. Now he was really ready for the show.

Sammy Davis Jr.'s voice introduced Sam warmly on tape. "Good evening, everybody. My name is Sammy Davis. I'd like to say, tonight I'm taking the opportunity to introduce to you a cat who's gonna set the town on its ear. He's a good friend, swinging artist, and one of the nicest people I know. So all you first-nighters at the Copacabana, here is the swinging Mr. Sam Cooke." Then René cued the band — the full sixteen-piece Copa Orchestra plus Sam's expanded five-man rhythm section (Sam had hired New York percussionist Sticks Evans for the engagement) — and they were off and running on the agreed-upon set.

It was, as Sam had explained to Bobby, a distinctly white-folks version of his standard show. A ringadingding approach to "Bill Bailey" took the place of "Cupid"; a swinging "Frankie and Johnny" replaced "Chain Gang," barely alluded to on opening night as part of the closing medley, then dropped altogether; instead of the anthemic "Having a Party," Copa patrons got a cheerfully up-tempo version of the new single, "Tennessee Waltz"; and Sam's hoarse, gospelized reinvention of "You Send Me" as preamble to "Bring It On Home to Me" gave way to a delicate linking of the song to "Try a Little Tenderness" and "(I Love You) For Sentimental Reasons," complete with flute obbligato.

But there were similarities as well, as Clif's rock-solid chording provided an underpinning for Bobby's playful leads, the rhythm section, locked in by weeks of demanding rehearsals, found the same driving grooves that would have propelled the more familiar material, and Sam's easy conversational delivery drew in the audience, drew in an entirely *different* audience, in much the same way that he had first wrecked house in all those makeshift storefront churches, with little more than his charm, his confidence, and his extraordinary storytelling ability to put him across.

It was, all in all, an unqualified triumph, even if the critics were not altogether unanimous in their praise. The *New York World-Telegram* opined that "Sam yells a lot but doesn't sing much." *Variety* maintained that "although he did well . . . he didn't quite achieve his aim," and the *New York Times* offered the additional caveat that while "[Mr. Cooke] has dignity, humility and feeling to go with a strong voice, the performance is not by a long shot all good." At the same time, it was remarked that Sam moved "like a panther," looked like "a young Belafonte," and showed "worlds of poise and savvy" and "a zingy, swinging style." But it was left to a female reporter for the Harlem-based *Amsterdam News* to capture the emotional impact for the woman at ringside.

"A dashing, handsome young man," wrote Sara Slack, "sent the women in the audience C-R-A-Z-Y from the moment he opened his mouth until he stopped singing fifty minutes later.

> Wearing black tapered pants set off with a black and white checked shortie Continental jacket, the [onetime] gospel singer sent women into lingering, swooning tizzies when he caressed the mike and began oozing "You Send Me." Coaching the girls back to the present with "Tennessee Waltz," suddenly off came his coat, off came his tie, and off went the ceiling when he began belting out "Twistin' the Night Away." . . . A singer of rare talent, Sam wound up by singing women back to dreamland with "(I Love You) For Sentimental Reasons." Retiring to ear-splitting applause and shaking hands along his exit route, Sam Cooke left them begging, begging and begging for more.

It was, said J.W., who was working the light cues, "almost like a sex act. I said, 'Lighten up, buddy. You got 'em.'" Or as fellow r&b singer Chuck Jackson, who had himself emerged from the gospel world, said of Sam's invariable approach to performance: "He never did get so far into a song that he forgot where he was. He would feel the spirit as much as anybody else, but he was always in control, and women loved it. There was an earnest in Sam, they loved the coolness about him. It's like women say, 'Some men make love, but they're just too fast,' [but] what Sam did just went on and on, [he] could hold out till the end!"

The house was full every night, because Allen and RCA made sure that it would be full, and they even guaranteed a good black representation by giving Crain a bloc of tickets to distribute to some of the social clubs uptown. Sam kept playing with the content and order of the show, but it remained a race-neutral mix of romance, sex, and — ironically — uplifting racial politics, in which, as *Variety* pointed out, "at no time does he make any political references but yet he scores his strongest impact with his long community-sing version of 'If I Had a Hammer,'" the song with which night after night the audience declared its love for "my brother and my sister, all over this world." Sometimes Bobby got so caught up in the show and how Sam worked the glamorous room, that he lost his place in the music. "He'd give me my cue, and everybody would be looking at me, and Sam would say, 'Bobby, give me my motherfucking song.' I said, 'Oh, man, I forgot.' 'Cause I'm watching him, I'm watching the people, you know. He'd say, 'Bobby, you don't drink, you don't smoke. You ain't got no excuse.' But I was just that engrossed."

Allen was no less engrossed. He was there every night, perched on the edge of the stage with a towel and a glass of water. René, for whom some years had passed since his last extended time on the road, was surprised at the number and diversity of Sam's friends and associates. He knew Sam as an urbane man about town, but he was a little taken aback by all the people for whom Sam bought liquor and all the hustlers and lowlifes on the fringes of Sam's world. Perhaps the most surprising visitor, though, was a young film executive in charge of 20th Century Fox's East Coast production department who appeared out of the blue and started talking to Sam about a movie career.

Earl McGrath, a nightclub habitué and music fan who would go on to become a prominent record company executive, was sitting in the back of a taxi at 7:30 in the morning after a night on the town. "I was feeling really terrible, and I looked up, and there was that sign, 'Sam's the Biggest Cooke in Town.' And I thought, God, that guy is so great-looking. And I just loved his work. So I went home and went to sleep, got to the office around noon, and called up Sam's agent at GAC."

He went to see Sam that night and was so impressed that he returned four or five times, with his wife, Camilla, and a group of people from the Fox office. "It was just a magical thing. Sam was wonderful and debonair and generous with the audience, and he made you feel like you were an intimate friend — I think everybody felt that, but he really worked [at] it, too, because he would call me up, and he got to understand what I thought was funny and so forth. He was a very, very sensitive person, one of the nicest people I ever met, and optimistic all the time, but he had a melancholic side that he would just sort of let roll over him. Something would go wrong, and there would be this little tiny pause where you could see him looking at it very carefully, and then, you know, just putting it aside — not out of his mind but just aside — because it was interrupting what he was doing.

"He was a natural, so I said, 'Look, Sam, why don't you do a screen test?' And he was so friendly and so sweet. He said, 'You really think I could do it?' And I arranged to shoot him — I didn't tell anybody, this was just to see how he photographed, and I would ask him a few questions, too — at the Fox studio, over on Ninth Avenue around Fifty-fourth, right after [he finished] his gig at the Copa."

Sam took it all in stride. It was all part of the readjustment of goals, the refurbishing of image that went along with any kind of career change. He was aiming at a different kind of audience now, Sam told a *New York Times* reporter, who evidently assumed that Sam was speaking of a difference based primarily on age, not race, in this instance perhaps fundamentally the same thing. "You know, those old cats," Sam said, falling right in, "they don't go out much. A lot of them are lonely. They *need* records. They need them worse than anybody. I'm going to sell them."

To Don Paulsen, a young freelance reporter and photographer, he mused more expansively on life, art, and the nature of success. His music, he said, consisted of a combination of elements, including blues, gospel, jazz numbers like "The Girl From Ipanema," and country — "every singer draws inadvertently from everything he's heard and liked."

Soul was "the capacity to project a feeling," and rhythm and blues represented "the most fervent sound in pop music." The Beatles had some of that fervor and, above all, real honesty of observation, but they would eventually discover that "once you get [people's attention], you can speak softly." For himself, he had learned that "there's only so much to be gotten out of life. [With success] I have less free time, but it's given me more sense of responsibility. I find I can't do things without thinking about them; it has made me more of an adult [who] can appreciate the various shadings and tones of life." As for future plans: "I want to go to Las Vegas. I'd like to do some movie roles. Someday I'd like to do a Broadway play."

Most of all, he said with the utmost conviction, "I have an intense desire to make all of my audiences happy."

A LLEN HAD ARRANGED for RCA to record the last two nights of the show, something that Joe D'Imperio supported over the strong opposition of his staff. The prevailing opinion in the a&r department was that a live Copa album would never be a good seller for this kind of artist. D'Imperio, however, insisted that what had led him to sign Sam in the first place was his belief that they had in Sam Cooke a pop artist of unlimited crossover potential. It was their own fault, D'Imperio said, if in the past they had ignored that potential because of his color. Now was the time to turn Sam Cooke into the next Belafonte, the next Nat "King" Cole — and selling albums was the place to start.

Al Schmitt, the longtime engineer on Sam's West Coast sessions and now, with the departure of Hugo and Luigi, his official "producer" at RCA, got a much better sound out of the room than Bob Simpson and Tony Salvatore had been able to achieve at the Harlem Square Club a year and a half earlier. That album had yet to come out and didn't appear likely to surface anytime soon, mainly because it had no place in the new scheme of things. It was, to Allen's way of thinking most of all, too much of the image they wanted to get away from, too much of a way of life that Sam wanted to leave behind. Sam in any case was, for the time being, thinking only of the present, and after a decent second show on Tuesday night (from which Al Schmitt planned to use at least the "You Send Me" medley), he put everything he had into the early show on Wednesday, July 8, the final night. What you hear is a summation of one side of the vision that had defined "Sam Cooke" ever since he first switched over to pop. It had been Bumps' prescription for success from the start ("a modern Morton Downey"), in different ways it had been René's and Alex's, and it had been Hugo and Luigi's, in full collusion with his own. The show ended with a medley of "Amen" (recently featured in the Sidney Poitier vehicle *Lilies of the Field*) and "This Little Light of Mine," his father's favorite song, followed by a full-throated big-finish version of Bob Dylan's "Blowin' in the Wind." And when he encored with Patti Page's "Tennessee Waltz," he completed the process, putting the crowd away with songs with which he was able to identify but, more important, which they could also claim as their own. It was not intended as a performance for the ages; as the *New York Times* critic wrote about another number in his Copa repertoire, "The way Mr. Cooke sings [it], a person who does not understand English would assume that it was a song about a little girl hippity-hopping down to the candy store to buy herself a lollipop." But the effect was exactly what he intended, Bobby and Clif and June were playing their asses off, and clearly no one in the audience that night could fail to be entranced by the sound of Sam's voice and the pure pleasure he found in the very act of communication. Patti Page wouldn't recognize her own song, Sam declared with a chuckle over the introductory vamp. And he was right.

Immediately after the last show, Jules Podell, the gruff Copa manager, presented Sam with the prized Copa cuff links and bonnet. The following day he sent a letter to Sam care of Allen Klein Associates, letting the performer know that he had just completed a deal with GAC to bring him back to the Copa for the next two years, and Allen took out a full-page ad in *Variety* two weeks later, highlighting a performance shot of Sam, Podell's letter, and a "Thank You, Mr. Podell" above the legend, "Direction: Tracey, Ltd."

Sam stayed in New York for a few more days, did his preliminary screen test for Earl McGrath, and purely by accident ran into Jess Rand, whose group, the Lettermen, was about to open at the Latin Quarter the following week. Jess was checking into the Warwick, to which he had introduced Sam six years earlier, and the desk clerk told him his client, Mr. Cooke, was in the bar. "Sam was drinking Manhattans, and I was drinking Scotch on the rocks. He said, 'Come on upstairs.' So I went to his room, and he started telling me about the Rolls-Royce. At that time, there was no building across the street, there was this half-empty lot, and the hotel used to park cars there, and he pointed out the Rolls to me.

I said, 'Why would anyone, especially a bookkeeper, just give you a car [like that]?' He said, 'No, he gave me that as a present.' I said, 'You own the car? You got the pink slip? It just doesn't make sense.' He gave me a look, like, 'Well, you're just mad,' and he smiled at me. You know, it's funny, he walked out on the Soul Stirrers, he walked out on William Morris, he walked out on me. And yet he just wanted everyone to like him."

H E WAS SCHEDULED TO OPEN at Club Harlem in Atlantic City in two weeks, but first he had business to take care of on the Coast. He conducted a Soul Stirrers session on the twentieth, came to a reluctant final decision with Alex to let the Sims Twins and Johnnie Morisette go, and committed to a brief tour with the Valentinos, in part to make up to them for the disappointment of having had their hit taken away from them.

"It's All Over Now" had entered the pop charts at the end of June but dropped off again two weeks later when a cover version by a new English group called the Rolling Stones was released. The Rolling Stones had heard the single at the beginning of June while paying a visit to New York DJ Murray the K ("the Fifth Beatle") at the start of their first American tour. Murray had gotten the record from Pete Bennett, Allen's independent promo guy, who was really pushing it in the pop market. The Rolling Stones picked up on the number right away. As their then twenty-year-old manager, Andrew Loog Oldham, said, "They were like an airplane without a parachute at that time. They hadn't mastered the writing of their own material, and [the song] really fit them like a glove" — and they recorded the song the following week at the Chess studio in Chicago. The record was rush-released by both their British and American labels, hitting the streets in England with an advance order of 150,000 on June 26, the day before the Valentinos debuted on the American pop charts.

The Womacks could scarcely believe it. Once again they had been betrayed by their brother's employer and hero, Sam. Bobby was no more sanguine about the situation. To Bobby, the Rolling Stones were a joke. "I kept saying to Sam, 'This guy [Mick Jagger] ain't no singer.' Because I'm comparing him to a real singer, like Archie Brownlee or June Cheeks. But Sam was hearing something completely different. He said, 'I won't see it, but you'll see it down the line. These guys are gonna change the industry.' I said, 'Let them get their own songs. They mean nothing to me.' But he said, 'No, Bobby, you don't understand what I'm saying. This song is gonna take you — you'll be part of history. You'll go over to England, man —' he [was] laughing, I *knowed* he was joking — 'they'll be knocking down doors to get to you.' But he was right, man. He was always in the future."

Even Alex didn't fully comprehend it at first. He knew they would all make money off the publishing — he was pretty sure Bobby would be happy when he got his first songwriter's check — but he didn't see the change coming like Sam did. As Bobby finally came to understand it: "Sam was just saying it was something new getting ready to happen in the business, and his music was too adult to be caught up in it, but ours was just —. He said, 'You all fit.' He said, 'If you stay with the two guitars and the long hair, you guys ought to be the first to get in.'"

S AM OPENED AT THE CLUB HARLEM on July 23, the same day that Allen and Joe D'Imperio signed an agreement on behalf of Tracey Ltd. and RCA authorizing the use of "A Change Is Gonna Come" on an album entitled *The Stars Salute Dr. Martin Luther King*. The stars included Louis Armstrong, Count Basie, Harry Belafonte, Nat "King" Cole, Brook Benton, Ray Charles, Lena Horne, Sammy Davis Jr., and Frank Sinatra, and all proceeds were to be earmarked for the Southern Christian Leadership Conference. Riots had broken out in Harlem the weekend before the Atlantic City opening, and racial strife continued to erupt throughout the week in one city after another along the East Coast. Race could not fail to be far from any thinking person's mind, as Lyndon Johnson signed the first comprehensive federal civil rights legislation in nearly a century on July 2 even as the search continued for the three civil rights workers who had disappeared at the start of the Mississippi voter-registration project dubbed Freedom Summer. "I now believe I know how it felt to be a Jew in Hitler's Germany," wrote black baseball pioneer Jackie Robinson, an Eisenhower Republican, of the recent Republican Convention that had nominated Barry Goldwater, while the Impressions' "Keep On Pushin'," written by Curtis Mayfield, the group's great falsetto lead, who had gone to school on Sam and the Soul Stirrers, was climbing the pop charts. "I can't stop now," Mayfield sang with a purity of tone that left no doubt as to where the singer or the Movement stood. And as far as that "great big stone wall" of prejudice that blocked his way, "I've got my pride / And I'll move it all aside / And I'll keep on pushing." When a reporter for the *Atlantic City Press* asked Sam if he was surprised at the increasingly volatile political atmosphere, he said he was only surprised "that the American public failed to anticipate it." After all, discrimination existed on every level of society. He continued to experience it himself. Then, perhaps as a sop to his "older" audience, he declared, "It's getting better. . . . Love will conquer violence."

It was the same show with virtually the same repertoire as he had presented at the Copa (his "hootenanny" treatment of "If I Had a Hammer" remained the highlight), but here the audience was looser, blacker, and, when Sam asked them to join in, they really had something to contribute. Sam told Clif and June to invite their families, and he had Charles chauffeur Philadelphia DJ Georgie Woods down to Atlantic City in the Rolls. The highlight of the week was always the 6:00 A.M. "Breakfast Show" on Sunday, which every entertainer and player in town, black or white, generally attended after all the other clubs had closed. Sam knocked out the elegantly dressed Sunday-morning crowd, eating their breakfast of grits and wings, but he did something else besides. "They came out of the kitchen," said Lloyd Price, who was playing the Riptide in nearby Wildwood, "the waiters, the waitresses, even the girls in the line, and he stood there with that big bright smile, took his coat off, and he *rocked* — you could actually feel the building shaking. He didn't have to dance, he didn't have no tricks — you know, we all had to have tricks — he just did the same thing he did in the church, and by the time he finished, I don't think there was a person sitting down in the room. I'd seen Sammy Davis there, I'd seen Billy Daniels, but this was one of the greatest events I'd ever seen in my life. I [thought], You know something? I must be doing something wrong."

Whenever he opened his mouth onstage, Sam told an informal press conference of local newspaper reporters midway through the two-week run, he was trying "to grab hold of someone's heart." He was, wrote Paul Learn in the *Atlantic City Press*, "more alive than most people. To him, jokes are funnier, the music more enchanting, the leaves on the trees more in bloom."

Like his friend Cassius Clay, the reporter wrote, "Cooke is a healthy young man who still squirms in his chair [and] will perch cross-legged on a divan, and when he moves, his body flows with tiger grace. He's happy as a boy pushing skyward on a swing."

On the subject of Cassius:

"He beat [Liston] once, and he'll beat him again. And do you know why? Because he makes Liston afraid of him."

Cooke bounced out of his chair to illustrate how Cassius scared the big lumbering Liston into losing.

"Liston has just showed up for the fight, see?" said Cooke in recounting the day of Clay's glory. "Cassius comes over to him, and he puts his head real close to Sonny's, and he says, 'I didn't think you were going to show up. I'm sure glad to see you. You're mine tonight, baby.'"

Cooke put his face close to a reporter's head and grinned fiendishly.

"That's how he scared Liston," said the . . . singer.

He added that it accounts in part for his [own] ability to communicate with his audience.

"I have no doubts about myself," he concluded. "I have no fear. Doubt will kill you. Fear will kill you. The worst enemies are doubt and fear."

H E SHOWED LITTLE EVIDENCE of either doubt or fear in the full-scale screen test that immediately followed the Atlantic City engagement. There had been universal enthusiasm at Fox about the way he photographed in the preliminary shoot, so Earl McGrath set up a dramatic audition in which Sam traded lines from a Clifford Odets play with an experienced Broadway actor. He acquitted himself well in a five-minute scene that focused, like all of Odets' best work, on issues of social justice. What impressed Earl most, though, was how comfortable Sam seemed with the camera. He was eating an apple in his scene and, McGrath noticed, got a piece stuck on his upper lip. Earl had seen veteran actors thrown by less, but Sam just reached up lazily with his tongue and flicked the apple away, as if it were just another small dramatic "bit" in his delineation of the character.

Sam took Earl and his wife up to Harlem while he was still in town, waving off any concerns they might have about the recent rioting and introducing them to the DJ Fat Jack Walker, who made them a big soul-food dinner. They went to a few bars, and everywhere they went, Sam was greeted like a long-lost friend. It was, Earl later came to think, a kind of lesson. "Sam was a very optimistic person, and when those riots happened, he was just saying, 'Everything's going to be all right.'" At the same time, Earl realized, he wasn't simply going to come right out and say it. "By taking us up to Harlem, he was *showing* us without proselytizing. He was pointing [us] in that direction, so the thoughts would be [our] own."

With Al Schmitt still in New York mixing the Copa tapes, Sam scheduled a double session at RCA's Twenty-fourth Street studios on the night of August 7. For the first session, from eight to eleven, he got a hot new arranger, Torrie Zito, who specialized in complicated string arrangements, to write a delicate, deliberately bossa nova–ized orchestral treatment of "I'm in the Mood For Love," the universal standard with which Louis Armstrong had had one of his biggest popular hits in the thirties. None of Sam's musicians played with the twenty-seven-piece ensemble, not even Clif, and if in the end the song came off as more mannered than successful, it was striking for its delicate instrumental voicings and bold vocal coloration.

The eleven o'clock to two A.M. session, with only his own rhythm section to accompany him, focused on almost as unlikely a choice. "He's a Cousin of Mine" had originated with a 1906 Broadway musical, *Marrying Mary*, written by two black songwriters, Chris Smith and Cecil Mack, and popularized by Bert Williams, the greatest of all the Negro blackface comedians and vaudevillians. Sam had first heard the song among the piano rolls, cylinder recordings, and old 78s in the collection of his and L.C.'s longtime friend the DJ Magnificent Montague. "He would go through my piano rolls," Montague said. "I have the original sheet music of 'Carry Me Back to Old Virginny' and 'In the Evening By the Moonlight,' so he knew that they were written by James Bland — a black man. He found out that most of your Tin Pan Alley hits were written by blacks. And he wanted to do an album."

He appeared, in fact, to be finally making a start at the program he had announced the previous year of "hit[ting] the trail on behalf of Negro writers . . . who are and have been idling on the shelf," but he didn't bother to clue in the band, who, with the possible exception of Clif, knew nothing of the origin of the song. Bobby had no idea what to make of it musically ("Play the guitar like a banjo," Sam said to him), but Sam had him convinced that the story — with its episodic narrative about talking your way out of a compromising situation by suggesting that the man or woman you happened to be with was actually your cousin — was a true one. "He was saying that this girl really was a cousin, and he wanted to fuck her," declared Bobby, who never noticed that Sam had reversed the storyline but played his guitar part persuasively nonetheless. The whole rhythm section acquitted itself admirably — it was the first time in all the years they had been together that June had played with Sam in the studio, and the addition of Sticks Evans on bongos only added to the eccentric flavor — as Sam put the song across with a sly wit and genuine relish that almost allowed it to be perceived as a contemporary number, despite its hoary origins.

He spent nearly the entire three-hour session on this one simple song, then gave Bobby an even odder assignment, with an insistent thick-toned lead on a new number called "The Piper," for which he had provided the words and melody of a children's song. "Up and down and through the town," Sam sang with curious wistfulness, "The piper plays today / Doors and windows open wide / To greet him on his way.

> *He's dressed all up*
> *In little boots*
> *And green and yellow clothes*
> *And when he plays his little heart*
> *Away your trouble goes*
>
> *Hi, everybody, I didn't come to stay*
> *I just came to let you know*
> *The piper's on his way*
>
> *Up and down and through the town*
> *The piper plays today*
> *Doors and windows open wide*
> *To greet him on his way*
>
> *Hi, everybody, I didn't come to stay*
> *I just came to let you know*
> *The piper's on his way*

Did he imagine himself as the Pied Piper? If so, he had clearly not recognized the implications of the fairy tale. Was it a song for Tracey and Linda, or was it a hastily dashed-off sketch of the uncomplicated role he would have liked to imagine for himself in the world, something like J. D. Salinger's Holden Caulfield, an incorruptible guardian and champion of innocence? Whatever his intentions, the song amounted to little more than a rough demo, the suggestion of another song it could only be imagined he might someday come to write. The whole double session, in fact, could scarcely be viewed as anything more than an experiment in diversity, but neither Sam nor his new a&r man was fazed in the least. "What was so great about Sam," said Al Schmitt, "was that he was willing to try anything. He had total control, but he was open to everything. I knew we were going to come out with something [that would] knock everybody on their ears."

In this case, they had to wait two weeks for all the elements to coalesce. Sam had returned to California by this time after headlining a big outdoor show, *Blues Under the Stars,* at Wrigley Field in Chicago on August 15. The show drew forty-five thousand people and included everyone from Muddy Waters, Buddy Guy, and Etta James to Motown stars Marvin Gaye and Little Stevie Wonder, but it was Sam who really incited the crowd, and, with Charles already en route to California in the Rolls, it was left to Duck to save him from the mob that broke through security lines and surged around him happily onstage. The Muslims pursued him no less ardently, as Cassius Clay and his wife, Sonji, who had just been married in Gary, Indiana, the day before, showed up with a large retinue of Black Muslims led by his new manager, Herbert Muhammad, the Honorable Elijah Muhammad's son. They were all over Sam, said his brother L.C., hustling his ass and telling him everything the Nation of Islam had done for the champ. "You didn't do nothing for Ali," Sam said indignantly. "Ali did for Ali, just like I'm doing for Sam. You wouldn't even be talking to me if I wasn't Sam Cooke." And with that, he turned his attention back to Ali and his beautiful new bride, a sophisticated twenty-seven-year-old woman of the world whom Sam knew from the clubs but who, after her introduction to Ali by Herbert Muhammad and their whirlwind romance that summer, had announced her intention to convert to Islam. "There are two types of artists, artists and con artists," Sam told Bobby and left little doubt as to which category he believed the official hierarchy of the Black Muslims belonged.

He called a session in Los Angeles five days later, once again with his own band, once again, surprisingly, to record a single song. The song was one he had given to the Sims Twins nearly two years earlier, a typical Sam Cooke composition built around a familiar phrase and then given a distinctive twist — but in the Sims' version, the song, "That's Where It's At," achieved none of the poignancy that Sam had imagined for it. Now, spurred on perhaps by the downhome flavor of the Chicago blues festival, and pricked no doubt by the rise of what was now widely referred to as "soul music," the strong gospel-based sound that had started to dominate the charts, he set out to create what could be taken almost as a template for that sound. "You've got to go back to what you know," he had told Don Covay, one of the most influential of the young soul songwriters, whose first big hit on his own, "Mercy, Mercy," had just been released. He had offered similar advice to Otis Redding and Solomon Burke, whose music reflected the same explicit embrace of a tradition that had long been represented, in different ways, by Sam, Ray Charles, Jackie Wilson, Clyde McPhatter, and James Brown — but never so explicitly as part of a "movement," never so unapologetically as an affirmation of identity. "Write about what you know, write about what you've experienced, write about what you observe," he told them. "Write about natural things, you've got to come out of the future and get back to the past, to what you knew when you were a little kid." Most important of all, he said over and over again with what each one took to be the fervor of true belief, "All you gotta do is be yourself."

That is what he now set out to do. Where the Sims Twins had given the song a bright, bouncy feel, Sam at first took it almost at a crawl, with a small four-piece horn section providing a steady choral-like backdrop, and Bobby's tremolo-touched lead providing more than a suggestion of the gospel sound. It didn't go smoothly at first. Sam's voice was a little raw, the horns couldn't get the off-kilter feel he was looking for, and he expressed uncharacteristic irritation at the rhythm section for rushing him ("They backwards to what I'm singing," he declared. "That's why I'm annoyed"). Most of all, though, he was frustrated at not being able to achieve the objective he had set for himself: the communication of unfiltered emotion. Finally, on the fourteenth take, it all began to come together as Bobby moved to a higher register and the band, at Sam's direction, picked up the tempo a little. The song remained as raw as Sam intended it, with the horns capturing some of the sweet-and-sour dissonance of a New Orleans marching band, and the drag of the tempo against intentionally ambiguous lyrics ("Your world turned upside down / You making not a sound / No one else around / That's where it's at") becoming a kind of implicit statement about mortality and the passage of time.

He continued for another twenty-four takes, proving once again his contention that the simplest effects were achieved only with the most arduous application of effort. Here arduousness yielded to almost painful deliberation, as he bore down for six more takes to create a ragged vocal overdub, seemingly spontaneous and out of synch, that suggested profound regret in the midst of romantic celebration. "Your heart beating fast," he sang, "You're knowing that time will pass / But hoping that it'll last" — and then the song's title, the last line of each verse and the single line of each chorus, providing a melancholy reminder, against the explicit manner in which the song would surely be taken, that this is all there is — this is how fragile and evanescent are our pleasures.

> You say, "It's time to go"
> And she says, "Yes, I know
> But just stay one minute more"
> That's where it's at

The chorus took it out, triple-, quadruple-tracked with only Sam's ironic laugh and a "pretty baby" thrown in to punctuate the fragmented reading of the single line, as the horns provided a soft pillow for vocals and guitar. It was as if in one moment Sam had summed up an entire chapter in his life and then, regretfully, made up his mind to move on. For at that moment, he knew it was time to go, even as he sought to linger for just one minute more.

2 | THE SHADOW WORLD

It changes. A lot of things change. Money is popping, and everything is happening, and it's hard to separate the difference. Everybody want a

*piece of the pie: you can spread it everywhere and have nothing. And
then you just like you were. You're slaving.*

— Sam to Bobby Womack, 1964

T HE VALENTINOS KEPT AFTER SAM about their upcoming session
all during their two-week tour together, which was billed as "Sam
Cooke and His Revue, Featuring the Valentinos." They wanted a full horn
section in the studio, just like all the other SAR acts got, and nothing Sam
said could dissuade them. The horns would just get in the way carrying
the background parts, Sam said. If they stuck with what they had, they
could compete with some of those new English groups like the Animals.
The Animals? Bobby said. He hated the fucking Animals, whose "House
of the Rising Sun," a gloomy minor-key version of the American folk
song, was currently number one on the pop charts. They were just another one of those English groups that couldn't sing. But Sam told him
he was going to have to lower his musical standards. He said, "Listen to
what the song is saying. It sounds like a haunted house." He said what
people were looking for was no more, and no less, than *communication;*
it wasn't a question of outsinging the other fellow anymore, like in the
gospel days, it was all about getting your message across. More and more
writers from behind the scenes were becoming artists, he told Bobby,
because "they don't sound as good, but the people believe them more."
And *that* was what was going to lead to the revolution that he saw coming: a day when the marketplace wouldn't distinguish between black
and white.

Sometimes, Bobby thought, Sam might have been better off if he
could have listened to his own advice. Three days before the Valentinos'
session, on September 16, he appeared on the premiere episode of
Shindig!, the first prime-time weekly show devoted to rock 'n' roll. He was
co-headliner with the Everly Brothers, and his appearance was widely
touted in the trades ("The Negro beat & blues singer . . . has rarely been
seen on network TV," *Variety* reported in an access of well-intentioned
enthusiasm), but rather than take advantage of the opportunity, he chose
to represent himself with a weird mélange of styles. While folk singers
Jackie and Gayle featured Sister Rosetta Tharpe's "Up Above My Head"
in their opening medley, and the rapidly rising white West Coast duo
who called themselves the Righteous Brothers showcased their own

black gospel sound, Sam sang two selections from his new supper-club fare, "Tennessee Waltz" and "Blowin' in the Wind," as the *Shindig!* Dancers, an outlandish collection of neatly scrubbed go-go girls clearly designed to appeal to a mainstream audience, pranced and ponied and, for the Dylan number, sedately mimicked ecstatic abandon. Sam's practiced gestures only enhanced the incongruity, particularly on "Blowin' in the Wind," as his right hand trailed off to show the way a cannonball might slide, his left fluttered to illustrate the song's central metaphor in a manner that appeared almost self-satirizing and certainly contradicted his heartfelt advice to Bobby to focus on words and message alone.

It was only with the show's closing number, an Everly Brothers' version of Little Richard's "Lucille" with the entire cast assembled onstage and the credits rolling, that Sam got untracked. The Everlys are standing alone at the mike, wailing away in harmony, when Sam comes trotting out with his guitar, finds a place in between the two brothers, and interjects some of the gospel fervor that was so conspicuously missing from his own performance. It is a curious moment, as Sam, ever watchful, seems willing to reveal this side of himself only as a kind of afterthought, but none of the reviewers seemed to notice, and Sam was already on to other things.

The tryout that Earl McGrath had promised him for an upcoming Twentieth Century Fox picture was scheduled for the week of October 5, and he and Alex flew into New York on the weekend, within hours of the birth of Alex's daughter, Adrienne. Sam read a scene from a recent Sidney Poitier film, taking on the role that Sidney had played with all of his customary aplomb. Earl was so confident that Sam would get the part that he had stills shot and directed the legal department to draw up a contract.

Sam met with Allen while he was in New York to discuss the immediate future. He was still pissed off about the new single release. He had wanted to put out "Yeah Man," the litany of dances set to the Valentinos' distinctive beat that he had recorded in March, but Allen had hated it. In fact, violating one of his own cardinal rules for managing — not for the first time, and not by just a little — he told Sam it was the worst fucking song he had ever heard in his entire life. "What the fuck do you know?" Sam shot back. It was the kind of stripped-down, simplified number he was convinced the kids would go for. But in the end he had allowed himself to be swayed by Allen's opinion, and now the single they had released, "Cousin of Mine," which Allen had insisted was a cute little song that they could sell pop, had shipped fewer copies than any single Sam had put out in three years, and they had thrown away "That's Where It's At" on the B-side.

It burned Sam up. He *knew* "Yeah Man" would have been a hit, but Allen had been right about so many other things, he told Alex, and the thing about it was, the fucker wouldn't back down, even if you put a gun to his head. Sam seemed to take Allen's obstinacy as a kind of challenge, he appeared to believe that if he could impress Allen, the whole world would be impressed. "That motherfucker doesn't tell me what I want to hear," he told Clif. "He tells me what I need to hear."

So far, almost everything Allen had promised had come true. The second $100,000 of Sam's $450,000 advance from RCA was scheduled to arrive on October 15, the *Live at the Copa* album was due out any day, and Allen reassured him that his Christmas booking at the Casanova Room at Miami's chi-chi Deauville Hotel was practically all set. Allen himself was off to England to make a deal with Mickie Most, the twenty-six-year-old manager and producer of the Animals, Herman's Hermits, and the Nashville Teens, the three groups that, after the Beatles and the Dave Clark Five (with whom Allen already had a deal), had dominated the British charts all fall. Allen was ready to guarantee a million dollars in front money for Most in exchange for a percentage of Most's management commission on all of his acts and, ultimately, ownership of the masters. He worried that Sam would be jealous, but Sam had neither the time nor the inclination. The question was no longer one entirely of theft or cooptation; Sam had long since come to recognize that these British groups were opening up another market for his music. Allen had told him that the Beatles wanted him on their show; the Rolling Stones' success with Bobby's song was bringing in money to Bobby and Kags. Allen could build an empire of his own as far as Sam was concerned, as long as he kept his deal with Sam front and center.

But he was still pissed off about "Yeah Man."

THERE WAS NO TIME to dwell on it, though, because, by the next week, Allen was in England, and Sam was out on tour with Jackie Wilson on what he had come to view as his valedictory to the whole Supersonic r&b world. It was billed, for once with little sense of hyperbole, as "The Greatest Show of the Year" and, occasionally, as "The Biggest Show Ever."

It included the Valentinos, the Upsetters, Hank Ballard and the Midnighters, Jimmy Hughes, Mitty Collier, and perennial Supersonic MC Gorgeous George with his own "orchestra," consisting of the drummer from the Royal Peacock and a flashy young guitarist he had picked up in Nashville and worked with off and on for the past year.

From the start, it was an incendiary combination. Every one of the supporting acts was capable of eliciting oohs and ahs from the crowd, but it was the two stars of the show that everyone came to see. They had not been out together since their original Supersonic tour in the spring of 1959, when Sam's insistence on closing the show, not to mention Jackie's spectacular showmanship and a recalcitrant band, had sabotaged both Sam's performance and his pride in a way that had taken a long time to get over. Now, with a polished rhythm section of his own and the crowd-pleasing theatricality of the Upsetters, Sam felt confident not only of his abilities but of his capacity to fuck with Jackie's head, if necessary, just like Cassius had fucked with Sonny Liston.

They opened in Mobile, and once again billing was a subject of contention, but this time, Alex said, he and Sam came prepared. "We had a clause in the contract about closing the show, and the very first night, Sam killed them, he just destroyed the house. So Johnny Roberts [Jackie's burly road manager, who had started out as an enforcer for the New York Mob] came up to me and said, 'What about Sam opening one night and Jackie another?' I said, 'Okay.' He said, 'Let's talk to Sam.' I said, 'You don't have to talk to Sam. Trust me.' So the next night in Knoxville Sam opened, and he just destroyed them, and Jackie came on, and after about three songs they started leaving. I went to the dressing room and [busted out] laughing. I said, 'Sam, they dismissing themselves.'"

Night after night it was the same. Jackie tried every trick in the book, J.W. said. "He would drag it out. He would have all the broads come up and kiss him." He would take off his shirt, work himself into a frenzy, do the splits, lie down on the edge of the stage. But then Sam would come out, J.W. said with relish, and "he would put the whip to them." By the time they reached Charlotte, Jackie was ready to hang out the white flag. "Man, you're killing me," he said to Sam. "You got me coughing up blood. What the fuck did you do?"

What made it different from the earlier tour was that Jackie seemed to finally come to an acceptance of his role in the new order of things. "Sam started singing million-seller after million-seller on my ass. I couldn't get over that," he told his own entourage. They were not at all alike. "Jackie was a party freak," said Hank Ballard, something of a party freak himself. "Sam didn't hang out too much. He would just get him a girl and a bottle and go to the room somewhere and freak out [himself]!" Jackie was "street," where Sam was reflective, Jackie had accepted Mafia "ownership" in exchange for immediate rewards, while Sam had always proudly asserted independence and self-control. Where they connected was onstage, where each made the other reach down for "that other thing." What finally won Jackie over was Sam himself. "Sam wasn't a jealous kind of fellow at all," he would later confide to L.C. "He always wanted to see you do good. I never could understand that, because I wanted to see the other guy mess up. But Sam just wanted to see you do your best." On the other hand, not even J.W. believed that Jackie was going to be subdued by either competition or kindness for long.

Over and over again, they topped each other — and themselves. In Richmond, toward the end of the tour, they played 7:30 and 10:00 P.M. shows at the thirty-two-hundred-seat Mosque Theater, with Sam closing the first half of the early show and the audience screaming for more. But then Jackie came out to close the second half, recalled Alan Leeds, an eighteen-year-old white college freshman who had just started deejaying on the local black radio station and would go on to become James Brown's longtime road manager, "and by the middle of his set, he was rolling across the lip of the stage, and women were pawing him to a pulp. He finished the show with the house lights up and the audience standing in the aisles, on their seats, and crowding the orchestra pit beneath the front of the stage [in] pandemonium."

To Alan Leeds and his friends, that was it, there was no way for Sam to beat that, but when, after another explosive set by Jackie, Sam closed the second show, he destroyed the audience with a medley of his hits, "then the band struck the intro to 'Twistin' the Night Away,' and without resorting to disrobing or even teasing the front rows too obviously, Sam managed to attract as many of the females in the audience as could possibly mount the stage. They tore *his* shirt off and God knows what else. The house lights went up, and local security pulled the curtain and prematurely ended the show. The last vision I had of Sam, he was being escorted backstage by his road manager and a bodyguard; his walk still seemed casual, and his face read somewhere between a smile and a knowing laugh."

For weeks afterward, Leeds and his friends were still talking about what they had witnessed. It had all the finality of the climactic game of a seven-game World Series, but what they failed to understand at the time, Leeds would later come to realize, was that the same thing was going on every night of the week — and sometimes, as in Richmond, twice a night. It was a cataclysmic experience that took place on an earthly plane, an earthly plane that required bills to be paid, payrolls to be met, and where, even at $1,500 a night and a percentage of the gate, you could do little more in the long run than make ends meet. It was not a world Sam was going to be sorry to leave behind. And yet it still thrilled him to be able to harness all that energy, it was like an electric current passing back and forth between him and every single member of the audience, as they sang his lines back to him amid all the clamor and celebration. It amazed him sometimes, the difference you could make in people's lives, if only for a moment, if only for a night. It was like the circus coming to town.

G ORGEOUS GEORGE WAS, AS USUAL, in charge of the after-show. The way it worked, there was always one club in town tied in with the promotion, and it was the MC's job to put out the word that the stars of the show would be there, so hold on to your ticket stubs, ladies and gentlemen, for reduced-priced admission. "That was my side hustle. Usually the man would slip me a hundred bucks to announce and didn't nobody know. You do that five, six nights a week — that's good money, man, 'cause the money I was making as MC I could put in my watch pocket. I would just tell [all the performers], 'Look, we ain't eat no fresh food except them sandwiches and stuff we been buying. And this man say he gonna have some barbecue and corn on the cob and chitlins.' So they say, 'Where is that, George?' And I say, 'He gonna send for us.' And when the bus pull up beside the club, that place be jammed."

In Greensboro, though, George slipped up. The promoter approached him at the Coliseum to propose the usual modest deal, but George, knowing that the Carlotta Club could seat up to fifteen hundred, held out for $150 up front plus a percentage of the door. George rode over with Sam and Jackie and was sitting in between the two of them when they pulled up in front of the club and found a line stretching around the block. "Then this big old greasy cat who was the manager come out and say, 'You can't hardly get in. But I'm gonna arrange for you and Sam and Jackie to come in the side.' And then he reach in his pocket and say, 'George, here's your money.' And he gave me a roll, man, all these

Gorgeous George onstage. *Courtesy of Gorgeous George*

twenties and wrinkled fives and ones, and Sam look at Jackie and Jackie look at Sam, and they caught me by the neck and said, 'Boy, you one smart little nigger. We ain't going in, motherfucker, unless we get half.' I laughed so hard, and they was laughing, too. But from then on, we split the money."

There was usually a band at the club, and everybody from the show did a song or two, but the after-party gave George a chance to shine, with his own guitarist backing him, who turned out to be the same kid Sam had met with Lithofayne Pridgon the previous year when he was in New York looking for a gig. George had run into the kid, a goofball from Seattle named Jimmy Hendrix, while passing through Nashville on one of the Supersonic package tours. Jimmy was playing at the Club Baron with a group called the King Kasuals, whom he had hooked up with after mustering out of the army in nearby Fort Campbell in the summer of 1962. George saw the advantage of getting someone to play behind him on the show for practically nothing and got the tour manager, Henry Nash, to take the kid on the bus as a kind of all-purpose factotum. Jimmy had continued to bounce around between New York and Nashville ever since, doing a little recording and touring with the Isley Brothers and joining George on various Supersonic tours over the past year. He was shy and reserved and seemed standoffish, which had not earned him a lot of popularity on the present show. In fact, he was very quiet, except in his eccentric dress (which had earned him the puzzled scorn of all the sharp jitterbugs on the bus as "some kind of beatnik nigger") and onstage, where he was so insistently flamboyant that George one night was prompted to declare, "Next time I catch you with that guitar in your mouth, you gonna eat it. It's my motherfucking show." No one was more put off by his unconventionality than the Womack brothers, who seemed to take his youthful naïveté, impressionable manner, and an unorthodox left-handed playing style that could have been plagiarized from their own as a personal challenge. One time Harry, the bass-playing brother, missed his money and immediately pointed the finger at Jimmy. "Look at that beatnik," he said, "he ain't got no money, he stole it." "Well, you don't know that," his brothers said, but Harry insisted that there was no doubt as to who was the culprit, he could tell just by the way Jimmy was looking at him, and later that night, when Jimmy was asleep, he threw his guitar out the bus window.

In St. Louis Jackie Wilson was arrested after first trying to get away by leaping out of a second-floor window while the rest of the troupe joined Sam onstage for the show finale. Everyone thought it was because of a woman, but actually it was a default on a $2,200 judgment that went back to Jackie's failure to show up for a club date in 1959. A large crowd watched him jump from the ledge outside his dressing room and get picked up by the police as soon as he started to run away, but everyone on the show would later recall either that Sam walked him down the aisle and out the door, or that Sam successfully fooled the cops into thinking *he* was Jackie by going out onstage and singing all of Jackie's hits, until Jackie was able to make his escape. In yet another variation of the story, all the performers joined hands to form a human shield and prevent the police from getting their hands on Jackie. But in every version Jackie got away scot-free. Which was understandable enough, given that he rejoined them in Nashville the following night after Henry Wynn posted $3,000 bond.

They were in Memphis on Election Day to play an integrated Ellis Auditorium, the same hall where Sam and Clyde McPhatter had refused to perform three years earlier because of its segregated seating policy.

Sam got a call on the afternoon of the show from popular Memphis DJ George Klein, requesting him to appear on Klein's new Dick Clark–styled TV *Talent Party,* on which guest stars lip-synched their hits. Sam was glad to oblige; Wink Martindale, an ex-Memphian and prominent West Coast DJ, had told him that George was a good guy, and a close friend of Elvis Presley besides. Sam got Jackie to do the show, too, and as he and George drove to the station together, he surprised the Memphis DJ by calling attention to various points of local interest along the way. How in the world had he gotten to know the city so well in such a short period of time? George asked. Sam shrugged. He had lived here for six months with the spiritual group he had been with before joining the Soul Stirrers, he said, as if it were a matter of common knowledge. Then he expressed admiration for George's sharp new Beatle boots, and George got his size and promised to send him a pair.

When they arrived at the studio, for some reason George asked Sam to do "Everybody Loves to Cha Cha Cha," maybe because Sam's 1959 hit remained a big Memphis favorite, maybe just because the station happened to have a copy of the record. Sam was running through the song, doing his best to match up the miming of words and gestures to recorded sound while George and Jackie watched. George couldn't help but notice that Jackie was softly singing along, and suddenly the idea struck him: Why not have the two of them do it together? Sam and Jackie were game, and in the televised performance, Sam has barely gotten through the second chorus when all of a sudden Jackie glides out gracefully and lip-synchs the next verse while Sam indicates eye-rolling surprise. They are a study in similarities and contrasts, each wearing tight, beltless continental pants and an open-necked shirt (Sam's striped, Jackie's black), but Sam's "natural" hairstyle is longer and nappier than we are accustomed to seeing, while Jackie's slick conk gives him the appearance of a bronze Elvis Presley. They take turns mouthing the words, and they take pure pleasure in each other's company, laughing, slapping hands, showing unabashed appreciation for each other's moves, as Jackie's twirls and athletic boxer's shuffle affectionately complement Sam's more carefully practiced steps. Both are unassailable pictures of youth; at the end they bow and make as if to exit, laughing and holding hands.

It's hard to know what to make of this picture. It is a moment that almost defies analysis (were they doing this solely at the behest of

George Klein? was it in its own way some sly commentary on the events in St. Louis just two nights earlier or, as Bobby Womack took it, the idea that "white folks think we all look alike"?). Whatever may have prompted their shadow show, it was in its own way a personification of the easygoing camaraderie and spirit of friendly rivalry that permeated the entire tour. It stands as the one permanently preserved moment of the good times that everyone enjoyed in the midst of a climate of inescapable ambiguity.

Alex left the tour the next day, encouraged by the thought that Lyndon Johnson's landslide victory over Barry Goldwater ensured some hope of progress in the struggle for civil rights, at least for a little while. He wanted to see his baby, just one month old now, and return to business matters he had been neglecting ever since Allen Klein's full-scale entrance into the picture fifteen months ago. With Tracey firmly established, it was time, as he saw it, to get the Los Angeles office back in order, hire a replacement for Zelda, set up some new SAR sessions, and let the distributors and DJs know that he and Sam were still in business.

Sam was no less set on his new course. The perils of the road had never been more clear-cut. Just days before, Ray Charles had been busted for heroin possession in Boston and Frankie Lymon jailed in New York on "dope charges." Little Willie John had gotten into a barroom fight in Seattle while they were playing Knoxville, and then he had gone and killed the fucker. Sam had Crain wire him money, but he was up on a second-degree murder charge and there was no telling what the outcome might be. There was no insulating yourself from the dangers. It didn't matter who you were or what you did, you were just a moving target. If you stayed out there, you were never going to be anything but a nigger, a nigger with money perhaps, a nigger with a fancy car or even, in Ray's case, your own plane, but a nigger nonetheless.

He had already told L.C. and Charles what he had made up his mind to do. Clif was the only one he was going to keep, but he wasn't going to leave anyone stranded. He was going to turn L.C. over to Montague, his brother's original producer, and if Montague couldn't get a hit on L.C., he just might buy the two of them a radio station. After all, they both loved to talk, and Montague had convinced Sam that station ownership was the logical extension of the communications empire he had already begun to build. Charles he was going to set up with a carwash and some real estate in Atlanta. It was time for Charles to settle down, he told his older brother, stay home with his wife and children, and Atlanta represented the future for black people in this country. He was going to send Bobby back to his brothers, he and Alex were putting their money on the Valentinos. He was going to buy his drummer and bass player new instruments, use them on sessions and the occasional live date, maybe even help June relocate to Los Angeles if he wanted to — but, unlike Clif, they would no longer be on a weekly draw. As far as Crain was concerned, he and Alex would find something for him to do. Crain remained obdurate about accepting any actual "job," but Sam wasn't going to walk away from the man who had first showed faith in him.

Barbara alone remained the problem. For the first time, he spoke to a lawyer about getting a divorce, but he couldn't really imagine going through with it. He was not going to write his will, because, he told Bobby, "When a woman start asking about a will, she will kill your ass." When Bobby remonstrated that this wasn't anything to joke about, "Sam would say, 'If I should die before I wake, bury me deep, put two bitches on each side of me.' And he would laugh." Bobby didn't like it when he talked like that. It was as if he had misplaced the happy-go-lucky quality that had always kept him from seeming sorry or slick. His one piece of advice for Bobby when he was in that kind of mood was: Never fuck with your fans. "He was pretty cold about it. He said, 'Every girl you go with [gets herself] a baby. Now you get you a high hooker. She knows exactly what you want, and how you want it, and all that. You can give her five hundred bucks, and she gone.' I said, 'Five hundred!' He said, 'I'm telling you, man, it save you a lot of grief.' "

B ARBARA WAS OUT almost every night with her bartender friend when he got home. If Sam ever came into a place she and her boyfriend might have been, he would purposefully ignore any evidence of her visit, to the point of angrily disputing anyone who might have the temerity to suggest they had seen her with the cat. "That ain't my wife, man," he said. "My wife don't do things like that." And he made it clear they had better back off — or be prepared to fight about it.

He scheduled a session with Al Schmitt to record "To Each His Own," one of his favorite Ink Spots ballads, along with a couple of dance originals like "Yeah Man," which had gotten a good response every time he threw it into the show on tour. The two numbers he worked up were "It's Got the Whole World Shaking," which he and Alex had cut on the

Sims Twins earlier in the year, and a new song called "Shake," inspired by Bobby Freeman's big summer hit, "C'mon and Swim." Sam had worn that record out, playing it again and again and pointing out to Bobby the groove that its producer, a young San Francisco DJ named Sly Stone, had laid down. "Man, I got to sing that song," he kept saying, but instead he wrote his own version, which directly recalled the original only in the little slide that Bobby threw in at the end. What they wanted to achieve, J.W. said, was straightahead energy, and that was what the song communicated, from Earl Palmer's opening drum roll to the melodic hook that René played on electric bass to Earl's dancing riff on toms, which functioned effectively as the lead instrumental voice for the song. "We thought we had started a whole new thing," said RCA a&r man Al Schmitt.

It was, certainly, a whole new thing for Sam, as unapologetic a pure rhythm number as he had ever cut, unmodulated by the kind of melodic touches that had accompanied even "Yeah Man" or "It's Got the Whole World Shakin'." It was the definition of what Sam kept telling everyone who would listen was the coming trend in popular music and r&b, something that, like James Brown's raw extemporizations, the Valentinos' and the Rolling Stones' rough-edged rock 'n' roll, was conveyed as much by rhythm and attitude as it was by vocal technique. It used to be, he explained, that sound brought attention to the lyric, but what you needed to do now was to find sounds — as opposed to words — that could emotionally move an audience. And that was precisely what he had achieved here.

With the session at an end, he and Alex turned their attention briefly to preparing "A Change Is Gonna Come" for single release. After ten months of listening to Allen sing its praises, Sam had finally agreed to revisit the song that had caused him so much inner turmoil and put it out as the B-side of "Shake." Now he and Alex set out to edit the song for radio airplay, in consultation with Al Schmitt. They needed to cut at least thirty seconds from its album length, and Sam was adamant that he didn't want to lose either the cascading overture or the coda at the end. What this pointed to was deleting the verse and chorus just before the bridge, which included one of Sam's most direct statements of social criticism ("I go to the movies / And I go downtown / Somebody keep telling me / Don't hang around"), but it permitted him to retain the bitter realization at the heart of the song ("I go to my brother / And I say,

'Brother, help me, please' / But he winds up knocking me / Back down on my knees"), along with the final verse and chorus, which served, however tentatively, as its underlying statement of redemption and belief.

With everyone in agreement on what had to be done, they left the actual editing to Al Schmitt and went off to the Gaiety Deli on Sunset with Clif, René, and Earl Palmer. Sam and Earl reminisced about Sam's first pop session in New Orleans, in 1956, just before Earl himself moved to L.A., joining Clif and René on the studio scene. It seemed like a lifetime ago to them all, and they talked about Jesse Belvin and the career he might have had if he hadn't been cut down by those racist mother-fuckers in Arkansas. Earl asked Sam and J.W. about the Copa, and they told him how great it had been. "A little nigger in the Copa!" said Sam with almost childlike delight. "A little nigger was in the Copa!" They talked about Mel Carter and his new deal with Imperial and how much they all missed the opportunity to watch Zelda tan. Some white girls came by to get Sam's autograph and practically fell all over one another as he signed their little pieces of paper, but he didn't pick up on it and just sent them on their way. It was well after midnight, the end to a nice relaxed evening in which much had been accomplished, and after they finished their drinks and sandwiches, J.W. got his cheesecake, and they all headed off in various directions of their own.

Sam had one more week at home before returning to Atlanta to play the Royal Peacock for Henry Wynn over the Thanksgiving weekend. It was *The Sam Cooke Show,* with the Valentinos and the Upsetters on the bill, a nice way to pick up some change and repay Henry a little for all of his kindnesses over the years. Four weeks later, he would be opening at the Deauville, then the Fairmont in San Francisco, and then — who could say for sure? The movies definitely, maybe even producing movies of his own. The Palladium in London. A one-man show at Carnegie Hall, delineating the development of Afro-American music in this country. Las Vegas. He doubted that he would be passing this way again.

Uncloudy Day

Oh, they tell me of a home far beyond the skies
They tell me of a home far away
They tell me of a home where no storm clouds rise
Oh, they tell me of an uncloudy day

THE WHOLE FAMILY flew into Atlanta the Tuesday before Thanksgiving for Sam's five-day engagement at the Royal Peacock. Sam, Barbara, and Tracey occupied a corner suite at the Holiday Inn, while Linda stayed with the Wynns, whose daughters, Claudia and Henrietta, took her to school with them. The last time Sam had come through town with Alex, they had run into Martin Luther King at the airport, pausing for a moment under the terminal's harsh fluorescent lighting to exchange greetings. Martin asked if Sam would perform at an SCLC benefit early in the new year, and Sam instantly agreed, and then they all hurried off to catch their respective flights.

This time Sam was determined to just make the most out of what amounted to an extended breakup party for the band. Every night the club was packed, and Barbara, who rarely came to the shows when she had the kids with her, was in regular attendance with Sam's friends, the Paschals, a wealthy black family with a restaurant, a hotel, and an upscale jazz club, who provided her with a babysitter for Tracey. Lotsa Poppa, whose new single paid explicit tribute to Sam with a gospel-laced medley of "That's Where It's At" and the Falcons' "I Found a Love," managed to catch the show, too, even though he had a gig of his own at the Magnolia. He came by on Saturday night in a powder-blue leather suit, and Sam had everyone turning their heads to look as he laughingly declared from the stage, "Boy, that's the first time I ever seen a big man

with a leather suit that color." Seventy-four-year-old Carrie Cunningham, who had opened the Royal Peacock fifteen years earlier after coming to town in the thirties as a circus rider with the Silas Green tent
show, was sitting at a front-row table. She was a tall, regal woman who
had known everyone on the entertainment scene over the last thirty
years, and Sam was in the middle of a laid-back, mellow kind of set when
he leaned over and dedicated his next song to Miss Cunningham and
Mr. and Mrs. Jefferson, the owners of the Forrest Arms Hotel. The song
was "A Change Is Gonna Come," and Lotsa would always remember it
because of the way it just tore the place up.

On the last night of the engagement, Sam threw a dinner for the
band and hit everybody with some money. He told them all to get Christmas presents for their wives and children and gave June his ticket to
Miami, where they would be meeting up in three weeks for the Deauville
date.

He had no special plans for his time at home. Mostly he looked forward to being able to just kick back and relax — listen to his music,
drink his Scotch, not even answer the phone. Bobby came by early in the
week, and Sam once again ran down all the reasons for sending him
back on the road with his brothers. He knew Bobby's feelings were hurt,
but it would be better all around. Bobby's brothers needed him, and now
that they would be headlining their own tour with L.C. and the Upsetters, Bobby would see — it might be hard at first, but he would see —
how much better it was. Sam was giving them the Checker and his old
limo for the tour. "It'll keep me from having to send L.C. money," he
joked. "Man, it's better for you all to work." When he sensed that Bobby
might not be altogether convinced, he said, "You know, I'd be selfish if I
kept you as a guitar player just so you could play for me. I have to realize
that, as a businessman, I have to turn certain things loose from my own
fancy."

On Sunday, December 6, he attended the *Ebony* magazine Fashion
Fair, and Cassius Clay's photographer friend, Howard Bingham,
snapped a picture of him holding hands and chatting animatedly with
Miss Omega Sims. The next night, there was a Johnnie Taylor SAR session at the RCA studio, but he didn't bother to attend. Johnnie had gotten even more of an attitude since his namesake (and he would argue his

With camera and XKE, 2048 Ames. *Courtesy of Joe McEwen*

2048 Ames. *Courtesy of Barbara Cooke and ABKCO*

rank imitator), Little Johnny Taylor, had enjoyed a smash hit with "Part Time Love" the year before. At first Johnnie wanted to call out the other guy, whose real name was Johnny Young ("I was the Johnnie Taylor that everybody knew"), but then he began getting gigs on the basis of the name confusion, and he adapted his own repertoire to the kind of Bobby "Blue" Bland–style blues that Little Johnny Taylor specialized in. After a while a large part of the public started believing that it was *his* hit, but that didn't stop him from running off his mouth about how Sam was holding him back. "Sam always trying to tell me how to sing a song? I know how to goddamn sing a song. That's one thing I know how to do." So Alex suggested to Sam that he might be better off leaving the session alone. Sam just laughed and said, "That crazy fucker. Don't he understand we don't give a shit as long as we go to the bank?" And he timed

his arrival at the studio to when they would be finishing up so he and Alex could take Johnnie out to the California Club, where Little Johnny Taylor was headlining and they could all listen to the blues and get drunk.

He didn't come into the office for the next couple of days. He told J.W. he had a cold, but Alex thought he probably just wanted to be by himself. Bobby came by the house the day before he and his brothers were planning to set out on tour, and Sam was still in bed in his silk pajamas and green terry-cloth robe in the middle of the afternoon. He told Bobby to go get his briefcase from the Ferrari and peeled off $500 from a wad of bills that Bobby thought might have added up to $10,000. He asked Bobby if that would be enough to carry them for a while, he didn't want them getting stranded, but Bobby said that was fine, only how come he had so much money just laying around in the car? Sam passed it off with a dismissive wave. It was money he had gotten from the Peacock and the Henry Wynn tour — he had been meaning to get to the bank, he just hadn't gotten around to it yet. Bobby nodded. Sam told him to take care of the cars and call when they got there, and Bobby said that he would.

On Thursday Sam had a dentist appointment, and he planned to stop off and see Jess Rand to wish him a belated happy birthday along with a happy tenth anniversary the following day. He called Alex and told him he would meet him at the California Club around ten o'clock that night, first he had to get together with René about some arrangements for the Deauville, and then he was scheduled to have dinner with Al Schmitt to discuss his plans for an upcoming blues album.

Lou Rawls saw Sam's Ferrari parked outside their dentist, *Sentinel* columnist Gertrude Gipson's brother-in-law Dr. D. Overstreet Gray's office, and he left a note on the windshield to come by the house afterward. Sam invited Lou to join Alex and him at the California Club, but Lou didn't think he'd be able to make it because the baby had been sick. Sam went in to see how his godson was doing, but the baby started crying as soon as he walked into the room, and they left him to his mother's care. Sam talked to Lou a little about the kind of blues album he was planning to cut, something like Lou's recent hit, "Tobacco Road," but more downhome — Muddy Waters, John Lee Hooker, nothing like he had ever done before. He told Lou to keep an eye out for good gutbucket material and invited him once again to come down to the club, but Lou didn't think he could make it unless the baby was feeling better.

Barbara grew increasingly irritated with her husband as he ran in and out of the house all day. She had plans of her own, and she just wanted him out of her hair. He got a call from Crume as he was about to go out for the evening. The custom-made Dodge motor home that Sam had helped the Soul Stirrers purchase the previous year had caught fire outside Atlanta, and the fire department had had to chop it up. Sam told Crume to stay put, he would wire money to the group at the Forrest Arms early the next morning so they could go on with their tour.

Barbara got on the phone with her sister Beverly as if she were planning to spend the evening with her. Sam knew damn well that wasn't what she had in mind and asked if she couldn't just stay home with the kids for once. She asked if *he* was going to stay home, and then they really got into it. They had reached a standoff when she said, "You just want me to sit here until you decide to go out, don't you?" To which he icily responded she could go out now if she wanted. But she knew he was furious because she had seized the initiative. He was supposed to be the one in control, he was supposed to be the one to bring up the subject first — it was ridiculous, but that's the way it always was.

"I'll probably be back early," she said as a small gesture of apology. It made no difference, he said, he wouldn't be there. As she was getting dressed, he came into the room and announced that he was leaving. At first he wouldn't even kiss her good-bye. But when she reminded him, he said, "Oh yeah, okay," and gave her a perfunctory smack on the lips.

He stopped by René's office, and they went over the arrangements, with Sam indicating how he wanted to change some of the instrumental voicings by humming the parts into René's tape recorder, then enunciating specific verbal instructions for each song in the show. Sam asked René if he felt like coming out to dinner, but René said he wanted to write out some of the changes first, maybe he would meet up with Sam and Alex at the California Club later.

Al Schmitt and his wife, Joan Dew, were waiting for him at the bar when he arrived at Martoni's, on Cahuenga just above Sunset. Martoni's had been his hangout ever since he met Jess, when Jess and Sammy had introduced him to the joint where Sinatra and all the top showbiz people hung out. It had represented a real step up the ladder when he first set foot inside the restaurant in his brand-new Sy Devore suit, nobody knowing him, trying to act like the coolest cat in the world, but now he could barely make his way to his table in the back dining room with all the people who clamored for his attention. Joan Dew thought he seemed a little distracted, but he spoke excitedly about coming off the road and how good the recent trip to Atlanta had been. He talked about the new album. This was the first Al had heard any specifics, and Sam talked about some of the musicians he wanted to use, blues musicians, but blues musicians who could play sophisticated, too. He invited Al and Joan to come out to the house over the weekend to go over material — he would barbecue some steaks, they could even stay over. Joan shuddered a little at the prospect. She was crazy about Sam, but she was the one who always got stuck with Barbara. She could never really find anything to say to her, and Barbara didn't seem much interested anyway, but if that was what Sam wanted, she would make the best of it, for Al's sake and for Sam's.

People kept stopping by the table, interrupting their conversation, and after a while, Sam, who had had three or four martinis already, drifted back to the bar. Al went to get him when their orders arrived but, on returning to the table, reported to Joan that Sam was surrounded by a coterie of friends and was having such a good time that he said not to wait for him, just go ahead with their meal.

The party at the bar included a broad assortment of music industry figures, from songwriter Don Robertson to Liberty promo man Jim Benci and Gil Bogus, who did promotion work for one of SAR's principal distributors. Sam was still ordering martinis, and after a while, at his instigation, the whole group started singing a selection of old favorites, including Sam's "Ain't That Good News" and the folk perennial "Cottonfields." There was a Eurasian-looking girl, twenty-one or twenty-two with a plump, pretty face, sitting with three men in a booth by the bar. Sam nodded to her — he had seen her around — and then one of the men, a guitar player he knew from the clubs, introduced her. Her name was Elisa Boyer, and she was staying at a motel over at Hollywood and LaBrea — she had been working as a receptionist, she said, but Sam knew she was a party girl, and it wasn't long before they cozied up together in the booth. Al and Joan stopped by on their way out to see if Sam might want to join them at the African Queen, where Al was going to check out a new RCA act. From there they were planning to go on to PJ's on Santa Monica. Sam said he'd probably catch up with them at PJ's as his hand rested lightly on the girl's shoulder.

Not entirely to their surprise, he hadn't shown up when they left PJ's around 1:30 A.M. He hadn't shown up at the California Club, either, where J.W. finally gave up, bought his little girl a Christmas tree from a guy with a raggedy stand outside the club, and went home. Sam did finally arrive at PJ's just around closing time, and he ran into a couple of old friends — but he got pissed off when a guy started talking to Elisa, and it was all she could do to get him out the door before he got into a fight.

THEY DROVE OUT SANTA MONICA, then turned onto the Harbor Freeway. Now that the evening's conclusion had been firmly established, Sam knew exactly where he wanted to go. He loosened his tie and stroked the girl's hair distractedly, murmuring how crazy he was about her, how much he loved her pretty, long hair. In the backseat lay a bottle of Scotch and a copy of the Muslim newspaper, *Muhammad Speaks*. He was high, and he was probably driving too fast, but there wasn't much traffic on the road and the wind felt good against his face.

The girl pestered him as they got farther and farther out of town. She didn't see why they couldn't go to some nice place in Hollywood instead of some out-of-the-way fleabag motel — where *were* they going? she kept asking him in between increasingly insistent pleas to slow down.

But Sam knew exactly where he was going — its remote location was part of its appeal. There were no gawkers, no celebrity stalkers, it was part of a strip of clubs and motels and liquor stores out by the airport, near where the Sims Twins lived and just down the street from the club they played all the time. It was cheap, it was convenient, but, more important, if you were a musician and liked to party, no one ever bothered you — that was the reason the Upsetters and lots of other entertainers stayed here whenever they were in town.

He turned off the freeway at the airport exit, got on Figueroa, drove a few blocks, and pulled into the parking lot of the motel, the Hacienda, with signs that announced, "Everyone Welcome, Free Radio TV, Refrigerators and Refrigeration Coming Open 24 Hours $3 up." It was 2:30 in the morning when he walked up to the glass partition at the left of the manager's office-apartment to register, leaving the girl in the car. The manager, a dark-skinned woman with a glowering, impassive look, just stared at him, giving no indication that she either recognized him or cared who he was. He looked like every other fool who arrived with his shirttails hanging out and a pleasantly dazed expression on his face. She saw the girl, too, and told him phlegmatically that they would have to register as Mr. and Mrs. Then she gave him the room key, and he drove around to the back, and he and the girl went into the room.

He tore off her sweater and dress, leaving her in her bra and panties and slip. He was acting a little rough, and she did her best to slow him down, but he was intent on something, and it seemed clear he wasn't going to be slowed by either entreaty or design. She went into the bathroom and tried the lock on the door, but the latch was broken and the window painted shut. By the time she came out, he was already undressed, and he groped for her, then went into the bathroom himself, saying he wouldn't be a minute. When he came out, the girl and his clothes were gone.

It is impossible to know exactly what happened next. All Sam had left in the way of clothing was his sports jacket and shoes. He pulled on the jacket, covering himself as best he could, then put the shoes on his feet and flung open the door. His head was thick with alcohol and rage, but evidently he thought he had seen her going toward the manager's office unit. Maybe he did. Or maybe in his befuddled state Sam just assumed there was nowhere else for her to go. He jumped in the car and pulled up in front of the manager's apartment, leaving the engine running as he banged loudly on the door. It was a long time before the woman answered — he could hear the sound of the TV inside, so he knew she was in there — but finally she came to the window and glanced balefully out at him. From her vantage point, she could see his bare chest underneath the fancy sports jacket — she wasn't interested in seeing any further. She stood there with her arms akimbo, glaring at him. Where was the girl? he kept on shouting, yelling his damn-fool head off. What did you do with her? She shook her head. She didn't know about no girl. Where's the fucking girl? he demanded. When she continued to indicate that she had no idea, and what's more, she didn't care, he said he didn't believe her and demanded that she let him in so he could see for himself. Call the police, she shrugged, if he was so damn certain. Let them sort it out. But she could see he wasn't going to go away. She had dealt with men in this state before. That was one of the reasons she had the gun. She checked its location on top of the two TVs stacked one on top of the other. Then she heard his shoulder working at the door, and before long the cheap stripping gave way and the door came off its hinges, and the man was standing there demanding that she give over the girl.

If the girl was, in fact, there, did she hide? Or was she really gone, as the motel manager, Bertha Lee Franklin, continued to insist and would insist to her dying day? Whatever the case, Sam was enraged. The girl had his clothes, and the girl had his money. Did she think he was just going to let her play him like that? He went back to the kitchen and the bedroom of the small apartment, and when he didn't find her there, he grabbed the manager, who, though she was only five foot six, at nearly one hundred ninety pounds outweighed Sam by a good twenty-five or thirty. He was so angry he could scarcely remember who he was. He shook the woman by the shoulders, as if he could wring the information out of her. She fought back, and they got into an awkward wrestling match and fell to the floor. She was biting and scratching, and when she finally got out from under him, she went for the gun. He must have realized immediately how desperate the situation was, but how many times had he been in situations no less desperate and emerged unscathed by dint of luck, pluck, or simply because *he was Sam Cooke?* There was a flash and a report as they struggled for the gun, and a bullet went into the ceiling. There was a second discharge, and he was still standing. The third bullet tore through both lungs, the heart, and lodged near his right shoulder blade, as blood splattered all over the woman's dress. "Lady, you shot me," he said with a combination of astonishment, bewilderment, and disbelief. In Bertha Lee Franklin's recollection, he ran at her once again, and she picked up a stick and hit him over the head with it so hard that it broke in two.

T HERE WERE TWO CALLS to the police in almost immediate succession. The girl called at 3:08 from a phone booth barely a block away. She said she didn't know where she was, that she had been kidnapped and it was too dark for her to ascertain her exact location. She was told to stay right where she was, an officer would come to her rescue. Less than ten minutes later, another call was logged at the Seventy-seventh Precinct house, this one from a Mrs. Evelyn Card, who said she owned a motel called the Hacienda and had been on the phone with her manager when she heard a guy break in the door of the manager's apartment. There had been a loud altercation, and then all hell broke loose, "and I think she shot him, I don't know." What was the location of the motel? the police dispatcher asked, and she told him it was Ninety-first and Figueroa, then returned to her description of the scene she had so conveniently witnessed on the telephone. There had been a lot of break-ins in the area lately; as a matter of fact, she had had some bastards try to hold her up tonight at Mary's Come In Motel, the establishment that she and her husband ran just a few miles up Figueroa from the Hacienda — the dispatcher cut her off and told her they would send out a car right away to take her statement.

B ARBARA WAS SITTING in the library waiting for Sam to come home. In spite of her promise to be in early herself, she had only gotten in around 2:30 or 3:00 — she had had certain things to work out with her bartender friend, and she knew damn well Sam wasn't going to be rolling in until the early hours. She didn't want to go to bed alone, though, so after checking on the children, she turned on the TV, made herself a drink, smoked a little pot, and curled up on the couch in the reading room while she waited for the fucker to come home. She was asleep when the phone rang a little before six. It was her sister Beverly, and she was momentarily confused as Bev started talking about how she had just gotten up and was getting dressed to go to work when she heard the news on the radio. She said, "Have you heard the news?" It was six o'clock in the damn morning, Barbara said. How in the hell was she going to hear any news? "Well, girl," her sister said, "is your husband at home?" Barbara just snorted. "Well, honey," her sister said, "he's dead."

Just then, the doorbell rang. Shaken, still unable to absorb what Beverly had said, she told her sister to hang on. It was the police, two police detectives — they flashed their badges and said, "Are you Mrs. Sam Cooke?" She nodded mutely. They said, "May we come in?" She nodded again. She said, "I'm on the phone, talking to my sister. Is my husband dead?"

The rest was a blur. She asked Beverly to come over as soon as she could and made herself a drink. She offered the police a drink, but they declined. They told her the details of the shooting, but it made no sense to her. He had been with some woman, but when he got shot, the woman wasn't nowhere to be found. She poured herself another drink. By this time the house was filling up with people, and the phone was ringing off the hook — it must have been all over the news. René and Sugar Hall were among the first to arrive, Alex and Carol and the baby, Clif, Lou Rawls, Sam's old manager, Jess Rand, and his wife, Bonnie, who had helped her decorate their first apartment — except for the pained expressions on their faces, it could have been a damned party. But she was unable to face any of them, she didn't want to talk to anyone on the phone — and while the two policemen looked on in some surprise, she took her drink and went out and sat by the pool, leaving them all to René and Sugar and her sister to deal with. At some point Linda came out and joined her. Her eyes were deep wells of sadness, and even though she was only eleven years old, Barbara knew she understood exactly what was going on. Just like Barbara had understood when she wasn't much older than eleven that she loved Sam Cook and she would love him till the day he died. And now he had. You never knew the twists that love could take — if she had been a better mother, maybe things would have been different, if she had been a better mother, maybe Vincent would still be alive, if Vincent were still alive, maybe Sam . . .

There was a big tree in the music room with a bunch of Christmas presents under it — Sam had just gone out and made a damn fool of her . . . again. He had been doing it all his life, from the time he went off and married that California bitch, left her and her baby on their own, and now, by the manner of his death, he had really outdone her once and for all in the world's eyes. They had all thought she wasn't good enough for him, Sam's friends and business associates, the Cooks with their damned prejudice-ass attitude, they had never thought she was good enough for their Sammy, and now he had gone and proved them all right. If there had been anything to the marriage, everyone would be saying, why couldn't she keep him at home? There was no way for her to answer back. She knew things about their all-American boy — but it was just like it had always been. Every time she tried to say anything, he always had the last word. He was just doing what he wanted to do. Everyone knew that. And her? She had never known what she wanted. Except Sam.

THE TWO POLICEMEN stuck around for most of the day, talking to everyone, getting all their gossip, opinions, and theories — it was almost, Barbara reflected, like a damn TV show. Crain was on his way from Chicago, along with her older sister, Ella — she trusted Crain more than the whole damn lot of them. Once they had gotten their business straight, he had always treated her with respect. He was like a longtime court servant loyal to them both, and she knew he'd help her get through some of the worst of it. He'd help out with the Cooks, too, serve as a kind of intermediary for her. She had spoken with the old man, and he had given her more of that cold-ass shit. He would be driving out with Charles, he told her. No, he wouldn't be staying with her. What would be the point? he said with his usual weird insistence on the literal. His son would not be there.

Charles, who lived with his wife and family in Detroit, had actually set out for California on his own as soon as he confirmed that it was not just another false rumor. At first he had thought it was going to turn out like the leukemia scare, but when he called Sam's house and the police answered, he knew it was true. So he gassed up the brand-new limo Sam had given him and stuck his pistol in his pocket and said, "I'm gonna kill that woman, Bertha Franklin." He had only gotten as far as St. Louis when the fuel line sprang a leak, and while he was getting it fixed, his mother called him on the car phone. She begged him to come back to Chicago for Reverend Cook ("I couldn't refuse my mother nothing"), and when she found out what he planned to do, she made him leave the gun behind. Then he embarked for California once again, his mind still roiling with thoughts of revenge. It couldn't have happened the way they said it did. Sam didn't have to pay for no pussy — and to get killed for it to boot? Sam wasn't no gangster, but he knew how to take care of himself. The more Charles thought about it, the more he was convinced that Barbara might have had something to do with it. And if he found out that she did, then he was going to kill her, too. Meanwhile, the old man sat beside him wearing his preacher's hat and light, plastic-rimmed glasses, his face almost expressionless, his spine stiffened with rectitude, not sharing his thoughts with anyone but his Maker. When they first got the call, his wife had turned to him and said piteously, "Oh, Brother Cook, what are we going to do now?" He just stared at her. Do? he said a little incredulously. They were going to do what they had always done. "I didn't depend on Sam taking care of me," he told Annie Mae, as if surprised that she would need reminding. They had always depended on God.

Allen Klein first heard the news on the radio. It was snowing hard in New York, and he felt as if the world had come crashing down around him, but he knew he had to keep going somehow, and when he couldn't get a flight out until the next day, he put together a statement that desperately sought to salvage whatever he could from the situation. "The story of Sam's death as reported is impossible," he declared, citing as one of his proofs the fact that "Sam was known to carry huge sums of money with him at all times and it is evident that someone is trying to cover up the [real] reasons for this tragedy." He didn't know if this was true, and he didn't care, he was just trying to deflect some of the attention from Sam's actions by suggesting that this was a man who had been killed not in an act of adultery but as the victim of a violent crime. "Sam was a happily married family man with deep religious convictions," the press release went on, "[he] was not a violent person, and the statements given out as to why he was killed are entirely inconsistent with the type of person he was. Out of respect to Sam and his wife and children, I would appreciate it if the press would withhold publishing hearsay information."

Barbara went down to the city morgue with her sister and Sugar Hall to identify the body. They had him up on a slab in a glass room all by himself — it was like out of one of those monster movies, Barbara thought, this couldn't really be happening to her. She wanted to touch him, it didn't even look like Sam, all cold and lifeless — he was so pretty, and now he was just this battered corpse — but the man said, "Can you see, Mrs. Cooke? Can you see him?" And she said, "Yeah, that's him." Except it wasn't — not really. They said they had to perform an autopsy to determine the cause of death, and when she questioned the need, they said by law they had to do it, whether or not she gave consent. She asked them who would perform the autopsy, and they said, "Well, you can have your doctor, if you want." So she called her doctor, and it turned out he had worked for the coroner's office while he was in medical school, and he agreed to do it. That way at least, she figured, she would find out what had really happened. She picked up Sam's keys, the $108 he still had on him, and the rest of his belongings, including the bottle of whiskey — good booze, she noted, just like Sam always drank. Then she and Sugar and Beverly went to the police lot to pick up the car, his latest pride and joy, and she slowly drove it home. He must have been drunk, she thought, drunk and confused — that was how he died, this man to whom propriety and control were always so important.

Meanwhile, at the Hacienda, a crowd had formed both out of curiosity and to voice its anger and disbelief. They started off singing some of Sam's songs, but the mood swiftly changed, and they began to call out Mrs. Franklin's name, demanding that she show herself while they shouted angry threats. Eventually, the *Los Angeles Sentinel* reported, "the police had to be called to maintain order, and the motel was later closed until further notice." It was as if the whole world had gone off its axis.

B ARBARA PICKED UP ALLEN at the airport the next day in the Rolls and offered to take him to lunch at Martoni's, but he declined, and they went to the office instead, then to the house, where Barbara anxiously pumped him for information. Sam had kept her in the dark about almost everything to do with his personal finances, and now she was desperate to find out. Allen could certainly understand her feelings, and he went over some of the details with her, but he didn't really feel comfortable with the situation, and he didn't really feel comfortable with the widow, either, whom he scarcely knew. Death always unsettled him, but he was unnerved by Barbara's sheer intensity, her near-ferocity, and the gulf in personality and manner between Sam and her.

There were going to be two funerals, she told him. Crain had convinced her of the necessity of that. There were just too many of Sam's fans, friends, and family — including Sam's own mother — who wouldn't be able to travel to L.A. So Barbara agreed and gave Crain money to take care of the arrangements. But they couldn't have either of the funerals until after the inquest was over. And in the meantime, she was going to have Sam's body available for public viewing at People's Funeral Home, here in Los Angeles, as soon as it was released by the coroner's office.

Crain hovered around her, diplomatically seconding whatever she said. The subject was Sam, but the real Sam had disappeared from the conversation. "It was a boy that got killed," Crain said at one point, and Barbara could barely restrain her disbelief. He wasn't a boy, she wanted to scream at him. He was a full-grown, motherfucking man, who should have had more fucking sense, who should have looked out better for them all. But Crain was, in almost every other respect, a comfort to her; unlike Alex, he had never had any real ambition except to serve. Allen she was not so sure of. Every time she looked at him, those beady little eyes shifted away, and she didn't know what he was thinking. He was going to get to the bottom of this, he kept assuring her, more and more emphatically. He was going to hire a private investigator, and he was going to find out the truth. Well, maybe so — but what good was the motherfucking truth going to do them now?

T HE BODY LAY IN STATE at People's, across from the Dunbar Hotel on Central, for three days. It was released by the coroner's office on Saturday night, with viewing scheduled to begin Sunday afternoon, but by one o'clock, traffic was tied up for blocks, with thousands of people lining the sidewalk and spilling out onto the street. Sam's body was laid out in a glass-lidded bronze coffin, with guards stationed at either end. The bruises on his face were clearly evident, and friends and fans were openly weeping. "It hurt us so to see his little curly lashes closed and all bruised up in the face," said the songwriting Prudhomme twins, who had given him "Rome Wasn't Built in a Day." "We went to view him and pray for him — our hearts were broken." A contingent of Black Muslims in dark glasses silently observed the proceedings, and nearly everyone who passed the coffin, as visiting hours extended well into the evening to accommodate the crowd, expressed skepticism about the official story of his death.

Allen and J.W. and Allen's lawyer all met with a private detective from the Beverly Hills Investigating Service on Monday morning at the Polo Lounge at the Beverly Hills Hotel. They went over their doubts and suspicions, the inconsistencies that not only surrounded the circumstances of Sam's death but challenged the faith they had all come to place in him. The papers were full of talk of conspiracy, the girl, Elisa Boyer, had been named a prostitute by police sources, and her version and the motel owner's version of just what had transpired were treated with almost universal disbelief. To the community at large it was almost as if this couldn't have happened because it shouldn't have happened, and Allen and Alex were caught up in similar feelings. And yet they knew Sam, and they knew something of Sam's circumstances, and almost in spite of themselves they harbored darker suspicions of their own. This was about a *business* transaction, after all, and the single question that had to be answered was: was anyone else involved? The agency operative, M. K. Pelletreau, outlined the way in which he would begin his investigation: he had an appointment with a Dr. Curfey, the coroner of Los Angeles County, set up for that afternoon. Through his previous work, he would develop contacts within the police department. And he would seek to develop additional undercover sources to learn something more about the girl, how she worked, who she worked with, and how it was she had come to meet the subject in the first place. He would report back to them in a few days.

B OBBY WOMACK WAS INCONSOLABLE. He didn't know what to do with himself. He and his brothers had arrived in Houston with the Upsetters for the start of the tour. They were just checking into their motel when they heard the news, and after calling J.W. to confirm that it was true, they headed straight home. Bobby was unable to contain himself — he just cried and cried, and by the time they got back to Los Angeles, the others were sick of having him around. Bobby, in turn, was shocked by what he viewed as the callousness of some of his fellow musicians. A bunch of them were riding back from the funeral parlor, "and I was crying so hard, I remember, somebody slapped me upside the head and said, 'Shut the fuck up.' Everybody was talking about what they were supposed to get, what Sam was going to give them, and then the motherfucker up and died. And I was just sitting there crying."

He went to Barbara and told her that Sam had bought them all new instruments just before they went out, and none of them, including Bobby, had even begun to pay him back. She looked at him, like, "What the fuck do you want me to do about it?" And he said, "I just wanted you to know." But Barbara was more out of it than she let on — she was unable even to focus most of the time. The Cooks had barely spoken to her when they arrived, the old man indicating what he thought of her by his icy disdain, that damned Charles practically accusing her of murder. The house was full of people, but she felt all alone, removed by a gauzy web of medication and mood from the day-to-day events that were taking place around her. Her sisters looked out for her and made sure the children were being taken care of. René and Sugar did the best they could to protect her from everyone else's needs and solicitude. Alexander's wife, Carol, was sweet, but the others all seemed to want something from her — Clif acted like it was him that had gotten killed, those damned Womack brothers were always underfoot, and people were coming around with food and shit that she didn't even want to look at, let alone touch. They all blamed her, she could tell, but the truth was, none of them could blame her more than she blamed herself. She kept thinking maybe it was because she hadn't been able to raise herself to Sam's expectations, maybe she had expected too much from him. One time she felt so cold she thought she was going to die. Her feet felt like they weren't even attached to her body, her breath grew short, and the only thing that saved her was the thought of her children. They would have no one to take care of them. "I can't die," she said, and her sisters started crying, even as they sought to comfort her. She was only twenty-nine.

THE CORONER'S JURY hearing on Wednesday was a cut-and-dried affair. It convened at 1:00 P.M. in room 150 at the austere Hall of Justice, with the coroner making his presentation to a seven-member jury consisting of four men and three women, and a Mr. Joe Barilla representing the district attorney's office. There was a crowd of fans outside hoping to gain admission when Barbara arrived with Crain and her sister Ella. Barbara was wearing a light-colored tweed suit with a white blouse, a fashionable broad-brimmed hat, and a hurt, almost wounded expression on her handsome, high-cheekboned face. Her sister and Crain sat on either side of her with Alex and Reverend Cook to Crain's right and the motel owner and manager seated in the row directly in front of her. She was barely audible in her brief testimony, merely reaffirming her identification of her husband's remains and correcting the coroner's statement of his age. Allen's lawyer, Marty Machat, was identified as her attorney, but he had nothing to add.

After the medical examiner's testimony and the report of the first investigating officer on the scene, the girl, Elisa Boyer, took the stand. She was bare-legged and wearing the kind of oversized dark-glasses-and-kerchief combination that made her look a little bit like Jackie Kennedy, or as if she had just been out for a ride. Her shiny black bangs peeked out from underneath the scarf, and she wore a belted sweater coat over a sleeveless drop-waist dress. There were gasps from the crowd and a growing wave of restiveness bordering on outright hostility as she recited her by now familiar story in a shrill, almost defiant, and unhesitating voice. When she reached the point where she spoke of being kidnapped against her will ("I turned to Mr. Cooke, and I told him, 'Please, take me home,' [but] he took me by the arm and he dragged me into that room"), the courthouse erupted with cries of protest, and the coroner, who served as both chief investigator and presiding officer, was led to announce, "There will be no demonstration or no outbursts. If there are, these people will be eliminated from hearing the inquest." Sam pulled her sweater off, she said, he ripped her dress — she was able to make her escape only after he had gone into the bathroom. She knocked on the manager's door, but evidently the manager didn't hear her, so she went around the corner, got dressed in the shadow of an apartment building, dumped Sam's clothes in the building's garage area, spotted a telephone booth, and called the police. "I had no idea that someone had shot Mr. Cooke," she testified. After the coroner had finished with her, the district attorney asked a few questions, and when he was through, Marty Machat attempted to address the witness. He only got as far as "May I —" when the coroner said to the witness, "You may be excused."

Bertha Franklin was then called to the stand. She moved slowly, still in pain, apparently, from the physical struggle she had undergone with the deceased. She wore a light-colored suit, a single strand of pearls, and harlequin dark glasses, but though she had had her hair done for the occasion, the impression that she gave was one of uncompromising gruffness, as she truculently regarded both the coroner and the courtroom. Was she willing to testify in the absence of counsel? she was asked. "I can if you want me to," she said. "I don't mind."

In her testimony she contradicted Elisa Boyer's and the investigating officer's accounts slightly — she had personally witnessed no resistance on Miss Boyer's part when the two of them arrived ("She didn't say a word") — but for the most part differed in no other significant respect from the previous witnesses. As for the happy coincidence of her having been on the phone at the exact moment that the man broke down the door, she indicated, after a momentary hesitation, that she was not engaged in conversation when he rented the room. "It was shortly after." It had been, she said, quite a struggle. She was still sore all over and was taking therapy treatments every other day. How far was Mr. Cooke from her when she fired the gun? "He wasn't too far. He was at close range." And how did she know she had struck Mr. Cooke? "Because he said, 'Lady, you shot me,'" she testified in a raspy, dismissively impassive voice. The dress that she had been wearing that night, all splattered with Sam's blood, was identified and put into evidence. A juror asked if she had a gun permit, and she said that she did. At the conclusion of her testimony, Marty Machat once again attempted to ask a question and was once again refused, and she was dismissed at 2:10 P.M.

After a ten-minute recess, just three additional witnesses were called: a motel resident who had occupied the room next door and thought there might have been a little bit of resistance, or disagreement, when the couple entered their room; the motel owner who had been on the phone with Bertha Franklin; and a police officer who recounted some of the details of the investigation. The motel owner, Evelyn Card, offered testimony that so precisely corroborated her employee's it might almost have seemed a pas de deux. She had heard everything, right up to the arrival of the police. She had employed Mrs. Franklin for three years, and they spoke on the phone every night. Through Officer Thomas' testimony it was established that both Miss Boyer and Mrs. Franklin had passed voluntary lie-detector tests. Photographs of the scene were introduced into evidence. Tape recordings of both calls to the police were played. All of the deceased's recovered possessions were enumerated: his clothing, an Omega wristwatch, the money clip with $108, and some change.

Once again the witness was dismissed by the coroner after the district attorney and members of the jury had concluded their questioning, but this time when Marty Machat raised his voice to object, the coroner momentarily conceded the point. "You may ask one, Mr. Macheck [*sic*]," he said.

"Did you, by any chance," he asked Officer Thomas, "trace the occupation of the girl, Lisa Boyer?"

"We are not concerned with the occupation of the girl, Mr. Macheck," the coroner interposed before the officer was able to answer.

After a couple more questions that yielded no more satisfactory response, Allen's lawyer asked, "Was anything else missing from the clothing that was not found, such as credit cards?"

"I understand," said Officer Thomas, "from members of his family and Mr. Alexander, that a card carrier, not the wallet, that he carries a bunch of credit cards in, also a driver's license. To my knowledge this has not been found." Was a search made of Miss Boyer by the police department? asked the coroner, his interest evidently piqued for the first time by this line of questioning. No, sir, was the officer's reply, and he was once again about to be dismissed, when the DA jumped in and asked if a search had been made of Miss Boyer's purse? Which, as it turned out, had been done, yielding only $20, Miss Boyer's driver's license, and some miscellaneous papers. None of the cash that Sam was said to have been carrying on him — the thousands of dollars that many people believed he always had on his person, or even the roll of bills that Al Schmitt's wife, Joan, would recall having seen at Martoni's — had turned up. But no further follow-up was undertaken, and after little more than two hours of testimony, the case was turned over to the jury, who deliberated for twenty minutes, then returned with a verdict of "justifiable homicide, committed by the said Bertha Franklin in protection of life and property." When polled individually by the press, the jurors indicated that the strongest evidence in favor of acquittal were the lie-detector tests but that the motel owner Evelyn Card's testimony helped quite a bit, too. Short of a filmed record of the event, what could be more persuasive than the overheard commission of a crime?

Allen and Marty Machat met with the private investigator later in the day at the Beverly Hills Hotel, while Alex prepared to fly to Chicago for the funeral. The investigation was beginning to yield results, but Allen was more and more uncomfortable with the direction it was taking. The PI, Mr. Pelletreau, had already turned up information about Sam's domestic situation that Allen wasn't sure he wanted to know — there was something about a bartender with whom the subject's wife had an ongoing relationship, and Pelletreau was convinced that the girl, Elisa Boyer, was a "professional roller" who operated with at least one known confederate and that, most likely, Sam had met her before. What wasn't clear was how this particular scene had gone down — or, almost as important, how it was *supposed to* have gone down. For Allen, finicky about appearances even under the best of circumstances, there was little doubt that the situation was going to get messier, but equally little doubt that, for the time being at least, they had to go on.

Barbara, Ella, Crain, and Barbara's two little girls all flew to Chicago with the body that night, with Allen, Alex, and Allen's lawyer arriving the following day. The family, led by Reverend Cook, was at the airport to meet the plane, along with a limo and hearse from the A.R. Leak Colonial Chapel at 7838 Cottage Grove. Leak had gotten the business because his son was married to the gospel singer Mavis Staples, and through Mavis he was able to reach the family first.

The mourners were out in front of the funeral home well in advance of the three o'clock start of viewing hours on Thursday. It was a freezing-cold day, with temperatures hovering around zero and the wind howling down the desolate streets, but this did little to discourage an estimated six thousand fans from standing in line for much of the afternoon in hopes of gaining admittance to the viewing.

Inside the funeral home the Cook family was visibly distressed at the job the Los Angeles mortuary had done. Sam's head was all bashed in, and it looked like all the bones in his hands, and maybe even his arm, were broken — he appeared neither peaceful nor at rest. They prevailed on the mortician to work on him some more, and then L.C. fixed his hair, and he was laid out, just as he had been in Los Angeles, in an elegant gray suit and tie, looking almost but not quite like the smooth, confident young man he had always been.

Comedian Dick Gregory, singers Dee Clark and Major Lance, Motown stars Marv Johnson and Smokey Robinson, the Soul Stirrers, and the Upsetters were just some of the prominent figures scattered among the ordinary citizens who stood in line. Muhammad Ali, who had flown in specially for the ceremony, arrived at midafternoon with his omnipresent manager and personal adviser, Herbert Muhammad, and expressed the feelings of almost everyone in the crowd when he declared loudly and repeatedly that if Sam had been a white singer, "if he had

Chicago, December 17, 1964. © *Ernest Withers. Courtesy of Panopticon Gallery, Waltham, Mass.*

been someone like Elvis Presley or one of the Beatles, the FBI would still be investigating and someone would be in jail." Philadelphia DJ and civil rights activist Georgie Woods, who stood in the cold for hours, vowed that he and other DJs would hire private investigators to make sure that "certain facts about this case [that] are being withheld from the public . . . are brought to light." As for the fans, they were there simply to be with Sam, and many were disappointed, the *Chicago Defender* reported, when they discovered that the coffin was covered with glass. "A blind woman who came to pay her respects and perhaps 'touch' her singing idol, was rammed against a door frame and had to be pulled over the entrance by funeral parlor employees. . . . The urgency of many to 'get a last look at Sam' resulted in near chaos with the young and old being crushed in the process. When the plate glass in a front door of Leak's Chapel gave way under the pressure of the crowd," the report went on, "Spencer Leak, a son of A.R. Leak Sr., shouted, 'There are just too many of them!'" An eleven-year-old girl set up a wailing that could not be stilled, and when reporters pressed for her identity, her mother volunteered that this was Denise Cooke, Sam's oldest daughter, and that she was Marine Somerville of Cleveland.

The funeral that evening was scheduled for eight o'clock, but a swelling number of mourners who had been unable to gain admission to the funeral home started lining up in front of the cavernous Tabernacle Baptist Church at Forty-first and Indiana by midafternoon. "It was the coldest night ever," said Soul Stirrer Leroy Crume, as policemen in earmuffs tried to control the huge crowd with bullhorns and ropes. Barbara and her daughters had to be lifted over the crowd to get in, while Allen Klein stood outside for a few moments but then couldn't bring himself to enter. L.C. was late, and when he told the police that he was Sam's brother, he was turned away at first because Charles had just talked his way in with the same explanation. L.C. was prepared to fight any number of policemen and die in the attempt, but finally a lieutenant who knew him from the neighborhood said, "Naw, that's L.C.," and they let him through. Once the family was assembled inside, it took almost forty minutes for attendants to show them to their seats. Annie Mae Cook, looking pale, almost ghostly in her black hat and veil, with an unutterable expression of despair on her face, could barely stand, as her sons and daughters surrounded her and her husband stood unbendingly erect at her side. Close to two thousand people crowded inside the overflowing church, with at least twice as many standing outside in the frigid cold, as Professor Willie Webb played the processional, "Precious Lord," over and over again and the congregation faced the giant mural dwarfing the pulpit and framed by vaulting arches on either side.

After greetings, brief Scripture readings, and prayer from various prominent ministers, including Reverend Clarence Cobbs of the twenty-thousand-member First Church of the Deliverance, the choir in alternating robes of black and white sang "Never Alone," and "nurses" dressed in white fanned through the crowd to attend to the inevitable faintings and emotional disruptions that were bound to occur.

"The world is better because Sam Cooke lived. He inspired many youths of all races and creeds," said Dr. Louis Rawls, no relation to the singer, who had just celebrated his twenty-third anniversary at Tabernacle Baptist and had lent his church to Reverend Clay Evans of Fellowship Baptist to accommodate the magnitude of the occasion. Like the other ministers, he had known Sam from childhood on, and, like the others, he alluded not just to the Highway QCs, listed in the program as honorary pallbearers, but to the family gospel group with which Sam had first begun, the Singing Children.

The Staple Singers sang the traditional "Old Rugged Cross," and Mavis Staples started crying at the outset and cried all the way through. The Soul Stirrers sang Crume's composition "His Precious Love," one of Sam's favorites, but only after Crume borrowed Pop Staples' guitar because he had forgotten his own. The congregation for the most part behaved with tearful decorum, although fistfights broke out from time to time outside the church.

"We must strive in the midst of our grief to build a world where men will not need to perish with their mature songs still unsung," preached Clay Evans, a young quartet singer himself when the QCs were starting out, whose small congregation Sam had joined while still with the Soul Stirrers almost ten years earlier. "We need not be afraid of anyone dying before his hour," Evans comfortingly intoned. "Some men have lived long, yet they've lived a short life." Sam, he implied, had packed a great deal into his few short years, into what must be considered a transitory experience at best, a "Great Park [in which] we are very much like children, privileged to spend a day."

After the eulogy the family took one last look at the body and was escorted out, leaving the mourning to the public, who lined up once again for a final viewing of their own. Barbara went back to her hotel on the north side by herself — her mother took the girls, and she had no interest in being around anybody else, not the Cooks, not old friends looking to recall happier times, not even Crain and his wife, Maude, who had been looking out for her ever since her arrival in town. She knew what it was like after a funeral, people getting drunk and speaking sentimentally about the deceased — and then all of a sudden the dead person was forgotten. Just gone. She wasn't ready for that. Not yet. She just felt so — alone. When she got back to her fancy hotel room, she took all the bedding off the bed and curled up in a corner on the floor and tried not to think of what was going to happen to her. She had a record company and a publishing company, and a partner and a business manager she didn't trust. She had all these people who were looking to her to save them, and she couldn't do a damn thing. Their leader was dead. And now she had to try to get some sleep before carrying the body back to Los Angeles in the morning.

THE FUNERAL DIRECTOR at People's told her he would do all he could to keep Sam's color, but the body was getting darker by the day — it was lucky the funeral and final interment were going to take place on Saturday. Barbara's old friend, the Reverend H.B. Charles, who by his own eagerness to take care of her and her baby when she first moved to Los Angeles had been unwittingly instrumental in finally getting Sam to marry her, had prevailed upon Barbara to allow him to perform the obsequies at his fashionable Mount Sinai Baptist Church. She wasn't sure why she agreed to it, she told a friend, she knew he just wanted the publicity, but he begged and begged her, and he did have one of the biggest churches in town.

The funeral was scheduled to begin at 2 P.M., but just the crush of people outside would have delayed its start, and Barbara's late arrival in the Rolls only extended the delay all the more. People began showing up at 9 A.M., and by noon, there were close to five thousand standing outside in the rain, as local residents flung open their windows and the sound of Sam Cooke's music eerily echoed from turntables and radios throughout the neat, well-kept-up neighborhood. "Long lines of convertible Cadillacs, Rivieras, and Thunderbirds," the *Afro-American* newspaper chain reported, "ladies in more mink and men in more silk than the Internal Revenue allows [arrived to give Sam] a regal send-off highlighted by brouhahas, rhubarbs, and enough wrinkled fenders to make any blues singer cry a new kind of blues."

It was yet another celebration from which Sam alone had been strangely excluded. All his friends were there, everyone he had known from the start, Alex and Crain, Bumps, René and Sugar, Oopie, Lou Rawls, Lou Adler, Paul Foster from the Stirrers, Jesse Whitaker from the Pilgrim Travelers, Johnny Thunder, Jess Rand, Al Schmitt and his wife, Joan, nearly every one of Sam's SAR artists, Ray Charles, and B.B. King. There were television crews invited by the Reverend Charles and loudspeakers set up to pipe the sound to the crowd outside. A lot of people were taken aback when the Womack brothers arrived, each dressed in an identical dark suit of Sam's, but Barbara had given them the suits, she explained to Sugar Hall, because they had nothing else to wear. Barbara herself arrived in a diamond-mink coat, with Crain, the kids, a uniformed nurse, and a white man she identified as her new financial adviser. He was, in fact, a vice president at the Wilshire-Robertson Bank of America, and Barbara needed his help to gain access to the Tracey account, which would otherwise have been frozen with Sam's death. A photographer who had been banned from the funeral home for snapping a picture of Sam in his casket was selling prints outside for twenty-five cents apiece.

Inside the church, after an organ prelude by Billy Preston, the Womack brothers, billed as "Sam Cooke's Musicians [with] René Hall Conductor, Clif White, Dir.," struggled tearfully to complete "Yield Not to Temptation," their first SAR release. Then Lou Rawls, ordinarily the most controlled of performers, sang "Just a Closer Walk With Thee" with unrestrained emotion, barely able to contain his grief or mask the anger he felt at Elisa Boyer, the woman he blamed for Sam's death. Zelda practically had to slug her way into the church in the middle of Lou's performance. She couldn't find a parking place, and when she arrived at the church door, she was met by some functionary who tried to block her entrance. She was not about to be denied, she told writer Daniel Wolff. "I had a fist," she said, "and I just flung [it]. . . . I was screaming. I was kicking." Nor did her efforts go unnoticed. "Every time things would get real solemn and quiet," said René Hall, "she'd push back these guards and force the door open and they'd snatch her back." It was, said René, a rare moment of comic relief, but when Johnnie Morisette started screaming, "I'm sorry, I'm sorry, Sam," and then began to weep uncontrollably, it triggered an hysterical reaction all through the church.

After a Scripture reading by Reverend Charles and a brief prayer, Bumps' longtime gospel protégé, Bessie Griffin, got up to sing, but she was barely able to get out of her seat before she was overcome with such intensity of emotion that she had to be carried out. There was momentary confusion, and then Ray Charles, sitting on the edge of the roped-off family section, stood up, the *Los Angeles Sentinel* reported, and "asked to 'see' the body of his slain friend for the last time." Standing by Sam's casket, he asked the crowd what they wanted him to do. "Sing!" the response came back. And he sat down at the piano and sang "Angels Keep Watching Over Me" as J.W. leaned over, gravely holding the mike.

"I gave my heart to it," said Ray, whose career almost perfectly mirrored Sam's, each encountering bitter criticism when he "crossed over," in Ray's case by introducing gospel sounds to a pop setting, in Sam's by embracing pop. "The song itself I loved, because it was so true. 'All night and all day / All day and all night / The angels keep watching over me.' You know, that says so much, and that's what I felt about him. I tried to sing it in such a way that he would be proud. Sam had a uniqueness about him. Nobody sound like Sam Cooke. I mean *nobody*. He hit every note where it was supposed to be, and not only hit the note but hit the note with feeling. Everything that came out of me that day was truly genuine. There was nothing fake about it, and somehow in my heart I felt he was listening."

"It was," said René Hall, the consummate a&r man, "the greatest gospel rendition I ever heard in my entire life." According to *Ebony*, "women fainted, tears rolled down men's cheeks and onlookers shouted," and the renditions of two more of Sam's gospel favorites by Bobby "Blue" Bland and Arthur Lee Simpkins, a forty-nine-year-old classically trained baritone whom Sam had known from his early days in Chicago, only added to the "genuineness," and genuine hysteria, of the moment.

After a lengthy sermon by Reverend Charles ("Sam Cooke has lived his life. He has made his contribution. If he had not died when he did, Sam Cooke would still have to die sometime"), the funeral ended as the skies grew even darker and the thousands of people lining both sides of West Adams Boulevard held up the two-hundred-car procession for a full forty minutes before it could get under way to Forest Lawn Memorial Park in Glendale, where Vincent, too, was buried. At the cemetery Barbara picked a rose from the casket, and four-year-old Tracey said loud enough for everyone to hear, "Oh, you're going to wake my daddy up," as they lowered the casket into the ground. "No," said Linda, clasping her little sister's hand and looking very hurt and very adult, "he's not going to wake up anymore." It was night, and the rain was still falling.

Afterward they all went back to the house, and Barbara met with Sam's musicians and explained that, while Sam had made no provision for them, she was going to give each a few hundred dollars, which she hoped would help, because there wasn't going to be any more. There was some grumbling, and some remonstrance about withholding taxes that hadn't been paid, but eventually, said June Gardner, "we split, and that was it. It was a beautiful operation, but the patient died."

It was the end of their world. For each of them it marked a bitter conclusion, but for no one more than Barbara. She was terrified of the future, and Sam had already begun to disappear. For all his faults, he had always taken care of her. Who was going to look out for her now?

Aftermath

WITHIN JUST A FEW DAYS of the funeral Barbara and Bobby Womack were in a full-blown relationship. As Barbara described it to her friend Gertrude Gipson for a headline story in the *Los Angeles Sentinel* one month later, "Bobby has been my constant escort for the last few weeks and has been seen with me at most of the functions I have recently attended." Despite rumors to the contrary, she was not yet married, she said, but she showed off "a very large and beautiful 'carat' on her left finger . . . a gift from the musician-vocalist," who, in an accompanying article, was described as bearing "a remarkable resemblance to the late Cooke as well as comparable mannerisms."

Bobby's first act even before entering into his new role was to throw Barbara's boyfriend out of the house after the funeral. He had come by to pay his respects and found the man, the bartender from the Flying Fox, wearing Sam's watch, ring, and robe. "I was like, 'This motherfucker's trying to fuck over my hero.' I told him to take off the watch. I said, 'Get the fuck out of here, and give me that robe, too, while you going.' He was a big guy. He could have floored me, and I would have never known what hit me. But at that point it didn't matter — it was the first time I really felt like a man. Barbara said, 'I like a man who speaks up. I'm impressed.' That was the quick move."

The next move was not immediately apparent to Bobby, but he could tell she was impressed enough to encourage him to keep coming around. From Barbara's point of view Bobby's company was not only welcome, it was necessary. She felt abandoned. Nobody cared about *her* — nobody really approved of her. And even though René and Sugar Hall and Alex

Barbara and Bobby. *Courtesy of Barbara Cooke and ABKCO*

and Carol still came by all the time, she could tell they were looking at her funny, they were trying to watch out in case she went off or something. Sam had made a laughingstock of her in front of the whole damn world. She took the children out of school — she didn't know when she would send them back — she just didn't want them to have to suffer the kind of ridicule that she sensed all around her. If her husband was going to get himself killed, why did he have to get killed in some fleabag ghetto motel? Why couldn't he have gone someplace with someone with a little more class? At least then he wouldn't have left her looking so ridiculous in everyone's eyes.

Then one night, right around Christmas, after René and Sugar Hall had left and the kids were asleep, Bobby started talking about how his brothers had decided to go back to Cleveland, but he wanted to stay out here. She explained to him that she couldn't do anything for him, she didn't know how she was going to get by herself, but he said that he knew he had some songwriter's royalties coming from Kags, she could just keep the money if she would let him stay and work with her. She reminded him that he was in a group with his bothers, but he said, "I don't have to be with my brothers." She gave him a long, assessing look, and then it hit her all of a sudden, how death and sexual attraction went hand in hand. He looked a little scared, but when she indicated her feelings, he didn't turn her down, and that was the beginning.

Bobby remembered it a little differently. In his recollection: "She called and said, 'Bob, I want you to come over here. Sam left something on a tape. It's some songs, and I don't want [anybody else] to hear what it is, and I don't know how to work the tape recorder . . . ' So — I'll never forget. It was in the early evening, and René and his wife was there — I wanted to get out there early, because I've always been scared of dead people, like they'll come back. Anyway, I'm trying to work the tape recorder [in Sam's little workshop/studio], and she's standing so close behind me I couldn't even move my arms, and I said, 'Damn, all you got to do is push right here, it's easy.' She said, 'You never look at me when I'm talking. You afraid of women, but you ain't that little boy no more. You got your chance now [to] be a big man.' I said, 'I just want to get this tape to work.'

"It was like *The Graduate*. She went back in the house and comes back in a red robe, full-length. She said, 'You seem like you're nervous to me.' I said, 'I'm not nervous. I think I might see Sam.' She said, 'Sam?' She said, 'Sam is dead.' I said, 'Yeah, but his spirit is all over the house.'

"Then she started saying, 'René, when are y'all gonna be leaving? 'Cause I'm tired.' Or something like that. So they was laughing and joking, like they knew what was happening, and I was really petrified. 'Cause I'm saying, This woman is hurt, and she's coming on to me to get revenge or whatever, but I'm caught up in the shit. At the same time, to be honest with you, I was thinking of all the times I wanted a woman and could never get one on the road, and I got the real one now. 'Cause you could not get no heavier than this. Let me show her what I know.

"So she was telling me, like, 'You afraid, you're scared.' I said, 'I'm not scared. You know how I feel about Sam.' So she said, 'Well —' And one thing led to another, and she said, 'Give me a kiss. I mean, a real kiss.' And she was more challenging. I didn't like it, because she was more dominant than I ever could have been. I felt like a kid again. She tells me to go in the bedroom. I said, 'No way. If I die, I want to die on the couch.' She finally talked me into coming in there, and the only reason I went in was because she said, 'I'm gonna cut out the light, and I hope you'll be comfortable in here.' But, you know, something weird happened, man. The next morning I woke up, and them front doors were wide open, big hardwood doors that were never open because [everybody] always went in the back — I thought he had came and opened the doors just to let me know he was there.

"I don't remember if it was that day, but it wasn't too long before she said, 'Bobby, people are going to be talking about us. Why don't you marry me?'"

PEOPLE *WERE* TALKING, and Bobby was causing trouble for at least a few of them in his efforts to take care of her. J.W. came by his place on Budlong before he had any idea that there was something going on between Bobby and Barbara. He told Bobby that the company still had money in the bank and that he wanted to invest it in Bobby and his brothers because, like Sam, he had faith in their talent and would do anything he could to keep them on the label. Instead of being flattered, Bobby went straight to Barbara, just as he had a week or two earlier about the new musical instruments Sam had bought for the band. After taking in the fact that Alexander was throwing money around that by all rights was at least half hers (and was attributable, she felt, almost entirely to Sam's creative contributions), she asked Bobby why he was telling her this. "Sam would have wanted me to," Bobby told her. "I just want to protect you from everybody, 'cause everybody is out to get you." After that, he said, "she totally trusted me."

Not surprisingly, Bobby's protectiveness was not taken in quite the same spirit by anyone else. For J.W., there was first disappointment, then disgust. For Sam's peers, who saw Bobby driving around in Sam's car, dressed in Sam's clothes and squiring Sam's wife, it was almost like the punchline of a dirty joke. Even Bobby's own brothers sought to distance themselves from him initially. "They said, 'The disc jockeys ain't gonna play our record 'cause you on it.'" The rumor was all over town that Bobby had been in bed with Sam's old lady when Sam got killed. "I was accused of all kinds of shit, and I was totally innocent. Everybody said, 'That little guy that he always would take [out with him], that he loved, has finally got his dream come true.' But I can understand them taking the attitude that they did. I [should] have done it differently."

The public outcry over Sam's death, meanwhile, continued unabated. Talk of conspiracy abounded, with newspaper headlines suggesting cover-up and conspiracy, speculation reported as fact, and otherwise straightforward accounts heavily interlaced with irony and disbelief. "The story goes that Sam Cooke picked Miss Boyer up in a Sunset Strip bar. The story goes . . . " was the way one ANP dispatch put it before acknowledging that "seldom in show business annals has there been so much unhypocritical postmortem expression of shock and regret." But amidst all the hand-wringing, there were stirrings that indicated that even Sam's adoring public might have to come to grips with an uncomfortable truth. The most commonly quoted reservation was one that first appeared in a syndicated series by A. S. "Doc" Young, "The Mysterious Death of Sam Cooke." "Sam was a swinging guy," an unidentified female friend of the family was quoted as saying, "but he couldn't keep away from those $15 tramps." Or as Bumps Blackwell put it more acerbically some years later, "I often said Sam would walk past a good girl to get to a whore."

The precise scenario of his death remained a matter of debate among Sam's friends and associates, but almost all could imagine how it *might* have happened, given Sam's temper and the sense of unbridled rage that could manifest itself when he felt that he had been wronged. "He'd come out charging," said one old friend. "He would *not* back down," said another. There was dark talk of the Mafia; René Hall developed an elaborate theory of a drug deal involving someone closely connected to Sam in which Sam tried to intervene. Those who were less close to him interpreted the death as everything from simple betrayal to outright murder, whether by those within his domestic circle or powerful forces outside his control ("He was just getting too big for his britches for a sun-tanned man," said one woman friend). Sam's sisters saw it not only as altogether implausible, totally uncharacteristic of Sam's way of life, but as irrefutable evidence of the same kind of spitefulness, envy, and racism that permeated society. Even Elvis Presley subscribed to a variant of this point of view. "You can only go so far," he told his spiritual advisor and hairdresser, Larry Geller. "Sam got out of line, and he was taken care of." But J.W. Alexander, Sam's partner and friend, came to see it as little more than a tragic accident, a senseless waste of a life, while Sam's brother L.C. announced that he was "preparing to step into the giant-sized entertainment shoes of his slain brother" just one week after the funeral, when he went into rehearsals for a memorial album and what would turn out to be a month-long memorial tour.

T HE INVESTIGATION that had been instigated by Allen Klein and J.W. Alexander in the wake of Sam's death was brought to an abrupt halt three days after Christmas. Even as the newspapers were trumpeting that "a crack organization of private investigators paid for by the slain singer's relatives" was about to crack the case, Allen decided to shut it down, not because he was satisfied with the results but because he was convinced that it was not going to lead anywhere useful. The investigation to date, the Beverly Hills P.I., Mr. Pelletreau, reported, had "clearly shown that the victim Sam Cooke was lured to the place where he died by trick and device and though the homicide was justifiable, the alledged [sic] kidnapping was pure fiction" — as any observer with common sense or knowledge of the street would surely have concluded by now. The report further stated that "Elisa Boyer is well known among the cheap nightclub hangers on as being a professional roller. Her regular modus operendi [sic] [is] to lure the victim into a cheap hotel room and after they are both undressed to tell the victim that it is her custom not to undertake the evening's entertainment until after her male partner has bathed. When he goes into the bathroom she then steals the clothes and takes off." It named her pimp, a well-known local musician, and implicated him not in the killing but in the social mechanics of the introduction and in the business arrangements that ensured his participation in the profits. As for the murder itself:

Elisa made two miscalculations, one when she grabbed the clothing, she missed the victim's coat, this made it possible for him to
leave the room. And two, she miscalculated the effect of the liquor
on the victim and the violent reaction that occurred when he discovered that she had taken him. There is little question in my mind that
were we to continue the inquiry we could prove this investigation beyond a reasonable doubt. . . . I do not know what your final intentions
are but I do know that if we do not tie up the facts in the very near
future, we are going to throw away our investment. . . . I am holding
the file open pending further instructions.

But Allen wasn't worried about throwing away his investment. He
was worried more about what the private investigator was uncovering, or
might potentially uncover, about Sam and Barbara's marriage. He didn't
know if Barbara was aware that Sam had spoken to Marty Machat about
possibly instituting divorce proceedings, he didn't really know (and he
didn't want to find out) where the business of the bartender would lead.
And when he brought up the matter of the investigation to Barbara, she
indicated not just her willingness but her eagerness to drop the whole
thing. She said, "Allen, I have two kids. There are two questions I'd like
to ask you. Can you get Sam out of the room with that woman? Can you
bring him back? I just don't want to put my children through this." As
Allen saw it, it was, in the end, her call.

However brave a front she might put on for the outside world, there
was an increasing sense of panic on Barbara's part. She didn't trust
Allen, she didn't trust Alex, she didn't even know where all the money
was — and she was afraid to admit it. Every morning she awoke with
nightmares. She was terrified about how she was going to manage. "I
just don't know, Bobby," she told her twenty-year-old protector. "We ain't
gonna be able to stay here long." He tried to tell her that Sam had always
said that publishing was the backbone of his business, but she wouldn't
listen — it was like she wasn't going to let Sam dictate to her from
beyond the grave. "Well, this is mine," she lashed out when Bobby
offered her advice. "You can't tell me what to do with it." And she
expressed her determination to sell it all as soon as she could.

She showed Bobby off all over town, heedlessly, it seemed, some
would say shamelessly. She brought him into the office and told Alexan-

der that Bobby was going to be occupying Sam's office from now on. "She said to me, 'I'm your partner now, and I ain't gonna be like Sam.' She said, 'Sam trusted you, you did everything, [but] I'm going everywhere that you go and make your deals, and Bobby gonna take over Sam's office.' I told her, 'I'm gonna take over Sam's office, and I'm gonna give Harold Battiste my office.' That was when she went to [her lawyer] Hecht." That was also, in effect, the end of their partnership, and J.W. began to quietly make plans to release all of his artists. As he saw it, he could still administer the publishing and back catalogue, and he could go into management for himself. And he planned to record a memorial album for Sam. He wrote a song called "Our Years Together," which would eventually become the centerpiece of the album. "When the evening shadows fall," he wrote:

That's when I remember most of all . . .
Dreams of finding happiness
The times of our searching for success . . .
I miss you more than words can explain
The joy I feel when others call your name

"Sam and I were just so fucking close," he said. "Doing the album was the only thing that really helped me."

JUST TWO WEEKS after denying that she was married to Bobby, on February 11 Barbara permitted *Sentinel* columnist Gertrude Gipson to reveal to the world the time and place of her upcoming wedding. In a story headlined "A Change Is Gonna Come For Barbara," it was stated that "barring any rumored complications which we won't even bother reporting," Barbara and Bobby planned to marry at the Los Angeles county courthouse on February 25, "two days after the final disposition of Barbara's late husband's estate." In an accompanying interview Bobby stated that Sam would have wanted him to do this and that the children were very fond of him and "think I look a lot like Sam." He was planning on reorganizing his group and getting out on the road right away, he told Gipson. And he did not believe that any of the "recent stories or headlines linking him with Barbara Cooke [would] in any way harm his work, at least he is hoping not. Nor does he feel that this will take away any happiness." Barbara's mother, on the other hand, said only, "I don't know anything about those people's business. . . . I just don't have anything at all to say."

Sam's new single, "Shake" (with the edited version of "A Change Is Gonna Come" on the B-side), was nearing the top of the charts when Barbara brought Bobby to RCA to meet with Sam's producer, Al Schmitt. Schmitt knew Bobby from Sam's sessions over the last year and a half, but he had never had much to do with him personally, and he was totally unprepared for the sight with which he was greeted. There the two of them were, dressed to the nines, Barbara as usual looking hard, remote, and glamorous, while Bobby was dressed head to foot in Sam's clothing. "The sports jacket, the slacks — it was all Sam's. I just went blank. I mean, I don't remember a thing after that. I thought, 'God almighty, it's only been a [couple of] months!'"

L.C. had already approached RCA himself with the idea of being signed. With his younger brother, David, he had traveled to New York and lunched with two RCA executives, who told him they might be interested if he could get Allen Klein to endorse the deal. But L.C. didn't know Allen Klein, and for all he knew, this was just a polite putdown on the record company's part, so he and David turned around and drove back to Chicago, and he started his memorial tour in the middle of January.

Actually, it was two tours. The first was headlined by Jackie Wilson, with the Upsetters as the backing band and L.C., billed as "Sam's good-looking singing brother," giving away free eight-by-ten "Memorial Souvenir" pictures of Sam, whose photograph at the top of the poster was identified only as "That 'Good Times' Singing Guy." The second tour, a mix of gospel and pop including Jerry Butler, the Impressions, Johnnie Taylor, the Soul Stirrers, and the present-day Highway QCs, served as a more explicit tribute to Sam, with Johnnie singing "Rome Wasn't Built in a Day," the Upsetters' "Johnny 'Guitar' Taylor" doing "Tennessee Waltz," the Soul Stirrers featuring Sam's best-known gospel hits, and L.C., of course, building his set around faithful but somehow over-the-top representations of such familiar numbers as "Wonderful World," "Good Times," and "Twistin' the Night Away." There was something almost spooky about the tour, a Supersonic Attractions package with the headliner undeniably present but unaccountably absent and his brother, like Bobby out in L.A., summoning up memories that arrived, bidden or unbidden, with eerie familiarity. "L.C. scared me," said Billy Davis, who had played with Hank Ballard and the Midnighters in the early days and now was back with Jackie, his boyhood friend. "He looked just like Sam. It was like seeing a ghost."

BERTHA LEE FRANKLIN, the woman who had shot Sam, made a claim against the estate for $200,000 on February 16. In the immediate aftermath of Sam's death she had gotten so many threats that she had been forced to move from the motel and temporarily go into hiding. In her lawsuit she sought $100,000 in punitive damages and $100,000 for the injuries she had suffered "as a result of wilful misconduct, assault and battery, recklessness, carelessness and negligence of the decedent."

Elisa Boyer had by now gotten two continuances of her trial on a prostitution charge stemming from a January 11 arrest at a Hollywood motel. After all the public debate about whether she was or was not a prostitute ("Although Miss Lisa Boyer has no police record," J.W. had stated unequivocally to the *Sentinel* just days prior to her arrest, "we have absolute evidence in hand which indicates that she is definitely a hooker"), she had named a price of $40 over the telephone and was then picked up by an undercover agent posing as a client at the "swank" Hollywood motel that had served as their assignation. She, too, had been forced to leave her old address following Sam's death, but the $300-a-month rent she was paying at her new apartment, with no evidence of gainful employment, was one of the elements that led to renewed questions about her means of support. The case was thrown out eventually by a municipal judge on the basis that the "telephone date" represented an infringement on protected constitutional rights ("What kind of a country would we have," the judge asked, "if a man could get into your house . . . under deception?") and constituted police entrapment. The arrest, however, bore out the point that J.W. and Allen Klein had been making all along: that Sam was the victim of a robbery, not the perpetrator of a crime, that he was killed, as Allen now publicly formulated the private investigator's findings, "searching not for a girl but for his missing driver's license and credit cards. . . . It just wasn't Sam's nature to chase women like that."

Bobby and Barbara showed up at the Los Angeles county courthouse a day early, on Wednesday, February 24, with their blood tests and license application. Bobby was wearing Sam's blue suit with black shoes and sunglasses; Barbara was dressed much as she had been at the inquest, in a lime green princess-style coat-and-dress ensemble, pearl necklace, and slouch hat. Linda and Tracey, René and Sugar Hall, and a tuxedoed Walter Hurst were all present as guests and witnesses. Television cameras were ready to record the event, but the application was "flatly refused," Gertrude Gipson reported in the *Los Angeles Sentinel*, because Bobby, just eight days short of his twenty-first birthday, did not have his parents' permission to marry. Barbara made light of the foul-up, but "according to reliable sources permission was denied by Womack's mother who allegedly stated she 'wanted no part of it.' " Bobby said, "Let's go to Cleveland anyway," and they took off with Barbara's two girls on a kind of pre-wedding honeymoon, to meet Bobby's and Barbara's families in Cleveland and Chicago, before returning to Los Angeles to finally wed on March 5, the day after Bobby's birthday. His brothers, evidently, were now reconciled to the marriage. Curtis Womack was quoted about the ceremony in the *Amsterdam News,* and the paper described the "big plans" Sam had had for the Valentinos and his intention "to invest a large sum of money into promotion for them. His widow, Barbara," the *News* commented drily, "apparently intends to pick up where Sam left off." Bobby followed up with an interview in which he declared that he and his brothers were currently negotiating with both RCA and Chess Records and would be recording in future as Bobby and the Valentinos, with Allen Klein serving as their manager.

THE COOK FAMILY'S ANGER only continued to grow. To one degree or another they all held Barbara responsible for Sam's death, and her marriage to Bobby was just the latest in a series of insults not only to Sam's memory but to their status as a family. In the absence of a will, no one had been taken care of, and they could hardly expect anything from Barbara, given her long-standing feelings about them and theirs about her. Annie May was broken-hearted, and her health visibly deteriorated as she mourned the loss of her "sweet," "thoughtful," "wonderful" child whose greatest desire as a boy "was to grow up and take care of his parents when we got old." Reverend Cook simply took his daughter-in-law's remarriage as proof that she had never been worthy of his son in the first place. Charles, on the other hand, continued to harbor thoughts of revenge.

His opportunity came sooner than he expected. Sam's niece Gwendolyn, Mary's daughter, was getting married on June 27, and Linda and Tracey had been invited to take part in the ceremony. Barbara had no interest in going, but Bobby was determined not to be run off. "Charles called and threatened me. He said, 'Hey, motherfucker, I know the real

Bobby Womack.' I say, 'Hey, I'm packing my clothes.' Barbara said, 'You fucking crazy. You know how Charles is. Charles will kill you.' I said, 'It ain't about Charles. I can turn and be in his position and understand how he feels if somebody marries his brother's wife. He just gonna have to get it off his chest. But I'm going to be famous. I ain't gonna be running. I'll show them who the motherfucker is.' But when I [did], them niggers tried to kill me."

They registered at the Evans Hotel, where Sam had always stayed, and Charles called and seemed surprised to hear Bobby's voice. "Man, you a bold nigger," he said. But Bobby replied, "No, I just want to do what's right." Charles said that he and his brother David were going to come by the hotel, and Bobby said that was fine. He was still trying to persuade Barbara that if she would just give the family some money, things would be better for them all, most of all for her and the girls. But she was adamant, she'd be damned if she'd give those Cooks any money after the disrespect they had shown her. "She told me, 'Honey, I'm gonna put on a robe.' And I knew she had a gun under the pillow — I told her not to bring it but I knew she did — and when she went in the bathroom, I took all the bullets out and put it back under the pillow. Then they came up, and Charles said, 'How you doing, Bobby?' And I said, 'I'm doing fine. I just come to try to straighten this thing out if we can' — and then he hit me. And he hit me again. And after that I don't remember nothing else. I mean, I remember hearing stuff, but I didn't feel nothing. I ain't talking about no easy beating — they broke my jaw, and my head must have been this big. And Barbara was saying, 'Stop hitting him, you're gonna kill him.' That's when she reached under the pillow. And I remember her pulling the gun out and firing, firing, firing. And she said, 'This motherfucker took the goddamn bullets out.' Then Charles took the gun from her and hit her in the jaw and knocked her down. And going out, he ran into the door and busted his head wide open."

There were headlines in the papers about "Cooke Family Feuds," and charges were filed against Charles for his pistol whipping of his brother's widow. The official story was that Charles had come to demand his royalties for "Chain Gang," on which he was still listed as coauthor, and that when Barbara found out what he was there for, "she became indignant [and] pulled a gun." Within a month, at Barbara's request, the charges were dropped, and Bobby turned out to be right; though he never actually won Charles over, he never had any trouble from him again. Bobby's brothers wanted to go to Chicago and make it a war, "but

I said, 'I jumped in this by myself, and I'm going to deal with it by myself.' Sooner or later everything gets old."

He had confidence in his talent. He knew that before too long he was going to make it. After all, Sam had believed in him, why shouldn't he believe in himself? Barbara was hot and cold about his ambitions. Sometimes she was tender with him. "She said, 'Why do you want to go on the road? Why don't I just build you a club, and you can sing there every weekend?' I said, 'Aw, baby, that won't be no challenge. I got to travel and all that. I got to make my own.' She said, 'Well, I'm not going to risk losing you like Sam. Sam used to be just like you. Square and clean, till he got out there on that road, and he just couldn't resist.'"

He would awaken to find her crying. Sometimes she would be screaming and hitting her head against the wall. He knew how much she thought about Vincent, he knew all about the little boy, Eric, she had tried to adopt. One day he said to her, "Why don't you just have another baby? We'll name him Vincent." He didn't really want a baby at this point, but he was willing to do it for her. So she went to the doctor and started taking hormone shots, and six months later she did get pregnant, and they did have a boy, and she named him Vincent.

In the meantime, against all of Allen's and everyone else's advice, she withdrew all of the money from the Tracey account, converted Sam's tax-free bonds into cash, and in July sued to dissolve the Kags Music Corporation. Bobby tried to tell her that she was going to undo everything Sam had worked for, "but at that point I was back in school again, and she was the boss." As he saw it, Barbara simply didn't know who to trust, and with Alexander and Allen off together in England to sign up the Rolling Stones and some of those other English groups, she had no idea, as Bobby said, who was "on her team."

In the end her lawsuit against J.W. succeeded only in creating a deadlocked corporation, and, faced with the tax bill that resulted from her conversion of all of her assets into cash, she sold her half of the company to Hugo and Luigi in June 1966 for the bargain-basement price of $75,000. Little more than six months later, when they found themselves deadlocked in much the same way as Barbara, primarily, they came to believe, due to the actions of the company's administrator, they sold their half to the administrator, Allen Klein, for what amounted to double the price they had paid. By the time that Allen bought out J.W. for $350,000 two years later, RCA had run out of new Sam Cooke tracks to issue, but his presence never ceased to be felt not just on the pop charts (where everyone from the Animals and Herman's Hermits to Simon and Garfunkel, James Taylor, and Aretha Franklin continued to interpret his songs) but as a symbol of an era that glowed with racial pride, ambition, and promise. When Martin Luther King was killed, Rosa Parks, the woman who had galvanized the Movement in 1955 when she refused to give up her seat on the bus, was sitting at home with her mother, and in the midst of their tears, holding each other and rocking back and forth, they played Sam's "A Change Is Gonna Come." Sam's "smooth voice," she said, "was like medicine to the soul. It was as if Dr. King was speaking directly to me."

For those closest to Sam, his words, his sayings, his drive and determination, that almost invincible optimism and beguiling good humor remained a beacon illuminating their way. His death was something with which many of them were unable to contend, but his life — and his spirit — were a rare glimpse of the kind of enlightenment to which each, in his or her own way, might momentarily aspire. Other than his brother L.C., he found his greatest disciple in Bobby, who did go on to the success that Sam had predicted for him, though not without the pitfalls that sometimes, in his more sentimental moments, he thought Sam might have helped him to avoid. As Bobby noted, Sam's greatest lesson was to cherish each moment. "I knew I loved it, but I didn't know I loved it that much. I couldn't even appreciate it [at the time]. You know, you get caught up in it till you're on a merry-go-round, but if I could say one thing to anybody in this business, it would be, 'Don't pass up a day when you could make something count. Do it to your fullest ability.' 'Cause you never go back to [those days] again."

For Barbara, after all the bitterness and recriminations, even today in the midst of her ongoing argument with Sam, it is the beginning that she always returns to, when snowflakes fell like crystals and diamonds as the two of them huddled together in Ellis Park. "That was our spot. It was so quiet and serene, with those beautiful lights [shining] on all that clean, soft snow. We'd walk around the park for hours and fantasize. We didn't have a dime between us, but you'd have thought I was the princess, and he was the prince. Every time a Cadillac went by, I'd say, 'That's our chauffeur. He's coming to take us [home] to our mansion.' Sam said, 'You're my love. I'll always love you — forever.' And I believed that till he died. Do you know that's everybody's ending? Everybody wants a happy ending. That's the way I see it."

Notes

THE MAJORITY OF THE INTERVIEW MATERIAL is my own, but I am indebted to John Broven, Rick Coleman, Ray Funk, Lee Hildebrand, Cilla Huggins, Dred Scott Keyes, David Kunian, Joe McEwen, Bill Millar, Opal Louis Nations, Michael Ochs, Ed Pearl, Lee Poole, Steve Propes, Ben Sandmel, and Doug Seroff for sharing their raw, and in many cases unpublished, tapes and transcripts, which are specifically acknowledged in the notes themselves.

At BMG (RCA) Glenn Korman, Jeff Walker, Rob Santos, and Vicky Sarro all went out of their way to help.

I can't imagine writing about Sam's years with the Soul Stirrers without having had the kind of access to the Specialty Records archives that Bill Belmont provided, along with the insightful commentary and interpretation supplied by both Bill and Billy Vera.

Allen Klein opened up the most extraordinary source of insight and information of all when he made available to me the complete archive of newspaper clippings, filmed television performances, AFM session sheets, original tape boxes and session tapes (interpreted by Teri Landi), legal documents, photographs, and contractual and booking information (the whole curated by Cheri Wild) that he has assembled over the years.

Many others contributed their time and resources, and I have tried to indicate my thanks and indebtedness in both these notes and the acknowledgments that follow.

What I have *not* done is to provide source notes for my own interviews, simply because in many cases I have interviewed people fifteen or twenty times (and frequently more) over the course sometimes of nearly as many years, and to attempt to separate out each strand of conversation would amount to a deconstruction of text, and an accumulation of source notes, that might equal the length of the book itself. So, where a quotation is not sourced, it can be assumed to come from one of my own interviews.

PROLOGUE: "THE QCS ARE IN THE HOUSE"

3 "There is no music like that music": James Baldwin, *The Fire Next Time*, p. 47.

4 "Mayor of Bronzeville": Albert G. Barnett, "R. H. Harris Elected Mayor of Bronzeville," *Chicago Defender*, November 10, 1945. Harris won by 87,800 votes "in the most bitterly contested election in Bronzeville history." The election was, in fact, a contest sponsored by the *Defender* "in an effort to have a Negro member of the community take an active part in

neighborhood affairs," with each sixty-cent ticket purchased to the election "frolic" at the Club DeLisa (which doubled as party site and polling place) worth one hundred votes.

4 "a new song": W. E. B. DuBois quoted in Mike Marqusee, *Redemption Song: Muhammad Ali and the Spirit of the Sixties,* pp. 93–94.

4 "a freedom . . . close to love": Baldwin, *The Fire Next Time,* p. 55.

5 It is at his signal: The specific description comes primarily from my interviews with Marvin Jones, augmented by Dred Scott Keyes' interview with Leroy Crume.

6 "He was just singing from his heart": Interview with Ann Thompson Taylor.

THE SINGING CHILDREN

9 the church split in two: The schism is delineated in Edith L. Blumhofer, *Restoring the Faith: The Assemblies of God, Pentecostalism, and American Culture,* pp. 77–78.

10 Mound Bayou, a self-sufficient all-black township: Information on Mound Bayou is derived from Neil R. McMillen, *Dark Journey: Black Mississippians in the Age of Jim Crow,* pp. 186–187, and *Mississippi: The WPA Guide to the Magnolia State* (originally published 1938).

11 Christ Temple Cathedral: Otho B. Cobbins, ed., *History of Church of Christ (Holiness) U.S.A. 1895–1965,* pp. 175–176.

13 "I worked up to one hundred and twenty-five": Daniel Wolff with S. R. Crain, Clifton White, and G. David Tenenbaum, *You Send Me: The Life and Times of Sam Cooke,* pp. 26–27.

14 "When they'd come back, the people would tell me": Reverend Charles Cook, at a press conference at the Waldorf-Astoria on his son's induction into the Rock 'n' Roll Hall of Fame, 1986.

14 "Brother, I made my money!": Wolff, *You Send Me,* p. 32.

21 He established his *own* business: The fence slat–selling business was also related by Sam, "with sparkling eyes and laughing," in the first part of a two-part profile by Ernestine Cofield, "Close Look at Sam Cooke: From 'Rags to Riches' Story of Young Chi Club Singer," *Chicago Defender,* October 18, 1958.

22 His teachers described Sam as "personable and aggressive": "Friends Doubt Singer's Death Story," *Chicago Defender,* December 14, 1964.

23 he was given a solo at the Christmas show: Don Nelsen, "A Successful Cooke," *New York Sunday Daily News,* July 16, 1961.

23 "We had to belong to a club to go to school": Ernestine Cofield, "Close Look at Sam Cooke," *Chicago Defender,* October 18, 1958.

25 "too old to be getting up there singing": Wolff, *You Send Me,* p. 39.

27 "singing around [different] places": Margurite Belafonte, "Eye to Eye with Sam Cook," *Amsterdam News,* December 21, 1957.

28 "He didn't bother about playing ball": Dred Scott Keyes interview with Reverend Charles Cook, 1995.

28 Then one day in the spring of 1947: In addition to my interview with Creadell Copeland, Barbara Cooke interview with Lee Richard, ca. 1984–1985.

"THE TEEN AGE HIGHWAY QUE CEES, RADIO AND CONCERT ARTISTS"

34 the "first all-Negro spiritual gospel concert": *Chicago Defender,* October 14, 1950.

35 "The competition was *very* strong": Dred Scott Keyes interview with J.W. Alexander, 1995.

35 an organization conceived as a kind of clearinghouse: Background on the formation of the National Quartet Convention (which is alternately referred to as either the National Quartet Union or Association) is derived primarily from my interview with R.H. Harris and Opal Louis Nations' interview with Abraham Battle as well as Kip Lornell's *"Happy in the Service of the Lord": Afro-American Gospel Quartets in Memphis*, pp. 84–85 in particular.

36 a focal point for the teenage gospel movement: Everyone recalls 3838 South State, and the hard-fought gospel "battles," but specifics on the day of the week, the size of the room, and the price of admission differ widely. For such a well-known venue, 3838 elicits a host of conflicting descriptions.

36 J.W. Alexander would always recall the first time he saw Sam singing: The one point of confusion here is whether or not this was a program that the Pilgrim Travelers headlined. J.W. recalled that it was, but more likely it was a drop-by situation, since both the Soul Stirrers and the Pilgrim Travelers had their own money-making programs to publicize. Gus Treadwell of the QCs remembered meeting J.W. at 3838, and J.W., whose recollections were almost invariably, and uncannily, accurate, believed that that first meeting came relatively early in Sam's tenure with the QCs, before R.B. Robinson started coaching them. In a ca. 1973 interview with *Blues & Soul* 124, he recalled a second meeting at a radio station broadcast some two years later, once again in passing. The Travelers appeared on the Soul Stirrers' radio show on WIND whenever they were in Chicago for a program, and by 1950 the QCs had a show of their own immediately following the Stirrers on the same station.

43 the all-star musicale at Holiness Community Temple in May: *Chicago Defender*, May 1, 1948. Gus Treadwell is listed as a guest artist, presumably to pad the bill. There is extensive background on the Gay Sisters in Opal Louis Nations, "The Gay Sisters," *Blues Gazette*, summer 1996.

45 "I just sat there, and I was spellbound": Daniel Wolff with S. R. Crain, Clifton White, and G. David Tenenbaum, *You Send Me: The Life and Times of Sam Cooke*, p. 52.

45 "He approached us at a church program": Which program this was remains a subject of speculation. Louis Tate simply told gospel researcher Ray Funk that it was "one of the major programs in Chicago." L.C. Cooke and Marvin Jones both recalled the occasion as a church program in Gary. Creadell Copeland spoke of playing Gary frequently prior to meeting Tate. Daniel Wolff, in his book *You Send Me*, posited that the meeting took place at the Soul Stirrers' September 26, 1948, program at DuSable, with the Flying Clouds and the Fairfield Four on the bill. The QCs were not advertised on that program, but that doesn't altogether rule out the possibility.

46 "He'd eat it, sleep it, walked it, talked it": Ray Funk interview with Louis Tate. This, and the Wolff interview quoted below, conducted by David Tenenbaum, are virtually identical in subject and language.

46 "He'd wake up at twelve [midnight], one o'clock, two o'clock": Wolff, *You Send Me*, pp. 60–61.

46 "he'd did his thing long enough": Wolff, *You Send Me*, p. 59.

47 its first state program of 1949: *Indianapolis Recorder*, May 14, 1949.

49 That was the summer . . . that they went to Memphis: Primary sources for the QCs' sojourn in Memphis were interviews with Reverend Gatemouth Moore, Essie Wade, Cornelia (Connie) Berry, Dan Taylor of the Southern Jubilees, and, of course, the QCs themselves. Also Ray Funk's interview with Louis Tate, Peter Lee, and David Nelson, "From Shoutin' the Blues to Preachin' the Word: Bishop Arnold Dwight 'Gatemouth' Moore," *Living Blues*, May/June 1989; Kip Lornell, *"Happy in the Service of the Lord"*; Louis Cantor, *Wheelin' on Beale: How WDIA-Memphis Became the Nation's First All-Black Radio Station and Created the Sound that Changed America*; and Doug Seroff's notes for the album *"Bless My Bones": Memphis Gospel Radio, The Fifties* (Rounder 2063) along with the album itself.

49 a public conversion onstage: " 'Gatemouth' Moore," *Ebony*, December 1949; see also Mike Streissguth, "Gatemouth Moore," *Goldmine*, July 31, 1998.

49 a revival at the . . . seven-thousand-seat home church, Mason Temple: *Memphis World*, July 29, 1949.

49 "the Memphis boy who skyrocketed to world fame": "Former Noted Blues Singer Returning to Memphis as Gospel Singer and Preacher," *Memphis World*, July 29, 1949; see also Nat D. Williams, "Beale Street's 'Gate'" in his "Down on Beale" column, *Pittsburgh Courier*, January 21, 1950.

51 a Women's Day program sponsored by R.H. Harris' wife: *Chicago Defender*, June 4, 1949.

51 Sam was taken with the singing of Cassietta Baker: Interviews with L.C. Cooke and Marvin Jones.

51 the Reverend Brewster . . . an extraordinary preacher and polymath: Information and quotes about the Reverend Brewster come primarily from Bernice Johnson Reagon, ed., *We'll Understand It Better By and By: Pioneering African American Gospel Composers*, particularly the section on Reverend Brewster, with contributions by Reagon, Horace Boyer, Anthony Heilbut, and William H. Wiggins Jr.

56 "The Teen Age Highway Que Cees, Radio and Concert Artists": *Chicago Defender*, March 25, 1950.

56 a "nasty book" that Sam had given to his girlfriend: Charles and L.C. Cooke, Barbara Cooke, Gus Treadwell, Roscoe Robinson, S.R. Crain in Wolff, *You Send Me*, and even Dan Taylor of the Southern Jubilees in Memphis described something of the circumstances of Sam's arrest, and most described the book itself — sometimes in graphic detail. Since in the end, though, I can't be sure who actually saw it, I've confined myself to the description in the court papers. Also, I'm not sure whether the Doolittle schoolgirl who was named in the complaint against Sam was a girlfriend or the sister of a girlfriend, since no mention is made in the court papers of a sister and at fifteen this young woman was older than Sam's steady girlfriend, Barbara Campbell. No one that I spoke to remembered the girl specifically. However, a sister kept being mentioned, so I have retained her, whether she is an echo or not.

56 "the obscene and indecent handwritten pamphlet": This description and all subsequent dates and data are from Municipal Court of Chicago Preliminary and Court Papers, February 23 and March 6, 1950, Case No. 26787.

57 "I get there and — no Sam": Dred Scott Keyes interview with S.R. Crain, 1996.

58 M. L. Itson's most egregious crime: All of the QCs, and L.C. Cooke, were voluble about Itson's perfidy, but the *Chicago Defender* in front-page stories on January 13, 1951 ("Rich Widow, 84, Missing, Seek Agent"), and January 20, 1951 ("Police Find Aged Widow in Basement"), specified not only Itson's crimes but the "rent racket" in general.

59 Harris had quit the Soul Stirrers: R.H. Harris told Lee Hildebrand in a 1984 interview that he left the group on October 16, 1950. He cited the same date to me and said that he introduced Sam onstage at DuSable before taking his leave — but there was no program at DuSable on October 16, though there was one in Meridian, Mississippi, on October 19. The Stirrers program at DuSable closest to that date took place on September 24, which Daniel Wolff cites as the departure date and is certainly plausible. Harris spoke at length in various interviews about taking Sam out on a series of programs in order to introduce him to Stirrers (and Harris) fans — but this almost certainly did not take place. Marvin Jones of the QCs was positive that no public announcement was made — there were simply rumors that Crain and Harris had had a fight — and I think that's as likely a scenario as any.

59 the group's original founding in Trinity: Historical background on the Soul Stirrers comes primarily from Ray Funk, "The Soul Stirrers," *Rejoice!* 1 (1), winter 1987; Funk's 1981 interview with S.R. Crain; Tony Heilbut, *The Gospel Sound: Good News and Bad Times;* Opal Louis Nations' liner notes for a forthcoming 2005 Soul Stirrers release on Acrobat; and numerous interviews and monographs, not all of which, it must be noted, agree in every particular. In his interview with Lee Hildebrand, R.H. Harris said that Crain sought him out and got his parents' permission for him to tour with the group for just two months. They arrived in California in November 1937 and then were stuck there for the next few months by a series of floods, which are documented in various histories of the area.

60 "art almost immune to criticism": Heilbut, *The Gospel Sound*, p. 82.

60 "as you get more records out on the SPECIALTY label": Art Rupe to S.R. Crain, June 6, 1950 (this and all subsequent Specialty correspondence comes from the Specialty archive).

61 "Harris really believed in what he was doing": Dred Scott Keyes interview with J.W. Alexander, 1995.

61 "The moral aspects of the thing just fell into the water": Heilbut, *The Gospel Sound*, p. 86. Crain contended, however, in his interview with Dred Scott Keyes, that Harris was no more religious than any of the Stirrers, or the average gospel singer, for that matter, and Harris, in fact, joined the Christland Singers, with whom he continued to travel and record, almost immediately after his departure from the Stirrers.

61 Others viewed the matter: Various opinions were expressed by L.C. Cooke, Leroy Crume, Lee Richard (in his interview with Barbara Cooke), J.W. Alexander, and Marvin Jones, along with other *ex post facto* views.

61 politics was at the bottom of it all: J.W. Alexander suggested, "Sometimes friends tell them [lead singers] they are so much better than anyone else in the group. That's how different religions split up, same principle."

61 the December 1950 issue of *Ebony:* "Gospel Singers: They Move Millions with Their Ringing Voices," *Ebony*, December 1950.

62 After trying out Paul Foster as first lead: Ray Funk interview with Paul Foster, 1981.

62 Crain invited Sam to his apartment: The best description of Sam's tryout comes from Crain in Wolff, *You Send Me*, p. 65, from which Crain's quotes are taken.

62 a second audition . . . with Reverend Leroy Taylor: Taylor sang baritone on the Stirrers' December 21, 1948, session for Aladdin and was listed as second tenor on the stationery the Soul Stirrers were using as late as June 1950. In his 1981 interview with Ray Funk, Reverend Taylor said, "I helped train Sam Cook [while] I was going to seminary" — but he made no mention of any tryout of his own. And he was one of the founders of the Christlands, which R.H. Harris would almost immediately join.

62 The next day Sam came back to the house: To show how close the timing was, Itson disappeared on December 2. Crain wrote to Art Rupe on December 6 that the Stirrers and Pilgrim Travelers, who had just sung on the Stirrers' Tennessee Day program at DuSable, would be going out on tour together in two days. When they did, Sam went with them.

63 "I told him: 'Anytime you can make a step higher'": Dred Scott Keyes interview with Reverend Charles Cook, 1995.

SOUL STIRRING

65 "The Soul Stirrers were very well named": "Salient points from ANR's [Arthur N. Rupe's] Talk, from tape," n.d., Specialty archives.

65 a day or two before the . . . scheduled March 1 recording session: Art Rupe said that it was always his custom to audition the group just before the session and pick out at least four songs for them to concentrate on.

65 the Soul Stirrers had been out on the Coast for the past two and one-half weeks: They played the Embassy Theater in Los Angeles on February 11 with the Christian Travelers of Detroit (this was advertised in the *Los Angeles Sentinel* on January 24), and J.W. Alexander spoke of playing Oakland immediately thereafter. I never thought to ask about additional stops on the tour. The Stirrers had had a program in Chicago on January 14. They were still there on January 21 (Crain signed for a letter), and Art Rupe wrote to them again on January 30 with reference to their forthcoming tour. "I hear you're coming out next week," he said, suggesting that this might make it a good time for a session. In some ways, then, it is probably more accurate to see the tour as prompting (and paying the Stirrers' way to) the session rather than the other way around.

65 Where was Harris? he demanded of Crain: The story and the controversy surrounding this session come primarily from my interviews with J.W. Alexander, Pilgrim Travelers' baritone singer Jesse Whitaker, and Art Rupe (by fax); Dred Scott Keyes' 1996 interview with S.R. Crain; and Ray Funk's and Lee Hildebrand's interviews with Paul Foster, 1981 and 1984 respectively. Art Rupe's interviews for the BBC television series *Too Close to Heaven: The Story of Gospel Music;* Barret Hansen, "The Specialty Story," *Hit Parader,* June 1969; and the documentary CD *In His Own Words: Art Rupe — The Story of Specialty Records* (Ace CD 542) provided valuable insights as well.

68 He had first come to California: Background on Art Rupe, as well as a perspective on his aesthetic views and business principles, comes primarily from Billy Vera's booklet for *The Specialty Story* (Specialty 4412), an indispensable five-CD box set. See also *In His Own Words: Art Rupe — The Story of Specialty Records.*

69 "Gospel was my favorite type of music": *In His Own Words: Art Rupe — The Story of Specialty Records.*

70 a 1939 composition called "Peace in the Valley": The history of this song is a curious one. The earliest gospel recording that I'm aware of is a 1949 version on the tiny Trilon label by the San Francisco–based Paramount Singers, led by Tiny Powell, with whom Paul Foster had sung extensively in the Bay Area before joining the Soul Stirrers. Sam's friend Roscoe Robinson had recorded the song with the Southern Sons for the Jackson-based Trumpet label in May of 1950 — but, according to Marc Ryan, *Trumpet Records: Diamonds on Farish Street,* p. 18, the masters burned up in a fire, and no copies of the record are known to have survived. Why the Stirrers recorded the song at this particular time will have to remain something of a mystery. It might have been Paul Foster's familiarity with it, or Sam's or Crain's, for that matter — it could very well have been a staple on the *live* gospel circuit in Chicago. The reason that country singer Red Foley recorded it some four weeks later and the song rapidly became an across-the-board standard (Foley's version went to number five on the country charts) is more discernible. Red Foley, like Nashville superstar Eddy Arnold, had a copublishing deal with Hill and Range Songs. Hill and Range was owned by two Viennese-born brothers, Jean and Julian Aberbach, who at this point operated primarily within the country-and-western market but would soon dominate much of pop publishing, particularly after forging a copublishing deal with Elvis Presley at the start of his career. In early 1951, according to Bar Biszick, Jean Aberbach's biographer, the Aberbachs made their first tentative foray into gospel music, setting up an incipient publishing deal with Thomas A. Dorsey that would not be completed until August 1952. In the meantime, it would appear, they set out to expand the market for gospel songs, probably in order to prove themselves to Dorsey and to further both his interests and their own. That appears to be the reason for the sudden revival of interest in a twelve-year-old song, and it certainly helped further the song's prominence in Elvis' repertoire (he introduced it on *The Ed Sullivan Show* in January 1957 and recorded it shortly thereafter). None of this impinged on the Soul Stirrers, though, whose record came out several weeks before Red Foley's. Interestingly, Crain wrote to Art Rupe on September 14, in response to a question about the song's authorship and publishing, and made reference to the differences between the Stirrers' and Foley's versions.

71 they had just sold twenty thousand copies: All sales figures, here and subsequently, are from the Specialty archives.

71 "You will think that we have gone crazy": "Pre-release information for Distributors, Salesmen, Dealers," entitled "A PROMOTION PLAN TO MAKE YOU MONEY" and sent out ca. October 1950.

71 Crain and Alex were adamant . . . that he should at least give Sam's version a chance: J.W. Alexander said that Rupe called several months later to apologize for his reluctance to let Sam record the song (see similar letter to Crain below).

72 "Put all the showmanship that you can in your voices": Art Rupe to John E. Myles and the Swan Silvertones, March 29, 1952.

73 Pine Bluff: The fact that this was Sam's first program with the Stirrers was attested to again and again by both J.W. Alexander and S.R. Crain. J.W. always said that it was in December 1950, and this is borne out by the correspondence cited above, which indicates that it must have been the weekend of December 10. I have been unable, however, to find any additional listings or correspondence regarding that tour (most gospel programs were promoted on the radio and by word of mouth), and while Bob Riesman's yeoman research in the Pine Bluff area, in pursuit of his forthcoming biography of Big Bill Broonzy, has yielded some tantalizing clues, I'm afraid concrete evidence of the actual date is still lacking.

73 "You could stand next to Archie onstage:" Dred Scott Keyes interview with J.W. Alexander, 1995.

73 "Perkins could make Archie jump offstage": Dred Scott Keyes interview with S.R. Crain. Viv Broughton quotes an unnamed gospel star describing how Archie would "jump all the way off that balcony, down on the floor — blind!" in *Too Close to Heaven: The Illustrated History of Gospel Music*, p. 87.

74 "Our Father" [was] the kind of hit: "Our Father" actually entered *Billboard*'s Juke Box R&B Chart at number ten on December 30, 1950, a *very* rare occurrence for a gospel recording.

74 "Archie could make an audience cry": Interview with Bobby Womack, who met the Blind Boys at a very young age at a church program.

75 Archie was the only singer out there who could make *him* cry: Interview with L.C. Cooke.

75 It was "devastating": Interview with Leroy Crume.

75 "It wasn't a matter of me fitting into Sam's life": Barbara Cooke interview with S.R. Crain, ca. 1984–1985.

75 "Sam started as a bad imitation of Harris": Tony Heilbut, *The Gospel Sound: Good News and Bad Times*, p. 88.

75 " 'Jesus Gave Me Water' — that's easy": Ray Funk interview with Paul Foster, 1981.

76 the boy's only true "guide and protector": Barbara Cooke interview with S.R. Crain.

76 "You could never get him up in the morning": Terry Gross interview with S.R. Crain, *Fresh Air*, National Public Radio, March 23, 1995.

76 "Fortunately [he] went over well": "Behind the Scenes with J.W. Alexander," *Blues & Soul* 124, p. 14.

76 a series of cheerfully hectoring letters: Art Rupe wrote to Crain on September 7, 1951, "We want to thank you for suggesting that we put out 'Jesus Gave Me Water' and keeping on us until we did."

76 "Jesus Gave Me Water" was the single most requested number: Crain to Art Rupe, May 8, 1951, in a letter that speaks of having just played Orlando and Palm Beach.

78 Sam "did it in a different way": Heilbut, *The Gospel Sound*, p. 88.

79 they had rehearsals twice a week: Much of the detail concerning the Stirrers' day-to-day practices is from Barbara Cooke's interview with S.R. Crain.

79 Crain became a proud "papa": S.R. Crain to Art Rupe, September 14, 1951.

80 "a well-educated Negro lady": Art Rupe in a letter to Brother Joe May, February 7, 1950.

80 "a young liberal who doesn't [just] preach liberalism": Lillian Cumber letter housed in the Barnett Collection, Chicago Historical Society, cited in Daniel Wolff with S. R. Crain, Clifton White, and G. David Tenenbaum, *You Send Me: The Life and Times of Sam Cooke*, pp. 91–92.

81 J.W. Alexander attempted to intercede: Letter from J.W. Alexander to Lillian Cumber, May 14, 1951.

83 "We are very proud of the group": Art Rupe to S.R. Crain, September 7, 1951.

83 "gospel singing is not only popular but very lucrative": Charles Hopkins, "Wax and Needle," *Chicago Defender*, October 13, 1951.

84 "a part of our American heritage": "Wax and Needle," *Chicago Defender*, November 3, 1951.

84 "more appropriate to more enlightened times": Jerry Wexler and David Ritz, *Rhythm and the Blues: A Life in American Music*, p. 62. Wexler wrote this, he says in his memoir, in a "turn-of-the-decade" essay for the *Saturday Review* but introduced the term in *Billboard* earlier in 1949.

85 "The public is crazy about them": S.R. Crain to Art Rupe, September 14, 1951.

86 The young fellow was twenty-year-old Lloyd Price: Background on the Lloyd Price session comes primarily from my interviews with Lloyd as well as Dave Booth, "Lloyd Price, Mr. Personality," *Goldmine*, December 17, 1991, which quotes from an interview by Ian Whitcomb. See also Bill Dahl, "Lloyd Price: 'Mr. Personality,' " *Living Blues*, September–October 1999; Seamus McGarvey, "Lloyd Price: Mr. Personality," *Juke Blues* 24; and Billy Vera liner notes to Specialty CDs *Lawdy!* and *Heavy Dreams* (Specialty 7010 and 7047).

87 "The white retail shops began to carry it": *In His Own Words: Art Rupe — The Story of Specialty Records.*

87 "As far as we can determine": Jerry Wexler and Ahmet Ertegun, "The Latest Trend: R&B Disks Are Going Pop," *Cash Box*, July 3, 1954.

90 Five thousand singers from all over: *Los Angeles Sentinel*, August 7, 1952.

91 Mahalia Jackson announced: "Mahalia Jackson Will Tour Europe With Her Famous 'Gospel Train,'" *Chicago Defender*, August 9, 1952.

91 [she] would sell out Carnegie Hall once again: John Hammond, "Gospel Singers' Progress from Churches to Carnegie," November 19, 1952 (no further information), in Opal Louis Nations' liner notes to the 3-CD *Mahalia Jackson: How I Got Over / The Apollo Sessions* (Westside 303).

92 the European tour he had announced: Galen Gart, *First Pressings: The History of Rhythm & Blues*, 1951, p. 38, datelined April 7.

93 Crain clucked that Sam was going to have to learn: Barbara Cooke interview with S.R. Crain.

THE FURTHER EDUCATION OF SAM COOK

94 "He just floated under": Daniel Wolff, with S. R. Crain, Clifton White, and G. David Tenenbaum, *You Send Me: The Life and Times of Sam Cooke*, p. 101.

94 Crain sometimes ascribed the transforming moment: Dred Scott Keyes interview with S.R. Crain, 1996.

95 "I am indeed very sorry": Art Rupe to S.R. Crain, February 9, 1953.

97 a "full-fledged trend": Jerry Wexler and Ahmet Ertegun, "The Latest Trend: R&B Disks Are Going Pop," *Cash Box*, July 3, 1954.

97 a detailed memo that covered everything: Billy Vera booklet accompanying the five-CD box set *The Specialty Story* (Specialty 4412), p. 8; also see *In His Own Words: Art Rupe — The Story of Specialty Records* (Ace CD 542).

97 He was paying money to get his records played: Billy Vera notes to Don and Dewey CD, *Jungle Hop* (Specialty 7008). Vera quotes from correspondence between Rupe and Alan Freed from 1953 to 1955, expressing for the most part Rupe's "disappointment" and disillusionment, and Vera cites payola as one of Art's principal reasons for eventually leaving the business.

98 he had produced, "I'd say ninety-five percent": *In His Own Words: Art Rupe — The Story of Specialty Records*.

98 They were out with the Five Blind Boys: J.W. Alexander to Art Rupe, April 25 and May 14, 1953.

98 set "attendance records": *Los Angeles Sentinel*, June 25, 1953.

98 A 1948 program in Newark: Lee Hildebrand and Opal Louis Nations, liner notes to *The Original Five Blind Boys of Alabama: The Sermon* (Specialty CD 7041). See also Geoffrey Himes, "The Five Blind Boys of Alabama," *No Depression*, May–June 2001.

99 as J.W. wrote to Art in April: J.W. Alexander to Art Rupe, April 25, 1953.

99 Clarence Fountain and the Blind Boys . . . took pretty much the same view: Their view is based primarily on my interviews with Clarence Fountain and Johnny Fields.

102 "She was a pretty girl": Wolff, *You Send Me*, p. 104.

102 Barbara, meanwhile, had had her baby: Linda Marie Campbell was born April 25, 1953.

102 he even married her: Barbara and Clarence married on October 5, just two weeks before Sam and Dolores Mohawk.

103 the substitution of Hawaiian steel guitar: The unnamed steel guitarist appears to have been someone unknown to Art Rupe, and perhaps even to the Soul Stirrers — at least that would be one reason why the combination was so unsuccessful. Possibly, Rupe came up with the idea in the hope of recapturing some of the fire, and some of the popularity, of the group's partnership with Willie Eason, the father of "sacred steel" guitar, on two 1947 Aladdin titles. In any case, it didn't work, and while the steel player was given a vocal audition of his own, nothing more seems to have been heard from him at Specialty, and it would be another two years before the Soul Stirrers had a guitarist of their own, when Bob King joined the group.

104 "a basketball team [who] when they throw a note": "Salient points from ANR's [Arthur N. Rupe's] Talk, from tape," n.d., Specialty archives.

104 "'Shake a Hand,' a common greeting among followers of spiritual and gospel music": Joel Friedman, "Hallelujah! Religious Field Growing Bonanza," *Billboard*, February 6, 1954.

104 a year-end gross of $100,000: Ibid.

106 "Sam was a man about town": Wolff, *You Send Me*, p. 107.

107 "I was the first": Tony Heilbut, *The Gospel Sound: Good News and Bad Times*, p. 122.

107 "we wound up with fifty cents": Ibid., p. 125.

107 The other Gales took a somewhat less charitable view: Their view, and my perspective on the group, come primarily from interviews with JoJo Wallace and Howard Carroll, as well as from Heilbut, *The Gospel Sound*, and Glenn Hinson, *Fire in My Bones: Transcendence and the Holy Spirit in African American Gospel*.

107 "I was the one": Heilbut, *The Gospel Sound*, p. 125.

108 Oakland gospel stalwart Faidest Wagoner: Wagoner's story comes from Lee Hildebrand's ca. 1992 interview, from which all quotes are taken. Also Doris Worsham, "Fete Planned for Musician," *Oakland Tribune*, November 25, 1978; Opal Louis Nations, "My Soul Concerto: The Story of the Apollas"; and biographical material supplied by Faidest Wagoner through Opal.

111 J.W. Alexander put Herman Hill and Associates . . . on retainer: Letter of authorization for payment to Herman Hill by Herald Attractions, March 17, 1954 (Specialty archives).

111 "a white piano installed in the trunk": *Jet*, July 1, 1954.

112 Mahalia Jackson was continuing to develop: See *Jet*, July 22, August 26, and September 30, 1954, among others.

112 a twenty-seven-year-old New Orleans–based bluesman named Eddie Jones: Information on Eddie Jones (Guitar Slim) and Johnny Vincent comes primarily from John Broven, *Walking to New Orleans: The Story of New Orleans Rhythm & Blues*, pp. 50ff., and Jeff Hannusch, *I Hear You Knockin': The Sound of New Orleans Rhythm and Blues*, pp. 177ff.

112 auditioned for him by the devil in a dream: Hannusch, *I Hear You Knockin'*, p. 182.

113 whose "predominantly [white] femme audience . . . went beserk": *Cash Box* (n.d.), as quoted in "In Memoriam," *Shout* 47, September 6, 1969. By far the best account of Hamilton's career is Peter Grendysa, "Never Walking Alone," published in both *Goldmine*, April 1979, and *Soul Survivor* 5, summer 1986.

113 "try to write words in the blues field": Art Rupe to Wynona Carr, April 14, 1955. Carr had written to Rupe as early as January 27 on the subject.

115 "Please release 'Nearer My God to Thee'": S.R. Crain to Art Rupe, undated but answered with a check dated February 22, 1955.

115 a follow-up letter a week later: This letter was dated February 28.

116 the controversy that J.W. deliberately ignited: The *Los Angeles Sentinel* reported on the controversy on October 6, 1955; the session was August 4.

118 "Well, let him get his head bumped": Wolff, *You Send Me*, p. 105.

119 Johnnie had been raised by an aunt: Background on Johnnie Taylor's early life, and his joining the QCs, comes primarily from my interviews with Creadell Copeland and L.C. Cooke; Barbara Cooke's interview with Lee Richard; John Broven and Cilla Huggins' 1989 interview with Johnnie Taylor; Lee Hildebrand liner notes to the three-CD career survey *Johnnie Taylor: Lifetime* (Stax 4432); and Pierre Daguerre, "L'Interview de Johnnie Taylor," *Soul Bag* 118.

120 That was the summer that . . . Bob King joined the group: Background information on Bob King is primarily from interviews with Howard Carroll, JoJo Wallace, and Edith King. Jerry Zolten originally put me onto the connection between Carroll and King, whose picture together appears in Zolten's book *Great God A'Mighty!: The Dixie Hummingbirds* under King's given name of Rudolf. Jerry also provided me with an introduction to Howard Carroll.

121 Dorothy Love and the Original Gospel Harmonettes: Although Dorothy Love became best known as Dorothy Love Coates (and all of her earlier, as well as her later, work has now been reissued under that name), she did not marry Sensational Nightingales bass singer Carl Coates until 1959.

121 Art recorded the program at the Shrine Auditorium: Rupe had been recording live gospel programs at Brother Joe May's urging for over three years at this point. He downplayed the significance of it in interviews. "It was very primitive," he told the BBC, "and I never really intended to put it out; I just wanted to double-check for myself audience response." Clearly, though, the aim was to capture some of the power and the glory that he heard in the music. That, certainly, is what one hears, all these years later, on the tracks that have finally been released, but I'm not aware that any of it came out at the time.

121 Bumps . . . was an indifferent musician but a tireless hustler: Bumps' Seattle background is detailed in Paul de Barros, *Jackson Street After Hours: The Roots of Jazz in Seattle*, where the Floyd Standifer quotes appear.

121 a working knowledge of Yiddish and an advanced degree in music: Bumps spoke of his "conservatory training" in various interviews, and it is cited in the *Melody Maker* article below.

121 "the sun was shining, everything was happening": Michael Watts, "Bumps Blackwell," part 1, *Melody Maker*, August 26, 1972. There is extensive background on Blackwell here, also in Michael Ochs and Ed Pearl's 1981 interviews with Blackwell, and an anonymous taped interview in the Specialty archives.

121 a singer named Sonny Knight: Information on Sonny Knight comes primarily from Bill Millar's 1981 interview. All quoted material is from that interview. His story appears in Millar, *Let the Good Times Rock! A Fan's Notes on Post-War American Roots Music.*

122 he had not up to this time recorded "spiritual" music: Bumps' assignment appears to have been designed as some kind of test — although it should be noted that previous live gospel recordings had been done by Ted Brinson, a bass-playing fixture on the L.A. r&b scene, who had his own home studio in his garage.

123 "We were making up songs to make folk shout": JoJo Wallace in Hinson, *Fire in My Bones*, p. 242.

123 "People were screaming, throwing purses": Wolff, *You Send Me*, p. 121.

123 "they didn't need us women": BBC interview with Dorothy Love Coates.

125 "Nearer to Thee," Crain said, was the group's "stick": Dred Scott Keyes interview with S.R. Crain. Subsequent quotes are from that interview.

127 "It was awesome, phenomenal": Wolff, *You Send Me*, p. 121.

128–129 a singer who . . . had sent Art a tape: The tape box arrived on February 17, 1955, according to Rick Coleman and Rob Finnis' notes to the three-CD Little Richard box set, *Little Richard: The Specialty Sessions* (Specialty 8508), p. 20. Additional sources are the Art Rupe interview in the Specialty archives; Barrett Hansen, "The Specialty Story," *Hit Parader*, June 1969; Michael Ochs and Ed Pearl's interview with Bumps Blackwell, 1981; "Gospel Singers in Coffee Houses," *Sepia*, March 1960; Charles White, *The Life and Times of Little Richard: The Quasar of Rock*; and my interview with Lloyd Price.

129 "Mr. Art Rupe," the singer announced: The announcement, and the songs, are included as the first two tracks of the three-CD set above. The difference between this audition tape and "Tutti Frutti," Little Richard's first Specialty single, provides an eye-opening picture of the revolution that Bumps, Art Rupe, and the New Orleans rhythm section wrought.

129 "that, coupled with a gospel sound and a little more energy, was the basis for [my] being interested": Rick Coleman, notes to Little Richard box set, p. 21. As Rupe says in this interview, he and Bumps listened to the audition tape together and then compared notes.

129 a judicious loan to the artist of $600: Buyout agreement, May 13, 1955, and correspondence with Little Richard's manager, Cliff Brantley, September 13 (Specialty archives).

129 "I had to literally make blueprints": Rick Coleman, notes to Little Richard box set, p. 22.

129 Bumps mailed back the session sheets: Letter from Bumps Blackwell to Art Rupe, September 17, 1955.

"LOVABLE"

130 he and Sam would wait in the reception area: Interviews with Jerry Wexler and Ahmet Ertegun.

132 "A lot of things was going on": Dred Scott Keyes interview with S.R. Crain, 1996.

137 doing some work for Don Robey: For purposes of dating, "Next Time You See Me" was recorded in Houston on May 7, 1956.

139 the White Citizens Council attack on Nat "King" Cole: This took place on April 10, 1956, and is documented in Daniel Mark Epstein, *Nat King Cole*, pp. 255ff.

139 "He was born there": "Backstage with Clyde Reid," *Amsterdam News*, April 21, 1956.

139 J.W. Alexander was reported . . . to have "electrified audiences everywhere": *Los Angeles Sentinel*, March 29, 1956.

141 he had to share his income equally: In a letter to S.R. Crain, February 16, 1956, Art Rupe stipulates that by prior arrangement all Soul Stirrers songwriting royalties are going to Crain, and that it is up to Crain to give Sam his.

143 Dorothy Love . . . took to calling him "Mr. Wonderful": BBC interview with Dorothy Love Coates.

143 the kind of pansexual hysteria: Sam Moore and Dave Marsh, *Sam and Dave: An Oral History*, pp. 26–27.

143 "This man was so smooth, so good": Daniel Wolff, with S. R. Crain, Clifton White, and G. David Tenenbaum, *You Send Me: The Life and Times of Sam Cooke*, p. 90.

144 "RETURNED BY POPULAR DEMAND": Advertisement, *Atlanta Daily World*, July 13, 1956. Additional ads and squibs for the program appeared on July 15 and 18.

146 "all them tricks that Harris was making": Ray Funk interview with Paul Foster, 1981.

146 an event "celebrating Herman Nash's six years of Gospel Promoting": *Atlanta Daily World,* August 19, 1956.

147 The presentation of a full gospel program had been introduced: Background on gospel at the Apollo and Thermon Ruth (including quotations) from Ted Fox, *Showtime at the Apollo: The Story of Harlem's World Famous Theater,* pp. 227–228, and Todd R. Baptista, *Group Harmony: Echoes of the Rhythm and Blues Era,* pp. 96–116, primarily.

148 he was offered no more than $1,000: Alex Bradford and his six Bradford Singers received $850.11 for the original December 1955 show, the Harmonizing Four $550, according to Apollo Theater records, Schiffman Collection, Archives Center, National Museum of American History, Smithsonian Institution.

148 "we will go into the Apollo, but when we do, we gonna get paid": The source for Crain's claim is, as indicated, Leroy Crume. There is no written record of what the Soul Stirrers got paid in August, but when they returned in December, they received $3,500, according to Apollo Theater records.

149 Fats Domino and Frankie Lymon were headlining: The Paramount's gross and Fats Domino's *Steve Allen Show* appearance are documented in Lee Cotten, *Reelin' & Rockin': The Golden Age of American Rock 'n Roll,* vol. 2, 1956–1959.

149 "the first black [-owned business] on the street": John Broven, "Bobby's Happy House of Hits," parts 1 and 2, *Juke Blues* 15 and 16. Also, Valerie Wilmer, "Echoes: Legends of the Back Streets," *Melody Maker,* November 18, 1978.

149 "If the rules are more important to you than the money": Wolff, *You Send Me,* p. 138.

149 the departure of his meal ticket: Galen Gart, *First Pressings: The History of Rhythm & Blues,* 1956, p. 72, which dates Bill Cook's announcement as June 2. See also Peter Grendysa, "Never Walking Alone," *Goldmine,* April 1979; and Roy Hamilton, "The Night I Couldn't Find God," *Sepia,* January 1958.

149 Bill Cook, in fact, was booked into the Apollo: *Amsterdam News,* September 8, 1956.

150 Cook cut demos on half a dozen of the "little songs": Bill Cook's composition "I'll Come Running Back to You" was titled "Just Call My Name" on the tape box from this session. The tape itself survived in fractured form. It was almost entirely recorded over, so you can hear only fragments of each song, with the exception of "The Time Has Come," which for some reason escaped intact. So far as dating is concerned, Rupe's check for studio time was sent to Bill Cook on August 21, which might make one think that the session was held prior to the Apollo engagement, were it not for the steady lineup of Soul Stirrers dates leading up to their week in New York. My assumption, then, is that the check represented a deposit on studio time paid out to Bill Cook in advance.

150 "Gospel songs intrigued me": "Gospel Singers in Coffee Houses," *Sepia,* March 1960.

150 his own inclination "to look down my nose": Interview with Bumps Blackwell, Specialty archives. All quotes through "You don't leave religion to sing" are from this interview.

151 An artist was someone "born and endowed with talent": Michael Ochs and Ed Pearl interview with Bumps Blackwell, 1981.

151 the first Soul Stirrers session for which he had had direct responsibility: Roy Porter, the drummer on this session, places Bumps in charge in his memoir, written with David Keller, *There and Back: The Roy Porter Story,* p. 94.

151 "So S.R. Crain was a little upset": Bumps Blackwell interview, Specialty archives.

152 "I had the voice, the confidence, and the equipment": "The Private Life of Sam Cooke," *Tan*, April 1958.

152 a low of 66,000: To indicate how precipitous a drop in income these 1955 figures represented, at their height in 1950 the Travelers sold a total of 392,000 records and earned $7,800 in royalties.

153 "I have never said you made a mistake": J.W. Alexander to Art Rupe, January 27, 1957.

153 In September he wrote to Art: J.W. Alexander to Art Rupe, September 12, 1956.

153 he wrote to him again at the end of the month: This letter is undated but notes that J.W. will be at the same address in Houston until October 3. The coincidence that he speaks of, the resemblance between Ray Charles' "Lonely Avenue" and Whitaker's "I Got a New Home," was no coincidence: they were the same song. "Ray idolized my baritone Jesse Whitaker," J.W. said. "I had a girlfriend who had an aunt who owned the Little Hotel for Visiting Friends in Dallas. Ray used to stay there [in the early days] and come to our concerts."

153 "It seems," Bumps wrote at the end of the year: Bumps Blackwell to J.W. Alexander, December 28, 1956.

154 Matassa, whose family had long owned a grocery store: In addition to my own interviews with Cosimo, John Broven's *Walkin' to New Orleans: The Story of New Orleans Rhythm & Blues* and Rick Coleman's research proved invaluable resources.

155 how Tony first came to Specialty: See Opal Louis Nations, "The Chicken Baby Man: The Story of Tony Harris," parts 1 and 2, *Blues & Rhythm* 115, 116.

155 Art came downstairs to the little rehearsal studio: Art Rupe told me that the idea for "Lovable" came from him brainstorming with Bumps and that Bumps engaged Tony and/or Sam to write new lyrics. He had no recollection of Bill Cook's involvement, but it is clear from Bill Cook's contemporary correspondence that Sam and Bill Cook had the idea long before the New Orleans session.

156 "I had a wonderful time, a wonderful life": "The Private Life of Sam Cooke," *Tan*, April 1958.

159 Dolores showed increasing signs of dissatisfaction and depression: Agnes Cook spoke of Dolores' sense of insecurity and displacemement in our interviews; see also Wolff, *You Send Me*.

159 Sam was about to become a father again: Much of the information on Sam and Connie Bolling's relationship comes from their son, Keith Bolling, and his wife, Pam, to whom I was introduced by Diane Brown.

159 a potential "moneydripper": Michael Ochs and Ed Pearl interview with Bumps Blackwell.

159 L.C. had just played Memphis with the Magnificents: In addition to my interviews with L.C. Cooke and Magnificent Montague, Johnny Keyes' *Du-Wop* provides a wonderful firsthand account.

159 "How come cullud girls would take on so": Nat D. Williams, "Down on Beale: 'Pied Piper' Presley," *Pittsburgh Courier*, December 22, 1956.

160 "I've got all of your records": Keyes, *Du-Wop*, p. 60.

160 "Dear Art," Bill Cook wrote: Bill Cook to Art Rupe, January 6, 1957.

160 "Hi Bill," Bumps responded: Bumps Blackwell to Bill Cook, January 18, 1957.

161 "Dear Mr. Rupe," he wrote from Detroit: J.W. Alexander to Art Rupe, January 22, 1957; Rupe's reply of January 24, and J.W.'s subsequent response, are all in the Specialty archives, as is Bumps' January 4, 1957, letter to Kylo Turner.

162 "just dumb and naive": Art Rupe quoted in Billy Vera's notes to *The Specialty Story* (Specialty 4412), p. 36.

162 He had checked up on Bumps' credentials: Responses to his inquiries from both the Cornish School and the Office of the Registrar at the University of Washington on September 26 and September 27, 1956, respectively, are housed in the Specialty archives. They show that Bumps studied theory, harmony, and piano at the Cornish School, mostly as a private student, over a period of roughly eighteen months. There was no record of attendance at the University of Washington.

162 He had stated emphatically: Handwritten memo by Art Rupe, ca. April 1, 1956.

163 "creatures of the Creator [with no] barrier": Art Rupe to Brother Joe May, April 30, 1951.

163 "you know that we are in your corner": Art Rupe to Brother Joe May, April 12, 1950.

163 he was "an intense guy": "Salient points from ANR's [Arthur N. Rupe's] Talk, from tape," n.d., Specialty archives. Rupe spoke of Sam as an "enigma" and "puzzle" in a BBC interview, and in similar terms to me.

164 he pointed to a picture of Harry Belafonte: Wolff, *You Send Me*, p. 132. Paul Foster spoke more on this subject in his 1984 interview with Lee Hildebrand.

164 To Morgan Babb . . . he declared: BBC interview with Morgan Babb.

164 to others, like Oakland piano and organ player Faidest Wagoner: Lee Hildebrand interview with Faidest Wagoner.

164 a "personable debut": *Billboard*, March 9, 1957. In this same issue, there is extensive discussion in Ren Grevatt's column, "On the Beat," of the "integration of the tastes of the majority into the minority," in other words, the merging of the r&b and pop markets.

166 "If this [record] doesn't make it": Bumps Blackwell interview, Specialty archives.

167 "Hi Bumbs": The letter is undated but clearly was written in the week preceding May 3.

168 a song he had been trying to get L.C. to record for Vee Jay: Interview with L.C. Cooke; L.C. said that Vee Jay a&r head Ewart Abner had no use for the song.

168 "I hit the ceiling": Bumps Blackwell interview, Specialty archives.

168 Crain telegrammed Art: S.R. Crain to Art Rupe, May 3, 1957.

169 Things clearly must have come to a head: Both Charles and L.C. Cooke and Leroy Crume all spoke to me about Sam's dissatisfaction with his songwriter's royalties. Art Rupe's February 16, 1956, letter to Crain alludes obliquely at least to the potential for misunderstanding. Daniel Wolff wrote about the group vote in *You Send Me*, p. 122, undoubtedly on the testimony of his coauthor Crain.

169 In the end, Sam got his way: Wolff wrote that Sam got his own songwriter's contract, presumably in February 1956, but I could find no evidence of this in the Specialty archives. I think there's little question, though, that an informal understanding at least was reached.

169 "I hated Bumps": Dred Scott Keyes interview with S.R. Crain, 1996.

170 he was "thinking about going out for himself": Lee Hildebrand interview with Paul Foster, 1984.

170 "He asked my opinion": Terry Gross interview with S.R. Crain, *Fresh Air*, National Public Radio, March 23, 1995.

170 His father told him he owed no loyalty to the Soul Stirrers: Dred Scott Keyes interview with Reverend Charles Cook, 1995; Reverend Cook at the Rock 'n' Roll Hall of Fame, 1986.

170 He had come to a parting of the ways: In Sam's initial filing for divorce, in November 1957, the date of separation is listed as May 24, 1957.

HOW HE CROSSED OVER

171 the escalating problems . . . with Little Richard: "He was very insincere in my opinion," Rupe told the BBC. According to Rupe, Little Richard was converted to the Seventh Day Adventist faith by former Specialty artist Joe Lutcher, who convinced Richard that it was "evil to sing pop." "As early as June 1957," Rob Finnis wrote in the notes to *Little Richard: The Specialty Sessions* (Specialty 8508), p. 15, "Richard hinted to reporters that he was planning to become an evangelist." But part of Art continued to wonder if it wasn't some kind of business or negotiating ploy.

171 Art had gone over the ground: Rupe expressed this to me and went into it further in Billy Vera's notes to *The Specialty Story* (Specialty 4412).

172 Sam had been staying: Bumps Blackwell interview, Specialty archives.

172 Clifton ("Clif") White: I have spelled Clif's first name in this way because he made the point very strongly to me that there was no second *f* in Clifton.

173 "The girls were nearly sitting out in the hall": Bumps Blackwell interview, Specialty archives.

173 The first song they did, "You Send Me": Clif White was very clear on the order of the songs in my interviews with him.

174 Sam signed a new contract . . . with a 1 percent royalty: A 1 percent royalty amounted to a penny a single on 90 percent of all records sold, which by standard record company practice allowed for a 10 percent dispensation of "free goods" to DJs and other interested parties. If a million singles were sold, in other words, income for the recording artist at that 1 percent rate would come to $9,000.

174 Sam also got a $400 advance: Royalty statement, June 30, 1957.

174 The songwriter's agreement stipulated that he would split his one-penny-per-side mechanical royalty: Royalty statements, December 31, 1957, and June 30, 1958. The second is drawn up with instructions not to pay out any money until the conclusion of the lawsuit in which Rupe, Sam, Bumps, and Keen Records were by then embroiled. But it includes a calculation of Sam's royalties at $.005 per side along with an alternate statement for L.C. Cooke at $.02 per side for L.C. and/or his publisher, should the court decide that he, and not Sam, had written the pop songs by Sam that Specialty had released. Little Richard had a similar deal, with Venice taking a 50 percent cut-in on his writer's share (see Charles White, *The Life and Times of Little Richard: The Quasar of Rock*, pp. 57–59).

175 The session was in full swing: The details of the session itself are based primarily on interviews with Art Rupe, Clif White, Harold Battiste, J.W. Alexander, Steve Propes' 1987 interview with René Hall, and the Bumps Blackwell interview in the Specialty archives. The documents that detail the legal outcome of the case are in the Specialty archives.

176 They were on the third or fourth take of ["Summertime"]: The order of the songs remains in dispute in the accounts of the various participants. Bumps, however, was adamant that they had completed "You Send Me" before Art walked in, and Rupe's remark to René Hall about the arrangement of "Summertime" tends to bear him out.

176 "something new in the creative world": Steve Propes interview with René Hall.

176 he launched . . . into a tirade: In addition to the sources listed above, see Stuart Colman, "The Many Sides of René Hall," *New Kommotion* 25, 1980, which has a good description by René of the tirade.

176 "You're going to try and turn everything into Billy Ward's Dominoes": This is from a BBC interview with René Hall.

176 "when I woke up, I had a different concept of the song": Michael Ochs and Ed Pearl interview with Bumps Blackwell, 1981.

177 "the classical frosting on the cake": Steve Propes interview with René Hall.

177 Sam . . . "just wanted to quit": Bumps Blackwell interview, Specialty archives.

177 they finished the session: In Bumps' interview in the Specialty archives, he has Art Rupe staying around and getting them to change their approach to Sam's "You Were Made For Me," with René supplying "that little jig beat" that Art liked so much on guitar. In Rupe's recollection, there was no question that he stayed till the end. AFM records show the session running half an hour overtime, going from 1:30 to 5 P.M.

177 "the ill feeling that was created by me critizing the session": *In His Own Words: Art Rupe — The Story of Specialty Records* (Ace CD 542).

178 "I began to feel that Bumps was functioning [more] as Sam's manager": This comes from Art Rupe's faxed communications to me. In notes from a telephone discussion with Little Richard on August 22, 1956, Rupe remarked with respect to Bumps' undependability: "He told Richard he wanted to start his own record company." Rupe forced Bumps to give up managing Richard not long afterward over that same question of loyalty.

178 an almost naked, covetous desire "for bread pure and simple": This is from "Salient points from ANR's [Arthur N. Rupe's] Talk, from tape," n.d., Specialty archives, but Art expressed the same sentiments on many other occasions, including in his faxed communications to me.

178 "Art just assumed he was superior": Bill Millar interview with Sonny Knight, 1981.

179 "I just felt, I'm not going to fool with these people": *In His Own Words: Art Rupe — The Story of Specialty Records.*

179 "I know I owe you money": Bumps Blackwell interview, Specialty archives.

179 "I knew I had ten thousand dollars coming": Bumps Blackwell interview, Specialty archives. Bumps went on to speculate that the total he was owed may have been closer to $50,000 ("In court I found out I had [actually] given up fifty thousand, which I didn't know at the time"), but I think he was more on track here.

180 "I figured, well, this stuff'll sell maybe a hundred, a hundred fifty thousand": *In His Own Words: Art Rupe — The Story of Specialty Records.*

180 he never told his wife: Bumps Blackwell interview, Specialty archives.

180 René told him about a businessman: Steve Propes interview with René Hall. Further information on the earliest inception of Keen Records comes from my interviews with Art Foxall, Bob Keane, J.W. Alexander, and John Siamas Jr.

181 The deal . . . put Bumps in charge: John Siamas Jr. specifically recalled the gospel component, which would explain J.W. Alexander's otherwise anomalous presence.

182 Bumps came out to the house for the first time: Bumps estimated the deal to have been made June 15 in a later lawsuit against the company.

182 They agreed on terms similar to Bumps' arrangement: The terms were spelled out in Bob Keane's June 8, 1958, telephone conversation with Art Rupe (annotated in the Specialty archives) and in Bumps' 1960 lawsuit.

183 a name for the label: According to Bumps Blackwell in part 2 of Michael Watts' *Melody Maker* profile, September 2, 1972, John Siamas Jr. came up with the name when he said, "It's keen, Dad."

183 The corporation had four principal investors: As with so many financial matters for which no written records have surfaced, this is subject to interpretation. My account largely follows John Siamas Jr.'s recollection of the financial arrangements, along with Bob

Keane's vivid sense of exclusion from what he understood his role in the company to be. With respect to John Siamas' uncles Andy and Paul Karras, there is some discrepancy in the spelling of the family name, but John Siamas Jr. says this is the correct spelling.

183 Sam spent the summer on the sofa: Information on Sam's two months of anxious waiting, as well as on his apprenticeship to Bumps and the kind treatment he received from him, comes largely from interviews with Rip Spencer and L.C. Cooke, in addition to Bumps' own interviews.

185 the burgeoning L.A. r&b community: Apart from Rip Spencer's patient elucidation of both the history and the spirit of the scene, historical perspective comes primarily from Steve Propes and Galen Gart, *L.A. R&B Vocal Groups 1945–1965;* Mitch Rosalsky, *Encyclopedia of Rhythm & Blues and Doo-Wop Vocal Groups;* and Bill Millar, *The Coasters,* pp. 86ff.

186 "he was like a big brother to all of us": Information and quotes on Jesse Belvin come primarily from Jim Dawson liner notes for the 1986 LP *Hang Your Tears Out to Dry* (Earth Angel JD-900); also Ray Topping liners for the 1991 CD *Goodnight My Love* (Ace 336).

186 "I'll bring Hollywood to the blacks": Tom Reed, *The Black Music History of Los Angeles — Its Roots: A Classical Pictorial History of Black Music in Los Angeles from 1920–1970,* p. 78.

187 "I could break a record": Dick "Huggy Boy" Hugg, as told to Jim Dawson, "Huggy Boy: The Voice of Dolphin's of Hollywood," *Juke Blues* 17.

188 "a self-sufficient community with two black-owned newspapers": Morris Newman, "New Riffs for a Street Linked to Jazz," *New York Times,* March 23, 1997.

188 Sam took acting lessons: Sam spoke of his acting training in interviews with the *Amsterdam News,* December 21, 1957, and the *Chicago Defender,* October 25, 1958, and it is referred to in the program book for the Howard Miller–promoted show at the Chicago Opera House in December.

188 he added a letter to his last name: Art Rupe, in his remarks on the Soul Stirrers in the Specialty archives, says Bumps Blackwell gave Sam the *e.* Bob Keane took credit for it in his conversation with me and said it was "for class." Bumps said he suggested it to give Sam an even number of letters between his two names in Daniel Wolff, with S. R. Crain, Clifton White, and G. David Tenenbaum, *You Send Me: The Life and Times of Sam Cooke,* p. 153. Both L.C. Cooke and his sister Agnes scoffed at the idea that Sam would care about the number of letters in his name. Sam signed his contract on September 7 with his still-legal name of "Cook."

188 Harry Belafonte . . . was reported to be looking at a $1 million gross: *Amsterdam News,* August 3, 1957.

189 Specialty [would] be losing "a lot of [its] spiritual artists": Sister Wynona Carr to Art Rupe, July 18, 1957.

189 He had acetates cut: Art Rupe specifies the date as July 29 in handwritten notes for his lawsuit against Sam and Keen.

189 Bumps jollied him along with paternal good humor: The tone is described by L.C. Cooke and Rip Spencer. Bumps liked to say (particularly in the interview housed in the Specialty archives) that he spent the entire summer recording Sam, searching in vain for a commercial hit, then, "three months later," suddenly recollected the two sides he had cut for Specialty. However, not only is there no record of any of these recording sessions with Sam, but Bumps, in fact, started distributing acetates for the single within a month of his arrival at Keen, then had the record mastered on August 28, prior to which there was no record company. Not to mention the fact that it is inconceivable that he would have forgotten something in which he believed so strongly and for which he had paid so dearly.

189 The phone lines of Hamilton's booking agency: *Los Angeles Sentinel*, July 25, 1957.

190 The Soul Stirrers themselves were beginning to wonder: The Soul Stirrers' situation was detailed in my interviews with Leroy Crume, Lee Hildebrand's interview with Paul Foster, and Lee Hildebrand and Opal Louis Nations' liner notes for the 1993 Soul Stirrers CD, *Heaven Is My Home* (Specialty 7040).

190 Little Johnny Jones, the lead singer of the Swanee Quintet: Biographical information on Little Johnny Jones is primarily from Opal Louis Nations' liners to a 1996 release, *Let's Go Back to God*, by Little Johnny Jones and the Johnny Jones Singers (Nashboro 4535).

190 The Soul Stirrers, "[he] told disappointed Atlanta gospel music lovers": Marion E. Jackson, "Soul Stirrers Vow to Carry On in Gospel Music Field," *Atlanta Daily World*, July 16, 1957.

191 Crume had gone to see him: According to Crume, the Stirrers approached the QCs' co-lead, Spencer Taylor, first, but Spencer said he couldn't join them until he had fulfilled a week's worth of scheduled QC engagements. When the group went to Johnnie Taylor, he was obviously burdened by no such constraint. Paul Foster, in his 1981 interview with Ray Funk, expressed his own reservations about Johnnie Taylor, which included sending him back to Chicago to learn a little humility shortly after he joined.

191 the Big Gospel Cavalcade: *Amsterdam News*, August 3, 1957, news item, and Jesse H. Walker, "Gospel Singing on the Move as Package Show Heads South," August 17; also "Singing for Sinners," *Newsweek*, September 2, 1957.

193 he lacked brains, talent, trustworthiness: "Excerpts from shorthand notes, Bob Keane telephone conversation, Sunday, June 8, 1958," Specialty archives.

193 Bob spoke with Andy Karras: From speaking with John Siamas Jr. and Bob Keane, and from other interviews of Keane's (including Howard DeWitt, "Bob Keane: The Oracle of Del-Fi Records," *Blue Suede News* 34, and Jim Powers, "Del-Fi Records," *Goldmine*, May 7, 1999; also Steve Propes' interview with Keane, 1984), this is my best understanding of the situation. Keane said, in his June 8, 1958, telephone conversation with Art Rupe, that he severed relations with Siamas on September 6 (a Friday). With regard to financial specifics, much testimony has been offered, but, perhaps understandably, I'm not sure how much light has been shed. The crux of the problem, clearly, is over the voice of the verb "owed." Bob Keane felt that he was owed something substantial; John Siamas felt just as strongly that Bob Keane owed the company something more than the investment of his labor. In the end the argument comes down to the usual misunderstanding over the placement of a decimal point, or several.

194 Bob Keane left the company . . . with a plan to start his own label: He did, approximately three months later, calling it Del-Fi after the Greek oracle at Delphi, who customarily spoke in riddles. Within a year he had had a huge double-sided pop hit with Ritchie Valens' "Donna" and "La Bamba."

194 Sam . . . laid down three tunes: The tape box specifies songs and date.

194 his 10 percent manager's cut: "Excerpts from shorthand notes, Bob Keane telephone conversation, Sunday, June 8, 1958," Specialty archives.

194 the release of the first two Keen singles: "You Send Me" (Keen 4013) was the label's first release, in early September 1957. The next appears to have been "Hey Team" (Keen 4001), with additional releases following more or less in sequential order, I believe, through 4012. The Andex label was begun at about this point at 2001 and merged in May with the

4000 series, which restarted at 4014. There were some additional variants, but if there was any numerical logic to it, I don't know what it is — nor does John Siamas Jr.

194 Dolphin's of Hollywood had been well primed: Bob Keane told me about bringing Sam around to Dolphin's. Rip Spencer said that Dolphin's was a regular hangout of theirs, and Lou Rawls spoke of frequent visits, which included the Harrison and Ross Funeral Home nearby, where one of the owner's daughters was crazy about Sam.

195 "Nobody," said René Hall . . . "realized how big the record was": This quote combines Hall's descriptions of the Elks Hall dance from interviews with the BBC and Steve Propes. Bob Keane spoke of Sam playing the dance not for money but for airplay.

196 It was an oversight, Bumps told him: In an October 21, 1957, letter to Higuera Music (Keen's publishing company), Art Rupe wrote: "We discussed this matter with your Mr. Robert 'Bumps' Blackwell several weeks ago, and he left us with the impression that he would straighten out this misunderstanding."

196 E. Rodney Jones played "Summertime": Wolff, *You Send Me*, p. 155.

198 "I can tell my listeners": *Time*, February 14, 1955.

198 Teresa Brewer may not have realized it: Bumps Blackwell interview, Specialty archives (I've changed the tense of the verbs to the present throughout); Crume, too, spoke of Sam being upset about Teresa Brewer's version, which went to number eight on the pop charts.

199 he . . . was about to have his own teen dance show: This was announced in September but did not actually go on the air until January.

199 "Somebody's kicking on the front door": Lex Gillespie interview with Doug "Jocko" Henderson, 1995, for the Smithsonian series produced by Jacquie Gales Webb for National Public Radio, *Black Radio: Telling It Like It Was*. Used by permission.

200 "he emaciated the house": Michael Ochs and Ed Pearl interview with Bumps Blackwell, 1981. Both here and in his interview in the Specialty archives, Bumps spoke of Sam appearing with the Stirrers, but it was in Philadelphia, not Washington, D.C. Crume had no question, though, that the chance meeting took place in Philadelphia, but Sam appeared with the group in D.C.

201 "I was sitting in my office with a guy named Paul Cantor": This, and subsequent passages about Sam's early days at William Morris, is based primarily on my interview with Larry Auerbach but is supported by interviews with Paul Cantor.

202 In Atlanta they . . . set up a show: Sam spoke of "running into" B.B. Beamon, and the $1,000 fee, in his interview with the *Amsterdam News*, December 21, 1957. The show was advertised in the *Atlanta Daily World*, October 10, 1957.

202 "The way they are treating my people": "Which Negro Celebrities Back Satchmo Blast at Ike," *Jet*, October 3, 1957.

202 "We don't take that jive": *The Carolinian* (ANP), November 9, 1957.

202 his . . . road manager suggested that he had spoken "in haste": *Kansas City Call* (ANP), November 1, 1957. Armstrong responded, according to *Jet*, October 3, 1957, by calling the white road manager, "whom I've respected for 20 years . . . a flunky [and] a menace to the colored people," while insisting that he would not retract a single word of his criticism — in which he called the president "two-faced" and "[having] no guts" and Governor Faubus "an uneducated Arkansas plowboy." He then "immortalized the report by scribbling the word 'solid' across the bottom and affixing his signature."

204 Sam was rebooked: The specifics of the public's response come from my interview with Larry Auerbach and Bumps' Specialty interview.

204 on October 21, he fired off letters: All letters in this and subsequent exchanges are in the Specialty archives, as is the "Hi Sweet" letter subsequently quoted.

208 Richard had dramatically announced that he was quitting show business: The best sources here are Damien Johnstone, "The Big Show: Rockin' Australia 1957," *Now Dig This* 37, April 1986 (reprinted from the Australian Rock 'n' Roll Appreciation Society), and Derek Glenister's thoughtful analysis, relayed via Bill Millar. Charles White's *Life and Times of Little Richard* also provides valuable insight.

209 "ANOTHER KEEN HIT": *Cash Box* ad, November 30, 1957.

209 a self-made man with the attitude that he had come into this world with nothing: Summarized and quoted from Art Rupe's notes on the back of John Siamas' December 5, 1957, letter to Rupe.

210 "In just three sensational weeks": "Meet Sam Cooke — He's the Most," *Norfolk Journal and Guide* (ANP), November 30, 1957.

213 "I'm going with Sammy-o": From interview with L.C. Cooke. The group's reaction comes from my interview with Leroy Crume and Lee Hildebrand's and Ray Funk's interviews with Paul Foster.

214 Tony played the Apollo . . . with a little record of his own: Tony Harris' hit, ironically, was on Art Rupe's ex-wife Lee's label, Ebb.

214 "None of my children have turned out badly": "Rock 'n' Roll Cinderella," *Sepia*, March 1958. I have added the dash at the end of the quote.

214 an extensive interview to one of the country's most prestigious black newspapers: Margurite Belafonte, "Eye to Eye with Sam Cook," *Amsterdam News*, December 21, 1957.

216 "If church people feel that Sam deserted them": Lillian Cumber quoted from her *Los Angeles Tribune* column in "Sam Cook Zooms to Fame," *Cleveland Call*, November 23, 1957.

217 He gave an interview to the *Philadelphia Tribune*: Malcolm Poindexter, "Sam Cooke's 'Baby You Send Me' Now Over 1,125,000 Mark," *Philadelphia Tribune*, January 4, 1958.

217 Connie Bolling, whose son, Keith: Much of the information on Keith Bolling and his mother, and the intensity of Sam's feelings, comes from my interview with Keith and his wife, Pam.

217 The sheriff and his deputies: Much of the specific detail of Sam's arrest is derived from Art Peters, "Singer Sam Cooke Fathered Her Child, Says Unwed Girl," a front-page story in the *Philadelphia Tribune*, March 25, 1958, along with the follow-up on April 1 by the same reporter, "Singer Sam Cooke Settles Baby Case for Over $5000."

THE BIGGEST SHOW OF STARS FOR 1958

218–219 Crain . . . strongly seconded Sam's demands: In his March 23, 1995, interview with Terry Gross on National Public Radio's *Fresh Air*, Crain said, "We *begged* Larry Auerbach . . . "

219 He spoke to Sam Bramson: This account is culled from my interviews with Larry Auerbach, Paul Cantor, and Jess Rand, which, perhaps needless to say, do not agree in every particular.

220 "the young man with the golden voice": *Philadelphia Tribune*, December 21, 1957.

220 headlining at the Crescendo: *California Eagle*, January 30, 1958.

220 "the red-haired vampire": *Miami Times*, August 18, 1958.

220–221 "He's cute as a button": "Topic A," *Time*, May 26, 1958.

221 "a wardrobe full of Ivy League clothes": "The Private Life of Sam Cooke," *Tan*, April 1958.

222 "Sam took Sister Flute:" Dred Scott Keyes interview with S.R. Crain, 1996.

223 "Bumps didn't know what he was doing": BBC interview with René Hall.

223 "Well, girls," the *Amsterdam News* announced: Jesse H. Walker, "Theatricals," *Amsterdam News*, March 8, 1958.

224 "Jules Podell told me": William Peper, "Sam Cooke Sings the Blues, Too," *New York World-Telegram*, February 6, 1964.

224 "We were pulling for him": *Houston Informer*, March 22, 1958.

224 Sam Cooke had "laid a golden egg": A. S. "Doc" Young, "The Big Beat," *Los Angeles Sentinel*, March 20, 1958.

224 "the handsome Negro lad with two hit records": *Variety*, March 12, 1958.

224 with Crain consoling him: Terry Gross' National Public Radio interview with S.R. Crain, *Fresh Air*.

224 "the pretty model with an amazing hair style": *Houston Informer* (ANP), March 15, 1958.

226 he ran into Barbara for the first time: In addition to Barbara's own recollections, her interview of Mildred Richard ca. 1984–1985 was particularly illuminating.

227 The Spring Edition of the Biggest Show of Stars: Background information on this tour, and the history of the package tour in general, comes from numerous *Billboard* and *Cash Box* articles culled by Galen Gart in *First Pressings: The History of Rhythm & Blues*, 1954–1958. "Top R&R Shows Compete for Talent," datelined February 17 in *First Pressings*, 1958, p. 15, details the situation in the spring of 1958.

228 an all-star gospel tour: *Variety*, December 25, 1957.

228 The result of this direct "competition": "Sharp Downturn in Grosses Plaguing Touring Packages," Gart, *First Pressings*, 1958, p. 47.

228 "for the first time in 'package show' history": *Norfolk Journal and Guide*, March 29, 1958.

229 the "fornication and bastardy" charge: *Jet*, April 3, 1958; see also *Philadelphia Tribune*, March 25, 1958.

230 Frankie Avalon was hailed: *Billboard*, April 21, 1958.

230 the number of notes to which he could draw out a single syllable: Bill Millar, *The Drifters*, p. 21.

231 the *Houston Informer* reported: *Houston Informer*, May 24, 1958.

231 her "sexy gestures": "Tweedlee Dee Girl," *Ebony*, April 1956. Chip Deffaa contributed the eye-rolling and finger-in-the-mouth details in his chapter on LaVern Baker in *Blue Rhythms: Six Lives in Rhythm and Blues*.

231 "If they can get permission from their respective record firms": *Los Angeles Sentinel*, April 17, *Norfolk Journal and Guide*, and *Chicago Defender*, April 19, 1958, *et al*. Sam wrote in "The Trouble I've Seen," *Sepia*, September 1958: "I've succeeded in interesting my friend, LaVern Baker, in joining me [in a gospel album, and] we may also have the voice of our friend, Clyde McPhatter." But in the end LaVern made her own album for Atlantic the following year with the Alex Bradford Singers.

233 "based on fear [and] hocus-pocus": Lee Hildebrand interview with Clyde McPhatter, 1972.

233 a lifetime membership in the National Association for the Advancement of Colored People: *Chicago Defender*, June 1, 1957.

233 he was pictured . . . mailing a box of records: *Memphis World* (ANP), January 1, 1958.

233 he railed quietly against the mistreatment: Colin Escott, *Clyde McPhatter: A Biographical Essay*, p. 33.

233 he and Clyde would sometimes fool around with country: In addition to Phil Everly pointing this out to me, George Hamilton IV also spoke of Sam and Clyde "strumming Hank Williams songs" and singing country in Spencer Leigh, *The Story of Pop*, p. 135.

234 Jake Richard induced Sam: Barbara Cooke interview with Lee Richard, ca. 1984–1985.

234 "The transition from gospel to pop tunes was easy": "Sam Cooke says all tours alike," *Richmond Afro-American* (ANP), May 17, 1958.

234 That same night the violence . . . exploded: The Boston riot and its aftermath are well recounted in John A. Jackson, *Big Beat Heat: Alan Freed and the Early Years of Rock & Roll*, pp. 192ff.

235 another keen "battle of songs": *Norfolk Journal and Guide*, May 31, 1958.

235 Prophet John the Conqueror: *Pittsburgh Courier*, March 29, 1958.

236 the label's new West Third Street location: The studio first shows up on an American Federation of Musicians (AFM) session sheet on August 6, 1958.

237 He had been cultivating a Latin dance sound: Raul Trana first appears on a February 4, 1958, session sheet.

237 He carried a blue spiral notebook: Jess Rand interview.

238 He was "stubborn": BBC interview with René Hall.

242 The July 4 *Larry Finley Show*: This was reported in *Billboard*, July 19, 1958, and various other trade items are included in Alan Clark, *Rock and Roll Legends* 3, p. 45 and *Rock and Roll Memories* 7, pp. 61–62.

243 Beamon, who . . . bought over $2 million worth of talent: *Atlanta Daily World*, November 6, 1958.

243 his divorce action with Dolores: Most of the information on the divorce settlement is culled from the divorce action itself, *Sam Cook v. Dolores Cook*, No. D 0529553, filed in California Superior Court, November 15, 1957.

243 a first-person article for *Sepia*: "The Trouble I've Seen," *Sepia*, September 1958.

244 "My mama won't tell me": L.C. Cooke described this scene to me. Barbara Cooke recounted it similarly. Barbara's story here and throughout is based on interviews with her.

246 he was entitled to something like $45,000: This is based on 1.7 million sales. All subsequent Specialty business calculations derive from documents in the Specialty archives, including Art Rupe's detailed notes with respect to both the case and his options.

246 Bumps was ruining Sam: "Excerpts from shorthand notes, Bob Keane telephone conversation, Sunday, June 8, 1958," Specialty archives.

247–248 his 25 percent ownership of the company would soon be . . . recognized: Bumps' expectations and complaints are detailed in his lawsuit, *Robert A. Blackwell v. John Siamas et al.*, No. 743709, filed in California Superior Court, April 15, 1960. His relationship with John Siamas and the company is described in Bob Keane's June 1958 telephone conversation with Art Rupe; his method of operation was borne out by the observations of everyone I spoke to around Sam and him in the Keen days.

248 "You taking care of all these other people's business": Charles and L.C. Cooke quoted Sam. Barbara Cooke and Jess Rand reinforced that this was Sam's view, as did J.W. Alexander. In the second part of Michael Watts' *Melody Maker* profile, September 2, 1972, Bumps stated, "The only argument he and I ever had was over money."

249 J.W. immediately released the news to the press: *Kansas City Call*, September 12, 1958.

251 the eight-piece band he had put together: Sam spoke early and often with Clif White about getting his own band. Much of the information about the band he put together, and their two subsequent tours, comes from Lee Poole's 1991 interviews with its musical director, Bob Tate. Tate didn't speak about the Cavalcade of Jazz date at the Shrine; instead, he retained a vague memory of playing Elks Hall. But since the first tour he went out on with Sam came two days after the Shrine show, and since the *California Eagle*, July 24, 1958, reported that each of the stars would be playing with his own orchestra, my assumption is that Sam's band debuted here.

254 Johnny Mathis had broken attendance records: *Houston Informer*, May 10, 1958.

254 "Sam Cooke's disk stature is of very uncertain value here": *Variety*, September 3, 1958.

254 The *Chicago Defender* . . . was burdened with no such doubts: Sam's two-week engagement at the Black Orchid was the impetus for a full-blown two-part profile of Sam by Ernestine Cofield: "Close Look at Sam Cooke: From 'Rags to Riches' Story of Young Chi Club Singer," *Chicago Defender*, October 18, 1958, and "Sam Cooke's Big Decision," *Chicago Defender*, October 25, 1958. Sam's performance is reviewed in the first, and both pieces include numerous photographs of his homecoming. All quotes, both direct and indirect, are from these two articles.

256 a "thoughtful thief": *California Eagle*, October 2, 1958.

256 "Sammy Davis wanted the role": *California Eagle*, October 9, 1958.

256 the William Morris Agency . . . had been affiliated with Sammy: According to Frank Rose's *The Agency: William Morris and the Hidden History of Show Business*, p. 162, the agency signed the Will Mastin Trio in 1945.

258 he promised his fans: *Atlanta Daily World*, September 23, 1958.

261 "one of the few ballsy things I ever did": Dick Clark and Richard Robinson, *Rock, Roll & Remember*, p. 136. The rest of the account is based on my interview with Dick Clark and coverage in the *Atlanta Constitution*, October 2–14, which reports on an ecstatic public reception of the show and makes no mention of any public threat.

263 an amateurishly printed souvenir book: I showed this to Jess Rand, but he had no recollection of it, nor did Lou Rawls. Unfortunately, I didn't get a chance to ask either S.R. Crain or J.W. Alexander.

264 "cheating and swindling" local telephone companies: *Atlanta Daily World*, November 2 and 15, 1958.

264 Eddie Cunningham got into a fight: *St. Louis Argus*, November 21, 1958.

265 There had been an accident: The account of the accident and the events preceding it was pieced together primarily from interviews with Lou Rawls, Clif White, J.W. Alexander, and Jesse Whitaker, Lee Poole's interviews with Bob Tate, and newspaper accounts in the November 11 and 18, 1958, West Memphis *Evening Times*, the November 15 *Tri-State Defender*, and the November 15 and 19 *Memphis World* — some of which are not infrequently in conflict. I'm not going to try to adjudicate, or seek to reconcile, all the conflicts but simply set down my best understanding of what happened, as borne out by both objective and subjective accounts.

266 he was just getting over a bullet wound: *Chicago Defender*, October 13, 1958.

SAM, BARBARA, AND LINDA

268 a big welcome-home Christmas party: In addition to J.W. Alexander's and Lou Rawls' specific recollections, Sam referred glancingly to the party (and the children) in a

1964 interview with journalist Don Paulsen, "You Have to Pay Your Dues," *Hit Parader,* January 1965.

269 "It was all I could do to concentrate": Darlene Love with Rob Hoerburger, *My Name Is Love: The Darlene Love Story,* pp. 37ff.

270 "simple on the surface": Leon Forrest, "A Solo Long-Song for Lady Day," quoted by Farrah Jasmine Griffin in her notes for the ten-CD set *Lady Day: The Complete Billie Holiday on Columbia* (Sony Legacy 85470).

272 "I said, 'What about Bumps?' ": There is no way to specifically date Jess Rand's recollection, but by April 1959 it had been announced in the trades that Jess was Sam Cooke's new manager (Galen Gart, *First Pressings: The History of Rhythm & Blues,* 1959, p. 53). In another version of the story, as Jess told it, it was Sam who first approached him, with Crain consummating the deal.

273 Sam celebrated his birthday: *California Eagle,* January 15, 1959.

277 He had played the Royal Peacock: *Atlanta Daily World,* January 15, 1959.

277 a BMI songwriting award for Sam's hit: According to the *Kansas City Call,* February 20, 1959, the awards ceremony was held at the Hotel Pierre in New York on February 25.

278 He formalized the partnership: BMI wrote to J.W. on March 10, 1959, with a new agreement stipulating that the three-man partnership would be recognized as dating back to December 1, 1958.

282 the Palms of Hallandale, a converted drive-in: The description comes from Gart, *First Pressings,* 1955, p. 55, and Etta James and David Ritz, *Rage to Survive: The Etta James Story,* p. 98.

282 Dolores had died in an automobile accident: *Fresno Bee,* March 23, 1959; *Los Angeles Sentinel,* March 26. According to the divorce papers, Dolores had been living in Los Angeles in August 1958, but the *Bee* had her in Fresno for the last two years of her life.

283 "The Grim Reaper has been shadowing [Sam]": *Birmingham News,* April 25, 1959.

283 He told Farley he had written some new spiritual numbers: J.J. Farley to Art Rupe, April 8, 1959.

283 a cute little routine that "ran the audience wild": *Amsterdam News,* April 25, 1959.

284 "a connoisseur of men": James, *Rage to Survive,* p. 89.

284 He . . . held out for a $2,500 guarantee: Sam ended up with $3,195 for the week under this arrangement, receiving half of the reported $1,388.45 gross over $20,000, according to Apollo Theater records, Schiffman Collection, Achives Center, National Museum of American History, Smithsonian Institution. Given that the show earned out its guaranteed advance, this is the same amount he would have received under the William Morris proposal, but I think Sam would have said that it was the principle that counted.

290 on some nights, "Sam would come out, and Boom!": "Eddie Floyd: Stax Is Back" (no further information available).

290 Jackie was her "teen idol": Gladys Knight, *Between Each Line of Pain and Glory: My Life Story,* p. 93; all additional quotes from Gladys Knight are from this source.

294 she signed a paper relinquishing all rights: The paper was dated July 8, 1959. It was signed by both Barbara, as Barbara Campbell, and Sam Cooke, without the *e.*

294 at last nearing a resolution of his legal problems: Documents and memoranda, Specialty archives.

294 Bumps . . . was to receive $10,038.70: Agreement between Specialty Records and Robert A. Blackwell, October 15, 1959.

295 "a new idea in entertainment programming": This "new idea" was written up in "Soundtrack with 'Chazz' Crawford," *California Eagle*, June 25 and September 24, 1959.

296 he had yet to receive even a statement: From the lawsuit filed as *B. Wolf v. Rex Productions, Inc.*, No. 732700, California Superior Court, October 19, 1959. All subsequent information on Sam's claims, and Keen/Rex's response, stems from these records.

296 anything against the Siamases: J.W. always referred to John Siamas as "an honest fellow."

296 "We should talk to them about recording": The story here is the way J.W. always told it. Leroy Crume's version is similar but somewhat more dramatic. Suffice it to say that in Crume's version Vee Jay offered the Soul Stirrers a $10,000 signing bonus, and the group was very much leaning toward that offer when Sam flew in to Atlanta to present his case. He balked, however, at speaking with the entire group, leaving that to Crume. In the end the result was the same.

297 "Recipients of letters . . . written on good stationery": Walter E. Hurst and William Storm Hale, *The Music Industry Book*, p. 3143.

297 The label was called SAR: J.W. credited Barbara with persuading Sam to drop the idea of including the others when they didn't pitch in. Interestingly, when the business was incorporated, on March 9, 1960, it was stipulated in the incorporation papers that stock could be sold or transferred only to Charles, Clif, or Jess Rand, in addition to the three principals.

300 "James W. Alexander," wrote Walter Hurst: Hurst, *The Music Industry Book*, pp. 3111, 3115.

300 a quick visit to New York: Little Anthony recounted how he had been using "a [set] closer with a gospel feel [and] George Goldner told me to put some lyrics to it," in Dennis Garvey, "Little Anthony and the Imperials," *Goldmine*, April 15, 1995. It was Goldner, said Anthony, who "sent over" Sam Cooke, because of the success that the Flamingos, another of Goldner's acts, had had with Sam's "Nobody Loves Me Like You."

302 he had been in Reno with Sammy Davis Jr.: Barbara recalled it as Las Vegas, but Sammy Davis Jr. played Mapes Casino in Reno from ca. August 26 to September 7.

302 his "pleasing and relaxed manner": *Variety*, July 8, 1959.

302 "You have to be more than just a straight singer": *Variety*, September 23, 1959. J.W. recalled this as the one time that Sam employed his full tap routine.

303 "one of the brightest and best-paced reviews": *Variety*, September 30, 1959.

303 The wedding on Sunday: I'm not sure if Sonny Vincent is the same as Sonny Benson, who is mentioned in the October 18, 1958, *Defender* story on Sam by Ernestine Cofield, "Close Look at Sam Cooke: From 'Rags to Riches' Story of Young Chi Club Singer." L.C. Cooke says that Sonny Vincent was Sam's friend but Duck was best man. The photo in *Sepia*, January 1960, shows Crain as best man. Barbara and her twin sister, Beverly, debated the guest list to no conclusion in my interviews with them. But I can say with assurance that other than myself no one much cared who the official best man actually was.

305 a four-star review: *Billboard*, November 2, 1959.

305 Alan Freed even played "Stand By Me Father": "On November 27, 1959, Alan Freed vanished from New York's airwaves," John Jackson wrote in *Big Beat Heat: Alan Freed and the Early Years of Rock & Roll*, p. 260. Like nearly everything J.W. told me in our initial interviews over twenty years ago, when I had no real idea of what he was talking about, this checked out almost perfectly to the day.

305 his first dramatic role: Davis appeared in "Auf Wiedersehen," on the *General Electric Theater,* in 1958, according to Donald Bogle, *Prime Time Blues: African Americans on Network Television.* He subsequently appeared in "Mission," a drama about the Buffalo Soldiers, which aired on Dick Powell's *Zane Grey Theater* at just about this time, according to Bogle.

306 so he could rehearse with Sammy: All of the details in this account are from my interviews with Jess Rand. The *Atlanta Daily World,* November 8, 1959, reported that Sammy was rehearsing for his new dramatic role while playing the Sands. He headlined at the Sands from November 4 to 24.

306 the harsh realities of show-business segregation: See "Las Vegas — The Swingingest City," *Sepia,* December 1960, and Wil Haygood, *In Black and White: The Life of Sammy Davis, Jr.,* p. 303. Las Vegas was finally desegregated in March 1960 in the aftermath of the filming of the first *Ocean's 11* (starring Frank Sinatra, Dean Martin, and Sammy Davis Jr.) at the Sands. The Sinatra-led Rat Pack undoubtedly played a role, with the Sands, partially owned by Sinatra, the first casino to end its segregated practices in the face of a publicity campaign led by Dr. James B. McMillan, the city's only black dentist, and Hank Greenspun, publisher of the *Las Vegas Sun.* The other casinos continued to hold out until March 25, the day before the first threatened demonstration. It was at this point that desegregation was generally declared under an agreement signed at the Moulin Rouge and subsequently referred to as the Moulin Rouge Agreement.

306 Hugo and Luigi . . . had been hired by RCA: "Victor A.&R. Policy Beams 'Open Door,'" *Billboard,* March 2, 1959.

307 he had been treated with racial condescension: Clyde Otis, Clyde McPhatter's friend and producer, and one of the only black record executives at the time, said of Clyde's views: "It was his militancy that made him have problems with Ahmet Ertegun and Jerry Wexler. Their perception of him was different than the way he wanted to be perceived" (Colin Escott, *Clyde McPhatter: A Biographical Essay,* p. 33). When I asked Ahmet Ertegun about this, he ascribed Clyde's views to eccentricity and "paranoia."

308 "for quick commercial consumption": *Cash Box,* October 10, 1959.

308 Siamas agreed to pay Sam a lump sum: Court documents, *B. Wolf v. Rex Productions, Inc.,* as above.

308 he had decided to do without . . . William Morris: Sam's resentment of William Morris was vividly recalled by Jess Rand and Sam's brothers. Dick Alen, the Universal Attractions agent to whom much of the William Morris booking was farmed out, recognized that sometimes "Sam and Crain would just book themselves. We cared and didn't care. You look the other way."

309 he would be touring with L.C.: *Jet,* November 5, 1959.

310 Sam gladly lent his name: *Atlanta Daily World,* December 6, 1959.

310 the crowd went wild: Paul Foster referred to this in his interview with Lee Hildebrand as "a cheerful welcome." Crume spoke extensively of Sam's continued popularity with the gospel crowd and of the many times he appeared with the group both to help them out and for his own satisfaction. In fact, it became such a commonplace occurrence that the group felt let down when Sam refused to join them onstage at the Met in Philadelphia not long after the Atlanta program — but Sam said he would just watch from the wings, it was time for them to do it on their own.

310 a Frank Interlandi work called *Suffragettes*: Sam continued his art collecting and extended his collection of Interlandis. His sister Mary referred to his having acquired a third "Indrisano" painting in an ANP item that ran in various weeklies toward the end of Octo-

ber 1960. You can see Sam's wall of paintings in pictures of both the Leimert Park apartment and the house in Los Feliz that he and Barbara later moved into. He remained an enthusiastic art collector, Barbara said, visiting the Beverly Hills art galleries frequently whenever he was at home.

311 Mary . . . came out at Sam's expense: *The Carolinian*, September 26, 1959, January 2, 1960.

313 he sent out a card: Jess Rand kindly made a copy of the card for me.

HAVING FUN IN THE RECORD BUSINESS

315 The two cousins sat facing each other: I should say that virtually my entire account
of Hugo and Luigi's colorful, and long-lived, partnership is based on my interviews with
Luigi Creatore alone, due to Hugo Peretti's death in 1986. The only interview with Peretti
of which I'm aware appears in Gerri Hirshey's 1984 *Nowhere to Run: The Story of Soul Music*, and, in the broadest terms, certainly, it can be said to echo Luigi's account — but I wish
I were able to supply something of Hugo's independent voice. Session tapes bear out his
integral role in the New York sessions and his absence from the Los Angeles one.

316 "The Great Creatore": Professor Harold Hill, the rascally hero of the musical comedy *The Music Man*, recalls that memorable day when "the Great Creatore, W. C. Handy,
and John Philip Sousa all came to town," in his signature number, "76 Trombones."

319 "Chain Gang" stemmed from a very specific scene that Sam and Charles had witnessed: The November 10, 1960, *Jet* refers to Sam having "collaborated with his brother
Charles" to write the song. As to its hybrid style, in "Recipe for Success," an article under
his own name in the 1962 *Radio Luxembourg Book of Radio Stars*, Sam writes that "Chain
Gang" was "a typical example of my retention of the spiritual style of singing."

322 Kylo showed up in a state of such insobriety: J.W. spoke to me often about Kylo
Turner, both his talent and his insufficiencies, and I listened to one of the instrumental
tracks, "Wildest Girl in Town," on which Kylo did overdub a vocal. Daniel Wolff, too, describes
how "impressed" Johnnie was with the string section in Daniel Wolff with S. R. Crain,
Clifton White, and G. David Tenenbaum, *You Send Me: The Life and Times of Sam Cooke*,
p. 225.

322 Sam ran into Johnnie Morisette: Nearly all the biographical material, and all of the
quotes, are from Tim Schuller, "The Johnnie 'Two-Voice' Story: Johnnie Morisette," *Living
Blues* 49, winter 1980–81. See also Opal Louis Nations, "Superman: The Johnnie Morisette
Story," *Rock & Blues News*, October–November 2000.

323 "Under the Personal Supervision of Sam Cooke": I have taken a bit of poetic license here. This credit is on Kylo Turner SAR 102, but Johnnie's single, when it came out
two release numbers later, simply said "Produced by Sam Cooke and J.W. Alexander." I'm
not sure what the credit for the Soul Stirrers record in between was, because I've never
seen it.

324 a full-page ad in *Billboard*: *Billboard*, February 15, 1960.

324 another lawsuit against the Siamases: *B. Wolf v. Rex Productions, Inc.*, No. 741782,
California Superior Court, March 16, 1960.

327 a "hot dispute with [the] dance managers": Paul C. McGee, "Auto Crash Kills Rock-
Roll Ace," *Los Angeles Sentinel*, February 18, 1960. See also "The Strange Flaming Death of
Jesse Belvin," *Sepia*, June 1960.

327 "Did Racism Kill Jesse?": *Norfolk Journal and Guide,* March 5, 1960.

327 "They try to knock us down": *The Carolinian,* April 2, 1960, et al. (ANP syndication).

327 nineteen-year-old drummer Leo Morris: Morris is today the noted jazz musician Idris Muhammad.

332 "Being on a major boulevard . . . made this a good address": Walter E. Hurst and William Storm Hale, *The Music Industry Book,* p. 3142.

332 unless he was on the road: The *California Eagle,* July 7, 1960, for example, made a point of informing its readers that J.W. Alexander was just back "from the east."

332 going pop just after her eighteenth birthday: *Norfolk Journal and Guide,* February 27, 1960. J.W. spoke a great deal about Aretha and Sam. So did Sam's brothers L.C. and Charles. Aretha herself appeared to be under the misconception that Sam was trying to get her to sign with RCA — or perhaps this is just a distortion of memory fostered by Columbia executive John Hammond's belief at the time. "I had been told . . . that Sam Cooke was determined to sign Aretha to RCA Victor," Hammond wrote in his autobiography with Irving Townsend, *John Hammond on Record,* p. 348. The result, he said, was that he "signed her quick." But there is no question that when Sam and J.W. thought about signing Aretha, it was to their own label, SAR.

332 "Crain lived in Chicago": Hurst, *The Music Industry Book,* pp. 3116–3117.

333 "a spoiled little brat": Etta James and David Ritz, *Rage to Survive: The Etta James Story,* p. 64.

333 "like a little kid playing grown-up": Hirshey, *Nowhere to Run,* p. 102.

334 the "chain of devilment": "Little Willie John Grows Up," *Tan,* February 1961.

335 Little Willie John was a gambling fool: In addition to his sister's more circumspect testimony, *everyone* spoke of Little Willie John's gambling proclivities, from Charles and L.C. to Billy Davis, Solomon Burke, and Etta James, who wrote in her memoir, *Rage to Survive,* about Willie terrorizing the tour manager, Nat Margo.

335 the airport reception that greeted them: *Jet,* August 11, 1960, as well as Idris Muhammad interview.

335 "I burn with ambition": "Boy Singer Makes Good," *New York Journal-American,* August 5, 1960.

337 the violence "that gave Negro concerts black eyes": Elgin Hychew, "Dig Me! . . . ," *Louisiana Weekly,* August 13, 1960.

337 a direct ban on all rock 'n' roll revues: Marcel Hopson, "2 Wounded in Wild Shooting Spree at City Auditorium," *Birmingham World,* July 20, 1960.

337 "The commotion started": "Jazz Concert Ends on Near-Riot Kick," *Louisiana Weekly,* July 23, 1960.

337 these "young people . . . who are willing to risk verbal abuse": "Clyde Hails Young Freedom-Seekers," *Norfolk Journal and Guide,* July 9, 1960.

338 "plans had been made to run a rope": *Norfolk Journal and Guide,* August 27, 1960.

338 "The SAM COOKE crowd . . . did not fully dig": Elgin Hychew, "Dig Me! . . . ," *Louisiana Weekly,* August 13, 1960.

340 Johnnie Taylor got into an automobile accident: Paul Foster told a somewhat different story to Lee Hildebrand, which involved Johnnie getting busted for smoking dope at the Evans Hotel as well as the automobile accident.

340 he preached his first sermon at Fellowship Baptist: Lee Hildebrand liner notes to the three-CD set *Johnnie Taylor: Lifetime* (Stax 4432); Paul Foster, in his 1984 interview with

Hildebrand, recalled Taylor's first sermon, in Shreveport, while he was still on the road with the Stirrers. "He worshiped his Book," Foster said.

340 "The Reverend Johnnie Taylor (Formerly with the Soul Stirrers)": *Atlanta Daily World*, September 4, 1960.

340 Paul Foster took over the lead: Foster spoke of this in his 1981 interview with Ray Funk. According to him, someone named "Felt" replaced Johnnie Taylor for a minute. This may well be the same person that Crume referred to as the "little Holiness guy."

340 Sam had an audition set up: Joe Ligon, like June Cheeks, is a little hard to figure for the Soul Stirrers sound. He was, and remains, a *hard* singer. In any case, his group, the Mighty Clouds of Joy, had its first Peacock Records session within a month and achieved stardom within a couple of years, becoming one of the biggest and most emotionally riveting quartets from the sixties to the present day.

341 "Well, we was at the Shrine": J.W. remembered it as the Olympic.

345 at once "relaxed and hectic": "Sam Still Cookin' on New RCA Victor Album," *Michigan Chronicle*, April 1, 1961.

346 where he had fucked up: Leo has continued to think to this day that it was Clif White who wanted him out. No one else I spoke to would venture an explanation.

347 Cassius Clay . . . jumped up onstage: *Louisville Defender*, September 29, 1960. Everyone remembers meeting Clay around this time — Sam's brothers, June Gardner, Lloyd Price, Billy Davis, Leroy Crume, and Norman Thrasher, to name a few — and everyone remembers him as a good, eager kid.

348 "Sam was in and out": Harry Bacas, "Top Tunes — 'Sad Mood,'" *Washington Sunday Star*, n.d.

349 "All people are alike to us": James Booker, " 'We Are All Brothers' (Exclusive): Castro Talks," *Amsterdam News*, September 24, 1960.

351 It was midnight when he arrived: François Postif, "New York in Jazz Time," *Le Jazz Hot*, December 1960. The translation is mine, with *much* help from Ellen Mandel. I should point out, too, that the explicit description of miming masturbation (to which Postif alludes only with reference to its "disgusting" nature), stems from my own observation of the act three or four years later, and my checking with Hank Ballard about it.

352 a female fan emerging from the crowd to punch him savagely: *The Carolinian*, November 12, 1960.

352 a former gospel singer named Theola Kilgore: J.W. introduced her to her producer, Ed Townsend.

352 a press release announcing that Sam would soon be interviewed: *California Eagle*, October 27, 1960.

352 "eye-popping splendor": "Royal Peacock, Treasure Island, Henry's Lounge Win Rave Notices," *Atlanta Daily World*, October 22, 1960.

352 Clyde had taken his place on a downtown picket line: *Jet*, December 15, 1960, has a picture of Clyde picketing with Martin Luther King Sr.; the *Chicago Defender*, December 9–16, 1960, has an article entitled "Clyde McPhatter Advises Kids in Dixie on 'Bias,'" which refers to Clyde giving several speeches on local campuses while playing the Peacock and cites his gift of NAACP memberships for Christmas. *The Carolinian*, November 19, 1960, quotes from a letter he wrote to his fellow performers, which I have used in part for the text of his unrecorded campus speech. *The Atlanta Daily World*, November 26, covered the renewal of the demonstrations after a lull.

352–353 many big-name stars were bypassing the Deep South: *Jet*, December 22, 1960.

354 "I ain't never gonna sing at the Waldorf": This comes from interviews with Luigi Creatore but is also quoted from Hugo Peretti, with only a slight variation, in Hirshey, *Nowhere to Run*, p. 114. "They're not my people," Sam says of the Waldorf clientele in this version. To which Hugo adds, "He would rather work."

ANOTHER COUNTRY

355 "she shot him twice": Art Peters, "Jackie Wilson Near Death" (two front-page stories), *Philadelphia Tribune*, February 18, 1961. Jackie did not return to the road until July. When he did, he practically caused a riot in his first scheduled performance, at the Uptown Theater, as he leapt offstage, according to the *Philadelphia Tribune*, July 4, 1961, and the fans, as usual, tore his clothes off. When he scrambled back onstage, though, he gave the audience a scare of its own, *Jet* magazine, July 20, 1961, reported, as he "coughed violently in the middle of a tune, swayed," then fell backward onto the floor before miraculously reviving and going on with the show.

356 the formation of Cooke-Rand Productions: *Variety*, February 1, 1961.

359 his long association with Sammy Davis Jr. and its bitter dénouement: This is alluded to in Wil Haygood, *In Black and White: The Life of Sammy Davis, Jr.*, p. 298.

360 "I am aware that owning a record company": *Radio Luxembourg Book of Record Stars*, 1962. See also Don Nelsen, "A Successful Cooke," *Sunday Daily News*, July 16, 1961, for Sam's early- and subsequently oft-stated intention to give himself over to his record company and leave the singing "to the younger fellows."

360 She went to work the following Monday: Payroll records show Zelda receiving her first paycheck on January 20, 1961, for $85.

362 "with no formal musical training whatsoever": BBC interview with René Hall.

363 a gospel duo Alex had discovered: The Sims Twins recalled that the gospel program on which they appeared also included the Mighty Clouds of Joy.

364 Kenneth mimicked the sound of the arrow: Steve Propes interview with the Sims Twins. René Hall volunteers the same description in his 1987 interview with Propes. Luigi Creatore and Al Schmitt recalled Sam making the sound, but this is impossible because there is an overlap beween his vocal and the whoosh even on the outtakes.

365 She gave up Kools for Kents: Aretha spoke of this in both our interview and in her autobiography with David Ritz, *Aretha: From These Roots*, p. 67.

365 she kept a scrapbook: Mark Bego, *Aretha Franklin: The Queen of Soul*, p. 27.

367 throwing up a partition for her: Ritz, *Aretha: From These Roots*, p. 92.

367–368 *The New Yorker, Playboy*, and Aristotle's *Poetics*: J.W. Alexander, Aretha Franklin, June Gardner, Jess Rand, and Barbara and Linda Cooke, among others, all attested to Sam's specific reading habits and cited individual titles. J.W. named Aristotle, *The New Yorker*, and *Playboy*; Linda and June both spoke of *War and Peace*.

369 "to carry on the fight for Negro rights": Juan Williams, *Eyes on the Prize: America's Civil Rights Years 1954–1965*, p. 114.

369 Ray Brown . . . explained that the show had been advertised: "Cooke and McPhatter Kept Quiet," *Memphis World*, May 20, 1961. It should be noted that Ray Charles refused to play Augusta, Georgia, on March 15, 1961, under similar circumstances, described fully in Michael Lydon, *Ray Charles: Man and Music*, pp. 196–197. The promoter sued, and Charles paid a $757 fine. Ray subsequently played Memphis on August 20 in what *Variety* referred to, in an August 23, 1961, front-page story, as the first fully integrated show at Ellis

Auditorium. "Policemen were all over the place," the August 26 *Memphis World* reported with full cognizance of Sam and Clyde McPhatter's earlier stand, "but they weren't needed. Old Man Segregation had gone for a swim in the muddy Wolf River."

371 "Sam Cooke, singer and idol of thousands": "Walker, Turner Paid Glowing Tributes: City Heads Present," *Memphis World*, May 20, 1961.

371 The city's two white newspapers reported: "2 Negro Singers Fail to Appear," *Memphis Press-Scimitar;* "Two Negro Stars Cancel Show Here," *Memphis Commercial Appeal,* both May 13, 1961.

371 Sam released his own statement: *Tri-State Defender,* May 20, 1961, and *passim.*

371 "Singers Say No to Jim Crow": *Amsterdam News,* May 27, 1961.

371 "Top Singers Spurn Segregated Audience": *Los Angeles Sentinel,* June 1, 1961.

371 "Singing Stars Balk": *Kansas City Call,* June 2, 1961.

371 "Clyde McPhatter, Sam Cooke Clip Memphis": *Houston Forward-Times,* May 27, 1961, with the same story in *New Jersey Afro-American,* June 3, and *Louisiana Weekly,* June 10, among others.

374 "one continuous floor show": *Los Angeles Sentinel,* June 15, 1961.

374 the Brook Benton–Dinah Washington hit: *Norfolk Journal and Guide,* July 8, 1961. In addition, the Prudhomme twins gave a full account of the evening in my interviews with them.

374 RCA had a full-page ad: *Cash Box,* June 4, 1961.

374 Jess' crazy friend Mike Santangelo: Almost all information on Santangelo comes, with great affection, from Jess Rand.

374 the *Hollywood Reporter* ran a similarly unsourced note: *Hollywood Reporter,* December 28, 1960.

375 "That's the sound of broken glass": I've never quite understood Jess' story. I did notice in still photographs that the cue card for the start of the show says in part: "That's the sound of a man named Sam Cooke. A modest" — but that appears to be an echo of the "Chain Gang" lyric, and, in any case, that's where the edge of the picture intrudes. The show's subtitle, incidentally, I assume was "Phenomenon," but it was printed as "Phenomena" more than once.

375 ten or twelve numbers: the *Hollywood Reporter,* June 13, 1961, anticipated ten; *Cash Box,* July 15, counted a dozen.

375 He talked about some of the artists: "'PM East' Solid Artist Showcase," *Billboard,* June 26, 1961.

376 "one of the few instances where a top Negro entertainer": *Hollywood Reporter,* June 13, 1961.

376 "the show was an unalloyed smash": *Billboard,* June 26, 1961.

377 They had originally met Sam: Both Bobby Womack and his oldest brother, Friendly Jr. (in his ca. 1984–1985 interview with Barbara Cooke), vividly recalled the incident. Friendly said that the promoter, William Turner, introduced them to the Stirrers. The Womacks were not nonentities in the gospel world, to which they had been introduced by their uncle Solomon Womack, one of the early members of the Swan Silvertones, whose spectacular falsetto lead, Claude Jeter, was a source of unending inspiration to Bobby in particular.

378 The Womacks caught up with Sam: Friendly Womack Jr. recalled many of the details in his interview with Barbara Cooke. So did Bobby and L.C. in our many conversations on the subject.

379 he was looking to score some money for himself: This gibes with Tony Heilbut's account of Sam's generosity toward Cheeks in Heilbut, *The Gospel Sound: Good News and*

Bad Times, p. 125. "The first $500 bill I ever had," said Cheeks, "Sam gave it to me. . . . [Of all the r&b singers] Sam's the only one treated me right."

381 "Soothe Me" . . . was just beginning to break into the charts: The record was referred to as "hitting nationally" in *Cash Box*, September 9, where it was also listed at number 32 on the "Looking Ahead" chart. SAR ran a small ad in the September 23 issue with a one-word text, "Tremendous!!!" The session to record "I'll Never Come Running Back to You" was held on August 15, almost certainly with J.W. alone supervising. It replaced "(Don't Fight It) Feel It" on the B-side of the single in September.

382 who was going to close the show: Both June Gardner and Lithofayne Pridgon recalled the specifics of this date.

382 This was how he earned his living: *New York Sunday News*, July 16, 1961.

383 "I feel that we left our discussions in New York": Letter from Bob Yorke to Jess Rand, June 8, 1961. In a March 1, 1962, intra-office communication, Yorke wrote: "The last time I talked to Sam was regarding a contract and terms which he subsequently refused. It was not a friendly conversation."

384 The lawsuit that they had filed: This was still *B. Wolf v. Rex Productions, Inc.*, No. 741782, California Superior Court, originally filed March 16, 1960. At the time of filing, Sam and J.W.'s claims amounted to only $13,000 in publishing and artist royalties due through December 31, 1959, but as the case wended its way through the courts, sales records were demanded for all of Sam's recordings through February 15, 1961. With the success of "Wonderful World" in particular, the new filing had the potential to triple the amount involved, and the trial was scheduled to start on October 2.

386 Sam had found a new home: In addition to interviews with J.W. and Barbara, probate records from California Superior Court, *In the Matter of the Estate of Glen Glenn, Deceased*, No. 433, 391, October 27, 1961, supplied the specifics of the purchase.

387 Lew Chudd had decided to bid against him: I've never understood why Lew Chudd got involved, and J.W.'s chuckle in response to my questions indicated that to him it was a matter of little consequence, perhaps not much more than a practical joke.

388 the record was reviewed in both *Billboard* and *Cash Box*: *Billboard*, November 27, 1961; the *Cash Box* review and squib were in the December 2 issue.

388 RCA finally called: The first written record of the deal that I could find in the RCA files was December 18, 1961, but clearly talks had preceded it. Bob Yorke's subsequent in-house correspondence indicates that Luigi Creatore served as Sam and Alex's go-between.

389 a new gospel-based show called *Black Nativity*: There is a tangled history to this, which is detailed in part in Arnold Rampersad, *The Life of Langston Hughes*, vol. 2, *I Dream a World*, pp. 347–354. My understanding of Jess Rand's part (and Sam's) — including Michael Santangelo's offer of a financial stake in the show to Jess if Jess would move east — comes from interviews with Jess Rand. In the end, said Jess with some asperity, "I got a thank-you, not a piece." The thank-you consisted of a note at the front of the program for all productions to the effect that the producer, Michael R. Santangelo, "had become interested in gospel songs four years before, through recording artist Sam Cooke, a former gospel singer, and his mentor, Jess Rand."

389 The Denise Somerville paternity suit: Court records, going back to the original filing in Cuyahoga County Juvenile Court in 1958, as Case No. 178794, along with the subsequent Agreement and Release.

390 Sam happened to catch a television show: The inspiration for "Twistin' the Night Away" is a well-known story that comes primarily from interviews with J.W. Alexander but is also told by Sam in Chris Roberts, "Doesn't That Gospel Music Just Swing!" *Melody Maker,* October 20, 1962.

392 "Barbara Cooke . . . is already down to a size (7)": Gertrude Gipson, "Candid Comments," *Los Angeles Sentinel,* January 4, 1962.

BOOGIE-WOOGIE RUMBLE

393 "it was kind of tense at times": Bill Dahl, "Dion: Forever the King of the New York Streets," *Goldmine,* March 9, 2001. Also, Dion DiMucci with Davin Seay, *The Wanderer: Dion's Story,* p. 81.

395 what had landed him in Newport: Charles Brown's Newport hegira, and the writing of "I Want to [alternatively, "I Wanna"] Go Home," is well covered in Rick Coleman's 1988 interview; a 1991 interview supplied by Howell Begle from *Charles Brown: A Life in the Blues* (Rounder DVD 11661–2074); Chip Deffaa, *Blue Rhythms,* pp. 124–127; Billy Vera 1999 liners to *Blue Over You* (Westside 610), a CD anthology of Brown's Ace sides; and John Anthony Brisbin, "Charles Brown: the *Living Blues* Interview," *Living Blues* 118, November/December 1994.

398 Johnnie was still debating: In John Broven and Cilla Huggins' 1989 interview with Johnnie Taylor, he said: "Bobby Robinson told me, 'He ain't gonna promote you.' And he was right about that." He expressed a more restrained ambivalence in his 1986 interview in *Living Blues* 153.

403 the Pla-Mor Ballroom in Cleveland: *Cleveland Call & Post,* August 26, 1961.

403 "We all cried": Barbara Cooke interview with Friendly Womack Jr. All subsequent quotes from Friendly are from this interview.

404 they signed their new contract: The contract was dated June 1, 1962.

405 He pitched the song excitedly: I had three principal interview sources for this account: June Gardner, Grady Gaines, and J.W. Alexander. No one could understand Dee Clark's reason for rejecting the song. Interestingly, Clark had already recorded "Cupid" (as an LP cut) and "The Time Has Come," one of Sam's earliest compositions, and went on to cowrite "TCB" with Sam not much later.

406 Barbara and Sugar Hall started to do a slow twist: Walter E. Hurst and William Storm Hale, *The Music Industry Book,* p. 3214.

407 "We were after the Soul Stirrers–type thing": Steve Propes interview with René Hall, 1987.

407 Rickwood Field employed "Negro citizens": *Birmingham World,* April 21, 1962.

408 "the word of the hour": J. Gillison: "They Call It 'Soul Music,'" *Philadelphia Tribune,* September 8, 1962.

408 "Oh, we all heard it": Gerri Hirshey, *Nowhere to Run: The Story of Soul Music,* p. 110.

408 Sam Cooke's *Twistin the Night Away Revue*: *Jet,* June 7, 1962.

410 Sam took Johnnie Morisette out on tour: Johnnie signed a contract with Malloy Management, the management division of Kags Music Corp., on April 24, 1962.

411 "I was living in California": Tim Schuller, "The Johnnie 'Two-Voice' Story: Johnnie Morisette," *Living Blues* 49, winter 1980–1981, p. 25 (condensed). All additional quotes from Johnnie Morisette are from this interview.

411 "Welcome NAACP Convention": *Atlanta Daily World,* July 1, 1962.

411 "he rushed feverishly to a closing, four-word slogan": Taylor Branch, *Parting the Waters: America in the King Years 1954–63,* pp. 598–600.

412 "I have always had a rather bright insight on business": Alphonso S. McLean, "Sam Cooke Wows 'Em in Savannah, Georgia, Show," *Chicago Defender*, July 24, 1962.

412 Sam was playing three nights at the Knight Beat: *Miami Times*, July 14, 1962.

415 Cook, a "popular and dynamic nationally known promoter": Joe Rainey, "Seen and Heard," *Philadelphia Tribune*, October 22, 1960.

415 "entertainer Johnnie Morisette [would] be affiliated": Paul McGee, "Theatricals," *Los Angeles Sentinel*, July 26, 1962.

415 "Well, partner, let's go to New York": J.W. said this took place just before Sam's tour of England in October. In Maureen Cleave's "Disc Date" in the London *Evening Standard*, Sam is referred to as "the owner" of a beer company — though, of course, it's entirely possible that this information was gleaned from a recent publicity release, not from the interview itself. The beer company offices were the subject of a numbers raid "a month" after Sam got involved, according to an article in the *Baltimore Afro-American*, November 18, 1962, cited in Daniel Wolff with S. R. Crain, Clifton White, and G. David Tenenbaum, *You Send Me: The Life and Times of Sam Cooke*, p. 251. Five months later, however, Cooke's Beer was still being advertised in the *Norfolk Journal and Guide*, April 13, 1963, as the beer that was "brewed with pure artesian well water" and could boast of "Sam Cooke, President." I don't know any way to resolve these contradictions except to say that J.W.'s testimony was almost always accurate to the day and that in any case, in terms of the *spirit* of the business' conclusion, we can certainly take J.W. at his word.

ANOTHER SATURDAY NIGHT

419 "Unconfirmed rumors swept the Eastern seaboard": Art Peters, "Sam Cooke Illness Rumor Hotly Denied," *Philadelphia Tribune*, August 11, 1962. Reports also showed up in the *Los Angeles Sentinel*, August 2; *Washington DC Afro-American*, August 25 and September 1; *Norfolk Journal and Guide*, September 8; and *Cleveland Call*, September 8, among others.

419 "one of the meanest and lowest canards": *Los Angeles Sentinel*, February 28, 1963.

419 Jerry Brandt was still vehemently denying: Chuck Stone, "Sam Cooke NOT Ill or Dying," *Washington DC Afro-American*, August 25, 1962 (lead front-page story). One week later the same reporter led with: "Sam Cooke is neither dying nor ill, says his New York office."

419 everything from "low salaries to lack of employment opportunities": William Barlow, *Voice Over: The Making of Black Radio*, p. 219. This is by far the best written source for an insight into the development of black radio, but much of its interview material comes from *Black Radio: Telling It Like It Was*, a Smithsonian series produced by Jacquie Gales Webb for National Public Radio, which is essential listening. My interviews with Jimmy "Early" Byrd, Larry McKinley, Georgie Woods, and Harold Battiste bore out much of the general import of these two sources and helped fill in some of the gaps.

419 "We partied until it was time to go to church": Barlow, *Voice Over*, p. 220. All other quotes from "Jockey" Jack Gibson are from the same source.

419 "It was just an idea of camaraderie": This is from my interview with Larry McKinley. Georgie Woods made the same point in almost identical words.

420 "You have to understand": Barlow, *Voice Over*, p. 209.

421 Crain had his money and briefcase stolen: *St. Louis Argus*, August 24, 1962; also UPI story, August 21.

422 "I was also informed by Sam": Oscar Alexander, "Diggin' Daddy-Oh!" *The Carolinian*, October 6, 1962.

423 right up until opening night he was uncertain: In addition to my interviews with Don Arden and J.W. Alexander, Charles White describes in *The Life and Times of Little Richard: The Quasar of Rock*, pp. 107–108, how Arden took out advertisements in the music press in September to reassure the public that "Little Richard has been booked purely as a rock artist," with further specifics on just which of his rock 'n' roll hits he would sing.

423 J.W. accompanied Sam to Arden's hotel: To be fair, Arden recalled this in one interview as a telephone conversation, in another as this meeting. But the impression Sam (and J.W.) made, both then and subsequently, was clear.

424 Richard was wearing what looked . . . like religious robes: Chris Hutchins, "Little Richard Is Amazing!" *New Musical Express*, October 12, 1962, described Little Richard's outfit as a "large, baggy white suit"; Arden remembered it as black monk's robes.

425 Most of the audiences were there for Richard: Various British fans have described the shows to me (and their own preference for Little Richard), including Bill Millar (Maidstone), and Dave Williams (Kingston). Charles White writes about the Mansfield show in *The Life and Times of Little Richard*, p. 113, and Brian J. Hamblin's letter to *Now Dig This!* 235 (October 2002) describes the Bristol performance. At the prompting of Val Wilmer, I spoke to Ian Pickstock, who recalled a much-of-the-night party that Sam and Richard had with the cast of *Black Nativity*.

427 "he *hypnotized* the audience": Dave Williams described a similar effect as Sam mesmerized "all these rockers" just by waving his handkerchief round and round.

428 Sam had simply "dreamed up" another hit: "As Sam Cooke Dreams Up a Song in London," *New Musical Express*," n.d.

428 Sam also spoke to *Melody Maker*: Chris Roberts, "Doesn't That Gospel Music Just Swing!" *Melody Maker*, October 20, 1962.

429 Dressed in "red-patterned pyjamas": Maureen Cleave, "Disc Date," *Evening Standard*, n.d.

431 At the heart of the new act: The attentive reader will note that the show I am describing is available on *Sam Cooke Live at the Harlem Square Club* (RCA [BMG] 5181). The reason I have used this with some confidence as my model is because J.W. Alexander was emphatic that this was the show Sam introduced at the Apollo. The brief reference in the *Philadelphia Tribune*, December 8, 1962, tends to bear out just how notable a departure the show was for Sam.

433 "his rapport with the femmes": *Variety*, November 7, 1962.

436 he played a WAOK benefit: This remains something of a mystery, as the tape never surfaced. When I met Zenas Sears in 1984, it certainly existed, but I don't know what has become of it since his death. Zenas recalled L.C. Cooke as being part of the show. An article by Thelma Hunt Shirley in the *Chicago Defender*, December 16, 1964, "Friends, Fans Chorus 'Sam Was a Good Guy,'" has a DJ named Ed Cooke, formerly of Atlanta, talking about a kids' benefit show there. Grady Gaines of the Upsetters recalled an Atlanta date being recorded, and J.W. remembered the show, though he thought it was at the Royal Peacock. William Morris' booking schedule has Sam playing the Rhythm Rink on November 13, 1962, but I could find no advertisement for it.

439 Olsie Robinson ("Bassy") walked out of a sound check: Everyone agrees that Bassy stopped playing for Sam, but no one can quite agree on the date or reason. Bobby Womack, Grady Gaines, Gorgeous George, and June Gardner all had their own take on the situation, but there is no question that Bobby started playing more and more regularly with Sam from late 1962 on.

440 they had less than $100 among them: Bobby, Friendly Jr., Cecil, and Curtis Womack all recalled the tour (Friendly in his interview with Barbara Cooke). Once again timing is something of an issue, and I have never been able to find a listing for the Birmingham show with Tall Paul on which Johnnie Taylor, the Sims Twins, and possibly Johnnie Morisette were also on the bill. But all of the Womacks appeared to agree that it was before their session in California in December 1962.

441 SAR Pictures had acquired the film rights: *Cash Box*, June 9, 1962. J.W. told me: "I got a guy named Phil Waddell to [put it out] that I had purchased an original story from him, but then the story broke so damn big I gave Phil some money and said, 'You [better] start writing something!'"

441 They had given up on Jess at this point: The change in Jess' role is indicated by Paul Cantor's attempt to recruit Sam as a client and Jess' total noninvolvement in the English tour. Jess, however, was never made aware of his change in status by either Sam or J.W.

442 with Linda frequently in tow: You can hear Linda slating Takes 11–13 of "I Wish You Love."

442 Aretha Franklin was playing the Alexandria: *Los Angeles Sentinel*, December 13, 1962. Other club dates cited are from the same issue.

442 "Sam (Mr. Feeling) Cooke, who left the gospel field": *St. Louis Argus*, December 21, 1962, et al. It was written up in *Variety* December 19.

442 "an entirely new program of song": *Los Angeles Sentinel*, December 27, 1962.

443 "undoubtedly the most sensational gospel show": *St. Louis Argus*, December 21, 1962.

444 "on a sort of freelance basis": *Billboard*, December 1, 1962. *Variety* reported the same story on December 5.

444 that was the end of the deal: By the beginning of April, Sam and J.W.'s friend Ed Townsend had moved east to take the job.

445 "I only ever travel with those I like": This and all other quotes from King Curtis are from Charlie Gillet's 1971 interview with Curtis, published in *The Sound* ("a newsletter for King Curtis record collectors" published by Roy Simonds) no. 4, June/July 1985. The interview was concluded in the following issue.

446 "Never had I read words that sounded so real": Magnificent Montague with Bob Baker, *Burn, Baby! Burn: The Autobiography of Magnificent Montague*, p. 52. All other quotes are from my interviews with Montague.

448 "he urged all tan performers to pay more attention": *Philadelphia Tribune*, June 15, 1963, as well as *Cleveland Call, Norfolk Journal and Guide*, and *Jet*, January 31, among others. The story was not attributed to the ANP in the weekly newspapers, but the simultaneity of publication (and replication of language) argue for its syndication in this manner.

449 "This innocent country set you down in a ghetto": James Baldwin, *The Fire Next Time*, pp. 21–22.

450 the "coldest New Year's Eve in history": *St. Louis Argus*, January 11, 1963.

451 "I shall return": *Chicago Defender*, January 10, 1963; *St. Louis Argus*, January 11. Like the initial announcement, this report was orchestrated in a manner that indicates its importance.

451 Hugo and Luigi had agreed to record Sam's live show: Luigi wrote to Mr. Stewart Goldman, vice president of the Harlem Square's ownership corporation, on January 2, 1963.

The contractual form letter that Goldman signed granted RCA permission to record the show, with no remuneration for the club.

453 whatever the sonic shortcomings: As J.W. said: "We could have had more crowd noise, but we were popping."

455 the BMI Awards dinner: The January 23 dinner was reported in *Variety*, January 23, 1963, and *Billboard*, January 26 and February 2.

457 It was as overt a disagreement: J.W. Alexander disagreed that there was ever any overt disagreement, but as likeable as he found L.C., he did not see him as very hardworking.

457 "[L.C.] didn't want to sing like him": BBC interview with René Hall.

SCENES FROM LIFE

1 | JOCKO'S PARTNER

464 "He couldn't lie if he wanted to": Lex Gillespie interview with Doug "Jocko" Henderson, 1995, for the Smithsonian series produced by Jacquie Gales Webb for National Public Radio, *Black Radio: Telling It Like It Was*. Used by permission.

468 an improbable . . . wish list of stars: *Variety*, February 27, 1963.

468 "Politicians and Dogs Nearly Steal State Theatre Show": In addition to this story by Chris J. Perry, see also Mark Bricklin, "Sam Cooke Tops, Trib Critic Says," and an unattributed "Battle Rages at Rock 'n' Roll Show," all in the *Philadelphia Tribune*, March 12, 1963.

471 complaining to Sam that Curt had the lead vocal: The Valentinos' second record, a re-release of "Somewhere There's a Girl" on Sam and J.W.'s new Derby label, was actually credited to Curtis and the Boys. According to Bobby: "I was trying to say, 'Don't let Curtis sing too many songs.' But Sam kept saying, 'Bobby, in later years you'll happen, but they'll play Curtis' record faster.'"

473 "Why doesn't Sam Cooke appear on television?": Darcy DeMille, "Just Ask Me," *Sepia*, April 1963. In fact, Sam had just appeared on Merv Griffin's about-to-be-canceled afternoon talk show on March 18.

473 "the excellent song material written" by Negro songwriters: "Sam Would 'Cook' Revival of Oldies," Pittsburgh Courier, April 13, 1963 (ANP).

2 | LESSONS OF THE ROAD

475 "Onstage there's nobody who could touch him": *Tri-State Defender*, April 27, 1963.

475 a new Prudhomme twins–authored . . . song: The song was "Nobody But Me," and it was listed in *Billboard* July 20, 1963.

476 his real [name] of "Little" Julius High: This appears to have been a short-lived reclamation of his given name, but Lotsa had just appeared as Little Julius High at the Uptown in Philadelphia with James Brown, March 22–31.

477 "Henry started calling me Gorgeous George [because] I was sharp": George steadfastly refuses to acknowledge any nominal connection to the popular white wrestler from the fifties Gorgeous George, whose flamboyant style was such an influence on Little Richard, James Brown, and Muhammad Ali. But perhaps he's right, for this Gorgeous George, too, is an original in every way.

490 Al Hibbler standing side by side with Dr. King: David L. Lewis, *King: A Biography*, pp. 183–184; *The Carolinian*, April 27, 1963; *Chicago Defender*, April 13–19. There is some disagreement about whether or not Hibbler actually went to jail. Some accounts have him being rejected for imprisonment because of his blindness.

490 "Well, now, Mr. Mayor": Taylor Branch, *Parting the Waters: America in the King Years 1954–63*, p. 722.

490 "Are Show Biz Folk Sincere?": *Norfolk Journal and Guide*, April 20, 1963; also *Philadelphia Tribune*, April 30, and I'm sure others.

490 an exclusive nightclub in Atlanta: His engagement at the Copa (*Atlanta's* Copa) was advertised in the *Atlanta Constitution*, March 15, 1963.

490 "the right to be treated like an American": *Norfolk Journal and Guide*, April 20, 1963.

490 Nat "King" Cole . . . defended "stars who shun[ned] Dixie picket lines": *Chicago Defender*, May 11–17, 1963.

491 Fats Domino . . . announced his own break: "Fats Domino Abandons Freedom Push: Will Take Segregated Dates," *Kansas City Call*, January 11, 1963 (ANP).

491 he rescinded his new policy: "Fats Domino Denies Break with NAACP," *Kansas City Call*, January 18, 1963; *Carolinian*, January 19 (ANP).

491 "treat[ing] King's campaign as a disturbing rumor": Branch, *Parting the Waters*, p. 710. My account of the Birmingham campaign is largely culled from Branch; David J. Garrow, *Bearing the Cross: Martin Luther King, Jr., and the Southern Christian Leaadership Conference*; and Lewis, *King: A Biography*.

491 "reporters saw no news": Branch, *Parting the Waters*, p. 744.

492 "both wasteful and worthless": Garrow, *Bearing the Cross*, p. 240, citing the *Birmingham World*, April 10.

492 the single word "freedom": Branch, *Parting the Waters*, p. 759.

492 "Do not underestimate the power of this movement": Ibid., p. 791.

492 "sabotaged by a few extremists on either side": Ibid., p. 800.

492 "the nonviolent movement coming of age": Lewis, *King: A Biography*, p. 196.

492 Brook Benton . . . had only recently played Clemson: Account of his Clemson engagement in the *Miami Times*, March 9, 1963.

493 "We're waking up": Morton Cooper, "Brook Benton Afraid He Can't Be Non-Violent," *Chicago Defender*, May 25–31, 1963.

493 "We're in the middle of a social revolution": Paul Learn, "Mixing Melody, Love Puts Sam Cooke on Top," *Atlantic City Press*, July 30, 1964. It's interesting that Dick Clark, a friend and great admirer of Sam's, described Sam as the "first angry black man" Clark had ever met.

494 he and Alex had figured out a way of operating: As Alex said: "Neither one of us looked militant. They didn't know quite [what to make of me], because I went into so [many] areas. They just look at me and assume maybe I was something else."

495 Sam would get a $15,000 guarantee: J.W. saw the new deal with BMI as the end of Jess Rand. From his perspective they had hired Allen Klein as an accountant, and Allen had come through. From this point on, Allen had their full trust. Concurrent with the BMI agreement, Allen prudently had L.C. Cooke sign over all interest in any of Sam's songs credited to him on May 29.

497 "the one and only black history [bookstore]": This was the Aquarian Bookstore and Spiritual Center (later shortened to the Aquarian Book Shop), which had been founded in 1941 by Alfred Ligon. Ligon, born in Atlanta in 1906 and a devotee of African-American culture, metaphysical philosophy, and the occult, financed the shop originally with the savings from his job as a waiter on the Southern Pacific. He and his wife, Bernice, who went to work for him in 1943, five years before they married, formed a lending library, a black Book-of-the-Month Club, and various other enterprises to keep the store going. Typical titles were *The Stolen Legacy* and *Black Gnostic Studies*. The bookstore became a well-known center for black activist political study in the mid-'60s. There is a fascinating oral history by Alfred Ligon at the Oral History Program, UCLA.

498 Barbara "had a custom outfit made": Gertrude Gipson, "The Sam Cooke I Knew," *Los Angeles Sentinel*, December 17, 1964.

499 according to the *Sentinel*'s "Theatricals" column: *Los Angeles Sentinel*, June 20, 1963. Gertrude Gipson's "Candid Comments," in the same issue, has Sam and Barbara at the pre-opening, with Barbara wearing the wig and mink stole, and Earl Grant not on hand, but I have assigned Barbara the same accoutrements for the show.

500 it was too late: Vincent's death is noted in many brief news stories, including the *California Eagle* and *Los Angeles Sentinel*, June 20, 1963, but I have relied for the most part on the accounts of those who were there.

INDEPENDENCE DAY

503 "the best sepian night club show I've ever seen": "A History of Kentucky Avenue," compiled by Nancy Loorie, Atlantic City Library (no further information available), provides both the quote from the 1947 *Daily News* column and a brief history of the club.

504 "tall, cool, cigarette holder–carrying Larry 'Good Deal' Steele": Masco Young, "The Grapevine" (syndicated column), *The Carolinian*, March 23, 1963.

504 as important to Atlantic City as the Miss America pageant: "Larry Steele's Smart Affairs," *Sepia*, September 1964.

506 "a prizefight is like a cowboy movie": Thomas Hauser, *Muhammad Ali: His Life and Times*, p. 58. Hauser's book, a mesmerizing oral history, has been an invaluable source throughout.

506 "The fight was a disgrace": Hauser, *Muhammad Ali*, p. 59.

506 "simultaneously we're hearing this voice in the middle of the casino": Hauser has a very similar altercation taking place *before* the fight in *Muhammad Ali*, p. 58.

507 they had a great three days in Vegas: Out on the Coast, Kapralik got Sam together with another Columbia artist, Johnny Mathis, and, he said, the two of them spent much of the evening singing spirituals and discussing the different turns that their careers, which dated back to almost exactly the same moment in time, had taken.

507 Bob Yorke . . . had lost his position of independence: Yorke left the company in the fall and went to Colpix about a year later, replacing Don Kirshner as head of a&r, according to *Variety*, October 16, 1964.

507 Joe D'Imperio was the new man in charge: Almost all of my biographical information on Joe D'Imperio, and my insight into his thinking, apart from my interviews with

Allen Klein, who both liked and admired him, comes from Jonny Meadow, a music-industry veteran, who had worked for Atlantic and was working for Hill and Range Songs at the time. Through Hill and Range, Elvis Presley's publisher, Meadow was in regular contact with D'Imperio, who became something of a role model and mentor to him and whose words and biography he is able to recapitulate in detail. Wherever Meadow's stories could be cross-checked against other accounts, they were always borne out. It wasn't quite like interviewing Joe D'Imperio, but it was close!

508 the formal mechanism by which Allen would be involved with the company: Clearly an understanding was worked out by mid-July, because the bill for the Valentinos' July 19 session at Bell Sound in New York was directed to A. Klein and Co.

509 "These are not the days for anonymous and quiet approval": Bob Hunter, "Handsome Crooner Takes Strong Stand," *Chicago Defender*, July 20–26, 1963. A. S. "Doc" Young, "Mathis to Raise $60,000," *Los Angeles Sentinel*, June 13, 1963, details how "one by one and two by two, Negro entertainers — the highest-paid group within the race — are joining the civil rights battle lines."

510 civic authorities suddenly discovered that the auditorium urgently needed painting: *Amsterdam News*, August 3, 1963; Brian Ward, *Just My Soul Responding: Rhythm and Blues, Black Consciousness, and Race Relations*, p. 298.

510 "[Sam's] Los Feliz area manse buzzed": Paul McGee, "Theatricals," *Los Angeles Sentinel*, August 29, 1963. See also Gertrude Gipson, "Candid Comments," in the same issue.

510 The March took place four days later: Much of the detail on the March is taken from Thomas Gentile, *March On Washington: August 28, 1963*, as well as Taylor Branch, *Parting the Waters: America in the King Years 1954–63*, David L. Lewis, *King: A Biography*, et al.

511 "I've Been 'Buked and I've Been Scorned": Mahalia Jackson gives her own eloquent reasons for picking this song in her autobiography, written with Evan McLeod Wylie, *Movin' On Up*, pp. 197ff.

511 "The button-down men in front": Gentile, *March On Washington*, p. 219, quoting Lerone Bennett in *Wade in the Water*.

511 a speech that . . . "carried every ear and every heart": Gentile, *March on Washington*, p. 241, provides this quote from William Martin Miller, *Martin Luther King Jr.*, pp. 166–167. David L. Lewis identifies Miller as a pacifist colleague of Bayard Rustin in *King: A Biography*, p. 72.

512 "Tell them about the dream": Taylor Branch, *Parting the Waters*, p. 882, cites as his principal source for Mahalia's exhortation a 1983 interview with New York labor leader and march organizer Cleveland Robinson. King himself in a November 1963 interview spoke of how he "took up the first run of oratory," Branch wrote, "that 'came to me.'" Others have suggested the "dream" was part of the prepared text.

512 "rhetoric almost without content": Lewis, *King: A Biography*, pp. 226–227.

512 It is impossible to calculate the full effect: The effect of the March, and the Movement, on Sam comes largely from interviews with J.W. Alexander, and, of course, from his frequent expressions of his views on race to Bobby Womack and others.

513 "I still feel that there is something more": CORE papers, 1941–1967, Manuscript Division, Library of Congress. Hamilton's sign-off to the letter was, "You'll never walk alone."

514 Allen and Alex were in the lobby afterward: The specific chronology of this adventure remains somewhat indeterminate. When, or whether, lunch actually took place is the crux of the disparity. I have tried to meld Allen Klein's, J.W. Alexander's, and Joe D'Imperio's (via Jonny Meadows) differing versions in the most plausible fashion, with J.W. supplying the shoeshine. Everyone agreed on the fundamental facts, though, as well as the execution and result of Allen's strategy.

516 a very belated reckoning: Again, without belaboring the point, Jess Rand's perspective and Sam and Alex's were altogether different.

516 a big rock 'n' roll show at the Sports Arena: Lee Cotten, *Twist & Shout: The Golden Age of American Rock 'n Roll*, vol. 3, 1960–1963, p. 514.

516 the new Buick Riviera he had gotten as a gift: Gertrude Gipson, "Candid Comments," *Los Angeles Sentinel*, June 20, 1963.

516 J.W. announced to the press: *Los Angeles Sentinel*, August 15, 1963.

518 "totally contrary to everything going on in the record business": Will Friedwald, *Sinatra! The Song Is You*, p. 367.

518 a partnership between Harry Belafonte and Nat "King" Cole: Daniel Mark Epstein, *Nat King Cole*, pp. 303–304, cites a February 4, 1960, *down beat* article and one in *Jet*, March 10, 1960, concerning the formation of a company that was probably dissolved by April.

520 "I thought Allen was not up to it": Other voices of opposition were Florence Greenberg, who had her own interest in Sam, Zelda Sands, of course, and Paul Cantor, who went to work for Greenberg in early 1963.

521 the Sweet Chariot, a brand-new gospel nightclub: Sam Chase, "Club's Smash Opening in New York Sparks Hope of Big Gospel Trend," *Billboard*, May 18, 1963.

521 "What murdered these four girls?" Branch, *Parting the Waters*, p. 891.

522 "He knows consciously what he's going to do": Don Paulsen, "An Exclusive Interview with Sam Cooke," *Rhythm & Blues*, February 1965.

523 A teenage white girl who saw the show: This was Flo Murdock, who went on to become a club booking agent.

523 five hundred black churchgoers were attacked: "Break Up Memorial March," *Louisiana Weekly*, September 28, 1963.

523 "dragged out of [his] church, clubbed to the ground": *Louisiana Weekly*, October 12, 1963.

523 "We congratulate the mixed crowd": Elgin Hychew, "dig me! . . ," *Louisiana Weekly*, September 21, 1963.

524 a four-page document which stipulated: This was dated September 26, and presented in the form of a letter to Tracy [*sic*] Limited c/o Allen Klein from the Radio Corporation of America (RCA Record Division). It was signed by Norman Racusin, Division Vice President and Operations Manager, for RCA, J.W. Alexander for Tracy, Kags, and Malloy, and Sam Cooke individually.

524 a song they had written together, "Memory Lane": This had been the B-side of Lou Rawls' first single for his new label, Capitol, the previous year.

525 30 percent of the 6 percent royalty: Just to give an idea of the actual amount of money involved, a single that sold one hundred thousand copies would generate a figure of roughly $100,000 (this is based on a $.98 retail price), on which Tracey's 6 percent (but not Sam's 5 percent) royalty would be calculated. Of the $6,000 total of royalties due, Sam would receive roughly $4,230, Tracey $1,770.

526 it was Sam who refused to back down: Interviews with Charles and Barbara Cooke. Also *New York Times* (UPI), October 9, 1963: "The police said the rock 'n' roll band leader, his wife and associates repeatedly blew the horn of their car, yelled and woke guests. . . . The police said remarks were exchanged between Mr. Cooke and the hotel manager." The October 12 *Shreveport Sun*, the black weekly, also had an extensive account.

526 $9,989.72 in coins and wrinkled bills: *Shreveport Journal*, October 8, 1963.

527 a bomb threat was called in: *Shreveport Times*, October 9, 1963.

527 a kind of myth grew up: In addition to the well-known, if apocryphal, story that Solomon Burke told in Gerri Hirshey's *Nowhere to Run: The Story of Soul Music* about Sam, Solomon, and the entire troupe being forced to disrobe and sing, Gladys Knight had Jackie Wilson humiliated in exactly the same manner by "some cops in Louisiana" in her autobiography, *Between Each Line of Pain and Glory.*

527 enough money in his briefcase "to buy the damn motel": This was B.B. King recalling the incident, but conceding that he wasn't there.

530 Zelda caught the first plane back to L.A.: Again, perhaps needless to say, Barbara's perspective on this incident is different from Zelda's, though it does include the gun, the firing, and her presumption of Zelda's interest in Sam.

530 "'Zelda' — Sam Cooke's gal Friday": *Cash Box*, November 16, 1963.

530 Crain, too, found himself unexpectedly on the outside: Sam was still speaking of Crain as part of SAR while on the English tour (Chris Hutchins, "Little Richard Is Amazing!" *New Musical Express*, October 12, 1962). Even at that point, though, change was clearly in the air, because it was on the English tour that Sam and J.W. first broached the idea of Kags Music Corp. backing Crain in his own agency.

531 "Several women in the audience became hysterical": Jesse H. Walker, "Theatricals," *Amsterdam News*, November 30, 1963.

531 "I had to consult Sam. He was working on a percentage": Glenn Douglass for ANPI, "'Was Just Beginning to Live,' Friends Say," *The Carolinian*, December 19, 1964. The percentage appears to have been on something like a fifty-fifty basis. Universal agent Dick Alen speculates that there was very likely a break point at which Sam's percentage increased to 60 percent, but in any case, if the theater were to do $30,000 at the box office over the course of the week, Sam stood to personally clear as much as $10,000 after paying all the talent on the show. Which stands in sharp contrast to the $3,000 King Curtis received the week before or Sam would most likely have agreed to just two years earlier.

531 "Negroes will mourn doubly the loss": *Los Angeles Sentinel*, November 28, 1963.

531 impromptu remarks to reporters: According to Karl Evanzz, *The Messenger: The Rise and Fall of Elijah Muhammad*, pp. 272–273, Malcolm was substituting for Elijah Muhammad, who saw his lieutenant's off-the-cuff response, however true it may have been to Elijah's own private opinion, as a public relations disaster and "a blatant act of defiance."

531 almost like a big brother: Hauser, *Muhammad Ali*, pp. 97–98.

531 a "likeable, friendly, clean-cut, down-to-earth youngster": Malcolm X with Alex Haley, *The Autobiography of Malcolm X*, p. 303.

532 "He saw greatness": Hauser, *Muhammad Ali*, p. 98. Malcolm even placed road manager Osman Karriem (Archie Robinson) with Clay. Alex Haley, coauthor of *The Autobiography of Malcolm X*, speaks in Hauser, *Muhammad Ali*, pp. 109–110, of "the adoration between Malcolm and Muhammad Ali."

532 it was on this trip, too: Here, once again, there's no reconciling of dates. Lithofayne Pridgon vividly recalled introducing Jimi Hendrix to Sam at the Apollo in 1963. Sam played the Apollo twice that year, and by Lithofayne's figuring, and mine, June was too early. This all made sense until I read Robert W. Fisher, *My Jimi Hendrix Experience,* a memoir in which Fisher, the leader of the Bonnevilles, out of Parsons, Tennessee, recalls a monthlong tour with Hendrix that ended December 22. Hendrix's arrival in New York in January 1964 is well documented and was clearly not his first time in the city. I suppose it's possible that he joined the Bonnevilles' tour a little late — but this is baseless speculation. And I'm afraid I'll have to leave it at that.

533 an evening of poetry and entertainment with Cassius Clay: *Los Angeles Sentinel*, December 12, 1963.

533–534 introducing Linda to Cassius: Barbara Cooke recalled Clay coming out to the house and inviting them to a Los Angeles mosque.

534 the cover of *Cash Box*: *Cash Box*, December 7, 1963.

LONG TIME COMING

537 "For people fighting for their freedom": George Plimpton, "Miami Notebook: Cassius Clay and Malcolm X," *Harper's*, June 1964.

538 a kind of glorified demo: Johnnie Morisette would record a song that Sam wrote called "Keep Smilin'," which was at least in the spirit, if not a direct reworking, of "Keep Movin' On," at his January 21, 1964, session.

541 "He was very excited": In addition to J.W.'s testimony, Lou Rawls, Leroy Crume, Bobby Womack, and Barbara Cooke each spoke of Sam's unreserved mix of excitement and concern when he played the song for them for the first time.

543 "It was part of my little civic thing": This is from Nick Spitzer's 2001 interview with Harold Battiste for his weekly NPR series, *American Routes*. The rest is from my interviews with Harold.

544 Arthur Prysock's celebrity-packed opening: *Los Angeles Sentinel*, January 23, 1964.

544 He caught the Soul Stirrers: The show was listed in the *Los Angeles Sentinel*, January 9, 1964. Bruce Bromberg was at the concert and vividly recalled Sam being introduced.

547 "I wanted it to be the greatest": BBC interview with René Hall.

551 an interview with the *New York World-Telegram*: William Peper, "Sam Cooke Sings the Blues, Too," *New York World-Telegram*, February 6, 1964.

551 "[He] said he would rather be the creative producer": "Sam Cooke Yearns for Creative Roll," *Cash Box*, February 15, 1964.

552 an NBC timekeeper marked down: NBC Master Books, Television–Motion Picture Collection, Library of Congress.

553 Douglas . . . had first met Sam: Mike Douglas, *I'll Be Right Back: Memories of TV's Greatest Talk Show*, p. 18.

555 a brief family vacation: Malcolm X with Alex Haley, *The Autobiography of Malcolm X*, p. 308.

555 "Cassius Clay Almost Says He's a Muslim": *Amsterdam News*, January 25, 1964.

555 The promoter threatened to cancel the fight: The complications that arose from Malcolm X's presence in Miami and Clay's public announcement of his religious affiliation are detailed in Thomas Hauser, *Muhammad Ali: His Life and Times*, pp. 64ff, 100; Taylor Branch, *Pillar of Fire: America in the King Years 1963–65*, p. 252; *The Autobiography of Malcolm X*, pp. 308ff; and Mike Marqusee, *Redemption Song: Muhammad Ali and the Spirit of the Sixties*, p. 77.

556 there was no doubt in Sam's mind that Cassius *was* going to shake up the world: Sam's feelings about Clay/Ali were expressed in Paul Learn, "Mixing Melody, Love Puts Sam Cooke on Top," *Atlantic City Press*, July 30, 1964; Brad Pye Jr., "Pretty Cassius Stung 'Like a Bee,'" *Los Angeles Sentinel*, February 27, 1964; and interviews with J.W. Alexander and Bobby Womack, among others.

556 "a clown never imitates a wise man": Plimpton, "Miami Notebook: Cassius Clay and Malcolm X," *Harper's*, June 1964.

556 the title of a *Look* magazine story: Nick Tosches, *The Devil and Sonny Liston*, p. 202. The NAACP's "disowning" of Liston is described on p. 159.

556 "Sonny Liston isn't the worst person in the . . . world": "Give Sonny Liston a Chance, Pleads Singer," *Norfolk Journal and Guide*, August 26, 1961 (ANS).

556 "An aura of artificiality surrounds Tuesday's . . . fight": Hauser, *Muhammad Ali*, p. 68, quoting Arthur Daley, *New York Times*, February 23, 24, 1964.

556 "This fight is the *truth*": *The Autobiography of Malcolm X*, p. 311.

557 genetic "tricknology": Karl Evanzz, *The Messenger: The Rise and Fall of Elijah Muhammad*, pp. 74–75.

558 they joined together in silent prayer: *The Autobiography of Malcolm X*, p. 312.

558 "the Mohammedan abroad believes in a heaven and a hell": Plimpton, "Miami Notebook: Cassius Clay and Malcolm X," *Harper's*, June 1964.

558 Cassius Clay won the fight right then and there: Pye, "Pretty Cassius 'Stung Like a Bee,'" *Los Angeles Sentinel*, February 27, 1964.

559 They sat in Malcolm's room: Branch, *Pillar of Fire*, p. 252, cites the FBI report. See also Hauser, *Muhammad Ali*, p. 106; *Autobiography of Malcolm X*, p. 312; Jack Olsen, *Black Is Best: The Riddle of Cassius Clay*, p. 150.

559 he had made him afraid: This is offered as Sam's analysis in both the *Los Angeles Sentinel*, February 27, 1964, and the *Atlantic City Press*, July 30, as above.

559 Jim Brown . . . appeared . . . more elated: *Los Angeles Sentinel*, February 27, 1964.

559 "Well, Brown," said Malcolm: Hauser, *Muhammad Ali*, p. 106.

559 "There are seven hundred fifty million people all over the world who believe in it": Quotes from the two press conferences are taken from Hauser, *Muhammad Ali*, pp. 82, 83, who in turn is quoting from the *Washington Star*, February 27, and *New York Times*, February 28, 1964.

560 the little bungalow in the North Miami ghetto: Plimpton, "Miami Notebook: Cassius Clay and Malcolm X," *Harper's*, June 1964.

560 his smart new chartered bus: *Jet*, March 26, 1964.

560 he gave an interview to the *Amsterdam News*: Les Matthews, "The 'Greatest One' Pays a Visit to the *Amsterdam News*," *Amsterdam News*, March 7, 1964.

561 he and Sam made the record: "Cassius Cuts a Disk, a Caper and a Defeated Sonny Liston," *New York Times*, March 4, 1964. Also photographs and session tapes plus interviews with Dave Kapralik, Horace Ott, and J.W. Alexander.

561 "I'm champion of the *whole* world": Marqusee, *Redemption Song*, p. 83. See also Hauser, *Muhammad Ali*, p. 101.

563 Malcolm's suspension from public speaking would be ended: Evanzz, *The Messenger*, p. 287.

563 an official announcement of the name change: Ibid., p. 286.

563 Malcolm announced his break with the Nation of Islam: Marqusee, *Redemption Song*, pp. 84–85.

563 the break was not of his own volition: Ibid., p. 87.

563 "morally bankrupt": Evanzz, *The Messenger*, p. 287.

563 "Did you get a look at Malcolm?": *New York Times*, May 18, 1964, as quoted in Hauser, *Muhammad Ali*, p. 109.

563 "That hurt Malcolm more": Hauser, *Muhammad Ali*, pp. 109–110.

565 Georgie Woods' "Freedom Show of '64": *Philadelphia Tribune*, March 21, 1964, reported under the headline "14,000 Jam NAACP Convention Hall Freedom Show; $30,000 Raised."

566 newly named head of SAR Productions: *Billboard,* June 6, 1964.

566 after a couple of rehearsals: There were no formal takes of the song, and no trace of it exists on the session tapes.

569 The only arrangement of René's that they would keep: René's bill for the arrangement is dated May 9, 1964.

569 he was planning to include very few of his hit songs: He *did* do "Good Times" as an encore at the outset of the Copa run.

569 The Upsetters were at the California Club: Advertised in the *Los Angeles Sentinel,* May 21, 1964, with Jackie Shane; *Sentinel* ad, June 11, with T-Bone Walker.

570 The Sims Twins had a regular gig: Advertised in the *Sentinel* April 9 and June 4, 1964, with Johnnie Morisette advertised April 16.

571 He . . . took up archery: Sam's GAC press release included among his hobbies sports cars, archery, and swimming.

571 RCA had kept up its end: There was a full page in *Cash Box,* June 20, 1964, advertising both the single and the album.

573 "the tallest figure of an entertainment personality": This, and other quotes and information, from press information sheet from Marvin Drager Inc., the public relations firm that Allen Klein hired.

573 "Technical difficulties kept the figure from being raised": *Record World,* June 27, 1964; see also *Cash Box,* June 27.

573 a late-night meeting with a British reporter: Ray Coleman, "Sam Seeks a New Twist," *Melody Maker,* July 4, 1964.

THE PIPER

1 | THAT'S WHERE IT'S AT

576 it was a disaster by any standard: This account of Sam's show at the Laurels is based on interviews with Allen Klein, Bobby Womack, Jerry Brandt, June Gardner, Al Schmitt, and Charles Cook. The one person missing is J.W. Alexander, and he never spoke of it in all our conversations — but then again, I never thought to ask. Everyone remembered it slightly differently. Al Schmitt recalled the first show as being terrible but couldn't remember why. For June it was just normal first-night jitters. To Charles Sam was impervious to any tensions or pressure; the show simply didn't reflect him properly. Jerry Brandt didn't recall René at all, and, twenty-five years after the fact, René, almost eighty at the time, vividly remembered the disaster of the opening as the motivating force for his redoing the show but appeared not to recall his absence from it. When I asked everyone about J.W., they all responded, Oh yeah, he must have been there — but no one could recall any specific role that he played, and, not knowing what it might have been, I couldn't invent one. Maybe he remained in California until the beginning of the week, maybe he had other business to attend to in the city, but unfortunately J.W. wasn't around to provide his own account by the time I noticed his absence.

579 "A lot of cats try to show off their arrangements": BBC interview with René Hall. All subsequent quotes are from that interview.

581 "Frankie and Johnny" replaced "Chain Gang": Sam slipped in a few bars of "Chain Gang" for his encore on the first night, but it was soon dropped from the show.

582 "Sam yells a lot but doesn't sing much": "Frank Farrell's New York — Day by Day," *New York World-Telegram*, June 25, 1964.

582 "although he did well . . . he didn't quite achieve his aim": *Variety*, December 16, 1964.

582 "[Mr. Cooke] has dignity, humility and feeling": Robert Alden, "Sam Cooke at the Copa," *New York Times*, July 7, 1964.

582 Sam moved "like a panther": *Long Island Press*, June 28, 1964.

582 "a young Belafonte" . . . "worlds of poise and savvy" . . . "a zingy, swinging style": Nick LaPole, *New York Herald Tribune*, June 28, 1964.

582 "A dashing, handsome young man": Sara Slack, "Sam Cooke Cooking in E. Side Setting," *Amsterdam News*, July 4, 1964.

583 a bloc of tickets to distribute: Daniel Wolff with S. R. Crain, Clifton White, and G. David Tenenbaum, *You Send Me: The Life and Times of Sam Cooke*, p. 306.

583 "at no time does he make any political references": *Variety*, July 1, 1964.

584 "You know, those old cats": *New York Times*, July 7, 1964.

584 To Don Paulsen, a young freelance reporter and photographer: Don Paulsen, "You Have to Pay Your Dues," *Hit Parader*, January 1965; Paulsen, "An Exclusive Interview with Sam Cooke," *Rhythm & Blues*, February 1965.

586 "The way Mr. Cooke sings [it]": *New York Times*, July 7, 1964.

586 a full-page ad in *Variety*: *Variety*, July 22, 1964.

587 a reluctant final decision . . . to let the Sims Twins and Johnnie Morisette go: Their contract releases came on August 1 and August 21 respectively. J.W. continued to work with the Sims Twins, as their manager and producer, after Sam's death.

587 an advance order of 150,000: *Music Business*, July 4, 1964.

588 *The Stars Salute Dr. Martin Luther King*: This was a project promoted by the New York PR firm Louis-Rowe Enterprises, Inc., for which former heavyweight champion Joe Louis provided the public face. Although all the proper clearances were made, in the end a ten-track album was released in early 1965 (Warner Bros. 1591) without the cuts by Sam, Ray Charles, or Frank Sinatra.

588 Riots had broken out: *Time*, July 31, 1964; David Garrow, *Bearing the Cross: Martin Luther King, Jr., and the Southern Christian Leadership Conference*, p. 342.

588 the search continued for the three civil rights workers: Michael Schwerner, Andrew Goodman, and James Chaney disappeared on June 21; their bodies were found on August 4.

588 "how it felt to be a Jew in Hitler's Germany": Jackie Robinson, "Murder, Hate, Violence Will Be Weapons of GOP" (syndicated column), *Mobile Beacon-Alabama Citizen*, July 25, 1964.

589 he was only surprised "that the American public failed to anticipate it": Paul Learn, "Mixing Melody, Love Puts Sam Cooke on Top," *Atlantic City Press*, July 30, 1964.

589 the same show: The highlighted repertoire comes from Ted Schall, "Nightly Whirl," *Atlantic City Press*, July 29, 1964.

589 their breakfast of grits and wings: This is Aretha Franklin's description.

590 "He beat [Liston] once": *Atlantic City Press*, July 30, 1964.

591 "hit[ting] the trail on behalf of Negro writers": "Sam Would 'Cook' Revival of Oldies," *Pittsburgh Courier*, April 13, 1963 (ANP).

593 his beautiful new bride: Jack Olsen, *Black Is Best: The Riddle of Cassius Clay*, pp. 112, 149, 152.

596 "The Negro beat & blues singer": *Variety*, August 19, 1964.

597 The tryout that Earl McGrath had promised him: In addition to my interviews with J.W. Alexander and Earl McGrath, the screen test is referred to in the *Herald Dispatch*, December 17, 1964; the *New York Daily News*, September 28; Earl Wilson's column in the *New York Post*, October 9; and *Billboard*, October 10.

598 "The Greatest Show of the Year": Poster for the New Orleans and Norfolk shows, October 24 and 31. "The Biggest Show Ever" comes from an ad in the *Birmingham World*, October 21, 1964.

599 "Man, you're killing me": J.W. Alexander is the direct source for the quote, but L.C. Cooke (who went out on tour with Jackie right after Sam's death), Hank Ballard, and Grady Gaines all confirmed Jackie's acknowledgment of how things had changed and how daunting an advantage Sam's seemingly endless procession of hits proved.

600 "Sam wasn't a jealous kind of fellow": This was to L.C. Cooke in Houston shortly after Sam's death.

603 joining George on various Supersonic tours: Jimi Hendrix spoke of these tours in various interviews and cited his experience playing with soul stars like Sam Cooke, Jerry Butler, the Impressions, and Solomon Burke. After scrutinizing those interviews, however, and having any number of conversations with Gorgeous George on the subject, I'm still unable to nail down specific dates. I do know that Hendrix joined Little Richard's band by early 1965.

603 In St. Louis Jackie Wilson was arrested: In addition to my interviews, this was covered by the *St. Louis Post-Dispatch*, November 2, 1964, and *Jet*, November 19.

605 Ray Charles had been busted: The front page of the November 5, 1964, *California Eagle*, read "Ray Charles Faces Boston Dope Charge" above the headline. The headline was "Johnny Mathis in Million $$ Bust-Up," while "Singer Frankie Lyman Held on N.Y. Dope Rap," was the third headline, beneath the main headline.

605 Little Willie John had gotten into a barroom fight: By far the best and most cohesive account of this sad final chapter in Little Willie John's life is Kim Field, "The Strange Story of Little Willie John: Fever and Fate," *Village Voice Rock & Roll Quarterly*, spring 1990.

606 "Now you get you a high hooker": In addition to Bobby Womack, Jerry Brandt, Hank Ballard, Lou Rawls, and Barbara Cooke all testified to both the practical considerations and Sam's personal predilections.

608 they . . . went off to the Gaiety Deli: In addition to my own interview with Earl Palmer on the subject, Tony Scherman's interview with Earl for his book, *Backbeat: Earl Palmer's Story*, was of great help.

608 The Palladium in London. A one-man show at Carnegie Hall: There are numerous press mentions of Sam's ambitions, including the *Atlantic City Press*, July 30, 1964, which specifies that the one-man show will focus on "American jazz"; Earl Wilson's syndicated column in the *Philadelphia Daily News*, August 31, which reports that a scheduled September 25 Carnegie Hall concert would be filmed to sell as a television special; and Ted Green, "Main Street," in the Allentown, Pennsylvania, *Morning Call*, October 20 re the Palladium. None of these events ever actually took place.

UNCLOUDY DAY

609 The last time Sam had come through town: In addition to J.W.'s vivid memory of the encounter, the *Los Angeles Sentinel*, December 24, 1964, referred in one of its many columns on Sam's life and death to a "series of benefits [Sam] had been mapping [out] for the civil rights movement."

611 Carrie Cunningham, who had opened the Royal Peacock: Biographical information on Carrie Cunningham comes from Herman "Skip" Mason Jr., *African-American Entertainment in Atlanta*, pp 21–23, and the memories of her granddaughter Delois Scott.

611 The song was "A Change Is Gonna Come": Grady Gaines recalled Sam uncharacteristically singing the song at around this time, and Gorgeous George did, too. Lotsa Poppa said it was the first time he had ever heard Sam sing it.

612 "I was the Johnnie Taylor that everybody knew": John Broven and Cilla Huggins 1989 interview with Johnnie Taylor.

614 he planned to stop off and see Jess Rand: Jess has said that Sam told him on this visit that he wanted to have a lawyer look into his business relationship with Allen Klein, but whether that was what Sam genuinely felt or he simply said it at Jess' prompting in order to make Jess feel better about the loss of a favorite client is impossible to say. There is certainly no question how Jess felt about Allen Klein, and he believes to this day that Sam would eventually have come back to him. Bumps Blackwell, too, spoke disparagingly of Allen in interviews without ever having met him and expressed his conviction that Sam would have come back to *him*, despite Sam's clear (and very early) disillusionment with Bumps' managerial approach and the notable skepticism of such intimates of Sam's as René Hall and J.W. Alexander on the subject. It is certainly *possible* that the implications of Allen Klein's ownership of Tracey were beginning to come home to Sam, and J.W. told me somewhat enigmatically that his own intention was to take more control of the business at this point. But nothing J.W. ever said in the fifteen years that I knew him, for all of his recognition of the unsentimental nature of business, ever indicated any mistrust of Allen Klein's character, business practices, or intentions. And Sam had just agreed to do a benefit performance for the orphanage where Allen had grown up. Most significantly, as Allen Klein himself has pointed out with full recognition that all managerial relationships are bound to end (as Jess Rand says, the client *always* leaves), everything was going well at this point, Sam had just gotten his second payment of $100,000, nothing had yet had a *chance* to go wrong. And Sam and Alex continued to retain unchallenged ownership of their label and publishing, which for both of them had from the beginning been the foundation of their business and remained (the publishing anyway) its most valuable asset.

614 the kind of blues album he was planning: Both Lou Rawls and Al Schmitt spoke of Sam's intention to record a "downhome" album. In his *Hit Parader* interview with Don Paulsen, Sam cited Muddy Waters and John Lee Hooker, along with Howlin' Wolf, as being among his favorite blues artists.

616 They drove out Santa Monica: There was an enormous amount of coverage of Sam's death, but the most reliable came in the various witness statements and descriptions (including those of the police) in the inquest. Louie Robinson, "The Tragic Death of Sam Cooke," *Ebony*, February 1965, and "The Inglorious Death of Sam Cooke," *Sepia*, February 1965, both had good summary stories; the *Los Angeles Sentinel* was thorough and, for the most part, accurate in its coverage, as were the *Chicago Defender, California Eagle*, and *Philadelphia Tribune*. Those periodicals also provided good reporting through the funerals. The stories in other papers were primarily rehashes, though nearly all had some local angle on Sam. But most of the particulars in all of the accounts are drawn from the inquest testimony (and the autopsy report), which, with the exception of exactly how the death occurred (i.e., were there really only two people in the room?) and, more particularly, why was Sam so exercised, appears to be unexceptionably accurate. Here the private investigator's report fills in some of the gaps. For all that went on afterward, Barbara Cooke's flat, straightforward, and highly detailed account of both events and motivation was altogether convincing and in keeping with other, necessarily more narrowly focused recollections by Bobby Womack, Beverly Campbell Lopez, J.W. Alexander, Carol Ann Woods, the Cook family, Allen Klein, and others.

617 the club they played all the time: The Sims Twins by this time had a weekly gig at the Sands; Beverly and Betty Prudhomme recalled going out to the club with Sam, as did Barbara Cooke. In addition to the Upsetters, who stayed there regularly, Hank Ballard recalled the Hacienda, as did Gatemouth Moore — and Rip Spencer of the Valiants referred to the area as "motel row," popular for both its inexpensive motels and restaurants.

622 "I didn't depend on Sam taking care of me": Dred Scott Keyes interview with Reverend Charles Cook, 1995.

625 a private detective from the Beverly Hills Investigating Service: Report of Investigator, Agency File No. 731. This was supplied by Allen Klein and is the source for all information deriving from the private investigation.

625 He and his brothers had arrived in Houston: Bobby Womack has always remembered it this way, from as early as a 1974 *Soul & Jazz* interview through all of his interviews with me. His brother Cecil, like Bobby, recalled that they had just arrived at their Texas motel when they got the news. Cecil also recalled L.C. Cooke being present, though L.C. has no recollection either of how he learned of Sam's death, where he was when he was told, or of the tour itself. In Upsetters leader Grady Gaines' memory, they had all just checked into their motel in Oklahoma City, but the December 11 issue of the Oklahoma City weekly, the *Black Dispatch*, advertises the show at the Golden Eagle Club for the following night (Saturday), with L.C. billed as the headliner.

629 None of the cash that Sam was said to have been carrying: Despite all the rumors, then and since, Barbara told the police at the time that Sam was carrying no more than $150 (*Ebony*, February 1965), and that is what she insists on today. In her recollection, Sam was always running out of money, because he rarely thought to carry much on his person.

630 The mourners were out in front of the funeral home: The vast majority of coverage of the Chicago funeral is from the *Chicago Defender*, primarily the week of December 19–25, 1964. The *Philadelphia Tribune*, December 22, and *Los Angeles Sentinel*, December 24, also had good firsthand accounts, and the Obsequies program provides quite a bit of detail.

631 Georgie Woods . . . vowed that he and other DJs would hire private investigators: Mark Bricklin, "Georgie Woods Vows to Learn True Facts of Singer's Death," *Philadelphia Tribune*, December 15, 1964. Georgie Woods also spoke of this in our interview. See also Brad Pye Jr., "Disc Jockeys Demand Investigation," *Los Angeles Sentinel*, December 24, 1964.

634 The funeral was scheduled to begin at 2 P.M.: In addition to my own interviews, the *Los Angeles Sentinel*, December 24, 1964, is the primary source of information. Once again the funeral Obsequies program supplies a good deal of detail, and Gertrude Gipson, in a follow-up to her moving December 17 recollection in the *Sentinel*, "The Sam Cooke I Knew," reflects on the funeral in her "Candid Comments" column December 24, suggesting obliquely that while "it was a wonderful tribute . . . on the other hand the disrespect that was given the family was certainly not at all fitting and proper."

634 "Long lines of convertible Cadillacs": *Richmond Afro-American* and *New Jersey Afro-American*, December 26, 1964.

635 "I had a fist": Daniel Wolff with S. R. Crain, Clifton White, and G. David Tenenbaum, *You Send Me: The Life and Times of Sam Cooke*, p. 332. Many of those present mentioned the drama of Zelda's entrance in their interviews with me, as did Zelda.

635 J.W. leaned over, gravely holding the mike: There is a photograph, and a story, "Crescendo of Songs for Sam" by Chester L. Washington, in the December 24 *Los Angeles Sentinel*. The rest is from my 2004 interview with Ray Charles.

636 "the greatest gospel rendition I ever heard": Steve Propes interview with René Hall, 1987.

636 a lengthy sermon by Reverend Charles: Paul C. McGee, "Rock 'n Roll Idol Given Giant Rites," *Los Angeles Sentinel*, December 24, 1964.

636 Barbara picked a rose: There is a picture on the front page of the *Sentinel*, December 24, 1964. The dialogue is from *Sepia*, February 1965.

AFTERMATH

639 "Bobby has been my constant escort": Gertrude Gipson, "Sam Cooke's Widow Denies Marriage to Young Musician" [subhead: "Admits New Ring"], *Los Angeles Sentinel*, January 28, 1965. The accompanying article, "Hey! Meet Mrs. C.'s 'Steady,'" by Paul McGee, was in the same issue.

642 For J.W., there was first disappointment, then disgust: Interviews as well as a veiled reference in A. S. "Doc" Young, "Sam Cooke's Death — It's Been a Year Now," *Amsterdam News*, December 18, 1965 (syndicated), where J.W. is quoted: "We brought him from Cleveland, gave him a place to live and eat . . ." In the same story, L.C. Cooke says, "Sam gave him a Jaguar to drive." In later life J.W. and Bobby would once again be friends, and Bobby showed a devotion to J.W. in his final days, even taking him out on the road as Bobby's "executive" road manager just before his death.

642 "The story goes that Sam Cooke picked Miss Boyer up": Glenn Douglass for ANPI, "Slaying of Sam Cooke Shocks Fans," *The Carolinian* and *Norfolk Journal and Guide* (under the title "'Was Just Beginning to Live,' Friends Say"), both December 19, 1964.

642 "Sam was a swinging guy": A. S. "Doc" Young, "The Mysterious Death of Sam Cooke," part 3, *Chicago Defender*, December 31, 1964 (syndicated). In *Sepia*, February 1965, and elsewhere, the same quote is used with modifications, the principal one being that it was "15-cent tramps" who were Sam's undoing.

642 "Sam would walk past a good girl": Wolff, *You Send Me*, p. 339.

643 J.W. Alexander . . . came to see it as little more than a tragic accident: Over and over, both in my discussions with him and in his conversations with others, J.W. saw it this way. Many others within the most immediate circle of Sam's acquaintance were in general agreement, though only infrequently on the record because of the heat that Sam's death (and all the talk of racial and Mafia conspiracy) continues to generate. J.W.'s point always had more to do with Elisa Boyer than with Sam. "I believe he went there by invitation," he said both on the record and off. What happened was in the nature of the sometimes happenstantial nature of life.

643 "the giant-sized entertainment shoes of his slain brother": Lee Blackwell, "Sam Cooke's Brother to Follow Him on Stage," *Amsterdam News*, December 26, 1964 (ANPI); "L.C. Cooke, Sam's Brother, Seeks to Step Into Dead Singer's Shoes," same story, same date, *Philadelphia Tribune*.

643 "a crack organization of private investigators": Dorothy Kilgallen, "The Voice of Broadway," *New York Journal-American*, December 28, 1964.

645 a song called "Our Years Together": J.W. gave permission for the lyrics to be printed in a NARA memorial program, August 6, 1965, and then again the following year. He announced his plans for a SAR memorial LP in January, as reported in the *Los Angeles Sentinel*, January 7, 1965, but nothing ever came of it due to the almost immediate disintegration of the label. His own double album, *Our Years Together* (one LP consisted of vocals by J.W., the other of instrumental arrangements under René's direction), did not come out until 1970.

645 a story headlined "A Change Is Gonna Come for Barbara": Gertrude Gipson, *Los Angeles Sentinel*, February 11, 1965; see also Brad Pye Jr., " 'Sam Would Want It,' " in the same issue.

646 L.C. had already approached RCA himself: L.C. told me this. Also I have an undated clipping from Bill Millar which refers to Sam's recent death and, with a New York dateline and headlined "Sam Jnr," states: "L.C., who is 28, told reporters that he has gone into rehearsal to cut an album in the near future."

646 "Sam's good-looking singing brother": Poster for Raleigh, North Carolina, show, January 22, 1965 (courtesy of Hank Thompson).

647 a claim against the estate for $200,000: Numerous newspaper stories, transcripts of Case No. 857058 in California Superior Court, filed March 25, 1965.

647 "Although Miss Lisa Boyer has no police record": "What Was Cooke's Date?," front-page story, *Los Angeles Sentinel*, January 14, 1965; "Nab Sam Cooke's 'Date' in Hollywood Vice Raid," *Sentinel*, January 21; *Jet*, January 28; Rudy Villasenor, "Judge Overturns Police Procedure on Call Girls," *Los Angeles Times*, May 13, 1965.

647 Bobby and Barbara showed up at the Los Angeles county courthouse: "Mrs. Cooke Controls 50G Estate," *Los Angeles Sentinel*, February 25, 1965, and Gertrude Gipson, "Barbara's Fiance Becomes of Age," *Los Angeles Sentinel*, March 4, 1965.

648 the application was "flatly refused": Getrude Gipson, *Los Angeles Sentinel*, March 4, 1965. *Jet*, March 11, 1965, "Barbara Cooke Sidetracked on Her Way to Altar with Guitarist," shows René Hall and a tuxedoed Walter Hurst and describes Barbara's and Bobby's ensembles.

648 "Womack's mother . . . allegedly stated she 'wanted no part of it' ": Gipson, "Barbara's Fiance Becomes of Age," *Los Angeles Sentinel*, March 4, 1965.

648 "Let's go to Cleveland anyway": "Mrs. Sam Cooke's Fiance 'Too Young to Marry,' " *Amsterdam News*, March 6, 1965.

648 to finally wed on March 5: The wedding itself was covered in "Barbara Cooke Marries Dead Hubby's Guitarist; Says Sam Would Approve It," *Los Angeles Sentinel*, March 11, 1965.

648 the "big plans" Sam had had for the Valentinos: "Sam Cooke's Widow Marries Guitarist," *Amsterdam News*, February 27, 1965.

648 Bobby followed up with an interview: "Mrs. Sam Cooke's Fiance 'Too Young to Marry,' " *Amsterdam News*, March 6, 1965.

648 the loss of her "sweet," "thoughtful," "wonderful" child: Thelma Hunt Shirley, "Friends, Fans Chorus 'Sam Was a Good Guy,' " *Chicago Defender*, December 16, 1964.

649 Charles had come to demand his royalties: "Cooke Family Feuds Over 'Chain Gang,'" *Amsterdam News*, July 17, 1965. Most of the detail comes from interviews with Bobby Womack, Barbara Cooke, and Charles, L.C., and other members of Sam's family. So far as credit for "Chain Gang" goes, Charles has never fully abandoned his claim of co-authorship, though he says it is of little consequence and it was certainly not his primary motivation for going to Bobby and Barbara Womack's hotel room that day.

649 the charges were dropped: "Sam Cooke's Widow Drops Beating Charge" (NPI), *Amsterdam News*, July 31, 1965, plus interviews as above.

650 in July [she] sued to dissolve the Kags Music Corporation: Daniel Wolff, with S. R. Crain, Clifton White, and G. David Tenenbaum, *You Send Me: The Life and Times of Sam Cooke*, p. 350, refers to court documents indicating that papers were filed in July, though I haven't found them. The *Amsterdam News*, October 2, 1965, reported that Barbara had filed a petition in Superior Court for the "dissolvement" of Kags.

650 a deadlocked corporation: My perception of the events leading up to Barbara's sale of her half comes from interviews with Allen Klein, J.W. Alexander, Barbara Cooke, Bobby Womack, and Luigi Creatore. Details of the sale — both sales — come from the legal documents and contracts.

651 Sam's "smooth voice . . . was like medicine to the soul": The quote is from Douglas Brinkley, *Rosa Parks*, p. 205. The description is from a conversation with Doug Brinkley.

Bibliography

Abbott, Lynn, and Doug Seroff. *Out of Sight: The Rise of African American Popular Music, 1889–1895.* Jackson: University Press of Mississippi, 2002.

Alexander, James W., Personal Manager also known as "The Silver Fox," and Walter E. Hurst, Esq. *How to Manage Talent.* Hollywood: 7 Arts Press, ca. 1985.

Allen, Tony, and Faye Treadwell. *Save the Last Dance for Me: The Musical Legacy of the Drifters, 1953–1993.* Ann Arbor, Mich.: Popular Culture, Ink., 1993.

Baldwin, James. *The Fire Next Time.* New York: Dial Press, 1963.

———. *Nobody Knows My Name.* New York: Dial Press, 1961.

———. *Notes of a Native Son.* Boston: Beacon Press, 1955.

Baptista, Todd R. *Group Harmony: Behind the Rhythm and the Blues.* New Bedford, Mass.: TRB Enterprises, 1996.

———. *Group Harmony: Echoes of the Rhythm and Blues Era.* New Bedford, Mass.: TRB Enterprises, 2000.

Barlow, William. *Voice Over: The Making of Black Radio.* Philadelphia: Temple University Press, 1999.

Bego, Mark. *Aretha Franklin: The Queen of Soul.* New York: St. Martin's Press, 1989.

Benjaminson, Peter. *The Story of Motown.* New York: Grove Press, 1979.

Berry, Jason, Jonathan Foose, and Tad Jones. *Up from the Cradle of Jazz: New Orleans Music Since World War II.* Athens: University of Georgia Press, 1986.

Blumhofer, Edith L. *Restoring the Faith: The Assemblies of God, Pentecostalism, and American Culture.* Urbana: University of Illinois Press, 1993.

Bogle, Donald. *Brown Sugar: Eighty Years of America's Black Female Superstars.* New York: Harmony Books, 1980.

———. *Prime Time Blues: African Americans on Network Television.* New York: Farrar, Straus and Giroux, 2001.

———. *Toms, Coons, Mulattoes, Mammies, & Bucks: An Interpretive History of Blacks in American Films.* New York: Continuum, 2002.

Bowman, Rob. *Soulsville U.S.A.: The Story of Stax Records.* New York: Schirmer Books, 1997.

Boyer, Horace Clarence. *How Sweet the Sound: The Golden Age of Gospel.* Washington, D.C.: Elliot and Clark Publishing, 1995.

Branch, Taylor. *Parting the Waters: America in the King Years 1954–63.* New York: Simon and Schuster, 1988.

———. *Pillar of Fire: America in the King Years 1963–65.* New York: Simon and Schuster, 1998.

Brewster House of Sermon Songs. *Tribute: The Life of Dr. William Herbert Brewster.* Memphis, Tenn.: The Brewster Theological Clinical Seminary and Leadership Training School, 1984.

Brinkley, Douglas. *Rosa Parks.* New York: Viking Press, 2000.

Broughton, Viv. *Too Close to Heaven: The Illustrated History of Gospel Music.* London: Midnight Books, 1996.

Broven, John. *Walking to New Orleans: The Story of New Orleans Rhythm & Blues.* Bexhill-on-Sea, Sussex, England: Blues Unlimited, 1974.

Brown, Geoff. *Otis Redding: Try a Little Tenderness.* London: Mojo Books, 2001.

Brown, James, with Bruce Tucker. *James Brown: The Godfather of Soul.* New York: Macmillan, 1986.

Brown, Ruth, with Andrew Yule. *Miss Rhythm: The Autobiography of Ruth Brown, Rhythm & Blues Legend.* New York: Donald I. Fine Books, 1996.

Bryant, Clora, ed. *Central Avenue Sounds: Jazz in Los Angeles.* Berkeley: University of California Press, 1998.

Butler, Jerry, with Earl Smith. *Only the Strong Survive: Memoirs of a Soul Survivor.* Bloomington: Indiana University Press, 2000.

Cantor, Louis. *Wheelin' on Beale: How WDIA-Memphis Became the Nation's First All-Black Radio Station and Created the Sound that Changed America.* New York: Pharos Books, 1992.

Charles, Ray, and David Ritz. *Brother Ray: Ray Charles' Own Story.* New York: Dial Press, 1978.

Chilton, John. *Let the Good Times Roll: The Story of Louis Jordan & His Music.* Ann Arbor: University of Michigan Press, 1994.

Cleaver, Eldridge. *Soul on Ice.* New York: Delta Books, 1968.

Clemente, John. *Girl Groups: Fabulous Females that Rocked the World.* Iola, Wis.: Krause Publications, 2000.

Cobbins, Otho B., ed. *History of Church of Christ (Holiness) U.S.A. 1895–1965.* New York: Vantage Press, 1966.

Cohodas, Nadine. *Queen: The Life and Music of Dinah Washington.* New York: Pantheon, 2004.

———. *Spinning Blues into Gold: The Chess Brothers and the Legendary Chess Records.* New York: St. Martin's Press, 2000.

Cooper, Ralph, with Steve Dougherty. *Amateur Night at the Apollo: Ralph Cooper Presents Five Decades of Great Entertainment.* New York: HarperCollins, 1990.

Cox, Bette Yarbrough. *Central Avenue — Its Rise and Fall (1890–c. 1955).* Los Angeles: BEEM Publications, 1996.

Craig, Warren. *Sweet and Lowdown: America's Popular Song Writers.* Metuchen, N.J.: Scarecrow Press, 1978.

Creatore, Luigi. *This World Is Mine.* New York: Rinehart & Co., 1947.

Cripps, Thomas. *Slow Fade to Black: The Negro in American Film, 1900–1942.* New York: Oxford University Press, 1977.

Darden, Robert. *People Get Ready! A New History of Black Gospel Music.* New York: Continuum, 2004.

Davidson, Bruce. *Time of Change: Civil Rights Photographs 1961–1965.* New York: St. Ann's Press, 2002.

Dawson, Jim. *The Twist: The Story of the Song and Dance that Changed the World.* Boston: Faber and Faber, 1995.

de Barros, Paul. *Jackson Street After Hours: The Roots of Jazz in Seattle.* Seattle: Sasquatch Books, 1993.

Deffaa, Chip. *Blue Rhythms: Six Lives in Rhythm and Blues.* Urbana: University of Illinois Press, 1996.

DjeDje, Jacqueline Cogdell, and Eddie S. Meadows, eds. *California Soul: Music of African Americans in the West.* Berkeley: University of California Press, 1998.

Douglas, Tony. *Lonely Teardrops: The Jackie Wilson Story.* London: Sanctuary Publishing, 1997.

Drake, St. Clair, and Horace R. Cayton. *Black Metropolis: A Study of Negro Life in a Northern City.* Chicago: University of Chicago Press, 1993.

Dr. John (Mac Rebennack) with Jack Rummel. *Dr. John: Under a Hoodoo Moon.* New York: St. Martin's Press, 1994.

Du Bois, W. E. B. *The Souls of Black Folk.* New York: Vintage Books, 1990.

———. *Writings.* New York: The Library of America, 1986.

Dyson, Michael Eric. *Mercy, Mercy Me: The Art, Loves & Demons of Marvin Gaye.* New York: Basic Civitas Books, 2004.

Epstein, Daniel Mark. *Nat King Cole.* New York: Farrar, Straus and Giroux, 1999.

Escott, Colin. *Tattooed on Their Tongues: A Journey Through the Backrooms of American Music.* New York: Schirmer Books, 1996.

Escott, Colin, with discography by Richard Weize. *Clyde McPhatter: A Biographical Essay.* Vollersode, West Germany: Bear Family, 1987.

Escott, Colin, ed. *All Roots Lead to Rock: Legends of Early Rock 'n' Roll.* New York: Schirmer Books, 1999.

Evanzz, Karl. *The Messenger: The Rise and Fall of Elijah Muhammad.* New York: Vintage Books, 2002.

Federighi, Luciano. *Le Grandi Voci Della Musica Americana.* Milan: Arnoldo Mondadori, 1997.

Fein, Art. *The L.A. Musical History Tour,* 2d ed. Los Angeles: 2.13.61 Publications, 1998.

Fisher, Robert W. *My Jimi Hendrix Experience.* New York: Vantage Press, 2003.

Fox, Ted. *In the Groove: The Stories Behind the Great Recordings.* New York: St. Martin's Press, 1986.

———. *Showtime at the Apollo: The Story of Harlem's World Famous Theater.* New York: Holt, Rinehart and Winston, 1983.

Franklin, Aretha, with David Ritz. *Aretha: From These Roots.* New York: Villard, 1999.

Freeland, David. *Ladies of Soul.* Jackson: University Press of Mississippi, 2001.

Freeman, Scott. *Otis! The Otis Redding Story.* New York: St. Martin's Griffin, 2001.

Garland, Phyl. *The Sound of Soul.* Chicago: Henry Regnery, 1969.

Garrow, David J. *Bearing the Cross: Martin Luther King, Jr., and the Southern Christian Leadership Conference.* New York: William Morrow, 1986.

Gart, Galen, and Roy C. Ames. *Duke/Peacock Records: An Illustrated History with Discography.* Milford, N.H.: Big Nickel Productions, 1990.

Gentile, Thomas. *March On Washington: August 28, 1963.* Washington, D.C.: New Day Publications, 1983.

George, Nelson. *Buppies, B-Boys, Baps & Bohos: Notes on Post-Soul Black Culture.* New York: HarperCollins, 1992.

———. *The Death of Rhythm & Blues.* New York: Pantheon, 1988.

———. *Where Did Our Love Go? The Rise & Fall of Motown Sound.* New York: St. Martin's Press, 1985.

Gillett, Charlie. *Making Tracks: Atlantic Records and the Growth of a Multi-Billion Dollar Industry.* New York: Dutton, 1974.

———. *The Sound of the City: The Rise of Rock and Roll.* New York: Outerbridge and Dienstfrey, 1970.

Goldberg, Marv. *More Than Words Can Say: The Ink Spots and Their Music*. Lanham, Md.: Scarecrow Press, 1998.

Goreau, Laurraine. *Just Mahalia, Baby: The Mahalia Jackson Story*. Waco, Tex.: Word Books, 1975.

Gribin, Dr. Anthony J., and Dr. Matthew M. Schiff. *Doo-Wop: The Forgotten Third of Rock 'n' Roll*. Iola, Wis.: Krause Publications, 1992.

Hamilton, Charles V. *The Black Preacher in America*. New York: William Morrow, 1972.

Hannusch, Jeff. *I Hear You Knockin': The Sound of New Orleans Rhythm and Blues*. Ville Platte, La.: Swallow Publications, 1985.

Haralambos, Michael. *Right On: From Blues to Soul in Black America*. London: Eddison Press, 1974.

Harris, Michael W. *The Rise of Gospel Blues: The Music of Thomas Andrew Dorsey in the Urban Church*. New York: Oxford University Press, 1992.

Haskins, James, with Kathleen Benson. *Nat King Cole*. New York: Stein and Day, 1984.

Haskins, Jim. *Queen of the Blues: A Biography of Dinah Washington*. New York: William Morrow, 1987.

Hauser, Thomas. *Muhammad Ali: His Life and Times*. New York: Simon and Schuster, 1991.

Haygood, Wil. *In Black and White: The Life of Sammy Davis, Jr.* New York: Knopf, 2003.

Heilbut, Tony. *The Gospel Sound: Good News and Bad Times*. New York: Simon and Schuster, 1971.

Hildebrand, Lee. *Stars of Soul and Rhythm & Blues*. New York: Billboard Books, 1994.

Hinson, Glenn. *Fire in My Bones: Transcendence and the Holy Spirit in African American Gospel*. Philadelphia: University of Pennsylvania Press, 2000.

Hirshey, Gerri. *Nowhere to Run: The Story of Soul Music*. New York: Times Books, 1984.

Hoare, Ian, with Clive Anderson, Tony Cummings, and Simon Frith. *The Soul Book*. New York: Delta Books, 1975.

Hoskyns, Barney. *From a Whisper to a Scream: The Great Voices of Popular Music*. London: Fontana, 1991.

———. *Say It One Time for the Broken Hearted: The Country Side of Southern Soul*. Glasgow: Fontana/Collins, 1987.

Houston, Cissy, with Jonathan Singer. *How Sweet the Sound: My Life with God and Gospel*. New York: Doubleday, 1998.

Hurst, Walter E., and William Storm Hale. *The Music Industry Book (How to Make Money in the Music Industry)*. Hollywood: 7 Arts Press, c. 1963.

Jackson, John A. *Big Beat Heat: Alan Freed and the Early Years of Rock & Roll*. New York: Schirmer Books, 1991.

Jackson, Mahalia, with Evan McLeod Wylie. *Movin' On Up*. New York: Hawthorn Books, 1966.

James, Etta, and David Ritz. *Rage to Survive: The Etta James Story*. New York: Villard, 1995.

Jasen, David A., and Gene Jones. *Spreadin' Rhythm Around: Black Popular Songwriters, 1880–1930*. New York: Schirmer Books, 1989.

Jenkins, Carol, and Elizabeth Gardner Hines. *Black Titan: A. G. Gaston and the Making of a Black Millionaire*. New York: One World, Ballantine Books, 2004.

John, Mertis. *My Life and Experiences in the Entertainment World*. Pittsburgh: Dorrance Publishing, 2001.

Jones, Hettie. *Big Star Fallin' Mama: Five Women in Black Music*. New York: Viking Press, 1974.

Jones, Leroi. *Black Music*. New York: William Morrow, 1968.

————. *Blues People: The Negro Experience in White America and the Music that Developed from It.* New York: William Morrow, 1963.

Keil, Charles. *Urban Blues.* Chicago: University of Chicago Press, 1966.

Keyes, Johnny. *Du-Wop.* Chicago: Vesti Press, 1987.

Lemann, Nicholas. *The Promised Land: The Great Migration and How It Changed America.* New York: Knopf, 1991.

Lewis, David L. *King: A Biography.* Urbana: University of Illinois Press, 1978.

Lornell, Kip. *"Happy in the Service of the Lord": Afro-American Gospel Quartets in Memphis.* Urbana: University of Illinois Press, 1988.

Lydon, Michael. *Ray Charles: Man and Music.* New York: Riverhead Books, 1998.

Magnificent Montague with Bob Baker. *Burn, Baby, Burn! The Autobiography of Magnificent Montague.* Urbana: University of Illinois Press, 2003.

Malcolm X with Alex Haley. *The Autobiography of Malcolm X.* New York: Grove Press, 1965.

Marable, Manning, and Leith Mullings, with pictures edited by Sophie Spencer-Wood. *Freedom: A Photographic History of the African American Struggle.* New York: Phaidon Press, 2002.

Marqusee, Mike. *Redemption Song: Muhammad Ali and the Spirit of the Sixties.* London: Verso, 1999.

Mason, Herman "Skip," Jr. *African-American Entertainment in Atlanta.* Charleston: Images of America, Arcadia Publishing, 1998.

————. *African-American Life in Jacksonville.* Charleston: Images of America, Arcadia Publishing, 1997.

McEwen, Joe. *Sam Cooke: The Man Who Invented Soul.* New York: Sire Books, Chappell Music, 1977.

McMillen, Neil R. *Dark Journey: Black Mississippians in the Age of Jim Crow.* Chicago: University of Illinois Press, 1990.

Merlis, Bob, and Davin Seay. *Heart & Soul: A Celebration of Black Music Style in America 1930–1975.* New York: Stewart, Tabori and Chang, 1997.

Millar, Bill. *The Coasters.* London: A Star Book, 1975.

————. *The Drifters.* London: Studio Vista, 1971.

————. *Let the Good Times Rock! A Fan's Notes on Post-War American Roots Music.* York, England: Music Mentor Books, 2004.

Miller, Wayne F. *Chicago's Southside 1946–1948.* Berkeley: University of California Press, 2000.

Moore, Sam, and Dave Marsh. *Sam and Dave: An Oral History.* New York: Avon Books, 1998.

Murray, Albert. *The Omni-Americans: New Perspectives on Black Experience and American Culture.* New York: Outerbridge and Dienstfrey, 1970.

Nager, Larry. *Memphis Beat: The Lives and Times of America's Musical Crossroads.* New York: St. Martin's Press, 1998.

Neville, Art and Aaron, Charles and Cyril Neville, and David Ritz. *The Brothers Neville: An Autobiography.* New York: Little, Brown, 2000.

Newman, Mark. *Entrepreneurs of Profit and Pride: From Black-Appeal to Radio Soul.* New York: Praeger Press, 1988.

Oldham, Andrew Loog. *Stoned.* London: Secker and Warburg, 2000.

————. *2Stoned.* London: Secker and Warburg, 2002.

Olsen, Jack. *Black Is Best: The Riddle of Cassius Clay.* New York: Dell Publishing, 1967.

Otis, Johnny. *Listen to the Lambs.* New York: W. W. Norton, 1968.

————. *Upside Your Head! Rhythm and Blues on Central Avenue.* Hanover, N.H.: University Press of New England, 1993.

Palmer, Robert. *An Unruly History of Rock & Roll*. New York: Harmony Books, 1995.

Passman, Arnold. *The DeeJays*. New York: Macmillan, 1971.

Poe, Randy. *Music Publishing: A Songwriter's Guide*, 2d ed. Cincinnati: Digest Books, 1997.

Pinkney, Bill, as told to Maxine Porter. *Drifters 1: Bill Pinkney: Celebrating 50 Years 1953–2003*. Las Vegas: BillMax Publishing, 2003.

Pomerance, Alan. *Repeal of the Blues: How Black Entertainers Influenced Civil Rights*. New York: Citadel Press, 1988.

Posner, Gerald. *Motown: Music, Money, Sex, and Power*. New York: Random House, 2002.

Propes, Steve, and Galen Gart. *L.A. R&B Vocal Groups 1945–1965*. Milford, N.H.: Big Nickel Productions, 2001.

Pruter, Robert. *Chicago Soul*. Urbana: University of Illinois Press, 1991.

———. *Doowop: The Chicago Scene*. Urbana: University of Illinois Press, 1996.

Raines, Howell. *My Soul Is Rested*. New York: Bantam, 1977.

Reagon, Bernice Johnson, ed. *We'll Understand It Better By and By: Pioneering African American Gospel Composers*. Washington, D.C.: Smithsonian Institution Press, 1992.

Redd, Lawrence N. *Rock Is Rhythm and Blues (The Impact of Mass Media)*. East Lansing: Michigan State University Press, 1974.

Reed, Tom. *The Black Music History of Los Angeles — Its Roots: A Classical Pictorial History of Black Music in Los Angeles from 1920–1970*. Los Angeles: LA Black Accent Press, 1994.

Ritz, David. *Divided Soul: The Life of Marvin Gaye*. New York: McGraw-Hill, 1985.

Roby, Steven. *Black Gold: The Lost Archives of Jimi Hendrix*. New York: Billboard Books, 2002.

Rosalsky, Mitch. *Encyclopedia of Rhythm & Blues and Doo-Wop Vocal Groups*. Lanham, Md.: Scarecrow Press, 2000.

Rose, Cynthia. *Living in America: The Soul Saga of James Brown*. London: Serpent's Tail, 1990.

Rose, Frank. *The Agency: William Morris and the Hidden History of Show Business*. New York: HarperBusiness, 1995.

Ryan, Marc W. *Trumpet Records: Diamonds on Farish Street*, rev. ed. Jackson: University Press of Mississippi, 2004.

Salem, James M. *The Late Great Johnny Ace and the Transition from R & B to Rock 'n' Roll*. Chicago: University of Illinois Press, 1999.

Salvatore, Nick. *Singing in a Strange Land: C. L. Franklin, the Black Church, and the Transformation of America*. New York: Little, Brown, 2005.

Sanjek, Russell. *American Popular Music and Its Business: The First Four Hundred Years*. vol. 3, *From 1900 to 1984*. New York: Oxford University Press, 1988.

———. *From Print to Plastic: Publishing and Promoting America's Popular Music (1900–1980)*. I.S.A.M. Monographs: Number 20. Brooklyn: Institute for Studies in American Music, 1983.

Scherman, Tony. *Backbeat: Earl Palmer's Story*. Washington, D.C.: Smithsonian Institution Press, 1999.

Schiffman, Jack. *Harlem Heyday*. Buffalo: Prometheus Books, 1984.

———. *Uptown: The Story of Harlem's Apollo Theater*. New York: Cowles Book Company, 1971.

Schwerin, Jules. *Got To Tell It: Mahalia Jackson, Queen of Gospel*. New York: Oxford University Press, 1992.

Shaw, Arnold. *Honkers and Shouters: The Golden Years of Rhythm & Blues*. New York: Macmillan, 1978.

———. *The World of Soul*. New York: Paperback Library, 1971.

Sidran, Ben. *Black Talk: How the Music of Black America Created a Radical Alternative to the Values of Western Literary Tradition.* New York: Holt, Rinehart and Winston, 1971.

Simonds, Roy. *King Curtis: A Discography by Roy Simonds.* Tyne and Wear, England: Now Dig This, 1984 (rev. 2004).

Smith, Joseph. *The Day the Music Died.* New York: Grove Press, 1981.

Smith, Suzanne E. *Dancing in the Street: Motown and the Cultural Politics of Detroit.* Cambridge, Mass.: Harvard University Press, 1999.

Smith, Wes. *The Pied Pipers of Rock 'n' Roll: Radio Deejays of the 50s and 60s.* Marietta, Ga.: Longstreet Press, 1989.

Spear, Allan H. *Black Chicago: The Making of a Negro Ghetto 1890–1920.* Chicago: University of Chicago Press, 1967.

Stange, Maren. *Bronzeville: Black Chicago in Pictures 1941–1943.* New York: The New Press, 2003.

Talty, Stephan. *Mulatto America: At the Crossroads of Black and White Culture: A Social History.* New York: HarperCollins, 2003.

Titon, Jeff Todd, ed. *Give Me This Mountain. Reverend C. L. Franklin: Life History and Selected Sermons.* Urbana: University of Illinois Press, 1989.

Tosches, Nick. *The Devil and Sonny Liston.* New York: Little, Brown, 2000.

———. *Unsung Heroes of Rock 'n' Roll.* New York: Scribner, 1984.

Tye, Larry. *Rising from the Rails: Pullman Porters and the Black Middle Class.* New York: Henry Holt, 2004.

Wade, Dorothy, and Justine Picardi. *Music Man: Ahmet Ertegun, Atlantic Records, and the Triumph of Rock 'n' Roll.* New York: W. W. Norton, 1990.

Waller, Don. *The Motown Story: The Inside Story of America's Most Popular Music.* New York: Scribner, 1985.

Wallis, Ian. *American Rock 'n' Roll: The UK Tours 1956–72.* York, England: Music Mentor Books, 2003.

Waltzer, Jim, and Tom Wilk. *Tales of South Jersey: Profiles and Personalities.* New Brunswick, N.J.: Rutgers University Press, 2001.

Ward, Brian. *Just My Soul Responding: Rhythm and Blues, Black Consciousness, and Race Relations.* Berkeley: University of California Press, 1998.

Ward-Royster, Willa, as told to Toni Rose. *How I Got Over: Clara Ward and the World-Famous Ward Singers.* Philadelphia: Temple University Press, 1997.

Warner, Jay. *The Billboard Book of American Singing Groups: A History, 1940–1990.* New York: Billboard Books, 1992.

Werner, Craig. *A Change Is Gonna Come: Music, Race & the Soul of America.* New York: Plume, 1999.

Wexler, Jerry, and David Ritz. *Rhythm and the Blues: A Life in American Music.* New York: Knopf, 1993.

White, Charles. *The Life and Times of Little Richard: The Quasar of Rock.* New York: Harmony Books, 1984.

Whiteside, Jonny. *Cry: The Johnnie Ray Story.* New York: Barricade Books, 1994.

Williams, Juan. *Eyes on the Prize: America's Civil Rights Years 1954–1965.* New York: Penguin, 1987.

———. *My Soul Looks Back in Wonder: Voices of the Civil Rights Experience.* New York: Sterling, 2004.

Withers, Ernest C., et al. *Pictures Tell the Story: Ernest C. Withers, Reflections in History.* Norfolk, Va.: Chrysler Museum of Art, 2000.

Wolff, Daniel, with S. R. Crain, Clifton White, and G. David Tenenbaum. *You Send Me: The Life and Times of Sam Cooke*. New York: William Morrow, 1995.

Wright, Richard, with photo direction by Edwin Rosskam. *12 Million Black Voices*. New York: Thunder's Mouth Press, 1988.

Young, Alan. *The Pilgrim Jubilees*. Jackson: University Press of Mississippi, 2001.

———. *Woke Me Up This Morning: Black Gospel Singers and the Gospel Life*. Jackson: University Press of Mississippi, 1997.

Younger, Richard. *Get a Shot of Rhythm & Blues: The Arthur Alexander Story*. Tuscaloosa: University of Alabama Press, 2000.

Zolten, Jerry. *Great God A'Mighty!: The Dixie Hummingbirds*. New York: Oxford University Press, 2003.

REFERENCE

Cotten, Lee. *Shake, Rattle & Roll: The Golden Age of American Rock 'n Roll*. vol. 1, 1952–1955. Ann Arbor, Mich.: Pierian Press, 1989.

———. *Reelin' & Rockin': The Golden Age of American Rock 'n Roll*. vol. 2, 1956–1959. Ann Arbor, Mich.: Popular Culture, Ink., 1995.

———. *Twist & Shout: The Golden Age of American Rock 'n Roll*. vol. 3, 1960–1963. Sacramento: High Sierra Books, 2002.

Gart, Galen, comp. and ed. *ARLD: The American Record Label Directory and Dating Guide, 1940–1959*. Milford, N.H.: Big Nickel Productions, 1989.

———. *First Pressings: The History of Rhythm & Blues, Special 1950 Volume*. Milford, N.H.: Big Nickel Productions, 1993.

———. *First Pressings: The History of Rhythm & Blues*. Vols. 1–9, 1951–1959. Milford, N.H., and Winter Haven, Fla.: Big Nickel Productions, 1991–2002.

———. *Rhythm & Blues in Cleveland, 1955 Edition*. Winter Haven, Fla.: Big Nickel Productions, 2003.

Hayes, Cedric J., and Robert Laughton. *Gospel Records, 1943–1969: A Black Music Discography*. Vols. 1 and 2. United Kingdom: Record Information Services, 1992, 1993.

McGrath, Bob. *The R&B Indies*. Vols. 1 and 2. West Vancouver, B.C.: Eyeball Productions, 2000.

Pavlow, Big Al. *Hot Charts Artist Index, 1940–1959*. Providence, R.I.: Music House Publishing, 1995.

———. *Hot Charts Title Index, 1940–1959*. Providence, R.I.: Music House Publishing, 1995.

———. *Hot Charts Yearly, 1950–1959*. Providence, R.I.: Music House Publishing, 1990–1992.

———. *The R & B Book: A Disc-History of Rhythm & Blues*. Providence, R.I.: Music House Publishing, 1983.

———. *The R & B Files, 1940–1949*. Providence, R.I.: Music House Publishing, 2001.

———. *The R & B Files, 1950–1959*. Providence, R.I.: Music House Publishing, 2001.

Whitburn, Joel. *Joel Whitburn's Pop Memories, 1890–1954: The History of American Popular Music*. Menomonee Falls, Wis.: Record Research, 1986.

———. *Joel Whitburn's Top Pop Albums, 1955–1992*. Menomonee Falls, Wis.: Record Research, ca. 1993.

———. *Joel Whitburn's Top Pop Singles, 1955–1993*. Menomonee Falls, Wis.: Record Research, 1994.

———. *Joel Whitburn's Top R&B Singles, 1942–1988*. Menomonee Falls, Wis.: Record Research, 1988.

A Brief Discographical Note

YOU REALLY CAN'T GO TOO FAR WRONG with Sam Cooke. All but his very worst records have something redeeming about them, if only the grace of that inimitable voice. But there is a core of material that can serve as an introduction to his work and that will hopefully lead the listener not just to additional Sam Cooke albums but to the wealth of gospel, pop, and r&b music that not only served as his inspiration but continues to be inspired by him.

Virtually all of Sam's gospel recordings with the Soul Stirrers are presented in a meticulously remastered three-CD set, *Sam Cooke with the Soul Stirrers* (Specialty 4437), which also includes his first pop sides, recorded under the name of Dale Cook in December 1956. There are two other Soul Stirrers CDs worth seeking out for the alternate takes (*Jesus Gave Me Water* and *The Last Mile of the Way,* Specialty 7031 and 7052), but the one other gospel album that is absolutely essential is *The Great 1955 Shrine Concert* (Specialty 7045), the live program that includes Sam's epic "Nearer to Thee" while also featuring the work of Brother Joe May, Dorothy Love Coates and the Gospel Harmonettes, the Caravans, and the Pilgrim Travelers, among others. You can get the Stirrers' part of the program on the three-CD set, but you owe it to yourself to absorb the full flavor of the program on this stand-alone album.

For an overview of Sam's career, from his gospel beginnings through "A Change Is Gonna Come," nothing can compare to *Portrait of a Legend* (ABKCO 92642), which, like the earlier (and now out-of-print) *Sam Cooke: The Man and His Music,* serves as a guide to Sam at his very best. It has nearly all the hits, and while every listener is bound to miss one or two personal favorites, the sound is a revelation and brings to life some of the most familiar numbers in ways that they may not have been heard since their first release.

Keep Movin' On (ABKCO 95632) focuses on Sam's recordings over the last year and a half of his life, and, while there are, inevitably, duplications with *Portrait of a Legend,* there are more than enough rediscoveries and surprises (including the never previously issued title track) as well as intimations of the diverse directions in which Sam's music was continuing to evolve. From my perspective "(Somebody) Ease My Troublin' Mind," Harold Battiste's "Falling in Love," and "There'll Be No Second Time," a rare Clif White composition, would alone be worth the price of admission, but there are in all fourteen tracks not included on the *Legend* CD.

Sam Cooke at the Copa (ABKCO 99702) is a portrait of a moment in time, and while Sam's supperclub act has never been the side that most appealed to me, with its new, vastly improved sound, this 2003 CD reissue suggests some of the rhythmic drive that accompanied even Sam's most innocuous, crowd-pleasing music. This was certainly the first time that I was ever able to hear the churning interaction between Clif White's and Bobby Womack's guitars, and, if nothing else, the album offers not just a snapshot of Sam's well-thought-out approach to a new audience and a new phase of his career but a rare opportunity to catch a set by his working band.

I've got to admit to some conflict of interest here. I wrote the liner notes for each of the last three albums, as I did for *Sam Cooke's SAR Records Story* (ABKCO 2231), the incomparable two-CD (one pop, one gospel) document of Sam and J.W. Alexander's record label, which incorporates demos by Sam and some of the Valentinos', the Sims Twins', Johnnie Taylor's, Johnnie Morisette's, and L.C. Cooke's best secular work, along with a full CD by the Soul Stirrers, R.H. Harris and the Gospel Paraders, and the Womack Brothers. An added bonus is having the chance to listen to Sam produce some of the sessions as he prods singers and musicians with precise, enthusiastic, and infectious direction.

Two other essential albums have recently been rereleased by Sony/BMG with the same kind of improved sound as Sam's three ABKCO releases. *Night Beat* (RCA/Sony BMG Legacy 828 766 9551), remastered once again at Bob Ludwig's Gateway studio, is the beautifully realized late-night blues album that Sam conceived of as a tribute to Charles Brown. *Sam Cooke Live at the Harlem Square Club, 1963* (RCA/Sony BMG Legacy 828 766 9552) is almost the exact opposite, except in the careful calibration of its effects. Completely remixed and remastered, it is raw, high-energy music punctuated by Sam's hoarse imprecations, King Curtis' saxophone, and the audience's uninhibited response. It is very much of a secular follow-up, a *worthy* follow-up, to Sam's contributions to *The Great 1955 Shrine Concert* and offers a unique glimpse of the every-night-of-the-week good times and good feeling of his show. And yes, I wrote the liner notes for both, the first in 1984.

Without getting into all the great gospel and r&b that preceded, accompanied, and followed Sam throughout his career, let me at least recommend the five-CD *Specialty Story* (Specialty 4412), which provides a slice of the r&b revolution that directly precipitated Sam into pop, with great tracks by Percy Mayfield, Lloyd Price, Guitar Slim, and Little Richard, among many others, along with a smattering of gospel and a genuine sense of the aesthetic that Art Rupe developed over a glorious ten-year run.

Anyone interested in *seeing* Sam in action should pick up the DVD *Sam Cooke Legend* (ABKCO 1004). Again, I've got to admit to a conflict of interest because of my involvement in the project, but it includes wonderful performance footage, from Sam's first, truncated appearance on *The Ed Sullivan Show* in 1957 to his September 1964 *Shindig!* booking, that historic moment when Cassius Clay called Sam into the ring, and a rare interview-and-song segment by Sam and Muhammad Ali, as well as extras that feature interview material by Aretha Franklin, Bobby Womack, Lou Rawls, and L.C. Cooke, among others.

There are so many other related albums and documentaries that I could recommend (including the indispensable civil rights documentary *Eyes on the Prize* and the BBC's *Too Close to Heaven: The Story of Gospel Music*), but I think I'll leave it there.

My one hope is to someday be able to put together an album that I conceive of as *The Unknown Sam Cooke*. This would include the one extant track from his original August 1956 pop session (with just a rehearsal pianist for accompaniment), several unissued tracks from his December 1956 session in New Orleans that I think far surpass the issued ones, early (1959) demos of his own songs for Kags, and some of the wonderfully loose, unissued cuts that Sam recorded at various SAR sessions over the years.

But that will have to wait for another day. For now there is plenty to listen to!

Acknowledgments

IN WRITING A BOOK over so long a period, and in thinking about it even longer, one incurs debts that one can never repay. Literally hundreds of people have helped me with my research and my interviews, and I thank them all. The following are just some of the people who gave me a hand over the weeks, months, and years:

Lynn Abbott, Ace Records, Lou Adler, Dick Alen, J.W. Alexander, Wynne Alexander, Hoss Allen, Herb Alpert, Andy Ambrose, Wally Amos, Angel, Don Arden, Mark Arevalo, Larry Auerbach, Bill Austin, Chuck Badie, Pat Baird, Hank Ballard, Todd R. Baptista, Jeff Barry, Harold Battiste, Howell Begle, William Bell, Bill Belmont, Ray Benson, Cornelia Lee Berry, Scott Billington, Bar Biszick, Keith and Pam Bolling, Julian Bond, Ed Boyer, Taylor Branch, Jerry Brandt, Robin Bratter, Doug Brinkley, Lonnie Brooks, John Broven, Diane Brown, Gatemouth Brown, Del Bryant, Solomon Burke, Rev. Jimmy "Early" Byrd, Trevor Cajiao, Dwight Cameron, Louis Cantor, Paul Cantor, Gary Cape, Elston Carr, Howard Carroll, Mel Carter, Ray Charles, Dick Clark, Jack Clement, Bob Cochran, Nadine Cohodas, Jim Cole, Ray Coleman, Rick Coleman, Alisa Coleman-Ritz, Stuart Colman, Agnes Cook-Hoskins and her husband, Joe, Rev. Charles Cook, Charles Cook Jr., David Cook, Hattie Cook-Woods, Barbara Campbell Cooke, L.C. Cooke and his wife, Rev. Marjorie, Linda Cooke, Dan Cooper, Peter Cooper, Creadell Copeland, Lee Cotten, Tommy Couch, Don Covay, Luigi Creatore, Barbara Crissman, LeRoy Crume, Chick Crumpacker, B.B. Davis, Billy Davis, Jim Dawson, Paul DeBarros, Francesco De Leonardis, Walter DeVennes, Joan Dew, Mitch Diamond, Scott Dirks, Rex Doan, Tony Douglas, Charles Driebe, Don Drowty, Cornell Dupree, Ronny Elliott, Ahmet Ertegun, Colin Escott, Simon Evans (Man in Japan Collection), Phil Everly, Ernie Farrell, Luciano Federighi, Art Fein, Dennis Ferrante, Johnny Fields, Bill Flanagan, Bruce Flett, Clarence Fountain, Kim Fowley, Art Foxall, Carol Fran, Aretha Franklin, Jeff Frederick, Jim Fricke, Gil Friesen, Ray Funk, Grady Gaines, Ceil Gallagher, June Gardner, Galen Gart, Gregg Geller, Larry Geller, Peter Gibbon, Lex Gillespie, Jeff Gold, Robert Gordon, Gorgeous George, Michael Gray, Milton Grayson, Pete Grendysa, Guitar Shorty, Jenessa Gursky, Taylor Hackford, Mark Hagen, Dawn Haggerty, Roy and Maria Hamilton Jr., Rosemary Hanes, Jet Harris, R.H. Harris, Tony Harris, Wil Haygood, Tony Heilbut, Lee Hildebrand, Dave Hoekstra, Harvey Holiday, Pete Howard, Peter J. Howard, Bones Howe, Dick "Huggy Boy" Hugg, Cilla Huggins, Buzzy Jackson, Chuck Jackson, John Jackson, Jim Jaworowicz, Mable John, Jimmy Johnson, Plas Johnson, Ray Johnson, Jeff Jones, Marvin Jones, Peter Jones, Ernst Jorgensen, Chuck Kaplan, David Kapralik, Clark Kauffman, Ernie K-Doe, Bob Keane, Emily Kelley, Dred Scott Keyes, Johnny Keyes, Marc Kidel, Merle Kilgore, Carolyn Brown Killen, B.B. King, Earl King, Edith King,

George Klein, Robin Klein, Jurgen Koop, Glenn Korman, Howard Kramer, Eric Kuhlberg, David Kunian, Art Laboe, Teri Landi, Joe Lauro, Eric LeBlanc, Beverly Lee, Dickey Lee, Alan Leeds, Malcolm Leo, Colin Levert, Andria Lisle, Leon Litwack, Beverly Campbell Lopez, Kip Lornell, Lotsa Poppa (Julius High), Michael Lydon, Magnificent Montague, Waldo Martin, Cosimo Matassa, Phyllis McClure, John McDermott, Joe McEwen, Charlie McGovern, Earl McGrath, Larry McKinley, Ricky McKinnie, Jonny Meadow, Bill Millar, Rev. Dwight "Gatemouth" Moore, Idris Muhammad, Flo Murdock, Opal Louis Nations, Ford Nelson, Chris Nichols, Gene Norman, Michael Ochs, Andrew Loog Oldham, Horace Ott, Earl Palmer, Mick Patrick, Norma Jean Patton, Al Pavlow, Ian Pickstock, Randy Poe, Lee Poole, Steve Popovich, David Porter, David Potorti, Lloyd Price, Lithofayne Pridgon, Steve Propes, Betty and Beverly Prudhomme, Mark Pucci, Jess Rand, Bill Randle, Lou Rawls, Rodgers Redding, John Richbourg, John Ridley, Ginger Rieder, Bob Riesman, Shelley Ritter, David Ritz, Don Robertson, Bobby Robinson, Roscoe Robinson, Jackie Ross, Tony Rounce, Art Rupe, Jayne Rush, Simon Rutberg, Ken Salinsky, Nick Salvatore, Tony Salvatore, Ben Sandmel, Zelda Sands, David Sanjek, Rob Santos, Vicky Sarro, Jeff Scheftel, Tony Scherman, Al Schmitt, Tim Schuller, Delois Scott, Hammond and Nauman Scott, Zenas Sears, Joel Selvin, Doug Seroff, Val Shively, Dick Shurman, John Siamas Jr., the Simms Twins, Roy Simonds, Bob Simpson, John Simson, Louis Skorecki, Fred Smith, Andrew Solt, Rip Spencer, Joe Sperry, Nick Spitzer, Mavis Staples, Roger Steffens, Wolf Stephenson, Alva Stevenson, Pat Sullivan, Beverly Tatum, Ann Taylor, Dan Taylor, Rico Tee, Rev. Amos Terrell, Hank Thompson, Norman Thrasher, Johnny Thunder, Ray Topping, Allen Toussaint, Ed Townsend and Betsy Buchanan, Gus Treadwell, Sid Trusty, Billy Vera, Essie Wade, Gayle Wald, Phil Walden, Jeff Walker, Kate Walker, JoJo Wallace, Alton and Maggie Warwick, Dionne Warwick, David Washington, Jacquie Gales Webb, Harry Weinger, Steve Weiss, Jerry Wexler, Mary Wharton, Jesse Whitaker, Charles White, Cliff White, Clifton White, Skippy White, Cheri Wild, Tom Wilk, Dave Williams, Greg Williams, Val Wilmer, Ernest Withers, Peter Wolf, Bobby Womack, Cecil Womack, Curtis Womack, Carol Ann Woods, Georgie Woods, Marshall Wyatt, Claudia Wynn, and Jerry Zolten.

I WISH I COULD SINGLE OUT each person for his or her own individual contributions, but enumerating them all would be impossible, and to choose some over others would be unfair. For me it's been an ongoing education in the widest variety of subjects, from the early development of gospel music to the passions of poster collecting, from the intricacies of personal memory to the detective work of documentation. I've spent so many rewarding hours in the company of so many from whom I've learned so much — to all, my heartfelt thanks.

I would be remiss, though, if I didn't thank the entire Cook family for their many kindnesses, their graciousness and hospitality, their generous sharing of home and memory.

I promised L.C. Cooke a page of his own — and he deserves it. I couldn't get a page, but this is his paragraph. He was my goodwill ambassador, my co-interviewer, my reliable guide to Chicago past and present, and an ever-cheerful chronicler and social director.

Bobby Womack, too, was an unflagging guide. As with L.C., we have been talking now for a period of twelve or thirteen years, and the conversation doesn't seem close to ending. Barbara Cooke and I met fairly late in the day, but she made up for lost time with her frankness, candor, unsparing self-honesty, and dedication to uncovering hard truths. And, of course, J.W. Alexander, who first inspired me to want to write the book when we met in 1982, is never far from my thoughts. We maintained a running conversation for fifteen years, and I wish he were still around not just to set me straight on questions I never thought to ask but to go out to lunch with at his favorite El Pollo restaurant. His widow, Carol Ann Woods, and daughter, Adrienne, have helped keep his spirit alive with both encouragement and advice, just as LeRoy Crume, the last of Sam's group of Soul Stirrers, has volunteered at every opportunity to take me down not just the broad highways but some of the unexplored byways of his friendship with Sam.

Everyone told his or her own story. The stories didn't always gibe; perspectives naturally differed. But I hope I've been able to suggest enough different voices, and a broad enough range of perceptions and responses, to be fair to all the various parties involved.

The book would certainly have been poorer for the absence of any of those voices, but without Allen Klein, I don't know that I would have been able to write it at all. Allen knew Sam only for the last year and a half of his life, and, like everyone else, he has his own point of view, but in addition to the business records he accumulated in his role as Sam's manager, he has over the years compiled an unparalleled archive of Sam's life and career. He provided me with unimpeded and unconditional access to this archive and was unstinting in his efforts to aid in the research without ever seeking to influence it in any way. My thanks to him, to Jody Klein and Iris Keitel, and to the entire ABKCO office for their help, their unfailing good will, and their enthusiasm for the project from start to finish.

Once again Kit Rachlis offered the most scrupulous, perceptive, and noninvasively confrontational editorial advice, and Alexandra Guralnick patiently read, transcribed, debated, and imagined the details of the story every step of the way. As always, thanks to Jake and Connie, Nina and Mike for their incalculable contributions. And thanks once again to Pamela Marshall not just for her cheerfully stringent approach to copyediting but for her occasional willingness to forsake consistency for feel, not to mention her enthusiasm for obscure Latinate debate. Working with Susan Marsh, whose passionate commitment to elegance of form and unswerving dedication to the text have guided the design of every book I have written since 1979, was, as always, an unalloyed pleasure. And I could say much the same about my editor, Michael Pietsch, whose honesty, loyalty, editorial insight, and friendship have served as guideposts for the last thirteen years.

It's a great team. I hope we can all do it again!

Index

Page numbers in *italic* type
refer to photographs.

A&M Records, 517
ABC (network), 207, 225,
    282
ABC Records, 307, 465,
    466–67
"Ac-cent-tchu-ate the
    Positive," 254
Ace Records, 395
Adams, Faye, 104
Adams, Joe, 90
Adderly, Cannonball, 408
Adler, Lou, 210, 235–37, 238,
    242, 274–75, 295, 361,
    392, 404, 456, *456*, 533,
    634; on Bumps
    Blackwell's downfall,
    236–37; Sam's first Copa
    show and, 222–23; as
    songwriter, 236, 279,
    324; wedding of, 571
AFO (All For One) Executives,
    420, 541–42, 543,
    546–549, 566
Afro-American, 634
Ahbez, Eden, 194
"Ain't Misbehavin'," 207
"Ain't That Good News," 535,
    537, 549, 565, 569, 616
Ain't That Good News, 571
Aladdin Records, 42, 60, 65,
    121, 207
Alen, Dick, 287–88, 384

Alexander, Adrienne, 597,
    605, 616, 620
Alexander, Carol Ann (née
    Crawford), 510, 540, 571,
    620, 626, 640
Alexander, J.W. (James
    Woodie), xiv, 61, 80, 94,
    99, 108, 115, 117, 130,
    178, 179, 187, 188, 189,
    211, 216, 224, 268, 272,
    273, 274, 329, 331, 352,
    414–15, 420, 431, 454,
    456, 457, 458, 470, 486,
    499, 504, 510, 521, 529,
    542, 549, 551, 577, 585,
    597, 598, 608, 614, 616;
    as advisor and scout for
    Art Rupe, 60, 67–68, 98,
    113, 152, 153; Barbara's
    dealings with, after
    Sam's death, 639–40,
    641–42, 644–45, 650;
    Black Muslims and, 557;
    Bumps Blackwell and,
    162, 248, 249, 385; BMI
    and, 357–58; in break
    with Keen, 304–5;
    business acumen of,
    81–82; Mel Carter and,
    501–2; "A Change Is
    Gonna Come" and,
    540–41, 547, 607; Charles
    Cook's relationship with,
    484–85; Chicago gospel
    scene described by, 35; at
    Clay-Liston fight, 554,

557, 558; S.R. Crain's
    relationship with, 484;
    *Jesus Be a Fence Around
    Me* and, 359–60; Keen
    masters and, 384, 386,
    387, 388–89, 404; Allen
    Klein's audits and,
    473–74, 495, 505, 508,
    514–15, 525–26, 691*n*;
    Klein's financial analysis
    and, 494; in lawsuit
    against Keen, 384, 386,
    685*n*; in legal battle with
    Rupe, 206, 247, 384;
    leukemia rumor and,
    419; Malloy Artists
    Management and, 441;
    market potential of
    gospel and, 84, 104;
    Johnnie Morisette and,
    322–23, 339, 396, 397,
    399–400, 402, 587;
    music publishing
    company started by, 249,
    267, 278 (*see also* Kags
    Music); nicknames of,
    67; onstage during
    Sam's finales, 522–23;
    personality and
    demeanor of, 67, 81, 82,
    299–300, 361; personal
    life of, 249, 540, 571, 597,
    605; Pilgrim Travelers
    and, 67, 73, 74, 81,
    91–92, 111, 116, 148, 152,
    153, 161–62, 169, 181,

Alexander, J.W. (James
  Woodie) (*continued*) 185,
  207, 236, 262, 264–67,
  278; Billy Preston and,
  460; racial prejudice
  and, 139, 512, 513, 522;
  Jess Rand's relationship
  with, 330, 356, 359; Lou
  Rawls' solo career and,
  278, 392; record
  companies started by,
  295–301, 330–32,
  359–61, 441 (*see also* SAR
  Records); on road with
  Sam, 262, 264–67, 451,
  455, 483–85, 522–23, 524,
  553, 599, 600, 605, 609;
  Rolling Stones' cover of
  "It's All Over Now" and,
  588; salary of, 566; Sam
  first heard by, 36, 655n;
  Sam's change from
  gospel to pop and,
  127–28, 137, 163, 165;
  Sam's Copa shows and,
  550–51, 580–81, 583;
  Sam's death and, 620,
  625, 627, 629, 630, 634,
  635, 639–45, 647, 703n;
  Sam's European tour
  and, 423, 424–25, 427,
  428; Sam's first dates
  with Soul Stirrers and,
  73–76; Sam's personal
  life and, 102, 118, 250;
  Sam's RCA sessions and,
  362, 405, 406, 407, 539,
  607; Sam's relationship
  with, 309, 401–2,
  483–84, 500, 505, 645;
  Shirelles and, 444; Sims
  Twins and, 363–64, 365,
  373, 384, 390, 391, 422,
  443, 587, 606–7; as
  songwriter, 249, 270,
  277–78, 280, 281, 348,
  364–65, 459; Soul
  Stirrers' recording
  sessions and, 70–71,
  95–96, 97, 111, 296–99,
  339, 343–44, 385, 460,
  546; Johnnie Taylor and,
  359, 374, 397, 410,

612–13; Tracey Ltd. and,
  517, 519, 528; Kylo
  Turner's SAR session
  and, 321–22; Valentinos
  (initially Womack
  Brothers) and, 379, 402,
  403, 404, 410, 415, 422,
  438, 440, 470, 471, 488,
  567, 605, 641–42; on
  William Morris' advice to
  Sam, 281–82
Ali, Muhammad, *see* Clay,
  Cassius
Allen, "Hoss," 419
Allen, Steve, 149, 216, 218,
  222
Allison, Jerry, 571
"All My Trials," 568
"All of My Life," 236
"All Right Now," 110–11
"Almost in Your Arms," 239
Alpert, Herb, 210–11, 236,
  237–39, 240, 279, 295,
  324, 361, 392, 404, 517
Alsbrook, Adolphus, 279
"Amen," 586
American Bandstand, 228
Amsterdam News, 139, 150,
  214–16, 223, 283–84, 371,
  531, 555, 582, 648
Anderson, Queen C., 49
Anderson, Robert, 4, 35, 460
Andex, 192, 207, 224, 280,
  671n
Andrews, Screw (né Frank
  Andriola), 393, 395
Andrews Sisters, 254
Angel, Lee, 220
Angelairs, 109
"Angels Keep Watching Over
  Me," 635–36
Animals, 596, 598, 651
Anka, Paul, 203, 227, 229,
  233
"Another Saturday Night,"
  460–61, 473, 482
Anthony, Tony, 467
"Any Day Now," 109, 116
Apollo Theater, Harlem, New
  York, 130, 147–50, 152,
  199, 340, 349, 422, 463,
  464, 467, 510; Sam's pop
  appearances at, 283–84;

302–3, 362, 431–33,
  434–36, 453, 454, 503,
  530–31, 677n, 688n; Soul
  Stirrers' performances
  at, 147–49, 156, 158–59;
  Valentinos' shows with
  James Brown at, 436–38,
  453
Aquarian Bookstore and
  Spiritual Center, Los
  Angeles, 692n
Archer Associates, 221
Arden, Don, 422–28, 430
Armstrong, Louis, 202, 490,
  513, 539, 588, 591, 672n
Arnett Cobb Orchestra, 217
"Arrivederci, Roma," 323
Arthur Godfrey Time, 220
Arthur Murray Party, 260–61
ASCAP, 356, 359
Atco, 300
Atlantic Records, 84, 88,
  130–32, 149, 189, 230–31,
  233, 300, 307, 383, 431,
  466
Atlas Records, 68–69
Auerbach, Larry, 200–202,
  203–4, 218–19, 221, 222,
  223, 254, 306, 311–12
Austin, Gene, 223
Austin, Sil, 289
Autry, Gene, 33
Avalon, Frankie, 227, 230

Babb, Morgan, 164
"Baby Workout," 495
Badie, Chuck, 542, 548–49,
  566, 567
Bain, Bob, 423
Baker, Cassietta (later
  Cassietta George), 51, 124
Baker, LaVern, 232, 243, 255,
  264, 317, 384, 503, 508,
  674n; in Biggest Show of
  Stars, 189, 227, 230, 231;
  stylistic traits of, 230, 351;
  in Supersonic tour with
  Sam, 348, 351
Baldwin, David, 230
Baldwin, James, xiii, 3, 4, 230,
  429, 449–51, 498, 509
Baldwin, Wilbur, 230

Ballard, Hank, 214, *326, 347,*
351, 472; Castro's visit to
Harlem and, 348, 349;
Aretha Franklin and,
367; in Supersonic tours
with Sam, 287–88, 289,
290, 293, 326, 365, 366,
599, 600; "The Twist"
and, 288, 390
"Ballgame, The," 113, 114
Barber, Keith, 73
Barlow, William, 419
Barris, Marti, 236, 242, 252
Barry, Jeff, 319
Bartholomew, Dave, 86, 87,
336
Basie, Count, 173, 250, 327,
588
"Basin Street Blues," 539,
549, 550, 552
Bates, Daisy, 369
Bates, L.C., 369, 370
Battiste, Harold, 175, 247,
346, 420, 541–43,
547–48, 645; as head of
SAR Productions, 566;
Soul Station #1 and,
542–43, 547–48, 566
Battle, Abraham, 35
Battle of the Blind Boys, 98
Beal, Eddie, 421
Beal, Evie Rawls, 249, 268
Beal, Marion Wooten "Keg,"
249, 266, 268
Beamon, B.B., 80, 145, 189,
202, 243, 257, 258, 262,
263, 286, 287
Beatles, 430–31, 555–56, 564,
574, 584, 598
"Beautiful Weekend," 195
"Be Bop a Lu La," 423
Beck, Maudie, 102, 376–77
Bee, King, 198
"Begin the Beguine," 223
Belafonte, Harry, 272, 344,
352, 429, 517, 520, 580;
civil rights movement
and, 188, 490, 509, 513,
588; Nat "King" Cole's
partnership with, 518; as
model for Sam, 164, 188,
220, 256, 335, 478
Belafonte, Marguerite, 214

*Belafonte Live at Carnegie
Hall,* 453, 455
Bell, Leard "Kansas City,"
251, 253
Bellevue Casino, Montreal,
302
Bells of Heaven, 322
Belvin, Jesse, 122, 185–86,
198, 277, 289, 326–27,
337, 608
Benci, Jim, 616
Bennett, Lerone, 511
Bennett, Pete, 553, 566, 587
Bennett, Tony, 222, 510
Bennett, Wayne, 523
Benton, Brook, 374, 492–93,
546, 588
Berlin, Irving, 251, 271, 272,
372, 539
Berry, Chuck, 189, 230, 235
Berry, Richard, 185
Best of Sam Cooke, The,
514
"Best Things in Life Are
Free, The," 580
"Be With Me Jesus," 115–16,
124–25
Bibb, Leon, 490
Big Beat (1958 tour), 228,
229–30, 234–35
Biggest Show of Stars, 353;
1957 editions of, 189,
228; 1958 edition of,
227–35, 286, 287; 1960
edition of, 347, 393
Big Gospel Cavalcade (1957),
191–92
Big Maybelle, 326
Big Record, The, 221
"Bill Bailey," 568, 581
Billboard, 84, 104, 164, 171,
196, 206, 212, 228, 230,
305, 324, 330, 376, 388,
444, 550, 551
Bingham, Howard, 611
Birmingham, Ala., 489–90,
491–92, 509, 521–22, 523
Birmingham Municipal
Auditorium, 139, 439–40
Black Muslims (Nation of
Islam), 333, 555; J.W.
Alexander's views on,
557; Cassius Clay (later

Ali) and, 555, 556–57,
558, 559–61, 593;
Malcolm X's rift with,
531, 555, 563; Sam's views
on, 532, 555, 593–94
Black Nativity, 389, 428, 685*n*
Black Orchid, Chicago,
254–55
Blackwell, Marlene "Little
Mama," 173, 180, 216,
242, 248, 252, 276–77
Blackwell, Robert "Bumps,"
123, 127–29, 130, 155,
167, 171–84, 172, 185,
186, 187, 188, 215, 216,
221, 240, 241, 242, 247,
250, 251, 257, 263, 276,
295, 308, 309, 525–26,
586, 634, 642, 667*n,*
701*n;* arranging skills of,
222–23; artists signed to
Keen by, 184, 189, 236;
background of, 121;
difficulties of, at Keen,
247–48, 271–72, 280; in
founding of Keen
Records, 180–83, 193,
215; hired by Specialty
Records, 121–22; Latin
dance sound and, 237;
Little Richard and, 129,
144, 151, 154, 162, 176,
177, 182, 207–8;
organizational
shortcomings of, 236–37,
261; Art Rupe and,
162–63, 166, 176–80,
207–9; Sam's agency
contracts and, 200–202;
Sam's change from
gospel to pop and,
127–28, 150–52, 153–54,
159, 160–61, 163, 166,
167–68, 169, 215; Sam's
crossover to white
audiences and, 218,
222–23, 224, 246; Sam's
dissatisfaction with, 270,
272; Sam's first album
and, 207, 235; Sam's first
Keen single and, 189,
194, 195, 196, 198–205,
212, 235; Sam's legal

problems with Specialty and, 204–5, 246, 294; Sam's record contracts and, 178–80, 194, 204–5; Sam's recording sessions and, 153–54, 171–77, 194, 239; SAR Records and, 300–301, 385; Specialty's release agreement with, 180, 204; Valiants' "Good Golly Miss Molly" and, 207–9

Blaine, Hal, 459

Blair, Sallie, 220–21, 283

Blake, Rev. Harry, 523

Blanchard, Edgar, 157

Bland, Bobby "Blue," 137, 139, 355, 479, 521, 522–23, 541, 636

Bland, James, 591

Blossoms, 269–70

"Blowin' in the Wind," 510, 512–13, 586, 597

Blues Under the Stars, 593, 594

BMI, 249, 277, 571; Allen Klein's audit and, 473, 474, 495, 691*n*; Sam's problem with, 356–59

BMI Awards dinners, 356, 455–56, *456*

Bobby (Womack) and the Valentinos, 648

Bohème, La (Puccini), 319

Bolling, Connie, 159, 217, 229, 244

Bolling, Keith, 217

Bond, Julian, 513

Bono, Sonny, 174, 247, 566

Booker, Ernest, 264

Boone, Pat, 428, 460

Bostic, Mrs. Earl, 498

Boudreaux, John, 542, 548, 549

Bowen, Jimmy, 465–66

Boyer, Elisa, 616–19, 625, 627, 628, 629, 630, 635, 642, 643–44, 647

Bradford, Alex, 96, 104, 111–12, 148, 159, 163, 247, 665*n*

Braggs, Al "TNT," 522–23

Bramson, Sam, 219

Branch, Taylor, 411–12, 491–92, 511

Brandt, Jerry, 413–14, 419, 423, 450, 454, 463, 474, 496, 505, 525, 534; at Clay-Liston fight, 554, 556–57; Allen Klein's dealings with, 520–21, 554; Sam's return to Copa and, 576–77, 579, 580

Brel, Jacques, 321

Brewer, Teresa, 198, 672*n*

Brewster, Rev. W.H., 49, 51–52, 62, 72, 85, 511

Bridges, Charlie, 35, 36

Briggs, Bunny, 302

"Bring It On Home to Me," 393–95, 404–5, 406–7, 413, 414, 422, 433, 454, 455, 458, 469, 473, 475, 479, 482, 569, 581

Brinson, Ted, 175, 187, 663*n*

British pop invasion, 564, 573–74, 587–88, 596, 598

Brooks, La La, 489

Brooks, Lonnie, 292

Brooks, Shelton, 473

Brown, Annie, 50

Brown, Charles, 393–95, 404–5, 406–7, 458, 459, 461, 528

Brown, Drew "Bundini," 559

Brown, James, 145, 333, 382, 433, 435, 488, 495, 523, 594, 600, 607; Liston supported by, 556; showmanship of, 438; Valentinos' tour with, 422, 436–38, 453

Brown, Jim, 559

Brown, Ray, 369

Brown, Roy, 346, 354

Brown, Ruth, 130, 231

Brownlee, Archie, 46, 48, 60, 73–75, 76, 98–99, 107, 114, 117, 123, 377

Bumps Blackwell Orchestra, 207, 251

Bumps Blackwell Rockin' Combo, 242

Bunche, Ralph, 336

Bundy, June, 230

Burke, Solomon, 393, 408, 411, 436–37, 475, 476, 478–79, 480, 594

Burks, Gene, 478

Butler, Jerry, 348, 474, 479, 480, 488, 646

"By and By," 75, 83

Byrd, Jimmy "Early," 105, 130, 196–97

Caddy Records, 180

California Eagle, 216, 256

Callender, Red, 322

Campbell, Barbara, *see* Cooke, Barbara

Campbell, Beverly (Barbara's sister), 39, 227, 304, 401, 500, 545, 570, 614, 620, 623, 626

Campbell, Ella (Barbara's sister), 39, 41, 226–27, 417, 621, 626–27, 630

Campbell, Linda Marie (Barbara and Sam's daughter), *see* Cooke, Linda Marie

Campbell, Lucie, 34, 96

Campbell, Mamie (Barbara's mother), 39, 92, 102, 633, 645–46

Camp Meeting of the Air, 51–52

"Camptown Twist," 396

"Canadian Sunset," 223

Cantor, Paul, 201, 441–42, 525, 694*n*

Capitol Records, 239, 295–96, 307, 362, 383, 392, 466, 518

Caravans, 51, 114, 124, 148, 191, 444

Card, Evelyn, 619, 627, 628, 629

Carmichael, Hoagy, 372

Carolinian, 422

Carpenter, Harry, 561–62

Carr, Sister Wynona, 113, 114, 156, 189

Carroll, Howard, 120

Carr's Beach, Annapolis, Md., 287–88

Carson, Johnny, 436, 549, 550, 552–53

Carter, Johnny, 27, 215

Carter, Mel, 460, 501–2, 516, 529, 530, 539, 608

Cash Box, 88, 113, 216, 308, 374, 384, 388, 528, 530, 534–35, 551

Casino Royal, Washington, D.C., 302

Castro, Fidel, 348–49

Cato, Charles, 287

Catskills, 574, 575, 576–80, 698*n*

Cavalcade of Jazz (1958), 243, 250–51

CBS, 225, 305–6

Central High School, Little Rock, Ark., 202, 233, 369

Central Record Sales, 180

"Chain Gang," 319–21, 344, 346, 348, 351, 356, 361, 363, 380, 569, 581, 649, 705*n*; BMI and, 357–58; impetus for, 319–20, 680*n*; recording of, 320–21, 325; response to, 338–39

"Chain Gang (The Sound of My Man)," 352

Challengers, 248

Chandler, Jeff, 222, 272–73, 321, 389

"Change Is Gonna Come, A," 550, 551–54, 569, 588, 611, 651; J.W. Alexander's response to, 540–41; edited for single release, 607–8, 646; René Hall's arrangement for, 547–48, 569; impetus for, 512–13; Allen Klein's response to, 550, 552–53; marketing of, 553–54; recording of, 547–48; televised performances of, 550, 551–53; Bobby Womack's response to, 549

Charles, Jimmy, 353

Charles, Ray, 112, 121, 129, 130, 144, 153, 159, 172, 230, 250, 251, 307, 320, 334, 414, 419, 434, 436, 458, 469, 495, 509, 520, 588, 594; arrest for heroin possession, 605; "Georgia on My Mind" and, 371–72; "I Got a Woman" and, 113, 120, 165, 372; at Sam's funeral, 634, 635–36; segregated performances refused by, 683*n*–84*n*

Charles, Rev. H.B., 634, 635

Checker, Chubby, 347, 353, 390, 490

Checker Records, 255, 277, 342, 359, 457

Cheeks, Julius "June," 95, 114, 119, 123, 146, 191, 340, 379, 438; performing with Soul Stirrers, 107–8, 110–11, 433, 544

Cher, 566

"Cherry Pie," 185

Chess, Leonard, 359–60

Chess Records, 277, 648

Chevelles, 183

Chicago Defender, 56, 58, 83–84, 188, 254–55, 440, 451, 492–93, 631–32

"Christ Is All," 73

Christland Singers, 78, 90, 110, 133, 134, 135, 145, 146

Christ Temple Cathedral, Chicago, 11–12

Christ Temple Church, Chicago Heights, 12–14

Chudd, Lew, 330–32, 373, 387

Church, Eugene, 185, 277

Church of Christ (Holiness), 9–10, 11, 17, 20, 25, 26, 46, 90

Church of God in Christ, 10

civil rights movement, 139, 188, 202, 233, 297, 327, 337–38, 352, 367, 489–94, 509–13, 523,

555, 588, 605; in Birmingham, Ala., 489–90, 491–92; connection between music and, 512–13; and Martin Luther King's speech at NAACP Convention, 411–12; March on Washington and, 509–12, 513; NARA's role in, 419–20; Pilgrim Travelers' show for, 139; and Sam's boycott of segregated show, 368–71; Sam's songwriting and, 512–13 (*see also* "Change Is Gonna Come, A")

Clark, Dee, 211, 220, 326, *326*, 334, 393, 405, 412, 475, 478, 630, 686*n*

Clark, Dick, 225, 228, 235, 260, 261, 282, 565, 691*n*

Clark, Don, 207

Class Records, 187

Claxton, William, 359

Clay, Cassius (later Muhammad Ali), 347, 505, 532, 533–34, *536*, 554–63, 589–90, 630; as Black Muslim, 555, 556–57, 558, 559–61, 563, 593; Liston's fight against, 531, 554–59, 590; Malcolm X rejected by, 563; marriage of, 593; name changes of, 560, 563; at Patterson-Liston fight, 506–7; personality and demeanor of, 555–56; Sam's record with, 534, 561, 562

Clay, Rudy, 505, 556–58

Cleave, Maureen, 429–30

Clemons, Barbara, 215, 255, 277

Cleveland, James, 114, 124

Cliques, 185

Clovers, 283

Club Elegante, Brooklyn, 218–20, 223, 254, 521

Club Harlem, Atlantic City, N.J., 503–4, 587, 588, 589
Club Riviera, St. Louis, 256
"C'mon and Swim," 607
Coasters, 185, 431, 439
Coates, Dorothy Love, *see* Love, Dorothy
Cobb, Arnett, 189
Cobbs, Rev. Clarence, 632
Cochran, James "Dimples," 27, 159, 215
Coefield, Brice, 183, 185, 189
Cohen, Myron, 223, 224
Cole, Nat "King," 27, 184, 194, 223, 239, 250, 256, 271, 272, 335, 352, 387, 539, 544, 546, 550, 551, 553; attacked on Birmingham stage, 139; Harry Belafonte's partnership with, 518; Capitol's royalty deal with, 307; civil rights movement and, 490, 509, 513, 588
Coleman, Ray, 573–74
Coleman Records, 48
Coles, Don, 545
Collier, Mitty, 599
Columbia Records, 112, 365, 521, 554, 561; Allen Klein's negotiations with, 505, 506, 517
Columbia Studio, 256
"Come, Let Us Go Back to God," 70, 85
"Come and Go to That Land," 103
Come Fly With Me, 323
"Come to Me," 288–89
Como, Perry, 303, 321, 362, 431, 453
Congress of Racial Equality (CORE), 469
Conic, Bishop J.L.I., 12, 46
Conic, Bishop M.R., 26
Connor, Eugene "Bull," 489
Consolers, 544
Cook, Agnes (sister), 78, 93, 197, 214, 215, 416, 643; childhood of, 12–13, 15,

17–18, 19, 20, 22, 23, 32–33; Highway QCs and, 32–33, 62–63; Sam's protectiveness of, 32, 89
Cook, Annie Mae (mother), 9–13, 10, 15–19, 27, 32, 37, 39, 48, 78–79, 90, 92, 93, 105, 118, 141, 214, 215, 244, 276, 286, 416, 500; as grandparent, 417–18; "Nearer to Thee" and, 126–27; Sam's death and, 622, 624, 632, 648
Cook, Bill, 137, 163–64, 168, 332–33, 358; Roy Hamilton and, 128, 130, 149–50, 159, 189; Sam's change from gospel to pop and, 128, 130–32, 149–50, 155, 158, 159, 160–61, 215, 332; Sam's demos and, 149–50, 167–68; as songwriter, 158, 206, 212
Cook, Charles, Jr. (brother), 23–24, 26–27, 43, 59, 93, 118, 141, 197, 215, 297, 308, 318, 409, 418, 434, 543, 580, 649–50; J.W. Alexander's relationship with, 484–85; Barbara's remarriage and, 648–50; in booking of Sam's dates, 308–9; "Chain Gang" and, 319–20, 649, 680n, 704n; childhood of, 10, 13–15, 16, 17, 18, 19, 22; gambling of, 335, 451; on road with Sam, 225, 266, 282, 289, 290, 292–93, 327–28, 335, 346, 347, 350, 366, 369, 371, 381, 413, 427, 436, 451, 455, 474, 482, 484–85, 487, 496, 526, 527, 589, 593; on road with Soul Stirrers, 89–90; Sam's death and, 621–22, 626, 632; Sam's reading habits and, 367–68; Sam's

retirement from road and, 605–6; stabbing of, 472, 474; Bobby Womack and, 485, 649–50
Cook, Charles, Rev. (father), 9–21, 10, 24, 27, 28, 32, 39, 44, 45, 78, 89, 92, 93, 105, 141, 178, 210, 211, 215, 215–16, 244, 276, 416, 429, 500, 586, 648; attitude toward racial prejudice and, 16, 26; entrepreneurial activities of, 14, 20; family relocated to Chicago by, 10–11; as grandparent, 417; as preacher, 9–14, 17, 18, 24, 25, 26, 46, 93; Sam and Barbara wed by, 302, 304; Sam's arrest and incarceration and, 56, 57; Sam's change from gospel to pop and, 156, 164, 170; Sam's death and, 621, 622, 626, 627, 630, 632; Sam's departure from Highway QCs and, 63–64; Singing Children and, 13–15, 20, 24; at Soul Stirrers performances, 90, 91; values instilled in Sam by, 63–64, 178–79, 336, 369, 493, 532
Cook, Dale, Sam's recordings under name of, 156, 164, 165–66, 206
Cook, David (brother), 26, 28, 89, 93, 105, 215, 264, 416, 646, 649
Cook, Dolores "Dee Dee" (née Mohawk, first wife), 101–2, 103, 106; death of, 282–83; Sam's marriage to, 105–6, 141, 159, 226; Sam's separation and divorce from, 170, 215, 243, 244; son, Joey, 105, 106, 159, 170, 282
Cook, Edna Gallmon, 146

Cook, Hattie (sister), 10,
12–13, 14, 18, 19, 21, 22,
24, 33, 93, 144, 215, 417,
643
Cook, Herbert G., 415
Cook, L.C., see Cooke, L.C.
Cook, Mary (sister), 10,
12–13, 14, 15, 17–18, 22,
24–25, 26, 93, 215,
245–46, 311, 643
Cook, Willie (brother), 9, 15,
24, 26, 39, 93, 156, 215
Cook County House of
Correction, 56–57
Cooke, Barbara (née
Campbell, second wife),
117–18, 244–45, 254, 293,
352, 376–77, 392, 398,
405, 406, 418, 442, 443,
454, 496, 499, 510, 535,
538, 540, 554, 557, 575;
"adopts" Eric, 544–45,
650; boyfriends of, 79,
117–18, 244–45, 246,
294, 301, 302, 570, 606,
619, 630, 639–42,
644–46; Cook family
and, 79, 92–93, 648–50;
credited as songwriter on
Sam's records, 262, 281,
293–94, 356–57, 358; Los
Angeles homes of,
310–11, 312, 313, 386–87,
389; married life of,
310–11, 328–29, 350–51,
381, 400–402, 409–10,
498, 500, 501, 503, 533,
542, 544–46, 570, 606,
614–15, 620–21, 644;
photographs of, 40, 269,
312, 313, 408, 462, 638;
relocated to Los Angeles,
245–46, 250, 251–52,
261–62, 274, 281, 286,
293–94; on road with
Sam, 350–51, 376,
381–82, 412, 482, 523,
526, 553, 609; Sam's
business affairs and, 311,
329, 332, 384, 441, 458,
535, 623–24, 633–34, 635,
636–37, 641–42,
644–45, 648, 650–51;

Sam's children with,
92–93, 102, 106,
328–29, 342–43, 376,
381, 389–90 (see also
Cooke, Linda Marie;
Cooke, Tracey Samia;
Cooke, Vincent Lance);
Sam's death and, 619–21,
622, 623–24, 626–27,
630, 633–35, 636–37;
Sam's jealousy and, 381,
390, 392, 409–10; and
Sam's marriage to
Dolores, 105–7, 283;
Sam's relationship with,
before marriage, 39–42,
48, 53–54, 78–79, 92–93,
102–3, 105–7, 226–27,
244–46, 250, 251–52,
253, 261–62, 274, 275,
285–86, 293–94, 651;
Zelda Sands' departure
from SAR Records and,
529–30; songwriting
award given to, 356;
Vincent's death and,
499–500, 501, 502, 503,
621, 644, 650; wedding
of, 301–2, 303–4, 678n;
on West Indies tour,
408–10, 409; and Bobby
Womack, 639–42,
644–46, 647–50; working
at Keen Records, 261
Cooke, L.C. (brother), xv, 7,
44, 46, 47, 56–57, 59, 62,
78, 82, 91, 92, 93, 105,
118, 119, 133–34, 142, 183,
206–7, 214, 215, 220,
298, 356, 369, 375, 396,
418, 451, 454, 593; J.W.
Alexander's relationship
with, 484, 485; Cadillac
given to, 275–76;
childhood of, 10, 12–16,
18, 19, 21–28, 32, 37,
38–39; credited as
songwriter on Sam's
records, 196, 204, 205,
207, 239, 247, 255, 262,
277, 294, 309, 356–57,
358, 691n; as drummer
for Soul Stirrers,

166–67; first Los
Angeles visit of, 275–77;
girlfriends of, 39,
197–98, 255, 277,
434–35, 454; memorial
tour and, 646–47; on
road with Aretha
Franklin, 366–67; Sam's
death and, 630, 632, 643;
Sam's girlfriends and,
39, 93, 224, 304; Sam's
reading habits and, 367,
368; Sam's relationship
with, 457; Sam's story
about name of, 429;
Sam's tour with, 309;
SAR Records session of,
342, 343, 434; singing
career of, 58, 90, 133,
144, 159, 160, 168, 255,
263–64, 277, 309, 339,
342, 422, 434, 436, 445,
446, 457, 516, 565, 605,
611, 643, 646–47; as
songwriter, 457; Womack
Brothers and, 379–80
Cooke, Linda Marie
(daughter), 102, 105, 106,
118, 141, 226, 227,
244–46, 261–62, 263,
268, 274, 275, 281, 283,
286, 293, 294, 301, 310,
387, 389, 408, 412, 442,
471, 513, 534, 545, 545,
568, 570, 648; Barbara's
remarriage and, 645,
647–48; in Chicago with
Cook family, 417–18; at
parents' wedding, 303–4;
relocated to Los Angeles,
245, 246, 251–52, 261; on
road with Sam, 350–51,
482, 523, 609; Sam's
death and, 620, 630,
632, 633, 635, 636, 640;
Sam's relationship with,
253–54, 311, 350, 401,
418, 497, 498; Vincent's
death and, 502; on West
Indies tour, 408, 409,
410
Cooke, Sam: acting career of,
188, 256, 272, 305–6,

321, 441, 583–84, 586, 590, 597, 608; agency contracts of, 200–202, 286, 308–9, 354, 564–65, 571; ambition of, 7, 15, 42, 164, 335–36, 344, 354, 383, 551, 565, 584–85; arrangements for, 222–23, 229, 238, 271, 318, 324, 362, 363, 435, 440–41, 458, 517, 539, 547–48, 569, 576, 578–79, 591; arrest and incarceration of, 56–57, 58; art collection of, 310, 679*n*–80*n*; awards won by, 356, 455–56; backup musicians for, 156, 157, 166, 167, 168, 172, 175, 176–77, 178, 194, 251, 279, 325, 339, 354, 409, 435–36, 439, 444–45, 541–42, 543, 567–68; birth of, 9, 10; black history as interest of, 446; in car accident, 265–66; change from gospel to pop, 127–28, 130–32, 136–37, 144, 149–61, 163–70, 197–98, 215, 234, 283, 379, 496, 565; childhood of, 7–28; children fathered by, 92–93, 102, 105, 106, 118, 141, 159, 205, 217, 229, 244, 261, 342–43, 381, 389–90 (*see also* Cooke, Linda Marie; Cooke, Tracey Samia; Cooke, Vincent Lance); Christmas card designed by, 313–14; control over masters of, 517, 518; coroner's jury hearing on, 626–29; death of, 616–30, 642–44, 647; *e* added to last name by, 188, 670*n*; early singing career of, 13–15, 19–20, 23, 24–26, 27, 30–34 (*see also* Highway QCs); educated about music business, 186–88, 249;

European tour of (1962), 422–31, *426*; fashion sense of, 210, 216, 221, 273, 429, 478, 499; female audience and, 51, 74, 82, 88–89, 91, 109, 117, 142–44, 242, 258, 259, 269–70, 283–84, 433, 454, 582–83, 600; first album of, 207, 271; first marriage of, 105–6, 141, 159, 170, 215, 226, 243, 244, 282–83 (*see also* Cook, Dolores "Dee Dee"); first pop record release of, 156, 160–61, 164–66; funerals for, 624–25, 630–36, *631*; generosity of, 300, 495–96; girlfriends of, 39–42, 48, 53–54, 78–79, 92–93, 101–3, 105–7, 118, 159, 217, 220–21, 224, 226–27, 229, 244–46, 250, 251–52, 253, 261–62, 274, 275, 281, 285–86, 355, 570; gospel concert of (New Year's Eve 1962), 442–43, 444–45, 450–51; hairstyles of, 144, 184, 210, 211, 216, 220, 407, 552, 604; Latin dance sound and, 237, 239, 296; leukemia rumor and, 419; live recording of, 451–55; Los Angeles homes of, 220, 242, 261, 273–74, 304, 310–11, *312*, *313*, 383, 384, 386–87, 389, 400, *612*, *613*; loyalty of, to family and friends, 309–10; management deals of, 272–73, 441–42, 498, 524–25, 701*n*; memorial album for, 645; musical training of, 30–31, 75, 76, 82, 85, 217, 221; in music publishing partnership, 267, 278, 280–81 (*see also* Kags Music); paternity suits against, 217, 229, 244,

381, 389; personality of, 19, 22–23, 28, 32, 37, 42, 45, 76, 78, 83, 88–89, 99, 101, 105, 117, 140–41, 143, 173–74, 195–96, 210–11, 218–19, 235–36, 269–70, 274–75, 282, 284–85, 328, 338, 347, 361, 400–401, 413, 468, 486–87, 496, 533; photography as hobby of, 255, 256; as producer, 339, 373–74, 398, 457; reading habits of, 140, 352, 367–68, 429, 446, 487, 497; record company started by, 295–301, 330–32, 359–61 (*see also* SAR Records); record contracts of, 174, 178–80, 193, 194, 204–5, 248, 296, 304, 306–8, 311, 376, 383–84, 429, 505, 506, 507, 517–21, 528, 534–35; recording sessions of (*see* Cooke, Sam, solo recording sessions of); recording under name of Dale Cook, 156, 164, 165–66, 206; religious upbringing and views of, 9, 20, 141–42, 275; retirement of, from road, 605–6; royalties of, 174, 178–80, 194, 296, 307, 308, 324, 356–59, 383, 384, 386, 429, 494, 495, 506, 514, 519–20, 524, 528, 668*n*, 694*n*; schooling of, 15, 22–23, 27–28, 42; second album of, 254, 260, 271; second marriage of, 301–2, 303–4, 678*n* (*see also* Cooke, Barbara); showmanship of, as gospel performer, 107–8, 142–44, 431–33, 454–55; showmanship of, as pop performer, 218–20, 222–25, 230, 254, 260–61, 281–82, 302–3,

Cooke, Sam (*continued*)
325, 427, 431–33, 436,
443–44, 454–55, 582–83,
584, 589; singing voice
and stylistic traits of, 33,
71–73, 74, 75–76, 78, 82,
85, 94–95, 96, 103,
108–10, 114, 115, 157–58,
194, 198, 231, 259, 345,
372–73, 407–8; as
songwriter, 115, 130,
136–37, 141, 151–52, 167,
169, 174, 192, 237–38,
268–69, 277–78,
280–81, 291, 318,
319–20, 343, 390–91,
428, 429–30, 455,
487–88, 497, 565, 594
(*see also specific songs*);
Soul Stirrers joined by,
59, 62–64, 65–68 (*see
also* Soul Stirrers); tap
routine of, 281–82, 302;
television appearances
of, 202, 203–4, 211–12,
216, 218, 222, 225,
260–61, 282, 305–6, 321,
352, 374–76, 436, 473,
533–34, 549, 550, 551–53,
565, 596–97, 604–5,
690n; temper of, 117,
285, 381, 409–10, 413,
642; white audience
sought by, 218–20,
222–25, 246, 254, 272,
569, 581; white Cadillac
convertible of, 225–26;
women on the road
and, 82, 105, 136, 184,
212–13, 243–44, 259,
263, 264, 265, 284, 285,
286, 291, 292, 328, 329,
335, 366, 412, 428,
434–35, 482–83, 496;
yodel of, 94–95, 96, 103,
108, 408
Cooke, Sam, solo recording
sessions of: August 1956,
149–50; December 12,
1956, 153–58, 159, 294;
April 1957, 167–68; June
1957, 171–77; August 23,
1957, 194; January 1959,

268–72; March 3, 1959,
279–80; July 24, 1959,
295–96; January 25 and
28, 1960, 318–21; March
1960, 323–24; April 13,
1960, 325; September 9
and 10, 1960, 342–43,
344–46; April 21, 1961,
361–65; May 19 and 20,
1961, 371–73; April 26,
1962, 405–7; August
1962, 421–22; December
14 and 15, 1962, 440–41;
February 1963, 458–61;
June 15, 1963, 498–99;
September 11, 1963, 517;
December 20–21, 1963,
537–40; January 28,
1964, 546–47; January
30, 1964, 547–48; March
25, 1964, 566; August
7–8, 1964, 591–93;
August 20, 1964, 594;
last (1964), 606–7; with
Bill Cook, 149–50,
167–68; for Keen
Records, 194, 239–42,
268–72, 279–80; moved
to Los Angeles, 361; for
RCA, 315, 318–21,
323–24, 325–26, 342–43,
344–46, 348, 361–65,
371–73, 389, 390–91,
405–7, 421–22, 440–41,
458–61, 498–99,
537–40, 546–48, 567,
591–93, 606–7; for
Specialty Records,
153–58, 159, 171–77, 294;
under Tracey aegis,
517–19, 528
Cooke, Tracey Samia
(daughter), 376, 412, 417,
497, 545, 545, 570, 648;
Barbara's remarriage
and, 645, 647–48; birth
of, 342–43; holding
company named for, 517;
on road with Sam,
350–51, 482, 609; Sam's
death and, 630, 632, 633,
635, 636, 640; Sam's
relationship with, 350;

401; Vincent's death and,
499–500, 502
Cooke, Vincent Lance (son),
392, 412, 440, 462, 497;
"adoption" of Eric after
death of, 544–45, 650;
birth of, 389–90; death
of, 499–501, 502, 503,
538, 621, 636, 644, 650;
Sam's doubts about
paternity of, 390, 392,
401, 501; Sam's
relationship with, 401
Cooke-Rand Productions,
356
Cooke's Beer, 415, 687n
Cooke's Tour, 323–24
Cookies, 496
"Cool Train," 499
Copacabana, New York, 473,
521, 550–51; recording of
Sam's show at, 585–86,
598; Sam's first
appearance at (1958),
219, 222–25, 235, 254,
281, 360, 553, 554; Sam's
return to (1964), 551, 554,
564–65, 567–69,
571–86, 572, 608
Copeland, Charles, 5, 28,
29–32, 38, 42–43, 44, 45.
See also Highway QCs
Copeland, Creadell,
"Bubba," 28, 29, 30, 31,
32, 33–34, 42–43, 44, 47,
54, 55, 63, 77–78, 119,
120, 197, 234. *See also*
Highway QCs
Copeland, Georgia "Babe,"
38
Copyright Act (1909), 174
Cornelius, Carter (Barbara's
stepfather), 92, 102
Cornelius, Don (Barbara's
stepbrother), 246
Cornelius, Mamie, *see*
Campbell, Mamie
Cornshucks, Little Miss, 281
Cosby, Harper, 567, 568, 576
Cosimo Recording Studios,
New Orleans, 154–55,
168
"Cottonfields," 616

"Couldn't Hear Nobody Pray," 380, 402, 403
"Cousin of Mine," 591–92, 598
Covay, Don, 434, 594
Crain, Maude, 79, 633
Crain, S.R., 77, 90, 91, 92, 96, 99, 104, 125, 127, 131, 147, 163, 178, 241, 274, 299, 346, 500, 583, 605; J.W. Alexander's rivalry with, 484; booking agency for SAR acts and, 441; in booking of Sam's dates, 309, 679n; Crume hiring and, 133–34; R.H. Harris' departure from Soul Stirrers and, 61–62, 65–67, 68; Highway QCs and, 57, 62; Kags Music and, 278, 508, 530; payments arranged for, 530; Jess Rand approached by, 272; robbed in hotel room, 421; Sam's change from gospel to pop and, 132–33, 163, 165, 168–69, 170; Sam's death and, 621, 624, 626–27, 630, 633, 634, 635; Sam's departure from Soul Stirrers and, 170, 190–91; Sam's joining of Soul Stirrers and, 62, 70–71, 73–74, 75; as Sam's mentor, 75, 76, 82, 85, 217, 221, 255; Sam's personal life and, 79, 93, 101–2, 103, 118, 145–46, 229, 245, 283, 303, 350–51, 410; Sam's relationship with, 116–17, 309, 484; Sam's retirement from road and, 606; as Sam's road manager, 213, 217, 218–19, 222, 224, 262, 264–65, 292, 300, 309, 350–51, 381, 408, 427, 441, 451, 455, 469–70, 474, 484, 526–27, 530; Sam's stylistic

breakthrough and, 94; SAR acronym and, 297, 332; singing backup for Sam, 413, 546; singing backup on SAR sessions, 402, 457, 546; Soul Stirrers founded by, 59; Soul Stirrers left by, 213; as Soul Stirrers' manager, 61–62, 79, 81, 120, 139, 140, 145–46, 148, 166–67, 169, 215, 377; Soul Stirrers' recording sessions and, 70–71, 72, 83, 85, 95, 115–16, 151–52, 339, 343. *See also* Soul Stirrers
Crawford, Carol Ann, *see* Alexander, Carol Ann
Crawford, Chazz, 256
Creatore, Giuseppe ("The Great Creatore"), 316–17
Creatore, Luigi, 315–21, *316*, 323, 339, 361, 384, *394*, 405, 414, 433, 434, 458, 461, 466, 538, 585, 586, 650, 685n; background of, 306, 315–18; *PM East/PM West* (television show) and, 374–75; Jess Rand's negotiations on behalf of Sam with, 306–8; recording of Sam's live show and, 451–53; Sam's recording sessions with, 315, 318–21, 323–24, 325–26, 342–43, 344–46, 348, 354, 361–65, 371–73, 389, 390–91, 396, 405–7, 421–22, 440–41, 461, 498–99, 538–39, 546, 548; Sam's "theme"-oriented albums and, 323–24, 372
Criner, John, 248
Crosby, Bing, 33, 94, 172, 254, 271, 281
Crume, Arthur, 133–34
Crume, Leroy, 94, 130, 131, 133–41, 145–49, 163, 225–26, 283, 296, 297, 299, 385–86, 450–51,

537, 544, 570, 614, 632; Jimmie Outler hiring and, 340–41; Sam's change from gospel to pop and, 136–37, 150, 155–56, 164, 165, 166, 169, 170; Sam's departure from Soul Stirrers and, 170, 191, 192; singing backup for Sam, 546, 547; as songwriter, 343, 535, 633; Soul Stirrers joined by, 133–35. *See also* Soul Stirrers
Crume Brothers, 133
Crystals, 431, 467, 469, 503
Cuban missile crisis (1962), 430
Cuffee, Jerry, 532
Cugat, Xavier, 221
Cumber, Lillian, 80, 81, 153, 216–17, 243, 499. *See also* Herald Attractions
Cunningham, Carrie, 611
Cunningham, Eddie, 213–14, 225, 258, 264, 265
"Cupid," 281, 362–64, 374, 380, 414, 581
Curfey, Dr. (coroner), 625
Curtis, King, 431, 435–36, 439, 444–45, 447, 452, 453, 455, 467–68, 469, 503
Curtis (Womack) and the Boys, 690n

Daley, Arthur, 556
"Danny Boy," 207
Dap Daddies, 155
Darin, Bobby, 252, 466, 470, 544
Dave Clark Five, 564, 598
Davenport, Ethel, 124
Davidson, Harold, 564
Davidson, Joyce, 375
Davis, Billy, 290, 326, 348, 370, 646–47; life on the road and, 291–92, 293, 349–50; on Jackie Wilson's rivalry with Sam, 288, 289

Davis, Sammy, Jr., 200, 222, 272, 273, 281, 285, 302, 305–6, 310, 352, 359, 471, 503, 581, 589, 615; acting career of, 256, 305, 306, 321, 679n; arranger for, used for Sam's Copa show, 569, 574, 576, 579; civil rights movement and, 490, 509, 511, 513, 588; Sam's relationship with, 250–51
Davis, Sammy, Sr., 302
Davis, Virginia, 142
Davis Sisters, 148, 159
Dawson, Jim, 186
Day, Bobby, 277
Dean, Walter, 506
Decca Records, 200, 207
Dee, Joey, 390
Dee, Sandra, 544
Defiant Ones, The, 256
Del Vikings, 214
Dennis, Fred "Diddy," 117–18, 226–27, 244–45, 246, 301
Derby Records, 441, 458
"Desire Me," 194
Devore, Sy, 176, 242, 404, 471
Dew, Joan, 615–16, 629
Diddley, Bo, 347
D'Imperio, Joe, 507–9; "A Change Is Gonna Come" and, 550, 551–52, 588; Allen Klein's negotiations with, 508–9, 514, 515, 517–20, 525, 528; personality and demeanor of, 507–8; Sam's return to Copa and, 564–65, 585
Dion, 347, 393, 521
discrimination, *see* racial prejudice
Dixie Hummingbirds, 107, 120, 148, 402, 444
Dixon, Luther, 444
Dolphin, John, 186–87, 249
Dolphin's of Hollywood, 180, 186, 187, 194, 672n
Domino, Fats, 86, 87, 113, 144, 149, 154, 158, 189,

278, 330–32, 335, 336, 338, 373, 460, 491, 508
Dominoes, 84, 175–76, 230, 234
Don and Dewey, 208
"(Don't Fight It) Feel It," 373–74, 381, 384, 431, 685n
"Don't Make Me Over," 469, 480
"Don't You Know," 306, 319
DooTone Records, 187
"Dorothy On My Mind," 339
Dorsey, Thomas A., 4, 20, 69–70, 297, 343
Dot Records, 465
Douglas, Mike, 553
Downey, Morton, 160–61, 166, 586
"Do You Remember?," 263–64, 457
"Dragnet for Jesus," 113
Drifters, 221, 230–31, 243, 326, 393, 475, 481
Drinkard Singers, 475
DuBois, W.E.B., xiii, 4
Dubs, 221
Dunbar, Paul Laurence, 446, 459
Dupree, Cornell, 451, 455
Duroff, Nate, 299
DuSable High School, Chicago, 35, 38, 61, 77–78, 83, 91
Dylan, Bob, 510–11, 512, 586

Eaglin, Snooks, 336
"Earth Angel," 185, 187
E.B. Marks Music, 319
Ebony, 61, 220, 221, 231, 464, 551, 611, 636
Eckstine, Billy, 84, 250, 271
Eddy, Duane, 347, 353
Ed Sullivan Show, The, 91, 202, 203–4, 211–12, 218, 473, 555
Eisenhower, Dwight, 202
Ellington, Duke, 271, 372
Ellis, Steve, 558–59
EMI, 388, 564
"End of My Journey," 96
Epic Records, 189

Epstein, Brian, 430, 564
Eric (Barbara's "adopted" child), 544–45, 545, 650
"Ernestine," 442
Ernie Freeman Orchestra, 222
Ertegun, Ahmet, 88, 130, 131, 149, 230, 307
Essex Productions, 518
European tour (1962), 422–31, 426; Little Richard and, 422–428, 433; Sam's interviews during, 428–30; Sam's showmanship in, 427; song inspired during, 428
Evans, Clay, 141–42, 633
Evans, Ray, 239
Evans, Sticks, 581, 592
Everly, Phil, 231, 571
Everly Brothers, 227, 231, 233–34, 596, 597
"Everybody Loves to Cha Cha Cha," 268–70, 278–79, 282, 283, 405, 604
"Every Day Every Way," 300
"Every Time I Feel the Spirit," 323

Fabares, Shelley, 571
Fairfield Four, 35, 42, 57
Falcons, 288, 609
Famous Blue Jays, 19, 30, 34, 35, 36, 71, 78, 90
Farley, J.J. (Jesse J.), 75, 77, 90, 114, 131, 134, 139, 147, 168, 213, 283, 296, 297, 310, 340, 544. *See also* Soul Stirrers
Farmer, Doris and Shirley, 43
Farmer, James, 509, 513
Farrell, Ernie, 501, 542
Faubus, Orval, 202
Faye, Marty, 198
"Feel It," 373–74, 381, 384, 431, 685n
Feld, Irvin, 221, 227–28, 229, 230, 287, 347, 564
Feld, Izzy, 227–28
Fellowship Baptist Church, Chicago, 141–42

Fields, Johnny, 99, 100, 143–44, 234
"15 Rounds for Jesus," 113
Film Daily, 467
Fire Next Time, The (Baldwin), xiii, 3
First Annual Summer Festival of Gospel Music (1955), 121, 122–28, 150
Fisher, Eddie, 515–16
Five Blind Boys of Alabama, 98–100, 104, 120, 146, 191, 236, 280, 436, 495–96; attitude toward change from gospel to pop and, 116; early career of, as Happyland Jubilee Singers, 48, 98–99; Sam's relationship with, 99–100
Five Blind Boys of Mississippi, 85, 90, 91–92, 94, 105, 110, 117, 142, 146, 148, 377; early career of, as Jackson Harmoneers, 46, 48, 98–99; records of, 83–84; Sam's early days with Soul Stirrers and, 73–75, 82; stylistic traits of, 73–74
Five Echoes, 119
"500 Miles," 568
"5" Royales, 348
Flairs, 185
Flames, 145
Flame Show Bar, Detroit, 255–56, 303, 376–77
Flamingos, 215, 278, 329
Floyd, Eddie, 290
Flying Clouds, 35, 42
Ford Startime, 353
Forest Lawn Memorial Park, Glendale, Calif., 636
"Forever," 156, 157, 158, 164, 206, 542
Forrest, Leon, 270
Foster, Paul, 60, 70, 72, 77, 79, 85, 91, 95, 96, 97, 114, 115, 131, 135, 138, 146, 147, 164, 188, 283, 296, 298, 299, 310, 516, 634; attitude toward change

from gospel to pop, 133; Cheeks' performances with Soul Stirrers and, 107, 108, 111; as lead singer, 62, 167, 340, 343, 344; Sam's departure from Soul Stirrers and, 170, 190; Sam's duets with, 124–27, 128, 407; on Sam's early days with Soul Stirrers, 75–76. *See also* Soul Stirrers
Foster, Stephen, 344
Fountain, Clarence, 99–100, 116, 117, 120, 164, 495–96
Four Lads, 214
Foxall, Art, 180–81
Foxx, Redd, 187, 217, 302
Foy, Eddie, 281, 282
Francis, Panama, 375
"Frankie and Johnny," 508, 581
Franklin, Aretha, 164–65, 203, 332, 365–67, 370, 442, 457, 651, 681n
Franklin, Bertha Lee, 618–19, 622, 623, 625, 627–28, 629, 647
Franklin, Rev. C.L., 114, 164, 332, 365, 366, 367, 507, 512
"Free At Last," 512
Freed, Alan, 149, 151, 185, 199, 228, 229–30, 234–35, 305, 439, 464
"Freedom Show of '64," 565
Freeman, Bobby, 607
Freeman, Ernie, 221, 222, 228, 250
Frizzell, Lefty, 234
Frye, Theodore, 142
Fuller, Blind Boy, 120

Gaines, Grady, 412–13, 439, 702n
Gale, Moe, 201
Gardner, Albert "Gentleman June," 350, 354, 368, 407, 408, 427, 430, 435, 480, 482, 496, 504, 552, 589, 611, 637; background of,

346; in first studio session with Sam, 592; hired as backup musician for Sam, 346–47; personality and demeanor of, 346–47; Sam's financial arrangements for, 535, 543, 606, 637; Sam's jealousy of Barbara and, 381; Sam's return to Copa and, 568, 569, 576, 586
Gas House Gang, 416, 417
Gay, Evelyn, 43, 166
Gaye, Marvin, 495, 516, 593
Gayle, Peter, 467
Gay Sisters (also Singers), 43
Geller, Larry, 643
General Artists Corporation (GAC), 564–65, 571, 586
General Electric Theater, 305–6, 321
George, Barbara, 420, 541
George, Cassietta (née Baker), 51, 124
"Georgia on My Mind," 372
Gershwin, George, 167, 173, 175–76, 251, 372
Getz, Stan, 575
Getz/Gilberto, 575
Gibbs, Georgia, 317
Gibbs, Richard, 298, 535
Gibson, "Jockey" Jack, 198, 419, 420
Gilberto, Astrud, 575
Gipson, Gertrude, 250, 273, 392, 442, 498, 533, 639, 645, 648
"Girl From Ipanema, The," 575, 576, 579, 580, 584
Glenn, Glen, 386, 387
"God Bless the Child," 271
Golden Chords, 155
Golden Gate Quartet, 20, 34
Golden Harps, 51
Goldmark, Goldie, 201
Goldsmith, Cliff, 237, 248, 347, 405, 460
Goldwater, Barry, 588, 605
"Good Golly Miss Molly," 207–10, 252

"Good Times," 535, 537–38, 539, 540, 571, 646

Gordy, Berry, 255, 288–89, 326, 420

Gordy, Gwen, 255

Gorgeous George (né Theophilus Odell George), 293, 456, 475–76, 479, 481, 496, 599, 602, 690n; after-show and, 601–3; on Castro's visit to Harlem, 348–49; sense of style of, 477–78

Gospelcade, 98–101

Gospel Caravan, 147–49, 152

Gospel Cavalcade, 98

Gospel Harmonettes, see Original Gospel Harmonettes

gospel music: emergence of rhythm and blues and, 84–85, 86–88; experience of, 122–24; market potential of, 83–84, 87, 104, 112–14, 116, 280; stylistic traits of, 4, 19–20, 31. See also specific performers and songs

Gospel Paraders, 402

Gospel Writer Junior Girls, 51

Gotch, Lee, Singers, 177, 206

Grant, Earl, 499

Grant, Jewell, 391

Gray, D. Overstreet, 614

Gray, John, 183, 204–5, 208, 294, 387–88

Grayson, Milton, 236, 281

Green, Freddie, 173

Green, Sonny, 39, 41

Green, William, 546

Greenberg, Florence, 444, 467, 468, 525, 529, 694n

Greenberg, Mary Jane, 444

Gregory, Dick, 490, 630

Griffin, Bessie, 295, 385, 635

Griffin, Merv, 690n

Guitar, Bonnie, 214

Guitar Shorty, 266

Guitar Slim (né Eddie Jones), 112, 113, 129

Gunter, Cornel, 185, 198

"Gypsy, The," 254

Hacienda Motel, Los Angeles, 617–19, 623, 702n

Haley, Alex, 563

Haley, Bill, 223, 225

Hall, René, 180, 186, 195, 216, 223, 248, 263, 268, 270, 297, 322, 398, 457, 504, 586, 608, 647–48; background of, 175–76; as backup musician, 175, 207, 342, 354, 607; "A Change Is Gonna Come" and, 547–48, 549, 550, 569; Sam's arrangements and, 175–76, 177, 206, 238, 271, 280, 321, 361, 362, 391, 405, 407, 421, 431, 458, 499, 537, 547–48, 549, 569, 579, 614, 615; Sam's death and, 620, 626, 634, 635, 636, 639–40, 641, 642; Sam's return to Copa and, 569, 579–80, 581, 583

Hall, Sugar, 216, 268, 392, 396, 405, 406, 635, 647–48; Sam's death and, 620, 623, 626, 634, 639–40

Halley, Michael, 545

Hamilton, George, IV, 227

Hamilton, Roy, 128, 130, 159, 189, 192, 252, 338, 478; civil rights movement and, 513; comeback of, 189; illness and premature retirement of, 149–50; Sam's tours with, 332, 333, 335; as Specialty Records artist, 112–13

Hampton, Lionel, 346, 354

Hancock, Hunter, 250

Haney, Carol, 221

Hank Moore Orchestra, 326, 327

Happyland Jubilee Singers, 48, 98–99. See also Five Blind Boys of Alabama

Harlem Square Club, Miami, 451–55, 460, 469, 585, 688n

Harmonettes, see Original Gospel Harmonettes

Harmonizing Four, 148, 159, 191, 665n

Harmony Kings, 47

Harper, Toni, 396

Harris, Eleanor, 553

Harris, Harlean, 220, 224, 355, 356

Harris, Jet, 423, 426, 426, 427

Harris, R.H. (Rebert), 48, 73, 77, 83, 108, 309; Christland Singers and, 78, 90, 110, 133, 134, 135, 145, 146, 657n; first heard by Sam, 25–26; National Quartet Convention and, 35–36, 47; Sam compared to, 33; on Sam's singing style, 78; SAR Records session of, 402; Soul Stirrers left by, 59, 60–62, 63, 65–68, 74, 75–76, 111, 169; stylistic traits of, 4, 25–26, 31, 33, 59–60, 94

Harris, Thurston, 221–22

Harris, Tony, 155, 214

Harry Fox Agency, 204, 465

Haskell, Jimmie, 517

"Having a Party," 414, 445, 455, 569, 581; recording of, 405–6; as Sam's closing number, 413, 433, 469, 482, 522–23, 531

Hecht-Hill-Lancaster, 517–18

Heilbut, Tony, 60, 61, 78, 107

"He'll Make a Way," 108–9

Henderson, Doug "Jocko," 199, 463–64, 466, 467–69, 473

Henderson, Herbert, 276

Hendrix, Jimmy (Jimi), 532–33, 602–3, 695n, 700n

Herald Attractions, 60, 80–81, 98, 104–5, 153, 162

Herman's Hermits, 598, 651

Hermosa Music, 270

"He's a Cousin of Mine," 591–92, 598

"He's Been a Shelter," 298, 516

"He's My Friend Until the End," 96, 97, 111

"He's My Guide," 128

"He's My Rock," 72

"He Understands, He'll Say, 'Well Done,'" 96

"Hey Hey, The Gang's All Here," 561, 562

"Hey Team," 194, 671*n*

Hibbler, Al, 304, 490, 691*n*

Hicks, Evelyn, 105

Hicks, Paula, 105

Highway Missionary Baptist Church, Chicago, 5, 31, 41, 44

Highway QCs, 5–6, 28–34, 30, 36–38, 42–59, 71, 73, 77–78, 133, 165, 170, 215, 255, 309, 344, 345, 633, 646; after Sam's departure, 119–20, 191, 197, 234, 411; formation of, 28–31; managers changed by, 45, 50, 54, 58–59; Memphis sojourn of, 50–53, 54; name of, 31; personnel changes in, 43–44; radio broadcasts of, 49–50, 51–52, 55; record deal sought by, 42, 48, 52; rivalries in, 48–49, 53; road tours of, 45–47, 49–53, 57, 493; R.B. Robinson and, 37–38, 42, 62, 63, 75; Sam's departure from, 59–64, 169; Sam's incarceration and, 56–57, 58; Sam's reunion with, 234; training of, 29–31, 38, 75

Higuera Music Publishing Co., 196, 204–5

Hils, Clifford, 459

Hines, J. Earle, 90

Hirshey, Gerri, 333

"His Precious Love," 633

Hit Kit, 308

Hits of the '50s, 323

Hodge, Alex, 185, 277

Hodge, Gaynel, 185, 186, 277, 322

Holiday, Billie, 254, 270–72, 279, 499

Holly, Buddy, 230

Hollywood Flames, 300

Holy Wonders, 58, 90

"Home," 539

Hooker, John Lee, 84

Hooven, Joe, 460, 539

Hopkins, Linda, 217

Horne, Lena, 490, 509, 588

Hoskins, Leroy "Duck," 23, 90, 91, 170, 188, 214, 215, 226, 255, 303, 304, 309, 376, 379–80, 416, 434, 593

Houseboat, 225, 239

"House of the Rising Sun," 596

Houston Informer, 224, 231

Howard, Camille, 69

Howard, Ira, 553

Howe, Bones, 392, 443, 571

Howe, Buddy, 564, 575, 576, 578, 579

"How Far Am I From Canaan?" 72–73, 74, 85, 86, 107–8

"How I Got Over," 511

Hoy, Raymond, 29, 39

Hugg, Dick "Huggy Boy," 180, 187, 242, 250

Hughes, Jimmy, 599

Hugo and Luigi, *see* Creatore, Luigi; Peretti, Hugo

Hulbert, Maurice "Hot Rod," 199, 463

Hunt, Tommy, 444

Hurricane Room, Wildwood, N.J., 508–9

Hurst, Walter E., 297, 300, 332, 391, 405, 648

Hutchins, Chris, 424, 425

Hychew, Elgin, 337, 338, 523–24

"I Ain't Gonna Cheat On You No More," 460

I Am the Greatest (Clay), 505, 531, 534

"I Can't Stop Loving You," 414

"I Cover the Waterfront," 254

"I Don't Want to Cry," 150, 156, 157, 167–68

"If I Got My Ticket," 566–67

"If I Had a Hammer," 580, 583, 589

"I Found a Love," 609

"I Gopher You," 278

"I Got a New Home," 153

"I Got a Woman," 113, 120, 165, 372

"I Have a Friend Above All Others," 96–97, 124

"I Know," 420, 541

"I'll Always Be in Love With You," 278, 300, 428

"I'll Come Running Back to You," 150, 158, 167, 168, 206, 212, 322, 665*n*

"I'll Never Come Running Back to You," 322–23, 381, 685*n*

"(I Love You) For Sentimental Reasons," 27, 194, 212, 223, 441, 581, 582

"I'm All Right," 300

"I'm in the Mood for Love," 591

"I'm Just a Country Boy," 344, 517

"I'm on the Firing Line," 70

Imperial Records, 154, 330–32, 373, 387

Impressions, 588–89

"I'm So Glad (Trouble Don't Last Always)," 115

"I'm Stickin' With You," 466

"I'm Thankful," 298

"I Need You Now," 167–68

Ink Spots, 27, 33, 94, 144, 230, 254, 481, 606

Interlandi, Frank, 310, 679*n*–80*n*

Isley Brothers, 444, 603

"It Must Be Jesus," 113

"It's All Over Now," 566, 567, 587–88, 598

"It's All Right," 431

"It's Got the Whole World Shaking," 606–7

Itson, M.L., 54–55, 56, 57, 58–59, 62
"I've Been 'Buked and I've Been Scorned," 510
"I've Got a New Home," 111
"I've Got Heaven On My Mind," 339
"I Want to Go Home," 393–95, 404–5
"I Want You to Know," 281
"I Wish You Love," 440–41

J. Walter Thompson Agency, 515
Jackie and Gayle, 596
Jackson, Chuck, 418, 444, 467, 469, 583
Jackson, Mahalia, 3–4, 34–35, 61, 70, 84, 91–92, 96, 112, 114, 128, 152, 197, 328, 352, 374, 531; Highway QCs and, 5, 512; at March on Washington, 511, 512
Jackson Harmoneers, 48, 98–99. *See also* Five Blind Boys of Mississippi
Jagger, Mick, 587
James, Etta, 284, 317, 333, 499, 593
Jamison, Agnes (née Cook), *see* Cook, Agnes
Jamison, Eddie, 214
Jan and Arnie, 252
Jan and Dean, 392
J&M Studio, New Orleans, 86, 113, 129, 154
"Jeanie With the Light Brown Hair," 345
Jefferson, Mr. and Mrs. (Forrest Hotel), 611
Jerry Lewis Show, The, 533–34
Jesse and Marvin, 185
Jessie, Obediah "Young," 185, 252
"Jesus, I'll Never Forget," 108
Jesus Be a Fence Around Me, 359–60
"Jesus Be a Fence Around Me," 343, 344, 360, 385
"Jesus Gave Me Water," 34,

70–72, 73, 74, 75, 76–78, 83, 86
Jesus Is the Light of the World, 49–50
Jet, 309, 352–53, 358, 367, 551
"Jim Dandy," 231, 351
Jimmy Dean Show, The, 225
Joe Parnello Trio, 254
John, "Little" Willie, 144, 145, 189, 213, 239, 250, 544; arrests of, 264, 605; as child in family gospel group, 88, 144; gambling of, 335; personality and demeanor of, 333–35, 350; Sam's relationship with, 334–35; Sam's tours with, 332, 333–35, 348, 350, 351–52, 521, 522–23; stylistic traits of, 333–34; Upsetters as backup band for, 251, 408, 412
John, Mable, 88–89, 255–56, 332–33, 334–35
Johnnie "Two Voice," *see* Morisette, Johnnie "Two Voice"
Johnny Canyon, 441
Johnson, Buddy, 147, 348
Johnson, Lonnie, 194
Johnson, Lyndon, 588, 605
Johnson, Marv, 288, 348, 350, 630
Johnson, Plas, 198
Johnson, Ray, 443, 458
Jones, Charles Price, 9
Jones, E. Rodney, 196
Jones, Gloria, 270
Jones, Helen "Sookie," 45, 48, 418
Jones, Jimmy, 159
Jones, Joe, 327, 346
Jones, Little Johnny, 190, 191
Jones, Marvin, 5, 30, 46, 55, 57, 58, 78, 418, 655n; early career of, 43–44; Highway QCs joined by, 44–45; on QCs' managers, 45, 46, 54; on QCs' Memphis stay, 50, 51, 52–53; on rivalry

within QCs, 48–49; Sam's move to Soul Stirrers and, 63, 77. *See also* Highway QCs
Jones, Quincy, 121
Jordan, Louis, 84, 221, 250, 535, 537
Jordan, Lowell, 386
"Joy, Joy to My Soul," 85
Juke Box Records, 69
Junior Destroyers, 23, 255, 309
"Just a Closer Walk With Thee," 635
"Just Another Day," 85, 86
"Just For You," 281, 296, 388–89

Kags Music, 329, 352, 441, 442, 475, 571, 598, 640, 695n; after Sam's death, 650; J.W. Alexander's passion for, 278; BMI and, 356, 495; Crain's role in, 278, 508, 530; demo sessions for, 280–81, 362; founding of, 249, 278; Keen Records and, 270, 324, 388; Allen Klein as administrator of, 508; offices of, 332; RCA's payment of royalties to, 494, 514, 519, 524, 528; Sam made partner in, 267, 278
Kalcheim, Harry, 353–54
Kapralik, Dave, 505–7, 521, 561, 692n
Karras, Andrew, 182, 183, 192, 193
Karras, Paul, 182, 183, 208
Karriem, Osman (formerly Archie Robinson), 557, 559
Kasem, Casey, 198
K-Doe, Ernie, 336, 338
Keane, Bob, 180–81, 188, 192–94, 207, 246, 670n, 671n, 672n
Keane, Elsa, 181, 182, 192

Keel, Howard, 553
Keen Records, 212, *240*, *241*,
    242, 271, 281, 392, 499;
    Andex subsidiary of, 192,
    207, 224, 280, 671*n*;
    Barbara's job at, 261;
    Bumps Blackwell's
    difficulties at, 247–48,
    271–72, 280; cash-flow
    problems of, 295, 304;
    demise of, 304, 308;
    expansion of, 207, 236;
    founding of, 180–83, 193,
    215; Bob Keane's
    departure from, 192–94;
    ownership of Sam's
    publishing and, 248,
    270; Art Rupe's legal
    dispute with, 193,
    204–10, 243, 246–47,
    262, 277, 294; Sam's
    acquisition of masters
    from, 384, 386, 387–89,
    404; Sam's break with,
    294–95, 296, 304–5,
    308; Sam's contract with,
    194, 248, 296, 304;
    Sam's decision to go
    with, 184, 189; Sam's
    first album for, 207, 216;
    Sam's first single for, 193,
    194–97, 198–205, 235
    (*see also* "You Send Me");
    Sam's lawsuit against,
    384, 386, 685*n*; Sam's
    recording sessions for,
    194, 239–42, 268–72,
    279–80; Valiants' "Good
    Golly Miss Molly" and,
    207–10; "Wonderful
    World" and, 279, 324
"Keep On Pushin'," 588–89
Kelso, Jackie, 391
Kennedy, John F., 352, 492,
    530–31, 532, 555
Kenny, Bill, 27, 33, 231
Kessel, Barney, 458, 460
Keyes, Johnny, 27, 160, 197
KFWB, 388
KGFJ, 187, 273
Kilgallen, Dorothy, 336, 352
Kilgore, Merle, 456

Kilgore, Theola, 352, 496
King, B.B., 50, 87, 113, 129,
    145, 159, 160, 393, 634
King, Ben E., 446, 447, 496
King, Bob, 120–21, 125, 128,
    133
King, Carole, 455
King, Earl, 336
King, Martin Luther, Jr., 493,
    555, 588, 609; address of,
    to 1962 NAACP
    Convention, 411–12;
    assassination of, 651;
    Birmingham church
    bombing and, 521–22;
    Birmingham
    demonstrations and,
    489–90, 491–92, 509;
    March on Washington
    and, 509, 511–12
King, Martin Luther, Sr., 352,
    682*n*
King Kasuals, 602. *See also*
    Jimmy Hendrix
Kingpins, 435–36, 439,
    444–45, 453. *See also*
    Curtis, King
King Records, 395
Kirk, Andy, 187
Kirk, Dick, 357–58
Kirshner, Donnie, 465, 466,
    692*n*
Klein, Allen, 464–70,
    504–6, 524–26, 528–29,
    533, 538, 549–55, 577,
    588, 597–98, 605, 646,
    648; audits conducted
    by, 465–67; background
    of, 464–65; BMI audit
    and, 473, 474, 495, 691*n*;
    British business interests
    of, 564, 571, 598, 650; "A
    Change Is Gonna Come"
    and, 550, 551–54; at Clay-
    Liston fight, 554–55,
    556–57, 558; Columbia
    approached by, 505, 506,
    517; deal negotiated with
    RCA by, 517–21, 524, 528;
    Jocko Henderson and,
    463–70; independent
    production concept and,

517–19; managerial
    responsibilities taken on
    by, 524–25; racial
    prejudice, resentment of,
    554–55; RCA audit and,
    473–74, 495, 498, 504–5,
    508, 514–15, 519–20, 524,
    525–26, 528; Rolls-Royce
    given to Sam by, 577,
    580–81, 586–87; Sam's
    agency contract and,
    564–65, 571; Sam's
    artistic freedom and, 538,
    540, 549–50; Sam's
    business dealings with,
    494–95, 504–5, 508,
    524–25, 565–66, 691*n*;
    Sam's death and, 622,
    623–24, 625, 629–30,
    632, 643–44, 647, 650;
    Sam's first encounters
    with, 468–70; Sam's
    relationship with,
    524–25, 552–53, 564,
    579–81, 597–98, 701*n*;
    Sam's return to Copa
    and, 554, 564–65, 569,
    571–81, 583, 585, 586;
    Vincent's death and, 502;
    "Yeah Man" and, 597–98
Klein, Betty, 468, 554, 557, 581
Klein, George, 604–5
Klein, Robin, 468, 502
Knight, Gladys, 289,
    290–91, 292
Knight, Marie, 217
Knight, Sonny, 121, 122, 178
Knox, Buddy, 465–66
KOWL, 90
KPOP, 195, 202–3
Kramer, Gary, 171
KTLA, 242

LaBaux, Walter, 79
Laboe, Art, 195, 202–3, 221,
    399
Lancaster, Burt, 510, 518
Lance, Major, 630
L&M cigarettes, 515
Lappas, Dino, 236
Larks, 147

Larry Finley Show, The, 242
Last Angry Man, The, 256
Lastie, Melvin, 420, 542
"Last Mile of the Way," 128
"Laughin' and Clownin'," 458, 459
"Lawdy Miss Clawdy," 86, 87, 88, 97
"Lead Me Jesus," 385–86
"Lead Me On," 355
Leak, A.R., Colonial Chapel, Chicago, 630–32
Learn, Paul, 589–90
Lee, Beverly, 444
Lee, Cornelia, 50
Leeds, Alan, 600–601
Lee Gotch Singers, 177, 206
Lettermen, 389, 586
"Let the Good Times Roll," 537
Levert, Clinton, 108, 281
Levy, Morris, 317–18, 466
Lewis, David Levering, 512
Lewis, Jerry, 285, 533–34
Lewis, Jerry Lee, 214, 230, 234–35, 393
Lewis, John, 509
Lewis, Willie, 284
Liberty Records, 404
Liggins, Jimmy, 69
Liggins, Joe, 69
Ligon, Alfred, 692*n*
Ligon, Willie Joe, 340–41, 682*n*
Liston, Sonny, 506–7, 531, 554–59, 590
Little Anthony and the Imperials, 300
"Little Red Rooster," 457, 458, 499, 544
Little Richard, 156, 220, 247, 250, 412, 439, 597; backing band of, 211, 251, 334; Beatles' dates with, 430–31; Bumps Blackwell's work with, 129, 144, 151, 154, 162, 176, 177, 182; "Good Golly Miss Molly" and, 207–10; oversize Bible of, 427–28; "retirement" from show business by, 171, 334, 668*n*; return to rock 'n' roll of, 422–25,

688*n*; Art Rupe's contract with, 171, 174, 178; Sam's European tour with, 422–28, 426, 430–31, 433, 458; showmanship of, 425–26, 433; Specialty left by, 189
Little Rock, Ark., 202, 233, 259, 326–27, 369
"Little Things You Do," 249, 270, 281
Little Walter, 113–14
Live at the Copa, 585–86, 598
Livingston, Alan, 518
Livingston, Jay, 239
London American Records, 207
"London By Night," 323
"Lonely Avenue," 153
"Lonely Island," 194, 263
"Lonesome Road, The," 223
"Look," 551, 556
"Lookin' For a Love," 403, 422, 472, 488
"Looking Back," 546
Look Up!, 207
Los Angeles County Fair (1957), 195–96
"Lost and Lookin'," 459–60
"Lost Someone," 438
"Louie Louie," 185
Louis, Joe, 507, 509, 558
"Lovable," 155–57, 159, 160, 164, 165–66, 168, 206, 460, 666*n*
Love, Darlene, 269–70, 277
Love, Dorothy, 121, 123, 143, 191, 663*n*
"Love I Lost, The," 150
"Lover, The," 342
"Lover Come Back to Me," 271
"Love You Most of All," 262
Lowe, Bernie, 200, 344
Lowe, Sammy, 342, 362
"Lucille," 425–26, 597
Lucy, Autherine, 139
Lyles, Cleo, 255, 303
Lymon, Frankie, 144, 149, 230, 605
Lynn, Mickey, 374

Mabley, "Moms," 468
Machat, Marty, 508, 515, 524, 528, 627, 628, 629–30, 644
Mack, Cecil, 591
"Made For Me," 388–89
Magnificent Montague, 330, 445–48, 449, 459, 473, 591; Africana collection of, 446; L.C.'s career and, 159, 255, 277, 445, 446, 457, 605; New York all-star show promoted by, 446–47; as rhyming jock, 196, 445; Sam's interview with, 447–48, 460
Magnificents, 159, 160, 168, 196, 197, 446
Magnolia Ballroom, Atlanta, 145, 202, 243, 258
Malcolm X, 349, 531–32, 537, 555–61, 563
Malloy Artists Management, 441
Malloy Music, 332, 519, 524, 528
March on Washington (1963), 509–12, 513
Marcus, Joe, 453
Marek, George, 414, 507, 534–35, 538
Margo, Nat, 287, 335
Marks, E.B., Music, 319
Marlo, George, 358
Marrying Mary, 591
Martin, Dean, 285, 321, 344, 501
Martin, Reba, 32, 48
Martin, Roberta, Singers, 4, 5, 35, 43
Martin, Sallie, 4, 35
Martindale, Wink, 604
Marvin and Johnny, 185
"Mary, Mary Lou," 223, 225, 260
Masingill, O.B., 150, 168
Mason, Charles Harrison, 9–10
Mastin, Will, 251
Matassa, Cosimo, 86, 113, 129, 154–55, 156–57, 168, 175

Mathis, Johnny, 188, 220, 254, 275, 501, 509, 544, 692n
May, Annette, 124
May, Brother Joe, 67, 83, 121, 123, 128, 148, 163, 197, 408
Mayfield, Clarence, 79, 93, 102, 117
Mayfield, Curtis, 588–89
Mayfield, Percy, 69
MCA, 181
McCardell, Rev. McKinley, 109
McCurn, George "Oopie," 242, 268, 392, 504, 516–17, 570, 571, 634; in Pilgrim Travelers, 185, 257, 264; singing backup for Sam, 421; single produced by Sam on, 404
McDaniel, Gene, 446
McGrath, Camilla, 584, 590–91
McGrath, Earl, 583–84, 586, 590–91, 597
McKinley, Larry, 419–20, 477
McNair, Barbara, 302
McPhatter, Clyde, 104, 129, 130, 144, 147, 243, 277, 323, 326, 594; Atlantic left by, 307; background and early career of, 230–31; in Biggest Show of Stars tours, 189, 227, 229, 230–34, 235; civil rights movement and, 337–38, 352, 368–71, 490, 494, 509, 679n, 682n; Sam's interest in private views of, 231–33; Sam's Supersonic tours with, 365, 366, 368–71, 422; stylistic traits of, 84, 230, 231
McSweeney, Judge John R., 56
"Mean Old World," 167, 459
Medlock, James, 25–26, 31
"Meet Me at Mary's Place," 546–47
"Meet Me at the Twistin' Place," 396–97, 402, 546

Mellonaires, 143
Melniker, Ben, 467
"Memory Lane," 524, 539
Memphis, Tenn., 50–53, 54, 368–71, 604–5
Mercury Records, 317, 323
"Mercy, Mercy," 594
Messner brothers, 121
MGM, 307, 467
Mickey and Sylvia, 221
Midnighters, *see* Ballard, Hank
Mighty Clouds of Joy, 340–41, 682n
Mike Douglas Show, The, 553
Milburn, Amos, 395
Millar, Bill, 230, 426
Miller, Don, 311
Miller, Gwendolyn, 311, 417, 648
Miller, Howard, 214
Miller, Mitch, 353
Miller, William Robert, 511
Millinder, Lucky, 84
Mills Brothers, 172, 229, 254
Milsap, Sam, 215
Milton, Roy, 69
Mr. Soul, 435, 440–41, 458
Mitchell, Guy, 207
Mitchell, Herman, 27
Mitchell, Sonny, 546
Mohawk, Dolores, *see* Cooke, Dolores "Dee Dee"
Monarch Record Manufacturing Plant, 299
"Money Honey," 104, 231
Monotones, 227
"Moonlight in Vermont," 207
Moore, Hank, 326, 327
Moore, Rev. Gatemouth, 49–50, 165
Moore, Sam, 143
Morisette, Johnnie "Two Voice," 334, 337, 375, 381, 396, 415, 439, 458, 471, 486, 516–17, 544, 546, 566, 570, 635; on road with Sam, 410, 411, 412; Sam's feelings for, 334, 516–17; SAR Records sessions of,

322–23, 330, 339, 396–97, 402, 442, 443, 461, 541, 543; stylistic traits of, 322
Morris, Leo, 327–28, 335, 338, 339, 346, 488–89
Most, Mickie, 598
Motortown Revue, 495
Motown Records, 326
Mt. Lebanon Singers, 230
Mount Sinai Baptist Church, Los Angeles, 634–36
"Move On Up a Little Higher," 3, 34
Muhammad, Elijah, 531, 555, 557, 561, 563
Muhammad, Herbert, 593, 630–31
Muhammad Speaks, 531
Murray, Bill, 370
Murray, Kathryn, 260
Murray the K, 587
Musicians Union strike (1948), 67
"My Babe," 114
"My Grandfather's Clock," 345, 499
My Kind of Blues, 372–73
Myles, Warren, 156

Nash, Henry, 602
Nash, Herman, 80, 145, 146, 190, 220, 385–86
Nash, Johnny, 460
Nashville Teens, 598
National Association for the Advancement of Colored People (NAACP), 233, 337–38, 352, 469, 491, 523, 556; boycott of segregated show and, 368–71; Martin Luther King's speech at 1962 Convention of, 411–12; Legal Defense Fund of, 565
National Association of Radio Announcers (NARA), 419–20, 510, 541
National Interdenominational Singers Alliance, 90–91

National Quartet
 Convention, 35–36, 47,
 90
Nation of Islam, *see* Black
 Muslims
NBC, 260, 353
"Nearer My God to Thee," 34,
 115
"Nearer to Thee," 115, 116,
 125–27, 145, 341, 343,
 443
Nelson, Ricky, 280, 332, 396,
 517
New Orleans, 336–37,
 523–24
New Pilgrim Travelers, 278
New Yorker, 449–51
New York Journal-American,
 335–36
New York Times, 527, 556,
 561, 582, 584, 586
"Night," 319
Night Beat, 458–59, 499, 528
Nightingales, *see* Sensational
 Nightingales
Nobleaires, 37, 57
"Nobody Knows the Trouble
 I've Seen," 459
"Nobody Knows You When
 You're Down and Out,"
 568
"Nobody Loves Me Like You,"
 278, 329
Nola Recording Studio, New
 York, 149, 168
"No One Can Take Your
 Place," 279–80
Norfolk Singers, 62
"No Second Time," 539
"Nothing Can Change This
 Love," 421–22, 433, 448,
 454–55, 569

Oberbeck, Rex, 182, 183, 192,
 208
Ocean's 11, 321, 679n
O'Flaherty, Terence, 375
"Oh Mary, Don't You Weep,"
 546
Okey Dokey, 87, 198
Oldham, Andrew Loog, 587
Old Ship of Zion, The, 147

"Ol' Man River," 207, 223,
 303
Olympics, 248, 347, 460
"One More River to Cross,"
 114, 116
One Night Stand, 451–55
"Only Sixteen," 280–81, 296
"Only Time Will Tell," 444
Oopie, *see* McCurn, George
 "Oopie"
Original Gospel
 Harmonettes, 67, 121,
 123, 128, 143, 159, 191,
 236, 280. *See also* Love,
 Dorothy
Orioles, 84, 96, 104
Orlons, 496
Osser, Glenn, 318, 324
Otis, Johnny, 211
Ott, Horace, 434, 440–41,
 458, 561
"Our Father," 34, 74, 83–84
"Our Years Together," 645,
 704n
Outler, Jimmie, 340–41, 343,
 344, 345, 386, 450,
 516–17, 546

Page, Patti, 221, 586
Paige, Grandmother
 (Barbara's grandmother),
 39, 41, 93, 301, 303
Palm Café, Harlem, New
 York, 284–85
Palmer, Earl, 175, 322, 363,
 391, 398, 399, 443, 548,
 570, 607, 608
Paramount Gospel Singers,
 339
Paramount Pictures, 305
Paris Sisters, 389
Parker, Colonel Tom, 581
Parker, Little Junior, 137,
 139
Parks, Rosa, 651
"Part Time Love," 612
"Party Doll," 466
Paschal family (Atlanta), 609
"Patsy, The," 305–6, 321
Patterson, Floyd, 506
Pauling, Lowman, 348
Paulsen, Don, 584–85

payola, 97–98, 171, 305, 419,
 464
"Peace in the Valley," 70, 75,
 76, 658n–59n
Peacock Records, 83, 85,
 110–11, 129, 137
Peale, David, 20
Pelletreau, M.K., 625,
 639–40, 643
Penguins, 185
"Peppermint Twist," 390
Peretti, Hugo, 315–21, *316*,
 323, 414, 433, 434, 458,
 466, 538, 585, 586, 650;
 absence from Sam's West
 Coast sessions, 361;
 background of, 306,
 315–18; Jess Rand's
 negotiations on behalf of
 Sam with, 306–8;
 recording of Sam's live
 show and, 451–53; Sam's
 recording sessions and,
 315, 318–21, 323–24,
 325–26, 342–43, 344–46,
 348, 354, 371–73; Sam's
 television show and, 375;
 Sam's "theme"-oriented
 albums and, 323–24,
 371–73
Perkins, Rev. Percell, 73–74,
 99
Pharaohs, 185
Phillips, Marvin, 185
"Pilgrim of Sorrow," 128
Pilgrim Travelers, 47, 55, 61,
 91–92, 124, 148, 185, 321,
 377, 537; Cadillac
 outfitted with piano for,
 111; car accident and,
 265–66; change from
 gospel to pop, 236, 257,
 264; civil rights
 movement and, 139;
 decline of, 152, 153,
 161–62, 278;
 incorporation of, 81; Lou
 Rawls and, 185, 224, 264,
 265, 266; records of, 60,
 67, 71, 83, 116, 128, 152,
 207, 224, 236; on road
 with Sam's pop act, 252,
 257–58, 262, 264–67; on

road with Soul Stirrers, 35, 38, 73–77, 90, 98, 104, 121, 169; stylistic traits of, 71–72, 73; Kylo Turner's departure from, 161–62

"Piper, The," 592–93

Pips, 289, 292

Platters, 137, 144, 164, 185, 220, 557

"Please Answer Me," 457

"Please Please Please," 145

Plimpton, George, 560

PM East/PM West, 374–76, 684n

Podell, Jules, 219, 224, 554, 564–65, 586

Pohlman, Ray, 443

Poindexter, Malcolm, 217

Poitier, Sidney, 256, 509, 510, 586, 597

Pollock, Dave, 294

Poppa, Lotsa, 411, 456, 476, 478–80, 609–11

Porter, Cole, 271

Portraits in Bronze, 295, 385

Postif, François, 351

"Pray," 344, 345

prejudice, *see* racial prejudice

Presley, Elvis, 159–60, 196, 197, 231, 307, 383, 414, 429, 551, 581, 604, 643

Preston, Billy, 424, 458, 460, 635

Price, Leo, 246

Price, Lloyd, 102, 129, 178, 220, 247, 326, 334, 347, 433, 468, 589; audition of, for Art Rupe, 86–87; civil rights movement and, 513; Allen Klein's audits for, 466–67; "Lawdy Miss Clawdy" and, 86, 87, 88, 97; Sam's first encounters with, 100–101

Pride, Freddie, 326

Pridgon, Lithofayne, xiv, 213, 220, 284, 285, 288, 349, 381–82, 434, 435, 503, 532–33, 695n

Prinz, Rabbi Joachim, 511

Progressive Moaners, 13, 14

Prophet John the Conqueror, 235

Prudhomme, Beverly and Betty, 195–96, 374, 397–400, 399, 460, 475, 546, 624

Prysock, Arthur, 326, 327, 337, 544

"Put Me Down Easy," 457

Pye, Brad, Jr., 559

Quartet Union of Indiana, 47–48

racial prejudice, 523, 560, 588–89, 643; James Baldwin's *New Yorker* essay and, 449–51; Jesse Belvin's death and, 326–27; Birmingham church bombing and, 521–22, 523; Cook family's experiences of, 16, 26; end of segregation in Las Vegas and, 679n; experienced by black entertainers in South, 80, 138–39, 228, 259, 261, 326–27, 336–37, 338, 353, 368–71, 480–81, 490–91, 522, 526–28, 683n–84n; Allen Klein's resentment of, 554–55; Little Rock school integration and, 202, 233, 369; Sam's ambition and, 335–36, 494; Sam's experiences of, 52–53, 57, 259, 261, 306, 336–37, 368–71, 369, 480–81, 493, 494, 522, 526–28, 554–55; segregated performances and, 228, 259, 327, 338, 368–71, 480–81, 490, 683n–84n; urban rioting and, 588, 590–91. *See also* civil rights movement

Racusin, Norman, 514, 515

Radio Four, 164

Radio label, 397

Radio Recorders, Los Angeles, 174, 189, 323

Ramsey, Thurman, 159

Rand, Bonnie, 310, 329, 389, 392, 620

Rand, Jess, 254, 274, 284–85, 352, 357, 361, 428, 433, 525–26, 586–87, 614, 615; J.W. Alexander's relationship with, 330, 356, 359; background of, 272–73; BMI and, 356–59; Sammy Davis Jr. and, 222, 250–51, 256, 272, 285, 305–6, 359; decorating of Sam's homes and, 310, 389; Keen masters and, 388; "My Grandfather's Clock" and, 345, 499; as PR man, 222, 223, 242, 250–51; recommendation of lawyer by, 295, 304; role in teaming of Sam with Hugo and Luigi, 306–8, 315; Sam's abilities assessed by, 272, 273; Sam's acting career and, 305–6, 321, 441; Sam's break with, 516, 689n; Sam's column ghosted by, 335–36; Sam's Copa show and, 222, 223, 225; Sam's dealings with William Morris and, 308–9, 311–12, 353–54; Sam's death and, 620, 634; Sam's management deal with, 272–73, 498, 677n; Sam's record contracts and, 306–7, 311, 376, 383–84; Sam's relationship with, 273, 284, 285, 309, 329–30, 356–59, 375–76, 389, 441, 473, 498, 516, 533, 587, 701n; Sam's television appearances and, 305–6, 321, 374–76; Vincent's death and, 501

Rand, Junior, 29

Randle, Bill, 196, 198

Randolph, A. Philip, 509, 511

Randolph, Jim, 250

Randy's Record Shop, Gallatin, Tenn., 71

Raul Trana and the Nicaraguans, 237

Ravens, 96

Rawls, Dr. Louis, 632–33

Rawls, Eunice, 280

Rawls, Lou, *66*, 91, 249, 259, 260, 274, 277, 504, 571, 614, 672*n*; as background singer on SAR Records sessions, 398, 399, 400; in car accident, 265, 266, 268; early career of, 37, 58, 90; family background of, 37; in Pilgrim Travelers, 185, 224, 264, 265, 266; on Sam in Highway QCs days, 6, 37, 58; Sam's death and, 620, 634, 635; singing backup for Sam, 396, 405, 406, 407; solo career of, 278, 392, 401–2, 442, 460, 544

Ray, Johnnie, 255

Razaf, Andy, 473

RCA Records, 316, 318, 319, 323, 345, 374, 380, 384, 436, 441, 444, 457–58, 473, 551, 571, 588, 598, 646, 648, 650, 681*n*; "A Change Is Gonna Come" and, 550, 551–52, 553–54; deal negotiated by Allen Klein with, 517–21, 524, 528; Joe D'Imperio's advancement at, 507–8; Hugo and Luigi's unhappiness at, 538; Keen masters and, 387, 388–89, 404; Klein's approach to Columbia and, 505, 506, 517; Klein's audit and, 473–74, 495, 498, 504–5, 508, 514–15, 519–20, 524, 525–26, 528; Jess Rand's approach to Hugo and Luigi and, 306–8; recording of Sam's live

show and, 451–53; Sam's contracts with, 307–8, 311, 376, 383–84, 429, 517–21, 528, 534–35; Sam's debts to, 457–58, 494–95, 514; Sam's dissatisfaction with, 458, 470; Sam's recording sessions for, 315, 318–21, 323–24, 325–26, 342–43, 344–46, 348, 361–65, 371–73, 389, 390–91, 405–7, 421–22, 440–41, 458–61, 498–99, 537–40, 546–48, 567, 591–93, 606–7; Sam's return to Copa and, 564–65, 583, 585–86; Sam's status at, 414; Tracey Ltd. and, 517–19

Reagan, Ronald, 305

Redding, Otis, 446, 594

Reed, Jimmy, 227, 446

Reese, Della, 306, 319

Regalettes, 498

Reisman, Sam, 295, 296, 304, 358, 386, 387–88

Reliable Jubilee Four, 165

René, Leon, 187, 473

René, Otis, 187, 473

René, Rafael "Googie," 187, 194–95

Renfro, Sister Jessie Mae, 142

Renoir, Jean, xiv

Rex Productions, 182–83, 184, 204–5, 209, 246, 278, 388. *See also* Keen Records

Reynolds, Debbie, 223, 239

rhythm and blues (r&b), 84–85, 86–88, 104; combining of gospel with, 112–14; crossover potential of, 87–88, 144, 171; gospel eclipsed by, 116. *See also specific performers and songs*

Rhythm and Blues Cavalcade of '58, 228, 235

Rhythm Orchids, 465–66

Richard, Charles "Jake," 5, 28–31, *30*, 48–49, 50,

52–53, 55, 59, 63, 119, 234. *See also* Highway QCs

Richard, Cliff, 423

Richard, Curtis, 29, 41, 43, 44

Richard, Lee, 28–31, *30*, 44, 46, 48–49, 50, 52–53, 55, 59, 63, 119, 120. *See also* Highway QCs

Richard, Mildred "Mook," 39, 41, 53, 226, 245

Richard, Reverend, 31, 44

"Riddle Song, The," 534, 539

Righteous Brothers, 516, 596–97

"Rip It Up," 176

Rivers, Johnny, 571

Roberta Martin Singers, 4, 5, 35, 43

Roberts, Johnny, 599

Roberts, Rip, 336

Robertson, Don, 616

Robey, Don, 85, 110–11, 129, 137

Robinson, Archie (later Osman Karriem), 557, 559

Robinson, Bobby, 149

Robinson, Dora Walder, 38, 106

Robinson, Eddie, 114

Robinson, Fabor, 397, 398

Robinson, Jackie, 336, 588

Robinson, Olsie "Bassy," 408, 439, 688*n*

Robinson, R.B., 37–38, 42, 62, 63, 75, 77, 90, 100, 106, 118, 131, 138, 140, 141, 146, 164, 169. *See also* Soul Stirrers

Robinson, Rev. Cleophus, 137

Robinson, Roscoe, 47–48, 377–78, 379, 380

Robinson, Smokey, 495, 630

Robinson, Sylvia, 221

Rocket Ship Show, 199

"Rockin' Good Way, A," 374

Rodgers, Jimmie, 203

Rodgers and Hammerstein, 112–13

Rogers, Jack, 194

Rolling Stones, 587–88, 598, 607, 650
"Rome Wasn't Built in a Day," 397–400, 410, 546, 547, 624, 646
Ross, Jackie, *396*
Ross, Roz, 463, 521, 554, 564
Roulette Records, 317–18, 466
Rowland, Steve, 280–81
Royal Peacock, Atlanta, 145, 277, 352, 411, 456–57, 599, 608, 609–10
Royal Teens, 227
"Run, Sinner, Run," 115
"(Run Along Home) Cindy, Cindy," 365
Rupe, Art, 65–73, 100, 101, 110–14, 182, 188, 263, 283, 312–13, 358, 525; J.W. Alexander as advisor and scout for, 60, 67–68, 98, 113, 152, 153; Bumps Blackwell hired by, 121–22; Blackwell's relationship with, 162–63, 166, 176–80, 207–9, 669n; Blackwell's release agreement and, 180, 204; booking agency set up by, 80–81 (*see also* Herald Attractions); defection of gospel groups and, 181, 189; early career of, 68–69; emergence of rhythm and blues and, 86–87, 88; "Good Golly Miss Molly" and, 207–10; R.H. Harris' departure from Soul Stirrers and, 65–68; in legal dispute with Sam and Keen Records, 193, 204–10, 243, 246–47, 262, 277, 294, 356, 384; Little Richard and, 129, 162, 171, 174, 176, 178, 189, 207–10, 247; marketing and production strategies of, 69, 71, 87, 88, 97–98, 104, 111–14,
128; Pilgrim Travelers and, 152, 153, 161–62, 181; Price's "Lawdy Miss Clawdy" and, 86–87, 97; remarriage of, 97; Sam's change from gospel to pop and, 127–28, 131–32, 149–50, 155, 156, 160, 161, 166, 168, 169; Sam's contracts with, 174, 178–80, 193, 194, 196, 204–7; Sam's solo recordings and, 149, 150, 156–58, 160, 168, 171–72, 174–77, 193, 194, 204–7; Sam's split with, 131–32, 178–80, 196, 204–7, 296; Soul Stirrers' recordings and, 60, 68, 69–73, 76, 83, 85–86, 95, 96, 97, 103–4, 110–11, 114, 115–16, 128, 247; views of Sam, 163, 178, 193, 205; Johnny Vincent's New Orleans–based operation and, 97, 112, 113. *See also* Specialty Records
Rupe, Leona, 97, 673n
Russell, Johnny, 397
Russell, Lew "Moondog," 194
Rustin, Bayard, 509, 511
Ruth, Brother Thermon, 80, 147, 148
Rydell, Bobby, 233, 347

"Sad Mood," 325, 348, 361
St. Louis Argus, 421, 443, 450
Salmas Brothers, 236
Salvatore, Tony, 453, 455, 585
"Sam Cooke . . . Man With a Goal," 344
Samson and Delilah (Saint-Saëns), 319
Sands, Zelda (née Samuels), 385, 391, 398, 403, 405, 458, 488, 500, 501, 516, 542, 565, 608, 635, 694n; background of, 360; birthday of, 443–44; at BMI Awards dinner, 455,
456, *456*; departure from SAR Records, 529–30, 605; hired by SAR Records, 360–61
Sands Cocktail Lounge, 570
Santangelo, Michael, 374–75, 389, 428, 685n
Sarkisian, Cherilyn (Cher), 566
SAR Pictures, 441
SAR Productions, 566
SAR Records, 318, 330–32, 359–61, 401–2, 429; AFO musicians as house band for, 543; after Sam's death, 644–45; Bumps Blackwell hired as producer for, 385; Mel Carter and, 460, 501–2, 516, 529, 530, 539; S.R. Crain's departure from, 332; expansion of, 441; financing of, 457–58, 494–95; first album put out by, 359–60; first pressings for, 299; genesis of, 295–97, 678n; R.H. Harris and, 402; Keen masters and, 388–89; Allen Klein's role at, 508, 565–66; label design for, 300; L.C. and, 342, 343, 434, 457, 516; Johnnie Morisette and, 322–23, 330, 339, 381, 396–97, 402, 410, 442, 443, 461, 516, 541, 543, 587; name of, 297, 332; offices of, 330–32, *331*, 385; party for artists of, 374; philosophy of, 359–60, 361, 473, 494, 551; Billy Preston and, 458, 460; Zelda Sands' departure from, 529–30, 605; Sands hired by, 360–61; Sims Twins and, 364, 365, 373–74, 381, 384–85, 390, 391–92, 396, 422, 442, 443, 516, 587, 607; Fred Smith hired by, 460, 501; Soul

Stations and, 542–43, 548–49, 566; Soul Stirrers and, 296–99, 305, 310, 332, 339–41, 343–44, 345, 359–60, 385–86, 450, 460, 512, 516, 544, 546, 587, 678n; Johnnie Taylor and, 359, 374, 397–400, 402, 410, 442, 458, 516, 611–13; Kylo Turner and, 321–22, 332; Valentinos (initially Womack Brothers) and, 377–80, 402–4, 410–11, 415, 422, 442, 566–67, 587–88, 596, 641–42

Saturday Night Beech-Nut Show, 225, 261, 282

Scandore, Joe, 521

Scepter Records, 440, 441, 444, 467–68, 529

Schiffman, Bobby, 149

Schiffman, Frank, 147–48, 284, 531

Schmitt, Al, 364, 405, 406, 414, 441, 507–8, 585, 591, 593, 606–7, 608, 614, 615–16, 646

Scott, Freddie, 521

Scott, George, 120

Scruggs, Bugs, 198

Sears, Zenas, 165, 292, 436, 453

segregation, *see* racial prejudice

Selah Jubilee Singers, 147

Selico, Ronnie, 279

Sensational Nightingales, 107, 110, 111, 119, 120, 146, 148, 191

Shabazz, Attallah, 532

Shadows, 423

"Shake," 607, 646

"Shake, Rattle and Roll," 459

Sharp, Dee Dee, 559

Sherman, Z. Charlotte, 310

"She's Wonderful," 460

Shindig!, 596–97

Shirelles, 444, 446, 467, 509

Shreveport, La., 526–28

Shrine Auditorium, Los Angeles, 121, 122–28, 150, 250–51

Shuttlesworth, Fred, 492

Siamas, Alex, 181–82, 296, 324, 358, 525

Siamas, John, 180–84, 198, 208, 212, 216, 236, 242, 324, 358, 525; background of, 181–82; Bumps Blackwell's deal with, 180, 181, 182; Blackwell's relationship with, 247, 271–72; Bob Keane's ouster and, 192–94; Keen's demise and, 308; ownership of Sam's publishing and, 248, 270; Art Rupe's copyright disputes with, 204, 208, 209–10, 294; Sam's break with, 296, 304–5, 307, 308; Sam's masters and, 387–88; "Wonderful World" and, 324. *See also* Keen Records

Siamas, John, Jr., 181, 182, 210, 212, 236, 308, 669n–70n, 671n

Silhouettes, 221–22, 227

Silver, Horace, 407

Simone, Nina, 509

Simpkins, Arthur Lee, 636

Simpson, Bob, 453, 455, 585

Sims, Omega, 611

Sims Twins (Bobbie and Kenneth Sims), 375, 384–85, 390, 410, 422, 439, 496, 516, 570, 617, 702n; recording sessions of, 373–74, 381, 391–92, 442, 443, 607, 685n; signed to SAR Records, 364; as Silver Twins, 364; singing backup for Sam, 363–65, 405, 407; "Soothe Me" and, 365, 373, 374, 381, 384, 396, 410, 685n; "That's Where It's At" and, 443, 594

Sinatra, Frank, 271, 281, 321, 323, 344, 501, 518, 588, 615, 679n

"Since I Fell For You," 348

Sing Along With Mitch, 353

Singing Children, 13–15, 17, 19–20, 23, 24–26, 27, 255, 633

Singleton, Shelby, 323

Slack, Sara, 582

Smalls, Tommy, 199

Smith, Chris, 591

Smith, Effie, 248

Smith, Eugene, 5, 43

Smith, Fred, 210–11, 237, 248, 347, 405, 407, 460, 501

Smith, Jimmy, 490

"Solitude," 271

Solomon, Lee, 554

"Somebody Have Mercy," 419, 431

"Someday You'll Want Me to Want You," 254

Somerville, Denise, 105, 381, 389, 632

Somerville, Marine, 93, 105, 632

"Something Within Me," 55–56

"Somewhere There's a Girl," 380, 403–4, 690n

"Somewhere There's a God," 380

"Somewhere to Lay My Head," 119–20

Songbirds of the South, 51

"Soothe Me," 365, 373, 374, 381, 384, 385, 396, 410, 685n

soul music, 407–8, 594

Soul Stations, 542–43, 548–49, 566

Soul Stirrers, 4–6, 19, 20, 25–26, 33, 34, 35, 52, 56, 57, 59–170, 77, 81, 95, 131, 146–47, 172, 215, 234, 243, 253, 255, 263, 309, 345, 375, 459, 630, 633; after Sam's departure, 189–92, 213, 247, 264, 283; as backup on Sam's recordings, 544, 546; business matters and, 79, 80–82, 86, 141, 148, 169, 174; June Cheeks' performances with,

107–8, 110–11, 433, 544; founding of, 59; founding of SAR Records and, 296–97; R.H. Harris' departure from, 59, 60–62, 63, 65–68, 74, 75–76, 111, 169; Highway QCs' relations with, 36, 37–38, 47, 55, 62; instrumental accompaniment of, 85, 103, 114, 120–21, 128, 166–67; *Jesus Be a Fence Around Me* and, 359–60; joined by Leroy Crume, 130, 133–35; joined by Bob King, 120–21, 133; joined by Jimmie Outler, 340–41; joined by Sam, 59, 62–64, 65–68; meticulous preparation and polish of, 103–4, 114; as model for Highway QCs, 30, 31, 44; motor home fire and, 614; Outler arrest and, 516–17; physical appearance of, 91; recording sessions of (*see* Soul Stirrers, recording sessions of); rehearsals of, 79, 82, 139; road tours of, 79–81, 82–83, 88–90, 98–101, 104–5, 121–28, 135–53, 155–56, 158–59, 165, 168–69, 377; rules for conduct of, 79, 139–40; Sam's change from gospel to pop and, 127–28, 130–32, 136–37, 144, 149–61, 163–70; Sam's departure from, 163, 164, 169–70, 190–91; Sam's first live performances with, 73–76; Sam's leadership role in, 116–17; Sam's New Year's Eve 1962 gospel concert with, 444, 450; Sam's return performances with, 192, 310, 679n; as SAR Records artists, 296–99,

305, 310, 332, 339–41, 343–44, 345, 359–60, 385–86, 450, 460, 512, 516, 544, 546, 587, 678n; sexual atmosphere created by Sam and, 142–44; stylistic traits of, 31, 59–60

Soul Stirrers, recording sessions of: March 1, 1951, 65, 69–73; February 1952, 85–86; February 27, 1953, 95–97, 104; July 10, 1953, 103–4; March 1954, 108–11; February 1955, 114–16; August 1955, 128; February 1956, 142, 151–53; April 19, 1957, 166–67; Sam's departure and, 247; for SAR Records, 297–99, 339, 343–44, 345, 460, 546, 587

"Soul Twist," 445
Sounds Incorporated, 423
Sour, Bob, 495
Southern Christian Leadership Conference (SCLC), 588, 609
Southern Jubilees, 50, 51
Southern Tones, 113, 120
Spaniels, 159, 215
Specialty Records, 35, 60, 65–73, 80, 81, 86, 97–98, 104, 155, 169, 181, 182, 185, 186, 189, 212, 236, 312–13, 322, 324, 337, 420; Bumps Blackwell hired by, 121–22; Blackwell's separation from, 178–80, 204; booking agency of (*see* Herald Attractions); and emergence of rhythm and blues, 86–87, 88; First Annual Summer Festival of Gospel Music and, 121, 122–28; in legal dispute with Sam and Keen Records, 193, 204–10, 243, 246–47, 262, 277,

294, 356, 384; proposal of, for Sam's first pop single, 160–61; Art Rupe's marketing and producing strategy for, 69, 71, 87, 88, 97–98, 104, 111–14, 128; Sam's break with, 131–32, 178–80, 196, 204–7, 215, 296; Sam's contracts with, 174, 178–80, 193, 194, 196, 204–7, 668n; Sam's sessions for, 153–58, 159, 171–77, 294; Soul Stirrers dropped by, 296; Soul Stirrers' sessions for, 65, 69–73, 85–86, 95–97, 103–4, 108–11, 114–16, 128, 142, 151–53, 166–67, 242; Valiants' "Good Golly Miss Molly" and, 207–10. *See also* Rupe, Art

Spector, Phil, 389
Spencer, Lou, 281, 282
Spencer, Sheridan "Rip," 183–85, 186, 252, 257, 672n
Spence Twins, 289, 290–91
Spiders, 154, 336
Spirit of Memphis Quartet, 35, 49, 50, 51, 53, 77, 98
"Stand By Me Father," 297–99, 305, 516
Standifer, Floyd, 121
Staples, Mavis, 143, 630, 633
Staples, Roebuck "Pop," 128, 633
Staple Singers, 128, 143, 402, 633
Stars Salute Dr. Martin Luther King, The, 588
State Theater, Philadelphia, 463, 467–70, 473, 475
Staton, Dakota, 336, 338
"Steal Away," 34, 280
Steele, Larry "Good Deal," 504
Steele, Silas, 35
Steiger, Rod, 203
Steve Allen Show, The, 149, 216, 218, 222

Stevens, Morty, 569, 574, 576, 579
Stewart, Sandy, 362
Stone, Sly, 607
Storm, Billy, 208, 209
"Stormy Monday," 523
Streisand, Barbra, 507
Strong, Barrett, 326
Stubbs, Joe, 288
Student Non-Violent Coordinating Committee (SNCC), 490, 510, 513
Student Voice, The, 513
"Sufferin'," 342
Suffragettes (Interlandi painting), 310
"Sugar Dumpling," 517
Sullivan, Ed, 91, 202, 203–4, 211–12, 218, 473, 503, 555
"Summertime," 167, 173, 174, 175–76, 181, 187, 189, 194–95, 196, 271, 303, 313
Super Attractions, 228, 287
Super Enterprises, 228
Supersonic Attractions, 286–87, 325, 348, 422, 456, 496, 646; origins of, 286–87; Sam's 1959 tour with Jackie Wilson for, 286, 287–93, 382; Sam's April 1960 tour for, 325, 326–28; Sam's June 1960 tour for, 332–35; Sam's October 1960 tour for, 348–52; Sam's May 1961 tour for, 365–71; Sam's April 1962 tour for, 393, 405, 407–8; Sam's spring 1963 tour for, 472–73, 474–89, 493–94, 495–96; Sam's 1964 tour for, 598–605
Swanee Quintet, 146, 190, 191, 444
Sweet Chariot, New York, 521
Swimmer, Saul, 467
"Swing Low, Sweet Chariot," 344

Tabernacle Baptist Church, Chicago, 632–33
"Take a Look at the Sensational Sam Cooke," 263
"Take Me for What I Am," 457
Talent Party, 604–5
Tamla, 288–89
"Tammy," 223, 239, 313
Tate, Bob, 251, 252, 253, 257, 258, 262, 263, 266, 290
Tate, Louis, 45–46, 47, 48, 49, 52, 53, 54, 58
Taylor, Dan, 50–51
Taylor, Johnnie, 119–20, 283, 298, 299, 344, 396, 439, 440, 566, 646; personality and demeanor of, 119; "Rome Wasn't Built in a Day" and, 397–400, 410; "Sam Cooke" sound of, 119, 191, 247, 305, 340–41; as SAR Records artist, 359, 374, 397–400, 402, 410, 442, 458, 516, 611–13; Soul Stirrers joined by, 191; Soul Stirrers quit by, 340
Taylor, June, 221
Taylor, Little Johnny, 612, 613
Taylor, Rev. Leroy, 62, 657n
Taylor, Zola, 220
"Teenage Machine Age," 236
"Teenage Sonata," 319, 321, 324
Teen Age Valley Wonders, 55–56, 57, 58
"Tenderness," 348, 364–65
Tenenbaum, David, 13, 26, 45
"Tennessee Waltz," 547, 571, 581, 582, 586, 597, 646
"Thank God It's Real," 395
Tharpe, Sister Rosetta, 84, 113–14, 596
"That Lucky Old Sun," 207
"That's All I Need to Know," 156, 157
"That's Heaven to Me," 167, 280

"That's It, I Quit, I'm Movin' On," 363
"That's Where It's At," 443, 594–95, 598, 609
"Things That I Used to Do, The," 112, 113
"Things You Do to Me," 174
"This Is the Night," 209, 252
"This Little Light of Mine," 580, 586
"This Train," 113–14
Thompson, Ann, 82–83
Thompson, Rev. Goldie, 82–83
Thunder, Johnny, 467, 475, 480, 481–82, 493, 634
Til, Sonny, 84, 104, 239
"Time Has Come (To Say Goodbye), The," 150, 404, 665n
Timmons, Bobby, 407
Tindley, Charles, 60, 297–98
Tiomkin, Dimitri, 467
"Tired of Living in the Country," 442
"Tobacco Road," 544, 614
"Today I Sing the Blues," 367
Todd, Nick, 214
"To Each His Own," 606
Tonight Show, The, 436, 549, 550, 551–53
"Too Close," 111–12, 159
"Touch the Hem of His Garment," 152–53, 442–43
Toussaint, Allen, 336, 338
Town Hill Club, Brooklyn, 325–26, 413
Townsend, Ed, 230, 242, 360, 471, 496
Tracey Ltd., 517–19, 524, 525, 588, 605, 635, 650, 694n, 701n
Trammel, Charles, 250, 273
Trapp, Mary, 546
Traveling Four, 155
Treadwell, Gus, 30, 43–44, 47, 48, 50, 52, 53, 55, 57, 77, 655n. *See also* Highway QCs
"Trouble I've Seen, The," 243–44

"Try a Little Love," 281, 296, 348

"Try a Little Tenderness," 281, 364–65, 581

Tucker, Sophie, 430, 554

Turks, 185

Turner, Big Joe, 459

Turner, Jesse, 368, 370–71

Turner, Kylo, 55, 73, 74, 76, 152, 161–62, 321–22, 332

"Tutti Frutti," 129

20th Century Fox, 583–84, 590

"Twist, The," 288, 347, 351, 390

"Twistin' in the Kitchen with Dinah," 396

"Twistin' the Night Away," 390–91, 392, 396, 397, 405, 414, 418, 431, 455, 534, 569, 582, 600, 646

Twistin' the Night Away LP, 414, 419, 517

Twistin' the Night Away Revue, 408–10

Tyler, Red, 156, 158, 346, 541–42, 548

"Under Paris Skies," 323

United Five, 88, 334

United Nations (UN), 561

United Recording Studio, Hollywood, 373, 391, 442

Universal Attractions, 201, 228, 235, 264, 286, 287, 309, 384, 411, 476

Universal Recorders, Chicago, 68, 100, 380

University of Alabama, 139

"Until Jesus Calls Me Home," 70

"Up On the Mountain," 159, 160, 446

Upsetters, 211, 251, 334, 348, 496, 569–70, 599, 608, 611, 617, 625, 630, 646; as Sam's backup band, 408, 410, 411, 412–13, 418, 431, 435, 439, 445, 474

Uptown Theater, Philadelphia, 463

Valentine, Patience, 385, 396, 442, 461, 503

Valentinos (formerly Womack Brothers), 410–11, 415, 422, 458, 470–72, 549, 605, 607, 640, 645; Bobby rejoins, 606, 611, 612–13; disappointed in Sam's decisions for their group, 567, 587–88; Friendly's departure from, 440; Jimi Hendrix disliked by, 603; move to California by, 440, 442, 470, 471–72; recording sessions of, 403–4, 442, 566–67, 596; rivalry among brothers in, 439, 470–71, 472, 567, 690n; Sam's death and, 625, 626, 634–35, 641–42, 648; showmanship of, 437–39; singing backup for Sam, 567; on tour with James Brown, 422, 436–38, 453; on tour with Sam, 436, 438–40, 468, 469, 470–71, 530, 587, 596, 599, 608; Womack Brothers renamed as, 404. *See also* Womack, Bobby; Womack Brothers

Valiants, 183, 189, 207–9, 210, 236, 252–53, 257, 392

Vaughan, Sarah, 317

Vee Jay Records, 119, 143, 159, 168, 296, 297, 678n

Venice Music, 174, 179, 193, 204–5

Vincent, Gene, 423, 426, 426

Vincent, Johnny, 97, 112, 113, 395

Vincent, Sonny, 303, 304, 678n

Vinton, Bobby, 554, 564

Wade, Brother Theo, 50, 263

Wade, Essie, 50

"Wade in the Water," 298

Wagoner, Faidest, 108, 109, 164

Walker, Albertina, 124

Walker, Fat Jack, 590–91

Wallace, JoJo, 107, 120, 123

Wallace, Mike, 352, 374, 375

Waller, Fats, 473

WAOK, 292, 436

Ward, Billy, 175–76, 230

Ward, Clara, 71, 92, 98, 146, 148, 152, 191

Ward Singers, 61, 71, 92, 98

Warwick, Dionne, 444, 446, 467, 469, 475, 480, 482, 493

Washington, Baby, 289, 521, 523

Washington, Dinah, 374, 508, 533

Washington, Rev. Frederick D., 80

Waters, Muddy, 84, 145, 593

Watley, Clarence, 436, 455, 457, 543

Watson, Johnny "Guitar," 207, 236, 252–53, 277, 289, 337, 443, 646

WDAS, 199

WDIA, 49–50, 51

WDIA Goodwill Revue, 159

Weathers, Mabel, 155, 213–14

Webb, Willie, 35, 114, 166, 632

WEDR, 165

Welch, Brother Clarence, 121

Wells, Mary, 495

Wendell Phillips High School, Chicago, 22–23, 27–28, 29, 42, 231

"Were You There (When They Crucified My Lord)?," 167, 443

"We Shall Overcome," 297

"Western Movies," 237, 248, 347, 405, 460

West Indies, 335, 408–10, 409

Westinghouse Network, 374

West Singers, 37

"We Wear the Mask" (Dunbar), 446, 459

Wexler, Jerry, 84, 88, 130–31, 149, 240, 307

"What'd I Say," 320, 469

"When a Boy Falls in Love," 281, 428, 460, 501, 516

"When Death Comes Creeping In Your Room," 115

"When I Lost My Mother," 98, 99

"When We Bow Our Knees at the Altar," 54–55

"When You Bow at the Cross in the Evening," 34

Whitaker, Jesse, 80, 81, 107, 111, 116, 117, 118, 264, 265, 278, 634

White, Clifton "Clif," 241, 251, 253, 277, 297, 454, 457, 470, 472, 489, 495–96, 535, 543, 589, 598, 605, 608; background of, 172–73, 185–86; as backup musician for Sam's recording sessions, 172–74, 175, 207, 239, 279, 280, 307, 325, 363, 405, 458, 460, 591; as backup musician for SAR Records sessions, 299, 321, 342, 380, 398, 399, 460, 546; in car accident, 265–66; on road with Sam, 211, 213, 222, 223, 224, 229, 254, 265, 290, 302, 327, 335, 346, 347, 350, 354, 427, 431; Sam's appearance on *PM East/PM West* and, 375; Sam's arrangements and, 222, 238, 271, 328, 362, 409, 539; Sam's death and, 620, 626; Sam's first meeting with, 173–74, 212; Sam's relationship with, 173–74; Sam's return to Copa and, 567, 568, 576,

582, 586; SAR Records session by, 396

White, Slappy, 503

White Citizens Council, 139, 490

Whitman, Slim, 332

"Why You Send Me," 246

Wilkins, Roy, 509

Wilks, James, 109

William Morris Agency, 207, 222, 256, 263, 413, 463, 564; booking of Sam by, 201–2, 204, 281–82, 284, 679*n*; Sam's contract with, 200–202, 354; Sam's Copa shows and, 225, 281, 554; Sam's dissatisfaction with, 308–9, 311–12, 353–54; Sam sold to Universal by, 286, 309. *See also* Auerbach, Larry; Brandt, Jerry

Williams, Barney, 566

Williams, Bert, 591

Williams, Dootsie, 187, 250

Williams, Larry, 337

Williams, Nat D., 159–60

Williams, Paul, 229

Williams, Ronnie, 80, 98, 161, 168–69, 340

Williams, Tommy "Buster," 322

Williams, Tony, 144, 164

Willie Webb Singers, 35

Willis, Chuck, 479

Wilson, Freda, 355

Wilson, Gerald, 499, 569

Wilson, Jackie, 227, 232, 234, 243, 255, 264, 319, 355–56, 393, 473, 495, 496, 594, 646, 647; arrested in St. Louis, 603; Kags song recorded by, 278, 300, 428; personality and demeanor of, 234, 600; racial incidents and, 326–27, 337, 480; Sam's 1959 Supersonic tour with, 286, 287–88, 289–90, 292, 308–9,

382; Sam's 1964 Supersonic tour with, 598–605; Sam's relationship with, 258, 286–90, 356, 599–601, 604–5; shooting of, 355, 683*n*; showmanship of, 234, 289, 303, 433, 599

WIND, 55

WINS, 228, 235

Winters, June, 316

"Win Your Love For Me," 239–42, 277

Without Each Other, 467

WLAC, 71

"Wobble, The," 457, 516

Wolff, Daniel, 102, 106, 143, 635

"Wolverton Mountain," 456

Womack, Bobby, xv, 108, 142, 143, 377, 378, 379–80, 392, 402, 403, 440, 442, 513, 593, 605, 607, 638, 651, 690*n*; as backup musician for Sam, 474, 535, 543, 567, 568, 576, 582, 583, 586, 591–92, 594, 611; Barbara's relationship with, 639–42, 644–46, 647–50; British pop invasion and, 587–88, 596; "A Change Is Gonna Come" and, 549, 550; Charles Cook and, 649–50; family life of, 485; Rolling Stones' cover of "It's All Over Now" and, 587–88, 598; on Sam's change from gospel to pop, 197; Sam's death and, 625–26, 634–35, 640–42, 702*n*; Sam's predictions of success for, 380, 587–88; Sam's relationship with, 439, 470–71, 472, 485–88, 567; Sam's return to Copa and, 567, 568, 569, 575, 576, 578, 579, 580, 581, 582, 583, 586; sent back on road with Valentinos by Sam, 606, 611, 612–13; songwriting and, 487–88, 538–39, 567; Soul Station #1 and, 549; on Supersonic tour with Sam, 474–75, 476–77, 481, 482–83, 485–88, 493–94, 496; on tour with James Brown, 436–38; Vincent's death and, 501; "Yeah Man" and, 567. *See also* Valentinos; Womack Brothers

Womack, Cecil, 377, *378*, 472, 567, 702*n. See also* Valentinos; Womack Brothers

Womack, Curtis, 377, *378*, 379–80, 403, 471, 472, 648, 690*n. See also* Valentinos; Womack Brothers

Womack, Friendly, Jr., 377, *378*, 403, 439–40, 470. *See also* Valentinos; Womack Brothers

Womack, Friendly, Sr., 142, 377, *378*, 379, 403, 470, 485

Womack, Harry, 377, *378*, 603. *See also* Valentinos; Womack Brothers

Womack, Shirley, 566

Womack, Vincent, 650

Womack Brothers, 142, *378*, 402–4, 684*n*; change from gospel to pop, 380, 402–3; renamed Valentinos, 404; signed to SAR Records, 377–80. *See also* Valentinos

Wonder, Little Stevie, 495, 593

"Wonderful," 142–43, 145, 152–53, 442; pop translation of ("Lovable"), 150, 155–57, 159, 160, 164, 165–66, 168, 206, 666*n*; pop translation of ("She's Wonderful"), 460

"Wonderful World," 279, 324, 335, 338, 356, 374, 384, 646, 685*n*

Woods, Georgie, 199, 420, 463, 464, 495, 565, 589, 631

WOV, 147, 199, 463

WWRL, 445

Wynn, Claudia, 292, 609

Wynn, Henrietta, 292, 609

Wynn, Henry, 145, 292, 293, 325, 332, 348, 352, 365, 369, 393, 404, 405, 456, 472, 473, 475, 476, 495, 496, 603; background of, 287; Gorgeous George and, 477; Sam's relationship with, 474, 608; Supersonic Attractions started by, 286–87. *See also* Supersonic Attractions

"Yeah Man," 567, 597–98, 606, 607

"Yield Not to Temptation," 635

York, Preston, 165

Yorke, Bob, 307, 383, 388, 473, 474, 498, 507, 692*n*

"You'll Never Walk Alone," 112–13

Young, A.S. "Doc," 224, 642

Young, Whitney, 509

"You're Always On My Mind," 339

"You're Workin' Out Your Bag on Me," 422

"You Send Me," 206, 207, 211–12, 216, 221, 228, 235, 263, 270, 282, 312, 318, 420, 445, 516, 671*n*; cover versions of, 198, 204, 543; demo of, 168; L.C. credited as songwriter on, 196, 204, 205, 247, 294, 309; live version of (1962–63), 431–32; promotion tour for, 198–204; recording and production of, 173, 174, 175, 182, 189, 542; responses to, 194–97, 201, 202; Art Rupe's legal actions and, 193, 204–5, 246–47; Sam's Christmas card and, 313–14; in Sam's 1964 Copa show, 569, 581, 582, 585; Sam's William Morris contract and, 200–202

"You Understand Me," 324

"You Were Made For All My Love," 356

"You Were Made For Me," 158, 167–68, 174, 447–48

Zavin, Theodora, 358, 495

Zito, Torrie, 591